Abstracts
of the
Proprietary Records
of the
PROVINCIAL COURT
of MARYLAND

1637–1658

Patent Record F & B (1640–1658)
Patent Record Z & A (1637–1651)
Patent Record A & B (1650–1657)

Vernon L. Skinner, Jr.

HERITAGE BOOKS
2011

HERITAGE BOOKS
AN IMPRINT OF HERITAGE BOOKS, INC.

Books, CDs, and more—Worldwide

For our listing of thousands of titles see our website
at
www.HeritageBooks.com

Published 2011 by
HERITAGE BOOKS, INC.
Publishing Division
100 Railroad Ave. #104
Westminster, Maryland 21157

Copyright © 2002 Vernon L. Skinner, Jr.

All rights reserved. No part of this book may be reproduced or transmitted in any form or by any means, electronic or mechanical, including photocopying, recording or by any information storage and retrieval system without written permission from the author, except for the inclusion of brief quotations in a review.

International Standard Book Numbers
Paperbound: 978-1-58549-796-6
Clothbound: 978-0-7884-8684-5

PREFACE

The probate court of Maryland for the greater part of the colonial period was call the Prerogative Court. Many of the features of the court, notably the terminology, were borrowed from the English Prerogative Court. Unlike the English court which was ecclesiastical, the Maryland court remained a civil court throughout its existence, although there were several attempts to put it under the control of the Bishop of London.

The Prerogative Court did not spring into existence, a full-fledged court. Like the other institutions of the Province, it was the product of a gradual evolution, influenced by the customs of the home country and the needs of the new. Its origin can be traced back to the Charter granted to Lord Baltimore in 1632. In it, he was given complete control over the colony, including authority in religious matters comparable to that of the Bishop of Durham. This, of course, included control over probate matters.

"Proprietary Records" is an artificial title which is ordinarily used to identify the earliest records of the colony. They are general record books covering all sorts of proceedings of the provincial government, especially records of the Provincial Court. These are the only source now existing of probate material for the period 1643-1657.

The Testamentary Proceedings contain probate material from 1657 to 1777.

> Hartsook & Skordas, Land Office and Prerogative Court Records

Abstracts of three of the libers of the Proprietary Record are included in this volume.

- Patent Record F & B - 1640-1658.
- Patent Record Z & A - 1637-1651.
- Patent Record A & B - 1650-1657.

The header at the top of each page indicates from the liber for the cited material. The appropriate folio number is cited down the left-hand side of the page. Two different dates are used:

- An underlined date, which is the date that the entry was actually recorded. These dates, for any particular liber, are generally chronological. But not always.
- An entry signified by the use of "Date:". This is the date for that particular citation, which may vary considerably from the recorded date.

Not just probate material has been included, but also depositions, deeds, and trials. All of this provides an interesting insight into early Maryland life.

> V. L. Skinner, Jr.
>
> 30 April 2002

Liber - Patent Record F & B - 1640-1658

f. 1   Petition of Capt. William Clayborne et. al. on Isle of Kent in Chesapeake Bay in VA

f. 2   made known to Sir John Governor of VA & Lord Baltimore & plantation in Sasquesahanough Country.

f. 3   ...

f. 4   at New Market. Date: 26 February 1637. Approved with advise of Mr. Horney. Signed: John Cooke.

f. 5   to be heard 1st Council Day after Easter. Signed: W. Cant, Tho. Coventrie, W. Manchester at Whitehall. 4 April 1638. Present: Archbishop of Canterbury, Lord Keeper, Lord Treasurer, Lord Privy Seal, Earl Marshall, Earl of Dorsett, Lord Cottington, Mr. Treasurer, Mr. Controller, Mr. Secretary Cooke, Mr. Windebanke.

Petition by Capt. Cleybourne et. al.

f. 6   ...

f. 7   ...

f. 8   Signed: Ex. T. Meantys.

Caecilius Lord Baltimore grants to his brother Leonard Calvert authority

f. 9   ...

f. 10 & as Chancellor, Chief Justice & Chief Magistrate.

f. 11 ...

f. 12 ...

f. 13 Jerome Hawley, Esq., Thomas Cornwallis & John Lewger (gentlemen) to be counsel.

f. 14 ...

f. 15 John Lewger to be Secretary.

f. 16 at London. Date: 15 April 1637. Signed: John Lewgar.

f. 17 August 1635. Transported by Mr. Thomas Greene for 1633: Mr. Thomas Greene for self & 2 servants Anam Benam & Thomas Cooper, in right of Mr. Ferfax, Mr. Smith, Thomas Wells.

8 August 1637. Transported by Mr. Thomas Copley & Mr. John Knolls: Robert Hedger, Luke Garnett, Walter King, Thomas Davison, Thomas Mathew, George White, Richard Cox, John Mackin, John Tue.

Richard Garnett, Sr. who transported his wife, Richard Garnett his son, & maid servant.

On 28 November 1637, in the Unity of Isle of Wight: Mr. John Lewger transported his wife, son John (age 9), Martha Williamson (maid servant), Ann Pike (maid servant), Mary Whitehead (maid servant), Benjamin Cobby, Phillip Linnis, Thomas Furston, Robert Serle (age 12), Robert Clark servant to Mr. Copley.

Mr. Jerome Hawley transported Mary & Ellen Jermogangout, Thomas Jermogan, Thomas Cullamore.

f. 18 Capt. Cornwaleys transported Charles Magnett, Stephen Gray, & Alice Moreman.

Thomas Franklin transported Mary Leefe, Thomas Pasmore, Joane Triggs, Frances Morgan.

Mr. Copley transported William Triggs (boy).

22 November 1638. Mr. Pulton, Mr. Morly.

Mr. Giles Brent & Mr. Fulke Brent his brother who returned in March following. Mrs. Margaret Brent & Mrs. Mary Brent who transported Mary Taylor (maid servant), Elisabeth Guesst (maid servant), Mary Lawne (maid servant), Elisabeth Brooks (maid servant), John Robinson, (N) Goodwin Blacksmith.

Mrs. Throughton transported Mr. Winifride (gentleman), Bridgett (N) (maid servant), Ann Elton (maid servant), John Sheercliff.

Liber - Patent Record F & B - 1640-1658

Transported at charge of Vicountesse Falkland: Joane Burgess (maid servant), Barnaby Jackson, Francis Thwaytes, James Moulins, Henry Adams.

Came to province on 13 March 1638: Mr. Richard Lee & wife, Mr. Owen Phillips, Mr. Egerton, youth servant to Marmd. Snow, Mr. Walter Broadhurst with 2 servants.

Came to province on 12 January 1637: Capt. Robert Wintour who transported Richard Brown, Arthur Webb, John Speed, Bartholomew Phillips, Thomas White, (N) Morgan, George Taylor (boy, age 15).

Mr. William Britton who transported his wife & William Nabbs (age about 60), wife (age likewise) of said Nabbs, William (his son, age 4),

f. 19 James Price, (N) Williams, William Suype, Thomas Rouney, Humphrey (N) (servant transported by Capt. Winter at charge of Mr. Giles Brent).

Came to province in April 1638: Marmaduke Snow, Thomas Gerrard (surgeon).

Came to province in October 1638: Baltasar Codd (Irishman), (N) Willis transported at charge of (N). Snow.

Richard Berwick demanded 50 a. Date: 8 May 1639. Signed: John Lewger Secretary.

30 April 1638. Entered by Capt. George Evelin for Manor of Evelinton in Baronie of St. Maries': Thomas Hebden, David Wickiliff, Randall Revell, James Cloughton, Hugh Howard, John Walker, Henry Lee, John Wortley, John Richardson, John Hill, William Medcalf, Phillip West, Edmond Parrie, Hoell Morgan, Matthew Roadham, Roger Baxter, Thomas Orley, William Williamson, Thomas Keane, Andrew Baker, Thomas Baker, John Hatche, Samuel Scovell.

Entered by John Lewger Secretary. Brought into province in 1637: John Lewger, Sr., Ann his wife, John Lewger (age 9), Martha Williamson (maid servant), Ann Pike (maid servant), Mary Whitehead (maid servant), Benjamin Cobbie, Phillip Linnie, Thomas Fursdon, Robert Serle (age 12), Xpofer Moreland, John Jones, Ann Norris, Humphrey Chaplin, Hugh Nash, Barth. Slater, William Stiles, Deborah (N), Ann Eglesfield, John Hatch, John Askue, Ann Reynolds.

Entered by Mr. Coply. Brought into province in 1633: Mr. Andrew White, Mr. John Althem, Thomas Statham, Robert Simpson, Mary Jennings, Mathias Sousa,

f. 20 John Hillierd, Robert Sherly, Mr. Rogers, John Hill, Christopher Carnock, John Bryant, William Ashmore, Richard Lusthead, Nicholas Hervey, Robert Edwards, Robert Edward [sic], Thomas Charinton, William Edwyn, Thomas Griysta, Richard Duke, Henry Bishop, Thomas Heath, John Tomson, James Thornton, Lewis Fremonds, Richard Nevill, John Hollis, Richard Cole, John Elkin, Thomas Hodges.

Brought into province in 1637: Mr. Thomas Copley, Mr. John Knoles, Robert Hedger, Luke Gardiner, Walter King, Thomas Davison, Franissco (N), Thomas Matthew, George White, Phillip Spurr, Richard Cox, Henry Hooper, William Empson, Edward Cottam, John Machin, John Smith, John Tue, Robert Sedgrave, James Compton.

John Lewger Secretary administrator of Peter Draper sold 1500 a. to Capt. Henry Fleet (gentleman). Date: 2 May 1644.

Said Henry Fleet demanded said 1500 a. & additional 500 a. for transporting 5 men. Date: 13 May 1644. Layout for Capt. Henry Fleet for 2000 a. Signed: Giles Brent.

Edmond Linnen demanded 50 a. for transporting self. Date: 22 October 1643.

f. 21 John Nott demanded land for transporting self & assigned land to Francis Posie. Date: 1 July 1643. Signed: Jo. Lewger.

Mary Trenton demanded 2000 a. per warrant dated 1 August 1638 at London & assigned to Nathaniell Pope. Date: 7 April 1643. Signed: Mary Troughton.

Nathaniel Orchard demanded 100 a. for transporting self in 1640. Date: 4 April 1643.

William Asiter demanded 300 a. for transporting self & 2 man servants in 1638 & assigned to Robert Kedger. Date: 27 March 1643.

Thomas Weston (gentleman) demanded. Date: 10 January 1642.

Liber - Patent Record F & B - 1640-1658

John Lewger demanded 50 a. for transporting maid servant Ann Pike in 1637 & assigned to her now husband John Pike. Date: 24 January 1642.

Anthony Penraddock, Esq. assigned of Mr. Edward Robinson, Esq. by his attorney Thomas Carey demanded 2000 a. for transporting 5 men. Date: 15 November 1642.

f. 22 William Durford demanded 150 a. at west side of mouth of Potomack for transporting self & son Joseph in 1640. Date: 12 November 1642.

Thomas Weston demanded 1200 a. for transporting self & 5 men in 1640: Richard Haniford, William Marshall, William Palmer, John Kelly, Jasper Collins. Date: 29 August 1642. Attested by: George Pye.

Thomas Weston demanded 100 a. for transporting William Hall & 50 a. assigned from George Pye. Date: 10 January 1642. Laid out for Mr. Thomas Weston on east side of St. George's Creek bounding land of: George Pye, Isaac Edwards, Henry Lee, Richard Nevett. [metes & bounds]

f. 23 Patent to Thomas Weston for Westbury Manor.

f. 24 Jane Cockshott (widow) requested patent for land granted Randall Revell who has surrendered the land. Date: 29 November 1642.

John Cockshott demanded 2000 a. for transporting in 1641: self, Jane his wife, Mary Cockshott, Jane Cockshott, Eleanor Clerk, Thomas Hardie, Gilbert Metcalf, Michael Hacker. Date: 5 July 1642.

Francess White demanded 1000 a. for transporting 5 men in 1641: Thomas Howard, John Howard, Rowland Mace, William Johnson, Thomas Lewis. Said Francess demanded 300 a. for transporting herself & 2 maid servants: Elisabeth (N), Julian (N), Jane (N). Date: 1 July 1642.

Margarett & Mary Brent demanded 1000 a.

f. 25 for transporting 5 men afore 25 March last: Thomas Tidd, Samuel Pursall, Francis Stower, John Stephens, John Delahay. Date: 25 April 1642. Margarett Brent assigned to John Brooke (Liber GG, Folio 241).

Thomas Pasmore demanded 200 a. for transporting 2 man servants in 1635: Thomas Price, Richard Williams. Date: 18 March 1642. Signed: John Lewger.

Thomas Copley, Esq. demanded 4000 a. for transporting self & 20 men in 1637: Thomas Matthews, George White, Edward Cottam, John Machin, Robert Hedger, Phillip Spurr, John Battam, Luke Garnett, Richard Cox, Charles (N) (a Welshman), John Tue, Walter King, Henry Hooper, Robert Sedgrave, Thomas Davison, William Empson, Nicholas Russell, James Compton, Edm. Tetersel, Richard Darsy. Date: 18 April 1642.

Richard Lusthead demanded 100 a. for transporting 1 man servant Edward Smith. Date: 6 April 1642.

f. 26 Thomas Copley, Esq. demanded 4000 a. for transporting persons in 1633. Date: 31 March 1641.

Thomas Petit demanded 200 a. for transporting self & wife. Arthur Hay demanded 100 a. John Gay demanded 100 a. Warrant to Thomas Petit for 200 a., Arthur Hay for 100 a., John Guy for 100 a. on north side of Patuxent River. Date: 7 March 1641.

7 March 1641. Thomas Cornwaleys, Esq. demanded 2000 a. for transporting 5 man servants in 1633: John Hallowes, John Holdern, Roger Walter, Roger Morgan, Josias (N) (drowned afterwards).

More demanded 3000 a. for transporting 15 man servants in 1635: Morris Freeman, Nicholas Guither, Richard Feriner, Edward Matthews, William Porescourt, Richard Cole, Xpofer Martin, John Norten older, John Norten younger, Richard Brown, Richard Brock, John Medley, Francis van Eynden, Walter Walterlin, Stephen Gray.

Warrant to Capt. Thomas Corwaleys, Esq. for 4000 a. on Potowmeck River upward of Port Tobacco Creek.

f. 27 4 March 1641. Warrant to John Cockshott (joyner) for 50 a. beyond Hill Creek called St. Joseph's Hill.

28 February 1641. Simon Richardson demanded 100 a. for transporting self. Granted for 100 a. in St. Clement's Hundred.

Liber - Patent Record F & B - 1640-1658

18 February 1641. Richard Hedger demanded 300 a. for transporting in 1640 self, his wife & 1 man servant Miles Ricketts & 100 a. assigned per William Asiter. Warrant on northeast branch of Herring Creek.

17 February 1641. Leonard Calvert, Esq. demanded 5000 a. for transporting 25 men in 1633: John Fridd (boy bought of Thomas Steg of VA in 1637), Thomas Cooper, Richard Smith, York (N) (boy sold to Thomas Bradnock), a purbline youth sold to Mr. Brainthwait, one called Small (N) sold to himself, Thomas Onley, Sam. Scovell, Nicholas Polhampton, Matthew Rodam, one that served the latter part of his time with Hales, William Harrington, Daniel (N) (Irishman), Will. Pinley, Samuel Barrett, Edward Ebbs, Thomas Mosse, 6 new hands bought of VA, Thomas Oliver (smith). 100 a. assigned to John Robinson (barber) & 50 a. to

f. 28 Richard Hills.

f. 29 ...

f. 30 Warrant to Mrs. Margarett Brent & her sister Mrs. Mary Brent

f. 31 for transporting 4 maid servants. Mrs. Margarett Brent assigned to James Clifton. Date: 12 October 1663. [Liber AA, Folio 324.]

Mrs. Margarett & Mary Brent transported on 22 November 1638 4 maid servants & 4 man servants: Thomas Ped, Mary Taylor, Samuel Pursall, Elisabeth Guesse, Francis Stower, Mary Lawne, John Stephans, Elisabeth Brooks.

Warrant to Mrs. Margarett & Mrs. Mary Brent bounding Mr. Giles Brent, Mr. Thomas Green, St. George's River, St. Andrew's Creek.

f. 32 [metes & bounds] Date: 7 October 1639. Signed: John Lewger. Mentions their brother Giles Brent, Esq.

f. 33 Giles Brent, Esq. demanded land for transporting 5 servants in 1637: Humphrey Fullford, James Price, William Knipe, Thomas Rowney, Thomas Williams. In 1638, 6 servants: John Warren, Devereux Godwin, Edward Berry, Richard Colesford, John Robinson, Richard Pinner.

Warrant to Capt. Giles Brent, Esq. for 60 a.

f. 34 [metes & bounds] bounding St. George's River. Date: 9 October 1639. Signed: John Lewger.

Patent to Giles Brent for land with his sisters Margarett Brent & Mary Brent.

Warrant to Mr. John Lewger for 2 manors of 3000 a.

f. 35 John Lewger demanded 200 a. on assignment from Capt. Thomas Cornwaleys, Esq. & 100 a. & 2 manors. Warrant for 200 a. on north side of St. John's Creek & Pope's Swamp, bounding Mill Creek, land of Phillip West (carpenter) called West's Valley, St. John's Brook.

f. 36 Warrant to Thomas Cornwaleys, Esq. for transporting self & 20 man servants in 1633. 200 a. assigned to John Lewger for transporting self & his wife & several servants.

f. 37 [metes & bounds], bounding St. John's Brooks, St. John's Creek.

Mr. Ferdinand Pulton demanded land for transporting in 1633 as assignee of Mr. Andrew White: Mr. Andrew White, Mr. John Altome, Thomas Statham, Robert Simpson, Henry Bishop, Thomas Heath, Lewis Fremond, Richard Thompson, Matthias Sousa (mulatto), Richard Luthead, William Ashmore, Robert Sherley. In 1634: Mr. Rogers, John Hill, John Briant, Nicholas Hervey, Xpofer Carnoll, a smith lost by the way. In 1635: John Horwood, James Thornton, Frannsco (N) (mulatto).

f. 38 As assignee of Mr. John Sanders in 1633: Benjamin Hodges, John Elkin, Richard Cole, Richard Nevell, John Marlburgh.

As assignee of Mr. Richard Gerrard in 1633: Thomas Munns, Thomas Grigston, Robert Edwards, John Ward, William Edwin.

As assignee of Mr. Edward & Frederick Wintour in 1633: black John Price, white John Price, Francis Rabnett, Thomas Smith, Richard Duke, Henry James, Thomas Charinton.

As assignee of Mr. Thomas Copley in 1633: Mr. John Knolls, Thomas Matthews, George White, Edward Cottam, John Machin, Robert Hedger, Phillip Spurr, John Smith (alias John Bettam), Luke Garnett, Richard Coxe, John Tue, Walter King,

Liber - Patent Record F & B - 1640-1658

Henry Hooper, Robert Sedgrave, Thomas Davison, William Empson, Nicholas Russell, James Compton, Edward Tetersell.

He brought in 1638: Walter Morley, Richard Darcy, Charles (N) (Welshman).

Ferdinando Pulton demanded 260 a. for transporting 26 men in 1633: Henry Bishop, Thomas Heath, Lewis Fremond, Richard Thompson, Richard Luthead, William Ashmore, Robert Sherley, Benjamin Hodges, John Elkin, Richard Cole, Richard Nevill, John Marlburgh, Thomas Munns, Thomas Grigson, Robert Edwards, John Ward, William Edwin, John Price, Sr. (alias black John Price), John Price, Jr. (alias white John Price), Francis Rabnett, Thomas Smith, Richard Duke, Henry James, Thomas Harington, Robert Simpson, Matthias Sousa. 140 a. for 28 other men: John Hill, John Briant, James Thornton, Thomas Matthews, George White, Edward Cottam, John Machin, Robert Hedger, Phillip Spurr, Richard Cox, Walter King, Henry

f. 39 Hooper, Robert Sedgrave, Thomas Davison, Nicholas Russell, James Compton, Edward Tetersell, Richard Darcy, Charles (N) (Welshman), a smith who died at sea, John Smith (alias John Bettam), Luke Garnett, John Tue, William Empson, Frannsco Peres. Ferdinand Pulton further demanded 10100 a. for transporting 25 men in 1633 & 2000 a. for transporting 10 of aforesaid 28 men.

9 November. Warrant to Mr. Pulton in north point of St. Inego's Creek, bounding St. Peter's Key, St. George's River for 120 a. Warrant bounding St. Peter's Key, Key Swamp in St. George's River, land of Mr. Giles Brent for 25 a. Warrant in St. Maries' Hill, bounding Hill Creek, St. Inego's Creek for 255 a. Warrant on Patuxent River, bounding

f. 40 Chesapeake Bay, St. Steven's Creek, St. Lewis Creek for 4500 a. Warrant on Patuxent River, bounding St. Lawrence Creek, St. Vincent's Creek, & Island of St. Thomas for 1000 a. Warrant on Patuxent River, bounding St. Augustine's Creek, St. Monica's Branch, Back River, Morley's Marsh for 3600 a. Warrant on St. George's River, bounding St. Inego's Creek, Trinity Creek, Back Creek,

f. 41 St. Luke's Creek for 2000 a. Warrant for St. George's Island for 1000 a.

Mr. Thomas Green (gentleman) demanded land for transporting self & 2 servants in 1633: Anam Benam, Thomas Cooper. And 1 servant in 1634: Thomas Wills. And assignee of Mr. Nicholas Firfax & William Smith. Warrant to Mr. Thomas Green as assignee of Nicholas Ferfax & William Smith for 55 a. Signed: Leonard Calvert. Survey for Mr. Thomas Green bounding Mrs. Margarett & Mrs. Mary Brent, St. Maries' Forrest, St. Maries' Hill, St. Peter's Creek, St. George's River

f. 42 for 55 a. Date: 15 October 1639. Signed: John Lewger. Patent to Thomas Green (gentleman) for transporting 3 servants & assignee of Nicholas Ferfex (gentleman) & William Smith [metes & bounds].

f. 43 Thomas Gerrard (gentleman) demanded land for transporting 5 man servants in 1638 & 1639: John Longworth, Peter Heyward, Samuel Barrett, Thomas Knight, Robert Brasington.

30 October 1639. Warrant to Thomas Gerrard (gentleman) for 1000 a. on north side of Potomack River near St. Clement's Island. Survey for Thomas Gerrard (gentleman) for 950 a., bounding St. Clement's Island, Potowmeck River, St. Patrick's Creek, St. Catherine's Creek. Date: 2 November 1639. Signed: John Lewger. Patent for Thomas Gerrard (gentleman) for

f. 44 St. Clement's Manor.

f. 45 ...

f. 46 Warrant to William Lewis for 30 a. on east side of St. Andrew's Creek. Survey for William Lewis for 30 a. on north side of St. Inego's Creek, bounding St. Andrew's Creek, St. Maries' Hill, land of Robert Clerk. Date: 4 December 1640. Signed: John Lewger.

7 January 1639. Warrant to Giles Brent (gentleman) for 1000 a., about Kent Fort & 1000 a. more. Signed: Robert Clerk. Survey for Giles Brent for 1000 a. near Kent Fort, bounding Chesapeake Bay, Northwest Creek. 1 September 1640.

f. 47 Patent to Mr. Giles Brent for Manor of Kent Fort in Isle of Kent,

f. 48 saving right to Giles Basha and Thomas Allen. Date: 5 September 1640.

f. 49 21 January 1639. Ralph Beane assigned 50 a. on Gerrard's Creek & in occupation of John Hillierd

Liber - Patent Record F & B - 1640-1658

f. 50 & William Broughe to Thomas Gerrard (gentleman). Signed: John Lewger.

29 January 1639. Thomas Gerrard (gentleman) demanded 200 a. for transporting 2 man servants in 1639: Christopher Moreland, John Jones. Warrant to Thomas Gerrard (gentleman) for 200 a. on north side of Gerrard's Creek late in occupation of William Brough. Survey for Thomas Gerrard for 243 a. on north side of Gerrard's Creek. Called Gerrard's Freehold. Date: 21 April 1640.

29 January 1639. John Wortley demanded 100 a. Granted near head of Wickliff's Creek.

f. 51 Survey for John Wortley on west side of Wickliff's Creek. Date: 22 October 1640. Signed: John Lewger.

8 February 1639. John Lewger demanded 200 a. on assignment from Capt. Thomas Cornwaleys, Esq. & 100 a. & 2 manors. Mr. Lewger as assignee of Capt. Thomas Cornwaleys received 100 a. about St. John's, 200 a. on West's Swamp & St. John's Creek, & 2 manors not to exceed 3000 a. on Patowmeck River between Herring Creek & land of Mr. William Britton. Date: 12 February 1639.

f. 52 Warrant about St. John's Creek, bounding West's Valley, land of Phillip West (carpenter), St. John's Creek. Date: 18 February 1639. Patent for St. John's Freehold to John Lewger (gentleman) for transporting self, his wife, child & servants, including assignment from Thomas Cornwaleys, Esq., bounding

f. 53 West's Swamp, St. John's Brook.

25 February 1639. Warrant to Nathaniel Pope for 100 a. on north side of St. John's Creek, bounding Pope's Swamp.

f. 54 Survey for Nathaniel Pope for land on west side of St. Maries' Bay, on southwest side of St. John's Creek, bounding land of John Lewger, Esq., Pope's Swamp, St. John's Brook. Date: 26 February 1639. Patent to Nathaniel Pope for Pope's Freehold in St. Maries' Hundred.

f. 55 25 February 1639. Abel Snow (gentleman, of London) on assignment from Justinian Snow demanded land, bounding St. John's Creek, Mattapanient Path, St. George's River, Portobacks Quarter. Patent to Abel Snow for land about Snow Hill. Date: 27 February 1639. Signed: John Lewger.

f. 56 Justinian Snow (gentleman, late of St. Maries', dec'd) confirmed to Abel Snow (gentleman, brother to said Justinian, of Cursitor's Office in London) for land about Snow Hill in St. Maries' Hundred

f. 57 saving rights to Thomas Gerrard (gentleman) & Nathaniel Pope (planter)

f. 58 called Manor of Snow Hill.

f. 59 ...

f. 60 28 March 1640. Robert Perrie (gentleman) demanded 100 a. for transporting self on merchant Bonaventure in 1635, & assigned to John Dandie. Signed: Robert Percy.

21 July 1640. John Dandie assigned land to Phillip West. Signed: John Dandie.

f. 61 Robert Percy (gentleman) demanded 5 a. for transporting self in 1635, & assigned to Robert Clerk (gentleman).

29 March 1640. Richard Garnett, Sr. demanded 100 a. for transporting self in 1637. Richard Garnett demanded 1000 a. for transporting self, wife, & 4 children & 2 servants in 1637. Date: 4 December 1640. Warrant to Richard Garnett for 1000 a. of manor on south side of Patuxent River. Date: 5 December 1640. Survey for Richard Garnett for land on south side of Patuxent River, bounding St. Laurence's Creek, manor of St. Gregories, St. Steven's Creek. Date: 6 December 1640.

f. 62 31 March 1640. Richard Garnett demanded land for transporting in 1637: self, wife Elisabeth, son Richard (age 21), son John (age 4), man servant Elias Beach (age 23), daughter Elisabeth (age 19), daughter Julian (age 6), maid servant Mary Derrick (age 19). Patent for Manor of St. Richard's.

30 March 1640. Mr. Gerrard demanded 1000 a. for transporting 5 men in 1635: Oliver Gibbons, William Pinly, Henry Smith, Thomas White, Thomas Morris. Survey for Mr. Thomas Gerrard for 1000 a. north of St. Clement's manor, including St. Catharine's Island.

f. 63 Thomas Gerrard demanded land for transporting in 1640: John Gerrard, John

Liber - Patent Record F & B - 1640-1658

Taylor, John Shanks, Richard Wright, Richard Boreman, Richard Walker, Francis Sutton, Thomas Doe. Date: 13 November 1641.

3 April 1640. Owen Phillips (gentleman) demanded 100 a. for transporting self in 1638. Warrant to Owen Phillips (gentleman) for 100 a. Owen Phillips assigned 100 a. to Peter Draper. Date: 4 April 1640. Signed: John Lewger.

2 April 1640. Leonard Calvert, Esq. demanded 100 a. for transporting 1 man servant James Hockly in 1633 & assigned to Peter Draper. Peter Draper demanded 100 a. for transporting self in 1633 & 100 a. on assignment from

f. 64 Leonard Calvert, Esq. on assignment from Owen Phillips (gentleman). Peter Draper (gentleman) demanded 1300 a. on assignment from Leonard Calvert, Esq. & 100 a. in his own name & 100 a. on assignment from Owen Phillips. Date: 10 April 1643.

28 April 1640. Warrant to Randal Revell for 100 a. on Green's Point for transporting self in 1636. Survey for Randell Revell for 100 a. in Green's Point in manor of West St. Maries', bounding on St. George's River, Oyster Creek, Thomas Surgeon's Creek. Date: 17 October 1640. Signed: Robert Clarke. Patent for said land.

f. 65 Randall Revell surrendered the patent to use of Jane Cockshott (widow). Date: 29 November 1642.

Randall Revell demanded 100 a. for transporting his wife Rebecca, & 50 a. for transporting his son John since 1634 & 100 a. for transporting 1 man servant Richard Nevill in 1641 & 100 a. on assignment from Thomas Letherborow & assigned to Richard Nevill. Date: 27 July 1641. Survey for Randol Revell for 300 a. on south side of Breton's Bay, bounding Randoll's Marsh. Date: 14 December 1641.

6 May 1640. Mary Throughton (widow) demanded 50 a. for transporting self & 6 servants in 1638.

f. 66 Warrant for 50 a. on or about St. Barbara's. Survey for Mrs. Mary Throughton near St. Barbara's, bounding St. Barbara's Brook, Mattapanient Path,

f. 67 land of Capt. Thomas Cornwaleys, Esq. Date: 29 May 1640. Signed: John Lewger.

f. 68 Leonard Calvert assigned 750 a. to Mr. Britton. Date: 29 October 1639. William Britton (gentleman) demanded 550 a. for transporting self & wife & 1 child & 3 man servants & 200 a. due to Thomas Nabbs for transporting self & his wife, assigned to said William Britton by his marriage to Mary daughter & heir to said Thomas

f. 69 transported in 1637. Servants: John Mansell, Richard Harris, James Jelfe. Date: 28 October 1639. Survey for William Britton (gentleman) for 1 neck of land (750 a.) on Patomeck River near Heron Island, bounding Patomeck River, St. Clement's Bay, Brittaine Bay, St. Nicholas' Creek. Date: 29 June 1640. Signed: John Lewger. Patent to William Britton for Manor of Little Brittain.

f. 70 16 July 1640. William Britton demanded 25 a. for transporting self & 4 others. Said William Britton assigned to Robert Clerk. Date: 26 July 1640.

Mr. Lewger received on assignment from Capt. Thomas Cornwaleys 100 a. & 100 a. on warrant, bounding West's Swamp, St. John's Creek. Also 2 manors not to exceed 3000 a. Date: 12 February 1639.

f. 71 25 July 1640. Baltasar Codd demanded 5 a. for transporting self in 1638 & assigned to Robert Clerk. Robert Clerk demanded 5 a. for transporting self in 1637 & 25 a. on assignment from William Britton (gentleman) & 5 a. on assignment from Robert Percy & 10 a. on assignment from Thomas Pasmore & 5 a. on assignment from Baltasar Codd & 100 a. Date: 16 July 1640. Robert Clerk assigned 100 a. to Phillip West. Date: 21 July 1640. Patent to Robert Clerk for 50 a., bounding St. Andrew's Creek, land of William Lewis, St. Maries' Hill.

6 June 1640. 50 a. laid out on

f. 72 St. Peter's Key for John Harris & Thomas Allen. Thomas Allen assigned to John Harris. Date: 15 July 1640. Survey for John Harris for a neck of land on St. Peter's Key. [metes & bounds] Date: 15 July 1640. Signed: Robert Clerk. John Harris assigned to Roger Oliver (marriner). Date: 15 September. Signed: John Lewger. Patent to Roger Oliver (marriner).

24 July 1640. Thomas Pasmore demanded 60 a.

Liber - Patent Record F & B - 1640-1658

f. 73 for transporting 6 man servants in 1634 & 20 a. for transporting 4 other servants in 1635. 1634: Thomas Price, Richard Williams, Henry Baker, Henry Tailor. 1635: John Armesby, Bryan Kelley, Thomas Thomas, Ananias Read. Thomas Pasmore assigned 10 a. to Robert Clerke. Date: 26 July 1649.

20 March 1640. Thomas Pasmore demanded 100 a. for transporting 1 man servant Henry Baker in 1635, & assigned to Anthony Rawlins. Warrant to Anthony Rawlins for 50 a. on Fresh Creek. Date: 4 September 1641.

21 July 1640. Phillip West (carpenter) demanded 100 a. in right of Robert Percy & 100 a. in right of Robert Clerk. Warrant to Phillip West for 100 a. on assignment from Robert Percy & 100 a. on assignment from Robert Clerke near plantation of

f. 74 William Broughe & John Prettiman. Date: 22 July 1640. Survey for Phillip West for 200 a. on west side of St. George's River, bounding land of William Broughe & John Prettiman, Frog Marsh, Oyster Creek. Date: 30 July 1640. Signed: Robert Clerk. Patent to Phillip West as assignee of Robert Percy (gentleman) who transported self in 1635 & assignee of Robert Clerk (gentleman) who transported self in 1637.

f. 75 11 August 1640. Walter Broadhurst (gentleman) demanded 300 a. for transporting self in 1638 & 2 man servants: Oliver Gibbons, William Pinley. Said Walter Broadhurst assigned to Mr. Thomas Gerrard. Date: 18 July 1642.

7 September 1640. Mentions Capt. William Brainthwait as Commander of Isle of Kent.

Robert Huett & Henry Bellamy demanded a confirmation of land of Crany Neck. Warrant to Robert Huett & Henry Bellamy for Craney Neck in Isle of Kent. Date: 24 September 1640. Survey for Robert Huett & Henry Belamy

f. 76 for 400 a.--1 neck of land called Craney Neck, bounding Craney Creek, Chesapeake Bay, Crany Pond. Date: 25 September 1640. Patent to Robert Huett & Henry Bellamy in freehold of Crany Neck. Date: 26 September 1640.

7 September 1640. Edward Comins (planter, of Isle of Kent) assignee of Thomas Pett demanded confirmation of land from Capt. Clapborne.

f. 77 Warrant to Edward Comins for land by grant of Capt. Clapborne to Thomas Pett. Date: 24 September 1640. Signed: Robert Clerk. Survey for Edward Comins for 100 a. in Isle of Kent, bounding Merson Freehold, Cany Pond, Chesapeake Bay. Date: 25 September 1640. Patent for Edward Comins. Date: 26 September 1640.

Thomas Keyne demanded Hog Pen Neck. Warrant to Thomas Keyne

f. 78 for Hog Pen Neck. Date: 8 September 1640. Survey for Thomas Keyne for Hog Penn Neck for 400 a., bounding Thicketty Creek, Hogpen Creek, Chesapeak Bay. Date: 9 November 1640.

Robert Philpott (gentleman, of Isle of Kent) demanded land he holds of Capt. William Clayborne. Warrant to Robert Philpott for land of Capt. Clayborne. Date: 24 September 1640. Survey for Robert Philpott for 350 a. in Isle of Kent, bounding Richard Thompson, Pinie Bay, Chesapeak Bay, Philpott's Creek, Long Point Creek. Date: 25 September 1640. Patent to Mr. Philpott

f. 79 for 600 a. Date: 26 September 1640.

Phillip Conner (planter, of Isle of Kent) demanded 100 a for transporting self. Warrant to Phillip Conner for 200 a. Date: 24 September 1640. Survey for Phillip Conner for 100 a., bounding Broad Creek, Chesapeak Bay, Conner's Creek. Date: 25 September 1640. [Warrant for resurvey granted to John Wright. Liber GG:251] Patent to Phillip Conner. Date: 26 September 1640.

f. 80 John Gresham (planter, of Isle of Kent) demanded 100 a. for transporting self. Warrant to John Gresham for 100 a. Date: 24 September 1640.

William Medcalf & Thomas Yewell (planters, of Isle of Kent) demanded land called Mattax Neck from Capt. William Clayborne. Said William demanded 100 a. for transporting self. Said Thomas demanded 50 a. for his service to Capt. William Clayborne. Warrant to William Medcalf & Thomas Yewell for 150 a. on Mattax Neck & 150 a. on Hog Pen Neck. Date: 24 September 1640. Survey for William Medcalf & Thomas Yewell for land in Mattapax Neck, bounding

f. 81 Mattapax Creek, Medcalf's Branch, Cedar Branch, Goose Harbour for 130 a. 1 other neck in Hog Pen Neck, bounding Pinie Bay, Long Creek, New Ordinary Creek for 150 a. Date: 25 September 1640.

Liber - Patent Record F & B - 1640-1658

f. 82 Patent to William Medcalf & Thomas Yewell. Date: 26 September 1640.

Richard Thompson (planter, of Isle of Kent) demanded a manor of 1000 a. for transporting self & 4 man servants in 1636: John Lee, William Smith, Richard Beckley, John Cocke. And for transporting wife, child, maid servant Dousbell Gladdus, & 2 other man servants: John Thompson, Herbert Smith. Called Poplars Island due from Capt. William Cleyborne. "Whereon he inhabited till in the year 1637, they were massacred by the Indians." Warrant to Richard Thompson (planter, of Isle of Kent) for a manor of 1000 a. due from Capt. Cleyborne. Date: 24 September 1640.

f. 83 [Restatement of warrant to Richard Thompson. Date: 6 November 1640.] Survey for Richard Thompson for 1000 a. called Popeler's Island & 430 a., bounding Manor of Kent Fort, Thompson's Marsh, Hog Creek, Chesapeak Bay, Howard's Creek. Date: 6 November 1640. Signed: John Lavger.

f. 84 Richard Purlivant demanded 100 a. for transporting self. Warrant to Richard Purlivant for 100 a. on Hog Pen Neck. Date: 24 September 1640. Survey for Richard Purlivant for 100 a. on Hog Penn Neck, bounding Hog Pen Creek, Thicketty Creek, Chesapeak Bay. Date: 25 September 1640. Patent to Richard Purlivant. Date: 26 September 1640.

f. 85 Thomas Hales (planter, of Isle of Kent) demanded land on grant of Capt. William Clayborne. Warrant to Thomas Hales. Date: 24 September 1640. Survey for Thomas Hales for 50 a., bounding Cedar Branch, Phillpott's Creek, Pinie Bay. Date: 25 September 1640. Patent to Thomas Hales for 50 a. Date: 26 September 1640.

William Brainthwaite (Commander of Isle of Kent) guardian of Katharine Smith (infant & heir of Henry Crawley (of Broad Creek, dec'd)) demanded plantation at Broad Creek

f. 86 whereas the said Henry Crawley was assignee of William Blizard who held it from Capt. William Clayborne. Warrant to Catharine Smith (infant of John Smith) for plantation of Broad Creek. Date: 24 September 1640. Survey for Katherine Smith for 250 a., bounding Katherine's Creek, Little Creek, Broad Creek. Date: 25 September 1640. Patent to Katherine Smith. Date: 26 September 1640.

John Smith (planter, of Isle of Kent) demanded 50 a. at Crayford that he holds. Warrant to John Smith. Date: 24 September 1640.

f. 87 Thomas Butler (planter, of Isle of Kent) demanded 600 a. for transporting self, his wife, 2 children, & 3 man servants: Charles Steward, Xpofer Thomas, Richard Smith. Warrant to Thomas Butler for 600 a. Date: 24 September 1640.

Thomas Butler demanded confirmation of his land. Warrant to Thomas Butler for land he has. Date: 24 September 1640. Survey for Thomas Butler for 50 a. on Isle of Kent, bounding Butler's Creek, Jones' Branch, Butler's Marsh, Cox's Bay. Date: 15 November 1640.

f. 88 Giles Basha (planter, of Isle of Kent) demanded a manor of 1100 a. for transporting self & 5 man servants: William Boate, William Wolfe, Walter Cottalls, Michael Scott, James Johnson. Warrant to Giles Basha for 1100 a. Date: 24 September 1640.

Giles Basha demanded confirmation of Peares Plantation. Warrant. Date: 9 December. Survey, Patent.

Robert Short demanded confirmation of Merson Freehold from Capt. Clayborne. Warrant to Robert Short for 50 a. called Merson Freehold. Date: 8 September 1640.

f. 89 Survey for Robert Short for 50 a. called Merson Freehold on Isle of Kent, bounding Merson Pond, [metes & bounds], land of Edward Comins, Chesapeak Bay.

Richard Purlivant (barber, chirurgeon) demanded 200 a. for transporting self. Warrant to Richard Purlivant for 200 a. Date: 8 September 1640. Survey for Richard Purlivant for 80 a. on Isle of Kent, bounding Beaver Neck Creek, [metes & bounds], Cane's Bite. Date: 5 November 1640.

f. 90 6 November 1640. John Abotts (planter, of Isle of Kent) demanded confirmation of 50 a. Warrant to John Abotts for 50 a. Date: 7 November 1640. Survey for John Abotts for 40 a., bounding Beaver Neck Creek, Andrew Basha, Abotts Swamp, John Abbott. Date: 8 November 1640.

f. 91 7 September 1640. Andrew Basha & James Cloughton demanded confirmation of 100 a. that they hold. Warrant to Andrew Basha & James Cloughton for 100 a. on west side of Isle of Kent. Date: 8 September 1640. Survey for Andrew Basha &

Liber - Patent Record F & B - 1640-1658

James Cloughton for 100 a. on west side of Isle of Kent on Beaver Neck Creek, bounding [metes & bounds], Abott's Swamp, Chesapeak Bay. Date: 6 November 1640.

7 December 1640. Robert Cooper demanded confirmation of his plantation. Warrant to Robert Cooper for his plantation. Date: 8 December 1640. Survey for Robert Cooper for land on west side of Isle of Kent, bounding Chesapeak Bay,

f. 92 Andrew Basha & James Cloughton, said Robert's land, Beaver Neck for 80 a. Date: 9 December 1640.

Capt. John Butler demanded confirmation of land he holds of Capt. Clayborne. Warrant to Capt. John Butler for land. Date: 8 December 1640. Survey for Capt. John Butler for 200 a., bounding Beaver Neck Creek, Chesapeak Bay, Thicketty Creek. Date: 9 December 1640. Said patent to John Abbott. Date: 25 September 1644.

7 September 1640. Thomas Allen demanded confirmation of land by grant of Capt. Clayborne.

f. 93 Warrant to Thomas Allen for land he holds. Date: 8 September 1640. Survey for Thomas Allen for 66 a. on south side of Northwest Creek, bounding Chesapeak Bay, Allen's Branch. Date: 9 December 1640.

Giles Basha demanded 100 a. for transporting self & demanded confirmation of Little Thickett which he has by grant from Capt. Clayborne. Warrant to Giles Basha for 200 a. Little Thickett on north side of Northwest Creek, bounding Hog Pen Creek, Chesapeak Bay, St. Giles' Branch, mannor of Kent Fort. Date: 8 September 1640.

f. 94 Survey for Giles Basha for Little Thickett for 200 a. Date: 9 December 1640.

William Cox demanded confirmation of land he holds. Memorandum: Gresham, Cox, Browne, Adams, Jo. Smith Burbage, Mr. Branthwait. Survey for William Cox for Cox's Neck bounding Blunt Point Creek, Hennes Bite, Chesapeak Bay, Cox His Bay for 1000 a. Date: 9 December. [Note: vide Patt. confir to Capt. Vaughan. Liber GG:419.]

3 April. Thomas Petts demanded confirmation of land he holds. Survey for Thomas Petts for land on east side of Isle of Kent, bounding Petts Branch, Butler's Creek, Alder Swamp for 100 a.

f. 95 Francis Brookes (of Kent) demanded patent of said land of Thomas Petts. Affirmed by Thomas Petts. Date: 12 February 1644.

5 March 1640. Thomas Adams (gentleman) demanded a manor of 1000 a. for transporting 5 servants since 1635: Henry Morgan, Edward Williams, John Phillips, Tho. Prosser, Walter Read. Warrant to Thomas Adams (gentleman) for mannor of 1000 a. on Purson's Point in Isle of Kent, called Prior's Mannor. Survey for Mr. Thomas Adams for Prior's Mannor on east side of Kent, bounding Prior's Creek, Chesapeak Bay, Adam's Bite.

25 September 1640.

f. 96 Thomas Cornwaleys, Esq. by his attorney Cutbeard Fenwick (gentleman) demanded confirmation of 2000 a. on west side of St. George's River granted to Capt. Henry Fleete on 9 May 1634 & sold to said Thomas. Mentioned: William Fitters, John Robinson (carpenter), Richard Lowe, Mich. Lucas, John Holdern. Warrant to Thomas Cornwaleys, Esq. for 2000 a. on west side of St. George's River called Mannor of West St. Maries', as assignee of Capt. Henry Fleet. Signed: Leonard Calvert. Survey for Thomas Cornwaleys, Esq. for 2000 a. on west side of St. George's River, bounding

f. 97 Wickliff's Creek, Oyster Creek, Phillip West. Date: 26 September 1640. Signed: John Lewger.

1 October 1640. Deed of 9 May 1634 to Capt. Henry Fleete for 4000 a. called Mannor of West St. Maries'.

Patent for 4000 a.

f. 98 sold to Thomas Cornwaleys except freeholds granted to Phillip West, John Robinson, Nicholas Cossin, Edward Parker, Randoll Revell. Date: 10 November 1640. Patent surrendered to Lord Proprietary by Thomas Cornwaleys. Date: 17 October 1640.

Liber - Patent Record F & B - 1640-1658

17 October 1640. Hutton Corbett demanded 100 a. as assignee of Thomas Stent who transported himself in 1636.

f. 99 Warrant to Hutton Corbett as assignee of Thomas Stent for 100 a. Survey for Hutton Corbett for 100 a. on west side of Wickliff's Creek, bounding David Wickliff, Hutton's Bite, [metes & bounds], Beane's Creek. Date: 22 October 1640.

9 October 1640. Robert Vaughan demanded 50 a. Robert Vaughan assigned to George Pye. Date: 12 October. Warrant to George Pye as assignee of Robert Vaughan for 50 a. Date: 9 November 1640.

f. 100 Survey for George Pye for 50 a. on west side of Wickliff's Creek, bounding Isaac's Creek, [metes & bounds], David's Well. Date: 12 November 1640. Patent to George Pye. Pye assigned to Thomas Weston who surrendered patent to Lord Proprietary. Date: 13 November 1640. George Pye demanded 100 a. for transporting self in 1637. Date: 24 January 1642.

4 October 1640. Thomas Charinton demanded 50 a. at appointment of Lieutenant General in 1636. Said Thomas Charinton assigned to Nicholas Cossin (Frenchman).

f. 101 Warrant to Nicholas Cossin for 50 a. in land formerly possessed by Thomas Charinton excepted from grant of Capt. Cornwaleys. Date: 6 October 1640. Survey for Nicholas Cossin (Frenchman) for 50 a. on east side of Wickliff's Creek, bounding Cossin's Bite, [metes & bounds], Charinton's Marsh. Date: 27 October 1640. Patent that Thomas Charinton (planter) in 1636 assigned land to Nicholas Cossin (Frenchman).

f. 102 15 June 1640. Edward Packer & William Nanfin demanded 100 a. for transporting self in 1637. Warrant to Edward Packer & William Nanfin for 100 a. Date: 4 October 1640. Survey for Edward Packer & William Nanfin for 100 a. on east side of Wickliff's Creek, bounding Packer's Bite, [metes & bounds], Winter's Creek. Date: 23 October 1640.

f. 103 9 October 1640. David Wickliff demanded 50 a. for transporting self in 1636. Warrant to David Wickliff for 50 a. on west side of Wickliff's Creek, bounding George Pye, Hutton Corbett. Date: 13 November 1640.

15 June 1640. Leonard Calvert, Esq. demanded 100 a. for transporting 1 servant. Said Leonard Calvert assigned to John Robinson (barber, chirurgeon). Warrant to John Robinson (barber, chirurgeon) for 100 a. Date: 16 June 1640.

f. 104 Survey for John Robinson (barber) for 100 a. near Wickliff's Creek, bounding [metes & bounds], Packer's Bite. Date: 22 October 1640.

20 October 1640. Henry Lee demanded 50 a.

f. 105 for transporting self in 1636. Warrant to Henry Lee for 50 a. Date: 3 December 1640. Survey for Henry Lee for 50 a. on west side of Wickliff's Creek, bounding The Hollow, [metes & bounds], Lee's Bite. Date: 4 December 1640.

10 February 1640. Thomas Hebden demanded 200 a. for transporting self in 1635 & his wife in 1640. Survey for Thomas Hebden for 200 a. on land he holds.

f. 106 4 February 1641. Thomas Hebden demanded 1000 a. on assignment from Mr. James Neale. Survey for Thomas Hebden (planter) for 1000 a. on west side of St. George's River, bounding Hebden's Hole, St. John's Creek, St. George's Creek, Weston's Creek, David's Well, Wickliff's Creek. Survey for Thomas Hebden (planter) for 700 a. on west side of St. George's River, bounding St. George's Creek, Beane's Creek.

f. 107 20 October 1640. Isaac Edwards demanded 100 a. for transporting self in 1637. Warrant to Isaac Edwards for 50 a. Date: 3 December 1640. Survey for Isaac Edwards for 50 a. on west side of Wickliff's Creek, bounding Henry Lee, Lee's Bite, [metes & bounds], Isaac's Creek. Date: 4 December 1640.

15 December 1640. Warrant to Mr. Secretary for 1000 a. on neck where town of New Patuxent stood.

f. 108 Survey for Mr. Secretary for 1000 a. where town of New Patuxent stood, on south side of Patuxent River, bounding St. Vincent's Bay, St. Vincent's River, St. Anne's Creek, Point Anne. Date: 18 December 1640. Patent to Secretary John Lewger (gentleman) for land called St. Ann's. Date: 19 December 1640. Patent surrendered by the Secretary. Date: 10 December 1642.

Liber - Patent Record F & B - 1640-1658

28 December. Jo. Harrington demanded 100 a. for transporting self in 1635.

Patent for plantation of Snow Hill for 1000 a. between St. John's Creek & Gerrard's Creek

f. 109 to Abel Snow (gentleman, of Cursitor's Office in Chancery Lane, London) called Mannor of Snow Hill. Abell Snow (gentleman, of Cursitor's Office, London) by his attorney Thomas Gerrard demanded 1000 a. Date: 9 February 1640. Warrant to Abel Snow (gentleman) for mannor of 1000 a. between St. John's Creek & Gerrard's Creek. Date: 10 February 1640. Survey for Abel Snow (gentleman) for land between St. John's Freehold & St. Maries' Bay, including Nath. Pope, St. George's River, Conception Mannor, freehold of

f. 110 Pork Hall for 1000 a. Patent to Abel Snow for Mannor of Snow Hill.

2 June 1639. Thomas Cornwaleys, Esq. demanded 4000 a. for transporting in 1633 10 man servants (as 2 mannors of 2000 a. each at St. Inego's): Thomas Beckworth, Matthew Burrowes, Samuel (N) that was brought from St. Xpofer's, Cutberd Fenwick, Richard Lee, William Fitter, John Robinson (carp.), William Browne, Stephen Gore, Stephen Sammion (?). Survey for Capt. Thomas Cornwaleys for 1 mannor of Cornwaleys Cross, bounding St. Inigo's Mannor, Trinity Creek,

f. 111 Back Creek, Governor's Creek for 2000 a. Survey for another mannor adjoining afsd. mannor on east, bounding Governor's Creek, St. Inigo's Creek for 2000 a. Date: 8 September 1639. Patent for Cornwaleys Cross & St. Elisabeth's.

Giles Basha demanded confirmation of plantation Peare's Plantation conveyed from John Peare (of Isle of Kent). Survey for Giles Basha for Peare's Plantation, bounding Oyster Creek, Chesapeak Bay, Basha' Branch for 75 a.

f. 112 Patent for land of John Peare to Giles Basha, to be holden of Mannor of Kent Fort in occupation of Giles Brent (gentleman).

Thomas Stent demanded confirmation of his land. Survey for Stent's Branch, Butter's Marsh, Cox's Bay.

19 June 1641. James Neale (planter) demanded 1000 a. for transporting self & 5 servants suite 1635: John Courte, Francis Pope, James Langworth, William King, Thomas Demar. Warrant to James Neale (gentleman) for 300 a. on west side of St.

f. 113 Catherine's Creek near St. Clement's Mannor, including St. Martha's Island & 700 a. on west side of Wighcocomaco Bay. James Neale, assigned his 1000 a. to Thomas Hebden. Date: 4 February 1641. Warrant to Thomas Hebden for 1000 a.

29 October 1642. James Neale (gentleman) demanded 2000 a. Survey for James Neale (gentleman) for 2000 a. on north side of Patowmeck River, bounding Wicocomoko River, St. Raphael's Creek, St. James' Creek.

15 July 1642. Robert Vaughan demanded 100 a. for transporting 2 women servants: Frances Brook, Mary Ford.

Grant for 2000 a.

f. 114 to James Neale (gentleman). Patent to James Neale (gentleman) for land
f. 115 called Wollaston Mannor. Date: 31 October 1642.

27 July 1641. Thomas Copley, Esq. demanded 400 a. for transporting 26 men in 1633 & another 28 men since. In demand of Ferdinando Pulton. Said Thomas also demanded 3000 a. Said Thomas assigned his right to Cutbert Fenwick (gentleman). Warrant to Cutbert Fenwick for 400 a. of town land & 4000 a. Survey for Cutbert Fenwick (gentleman) for town land near chappell at St. Maries', bounding St. Peter's freehold, Mr. Giles Brent (gentleman), Key Swamp,

f. 116 for 25 a. Also town land on north point of St. Inigo's Creek, bounding St. Peter's Key, St. George's River, Marrill's Point for 120 a. Also town land about St. Maries' Hill, bounding Hill Creek, St. Inigo's Creek, [metes & bounds] for 255 a. Also a mannor on east side of St. George's, bounding St. Inigo's Creek, Trinity Creek, Back Creek,

f. 117 St. Luke's Creek, Cornwaleys Cross for 2000 a. Also, an island on west side of St. George's River called St. George's Island for 1000 a.

Thomas Copley, Esq. assigned his right to Cutbert Fenwick (gentleman) for 400 a. of town land. Said Thomas Copley, Esq. transported 26 men in 1633 & granted 3000 a. in 2 parcels as neck of 2000 a. & island of St. George's as mannor called St. Inigo's to said Cutbert. Fenwick.

Liber - Patent Record F & B - 1640-1658

f. 118 2 August 1641. Thomas Copley, Esq. demanded 400 a. for transporting 4 men in 1633. Said Thomas assigned to John Lewger. Survey for John Lewger for 400 a., bounding Piscattaway Creek, Lyon of Jude, East Marsh.

4 August 1641. Richard Hills (planter) demanded 50 a. on assignment from Leonard Calvert, Esq. Survey for Richard Hills for land near New Towne Marsh, bounding William Thomson, Dixon's Hollow

f. 119 for 50 a. Date: 14 December 1641. Note: included in grant to John Medley for Medley.

6 August 1641. Richard Loe (planter) demanded 100 a. for transporting self in 1640.

9 August 1641. James Johnson demanded 100 a. for transporting self. Warrant to James Johnson for 100 a.

f. 120 on St. George's Creek at Beane's Point. Date: 7 October 1641. Survey for James Johnson for 100 a. on Beane's Point, bounding St. John's Creek, St. George's Creek, Johnson's Bite, James' Marsh. Date: 23 October 1641.

20 August 1641. Richard Nevill demanded 50 a. on assignment from Randoll Revell & 50 a. on assignment from John Medley. Warrant to Richard Nevill for 50 a. Survey for Richard Nevill for 100 a. on Medley's Branch, bounding [metes & bounds], Richard's Branch, Nevett's Creek. Date: 10 December 1641.

f. 121 13 August 1641. Leonard Calvert, Esq. demanded 6000 a. for transporting 15 men in 1633 & 100 a. of town land: Peter Draper, Robert Pike, James Hockley, Richard Gilbert, John Ashmore, Thomas Allen, Charles Middleton, John Halfhead, Evan Watkins, Richard Hills, John Nevill, Lodowick Price. Survey for Leonard Calvert, Esq. for 100 a. of town land nearest Governor's Field, bounding St. George's River, St. Maries' Bay, Mill Brooke, freehold of St. Peter's, chappell land. Also land, bounding Trinity Bay, Norton's Creek, Cauther's Creek, James' Creek,

f. 122 Deep Creek, Chesapeak Bay, Patowmeck River for 3000 a., subdivided in 3 mannors:
1. Trinity Mannor, bounding Trinity Bay, Norton's Creek, James' Branch, Broad Creek, Patowmeck River for 600 a.
2. St. Gabriel's Mannor, bounding Trinity Mannor, James' Branch, Deep Creek, Oister Creek, Patowmeck River for 900 a.
3. St. Michael's Mannor, bounding St. Gabriel's Mannor, Patowmeck River, Chesapeak Bay, St. Michael's Point for 1500 a.

f. 123 24 January 1642. William Broughe demanded 100 a. for transporting self in 1636 & 100 a. for transporting 1 man servant in 1638: Francis Thwaite. Warrant to William Broughe for 100 a. in Brittain's Bay. Survey for William Broughe for 200 a. in Poplar Neck, bounding Britton's Bay, Poplar Creek, Broughe's Branch, [metes & bounds]. Date: 25 November 1642.

f. 124 14 August 1641. William Tompson demanded 200 a. John Medley demanded 200 a. for transporting 2 men in 1637: Richard Brook, James Moulins. John Medley assigned 50 a. of above to Richard Nevett. Date: 10 December 1641. Survey for John Medley for 100 a. in Pacocomicok Point, bounding Pacocomicok Creek, Medley's Branch, Medlies' Hollow, Patowmeck River. Also 50 a. near head of Nevett's Creek, bounding Indian Hollow, [metes & bounds] Richard's Hollow, Nevett's Creek. Date: 14 December 1641.

25 August 1641. William Hawkins demanded 200 a. for transporting self & his wife in 1640.

f. 125 Said William Hawkins assigned his 200 a. to Thomas Bushell. Date: 24 January 1641. Said Thomas Bushell assigned his right to John Lewger (gentleman). Date: 16 April. Said John Lewger re-assigned the 200 a. to Thomas Bushell.

25 August 1641. Richard Dixon demanded 100 a. for transporting self in 1640. Said Robert Dixon [sic] assigned his right to William Thomson. Date: 1 December 1643.

25 August 1641. Thomas Leatherborow demanded 100 a. for transporting self in 1638. Said Thomas assigned his right to Randoll Revell.

John Lewger demanded 400 a. for transporting 4 man servants: Alexius Pulton, John Askew, William Stiles, Bartholomew Slater.

18 October 1641. Cyprian Thorowgood demanded 100 a. for transporting self.

Liber - Patent Record F & B - 1640-1658

24 January 1641. Richard Banks & William Wright demanded 200 a. for transporting selves. Warrant to Richard Banks & William Wright for 200 a. in Poplar Neck, between Herring Creek & New Town. Survey for Richard Banks & William Wright for land on north side

f. 126 of Patowmeck River called Popler Hill, bounding Popler Creek, Wright's Fresh, Bank's Branch for 200 a.

10 November 1641. Thomas Bushell demanded 100 a. for transporting self in 1640 & 200 a. by assignment from William Howkins. Warrant to Thomas Bushell for 100 a. on neck called Mepatiston on east side of St. George's Creek. Warrant to Thomas Bushell for 300 a. on Brittaine's Bay. Date: 24 January 1641. Survey for Thomas Bushell for 100 a. on south side of Bretton's Bay, bounding Blount Point, Lee's Creek. Date: 24 January 1642.

f. 127 Said Thomas Bushell assigned his interest in said land to Henry Lee.

4 November 1641. John Lewger demanded 100 a. for transporting John Hatch. Said John Lewger assigned his right to John Hatch & John Thompson. Survey for John Hatch & John Thompson for 100 a. on west side of St. Clement's Bay, bounding Thompson's Hollow, Hathe's Creek. Date: 7 February 1642.

William Hull (marriner) demanded 100 a. for transporting self. Warrant to William Hull for 100 a. on any point on St. George's Creek. Date: 19 March 1641.

f. 128 11 December 1641. Thomas Gerrard (gentleman) demanded 4000 a. for transporting self & 20 men in 1637, 1638, 1640: John Longworth, Peter Heyward, Samuel Barratt, Thomas Knight, Robert Brasinton, Richard Scotsford, John Ashton, Oliver Gibbons, William Pinley, Henry Smith, Thomas White, Thomas Morris, John Gerrard, John Taylor, John Shanks, Richard Wright, Richard Boreman, Richard Walker, Francis Sutton, Thomas Doe. And 2000 a. on assignment from Mr. John Lewger. Survey for Thomas Gerrard (gentleman) for land, bounding Patowmeck River, Wicocomoco River, St. Clement's Bay, Gerrard's Creek, Fresh Creek. Also St. Clement's Island in Patowmeck River, St. Catherine's Island at mouth of St. Catherine's Bay, St. Margarett's Island near mouth of Wicocomoco River. Total of 6000 a. Patent for transporting 20 men & on assignment of 2000 a. from Mr. John Lewger, Esq., saving to John Hatch, & John Thomson the 100

f. 129 a. they possess, to Thomas Gerrard called St. Clement's Mannor.

10 December 1641. John Lewger demanded 2000 a., & assigned his right to Mr. Gerrard.

4 February 1641. Richard Cole demanded 50 a. on assignment from Mr. Thomas Coply & 50 a. on assignment from Walter Beane. Thomas Copley certifies that he transported Richard Cole & assigned 50 a. to him.

13 December 1641. Marks Pheipo & Nicholas Keytin (Irishmen) demanded 200 a. for transporting selves.

17 December 1641. Nicholas Hervey demanded a mannor of 2000 a. on south side of Patuxent River for transporting self, his wife, & five others: 3 man servants: Richard Beard,

f. 130 Henry Spink, John Chair. 1 boy: Robert Ford. his daughter Frances Hervey. Patent to Nicholas Hervey for mannor of 1000 a. next to St. Richard's Mannor. Date: 17 December 1641. Warrant to Nicholas Hervey (planter) for 1000 a. on south side of Patuxent River, bounding St. Laurence Creek, Back River, Patuxent River, path of Patuxent, St. Francis' Branch. Patent to Nicholas Hervey who transported self, his wife, 5 other person in 1641. Date: 2 December 1642.

28 December 1641. John Robinson (carpenter) demanded 200 a. for transporting 2 man servants: Richard Baxter, John Michell. John Hatch demanded 50 a. on assignment from John Lewger Secretary.

f. 131 4 February 1641. Walter Beane demanded 200 a. for transporting self & 1 man servant: John Cole. Said Walter assigned his interest to Richard Cole. Warrant to Walter Beane for 150 a. on St. George's Creek.

12 January 1641. Giles Brent (gentleman) demanded 1000 a. on assignment from Leonard Calvert, Esq.

18 March 1643. Warrant to Nicholas Hervey for 1000 a. on south side of St. Jerome's Creek's mouth.

f. 132 12 February 1641. Thomas Pursall demanded 200 a. for transporting self & 1 man

Liber - Patent Record F & B - 1640-1658

servant: James Linch. Warrant to Thomas Pursall for 200 a. about Herring Creek.

<u>19 March</u>. John Rutlidge demanded 100 a. for transporting self in 1640. Warrant to John Rutlidge for 100 a. on St. George's Creek.

Appointment to William Brainthwait as Commander of Isle of Kent. Date: 22 October 1638.

f. 133 <u>2 November 1638</u>. William Lewis (planter) contracted to marry Ursula Gifford.

<u>23 November 1638</u>. Robert Smith (gentleman) contracted to marry Rose Gilbert.

f. 134 <u>24 November</u>. Roger Moy (planter) contracted to marry Ann Phillipso.

<u>26 November</u>. Francis Gray (carpenter) contracted to marry Alice Moreman. Signed: Francis Graye.

Appointment on 22 October 1638 of my kinsman William Brainthwait (gentleman) as commander of Isle of Kent. Signed Leonard Calvert, Esq.

f. 135 Certificate to John Harrington

f. 136 to arrest persons unlawfully trading with Indians. Date: 6 March 1638.

Certificate to Cutbert Fenwick (gentleman) & John Hollis (marriner) to arrest persons unlawfully trading with Indians.

f. 137 <u>14 March 1638</u>. Commission to Andrew Chappell & Thomas Morris to trade with Indians.

<u>13 April</u>. Certificate to Thomas Boys to arrest persons unlawfully trading with Indians.

<u>23 May 1639</u>. James Courtney (planter) contracted to marry Mary Lawne.

Commission to Giles Brent, Esq. as Captain.

f. 138 <u>1 June 1639</u>. John Hollis contracted to marry Restituta Tue. Signed: John Hallowes.

<u>2 June 1639</u>. Cutbert Fenwick & Robert Perry witnessed

f. 139 the marriage of John Hollis & Restituta by Mr. Thomas White.

Notice to examine Anne Moy wife of Roger Moy (planter).

Certificate to Andrew Chappell to trade with Indians. Date: 11 June 1639.

Certificate to Nicholas Hervey to act against Maquantequat Indians,

f. 140 to go to town of Aquascack in Patuxent River regarding killing of men of boat of Andrew Cotton. Date: 3 January 1639.

Commission of Capt. Giles Brent, Esq. as commander of Isle of Kent,

f. 141 to be assisted by William Brainthwait (gentleman), Capt. John Boteler, Thomas Adams (gentleman) inhabitants of said Island. Date: 3 February 1639.

f. 142 Commission to John Robinson as constable of St. Clement's Hundred, consisting of St. Clement's Isle & land between Herring Creek & St. Catherine's Creek. Date: 16 March 1639.

Note to Thomas Gerrard (gentleman). Land of St. Clement's Isle & Heron Isle & land on north bank of Patowmeck River between Herring Creek & St. Catherine's Creek as St. Clement's Hundred.

f. 143 <u>20 March 1639</u>. Certificate to William Brainthwait to trade with Indians.

<u>30 April 1640</u>. John Robinson, (constable of St. Clement's Hundred) appointed as coroner.

f. 144 Certificate to Thomas Games (also Thomas James, marriner) to trade with Indians. Date: 5 May 1640.

Certificate to Henry Bishop

f. 145 to arrest persons unlawfully trading with Indians. Date: 13 July 1643.

Page 15

Liber - Patent Record F & B - 1640-1658

f. 146 16 November 1640. William Brough & John Wortley brought before Lt. Robert Vaughan & appointed viewers.

Thomas Adams (gentleman, of Isle of Kent) pardonned.

f. 147 8 April 1641. Cyprian Thoroughgood (gentleman) appointed high sheriff of St. Maries' Co. Oath by said Cyprian. Signed: Cy. Thorowgood.

8 May 1641. Notice to Giles Brent (gentleman) as commander of Isle of Kent regarding cause between Thomas Bradnock & Henry Bellamy.

f. 148 Leonard Calvert, Esq. Lt. General to go to VA, appoints Capt. Thomas Cornwaleys, Esq. as Lt. General.

24 June 1641. Richard Thompson (also Richard Thomson, of Isle of Kent) contracted to marry Ursula Bish.

f. 149 16 October 1641. John Orms contracted to marry Frances Griffin.

f. 150 28 June 1642. Francis Stour contracted to marry Deborah Paulus.

24 March 1641. John Langford (gentleman) appointed Surveyor General.

f. 151 Petitions in 1641 before Leonard Calvert, Esq., John Lewger Secretary, et. al., by: John Lewger, Esq., Capt. Thomas Cornwaleys, Esq., Thomas Copley, Esq., Cutbert Fenwick (gentleman) & John Hallowes (marriner), John Robinson (barber chirurgeon), William Asiter (tailor), Robert Nicholls (victualler), Thomas Tidd, Mrs. Margaret Brent, Thomas Tidd servant to said Mrs. Margaret Brent, Thomas Pasmore (carpenter), Thomas Baldridge (planter), William Broughe (planter), Thomas Morris (chirurgeon), Christopher Martin, Joseph Edloe administrator of Christopher Martin (tailor)

f. 152 & Ann Smithson (widow) vs. Bryan Kelley, Baltasar Codd & Cornelius OSulivt. (planters, Irishmen of St. Maries').

f. 153 23 June 1642. Robert Evelin appointed to command English at Piscataway.

f. 154 William Blount appointed Captain of St. Maries' Co.

f. 155 2 July 1642. William Macfenin appointed serjeant of St. Maries' & St. George's Hundreds.

16 July 1642. Simon Demibel or Henry Bishop to hear complaints.

f. 156 2 August 1642. Commission to Mr. Giles Brent as commander of Isle of Kent & William Luddington & Mr. Richard Thomson to be joined with him.

f. 157 18 August 1642. Commission to Capt. Cornwaleys for action against enemies.

f. 158 23 August 1642. Letter to Governor of VA regarding massacre of John Angood & 4 others. Presented by Col. Trafford for aid on Isle of Kent. Cites revenge on Nanticoque Indians for death of Rowland Williams of Accomack.

f. 159 25 August 1642. Letter to Henry Bishop.

f. 160 28 August 1642. Notice for arming of St. Michael's Hundred, to house of Thomas Steerman & Lt. Thomas Baldridge to be in charge. St. George's Hundred, to house of Mr. Weston, defensible by George Pye (late burgess).

f. 161 ...

f. 162 8 January 1648. Thomas Gerrard, Esq. & Walter Brodhurst to discharge William Empson.

25 January 1650. Francis Martin sold chattel to Marke Blomefield. Witness: John Sturman.

Notice for my brother Capt. William Hawley,

f. 163 cites brother Jerome, brother Henry. Signed: Ja. Hawley. Date: 20 July 1649. Came James Hawley, Esq. (of New Branford, Middlesex). Jerome Hawley, Esq. (of London) acknowledged before Sir John Finch (Lord Chief Justice of Common Pleas) bound to said James Hawley

f. 164 money, citing note between said James & afsd Jerome Hawley. William Hawley (gentleman, of VA) to be attorney.

f. 165 Date: 18 July 1649. Signed: Ja. Hawley. Witnesses: Henry Hawley, Stephen

Liber - Patent Record F & B - 1640-1658

Bolton, Thomas Leigh.

Persons arriving 30 June 1650 by Robert Brook, Esq.: Robert Brooke, Mary his wife, his children: Baker Brooke, Thomas Brooke, Charles Brooke, Roger Brooke, Robert Brooke, John Brooke, William Brooke, Francis Brooke, Mary Brooke, Anna Brooke.

f. 166 Man servants: Marke Lovesay, Marke King, William Jones, James Leigh, John Chifford, Benjamin Hammond, Robert Sheale, William Bradney, Phillip Harwood, Thomas Joyce, Henry Peere, Thomas Elstone, Edward Cooke, Ambrose Biggs, Richard Robinson, Anthony Kitchin, Robert Hooper, William Hinson, John Barock, David Bowen, Henry Robinson. Maid servants: Ann Marshall, Katherine Fisher, Elisabeth Williamson, Margarett Watts, Abigael Mountague, Eleanor Williams, Agnes Neale.

22 July. Robert Brooke, Esq. & his 2 sons Baker Brooke & Thomas Brooke took oath of fidelity. Robert Brook, Esq. & Mr. William Eltonhead took oath of counsellors.

16 August 1650. Thomas Copley, Esq. demanded land for transporting in 1633: Mr. Andrew White, Mr. Jo. Altain, Thomas Statham, Robert Simpson, Mary Jennings, Henry Bishop, Richard Lusted, Thomas Heath, William Ashmore, Robert Sherley, Jo. Hilliard, Mathias Zause, Fra. Molita, Lewis Freman, James (N) (killed at Mattaponie). In 1634: Mr. Francis Rogers, John Hill, Richard Harvey, Xpofer Carnoll, John Bryant. Thomas Copley, Esq. demanded 20,000 a. Certain names delivered by Thomas Copley, Esq. were servants of Mr. Andrew White, Esq.

f. 167 & the gentleman afsd transported at least 60 persons. Date: 25 August 1650. Signed: Thomas Green.

Mr. Hatton. Luke Gardiner desired testimony. Signed: Thomas Green.

Maj. Bufkin to pay Thomas Gerrard (gentleman). Signed: Jo. Hallowes.

Received of Levin Bufkin per note of John Hollis. Date: 10 March 1650. Signed: Thomas Gerrard. Witness: William Stone.

Luke Gardiner demanded land for transporting Richard Gardiner his father & his

f. 168 wife (dec'd), Richard, self, John Gardiner his son, Elias Beach man servant, Elisabeth & Jullian Gardiner their daughters, Mary Derrick in 1637. For transporting Luke & Julian his sister after they were forced out in 1647 & 50 a. due Richard Lustick servant to Mr. Copley who married Luke Gardiner's sister dec'd who survived her husband.

30 July 1650. William Stone, Esq. to Mr. Edward Lloyd (gentleman): appointment as commander of Anne Arundel Co. Also appointment of Mr. James Homewood, Mr. Thomas Meares, Mr. Thomas Marsh, Mr. George Puddington, Mr. Matthew Hawkins, Mr. James Merryman, & Mr. Henry Catlyn as commissioners.

f. 169 ...

f. 170 29 July 1650. Appointment of Mr. Edward Lloyd. Signed: William Stone.

Appointment of Capt. Robert Vaughan. Signed: William Stone.

20 March 1650. Giles Brent, Esq. transported & claimed land

f. 171 at request of Mrs. Margaret Brent his sister & attorney. Servants sent with Capt. Winter about 1636: Humphrey Hutford, James Price, Thomas Williams, Thomas Rowney, William Simpe. About 1637: John Warren, Devereuxand Goodwyn, John Robinson, Richard Pinner, Edward Berry. About 1638: Richard Cotesford. About 1641: William Perfett, John Ayres, Thomas Tilsley, Thomas Fidler, William (N), William Cavert, William Bowman, Garrett Fitzwalters, Phillip Garreson, Xpofer Atkins, Henry Topping, Cornelius (N).

Francis Gray (of Apomattox) assigned his rights to 500 a. to Luke Gardiner. Witnesses: William Johnson, Abraham Jenman.

Nicholas Bannester assigned his rights to 200 a. for transporting self & wife to Bartholomew Phillips. Date: 19 March 1650. Witness: William Asitor.

Robert Holt assigned his right to 400 a. to George Manners. Date: 19 December 1650. Witness: William Eltonhead.

f. 172 Warrant to Anthony Rawlins for 100 a. Date: 25 January 1650. Signed: Richard Browne.

Liber - Patent Record F & B - 1640-1658

<u>19 May 1651</u>. Court. Attendees: William Stone, Esq. (Governor), Thomas Hatton (gentleman, Secretary).

Motion by Benjamine Gill attorney for Mr. James Neale.

<u>20 June 1651 at St. Maries'</u>. Court. Attendees: Governor, Robert Brooke, Esq., Thomas Gerrard, Esq., Capt. John Price, Mr. Thomas Hatton (Secretary).

Lt. William Lewis acknowledged debt to Friendship Tongue.

f. 173 Lt. William Lewis acknowledged debt to Robert Hager.

<u>21 June 1651</u>. Lt. William Lewis acknowledged judgement to George Manners.

Thomas Hamper acknowledged debt to Walter Beane. Witness: Thomas Hatton.

Motion by Walter Beane & Walter Pakes administrators of William Smithfield. Date: 29 December 1648.

f. 174 Francis Brook vs. Mrs. Margarett Brent attorney for Capt. Giles Brent. Cites certificate of Capt. Robert Vaughan. Date: 3 April 1651. Per Robert Vaughan (gentleman).

Motion of Henry Morgan by Francis Brookes his attorney for relief of charges when he was sheriff of Kent by imprisonment of Thomas Bradnox.

f. 175 Henry Morgan appoints Francis Brookes his attorney in suit between Mr. Giles Brent & Thomas Bradnox. Signed: Walter Smith.

William Smith vs. Capt. William Mitchell by his attorney Mr. Cutbert Fenwick. Defendant is from Bedfordshire.

f. 176 ...

f. 177 Francis Brookes & his wife vs. Capt. William Mitchell. Motion by Mr. Cuthbert Fenwick.

Thomas Ashbrook vs. Nathaniell Hunt. Date: 7 November 1651.

Francis Brook attorney for Henry Morgan vs. John Wade (chirurgeon).

f. 178 Anthony Rawlings vs. Edward Hudson.

Motion of Mrs. Susan Warren, with child by Capt. William Mitchell. Mr. Cuthbert Fenwick by Capt. William Mitchell on allowance from his estate.

f. 179 Mr. Cuthbert Fenwick vs. John Nunn.

Thomas Gerrard, Esq. vs. Lt. William Lewis. Cites former award by Thomas Copley, Esq.

f. 180 John Walton vs. William Smoote.

William Hardwick vs. Francis Brookes.

f. 181 Lt. William Lewis to pay Paul Simpson. Witness: Thomas Hatton.

<u>20 August 1651</u>. Mrs. Ann Cowper (widow of Walter Cowper (gentleman)) awarded his estate.

<u>26 September</u>. Mr. Friendship Tongue requested no patent be given to Henry Pountney.

<u>2 October</u>. Mr. John Lawson registered a cattle mark.

f. 182 <u>29 April 1651</u>. Mr. Henry Howper (also Henry Hooper, planter) vs. Mr. Zephaniah Smith (planter). Said Henry paid debt to said Zephaniah & Capt. William Lambe. References a deed between Robert Simpkin & said Zephaniah. Robert Knight (age 16, servant to said Zephaniah) assigned to said Henry. Said Zephaniah also assigns bills from Thomas Welds.

f. 183 Signed: Zeph. Smith. Witness: Thomas Hatton.

<u>5 June</u>. George Mackall & Robert Crane are 2 servants of Mr. Wilkinson.

Benjamine Gill acknowledged debt to Lord Baltimore. Date: 20 June 1651. Witness: John Medcalf.

Liber - Patent Record F & B - 1640-1658

f. 184 Richard Bennett of Popler Hill with John Taylor & his wife Sarah (mother of said Richard) sold to Mr. Thomas Hatton chattel intended by said Sarah to Sarah Bennett my daughter & increase to other of my children. Mentions: son Thomas Bennett, son Richard Bennett. Date: 16 July 1651. Signed: John Tailor, Sarah Tailor, Thomas Hatton.

Payment by Thomas Hatton.

f. 185 Signed: Richard Bennett, John Taylor, Sarah Taylor. Witnesses: James Johnson, Edward Williams.

James Johnson (planter, of Popler Hill) received from Mr. Thomas Hatton. Witnesses: Richard Bancks, Barbara Johnson.

16 July. Capt. Francis Pott (of Accomack, VA) made a gift to Thomas Hatton son of Thomas Hatton Secretary.

f. 186 6 July 1651. Thomas Motham (gentleman, clark, Six Clarks Office in Chancery Land, London, now dec'd) gave to his godson Thomas Hatton the younger (b. 14 March 1642).

f. 187 29 July. Robert Hatton son of Mr. Thomas Hatton Secretary registered a cattle mark. Mentions his brother Thomas.

William Hatton nephew of Mr. Thomas Hatton Secretary registered a cattle mark.

Richard Hatton nephew of Mr. Thomas Hatton Secretary registered a cattle mark. Mentions his brother William.

Mr. John Wade (chirurgeon) registered a cattle mark.

12 April 1651. Barnaby Jackson gave to his godson Barnaby Edlowe son of Joseph Edlowe. Witness: Thomas Hatton.

14 April. Paul Simpson vs. Richard Brown (prisoner).

20 May. William Johnson registered a cattle mark.

19 May 1651. John Nicholls gave

f. 188 to John Evans son of William Evans (dec'd) & his then wife now wife of said John Nicholls. Witness: Thomas Hatton.

Walter Guest acknowledged debt to John Hatch. Witness: Thomas Hatton.

Lewis Froman registered a cattle mark.

23 June. Thomas Green, Esq. of St. Maries' at request of his wife Winifred Green & affection for my children Thomas Greene, Leonard Green, Robert Green, & Francis Green (son), assign to Henry Adams & James Langworth all my estate.

f. 189 Payment to my friend Thomas Copley, Esq. Children under age 18.

f. 190 ...

f. 191 ...

f. 192 Date: 18 November 1650. Signed: Thomas Greene. Witnesses: Richard Willan, Alice Smith.

23 June. Robert Newchant (of New Town) binds his crop to Mr. George Mee. Signed: Robert Newchan. Witnesses: Thomas Innes, James Lindsey.

Walter Smith, age 28, deposed on 2 October 1651 that Mary Risbrook (widow) was very sick & requested Francis Lumbard

f. 193 to come. She gave her godson chattel & Mr. Pasmore chattel. Witness: Robert Vaughan.

Thomas Pasmore, age 78, deposed on 2 October 1651 that Mary Risbrooke said that Francis Lumbard was to receive her estate. Witness: Robert Vaughan. Date: 9 October. Administration of estate of Mary Risbrook (of Isle of Kent) granted to Francis Lumbard.

Motion by Walter Beane & Walter Pakes administrators of estate of William Smithfield.

f. 194 21 June 1651. Signed: Thomas Hatton.

Liber - Patent Record F & B - 1640-1658

Joseph Edlowe administrator of Robert Wiseman. Date: 20 October 1651. Signed: Thomas Hatton.

f. 195 18 October. On 18 April 1649, Isaac Iluice received of John Salter.

Andrew Watson registered a cattle mark.

22 October 1651. Edward Hall posted bond for Rebecca Manners widow & administratrix of George Manners.

Lord Baltimore revokes commissions to his brother Leonard Calvert, Esq. & Giles Brent, Esq.

f. 196 Said Leonard Calvert appointed Lt. General, Admiral, Chief Captain, Commander,

f. 197 Chancellor, Chief Justice, Chief Magistrate.

f. 198 ...

f. 199 ...

f. 200 ...

f. 201 ...

f. 202 ...

f. 203 ...

f. 204 Date: 18 September 1644.

Leonard Calvert, Esq. appoints Capt. Edward Hill as governor. Date: 30 July 1646, in VA.

f. 205 Sworn to Oath of Fidelity on 2 January 1646: Mr. Lewger, Mr. Gerrard, Mr. Green, Francis Gray, John Hampton, John Hatch, Francis Pope, William Tompson, Mr. Bretton, Nath. Pope, Thomas Sturman, John Hollis, John Tue, Walter Beane, (N) Nevett, John Nevill, William Wright, John Norman, Rowland Maze, John Thompson, Robert Edwards, Walter Broadhurst, James Walker, John Hilliard, Henry Spink, William Perfaite, Francis Sherwood, John Gore, Nath. Jones, William Brough, Thomas Thomas, Walter Pakes, John Jarbo, Mr. William Eltonhead, John Mansell, Fra. Posey, John Wheatley, William Hungerford, Stephen Salmon, Thomas Petite, Thomas Mitchell.

In 1647: Richard Brown (27 June), Robert Kedger, Thomas Waggott (3 July), William Wheatley (18 July), Thomas Bushell (24), John Harwood (31), John Grimesditch (1 August), John Paulett (20 August), John Deara (20 August), James Johnson (3 September), John Courts (12 September), John Walton (22 September), William Yewell (22 December), Christopher Russell (12 November), Robert Ward (14 February), Robert Smith (4 March).

In 1648: Thomas Asbrook (15 July), John Asbrook (15 July), Thomas Warr (4 August), George Manners (4), Mr. Richard Brown (17 November), William Edwin (15 December), John Shertcliffe (15 December), James Langworth (15 December), Phillip Land (20 December), Mr. Cuth. Fenwick (9 February), James Hare (15 March), John Ashley (15 March), Ralph Beane (15 March).

14 January 1646. Henry Hooper (chirurgeon) acknowledged debt to John Hallows.

f. 206 Rent in arrears:
- St. Michael's Mannor - Thomas Butler (dec'd).
- St. Gabriel's Mannor - Henry James (dec'd).
- Trinity Mannor - John Langford (dec'd), Robert Smith.

William Stephanson demanded wages of Robert Smith.

13 January. Court apprised of reviling speeches of William Pinly at home of John Hallows what he should say to Robert Douglas (messenger from governor).

f. 207 Nathaniel Pope demanded of John Dandy.

Edward Packe demanded of John Dandy.

John Pritchard demanded of Barth. Lewis.

14 January. Marks Pheipo deposed he paid to sheriff for use of Mr. Giles Brent per Nathaniel Pope.

Liber - Patent Record F & B - 1640-1658

Edward Packer deposed he received of Nathaniel Pope at suit of Fulk Brent.

Bartholomew Rench acknowledged debt to John Hallowes.

f. 208 Thomas Green, Esq. demanded of William Hardedige.

4 February. Thomas Green, Esq. demanded of William Pinly.

John Grimesditch demanded 100 a. for transporting self in 1644.

Charge against Thomas Sturman, John Sturman, Francis Gray, John Hamton, Robert Smith, & Thomas Yewell. They were lately pardoned of crimes of rebellion & sedition, & have fled the province & assembled at house of John Mottram & others of Checkacoan enemies to Lord Proprietary

f. 209 & spoke of Capt. Wyatt coming with commission & Capt. Clayborne coming with commission to support the rebellion in Kent. Signed: Jo. Lewger.

f. 210 Examination of Edward Thomson. Date: 18 January 1646. At his house in Chickacoan, Sam. Tailor said that the Speaker Francis Gray said they were the chief cause & their death (Capt. Price & Thornbury & Hebdon) vowed.

Vessel out of VA by Ralph Beane.

f. 211 19 January 1646. To: Mr. William Bretton.

Thomas Sturman, Francis Gray, John Hampton, Robert Sedgrave, & John Sturman owe to Lord Proprietary if they leave St. Maries' Co. or communicate with John Mott, Thomas Yewell, Thomas Lewis, or Robert Smith.

Capt. John Hamton responded to query of William Lewis.

Robert Smith, Thomas Yewell, & Thomas Lewis have fled the province.

f. 212 Marks Pheipo administrator of Samuell Pursall (late of VA) demanded of John Hallowes.

Return of William Lewis of warrant received of Mrs. Baldridge at St. Inigo's house.

f. 213 Warrant to William Lewis for rents. Date: 29 January. William Lewis summoned: Richard Banks, William Thomson, Jo. Medley, William Asiter, Walter Beane, Ja. Johnson, Mr. Britton, Mr. Gerrard, Rich Nevitt, Jo. Mansell.

25 January. Francis Posie demanded of William Smithfield. Francis Posie demanded of Thomas Moss. Ralph Beane demanded of John Cook.

1 March. Warrant to Capt. Price. Mentions: Barth Phillips & Marm. Walgrave.

Assurance to Robert Smith & Thomas Yewell of pardon.

Robert Edwards demanded of Richard Hills administrator of John Longworth.

John Sturman, William Hardige, & Francis Gray licensed to go to Chicacoan.

f. 214 Notice to Mr. Hollis by Thomas Speak.

Warrant to Walter Waterlin to search house of Antho Rawlins for goods of John Hallowes.

Robert Sharp demanded of Cyprian Mallot. Robert Sharp demanded of Thomas Knight.

Robert Kedger per Walter Pakes demanded of Nath. Pope.

Dorothy Baldridge demanded of Richard Duke.

Henry Hooper (chirurgeon) appointed to serve as chirurgeon.

Mary Clocker demanded of Francis Gray.

Nath. Pope demanded of Blanch Oliver.

f. 215 Mary Clocker deposed that Nathaniel Pope did promise to Blanch Oliver. Date: 1 March 1647.

Robert Kedger vs. Nathan Pope.

Liber - Patent Record F & B - 1640-1658

Thomas Hebden demanded of administrator of John Cole.

Nath. Pope vs. Tho. Jackson.

Nicholas Gwither demanded of Nath. Pope for voyage to VA in 1645.

f. 216 Ralph Beane demanded of John Cage.

Robert Sharp vs. Tho. Knight.

William Broughe demanded of Antho Rawlins.

George Rutland demanded of John Hallowes due of Capt. Hill.

William Wheatley demanded of Francis Ancketill & James Langworth.

William Brough vs. Antho Rawlins. Payment to Edward Packer.

Antho Rawlins demanded of William Brough.

Thomas Sturman, Will. Pinly, Jo. Powell, David (N) (a Welshman), & Arthur Whittington's man licensed to go to VA.

Barneby Jackson demanded of Nath. Pope.

f. 217 Thomas Jackson demanded of John Hampton.

Francis Pope demanded of William Smithfield as executor of John Phillips.

George Rutland demanded of John Kemp (of VA).

William Brough demanded of John Mansell. William Brough demanded of William Brown.

George Rutland demanded of Robert Smith assigned from Richard Hobin.

John Salter demanded of Thomas Waggott. Marks Pheipo administrator of Tho. Pursall demanded of John Hampton. Marks Pheipo administrator of Thomas Pursall demanded of Francis Gray administrator of James Cauther. Marks Pheipo administrator of Tho. Pursall demanded of John Hallowes administrator of Ja. Wavill.

8 February. Marks Pheipo administrator of Thomas Pursall vs. Francis Gray administrator of James Cauther.

f. 218 Marks Pheipo administrator of Tho Pursall vs. John Hamton.

John Hampton at request of Christopher Chamberlaine made oath that in VA the deponent received of Edward Moulson about 9-10 years ago. Nicholas Clerk for account of Edward Moulson.

6 March 1646. Francisco Van Eynden demanded of Richard Hobin. Francisco Van Eynden demanded of John Nunne.

John Hampton deposed at request of Marks Pheipo that John Hallowes owed Thomas Pursall.

Job Mayne demanded of Henry Brookes.

Blanch Oliver administratrix of Robert Dixon demanded of: Richard Nevett; William Thompson; John Modly.

f. 219 Leonard Calvert, Esq. transported men in 1633 & is granted Governor's Field, bounding on St. Maries' Bay, Mill Creek, freehold of St. Peter's & Chappell Land, St. George's River for 100 a. Also, 600 a., bounding Trinity Bay, Norton's Creek, James' Branch, Patowmeck River. Also, 900 a., bounding Broad Creek, James' Creek, Deep Creek, Oyster Creek, Patowmeck River.

f. 220 Also, 1500 a., bounding Deep Creek, Oyster Creek, Patowmeck River, Chesapeak Bay, St. Michael's Point. First parcel is Trinity Manor. Second parcel is St. Gabriel's Manor. Third parcel is St. Michael's Manor. Date: 30 August 1634.

f. 221 Ralph Beane demanded of Joseph Cardell goods bought by Thomas Severne.

f. 222 25 February. Restituta Hallowes wife of John Hallowes appeared to answer suit by Marks Pheipo. Subpoena to Edward Packer. Nicholas Keylin demanded of Francis Gray, for self & as administrator of James Cauther. In presence of Jo. Piles (attorney for defendant).

Liber - Patent Record F & B - 1640-1658

Subpoena of John Hallowes defendant to Marks Pheipo for Mary Ford to testify.

Richard Nevett, per demand of Blanch Oliver, agreed to demand.

William Thomson, per demand of Blanch Oliver, agreed to demand, & defendant due from Robert Dixon.

Mary Ford deposed, per attorney of Jo. Hallowes, that she was at house of James Cauther on March 6 years ago, & saw Edward Hen (servant to James Cauther) brought chattel he had of J. Hallis for Thomas Pursall.

Ralph Beane fined on estate of John Cole.

f. 223 William Asiter fined on estate of Richard Cole.

Tho. Greene recovered of William Thomson against estate of Thomas Willis (fugitive).

Richard Nevett, per John Medley, recovered against estate of Thomas Willis (fugitive).

William Browne, after paying Mr. Lowe & Mr. Green & Richard Nevett, to have patent of Thomas Willis. Richard Nevett acknowledged receipt.

Marks Pheipo recovered against estate of John Wavell.

Edward Packer assumed for Jo. Hollis chattel to be recovered by George Rutland for Jo. Kemp (of VA).

Marks Pheipo demanded of Francis Gray administrator of James Cauther for use of Thomas Pursall received from John Hallowes.

Geo. Rutland vs. Jo. Hollis.

George Rutland demanded of Capt. Edward Hill due from Richard Hobie.

Warrant to Richard Nevett for 100 a.

George Rutland demanded of Tho. Petit due from Richard Hobie.

George Rutland attorney of (N) Bridges demanded of John Nevill.

f. 224 Will of Thomas Weston exhibited by John Hausford administrator. William Marshall to appraise the estate.

Nicholas Cossin demanded of James Neale.

Ralph Crouch, per John Pile, deposed that about October 1644, he lade aboard the ship Reformation, master Richard Ingle, in Thames River, London, goods from Thomas Clerk (also Thomas Clark).

f. 225 Zephaniah Smith to bring to court at Kent a petition from court at Annarundel.

Cuthbert Fenwick vs. John Nunn. Oath by Mr. Gwyther. Payable on 10 November 1647.

Proof by John Merriday shipwright for vacating a bond to Thomas Hales & Roger Pollin.

Roger Pinner (marriner of VA), age 36, deposed on 31 July 1651 that last November on the Ann in Chesapeak Bay in VA between Pyankatauck & Rappannock, a small boat borrowed from John Merriday boatwright was lost of Thomas Hales & Roger Pollin.

f. 226 Richard Gripwood (planter), age 16, deposed on 31 July 1651 that he was aboard the vessel named by Richard Pynner when board was lost. Signed: Thomas Hatton.

To: Capt. William Stone (Governor of MD). Received letter by Mr. Copley. I will take advise of my brother.

f. 227 I have been forced to provide myself by my brother in VA. Date: 22 July 1650. Signed: Margaret Brent.

To: Capt. William Stone. My brother is extremely sick. Date: 28 August 1651. Signed: Margarett Brent.

To: Capt. William Stone. I took advise of my brother. Signify to me or to Mr. Bretton. Date: 10 July 1651. Signed: Margaret Brent.

Page 23

Liber - Patent Record F & B - 1640-1658

f. 228 Thomas Johnson (merchant) testified to agreement between Mrs. Margarett Brent & Capt. William Stone for house & 100 a. belonging to Gov. Calvert (dec'd). Date: 20 May 1650. Before: James Homewood (magistrate).

f. 229 Elisabeth Parry, age 26, deposed on 22 October that she was present when Mrs. Margaret Brent made bargain with William Stone, Esq. for house formerly of Leonard Calvert, Esq. (dec'd). Witness: Robert Vaughan, William Eltonhead.

William Stone, Esq. vs. Mrs. Margarett Brent.

f. 230 Mentions depositions of Thomas Johnson & Elisabeth Parry.

f. 231 3 November. George Manners voided a bill of Henry Pountney due Skipper Abraham. Date: 19 April 1651. Witness: Friendship Tongue.

13 November. Mr. Phillip Land demanded from estate of Thomas Maidwell.

14 November. Blanch Howell, wife of Humphrey Howell, as widow gave to

f. 232 Mary Harrison daughter of said Blanch & John Harrison (dec'd). Mentions William Oliver son of said Blanch & Roger Oliver (dec'd). Witness: Thomas Hatton. Signed: Blanch Oliver.

6 November 1651. Motion by Rebecca Manners widow & administratrix of George Manners.

Depositions taken by Mr. John Sturman.
- Robert Holt deposed on 3 November 1651 that Dorothy his wife threatened him & Edward Hudson compacted with said Dorothy.
- Andrew Watson deposed that July/August 1650, he was at house of Edward Hudson & saw said Edward & Dorothy wife of Robert Holt go to be together.

f. 233 ...
Dorothy & Edward told deponent that Robert Holt was dead. Date: 3 November 1651.
- Rose Smith, age 42, deposed that September last that wife of Robert Holt indicated that she would kill him. Date: 4 November 1651.

Depositions taken by Lt. Nicholas Gwyther.
- George Dolty, age 24, deposed that he came to house where Edward Hudson & wife of Robert Holt lived. Date: 6 November 1651.
- Humphrey Howell, age 57, deposed that in June 1650 he went to house of Edward Hudson & Dorothy wife of Robert Holt lay in the bed.

f. 234 ...
Date: 6 November 1651.
- John Medcalf (gentleman) deposed that he heard Dorothy Holt curse her husband & her son Richard. He knew nothing between Edward Hudson & said Dorothy. Date: 6 November 1651.
- Henry Cox deposed on 6 November 1651 that he lived in house with Robert Holt & Edward Hudson from August to mid-October & knew of no grievances. Nor did Edward Hudson & Dorothy wife of Robert Holt bed together.
Edward Hudson & Dorothy wife of Robert Holt were arrested & brought to court. Depositions by Andrew Watson, Rose Smith, George Dolty, Humphry Howell, Mr. John Medcalf, & said Robert Holt. Edward Hudson to be punished.

f. 235 Dorothy Holt to be punished.

f. 236 11 March 1650. Act to increase fees for secretaries & clerks. Complaint by Thomas Hatton (gentleman).

f. 237 ...

f. 238 ...

f. 239 12 October 1651. John Jarbo to pay John Pille.

f. 240 Witnesses: James Longworth, William Thompson. Satisfaction on 22 September 1657. Witness: Thomas Turner.

3 November. William Marshall acknowledged debt to the estate of Mr. Thomas Weston.

25 November. William Assiter demanded from the estate of George Manners. William Stone, Esq. demanded from estate of Stephen Samon. Lt. Nicholas Gwyther demanded from estate of George Manners.

Liber - Patent Record F & B - 1640-1658

2 December. John Dandy demanded from estate of George Manners.

3 December 1651. Edmond Wormell (gentleman) deposed that he was present when Mrs. Katherine Hunt made her will on 6 July.

f. 241 Signed: Thomas Hatton.

4 December. Arthur Turner the younger registered a cattle mark.

22 December. Michael Bousey register a cattle mark.

2 December 1651. Court. Attendees: William Stone, Esq. (Governor), Thomas Gerrard, Esq., Capt. John Price, Mr. John Pile, Mr. Thomas Hatton.

William Stone, Esq. vs. Walter Pakes administrator of Stephen Salmon.

William Stone, Esq. vs. Rebecca Manners widow & administratrix of George Manners by her attorney Edward Hall.

John Nicholls demanded from estate of George Manners. Edward Hall attorney for administratrix acknowledged debt.

f. 242 Mr. George Mee demanded from estate of George Manners. Edward Hall attorney for Rebecca Manners administratrix.

John Meredith vs. Mr. William Daynes by his attorney George Mee. Defendant had heard Thomas Gutridge (VA) say the plaintiff had a black bastard in VA by one of his Negroes.

f. 243 John Meredith (shipwright) vs. Thomas Hall & Roger Pollin. Bond cancelled.

Mr. John Sturman vs. Mr. Thomas Daynes by Mr. Henry Coursey his attorney & said Daynes vs. William Johnson & Luke Gardiner.

f. 244 Jurors: Lt. Richard Banks, Richard Nevitt, Mr. John Lewger, Anthony Rawlins, John Nunne, Owen James, Richard Willan, Henry Adams, John Meredith, Robert Smith, Richard Lloyd, Walter Pakes.

f. 245 William Smoot vs. James Johnson.

John Meredith, age 27, deposed on 23 December 1651 that he delivered a note to Mr. Daynes from Mr. John Sturman regarding a servant's time.

f. 246 Servant was hired to go to William Johnson. Cites said Daynes & his cousin Mee.
- Mr. George Mee deposed that he received the note. Date: 30 September 1651.
- Edmond Lindesey, age 26, deposed on behalf of William Johnson regarding the servant. Date: 3 December 1651.

f. 247 ...
- Edward Turnor, age 20, deposed on 3 December 1651 regarding the servant.

John Pille sold to his brother Jarbo his house & land & chattel.

f. 248 Date: 12 October 1651. Witness: James Langworth.

John Prince, age 35, deposed on 2 December 1651 that he was present when George Manners & George Mee settled accounts 2 days before the death of Manners. Signed: Thomas Hatton.

John Prince, age 35, deposed on 2 December 1651 that Henry Potter had chattel from Mr. Eltonhead per George Manners. Signed: Thomas Hatton.

12 February 1650. William Mitchell, Esq. & Robert Kadger agreed that Kadger to pay before his departure for Holland.

f. 249 Robert Kadger assigned to William Mitchell, now in the hands of Edward Hall, & deliver to Richard Hodgkins, & to be delivered to said Mitchell on return from England. William Mitchell assigns to Kadger the servant Vincent Atcheson. Witnesses: William Eltonhead, Richard Hodgkins, John Henshawe.

f. 250 William & Thomas Daynes (merchants of VA) appoint Henry Coursey as attorney to collect sums due them as administrators of Mr. William Cooper & Mrs. Ann Cooper. 3 November 1651. Witnesses: Cornelius Loyd, William Wells.

1 January 1650. William Stradder vs. Walter Cooper (gentleman). Witnesses: Joseph Manning, Abraham Pope.

Liber - Patent Record F & B - 1640-1658

f. 251 8 January 1651. John Shertcliff registered a cattle mark for his daughter Anne, a gift from Ann now wife of Lt. William Evans.

Capt. William Stone, as attorney for my sister Mrs. Margarett Brent, notice. Date: 5 January 1651. Signed: Giles Brent.

10 January 1651. William Harwich (of Nominy) appoints John Sturman as attorney, as well for Zephaniah Smith. Witnesses: John Wade, Thomas Yaulle.

Mrs. Katherine Hebden demanded from estate of George Manners.

20 January. George Dolty demanded from estate of George Manners.

21 January. John Nicholls was given continuance on estate of Thomas Maidwell.

28 January. John Medley registered a cattle mark.

f. 252 Francis Vanender assigned to Mr. Thomas Hatton chattel due from Capt. Robert Vaughan, Zachary Wade, Mr. George Puddington, Mr. James Cox, & Phillip Hyde. Date: 17 February 1651. Witnesses: John Metcalf, Nicholas Gwyther.

20 January 1651. Court. Attendees: William Stone, Esq. (Governor), Mr. Thomas Hatton (Secretary), Capt. John Price, Mr. William Eltonhead.

Henry Adams one of trustees of Thomas Green, Esq. (dec'd) vs. Mr. Phillip Land.

William Harwich by his attorney John Sturman vs. Mr. Phillip Land. Mentions bill assigned by Francis Vanenden to Mr. Hallowes in 1648. Satisfaction received. Date: 1 September 1652. Signed: Thomas Hatton.

f. 253 Satisfaction acknowledged. Date: 22 November 1652. Signed: William Hardich. Satisfaction by Mr. Hatton on debt from Phillip Land. Date: 2 March 1653. Signed: William Hardich.

Motion by John Hatch attorney for William Andrews, Esq. By order of 20 March, Robert Brooke, Esq. adjudged to pay Mr. Andrews. Lt. Nicholas Gwyther authorized for sheriff's business in Charles Co.

Motion by Mr. Thomas Hatton. An Act of Assembly dated 29 April 1650, there is an exception for orphans under age 16.

f. 254 ...

f. 255 ...

f. 256 ...

f. 257 Thomas Bushell vs. Friendship Tongue. Concerns a servant which defendant & George Manners (dec'd) agreed to deliver by 25 December per bill dated 22 July 1651.

William Stone, Esq. vs. administratrix of George Manners. Motion by Rebecca Manners widow & administratrix of George Manners.

Thomas Hatton (gentleman) assignee of Anthony Rawlins vs. administratrix of George Manners. Cites Rebecca Manners administratrix.

f. 258 Edward Hall vs. widow Manners. Payment due from estate of George Manners.

John Hatch vs. widow Manners. Payment due from estate of George Manners.

John Hatch attorney for skipper Abraham Johnson vs. Henry Pountney.

Henry Pountney vs. widow Manners. Cites debt to estate of George Manners which John Hatch attorney for skipper Abraham Johnson obtained judgement.

f. 259 Nicholas Cawseen vs. William Smoote. Cites deposition of Capt. Francis Morgan (of York Co. VA). Date: 24 November 1651. Witness: Rob. Bouth.

Capt. Edward Hill by his attorney John Hallowes vs. widow Manners. Cites chattel delivered to George Manners by Mr. Copley. Nicholas Keeting deposed.

f. 260 George Mee vs. widow Manners. Payment due from estate of George Manners & proved by oath of John Prince. Cites Rebecca Manners administratrix.

Mr. Thomas Daynes by his attorney George Mee vs. Rebecca Manners (widow).

Liber - Patent Record F & B - 1640-1658

Walter Beane vs. widow Manners. Payment due from estate of George Manners.

Abraham Johnson (marriner) by his attorney John Hatch vs. Rebecca Manners (widow). Payment due from estate of George Manners.

f. 261 Capt. William Mitchell by his attorney Mr. Cuth. Fenwick vs. Rebecca Manners (widow). Payment due from estate of George Manners.

Mr. Andrew Painter by his attorney John Sturman vs. widow Manners. Payment from estate of George Manners.

Capt. Jo. West & Capt. Robert Abell by his attorney Mr. Cuth. Fenwick vs. David O'Doughorty.

William Johnson vs. Thomas Daynes by his attorney George Mee.

Mr. William Eltonhead vs. Henry Potter. Payment from defendant & estate of George Manners. Oath by John Prince.

f. 262 Michaell Baisey vs. John Meredith. Defendant has absented from Province. Deposition by Mr. George Mee.

f. 263 Mr. Richard Blunt by his attorney Mr. Henry Coursey vs. Thomas Copley, Esq. Mentions Nicholas White (runaway servant of complainant) who lived in VA. Servant has absented himself. Mr. Henry Roch attorney for complainant. Note regarding my servant Nicholas White & the servant of Arthur Alling. Date: April 1650. Signed: Richard Blunt.

f. 264 Mr. Richard Blunt, age 36, deposed that there was no agreement with Mr. Thomas Copley nor did deponent authorize Henry Roch. Date: 15 January 1651.

Marke Livesey deposed he was at house of Thomas Copley, Esq. when said Copley stated to Mr. Richard Blunt regarding Nicholas White. Date: 15 January 1651.

The Governor testified that Henry Roach came for a runaway & the servant could not be taken until an oath of Dr. Taylor. Date: 21 January 1651. Signed: William Stone.

Ralph Crouch (gentleman) deposed that he heard

f. 265 Jeremy (N), servant to Mr. Copley, tell Mr. Richard Blunt that Nicholas White lived at Gaughouse belonging to Mr. Copley. Jury: Mr. Phillip Land, Serj. Marks Pheipo, William Johnson, Mr. George Mee, Martin Kirke, John Prince, Edward Hall, Serj. James Lindesey, William Edwyn, John Nicholls, Friendship Tongue, Serj. George Dolty.

Mr. Richard Blunt by his attorney Mr. Henry Coursey vs. Thomas Copley, Esq.

Mr. John Wade (chirurgeon) vs. John Nicholls administrator of Thomas Maidwell. Charges for passage of said Maidwell from England.

f. 267 Paul Simpson by his attorney Francis Brookes vs. Lt. William Lewis.

Henry Pountney vs. Robert Holt. Cites defendant, Richard Ware, & Edward Hudson.

Mr. George Mee fined for striking Nicholas Keeting.

William Smith vs. Capt. William Mitchell by his attorney Mr. Fenwick.

f. 268 Mr. Cuthbert Fenwick to deliver chattel.

William Smith vs. Capt. William Mitchell by his attorney Mr. Fenwick.

Mr. George Mee deposed that Dr. Waldron bought a ring of wife of Francis Brookes.

Martin Kirk, age 35, deposed that George Manners came to his house & that his mate Friendship Tongue had nothing to do with boy named John Kirk. Date: 21 June 1651.

John Prince, age 35, deposed that the deponent was at the house of George Manners & heard said Manners say that Mr. Friendship Tongue had nothing to do with boy named John Kirke. Date: 21 June 1651.

f. 269 Henry Pountney authorized Nicholas Gwyther to be his attorney.

Liber - Patent Record F & B - 1640-1658

John Nevill & Xpofer Carnoll sold to Richard Bennett land Thomas Poteet's, bounding Poplar Hill Creek. Date: 23 March 1650. Signed: John Nevill, Christopher Carnoll. Witnesses: John Wade, John Hatch.

12 February. Paul Simpson made over his estate in MD or VA to Thomas Copley, Esq. (of St. Inego's). Date: 4 November 1651. Witness: Ralph Crouch.

f. 270 Francis Langfield daughter of John Langfield (dec'd, of Little Creek in parish of Lynhaven, County of Lower Norfolk) appointed Richard Foster (planter, of Lynhaven) as her attorney in VA. Date: 8 February 1651. Witness: Thomas Jackson.

21 February. Mr. Leonard Strong was granted administration on estate of Thomas Tynney (of Providence, Anne Arundel Co.).

f. 271 John Nunne was granted administration on estate of Phillip Auther. Appraisers: John Medley, Walter Pakes.

6 March. Mr. Peter Sharp (chirurgeon) was granted administration in right of his wife Judith widow of Mr. John Garie (of Anne Arundel Co.) Certified by: Edward Lloyd, Tho. Mears, Tho. Marsh. Date: 27 February 1651.

9 March. Henry Fox demanded from the estate of Joseph Cadle.

11 March. William Boarman appointed Mr. John Medcalfe as his attorney.

17 March. Charles Maynard demanded from the estate of Joseph Cadle.

John Shertcliffe demanded from the estate of Joseph Cadle.

19 March. Bill of Joseph Cadle to Thomas Thomas. Date: 29 June 1650. Witness: Charles Maynard.

f. 272 Matthias Bryan for Thomas Thomas demanded from the estate of Joseph Cadle.

22 March 1651. Michael Baysey (also Michael Baisey) acknowledged a judgement to William Boreman. Witness: Tho. Hatton.

John Mannsfield demanded from the estate of Joseph Cadle.

20 March 1651. Court. Attendees: William Stone, Esq. (Governor), Robert Brooke, Esq., William Eltonhead, Esq., Capt. John Price, Thomas Gerrard, Esq., Mr. John Pille, Mr. Tho. Hatton.

Thomas Chynne (marriner) vs. William Edwyn. Plaintiff is one of the mates of Capt. Thurston.

Mr. John Lawson vs. William Edwyn.

f. 273 James Langworth, age 22, deposed on 18 February 1651 that yesterday Phillip Auther was in deponent's house in Newtown with Mr. Robert Clarke, Richard Willan, & Mary wife of John Greenway. Deponent shot & killed Phillip Auther.

f. 274 Mr. Robert Clark & Richard Willan deposed on 18 February 1651 that they were present when Phillip Auther was killed in house where James Langworth & John Greenway dwell.

Mary wife of John Greenway deposed on 20 March 1651 that on 17 February, Mr. Robert Clark was in the house where the deponent lived & where Phillip Author was killed by James Langworth.

f. 275 Jury: Lt. Richard Bancks, Lt. William Evans, Mr. Phillip Land, Edward Cotton, William Whittle, Mr. John Lawson, Mr. John Lewger, Henry Cox, William Edwyn, Mr. Francis Brookes, John Shertcliff, Walter Pakes.

f. 276 Verdict: Phillip Auther was accidentally shot by James Langworth. Robert Clark & James Langworth were fined. Date: 10 April 1653.

Thomas Thomas by his attorney Matthias Bryon vs. Lt. Richard Bancks executor of Joseph Cadle.

Rebecca Manners executrix of her husband George Manners vs. Nichas Keeting. Cites judgement of George Manners against Thomas Warr & Marks Pheipo was bound to said Warr.

Mr. Francis Brookes deposed on 20 March 1651 that he heard Thomas Maidwell (dec'd) say that Mr. John Wade paid his passage from England.

Liber - Patent Record F & B - 1640-1658

f. 277 22 March 1651. Court. Attendees: William Stone, Esq. (Governor), Robert Brooke, Esq., Thomas Gerrard, Esq., Capt. John Price, Mr. Thomas Hatton.

Thomas Warr vs. Mr. Richard Harris. Cites bill of William Scott (of VA). Cites John Hilliard (servant).

Robert Kedger vs. Capt. William Mitchell. Cites Vincent Acheson (servant).

f. 278 Francis Vanenden vs. Capt. William Mitchell.

f. 279 William Marshall vs. William Edis. Cites bill in hands of Mr. Husbands.

Capt. William Mitchell vs. Mr. Phillip Land.

Mr. Thomas Daynes executor of Mrs. Ann Cooper by his attorney Mr. Henry Coursey vs. Edmund Lindsey.

John Shertcliff vs. Lt. Richard Bancks executor of Joseph Cadle.

f. 280 Richard Willan, age 30, deposed on 11 March 1651 that he was at house of Joseph Cadle with John Shertcliff about 11 February. Witness: Mr. John Pille.

Charles Maynard, age 31, deposed on 15 March 1651 that he took chattel to John Shertcliff for Joseph Cadle. Witness: John Pille.

Ann, age 30, wife of John Dandy deposed on 22 March 1651 about the bill of Mr. John Wade to Thomas Maidwell.

John Wade (chirurgeon) vs. John Nicholls administrator of Thomas Maidwell. John Cage deposed that he heard Thomas Maidwell say that plaintiff paid for his passage.

f. 281 Henry Adams trustee of Thomas Green, Esq. (dec'd) vs. Phillip Land. John Wheatley deposed that Mr. Phillip Land paid deponent for Thomas Green, Esq. (dec'd).

Mary wife of Daniel Clocker deposed on 22 March 1651 that not long after the arrival of Capt. William Mitchell in 1650, the deponent told Mrs. Susan Warren (alias Mrs. Williams) that she heard she was pregnant.

Richard Hoskins, age 30, deposed on 22 March 1651 to the validity of the deposition of Mary Clocker.

Martha Webb, age 22, deposed on 22 March 1651 that when she lived with Capt. William Mitchell at St. Thomas that

f. 282 Mrs. Susan Warren (alias Elisabeth Williams) slept with Capt. Mitchell & that Mrs. Williams is now pregnant.

25 March 1651. Court. Attendees: William Stone, Esq. (Governor), Robert Brooke, Esq., William Eltonhead, Esq., Mr. John Pile, Mr. Thomas Hatton.

Deposition that Mrs. Mary Brent for herself or her brother Capt. Giles Brent or her sister Mrs. Margaret Brent has had killed cattle on Isle of Kent. Mrs. Mary Brent also had beef transported to Mr. Thomas Matthews. Date: 31 January 1651.

f. 283 William Boreman deposed on 4 February 1651 that the deponent was employed by Capt. Giles Brent to kill cattle at Kent & at the direction of his sister Mrs. Mary Brent with the help of John Deer. Cites Mrs. Margaret Brent (sister), Mr. Matthews.

Thomas Hatton (gentleman) Attorney General for Lord Proprietary vs. Mrs. Margaret Brent. Cites that Mrs. Mary Brent for herself or her brother Capt. Giles Brent or her sister Mrs. Margaret Brent killed cattle at Kent.

f. 284 Paul Simpson (marriner) & Phillip Land deposed that on 20 February 1651, they viewed beef brought by Mrs. Mary Brent from Isle of Kent.

Thomas Hatton (gentleman) Attorney General for Lord Proprietary vs. Mrs. Mary Brent. Cites that Mrs. Mary Brent for herself or her brother Capt. Giles Brent or her sister Mrs. Margaret Brent killed cattle at Kent. Cites Mr. Thomas Matthews attorney for Mrs. Mary Brent.

f. 285 William Foxery vs. William Batten. Defendant bought chattel of plaintiff 3 years ago & paid him in VA.

Liber - Patent Record F & B - 1640-1658

Levin Bufkin, Esq. appoints Cuthbert Fenwick (gentleman) as his attorney. Date: 21 March 1650. Witnesses: William Mitchell, Obedience Robins.

f. 286 Francis Vanenden (planter, of St. Inego's) is bound to William Assiter (taylor, of Newtown) & makes over chattel in hands of William Boreman. Date: 14 March 1651.

f. 287 William Assiter, age 38, deposed on 21 January 1651 at the request of John Nunne that about 4/5 years ago, Mr. Cuthbert Fenwick demanded payment & was paid. Mr. Fenwick was bound for VA. Witness: William Bretton.

Christopher Walter, age 12/13, deposed on 25 October 1651 that he was present when Thomas Lisle fell out of a tree on the plantation of this deponent's master John Halfehead & later died.

Thomas Hamper, age 23, deposed on 25 October 1651 that he was at plantation of John Halfehead & heard Christopher Walter call "Master" & saw Thomas Lisle lying under a tree.

f. 288 John Halfehead, age 45/46, deposed on 25 October 1651 that, according to Thomas Hamper, he went to see Thomas Lisle under a tree, who soon died.

f. 289 Notice on late payments of rents in St. Maries' Co., due at house of Attorney General Thomas Hatton. Date: 2 December 1651. Signed: William Stone.

f. 290 24 March. Col. Francis Yardley registered a cattle mark.

Mrs. Eure (his lordship's sister) registered a cattle mark.

George Raper registered a cattle mark.

William Boarman registered a cattle mark.

Estate of Thomas Tinney was sold. Date: 21 June 1652. Signed: Leo. Strong administrator.

f. 291 ...

f. 292 Yoacomoco Indians & Matchoatick Indians et. al. cited as hunting. Capt. John Price allowed to levy soldiers.

f. 293 Date: 9 August 1652. Signed: William Stone. Phillip Land proclaimed the proclamation.

Phillip Land & Henry Fox bound to Lord Baltimore in case Walter Peakes (of St. Maries' Co.) breaks the peace. Date: 12 October 1652.

12 November 1652. John Taylor registered a cattle mark.

20 November 1650. Court. Attendees: Governor, Mr. Green, Mr. Brookes, Capt. Price, Mr. Secretary.

Mr. William Eltonhead vs. George Manners.
- Martin Kirke deposed that last September Mr. Eltonhead was discussing with Francis Antell, regarding plundering.

f. 294 ...
- Cites Mr. Mottram & the Governor.
- Ales wife of Martin Kirk deposed that last September at the house of Mr. Eltonhead he was discussing with her husband about plundering. Cites Mr. Motram & the Governor.
- Elisabeth wife of Henry Potter deposed that she heard Mr. William Eltonhead say regarding plundering. Cites Mr. Mottram & the Governor.

William Jones, Phillip Harwood, & Anthony Kitchin (servants to Robert Brooke, Esq.) deposed on 19 March 1651 that John Clifford (another servant of Mr. Brookes) has been absent about 27 February, & Mr. Thomas Brooke sought him.

f. 295 Cites 2 eldest sons of Mr. Brooke.

f. 296 Cites Davy Bowen (another servant). Date: 19 March 1650.

f. 297 22 April 1652. Court. Attendees: Mr. Robert Brooke, Esq., Lt. Richard Banks.

Thomas Munns vs. Nicholas Cuszeen.

William Marshall vs. William Edis. Defendant made payment by Mr. Richard Husbands.

Liber - Patent Record F & B - 1640-1658

Mr. Henry Adams one of trustees of Mr. Thomas Green (dec'd) vs. Mr. Phillip Land.

Francis Vanenden vs. Capt. William Mitchell. Cites Mary wife of Auther Glayhay.

f. 298 Jury: Mr. Edward Packer, Mr. Paul Simpson, Mr. Walter Beane, Mr. William Marshall, John Cage, Nicholas Caszeene, Henry Fox, Mr. John Wade, Mr. Francis Brooke, Mr. Phillip Land, Henry Adams, Mr. John Metcalfe.

Mary wife of Arthur Glahay deposed on 14 March 1651 that she was present when Francis Vanenden sold chattel to Capt. Mitchell.

f. 299 Mrs. Susan Warren vs. Capt. William Mitchell.

Henry Cox was granted administration on estate of Robert Ward (of St. Maries' Co.), he having married the widow. Widow is now dec'd, leaving 3 small children by Ward.

Mr. Robert Clark by his attorney Mr. John Metcalf vs. Thomas Hamper. Cites bill of Capt. William Stone assigned to complaintant.

Mr. John Metcalf vs. Suppar Jacob Dirrickson by his attorney John Hatch.

f. 300 William Scote was granted administration on estate of William Bloff (also William Broff, of St. Maries' Co.) in right of Sarah his wife late the widow.

23 April. Court. Attendees: same as previous day.

Mr. Thomas Daynes, age 32, deposed on 23 April 1652 that he paid Dr. Waldron sum which the deponent & Mr. Daynes his brother had formerly given note to Mr. Henry Coursey our attorney to pay, & since paid said Waldron in the hands of Esq. Ludlo.

Mr. Francis Brooke, age 38, deposed that Thomas Medwell desired him going with Mr. Land to Newtown to speak to Mr. John Wade (chirurgeon). Cites Lt. Evans.

f. 301 Mr. John Wade vs. John Nichols administrator of Thomas Medwell. Cites that Thomas Medwell came from England.

Inventory & accounts on estate of Thomas Medwell per Mr. Wade. Date: 23 April 1652. Received from: John Nevell, Edward Packer.

f. 302 Payments to: William Edwn, Capt. Stone.

Mr. Phillip Land informed the court of ruling regarding Mr. Nicholas Gwyther high sheriff.

Mr. Thomas Hatton Attorney General to Lord Baltimore vs. Mrs. Mary Brent. Cites Capt. William Clayborne.

William Smith vs. Capt. William Mitchell.

f. 303 Said Smith is servant to defendant before leaving England. Cites Mr. Hatton. Said William Smith is age 61, "seduced from his country wife & children".

f. 304 At request of Mr. Thomas Hatton, Lt. Nicholas Gwyther is authorized. Date: 22 April 1652. Signed: Robert Brooke, Richard Banks.

George Mee discharges John Allen of further service by vertue of indenture to Mr. Walter Cooper (of Island of Barbadoes) & Mr. Edmond Hunt of same place. Date: 29 April 1651. Witnesses: Thomas Sturman, John Sturman.

Walter Beane (planter) bound himself

f. 305 to estate of William Broof, appraised by John Wade (chirurgeon) & John Taylor. Date: 20 May 1652. Witness: Henry Coursey.

22 June 1652. Court. Attendees: Mr. Robert Brooke, Lt. Richard Banks.

Mr. Phillip Land vs. John Nicholls administrator of Thomas Medwell.

Mr. John Nicholls vs. John Hatch attorney to skipper Jacob Derickson.

f. 306 John Hatch vs. John Danbe.

Walter Beane vs. John Danbe.

Liber - Patent Record F & B - 1640-1658

Walter Beane vs. John Bellame.

f. 307 George Ackcrek vs. John Vallane.

John Slingsby, age 35, deposed that at Christmas, he went to house of John Vallane & was shown pigs that were later marked with mark of Walter Beane.

Mr. William & Thomas Daynes by their attorney Mr. Henry Coursey vs. John Danbe. Cites a bill of William Johnson.

John Slingsbie vs. John Danbe.

Edward Hall administrator of George Manners.

f. 308 John Mansfield made over to John Hatch the following: William Bradley, Benjamine Hammon, & chattel.

Francis wife of Walter Peakes gave her godchild John Nevitt (under age 16) chattel.

Walter Beane vs. Ser. Richard Banks administrator of Joseph Cadle.

Robert Brooke, Esq. vs. Mr. Walter Peakes administrator of Steven Samson.

f. 309 Mr. Walter Beane attorney to William Scote administrator of William Brough vs. Humphrey Atwixe.

Mr. Francis Brookes vs. Mr. John Danbey. Cites defendant was bound to Esq. Littleton (of Accomack). Complainant paid William Stone, Esq.

f. 310 Phillip Land vs. Edward Claxton.

Received on a bill of John Mansfield & John Norman. Signed: Robert Brooke.

Lt. William Lewis vs. Paul Simson.

Received of Humphrey Atwick. Date: 18 March 1650. Signed: William Brough.

Thomas Cole, age 34, deposed on 23 June 1652 about a bond from Mrs. Susanna Warren to Capt. William Mitchell in their voyage coming to VA.

f. 311 In Portsmouth, Mrs. Warren desired the deponent to lend her money.

Mary wife of Daniel Clocker deposed on 23 June 1652 that in August 1651 that Mrs. Susanna Warren gave birth to a stillborn; Dr. Waldron called by Mrs. Fenwick.

f. 312 John Mansfield, age 36, deposed on 23 June 1652 that he sold 200 a. to Joseph Cadle & Robert Tutty, mates living together at Mr. Thompson. Said Cadle was forced out of the country. Deponent & Tutty went to house of William Brough. Said Cadle returned.

Mr. Edmund Wormell by order of Capt.

f. 313 William Stone, Esq. (Governor) paid Mrs. Margaret Brent. Date: 23 January 1651. Witnesses: John Lawson, Rich. Bankes, John Taylor, Rich. Watson.

Richard Trewe (also Richard Trew, of Anne Arundel Co., shipwright) was bound to chattel to Edward Lloyd. Cites bond to Nicholas Gwyther & William Boreman of 30 June 1652. Witnesses: Robert Vaughan, William Fuller.

f. 314 Susan Warren (widow), age 21, deposed on 18 June that Capt. Mitchell aided her.

Phillip Land, age 45, deposed on 21 June 1652 that on 28 May last he heard Mrs. Joane Mitchell wife of Capt. William Mitchell comment on heaven.

Thomas Cole, age 32, deposed on 22 June 1652 that when he was in England, he was at chamber of Mr. Edward Plowden when asked about Capt. Mitchell going to VA.

f. 315 Joane Toast (the pretended wife of Capt. William Mitchell) deposed on 29 June 1652 that they were married by Mr. Wilkinson & slept together.

William Wilkinson, age 50, deposed on 1 May 1652 that on 10 April last he went to house of Capt. Mitchell & married Capt. Mitchell to a young woman with John Baily as witness.

Liber - Patent Record F & B - 1640-1658

John Baily, age 33, deposed on 18 June 1652 that on 10 April last his master Capt. Mitchell called him to his chamber. Mr. Wilkinson was present. Capt. Mitchell was married to a young woman.

f. 316 William Smith (gentleman), age 60, deposed on 29 March 1651 that about 1 year ago he was in company with Capt. Mitchell at his lodging in the Strand near the Savoy when Capt. Mitchell desired the deponent to call his (the deponent's) daughter, whom Capt. Mitchell intended to take to these parts, as Mrs. Elisabeth Williams or Betty Williams, and the reason that Capt. Mitchell gave as he had a sister or friend by that name whom he dearly loved. The deponent's daughter is Susan Warren, having been formerly married to Humphrey Warren.

f. 317 William Hamstead (planter), age 23, deposed that before coming to these parts, the deponent was a servant to Capt. William Mitchell in the Strand near London.

Susan Warren (widow) deposed on 22 June that Capt. Mitchell would have married her in England, except he was married. The deponent saw Capt. Mitchell buy some drugs for his wife.

f. 318 Susan Warren (widow), age 21, deposed on 24 April that when Capt. Mitchell perceived she was pregnant by him, he prepared some drugs for her. Signed: Susanna Warren.

Susan Warren (widow), age 21, deposed on 24 April that of when Capt. Mitchell heard

f. 319 she had given birth & that the child was his. And the deponent was told that his wife was dec'd. Signed: Susanna Warren.

Mary wife of Daniel Clocker deposed that she was midwife to Susan Warren, who said the father was Capt. Mitchell and he had given her drugs to destroy it. Given to Robert Brooke in presence of Mrs. Fox. Date: 28 June 1652.

Anne wife of William Hempted deposed on 27 June 1652 that at Deale, when the deponent was coming towards VA, the deponent heard the wife of Capt. Mitchell urge William Hampsted to buy drugs.

f. 320 Mrs. Mitchell had a fit & was in a coma. Mrs. Dorrington indicated she wouldn't recover. Capt. Mitchell replied that she had been like that for hours before.

Martha Webb, age 22, deposed on 27 April 1652 that she was at the house of Capt. Mitchell before his going to England. Neither Capt. Mitchell nor Susan Warren were sick. Deponent left the room & when returned, Capt. Mitchell was well, but Susanna Warren was sick.

f. 321 William Hamsted, age 23, deposed on 19 January 1651 that he heard Capt. Mitchell at Deale tell his wife Mrs. Mitchell that Mrs. Warren (alias Betty Williams) had sent chattel & a servant Marke Webb. The chattel belonged to Mr. Smith father of Mrs. Warren.

f. 322 On arrival, Capt. Mitchell ordered his chattel separated from those of Mrs. Warren & Mrs. Boulton.

Anne Hamstead, wife of William Hamstead, deposed on 20 June 1651 that at Portsmouth in England, she saw Capt. Mitchell borrow money from Mrs. Susan Warren (alias Mrs. Elisabeth Williams)

f. 323 for passage. Capt. Mitchell indicated the money was for passage of her servant Martha Webb.

f. 324 On departure of William Smith, Capt. Mitchell remarked "that if he was a freeman". Mrs. Mitchell wife of Capt. Mitchell asked if Mrs. Williams came by her own means or if she & her father were brought.

f. 325 Richard Hoskins (gentleman) deposed that at the house of Mr. William Eltonhead in May a year ago, he was talking with Elisabeth Williams (alias Susan Warren) concerning Capt. William Mitchell. Before Capt. Mitchell went to England, the deponent was offered in the presence of George Manners & Mr. Friendship the said Elisabeth Williams. Date: 22 June 1652.

f. 326 John Baily deposed that sometime after Capt. Mitchell arrived, he heard Elisabeth Williams (alias Susan Warren) say that she was get revenge on Capt. William Mitchell.

30 June 1652. Court. Attendees: William Stone, Esq. (Governor), Thomas Hatton (Secretary), Robert Brooke, Esq., Col. Francis Yardley, Mr. Job Chandler, Mr. Richard Preston.

Liber - Patent Record F & B - 1640-1658

Since Susquehanna Indians desire peace, the following are authorized to negotiate a treaty: Richard Bennett, Esq., Mr. Edward Lloyd, Capt. William Fuller, Mr. Thomas Marsh, Mr. Leonard Strong.

f. 327 Complaints by inhabitants of Isle of Kent vs. Capt. Robert Vaughan. Mr. Thomas Marsh appointed commander of Isle of Kent.

25 June 1652. Court. Attendees: same as previous day.

f. 328 Petition by Capt. William Mitchell. Imprisoned by warrant of Robert Brooke, Esq.

f. 329 Charges vs. Capt. William Mitchell.
1. atheist.
2. adultery with Susan Warren.
3. murder of child by Susan Warren.
4. since late wife's death, lived with now pretended wife Joane.

f. 330 Grand jury: Mr. Cornelius Lloyd, Mr. Edward Lloyd, Capt. William Fuller, Mr. Robert Clark, Mr. Thomas Marsh, Capt. John Barriff, Mr. Francis Lloyd, Mr. Thomas Daynes, Mr. William Nugent, Lt. William Lewis, Mr. Henry Hooper, Mr. Thomas Hudson.

30 June 1652. Court. Attendees: Governor, Secretary, Col. Francis Yardley, Mr. Job Chandler.

Mr. Thomas Hatton His Lordship's Attorney General brought charges against Susan Warren (widow): adultery with Capt. William Mitchell.

f. 331 Oaths of Mary Clocker & Richard Hodgkins. Susan Warren punished. Capt. William Mitchell punished.

f. 332 Susan Warren vs. Capt. William Mitchell. Deposition of William Hampstead & his wife. Depositions of (N) Henshaw & (N) Hoskins set aside (servants of defendant).

Motion by Col. William Cleyborne & order between His Lordship's Attorney General & Mrs. Mary Brent.

f. 333 John Carrington & Nicholas Whight servants to Lawrence Starkey, Esq. ordered arrested. Date: 13 July 1652. Signed: William Stone.

14 July 1652. Court. Attendees: Governor, Col. Francis Yardley, Mr. Thomas Hatton, Mr. Job Chandler.

Lawrence Starky, Esq. by his attorney Mr. Thomas Matthews vs. John Carrington & Richard Whight.

f. 334 Defendants alleged discharge by Thomas Copley, Esq. (dec'd).

William Scott (marriner) appointed by Walter Beane as attorney. Mentions estate of William Brough. Date: 23 April 1652. Witnesses: John Lawson, Cr. Carnoll.

f. 335 William Scott & Sarah Scott sold to William Beane all chattel & land of Mr. Brough (dec'd). Date: 22 May 1652. Witnesses: Jo. Hatch, Ben Cowell.

Thomas Warr & Nathaniell Hunt (both of Mattapania of Patuxent River) bound themselves to Richard Trewe shipwright. Date: 17 September 1652. Witnesses: Henry Falconer, Thomas Hamper.

f. 336 Mr. Richard Harris (merchant) registered a cattle mark.

Mr. Richard Harris deposed that yesterday he was at house of Thomas Warr. Only John Read was present. Having heard that Richard Trew sold said Warr & Nathaniel Hunt a sloop, he supposed that Warr & his wife & Nathaniel Hunt were gone out of province. Date: 21 September 1652.

Paul Simpson (marriner) deposed that he believed his life in danger due to Walter Peakes. Date: 29 September 1652.

Geoffry Oliver, age 48, deposed on 29 September 1652 that about 5/6 weeks ago, the deponent was at the house of Walter Pakes & saw said Peakes strike Mr. Paul Simpson.

f. 337 Francis Martin registered a cattle mark. William Martin (son of Francis Martin) registered a cattle mark. Lodowick Martin (son of Francis Martin) registered a cattle mark.

Liber - Patent Record F & B - 1640-1658

Martin Kirk registered a cattle mark.

Martin Kirk sold 200 a. St. Jerome's Thickett to Francis Martin. Date: 20 August 1651. Witnesses: Thomas Ashbrooke, John Prince.

f. 338 Francis Anketill sold chattel. Cites George Manners. Date: 2 April 1640. Witnesses: Henry Pounsney, Nicholas Keating.

William Whittle & Walter Peakes were appointed appraisers of estate of Joseph Cadle. Cites 150 a. Date: 24 November 1652.

William Evans sold to Thomas Thomas chattel. Date: 19 October 1651. Witnesses: William Hungerford, Jeziph Cadle.

Thomas Thomas registered a cattle mark.

Paul Simson (planter) & Walter Peakes (planter) release all suits against one another. Date: 2 November 1652. Signed: Paul Simpson, Walter Peakes. Witnesses: Giles Brent, Richard Ware.

f. 339 20 November 1652. Court. Attendees: Governor, Col. Francis Yardley, Mr. Thomas Hatton, Mr. Job Chandler.

Complaint of Mary Jones against her master & mistress Mr. William Eltonhead & Mrs. Eltonhead.

Capt. Thomas Cornwallis vs. Mr. John Pile. Cites debt

f. 340 from Mr. Cuthbert Fenwick, who expected to recover from Argol Yardley, Esq.

Raph Harellton, age 21, deposed on 12 November 1652 that Paul Simpson came to the house of his master William Lewis at Porttobacke about 1 November 1651.

f. 341 Cites Mr. Copley as master.

f. 342 Capt. William Mitchell deposed that he never received any servant from Levin Bufkin, Esq. Date: 25 November.

John Sturman deposed on 23 November that he was with William Cole, William Bence, & Thomas Simons about November 1651, regarding a bill of William Bence to Thomas Simons.

William Stevenson vs. Walter Beane. Deposition by Humphrey Atwix on 24 November 1652.

Walter Gest received of Walter Pakes for Steeven Salman. Date: 14 November.

f. 343 Thomas Hatton (gentleman, Secretary) granted to Margaret Hunt widow of Francis Hunt (of Kent Island) administration of estate & appraisal by 2 persons appointed by commissions or Capt. Robert Vaughan. Date: 24 November 1652.

Thomas Hatton (gentleman, Secretary) granted to Mary Geathar widow of John Geathar (of Anne Arundel Co.) administration of estate. Date: 24 November 1652.

f. 344 Edward Claxton deposed that in March/April 1650, the deponent was hired by Mr. Francis Brookes, brought items from Kent to St. Maries', landing where John Dandy lived. Date: 22 November 1652.

Humphrey Atwixe, age 29, deposed on 24 November 1652 that Mr. Brough took chattel of William Stevenson adjudged by Walter Beane & said Brough to belong to Brough.

f. 345 John Cage deposed that he heard Mr. Cuthbert Fenwick tell Mrs. Hebden about 3 years ago that he received payment from Capt. Vaughan & William Whealey.

Francis Brooks assigned to John Dandy, to save him from a debt to Nathaniel Littleton, Esq., bills from: Mr. Phillip Conners, Richard Hoults, Francis Lumbard, William Jones, Christopher Chambers. And cattle in possession of William Edwyn. Date: 3 August 1649. Witnesses: John Wade, Tho. Medwell.

Major Bufkins is debtor to Capt. Mitchell. Signed: William Mitchell.

f. 346 Capt. Thomas Cornwallis registered a cattle mark.

Mr. Richard Husband is cited as master of The Hopeful Adventure. Date: 26 December 1648. Cites: bill of lading.

Liber - Patent Record F & B - 1640-1658

William Osbaston, age 26/7, deposed on 20 November 1652 that about 4 years ago, he heard Edward Hall say he sold to Henry Potter 1/2 plantation where the two lived.

f. 347 Richard Bennit is bound to Richard Banks for chattel & plantation formerly of Jozyph Cadell. Date: 1 December 1652. Witnesses: John Thimbleby, Henry Medlap.

f. 348 To Capt. William Stone (Governor) & Council from inhabitants of County of Isle of Kent. Cites disturbances by Eastern Shore Indians. Mentions: Capt. Gugnis. Signed: Henry Morgon, Phillip Conner, John Phillips, Thomas Ringgold.

f. 349 25 November 1652. Court. Attendees: William Stone, Esq. (Governor), Col. Francis Yardley, Capt. John Price, Mr. Thomas Hatton, Mr. Job Chandler.

Cites petition by Mr. Phillip Conner, Mr. Thomas Ringgold, Mr. Henry Morgon, & Mr. John Phillips. Mentions: Thomas Cornwallys, Esq.,

f. 350 house late of Thomas Warr,

f. 351 Capt. William Fuller, William Tompson servant to John Jarbo,

f. 352 command authorized to Capt. William Fuller. Mentions: William Stone, Esq. (Governor).

f. 353 Date: 29 November 1652. Signed: William Stone.

f. 354 Master Richard Prestone (commander of North side of Patuxent River) is authorized to raise men for arms. Mentions: plantation late of Thomas Warr, Capt. William Fuller. Date: 2 December 1652. Signed: William Stone.

f. 355 Order to support Capt. William Fuller.

f. 356 Order for

f. 357 William Thompson servant to John Jarbo with tools from John Dandy to support Capt. William Fuller.

f. 358 22 November 1652. Court. Attendees: Governor, Col. Francis Yardley, Mr. Thomas Hatton, Mr. Job Chandler.

Capt. Thomas Cornwallis, Esq. vs. Mrs. Katheren Hebden (widow) by her attorney William Marshall. Mentions: estate of Thomas Hebden.

f. 359 Payment made to Mr. Cuthbert Fenwick.

Thomas Simons acknowledged a bill made to Francis Martine dated 5 May 1651.

Mr. William & Thomas Daines by their attorney Henry Coursey vs. John Nicholls. Mr. Guyther received payment & Mr. Wilkinson was witness.

23 November 1652. Court. Attendees: Governor, Col. Francis Yardley, Capt. John Price, Mr. Thomas Hatton, Mr. Job Chandler.

Mr. Thomas Marsh demanded per bill of Richard True.

f. 360 Richard True petitioned for relief in escape of Thomas Warr & Nathaniel Hunt.

f. 361 Motion by Mr. Thomas Hatton for Mr. Edward Lloyd (commander of Anne Arundel Co.) who was surety to said True for payment to Nicholas Guyther & William Boreman.

Motion by Mr. Thomas Hatton to be relieved of payment due from estate of

f. 362 Thomas Hamper. Mr. William Eltonhead hired a servant of said Hamper.

Thomas Simons vs. William Cole. Complainant desires relief from bill of William Bence which defendant took to pay as deposed by John Sturman.

Motion by Col. Francis Yardley for an account of estate of Capt. Richard Husbands (mariner). Mr. Edward Packer is attorney for said Husbands.

William Cole vs. Henry Potter & ux.

Thomas Bushell was fined. Date: 1 April 1653.

f. 363 William Smith vs. Capt. William Mitchell.

Liber - Patent Record F & B - 1640-1658

John Sturman vs. Henry Bishop.

Paul Simpson vs. Walter Pakes.

f. 364 Capt. John West & Capt. Robert Abell by their attorney Mr. Thomas Gerrard vs. David Odoughorty.

Edward Scurfield by his attorney William Edwin vs. Nicholas Cawseene.

Motion of Benjamin Gill regarding chattel attached in hands of Walter Packes of Thomas Thornborough for rent of plantation of Mr. Neale.

24 November 1652. Court. Attendees: Governor, Col. Franc. Yardley, Capt. John Price, Mr. Thomas Hatton, Mr. Job Chandler.

William Whittle & Walter Pakes appointed appraisers of estate of Joseph Cadle at Newtowne.

Lt. William Lewis vs. Paul Simpson.

f. 365 William Stevenson vs. Walter Beane administrator of Mr. William Brough. Defendant is attorney of William Scott & his wife Sarah late widow. Deposition of Humfry Atwicks.

Administration

f. 366 granted to Walter Beane on estate of (N) Brough.

Lt. Richard Banks & Walter Pakes appointed appraisers of estate of Mr. William Brough.

John Ashcombe vs. Ismael Wright.

Francis Vandan vs. William Boreman.

Motion by Zephania Smith for chattel

f. 367 he bought of Thomas Hamper. Mr. William Eltonhead alleged chattel sold to Mr. Richard Hodgkins.

Capt. Thomas Cornwallies vs. William Smote. Jury: Mr. Thomas Mathews, Lt. Richard Banks, Ser. Mark Phepo, Mr. John Manfeeld, Mr. Walter Peakes, Mr. Walter Beane, Mr. Charles Manyard, Mr. Robert Cedger, Mr. John Nicholas, Mr. Francis Poesey, Mr. John Medley, Mr. George Mee.

f. 368 William Hardwich vs. William Empson.

John Dandy vs. Mr. William Newgent.

Capt. Thomas Cornwallis, Esq. vs. Mrs. Kathorne Hebden by her attorney William Marshall. Deposition of John Cage

f. 369 that he heard Mr. Cuthbert Fenwick say he received of Capt. Robert Vaughan, of William Wheatley, of Richard Willane. Thomas Cornwallis, Esq. acknowledged satisfaction. Date: 2 March 1653. Signed: Thomas Cornwalleys.

25 November 1652. Court. Attendees: Governor, Col. Francis Yardley, Capt. John Price, Mr. Thomas Hatton, Mr. Job Chandler.

Complaint of Robert Kedger by his attorney Capt. William Mitchell against estate of Mr. Thomas Gerrard

f. 370 when Mr. Land was sheriff. Mr. Land paid debt to Mr. William Bretton attorney for Mr. Thomas Gerrard.

Charles Maynard vs. Lt. Richard Banks administrator of Joseph Cadell.

Jo. Maunsell vs. Rich. Banks administrator of Joseph Cadell. Deposition of Charles Maynard.

William Whittle acknowledged judgement to Mr. Thomas Hatton on account of Capt. Robert Vaughan due him from John Salter.

Motion of Capt. William Mitchell regarding bill against estate of George Manners.

f. 371 Motion by Edward Hall husband to administratrix.

Liber - Patent Record F & B - 1640-1658

Mr. Francis Brooks vs. John Dandy. Complaintant made chattel over to defendant for bill to Col. Littleton.

Mr. Francis Brooks vs. Monjoy Evelin.

f. 372 William Empson acknowledged judgement for payment to Mr. Phillip Land & Henry Fox.

Motion of Thomas Cornwalleis, Esq., William Eltonhead, Mr. Cuthbert Fenwick, et. al.

Phillip Hide vs. Mr. William Eltonhead.

Capt. William Mitchell vs. Maj. Leavin Bufkin by his attorney Mr. Cuthbert Fenwick.

f. 373 Deposition by Richard Hodgkins.

Letter To Governor regarding inhabitants of Kent. Date: 13 December 1652. Signed: William Fuller.

f. 374 Letter to Capt. William Fuller. Date: 18 December 1652. Signed: William Stone.

Regarding commissions of Mr. Edward Lloyd (commander of Anne Arundel Co.) & Capt. Robert Vaughan (commander of Isle of Kent Co.).

Commissions to Mr. Edward Lloyd (commander of Anne Arundel Co.) & Capt. Robert Vaughan (commander of Isle of Kent Co.).

f. 375 dated 29 July 1650 augmented

f. 376 & Mr. Robert Clarke Surveyor General. Date: 18 December 1652. Signed: William Stone.

Francis Vanenden bound himself to William Boreman. Date: 24 September 1650. Witnesses: John Metcalfe, Friendship Toung.

William Boreman & Francis Vanenden bound themselves to each other to stand to award of Capt. William Mitchell & Mr. Francis Brooks. Date: 21 January 1652. Witnesses: Richard Hotchkins, Walter Hall.

f. 377 Richard Ingle (of Wapping, County Middlesex, mariner) assigned to Thomas Cornwallis (also Thomas Cornwallies, gentleman) all chattel.

f. 378 Date: 8 September 1647. Witnesses: Fran. Manestry, William Eltonhead. Notary: John Browne.

Inventory of papers received of Capt. Ingle for goods & debts in VA & MD: Nathaniell Pope, Mr. Gerrard, Barnaby Jackson, Thomas Baldridge, John Sturman, Thomas Bradnox, Capt. William Stone for receipt of bill of Argall Yardley, Esq. & Mr. William Andrews, Capt. William Roper, John Hinman, John Hollowes & John Wavell,

f. 379 Dr. Waldron, Mrs. Wheatley (of Accomack), Mr. William Brainthwaite, Capt. Stone for goods received of Mrs. Wheatley & of Capt. Ingle, Capt. William Roper since in hands of Capt. William Stone. Date: 25 November 1646.

Michael Baisey who married widow of Anthony Rawlings gave chattel to John Rawlings eldest son of said Anthony. Date: 28 January 1652. Witness: Tho. Hatton.

Administration granted to Henry Coxe on behalf of children of Robert Ward (dec'd). Said Coxe married widow (also dec'd). Date: 7 January 1652.

Indenture of 1 November 1643 between Thomas Gerrard (of St. Clement's Hundred) & Cornelius Canedy (brickmaker). Witnesses: William Bretton, John Shurtcliffe.

f. 380 Thomas Gerrard had 1 servant Cornelius Canedy (now runaway per writ of Governor of VA). Said Thomas sold to Morrene Delammonda (chirurgeon, of VA) all rights to said servant. Date: 28 February 1643. Witnesses: James Francis, Crersyen Cuersyaente.

f. 381 Susan Warren deposed on 19 January 1652 that Mrs. Ann Boulton now wife of Mr. Francis Brookes dwelling with Capt. William Mitchell, deponent was present when Mrs. Boulton delivered chattel to said Capt. William Mitchell.

f. 382 Francis Vanenden deposed on 25 January 1652 that about 3 years ago Francis

Brooks gave the deponent use of chattel, & later directed the deponent to deliver that chattel to John Dandy.

f. 383 Edward Hall & his wife Rebecca administratrix of her former husband George Manners appointed Mr. Henry Coursey as their attorney. Date: 25 January 1652. Witness: Tho. Hatton.

William Edde deposed that mid-October last, he was requested by Mr. George Mee to tell Richard Games servant to John Cornelius that Mr. Mee expected the servant returned to him. Date: 22 January 1652.

Garrat Bary deposed on 22 January 1652 that about 6 months ago, he was with John Roads now a servant to Mr. George Mee & inquired of the health of said Roads.

Tho. Gregory deposed on <torn> January 1652 that John Cornelius was to deliver to Mr. George Mee an able man.

f. 384 Thomas Methin, age 45, deposed on 24 January 1652 that he saw no disability in John Roads.

20 January 1652. Court. Attendees: William Stone, Esq. (Governor), Robert Brooks, Esq., Capt. John Price, Mr. Tho. Hatton, Mr. Job Chandler, Mr. Richard Preston.

Francis Brooks vs. Monjoy Evelin. Complainant desires relief of a debt a servant of the defendant in possession of Thomas Gerrard, Esq. had been attached. Cites note by the defendant to Levin Denwood. Mr. Mathew Stone demanded payment on that note.

f. 385 Mr. John Ashcomb vs. Ismaell Wright.

Thomas Bennett, against whom a special warrant was issued for his apprehension as a servant of Mr. Peter Langdell (clarke), appeared in court. Thomas Gerrard, Esq. is attorney for Mr. Langdell.

Thomas Cornwallis, Esq. vs. Thomas Gerrard, Esq. Cites chattel assigned to the complainant by Capt. Richard Ingle.

f. 386 Complaint of Thomas Cornwallis, Esq. vs. Mr. Thomas Gerrard (gentleman). Cites Richard Ingle (marriner), Capt. William Stone (now Governor of this Province).

f. 387 Thomas Cornwallis, Esq. vs. Thomas & John Sturman. Complainant is attorney & assignee of Richard Ingle (marriner).

f. 388 Thomas Cornwallis, Esq. vs. John Sturman.

William Stone, Esq. (Governor) vs. Mr. William Battan.

Robert Taylor, age 30, deposed on 20 January 1652 that James Morphew was drinking at the home of Mr. Battan.

John Tompkinson, age 35, deposed on 20 January 1652 that James Morphew (servant or overseer to William Stone, Esq.) was drinking at the home of Mr. Battan.

f. 389 Mr. John Abbington vs. Mr. James Knott.

Robert Taylor vs. Robert Brook, Esq.

21 January. Court. Attendees: Governor, Mr. Robert Brooke, Capt. John Price, Mr. Thomas Hatton, Mr. Job Chandler, Mr. Richard Preston.

f. 390 William Stone, Esq. (Governor) vs. William Empson. Referred to Mr. John Hatch, Lt. William Lewes, John Maunsell.

Thomas Symonds vs. William Cole.

f. 391 William Empson fined.

John Cornelius fined.

John Hallowes attorney for Capt. Henry Fleete by Edward Packer his attorney vs. Mr. William Eltonhead.

Thomas Gregory acknowledged judgement to Thomas Cornwallis, Esq. et. al.

Thomas Connerye appointed Mr. Friendship Tounge as his attorney. Date: 17 January 1652. Witness: Cuthbert Fenwick.

Thomas Cornwallis, Esq. vs. Walter Beane administrator of William Brough.

Richard Bennett, Esq. (Governor of VA) by his attorney Mr. Thomas Hatton vs. James Linsey. Cites bill from Epaphroditus Leveson to defendant & assigned to complainant.

f. 392 Thomas Connery by his attorney Friendship Toung vs. Edward Claxton by his attorney Mark Phepo. Cites bill of Edward Claxton to Edward Hudson attorney of Robert Holt & assigned by Holt to Connery. Satisfaction on 28 February 1652.

Mr. Thomas Hatton (His Lordship's Attorney General) cites question of rents. Capt. Cornwallis, Mr. William Eltonhead, et. al. were present.

f. 393 Motion by William Smoote to be relieved vs. Capt. Thomas Cornwallis.

Mr. George Mee vs. Mr. John Cornelius. Jury: Mr. Phillip Land, Mr. Thomas Mathewes, Mr. Richard Hodgkins, Mr. Friendship Toung, Ser. Marks Pheypo, Mr. William Whettle, Mr. Andrew Wardner, Lt. William Lewis, Mr. Nicholas Cuzeen, John Maunsell, Mr. Fra. Brooks, Mr. Walter Hall.

f. 394 Mary wife of William Edwine deposed on 20 January 1652 that Goodman Hoult had chattel at her husband's home. Deponent asked Fra. Brooks why the suit against her husband; the reply was: chattel belonged at that time to John Dandy.

f. 395 <u>22 January 1652. Court.</u> Attendees: Governor, Mr. Hatton, Mr. Chandler, Mr. Preston.

William Eddey deposed that 6 months ago George Mee & John Cornelius made a verbal agreement.

Mr. Richard Hodskins deposed that Thomas Hamper sold the deponent chattel in May 1651.

f. 396 Michael Basey vs. Hen. Cox & John Boulton.

Mr. Richard Hoskins deposed that when he was in the service of Capt. William Mitchell, that William Smith was one of Mitchell's servants.

John Bailey deposed on 22 January 1652 that William Smith was at home of Mr. Hatton, & challenged the ownership of chattel, bought the chattel with money from Capt. Michell. The deponent also was at the home of Mr. Phillip Land during his wedding dinner. Ownership question posed to Mrs. Williams.

f. 397 John Wheeler, age 21, deposed on 22 January 1652 that William Smith told the deponent on board a ship at Debtford, that said Smith was a servant to Capt. Mitchell.

George Howes, age 23, deposed on 22 January 1652 that he was aboard the ship Thomas & John at Debtford. William Smith had clothes for servants of Capt. William Mitchell (deponent's then master).

<u>24 January 1652. Court.</u> Attendees: Governor, Mr. Hatton, Mr. Chandler, Mr. Preston.

Marks Phepo vs. Edward Hall.

f. 398 Edward Scurfeeld by his attorney William Edwin vs. Mr. Nicholas Cuseen, Capt. William Mitchell is defendant's attorney. Cites note of complainant as attorney for Thomas Muns.

Nicholas Cawseen deposed

f. 399 that Thomas Muns did agree that in the deponent's payment said Muns would deliver chattel. Edward Scurfield attorney for said Munns & witnessed by Mr. Robert Clarke dated 14 March 1650.

Mr. William Eltonhead deposed on 24 January 1652 that he was at the home of Capt. Mitchell not long before he went to England. Capt. Mitchell asked Mrs. Williams (alias Mrs. Warren) to set aside her father's belongings & he would inquire of Mrs. Mitchell concerning them.

Motion of Thomas Ward (chirurgeon) who married the widow of Edward Commins concerning the sale of part of her land to Joseph Weeks. The widow was asked if she could sell the land from her children by said Commins.

f. 400 Capt. Robert Vaughan deposed that on demand of payment for use of William Stone, Esq. by deponent from William Jones (of Isle of Kent, dec'd), Jones acknowledged the bill.

Liber - Patent Record F & B - 1640-1658

Friendship Toung attorney for Thomas Connerye assigned to Thomas Cornwallis, Esq. judgement against Edward Claxton. Witness: Tho. Hatton.

f. 401 William Cole vs. Henry Potter & ux. Defendant's wife "lyeth in childbed".

Fracis Brooks vs. John Dandy.

William Smith vs. Capt. William Mitchell.

Mary Jones, age 20, deposed that 3 years ago she went to house of Martin Kirk & heard Elisabeth Potter & Martin Kirk & his wife that they found a way to pay (N) Eltonhead. Called them Papist dogs. Cites Capt. Halley.

Mr. Henry Coursey is authorized as attorney for Capt. Robert Vaughan in suit of William Whittle.

f. 402 Date: 28 January 1652. Witness: Tho. Hatton.

Thomas Warr (carpenter) sold 200 a. to James Knott (gentleman, of VA) bounding land of Luke Gardiner. Date: 22 October 1651. Witness: William Stone.

Petition regarding scarcity of corn.

f. 403 Date: 24 January 1652. Signed: William Stone.

William Hampstead registered a cattle mark.

5 February. Mr. Job Chandler registered a cattle mark.

10 February. Mordecue Hammond (son of John Hammond (of VA)) registered a cattle mark, with cows in possession of William Pakes.

26 February 1652. Henry Bullen (of North Patuxent) registered a cattle mark.

1 March 1652. Accounts from Co. of Isle of Kent. Margaret Hunt widow & administratrix of Francis Hunt. Payments to: Mr. Thomas Marsh, Elisabeth Busbie. Margaret Hunt widow & administratrix of Francis Hunt paid accounts. Date: 7 March 1652.

f. 404 Capt. George Evelin, Esq. received of Mrs. Temperance Jay in VA.

f. 405 Date: 11 October 1649. Witnesses: Tho. Scott, Sam. Cooper, John Foxe.

11 March. Lt. William Lewes is indebted to Capt. William Stone.

f. 406 Date: 9 March 1652. Witnesses: Edward Robinson, Edward Mounkes.

11 March 1652. Court. Attendees: William Stone, Esq. (Governor), Capt. John Price, Mr. Thomas Hatton.

Mr. Thomas Hatton (Secretary) informed the court that Mr. Francis Lumbard, (sheriff of Kent Co.) owed payment. Cites Mr. Thomas Marsh (merchant), Capt. Robert Vaughan (commander of the Isle of Kent).

f. 407 Thomas Ward (chirurgeon) vs. Mr. Thomas Ringold & Henry Clay.

f. 408 Thomas Ward vs. Mr. Thomas Ringould.

f. 409 Isaack Ilive, age 37, deposed on 29 January at Court of Kent that he was present with Capt. Robert Vaughan & Thomas Pott & heard Thomas Ward speak of wife of Henry Clay.

Capt. Robert Vaughan affirmed Isaack Ilive & Thomas Ward.

Thomas Pett affirmed.

Henry Clay sued Tho. Ward for slander.

f. 410 Cites deposition of Mr. Thomas Ringould.

Motion of Thomas Ward (chirurgeon) regarding actions with Joseph Weeks & a servant. Ward has a charge of wife & children.

f. 411 Servant belonged to children of Mr. Commins (dec'd).

Henry Potter, age 32, deposed on behalf of Marks Pheypo vs. Edward Hall. Date: 8 February 1652. He stated that in Winter 2 years ago, Edward Hall & Martin Kirke & the deponent were together.

Liber - Patent Record F & B - 1640-1658

23 March. Richard Bennett registered a cattle mark.

f. 412 Release of Mr. Joseph Manning on a bill to Mr. William & Thomas Daines administrators of Mr. Walter Coopar. Date: 9 January 1652. Signed: Henry Coursey. Witness: Tho. Hatton.

James Linsey attorney of Cornelius Canoda petitioned in suit against Thomas Gerrard, Esq. Signed: John Lewger.

John & Richard Sturman bound themselves for William Handwich in suit against Thomas Cornwallis, Esq. Date: 24 March 1652. Witness: Tho. Hatton.

f. 413 Thomas Gerrard, Esq. was authorized to determine designs of the Indians. Date: 24 March 1652.

22 March 1652. Court. Attendees: William Stone, Esq. (Governor), Robert Brooke, Esq., Capt. John Price, Mr. Thomas Hatton, Mr. Job Chandler, Mr. Richard Presto.

Mr. Hugh Lee vs. Henry Potter. For payment to Mr. William Witby (of VA) for passage from VA to MD of defendant.

Daniell Clocker vs. Tho. Cornwallis, Esq.

f. 414 Thomas Cornwallis, Esq. vs. Thomas Gerrard, Esq.

Thomas Gerrard, Esq. vs. Mr. Cuthb. Fenwick.

John Nunne by his attorney Mr. Henry Coursey vs. Mr. Cuthbert Fenwick.

Marks Pheypo, age 35, deposed that Mr. Cuthbert Fenwick 4/5 years ago requested the deponent to set him aboard a sloop of Capt. Burbage.

f. 415 Robert Taylor by his attorney John Hamleton vs. Robert Brooke, Esq.

Phillip Harwood, age 35, deposed on 20 February 1652 that last November the deponent was servant to Mr. Robert Brooke. One of Mr. Brooke's children came with a report. Tho. Brooke & John Taylor went to investigate. Before: Richard Preston.

f. 416 Ishmaell Wright deposed on 16 March 1652 that as a servant of Robert Brooke, one of the children came with a report, & Thomas Brooke & John Taylor went to investigate. Before: Richard Preston.

John Taylor, age 23, deposed on 20 February 1652 that when he was at house of Mr. Robert Brooke, one of his children came with a report. Thomas Brooke & the deponent went to investigate. Before: Richard Preston.

f. 417 Andrew Scot deposed on 20 February 1652 that Mr. Robert Brooke would give satisfaction to his master Robert Taylor. Before: Ri. Preston.

John Taylor & John Gramer deposed on 20 February 1652 that Mr. Brooke said to Robert Taylor if he could prove ownership, he would pay. Before: Ri. Preston.

Mr. John Henry & William Coursey vs. Mr. Thomas Daines by his attorney Geo. Mee.

Thomas Gerrard, Esq. vs. Mr. Cuthbert Fenwick. Defendant was attorney for Capt. Richard Ingle.

f. 418 Capt. Cornwallis (also Thomas Cornwalleyes) demands satisfaction.

William Whittle vs. Capt. Robert Vaughan by his attorney Henry Coursey. Cites chattel from Mrs. Margaret Brent which defendant took forcibly from John Salter.

Edward Hall & his wife Rebecca administratrix of Geo. Manners by their attorney Henry Coursey vs. William Hardwich.

f. 419 Robert Taylor (of Patuxent) made complaint of Mr. Robert Brooke, Esq. (of Patuxent).

23 March 1653. Court. Attendees: same as previous day.

Capt. William Mitchell vs. Henry Cox.

f. 420 William Batten authorized Mr. Thomas Hatton (Secretary) to mediate between him & Governor. Date: 21 January 1652. Witness: Henry Coursey.

Petition of Robert Brooke, Esq. against Mr. Cuthbert Fenwick for killing some chattel. Some chattel ran to land of John Medley (of Newtown).

Robert Brooke, Esq. vs. Mr. Cuthbert Fenwick.

f. 421 Anthony Kitchin, age 21, deposed on 22 March 1652 that last April the deponent was going with his master Robert Brooke, Esq. to the house of Mr. Cuthbert Fenwick, when the deponent's master desired Friendship Toung, Mr. Fenwick's overseer, to show him some chattel.

Thomas Cole, age 34, deposed on 23 March 1652 that in February a year ago, some chattel came to land of Mr. Fenwick where Mr. Fenwick, Mr. Eltonhead, some servants & the deponent lived.

f. 422 Considering the danger of the Indians, Capt. Cornwallis & Mr. Gerrard enlisted the services of Mr. Brooks, one of his sons, & John Shanks. Mr. Brooks & Mr. Preston are to notify Capt. John Price of activities.

Motion of Robert Brooke, Esq. indicating that William Stevens & Thomas Thomas have procured surveys on south side of Patuxent River without warrants. Mentions: Mr. Clarke (surveyor), Mr. Fenwicke, & Peter Johnson.

Mr. John Ashcombe vs. Ismeall Wright.

f. 423 Mentions Mr. Robert Clarke (Surveyor General).

Thomas Bushell appointed Capt. William Mitchell as his attorney in cause with Mr. Cuthbert Fenwick.

Capt. John Price deposed on 23 March 1652 that Humphrey Atwixe had chattel which William Marshall gelded & then went to Owen James.

f. 424 Henry Pountnell vs. Marke Blomfield.

Capt. William Mitchell vs. Mr. Robert Clarke.

Mrs. Kathorne Hebden by her attorney William Marshall vs. Richard Bennit. Mentions Governor Calvert.

Thomas Bushell vs. Friendship Toung & Mr. Cuthb. Fenwick.

f. 425 Motion of Henry Hide servant to Mr. Laurence Starkey for relief. Mr. Fenwick is attorney for Mr. Starkey.

Mr. Thomas Hatton (His Lordship's Attorney General) vs. Seigar Jacob Dirickson by John Hatch. Cites bill from Thomas Warr to said Dirickson, assigned to Thomas Greene, Esq. (dec'd).

f. 426 Mr. Thomas Hatton (His Lordship's Secretary) vs. Skyper Jacob Derickson by his attorney John Hatch.

Cornelius Canada vs. Thomas Gerrard, Esq. Plaintiff was servant to defendant.

Petition of Robert Brooke, Esq. that 1000 a. at Mattaponia are lost to Indians.

f. 427 Governor indicated other land, now occupied by William Stevens & Thomas Thomas. William Stevens has 400 a. adjoining John Ashcomb & Tho. Thomas has another 400 a. adjoining William Stephens.

Capt. William Stone received payment from Henry Potter. Date: 21 March.

Henry Potter registered a cattle mark. On 27 October 1653, Henry Potter purchased cattle.

f. 428 Walter Waterlin registered a cattle mark.

Robert Smith registered a cattle mark.

John Sturman registered a cattle mark.

24 March 1652. Court. Attendees: same as previous day.

John Sturman attorney for Zephania Smith vs. Henry Bishop.

Robert Smith demanded of Humfry Atwicks administrator of William Stephenson.

Motion by Mr. Henry Coursey on behalf of Capt. William Hawley regarding issue of Capt. Thomas Cornwallyes & Mr. Robert Clarke of the titles of Mr. Jerome

Liber - Patent Record F & B - 1640-1658

Hawley (dec'd) & upon reading deed of Mr. James Hawley, request warrant for 6000 a.

f. 429 Robert Brooke, Esq. vs. Capt. William Mitchell.

Petition of Robert Brooke, Esq. that he supplied Capt. William Mitchell's people as per Mr. Henshome, Mr. Geary, & Richard Hoskins & requests payment.

William Smith vs. Capt. William Mitchell & Capt. William Mitchell vs. William Smith. Cites that Smith was a servant of Mitchell.

f. 430 Vincent Atcheson deposed on 22 March 1652 that

f. 431 when he was at Debtford, the deponent met with William Smith. Said Smith said he was a servant of Capt. Mitchell.

Thomas Gerrard, Esq. deposed on 22 March 1652 that he was with the Governor & some of the Council when a letter produced by William Smith was read, regarding suit with Capt. Mitchell.

f. 432 William Smith asks pardon of Capt. Price, regarding his comment on ship of Mr. Husbands about the suit with Capt. Mitchell.

Complaint of Thomas Cornwallis, Esq. vs. Thomas Sturman & John Sturman (coopers) & William Hardwich (taylor). Cites his attorney Cuthbert Fenwick (gentleman), Richard Ingle (marriner).

f. 433 Thomas Cornwalleyes, Esq. vs. Thomas & John Sturman & William Hardwick.

Thomas Cornwallis, Esq. vs. Thomas & John Sturman.

f. 434 Thomas Cornwallyes, Esq. vs. John Sturman.

John Carington vs. Mr. Laurence Starkey by his attorney Mr. Fenwick.

Mr. Thomas Carpenter, age 47, deposed on 24 March 1652 that on 18 October last at St. Inego's, John Carrington demanded his freedom of Mr. Laurence Starkey.

Petition of John Carrington (planter).

f. 435 Demands of Mr. Laurence Starkey his last master.

Mr. Francis Brookes by his attorney Capt. William Mitchell vs. John Dandy. Complaintant was directed to procure note of Col. Nathaniell Littleton.

f. 436 Capt. William Mitchell vs. Lt. Nicholas Gwyther (sheriff). Cites Lt. Richard Banks,

f. 437 one of children of plaintiff, Mr. Robert Brooke, Capt. John Price, Mr. Job Chandler, the Secretary.

The Governor remitted payment charged to Capt. William Mitchell.

Capt. William Mitchell vs. Robert Brooke, Esq.

William Jones, age 25, deposed on 22 March 1652 that 2 years ago, Edward Philpott (wheelwright, servant to Capt. William Mitchell) was at work at the of Robert Brooke, Esq. (deponent's master).

f. 438 Bill of John Nunne (gentleman, of Newtowne) for payment to Paul Sympson (gentleman, of Newtowne). Date: 1 June 1652. Signed: John Nunn. Witnesses: Robert Jones, William Stephenson.

10 April 1653. Court. Attendees: Governor, Mr. Job Chandler.

Mr. John Hallowes vs. Lt. William Lewis.

Francis Vanenden deposed on 11 April 1653 about an order against Capt. William Mitchell.

f. 439 Capt. William Mitchell vs. Thomas Cole. Mentions suit of Francis Vanenden dated 22 April 1652, Henry Fox.

Henry Foxe acknowledged judgement to Mr. Thomas Hatton (His Lordship's Attorney General) for payment in part of fine due Capt. William Mitchell. Mentions payment by Thomas Cole.

f. 440 Mr. Thomas Hatton (Secretary) cited expenses of his sister-in-law & her

Liber - Patent Record F & B - 1640-1658

children (late wife & children of Mr. Richard Hatton (dec'd, brother)) & released Lt. Richard Banks & his wife Margarett late widow of said Richard Hatton. Date: 1 December 1652. Witness: Henry Coursey.

Mr. Thomas Hatton (Secretary)

f. 441 demanded from John Nun. Date: 4 April 1653.

<u>7 June.</u> William Stone, Esq. (Governor) demanded of estate of John Nunn on assignment from Mr. Phillip Land.

Luke Gardiner demanded of estate of John Nunne.

<u>8 July.</u> John Baily registered a cattle mark.

William Cole registered a cattle mark.

John Chandler (gentleman) sold to Mr. Thomas Hatton (Secretary) chattel for him & for Richard Hatton (son of said Thomas) & William Hatton (nephew of said Thomas). Date: 1 August 1653. Witnesses: Henry Coursey, John Metcalfe, Phillip Land.

f. 442 Lt. William Lewis sold to Mr. Thomas Hatton (Secretary) chattel. Date: 23 August 1653. Witness: William Hatton.

Bill from John Nunne to Lt. Richard Banks. Date: 2 May 1652. Signed: John Nun. Witness: Edmund Warmell.

Richard Banks deposed that said John Nun did not pay bill prior to Nun's death. Date: 24 April 1653.

Lt. Richard Banks demanded of estate of John Nunn. Date: 4 April.

Robert Jones servant to John Nunn (dec'd) demanded chattel.

Bill from John Nunn to Ralph Beane. Date: 2 March 1649. Witness: William Robines.

f. 443 Bill from Phillip Auther & John Nunn to Walter Beane. Witnesses: Richard Bralley, Tho. Bushell.

Bill from John Nunne to John Wade (chirurgeon). Date: 1 April 1651. Witness: William Parfitt. John Wade assigned his right to Mr. Walter Beane.

Walter Beane administrator demands from estate of (N) Nun. Date: 1 April.
- Account of John Bailye.

f. 444 ...
- Chattel for his man Ro. Jones.
- Assignment from William Marshall.

Date: 11 April. Signed: John Baily.

Bill from John Nunn (of Newtowne Hundred) to Robert Duglas (of Wichocomoco). Date: 6 February 1650. Witness: Walter Gest. Robert Duglas assigned to Capt. John Price. Date: 10 February 1650. Witnesses: Miles Cooke, Richard Banks. Capt. John Price demands from estate of John Nunn.

Bill from John Nunn to John Thimbleby. Date: 15 May 1652. Witnesses: Henry Bishop, Robert Sheld. John Thimbleby demanded from estate of John Nunn. Date: 4 April.

Bill from John Nunn

f. 445 to John Pille. Date: 2 February 1652. Witness: John Medley. Mr. Pile demands from estate of John Nunn. Date: 4 April.

Bill from John Nunn to John Medley. Date: 12 February 1649. Witness: John Thimbleby.

Bill from Phillip Allser & John Nunn to John Medley. Signed: Phillip Allder, John Nunne. Date: 12 February 1649. Witness: John Thimbellby. John Medley demands from estate of John Nunn. Date: 4 April.

f. 446 Mr. Phillip Land & Henry Fox demanded from estate of John Nunn. Date: 4 April.

Mr. Paul Simpson demanded from estate of John Nunn. Date: 4 April.

Liber - Patent Record F & B - 1640-1658

Walter Peaks acknowledged payment to John Dandy. Witness: Edward Packer.

Richard Spanne gave to youngest child of John Shurtcliff cattle. Should child die under age, then cattle to wife of John Shurtcliff. Date: 22 January 1651. Witnesses: William Evans, Charles Maynard.

Capt. John Hallowes discharged Thomas Baker of bill. Date: 16 April 1652. Witnesses: Rich. Browne, Thomas Bennett.

Robert Brooke, Esq. acknowledged judgement to Mr. Phillip Land & Henry Fox for payment. Date: 7 June 1653.

f. 447 Capt. John Price acquits Thomas Hatton (Secretary) of all accounts. Date: 14 August 1653. Witnesses: William Coursey, Henry Adams.

Thomas Gerard (also Thomas Gerrard, gentleman) is indebted to William Mitchell, Esq. If said Mitchell should die,

f. 448 Thomas Gerrard is to deliver to children of said William Mitchell. Date: 24 April 1652. Witnesses: William Bretton, Roger Isham.

William Mitchell, Esq. appointed William Johnson & Henry Foxe as attorneys for self & children. Date: 25 April 1653. Witnesses: Mathew Stone, Thomas Stone.

Thomas Cornwalleys, Esq. conveyed to Cornelius Canada 300 a. on south side of Putuxent River, bounding land of Nicholas Harvey.

f. 449 Date: 23 November 1652. Witnesses: Marke Phepo, Richard Hotchkyes.

f. 450 7 June 1653. Court. Attendees: Capt. William Stone, Esq. (Governor), Thomas Gerrard, Esq., Capt. John Price, Mr. Thomas Hatton, Mr. Richard Preston.

Mr. Phillip Land deposed on 7 June that he heard Mr. Francis Brookes had bought of Capt. William Mitchell. Mrs. Ann Boulton is now wife of said Brookes.

Mr. Francis Brookes & ux vs. Capt. William Mitchell by his attorney Henry Fox & Capt. William Mitchell by his attorney Henry Fox vs. Mr. Francis Brooks. Mentions: Major Wildman, Mr. Phillip Land.

f. 451 Testimony regarding Capt. Mitchell & Mrs. Ann Boulton now wife of Francis Brookes. Signed: John Wildman. Date: 14 February 1652 London.

Ann Beach (widow) vs. Francis Vanenden.

f. 452 Stanhop Roberts vs. Mr. Robert Clarke (surveyor). Cites land of Barnaby Jackson, Francis Brookes.

f. 453 Walter Peakes vs. John Hamond. Cites bill of Hugh Lee to defendant.

Motion of Mr. Thomas Hatton (His Lordship's Attorney General) on estate of William Bounday. William Stephens requested administration. James Veich to take effects into custody for His Lordship.

f. 454 Zephania Smith vs. Mr. William Eltonhead. Motion of William Stephens on behalf of plaintiff.

Cornelius Cannaday vs. Tho. Gerrard, Esq.

f. 455 8 June 1653. Court. Attendees: same as previous day.

William Edwine vs. Miles Cooke (mariner). Mentions Capt. Richard Husbands.

Miles Cooke (marriner) vs. Capt. Richard Husbands (marriner) by his attorney Edward Packer. Plaintiff desires satisfaction ordered to pay William Edwin.

Motion of Mr. John Hamond on behalf of wife of Robert Taylor.

f. 456 William Smith vs. Capt. William Mitchell. Motion of Mrs. Susan Warren (daughter & assignee of plaintiff). Mrs. Warren to have credit with Capt. Cornwallyes.

Mr. Joseph Manning (merchant) vs. Mr. Tho. Webb (merchant). Motion by Tho. Gerrard, Esq. on behalf of plaintiff. Attachment from plaintiff's suit to be placed in hands of Mr. Eltonhead.

Tho. Cornwallyes, Esq. vs. Tho. Gerrard, Esq.

Liber - Patent Record F & B - 1640-1658

Robert Taylor vs. Robert Brooke, Esq. Jury: Mr. William Bretton, Mr. Luke Gardiner, Mr. William Boreman, Mr. William Johnson, Mr. John Lawson, Mr. Tho. Mathews, Mr. William Edwin, Mr. Stanhop Roberts, Mr. John Cornelius, Mr. Tho. Bushell, Mr. William Smith, Mr. John Nicholls.

f. 457 Robert Taylor vs. Robert Brooke, Esq. John Hambleton deposed.

f. 458 Date: 23 April 1653. Ismaell Wright, John Taylor, & Phillip Harwood viewed the chattel of Robert Taylor vs. chattel killed at plantation of Robert Brooke, Esq. Before: Ri. Preston. Answer of Robert Brooke, Esq. to petition of Robert Taylor. Cites several courts appointed by Mr. Preston.

f. 459 Capt. Henry Fleete by his attorney Mr. John Hallowes vs. Mr. William Eltonhead. Capt. Henry Fleete appointed John Hallowes as his attorney to receive the debt. 2 August 1652. Witness: Jo. Due.

Thomas Gerrard, Esq. vs. Mr. Cuthbert Fenwick. Mentions: Capt. Thomas Cornwalleys.

Mr. Francis Brookes fined.

f. 460 Thomas Gerrard, Esq. vs. Mr. Cuthbert Fenwick.

Mr. Cuthbert Fenwick vs. Capt. William Mitchell.

Robert Taylor vs. Mary Ketchmay.

Mr. Joseph Manning (merchant) vs. Cloves Mace.

Walter Pakes, age 43, deposed on 7 June that

f. 461 Edward Cotten (also Edward Cotton, dec'd) had satisfied a debt to John Warren.

9 June 1653. Court. Attendees: Governor, Mr. Thomas Hatton, Mr. Richard Preston.

Edward Packer vs. George Mee.

John Carrington vs. Laurence Starkey, Esq. Cites deposition of Thomas Carpenter.

Robert Brooke, Esq. vs. George Ketchmay & Henry Ketchmay. Request for chattel to be viewed by John Grammer & Peter Johnson.

f. 462 MM Henry, John, & William Coursey vs. Mr. Thomas Daynes.

Markes Pheypo acknowledged satisfaction from Capt. Robert Vaughan payable to him & William Chappell. Witness: Tho. Hatton.

The Governor appointed Mr. John Metcalfe as high sheriff of St Maries' Co.

Petition of Robert Brooke, Esq. Cites petition of William Batten which caused payment to Henry Ketchmay & George Ketchmay his brother & master. Mentions: Peter Johnson.

f. 463 Miles Cooke deposed that he heard Benjamine Cowell say to Mr. Husbands that he received from Mr. Pills chattel for use of Mr. Richard Thurstone on board ship Hopefull Adventure who command was Mr. Richard Husbands. 8 June 1653.

John Hallowes (gentleman), age 40, deposed that before Ralph Beane went to England, the deponent paid said Beane for use of John Dandy. Before: Tho. Baldridge.

f. 464 Mr. Hallowes deposed that he paid fee in 1650. Date: 7 June 1653.

John Nunn was bound to Henry Fox. Date: 31 March 1651. Witness: Phillip Land. Henry Fox assigned said bond to Edward Packer. Date: 25 April 1651. Witness: Phillip Land. Edward Packer (gentleman) assigned said bond to Mr. Walter Beane. Date: 1 January 1652. Witness: Henry Coursey. Walter Beane administrator demanded of estate of John Nunn.

John Nunn was bound to Phillip Land. Date: 12 February 1650. Witness: Jeffry Oliver. Phillip Land assigned said bond to Nicholas Cuzeene. Date: 16 October 1651. Nicholas Cuzeene demanded of the estate.

f. 465 Ann Johnson, age 34, deposed on 30 April 1653 that she & Sarah Goulson were at the house of Robert Taylor on 24 December at the labor of said Taylor's wife. The following Sunday, the deponent came with her sister Alice Griffin. Mary

Liber - Patent Record F & B - 1640-1658

Taylor said it was not her brother's child. On Monday, the deponent asked Margaret Browne whether Robert Taylor said that he would turn his wife & the bastard out. Mentions: Edward Brisley.

f. 466 Mary Taylor had offended God & wronged her husband & children. Her cousin & the deponent urged her to identify the father of the child, as (N) Catchmey.

f. 467 She was 3/5 weeks pregnant when she came from VA. Robert Taylor said he would get a warrant from Mr. Preston.

f. 468 Signed: Ann Johnson. Before: William Stone, Rich. Preston.

Margaret Brome, age 24, deposed that on 24 December 1652 when her cousin Mary Taylor gave birth, Mrs. Johnson presented the child to Robert Taylor & he refused it. Cites: Mrs. Johnson, Sarah Goulson, & Alce Griffine (sister of Mary Taylor).

f. 469 Mrs. Johnson indicated it was like a Ketchmay.

f. 470 Signed: Margret Broome. Before: William Stone, Richard Preston.

Andrew Scot, age 30, deposed that Mary Taylor bid for Mr. Catchmay to take his child. Date: 7 May 1653. Signed: Andrew Scotte. Before: Ri. Preston.

Henry Pope, age 32, deposed that Andrew Scott told the deponent that his dame Mary Taylor bid Mr. Catchmay to take his child. Date: 2 May 1653. Before: Rich. Preston.

f. 471 Sarah Goulson, age 30, deposed that she was at the house of Mrs. Johnson, when Anne Pope sent for Mrs. Johnson. Mrs. Johnson told Mary Taylor that Mr. Catchmay was the father of the child; Mary Taylor denied it. Signed: Sara Goulson. Date: 7 May 1653. Before: Ri. Preston.

Sara Goulson, age 30, deposed that going to the house of Robert Taylor 3/4 days after his

f. 472 wife gave birth, when his wife said the father was Mr. Catchmey. Date: 7 May 1653. Before: Ri. Preston.

Mary Catchmey, age 25, deposed that she heard Geo. Catchmey say that he was at the house of Robert Taylor and Mary Taylor presented him with her child & Catchmey denied it. Robert Taylor went to house of John Grammer.

f. 473 Robert Taylor went to VA & to the house of George Catchmey.

f. 474 Deponent asked her brother Geo. Catchmey if he had been with her [Mary Taylor]. Mentions Thomas Davis the cooper [a rogue]. Date: 7 May 1653. Before: Rich. Preston.

Peter Johnson, age 42, deposed that he went to the house of Robert Taylor after his wife had given birth, & spoke about the birth.

f. 475 Mr. Catchmey came to the deponent's house a day or so later. Date: 7 May 1653. Before: Ri. Preston.

Cornelius Abraham deposed that last January, in going to VA, he met Geo. Catchmey at Cedar Point, who requested passage to VA. They discussed Robert Taylor, his wife, & the child. Date: 6 April 1653. Before: Ri. Preston.

f. 476 William Phillips, age 19, deposed that he heard Sarah Goulson talk to Mrs. Johnson. Mrs. Johnson said that Mrs. Osborne had sent to New England for chattel for her. Mrs. Johnson spoke of Mary Taylor & (N) Catchmey. Date: 7 May 1653. Before: Ri. Preston.

f. 477 John Tennis, age 25, deposed that he was at house of Mrs. Johnson & heard that there was a disagreement between Mrs. Johnson & Mary Taylor. Date: 7 May 1653. Before: Ri. Preston.

William Gramall, age 30, deposed on 7 May 1653 that Mrs. Johnson spoke of Mary Taylor & Mr. Catchmey. Before: Ri. Preston.

Francis Walton, age 47, deposed that he was

f. 478 at the house of Henry Catchmey & Mary Catchmey & the deponent were talking about Mr. Catchmey & Mary Taylor. The deponent said he believed his master would take the side of Robert Taylor. Date: 7 May 1653. Before: Ri. Preston.

Liber - Patent Record F & B - 1640-1658

William Hanington, age 21, affirmed to what Francis Walton said. Date: 7 May 1653. Before: Ri. Preston.

George Rapier (musician) sold to John Carrington (planter) chattel & 100 a. opposite land owned by Capt. Brent, being .5 of the land laid out by Mr. John Lewger (Deputy Surveyor). Date: 9 August 1653. Witness: Henry Coursey. Acknowledgement by John Carrington. Date: 9 August 1653. Witnesses: Henry Coursey, Thomas Robinson.

f. 479 Gift to Ann Hamon wife of John Hamond & her 4 children: Mordecay, Bernard, Ann, Daniell. Date: 28 December 1652. Signed: Gervis Dodson. Witnesses: William Hardie, Richard Sharpe. Received: 20 June 1653. Signed: John Hamond. Witness: Tho. Hatton.

1 August 1653 in Kent Co. Court. Attendees: Mr. Thomas Ringgould, Mr. Thomas Bradnox, Mr. Henry Morgan, Mr. Joseph Weeks, Mr. John Russell.

Francis Bright accused John Smith, Jr. of felony.

f. 480 Signed: Thomas Hatton.

Examination of John Smith, Jr. by Fra. Bright (of Isle of Kent). John Smith is servant of Fra. Bright.

f. 481 Referred by Mr. Thomas Hynson & John Ellis.

Henry Bishop made over chattel to John Medley & John Thimbleby. Date: 14 August 1653. Witnesses: John Metcalfe, Robert Greene.

Andrew Wardner registered a cattle mark.

Mr. Symon Oversea (merchant) registered a cattle mark.

26 September 1653 at St. Maries'. Court. Attendees: William Stone, Esq. (Governor), Capt. John Price, Mr. Thomas Hatton (Secretary).

Mr. John Hamond for wife & children vs. Walter Pakes.

f. 482 Chattel due from Gervis Dodson to Ann wife of complaintant & her 4 children.

Mary Warron (widow) deposed that on Thursday in last week in July, 4 Indians came into the house of Capt. Daniell Gookins on South River in Anne Arundel Co. The deponent's husband Jacob Warron, the deponent, & their son Jacob (age 7), all servants to said Gookins, were there. Her husband Jacob was killed,

f. 483 & her child.

Indictment of 2 Indians by Mr. Thomas Hatton (His Lordship's Attorney General). The 2 Piscataway Indians, & Indian Couna-weza, murdered Jacob Warron, a Negro servant of Capt. Daniell Gooken, & a child of said servant (age 7).

f. 484 Indians confronted by Mary Warron, Negro woman, & sent down by the Emperor Warcope. Jury: Mr. Cuthb. Fenwick, Mr. William Bretton, Lt. Nicholas Gwyther, Mr. John Sturman, Mr. Edward Packer, Lt. Richard Banks, Mr. Phillip Land, Lt. William Evans, Mr. John Lawson, Mr. Richard Hoskins, Mr. William Johnson, Mr. John Medley, Mr. Richard Willan, Mr. Henry Adams, Mr. Robert Cadger, Mr. John Nicholls, Mr. Daniell Clocker, Mr. James Langworth, Mr. John Thimbleby, Mr. William Edwine, Mr. John Taylor, Mr. John Hammond, Mr. Zachary Wade, Mr. Tho. Sympson.

f. 485 Paul Sympson & Walter Peakes agreed to

f. 486 partnership.

f. 487 Date: 20 September 1653. Signed: Paule Sypson. Witnesses: John Hammond, Richard Ware.

Paul Sympson authorized Walter Peaks as his attorney. Date: 20 September 1653. Signed: Paule Sympson. Witnesses: John Hammond, Richard Ware.

f. 488 Lt. Richard Banks gave to Richard Hatton (nephew to Mr. Thomas Hatton (Secretary)). Said Richard Hatton is son to wife of said Banks. Date: 17 October 1653.

f. 489 4 October. William Stone, Esq. (Governor) sold to Col. William Whittington (of Northampton Co. VA) all land in Northampton Co. Cites land sold to: James Davis, Urmston Foster, Mr. Cowdrey, Richard Nottingham,

Liber - Patent Record F & B - 1640-1658

f. 490 William Sachell. Date: 3 October 1653. Witnesses: Tho. Hatton, Francis Pott.

27 October. Henry Potter gave to his wife Elisabeth Potter chattel. Witness: Tho. Hatton.

Henry Potter gave to his daughter Awdrey Potter chattel. Witness: Tho. Hatton.

Edward Hall (planter) sold

f. 491 to Henry Potter (planter) one-half plantation (75 a.) where Hall lived. Date: 24 March 1652. Witnesses: William Mitchell, Tho. Bushell.

William Eltonhead (gentleman) discharged Henry Potter of all debts. Date: 1 May 1651.

f. 492 William Stone, Esq. (Governor) discharged Mr. Thomas Hatton (Secretary) of all debts. Date: 1 August 1653. Witness: Henry Coursey.

22 November. William Stevens demanded of estate of James Allen.

Tho. Hatton, at the direction of Lord Baltimore, sold to Mrs. Eure chattel, bought of Richard Bennett (also Richard Bennit). Date: 31 March 1653. Witnesses: William Stone, Henry Coursey.

2 December. Thomas Howard registered a cattle mark.

f. 493 Bill of Paul Sympson (gentleman) to Thomas Wilford (gentleman). Date: 19 October 1654. Witnesses: John Mottrom, Francis Clay. Thomas Wilford (gentleman, of County Northumberland) received of Paul Sympson (gentleman).

f. 494 Date: 19 October 1653. Witnesses: John Mottrom, Francis Clay.

Richard Thurston (marriner, of Boston, New England) appointed "my loving brethren" Charles Thurston & Robert Lord (marriners, of Boston) as attorneys. Date: 27 October 1653. Witnesses: Anthony Binge, James Hitchcocke, Nathaniell Gowther.

f. 495 William Smith appointed his daughter Susan Warren as his attorney. Date: 31 May 1653. Witnesses: John Metcalfe, Walter Hall.

f. 496 Proclamation. Date: 7 November 1653. Signed: William Stone.

Proclamation on motion of Thomas Cornwallis, Esq., Mr. Mr. Eltonhead,

f. 497 et. al., per information from Mr. Thomas Hatton, Marks Pheypo, Nicolas Keating, Martin Kirke, et. al. Date: 15 December 1653. Signed: William Stone.

f. 498 12 January. John Taylor sold to Robert Jones chattel. Date: 23 March 1652. Witness: Richard Watson.

Robert Jones registered a cattle mark.

John Bugbye, age 27, deposed that he went to the house of John Day last January when Edward Brisley came to discuss business. Mentions: Mr. Preston. Date: 7 January 1653. Before: Robert Brooke.

John Day, age 34, deposed in suit between Edward Brisley & Mr. Preston, that

f. 499 last January, Edward Brisley & Mr. Preston were discussing business. Date: 9 January 1653. Before: Robert Brooke.

William Walworth, age 22, deposed that the testimony of John Day was correct.

William Ewen, age 45, deposed that last January at the house of John Day, the deponent & Edward Brisely were discussing business regarding Mr. Preston. Date: 9 January 1653. Before: Robert Brooke.

f. 500 Indenture between Thomas Copley, Esq. (of St. Inego's) & Humphry Howell, Blanch Howell his wife & Mary Harris (daughter of said Blanch). Date: 8 August 1648. Witnesses: Robert Jerry, Thomas Mathews.

f. 501 Thomas Cornwallyes, Esq. (of Cornwalleys Cross) sold to Humphry Howell (of St. Inego's) 100 a., bounding Portoback Quarter.

f. 502 Date: 13 October 1653. Witnesses: Richard Hotchkeyes, John Nicholes.

11 January. Administration was granted to Henry Pope who married Ann late widow of Thomas Balmer (of Putuxent).

Liber - Patent Record F & B - 1640-1658

10 January. Edward Gibons (merchant, of Boston, New England) appointed Mr. Daniel Hoare

f. 503 (merchant, of London) as his attorney. Date: 11 October 1653. Witnesses: Peter Brackitt, John Richards.

31 January. John Cage registered a cattle mark.

f. 504 Thomas Baker registered a cattle mark.

William Empson registered a cattle mark.

1 February 1653. Court. Atendees: Governor, Secretary.

Proclamation regarding estate of John Stringer (carpenter), per information from Mr. William Wilkinson (clerke).

2 February. Bill from John Stringer to Capt. Richard Husbands. Date: 25 January 1652. Witness: Edward Packer.

f. 505 Thomas Cager demanded from the estate of John Stringer due to Mr. Peter Langsdale (clark).

Mr. Edward Packer attorney for Capt. Richard Husbands demanded from the estate of John Stringer.

Mr. William Allen (merchant) demanded from the estate of John Stringer.

Mr. Phillip Land demanded from the estate of John Stringer.

Walter Waterling demanded from the estate of John Stringer.

Robert Holt (planter in St. George's Hundred) bound himself to Mr. Nicholas Cawseen. Date: 28 January 1653. Witnesses: Ralphe Crouche, Zachay Zacharis.

f. 506 4 February. Mr. Mathew Stone demanded for himself & for Mr. John Stringer from the estate of John Stringer.

Col. Francis Yardley demanded from the estate of John Stringer.

6 February. Mr. William Wilkinson demanded from the estate of John Stringer

f. 507 for goods delivered to Capt. Webber & Mr. Allen, Mr. William Wilkinson to John Stringer.

Fracis Brookes demanded from the estate of John Stringer.

6 February 1653. Court. Atendees: Governor, Capt. John Price, Mr. William Eltonhead, Mr. Thomas Hatton.

Mr. William Wilkinson brought accounts of the estate of John Stringer. Motion by Mr. William Allen (merchant) & Capt. Thomas Webber, William Edwyn (also William Edwin), et. al. Cites William Wareing (carpenter).

f. 508 John Johnson & Thomas Adams vs. Col. Francis Yardley & Nathaniell Batts. Mentions: Mr. Charles Thurston.

f. 509 13 February. John Cornelius (planter) acknowledged a debt to Col. Francis Yardley

f. 510 before Capt. William Stone, Esq. (Governor). Date: 23 November 1651. Col. Francis Yardley assigned to Capt. Thomas Corwalleys. Date: 23 November 1651. Satisfaction on 13 February 1653.

15 February 1653. Court. Atendees: Governor, Secretary.

Estate of John Stringer. Mr. William Allen (merchant) claiming for himself & for Capt. Richard Husbands as greatest creditors. Motion of William Warren regarding bills by John Baily.

f. 511 Motion of Thomas Bennett regarding bills by Richard Bennett & John Mills. Mentions: Mr. William Allen, Capt. Thomas Webber. Motion of Mr. William Wilkinson who produced the account of the estate.

f. 512 List of goods sold to John Stringer per Mr. William Allen.

f. 513 List of goods delivered on 7 February 1653 to William Allen. List of goods delivered to Capt. Webber.

Liber - Patent Record F & B - 1640-1658

f. 514 George Willard (planter) assigned to Arther Wright (planter) chattel. Signed: George Willarde. Witnesses: John Hamelton, John Kale.

Proclamation. Date: 7 February 1653. Signed: William Stone.

f. 515 Henry Bishop deposed that last Christmas, Mary wife of William Edwyn received from William Stills chattel formerly belonging to deponent as per Walter Pakes.

f. 516 A fortnight later, Daniell Clocker came to the deponent's house. Date: 6 December 1653.

William Eltonhead, Esq.

f. 517 sold to Henry Potter chattel. Date: 3 March 1653. Witness: William Bretton.

3 March 1653. Received by William Eltonhead of Henry Potter: Imp: Mr. Anketell, to John Dandy for my use, Mr. Clarke for my use William Johnson for my use.

Henry Pountnell (carpenter) sold to Henry Potter chattel. Date: 4 February 1653. Witnesses; Andrew Wardnor, John Prince.

Walter Guest registered a cattle mark.

Thomas Connery acknowledged judgement to Thomas Cornwalleys, Esq.

f. 518 Francis Posey (planter) bound himself to Edward Swan chattel. Said Edward Swanne is bound with said Fra. Posey to Walter Beane. Witnesses: John Hatch, William Marshall.

Walter Peakes acquits Paul Sympson (gentleman) of all actions. Date: 3 January 1653.

f. 519 Witnesses: Tho. Willsfoard, Bridgit Willsfoard. 25 January 1653 recorded by Tho. Willsfoard Clerk Northb.

4 March 1653. Mr. Daniell Barwyck acknowledged judgement to Mr. Phillip Land. Signed: Daniell Barwicke. Mr. Phillip Land acknowledged satisfaction from Capt. Daniell Barwick. Date: 25 May 1654. Witness: Tho. Hatton.

Richard Recklesse acknowledged judgement to Lt. Nicholas Gwyther for use of Capt. William Hawley.

Raph Crouch executor of Henry Hooper (chirurgeon) assigned right of judgement to Mr. Cuthbert Fenwick. Date: 3 March 1653. Witnesses: Mathew Stone, Thomas Stone.

Capt. Thomas Webber (master of the Mayflower of London) et. al., took as a prize a ship in St. George's River. Date: 18 January 1653. Signed: William Stone.

f. 520 Mr. Symon Oversea (also Symon Oversey, merchant, Englishman, inhabitant of VA & MD) is not be molested. Date: 24 January 1653. Signed: William Stone.

Mr. Job Chandler took oath as a counsellor. Date: 11 February 1653.

f. 521 1 March 1653. Court. Attendees: William Stone, Esq. (Governor), Mr. Thomas Gerrard, Capt. John Price, Mr. Thomas Hatton, Mr. Robert Clarke.

Henry Bishop deposed that mid-November last, Mr. John Hammond delivered a note to the deponent to be delivered to Paul Sympson, believed to be living on VA side of Patomock River. The deponent returned the letter to said Hammond. The letter was later read to Walter. Pakes.

Mr. Robert Clarke took oath as a counsellor.

Robert Cadger complained against Ann Harlow his servant.

f. 522 Said Ann Harloe is to serve extra time to pay for expenses to Henry Fox.

Thomas James acknowledged judgement to Thomas Cornwalleys, Esq.

Phillip Land the younger, son of Phillip Land the elder, registered a cattle mark.

Tho. Burbage authorized Capt. Thomas Cornwalleys, Esq. as his attorney. Date: 9 May 1653. Witness: John Barber.

Liber - Patent Record F & B - 1640-1658

Col. Thomas Burbage by his attorney Capt. Thomas Cornwalleys, Esq. vs. Thomas Gerrard, Esq. Cites bill paid to Alexander Williamson by plaintiff for the defendant. The defendant

f. 523 directed Lewis Burwell to pay the complainant.

Col. Thomas Burbage by his attorney Thomas Cornwalleys, Esq. vs. William Smoote.

f. 524 Lord Baltimore by his Attorney General vs. Marks Pheypo, Nicholas Keeting, & Martin Kirke.

Walter Beane vs. Paul Sympson.

Motion of Thomas Cornwallyes, Esq. alleging he paid Nicholas Cawseene by appointment of William Smoote.

Thomas Cornwalleys, Esq. vs. Thomas & John Sturman. Defendant John Sturman is the son of defendant Thomas Sturman. Arbitration by William Stone, Esq. (Governor) & Mr. Thomas Hatton (Secretary).

Major Edward Gibons by his attorney Mr. Daniell Hore vs. John Nicholls.

f. 525 John Nicholls vs. Phillip Land.

2 March 1653. Court. Attendees: William Stone, (Governor), Mr. Thomas Gerrard, Mr. William Eltonhead, Capt. John Price, Mr. Tho. Hatton, Mr. Robert Clarke.

Walter Beane administrator of John Nunn. Accounts. Payments to: Secretary, sheriff, Mr. Piles, Robert Jones (servant to dec'd), John Baily,

f. 526 John Baily assignee of William Marshall, William Stone, Esq. (Governor), Lt. Richard Banks, Capt. John Price on bill to Robert Duglas, John Medley,

f. 527 William Marshall, Walter Beane (administrator) assignee of Thomas Dynyard, Luke Gardiner, John Thimbleby, Mr. Phillip Land & Henry Fox,

f. 528 Nicholas Cawseene assigned to Phillip Land, Robert Jones (50 a.).

Mr. Cuthb. Fenwick formerly attorney for Mr. Thomas Bushrode acknowledged that he gave Mr. Mary Brent receipts from her brother Capt. Giles Brent.

Mr. Edward Packer vs. Mr. Richard Hoskins.

Motion of Mr. Edward Packer

f. 529 as attorney for Capt. Richard Husbands the greatest creditor to estate of John Stringer. Mentions: Mr. William Allen.

Mr. Georg Mee demanded from the estate of John Stringer.

John Buttrice vs. John Cornelius.

Henry Medley, at the request of Mrs. Cornelius, deposed that a year ago he saw a ring in the hands of Mary Hatton that John Buttrice gave her. Date: 2 March 1653. Before: Thomas Hatton.

Lt. William Lewis was arrested at the suit of William Hardwick. Edward Packer is the attorney for said Lewis.

Mr. John Metcalfe (sheriff) deposed that Lt. Lewis authorized Mr. Edward Packer as his attorney in the suit against Mr. William Hardwick.

f. 530 Mr. William Hardwick vs. Lt. William Lewis. Mr. Edward Packer is attorney for plaintiff.

Arthur Wright deposed that he did not know that Mr. Cuthb. Fenwick ever killed chattel of Mr. Robert Brookes.

Ralph Hazelton, age 23, deposed on 26 February 1653 that he went with Mr. Cuthb. Fenwick. Mentions: Mr. Eltonhead & Mr. Fenwick. 3/4 weeks later, the deponent

f. 531 was sent by Friendship Toungue. Before: Job Chandler.

Motion of Mr. William Wilkinson regarding the estate of John Stringer.

Liber - Patent Record F & B - 1640-1658

Thomas Bennett, at the request of Walter Waterlyn, deposed that Mr. Stringer last November received chattel of said Walter, promising to deduct it from the bill of Capt. Cornwalleys.

Petition of Richard Moore regarding threats by Michael Baisey.

f. 532 Ordered the survey of the land of the children of Anthony Rawlings (mentioned in the above petition) be perfected.

Walter Pakes acknowledged judgement to Mr. John Hallowes.

Mr. Cuthb. Fenwick vs. Henry Fox attorney for Capt. Mitchell. Plaintiff sent chattel via Capt. Mitchell to Holland, whereupon Capt. Mitchell was to pay Mr. Lawrence Coughan (of Amsterdam). Capt. William Mitchell acknowledged transporting the chattel. Date: 4 March 1651. Witness: William Eltonhead.

f. 533 William Boreman vs. Mr. Robert Clarke. Mr. Robert Clarke is debtor to William Boreman for voyage from Accomack.

William Stone, Esq. (Governor) vs. Arthur Lehay.

3 March 1653. Court. Attendees: same as previous day.

Walter Beane deposed that John Slingsby worked for deponent about 2.5 years ago, for which William Stephenson was to pay.

f. 534 Motion of John Slingesby for payment from the estate of William Stephenson by Humfrey Atwicks administrator.

Thomas Cornwalleys, Esq. vs. Arthur Lehay. Cites defendant's payment to Mr. Weston.

James Lindesey vs. Thomas Bushell.

Mr. Francis Brookes vs. Mr. Paul Sympson. Cites bill in the hands of John Medley.

To: Thomas Hatton, (Secretary) cites service to him & Mrs. Hatton, & Goodman Medley is to pay Hatton, attachment of Mr. Wilford.

f. 535 Date: 24 February 1653. Signed: Paul Sympson. On 3 March 1653, John Medley to pay for Mr. Hatton. Before: William Eltonhead, Robert Clarke.

Mr. Arthur Turnor acknowledged a debt to Mr. Thomas Hatton (Secretary) per the account of John Hatch for a debt of Skipper Jacob Derrickson.

Thomas Cager vs. Mr. Peter Landesdesdale. Cites chattel in the hands of John Stringer.

Thomas Connery vs. Mr. Henry Hooper. Motion of defendant by James Veich.

Petition of Thomas Connery. Petitioner came from VA by persuasion of Henry Hooper.

f. 536 Robert Richins vs. Robert Warren. Petition of Robert Richins, who was servant to Robert Warren.

Mr. Robert Clarke vs. William Boreman. Complaintant cites John Abbott his servant, who went with defendant 2 years ago to VA.

f. 537 Francis Posey acknowledged a judgement to Henry Fox.

Motion by Mrs. Mary Brent for Capt. Giles Brent her brother. That Mr. Francis Brookes on 20 June 1651 obtained a judgement against her brother. Motion by Mr. Hatton His Lordship's Attorney General.

f. 538 Symon Groves (tob. rowler, of New England) appointed Daniell Clocker (planter) as his attorney. Date: 3 April 1652. Witnesses: Edm. Wormell, Henry Coursey, Phillip Land.

Symon Groves by his attorney Daniell Clocker vs. William Edwyn. Mentions deposition by Henry Bishop.

Petition by Robert Taylor that John Hambleton is indebted to petitioner. Petition of Robert Taylor that his maid servant is pregnant; father is thought to be

f. 539 John Hambleton. Petition of Robert Taylor vs. John Hambleton.

Liber - Patent Record F & B - 1640-1658

Ales Harris, age 30, deposed that when she was coming from Green's Rest, she saw in St. Peter's Field chattel of Zachary Wade, which John Dandy said was his.

Petition of William Harrison on behalf of George Abbott (merchant) that John Hambleton is indebted to Mr. Abbott

f. 540 on petition of attorney of George Abbott vs. John Hambleton.

Robert Newman vs. Francis Poesey.

Paul Sympson vs. Francis Posey.

Mr. John Hallowes vs. Mr. Cuthb. Fenwick.

Peter Johnson vs. John Tennison & ux.

4 March 1653. Court. Attendees: same as previous day.

Thomas Cornwallis, Esq. attorney for Mr. John Hallowes attorney for Capt. Henry Fleete acknowledged satisfaction of 8 June judgement whereby Mr. William Eltonhead was to pay Capt. Fleet.

f. 541 Walter Pakes acknowledged judgement to Gov. William Stone, Esq.

William Whittle vs. Capt. Robert Vaughan by his attorney Henry Coursey.

Motion of John Hamond attorney for Mary wife of Robert Taylor. Offense occurred in VA.

f. 542 Petition of John Hamond that petitioner & his wife were going to Putuxent, when they arrived at the house of Mr. Fenwick.

Mr. John Hamond vs. Mr. Cuthb. Fenwick. Chattel sent by defendant to plaintiff via William Wareman.

Edward Brisley vs. Mr. Rich. Preston.

f. 543 Robert Taylor vs. Henry Ketchmey & ux.

Petition of John Hamond that petitioner bought chattel of Phillip Land.

Mr. John Hamond vs. Mr. Phillip Land. Concerning petition. Satisfaction on 11 April 1654.

f. 544 Devoreux Goodwyn by his attorney Mr. Mathew Stone vs. Mr. Lawrence Starkey by his attorney Mr. Fenwick.

Thomas Cornwalleys, Esq. vs. Thomas Gerrard, Esq. Concerns debts in VA of Richard Ingle (marriner) made over to plaintiff in 1647 by deed in England.

f. 545 Thomas Cornwallis Esq. vs. Phillip Land & Henry Fox.

f. 546 Henry Fox vs. Phillip Land. Mentions arbitrators: Mr. Cuthb. Fenwick & Mr. Henry Coursey.

Walter Pakes acknowledges judgement to Mr. Symon Oversey.

Motion of Mr. Symon Oversey for attachment against estate of Paul Sympson.

Walter Pakes acknowledges judgement to Thomas Cornwalleys, Esq.

Motion of Mr. William Eltonhead, Henry Fox disclaiming to be attorney for Capt. William Mitchell.

William Scott (mariner) deposed that when Col. Francis Yeardley departed the Province, at the house of Mr. Edward Packer, that when he arrived at his house at Lyme Haven, he & some of

f. 547 his servants would build him a house, to entertain his family when they came, & to come back & fetch the rest of his family.

Petition of William Scott that Col. Francis Yardley is indebted to petitioner.

Francis Yardley authorized Mr. Edward Packer as his attorney. Date: 30 November 1652. Witness: Job Chandler.

Liber - Patent Record F & B - 1640-1658

William Scott (mariner) vs. Col. Francis Yardley by his attorney Mr. Edward Packer.

Walter Pakes vs. John Hamond.

f. 548 Petition of Walter Pakes that the petitioner sold to John Hamond his plantation & is unpaid.

Mr. Henry Coursey et. al. vs. Mr. Thomas Daynes.

Mr. William Nugent vs. Richard Watson.

Mr. William Eltonhead vs. Richard True.

Capt. Thomas Cornwaleys vs. Francis Martin.

Walter Beane vs. Mr. Thomas Mathews administrator of Edward Cotton.

Motion of William Stone, Esq. (Governor) for extent on land of Mr. Thomas Weston.

Motion of Mr. Thomas Hatton (His Lordship's Secretary) concerning

f. 549 pay of soldiers out of Dutch Custome.

John Domall vs. William Ewens.

Motion of Mr. Phillip Land for warrant against Richard Recklesse.

Petition of William Ewens regarding suit by John Domall.

6 March 1653. Court. Attendees: William Stone, Esq. (Governor), Mr. Thomas Gerrard, Capt. John Price, Mr. William Eltonhead, Mr. Richard Clarke, Mr. Thomas Hatton.

Motion of Marks Pheypo & suspicion that Col. Francis Yardley will remove from Province, said Colonel summoned.

f. 550 Mr. Job Chandler empowered to appoint officers as necessary to stop removal.

Richard Foster appointed Nicholas Gwyther as attorney. Date: 1 March 1653. Witness: David Thomas.

Petition of Cornelius Saunders, carpenter of ship of Mr. Hanneford, by his attorney Mr. Henry Coursey, that the petitioner sold to Nathaniell Batts, interpreter for Col. Yardley, as per note to Richard Foster.

Cornelius Sanders by his attorney Mr. Henry Coursey vs. Rich. Foster by his attorney Mr. Nicholas Gwyther. Concerning sale to Nathaniell Batts.

f. 551 Thomas Cornwalleys vs. Thomas & John Sturman. Arbitrations between Capt. Thomas Cornwalleys, Esq. & Mr. John Sturman & his father Mr. Thomas Sturman. Signed: William Stone, Thomas Hatton.

John Deare, age 31, deposed on 18 March 1651 that Christmas last Mrs. Mary Brent caused on Kent Island unmarked cattle to be killed,

f. 552 & a marked one of Mr. Cox, & of Mr. Geiries (also Mr. Geiry). Witness: Robert Vaughan, Nicholas Brown.

Year 1654.

John Maning (merchant, of Norwich in County Northfolk, England) binds to Richard Cooke & Daniell Hoare (both merchants of Boston, New England). Date: 12 December 1653. Witnesses: John Sanford, Elisha Cooke.

f. 553 Recorded at Boston 10 November 1653. Signed: Nathaniell Sowther.

Charles Freeman attorney for Mrs. Elisabeth Freeman per Capt. Brigges Freeman acknowledged receipt of all goods to said Elisabeth from Mr. Richard Harris. Date: 30 March 1654. Witnesses: John Billingsley, John Read, John Lone.

Ben. Cowell received on 5 May 1652 for Miles Cooke assignee of Capt. Thurstone of John Pills payment due from Mr. Thomas Copley.

William Scott deposed, on a motion of Marks Pheypo, of contemptuous demeanor of Col. Francis Yardley.

Liber - Patent Record F & B - 1640-1658

f. 554 20 March 1653. To: William Lewis, George Dolty, Edmond Lindsey.

William Scott (mariner) deposed that 2 years ago Capt. Richard Husbands was here with his ship & deponent was boatswain, Mr. Thomas Hatton

f. 555 (Secretary) demanded compensation for damaged goods. Date: 3 February 1653.

Lawrence Starky, Esq. deposed that last Spring for consideration received of Mr. Thomas Hatton (Secretary) sold chattel formerly of Mr. Copley. Date: 24 September 1653. Witness: Thomas Carpenter.

f. 556 Richard Foster deposed on 24 March 1653 that he can't say whether Nathaniell Batts had any estate, but said the truck was his.

Thomas Ringe was bound to John Taylor. Date: 10 April 1654. Witness: William Britten.

Richard Husbands (marriner, of Wappin County Middlesex) appointed Edward Packer (planter) as his attorney. Date: 16 May 1652. Witnesses: Miles Cooke, Benja. Cowell.

f. 557 Lt. William Evans & John Jarbo made over 100 a., with the consent of Walter Pakes, to Ann Hamond wife of John Hamond & her 4 children: Mordecai, Ann, Bardnard, Daniell. Date: 21 September 1653. Witnesses: Walter Pakes, John Hamond.

John Hamond acknowledged chattel from Gervis Dodson & promised by Walter Pakes. Date: 1 October 1653. Witness: John Pille.

f. 558 Administration granted to Mr. Edward Packer attorney for Capt. Richard Husbands (marriner) of estate of John Stringer. Date: 9 March 1653. Walter Waterling & John Nicholls were appointed to appraise estate of John Stringer (carpenter). Date: 11 May.

Daniell Hoare received of Mr. Thomas Hatton (Secretary) payment for Maj. Edward Gibbons. Date: 6 February 1653. Witnesses: Henry Coursey, James Veitch, Tho. Marsh.

Capt. Thomas Adams (marriner) having purchased a plantation in MD & planning to trade between English inhabitants of MD & those of Swedish Nation on Delaware Bay, is authorized. Date: 18 March 1653. Signed: William Stone.

f. 559 Lewis Froman, age 29, deposed on 8 August 1653 that 4-6 weeks after Mr. Robert Brookes was seated in Patuxent River, the deponent (being then a servant) was to interpret with the Indians regarding the killing of hogs.

f. 560 Robert Sheale, age 25, deposed that he was a servant to Mr. Robert Brooke, regarding the killing of hogs. Date: 23 March 1654. Thomas Gerrard, Esq. acknowledged receipt of payment from Mr. Cuthbt. Fenwick. Witness: William Bretton.

Mr. Thomas Belcher (of Anne Arundel Co.) was granted a license for an inn or ordinary. Date: 17 April 1654. Signed: William Stone.

f. 561 Mr. Thomas Hatton (Secretary) per request of Francis Brookes (gentleman) agreed to cancel bills of Edward Claxton. Date: 17 April 1654.

Luke Gardiner was charged with teaching Roman Catholicism to Elinor Hatton (daughter to wife of Lt. Richard Bancks & niece to Secretary). Date: 3 April 1654. Signed: William Stone.

f. 562 10 April 1654. Michael Baisey acknowledged judgement to Mr. Henry Coursey.

Thomas Mathews gave chattel to Peter Pakes. Date: 10 April 1653. Witness: Barnaby Jackson.

Charles Thurston (marriner) attorney for Mr. Richard Thurston (marriner) acknowledged satisfaction of Mr. Thomas Hatton. Witness: William Stone.

f. 563 10 April 1654. Court. Attendees: William Stone, Esq. (Governor), Capt. John Price, Mr. Thomas Hatton (Secretary).

Mr. Thomas Hatton (His Lordship's Attorney General) declared against Luke Gardiner for detaining his niece Elinor Hatton (age 12) to teach her Roman Catholicism.

John Norman vs. Edward Bowles. Mr. John Metcalfe (sheriff) moved for the defendant.

Liber - Patent Record F & B - 1640-1658

f. 564 Lawrence Ward (of Nansauwm VA) appointed Mr. Richard Collet as his attorney. Date: 8 December 1653. Witness: William Mego.

Richard Collett attorney for Mr. Ward petitioned regarding a debt owed by Robert Taylor.

Mr. Lawrence Ward by Mr. Richard Collett vs. Mr. Robert Taylor.

John Davis (of Chuckatuck) appointed Mr. Richard Collett (of Putuxent) as his attorney. Date: 10 November 1653. Witness: George Ketchmay, William Long.

f. 565 Richard Collett attorney for John Davis petitioned regarding a debt owed by Robert Taylor.

John Davis by his attorney Rich. Collett vs. Robert Taylor. Payment to be valued by Mr. Richard Harris & John Halfhead.

John Waughop vs. Andrew Watson by his attorney Edmond Lindesey.

Andrew Watson (planter) appointed Edmond Lindesey as his attorney. Date: 1 April 1654. Witness: James Lindesey.

f. 566 Lt. Nicholas Gwyther vs. Andrew Watson by his attorney Edmond Lindesey.

Andrew Watson by his attorney Edmond Lindesey acknowledged judgement to Mr. Edward Packer.

Thomas Batchelor petitioned that he was arrested at the suit of Capt. Cornwallis & Henry Fox & was sick & not able to come.

f. 567 Thomas Cornwalleys, Esq. vs. Thomas Batchelor.

Henry Fox vs. Thomas Batchelor.

Accounts of estate of Mr. James Neale debtor in 1647. Payments to: Mr. Nicholas Cawseene, Mr. John Hallowes, Mr. Gerrard, Capt. Cornwalleys, Col. Yardley, Francis Posey, Mr. Metcalfe, accountant. Signed: Benjamin Gill.

Motion by Mr. Benjamin Gill for an extent on the land of Mr. James Neale called Wollaston Manner 2000 a.

f. 568 Walter Beane, John Hatch, James Lindesey, & Arthur Turner to value the land for Benjamin Gill.

Mr. Edward Packer administrator of John Stringer vs. Humfrey Howell. John Nicholls & Walter Waterling appraisers of the estate.

f. 569 Walter Waterling vs. Edward Packer administrator of John Stringer. Cites oath of Thomas Bennett, payment for Thomas Symonds.

William Whittle is bound to Joseph Manning. Date: 26 February 1652. Witness: Cuthb., Tho. Hayward.

William Whittle acknowledged payment to John Danby. Date: 2 March 1653. Witness: William Bretton.

Motion of John Danby on judgement against William Whittle as before Mr. William Bretton.

f. 570 Account of Mr. Thomas Hatton (Attorney General) of Dutch Custome. Mentions: Mr. Greene, Hans Jacobsen, Jacob Derrickson, Mr. Metcalfe, Lt. Richard Bancks, Thomas Warr, John Hatch, John Halfhead.

f. 571 <u>11 April 1654. Court.</u> Attendees: same as previous day.

Mr. John Pile deposed on 11 April 1654 that 9/10 years ago Argall Yardley, Esq. (of Northton VA) gave deponent a bill engaged to pay Capt.

f. 572 William Stone, Esq. for use of Thomas Cornwallis, Esq.

Mr. Nicholas Gwyther, age 28, deposed on 11 April 1654 that he was a servant to Thomas Cornwalleys, Esq. when Thomas Harrison came to the Province in 1641 as a servant. Before the arrival of Richard Ingle in 1644, when said Harrison was sent by Cuthbt. Fenwick attorney for said Capt. Cornwalleys with Edward Mathews his fellow servant to assist Andrew Monroe. After that, said Harrison, with the help of said Ingle, fled the Province & deponent met him in Accomack.

f. 573 Mr. William Nugent vs. Richard Watson. Jury: Mr. Thomas Mathew (also Thomas

Mathewes), Walter Beane, John Medley, William Marshall, William Lucas, Walter Waterling, Henry Adams, Barnaby Jackson, William Brown, Walter Pakes, Robert Macklyn, John Martyn.

f. 574 Lt. William Lewis deposed on 10 April 1654 that Richard Watson told him that Watson was to build a house for Mr. William Nugent who was to give him or John Taylor right to 300 a. The house was built on land of Mr. Starkey at Portoback Creek.

Edmond Lindesey deposed on 10 April 1654 that a week before Christmas a year ago, he stopped at the house of Mr. William Nugent & saw Mr. Nugent's man, Robert Nugent, & Richard Watson.

Marks Pheypo vs. Col. Francis Yardly by his attorney Edward Packer.

Thomas Cornwalleys, Esq. vs. Col. Francis Yardly.

f. 575 John Tompkinson entered a judgement at suit of Capt. Thomas Cornwalleys. Date: 30 March 1654. Witnesses: David Thomas, Tho. Miller.

Thomas Cornwalleys, Esq. vs. John Tompkinson.

Ales Bushell requested a motion concerning her affairs with Mr. Fenwick. Date: 8 April 1654.

Ales Bushnell (widow) vs. Mr. Cuthbt. Fenwick. Plaintiff is widow of Thomas Bushnell. The house of Henry Fox was appointed as a prison for said Fenwick.

Robert Taylor vs. John Hambleton.

f. 576 Robert Taylor vs. John Hambleton.

Robert Taylor vs. Henry Ketchmay.

Motion of Mr. John Hamond attorney of Mary wife of Robert Taylor.

Capt. John Barriffe vs. Lt. William Lewis. Cites bill left with Mr. Edward Packer.

Mr. Henry Coursey et. al. vs. Mr. Thomas Daynes.

f. 577 Devereux Goodwyn vs. Mr. Lawr. Starkey.

Richard True confessed to a judgement to Mr. Thomas Hatton (Secretary) assigned to said Hatton by Lt. Nicholas Gwyther due on a bill of him & William Boreman.

John Dandy vs. Edward Claxton by his attorney Marks Pheypo. Cites a bill of Lt. Nicholas Gwyther assigned to plaintiff & account of Michael Baisey due to the plaintiff.

Mr. John Hamond vs. Mr. Cuthbt. Fenwick. Cites chattel delivered to William Warman.

George Ketchmay (of VA) appointed Mr. Richard More (of Putuxent) as his attorney. Date: 9 November 1653. Witnesses: Thomas Buckston, Daniell Ellesmore.

f. 578 Petition of Richard More attorney for George Catchmey. Cites attachment issued per Robert Brooke, Esq. Mentions: Henry Catchmey.

Robert Brooke, Esq. vs. George Ketchmey by his attorney Richard Moor.

William Boreman (gentleman) appointed Richard Hotchkeyes as his attorney. Date: 6 April 1654. Witness: Robert Guest.

Tho. Baker appointed Henry Fox as his attorney in suit against William Boreman. Date: 30 March 1654. Witness: John Metcalfe.

William Boreman by his attorney Nich. Hotchkeyes vs. Tho. Baker by his attorney Henry Fox. Cites testimony of Mr. Nicholas Gwyther.

f. 579 John Wakefield appointed Robert Richins as his attorney in suit of Hubart Paty.

Hubart Paty vs. John Wakefield.

Motion of Thomas Connery, summoned as a witness on behalf of Hubart Paty (also Hubart Patty) vs. John Wakefield.

Liber - Patent Record F & B - 1640-1658

Mr. Phillip Land vs. Mr. Edward Packer administrator of John Stringer.

Motion of Henry Pountney, summoned on behalf of Richard Ware at suit of Capt. Thomas Cornwallyes.

Motion of Mr. Nicholas Gwyther for attachment to estate of George Roper. Said Gwyther to give notice to widow Roper.

f. 580 Mr. William Eltonhead vs. Richard True.

Motion of John Medley for allowance of charge in keeping Mr. Robert Greene.

Walter Beane vs. John Dandy.

Robert Richins vs. William Turner. Defendant to detain payment due from Robert Warren.

Thomas Connery vs. Mr. Henry Hooper.

Tho. Batchelor vs. Cloves Mace.

Richard Lloyd (planter, of St. Clement's Hundred) appointed Mr. William Johnson (of St. Clement's Hundred) as his attorney in suit against Mr. Paul Sympson. Date: 21 November 1653.

Paul Sympson vs. Richard Lloyd by his attorney William Johnson.

f. 581 William Stephens (of Putuxent) registered a cattle mark. John Stephens son of said William registered a cattle mark.

John Wheatley, age 49, deposed on 18 April 1654 that about 12 years ago, the deponent & Thomas Harrison came to the Province from England with Thomas Cornwallies, Esq. Said Harrison was a servant to Cornwallies. For 1st year, said Harrison was hired out to Randoll Revell. After that, he was returned. When Capt. Cornwallis returned to England, he was left with Mr. Cuthbt. Fenwick until the arrival of Richard Ingle (marriner) in the Province (about February 1644).

f. 582 Cuthbt. Fenwick (gentleman), age 40, deposed that he knew Thomas Harrison who arrived with Thomas Cornwallis, Esq. about December 1641. Said Cornwallis bought of Richard Ingle (marriner). He was hired out to Randoll Revell (cooper) for 1 year & returned to Tho. Cornwallis until his departure for England,

f. 583 then left in custody of deponent. Mentions: Richard Harvy (taylor, servant to Cornwallis). Deposition of George Meredith is cited as false. Date: 18 April 1654.

Cuthbt. Fenwick (gentleman), age 40, deposed that as attorney for Tho. Cornwallis, Esq. when he went to England in 1643, he knew of bill of Argall Yardley, Esq. for the use of Mr. John Pile left in the hands of Capt. William Stone.

f. 584 Cuthbt. Fenwick (gentleman), age 40, deposed that a bill of Capt. Giles Brent to James Cauther was assigned to him from Francis Gray executor of said Cauther. Date: 18 April 1654.

Motion of Mr. Thomas Hatton (His Lordship's Attorney General) regarding receipts concerning Dutch Custom:

f. 585 ...
- Thomas Copley, Esq. Date: 23 December 1651. Witness: Ralph Crouch.
- Mrs. Margaret Brent assignee of Stephen Salmon. Date: 1 October 1651. Witnesses: Giles Brent, John Rookewood.
- Stanhop Roberts. Date: 4 June 1652. Witness: Henry Coursey.
- Marks Pheypo for self & Nicholas Keeting. Date: 27 September 1651. Witness: James Lendshy.
- Nicholas Keeting for self

f. 586 ...
 & Marks Pheypo. Date: 4 November 1651. Witnesses: Tho. James, Nicholas Gwyther.
- John Villane. Date: 26 November 1650. Witness: Nicholas Gwither.
- Henry Adames. Date: 7 June 1651. Witness: John Buttery.
- William Smoote. Date: 20 June 1650. Witness: John Lawson.
- Katheren Hebden in right of Thomas Paine (foot soldier, dec'd). Date: 30 August 1651. Witness: Tho. White.

Liber - Patent Record F & B - 1640-1658

f. 587 ...
- Nicholas Gwither. Date: 15 October 1651. Witness: William Smith.
- Henry Adams & James Langworth in trust of estate of Thomas Green, Esq. (dec'd). Date: 18 October 1651. Witness: John Mansell.
- John Jarbo. Date: 21 November 1651. Witness: John Pille.
- John Dandy. Date: 21 November 1651. Witness: Patrick Forrest.

f. 588 ...
- Robert Willan. Date: 8 January 1651. Witness: Nicholas Gwither.
- Henry Pountney. Date: 15 January 1651. Witness: John Halfhead.
- Ralph Crouch (gentleman) administrator of Henry Hooper. Date: 12 February 1651. Signed: Raphe Crouch. Witness: Phillip Land.
- Lt. William Lewis. Date: 4 July 1652. Signed: William Lewes. Witness: William Nugent.
- Cuthbt. Fenwick (gentleman). Date: 9 July 1652.

f. 589 John Martin cites heifer he had of Thomas Harris. Date: 1 May.

Francis son of Mr. Francis Brookes the elder & Ann his wife (dec'd) registered a cattle mark. Date: 23 May.

John Ashcomb (of Putuxent) registered a cattle mark. Date: 28 April 1654.

28 April 1654. Court. Attendees: Governor, Secretary.

Mr. Francis Brookes vs. Capt. William Mitchell.

f. 590 29 April 1654. Attachment issued against estate of Capt. William Mitchell at suit of Mr. Francis Brookes.

Proclamation of Protectorate of Oliver Cromwell. Date: 6 May 1654. Signed: William Stone.

f. 591 24 May. Thomas Cornwallis, Esq. demanded from estate of Francis Poesey (dec'd).

John Medley (of Newtowne) is bound to Paul Simpson (gentleman). Date: 7 November 1653. Witnesses: John Thimbleby, Robert Greene. Paul Sympson assigned his right to Tho. Willford. Date: 8 November 1653. Witnesses: Richard Cole, Robert Greene.

John Stringar is bound to John Biskoe. Date: 19 May 1653. Signed: John Stringer. Witnesses: Tho. Bennett, Marke Bloomefield. John Biscoe assigned his right to Walter Waterline. Date: 25 April 1654. Witness: William Obesto.

f. 592 Edward Cole assigned his right to a tract of land to Robert Douglas. Signed: Edward Coles. Witness: Henry Coursey.

John Hallowes (gentleman) released Thomas Cager of all bills. Witness: William Bretton.

John Allen is bound to George Mee for one man servant. Date: 28 April 1652. Witnesses: William Hawley, William Eddce.

30 May. William Whittle (planter) assigned chattel to Thomas Cornwallis, Esq. Date: 12 April 1654. Witnesses: Cloves Mace, Richard Hotchkeys.

f. 593 Henry Fox received satisfaction from Thomas Cornwallis for following judgements:
- William Johnson, Luke Gardiner, & estate of Capt. William Mitchell.
- Francis Poesey.
- Thomas Batchellor.
- John Waughop.
- Richard Foster.
- John Coleman.

Date: 27 May 1654. Witnesses: Richard Hotchkeys, W. Sinclair.

f. 594 Andrew Painter (marriner, of London) acknowledged receipt of chattel from Walter Waterling. Date: 13 February 1650. Witnesses: John Bisco, William Osbaston.

Thomas Burbage deposed, taken by Col. Cornelius Lloyd, that the deponent has not received payment from Mr. Thomas Gerrard. Date: 14 May 1654 in VA. Witnesses: Cornelius Lloyd, William Daines.

John Crabtree appointed Phillip Land as his attorney. Date: 7 June 1654. Witnesses: William Eale, William Hughs.

Liber - Patent Record F & B - 1640-1658

f. 595 Proclamation. Date: 23 May 1654. Signed: William Stone.

f. 596 Mr. Nathaniell Pope by his attorney William Johnson demanded from the estate of Francis Posey (dec'd). Date: 23 May.

23 May 1654. Court. Attendees: Governor, Capt. Price, the Secretary, Mr. Clarke.

Thomas Cornwalleys, Esq. vs. Nicholas, John, & Peter Miles.

John Norman vs. Edward Bowles.

William Stone, Esq. vs. Capt. Tho. Wilson.

24 May. Court. Attendees: Governor, Mr. Gerrard, Capt. Price, the Secretary, Mr. Chandler, Mr. Clarke.

Robert Hooper, servant to John Danby, deposed on 23 May 1654 that he was sent last winter to Edward Claxton, if he is to pay to deponent's master on account of Michael Baisey.

f. 597 John Bowcock, age 20, deposed on 24 May 1654 that in last February, he went with his master John Danby to the house of Nicholas Keeting, where his master met with Edward Claxton & his wife & said he had a bill of said Claxton, assigned from Nicholas Gwither.

Edward Claxton appointed Francis Brookes as his attorney in suit against John Danby. Date: 23 May 1654.

John Danby vs. Edward Claxton by his attorney Fr. Brookes. Cites a bill from defendant to Nicholas Gwither & an amount due on account from Michael Baisey.

f. 598 Mr. Mathew Stone vs. Edward Packer administrator of John Stringer. Cites a bill to Seabrant Derickson.

John Stringer (carpenter, of Accomack Co.) is bound to Seabrant Derrickson (merchant, of Edam). Date: 6 May 1651. Witness: Mathew Stone.

Mr. John Stringer is requested to make payment to "my brother" Mathew Stone if not already paid to Mr. Eltonhead. Signed: John Stringer. Date: 8 January 1653.

John Stringer (chirurgeon) by his attorney Mr. Mathew Stone vs. Edward Packer administrator of John Stringer (carpenter).

f. 599 Devoreux Goodwyn vs. Lawrence Starky, Esq. Cites the estate of Thomas Copley, Esq. (dec'd).

Thomas Cornwallis, Esq. vs. John Tompkinson.

Petition of Walter Pakes regarding the suit vs. John Hamond.

f. 600 Walter Pakes vs. Mr. John Hamond. Defendant paid Mr. Phillip Land. Cites that defendant is attorney for plaintiff in suit against Paul Sympson.

Mr. John Hamond vs. Mr. Cuthbt. Fenwick.

Capt. Henry Fleet by his attorney Mr. John Hallowes vs. William Edwyn. Cites a bill to Thomas Francklyn (dec'd).

f. 601 Plaintiff is administrator for said Francklyn.

Capt. Henry Fleet administrator of Tho. Francklin appointed John Hallowes as his attorney. Date: 30 July 1652. Signed: Henry Fleete.

Thomas Connery vs. Henry Hooper.

Thomas Batchelor vs. Cloves Mace.

25 May. Court. Attendees: same as before, except Mr. Gerrard is absent.

Thomas Batchellor on account of Samuel Parker acknowledged a judgement to John Danby on a bill from said Parker to Danby by assignment from John Waltom.

Thomas Batchelor acknowledged a judgement to Henry Fox.

Henry Fox vs. Capt. William Mitchell by his attorney William Johnson.

Liber - Patent Record F & B - 1640-1658

f. 602 Cites Mr. Fenwick. William Johnson & Luke Gardiner are sureties for debt. At motion of William Johnson, Henry Fox relinquished PoA from Capt. Mitchell.

Mr. Francis Brookes vs. Capt. William Mitchell by his attorney William Johnson. Depositions by John Wildman, Esq. & Elisabeth Bolton taken in England were entered for proof of agreement between Capt. Mitchell & late wife of said Brookes. Deposition of Susan Warren.

f. 603 Account of Francis Brookes to Capt. Mitchell. Cites wares for Martha Webb.

John Wildman, Esq. at Westminster, County Middlesex, deposed that he was present when Capt. William Mitchell hired Ann Boulton to be his servant & that

f. 604 she would be the governess to his children & family. Date: 1 December 1653. Witnesses: Edw. Eltonhead, Sheffield Stubbs.

Elisabeth Bolton, (widow, of Parish of St. Martin's-in-the-Fields, County Middlesex), age 50, deposed that she was present when Capt. William Mitchell hired her daughter Ann Bolton to be his servant & she was to be governess to his children & family. Signed: Elisabeth Boulton. Date: 1 December 1653. Witnesses: Edward Eltonhead, Sheffield Stubbs.

f. 605 Col. Francis Yardley vs. Capt. Richard Husbands by his attorney Edward Packer.

Thomas Cornwallyes, Esq. vs. Col. Francis Yardley.

Marks Pheypo vs. Col. Francis Yardley. Cites defendant's plantation in VA.

f. 606 Edward Parker attorney for Col. Francis Yardley vs. Richard Hotchkeys & William Boreman.

Lt. Nicholas Gwither requested an attachment to estate of George Rapier.

Henry Fox deposed on 24 May 1654 that last March, he was aboard a boat belonging to Col. Yardley & heard said Col. say to Mr. John Johnson that their differences were ended.

Mr. John Metcalf deposed on 24 May 1654 that Henry Fox deposed correctly.

Mr. Phillip Land deposed on 24 May 1654 that Henry Fox deposed correctly.

f. 607 Proclamation that Capt. Thomas Webber (master of the Mayflower of London) forcibly took the ship Maid of Gaunt & chattel of Mr. Symon Oversey (merchant). Date: 12 June 1654. Signed: William Stone, Thomas Hatton.

15 June. Henry Bishop (planter) is bound to John Greenwell. Date: 9 June 1654. Witnesses: William Johnson, James Langworth, Thomas Simpson.

f. 608 William Marshall (planter, of Pasquascutt, St. Mary's Co.) gave chattel for maintenance of a minister in Neck of Wicocomoco. Overseers appointed: John Hatch, Edward Boules, Francis Pope. Date: 3 June 1657. Witnesses: John Cage, John Douglas.

f. 609 Thomas Cornwallis, Esq. sold to Cornelius Cannedy (brickmaker) land on south side of Putuxent River, pt. of Resurrection Manner. Date: 10 March 1653. Signed: Thomas Cornwalleys. Witnesses: Robert Clarke, Geo. Read.

f. 610 Mr. William Lucas registered a cattle mark.

23 June 1654. Mr. Phillip Land registered a cattle mark for Phillip Land the younger his eldest son.

f. 611 Mr. Henry Corbyn (merchant, of London), age 25, deposed on 23 June 1654 that on board the Charity of London, Mr. John Bosworth (master), about 3 weeks before arrival, there was a rumor that the passenger Mary Lee was a witch. Cites consultation with Mr. Chipsham & the deponent. Signed: Henry Corbyne.

f. 612 Francis Darby (gentleman), age 39, deposed on 23 June 1654 that he was aboard the Charity of London, Mr. John Bosworth master, & cites the day Mary Lee was put to death for being a witch.

f. 613 20 June. Christopher Rushell registered a cattle mark. William Rushell son of Christopher Rushell registered a cattle mark.

Robert Hanley registered a cattle mark.

23 June 1654. John Bosworth (commander of the Charity of London) engaged on account of Mr. Henry Meese (merchant).

Liber - Patent Record F & B - 1640-1658

f. 614 Mr. William Allen (merchant) deposed that several accounts regarding the estate of John Stringer (carpenter) were true. Date: 4 July 1654.

3 July 1654. Proclamation. Lord Baltimore on 28 September 1653 discharged Robert Brooke, Esq. as Commander of Charles Co. from the Council. The Governor erected Calvert Co.,

f. 615 & Mr. Richard Collett is appointed high sheriff.

Edward Pearse (ship carpenter) deposed that about 1 year ago, John Winbridge was quartermaster to Capt. Tillman, Capt. Tillman told Walter Waterling that if he died unmarried, he forgave said Waterling of his debt.

Richard Moore, sick, called his wife Jane Moore & remade his will, making her sole executor [sic] & to dispose amongst her children as she desired. In presence of: Richard Manship & his wife Elisabeth Manship.

Jane Moore, wife of Richard Moore (dec'd), bound 400 a. over to her 3 sons: Richard Moore, Roger Moore, Timothy Moore. They are to be of age at

f. 616 18 & the maids at age 15. Mentions: 7 children. Witnesses: Richard Recklesse, Geaye White.

Peter Godson (chirurgeon) intending to marry Jane Moore (widow, of Calvert Co.) agrees not to interfere with the estate of Richard Moore (dec'd) her late husband. Date: 6 July 1654.

16 July 1654. Court. Attendees: William Stone, Esq. (Governor), Capt. John Price, Mr. Thomas Hatton (Secretary).

Motion by Mr. Richard Welles concerning John (N) & Ellen (N) his Irish servants. Said John brought to court by Henry Fox on warrant from house of Nicholas Keeting, he alleging said Ellen is his wife.

f. 617 Robert Chipsham (merchant) deposed that William Wright of Poplar Hill did agree to pay the deponent. Date: 15 July 1654.

William Allen (merchant, of Mayflower of London) appointed Thomas Mathews (gentleman) as his attorney. Date: 2 April 1654. Witness: Daniell Hore.

f. 618 To: Mr. Thomas Mathews. William Allen is indebted to Mr. Thomas Hatton. Date: 4 July 1654. Witness: Mathew Stone.

8 August 1654. Commission for Administration of Justice, settled in name of the Lord Protector, given Richard Bennett, Esq. & Col William Clayborne for settling MD & VA. Council left in the hands of Capt. William Stone, Mr. Thomas Hatton, et. al.

f. 619 ...

f. 620 For conservation of peace in MD, Capt. William Fuller, Mr. Richard Preston, Mr. William Durand, Mr. Edward Lloyd, Capt. John Smith, Mr. Leonard Strong, Mr. Lawson, Mr. John Hatch, Mr. Richard Wells, & Mr. Richard Ewen

f. 621 are to be commissioners. Mr. William Durand is to be Secretary to the Commission. Date: 22 July 1654. Signed: Ri. Bennett, William Claiborne. Witness: William Durand (Secretary).

Mr. Thomas Hatton is to deliver all records to Mr. William Durand. Date: 22 July 1651. Signed: Ri. Bennett, W. Claiborne.

Thomas Cornwalleys, Esq. (of the Crosse) appointed

f. 622 Richard Hodgkeys as his attorney. Mentions: Capt. William Stone (Governor). Date: 13 July 1654. Witnesses: W. Sinclare, Rob. Guest.

f. 623 16 October 1654. Court. Attendees: Capt. William Fuller, Mr. Rich. Preston, Mr. William Durand, Mr. Edward Lloyd, Mr. Leon. Strong, Mr. Rich. Euing.

John Ashcomb vs. estate of Tho. Trumpeter.

Peter Godson was allowed payment from estate of Thomas Trumpeter.

Bartho. Herringe, age 40, deposed that Peter Godson & Richard Manship met, & Manship asked Godson whether he would prove his wife a witch.

John Killy, age 25, deposed that at the house of Phillip Hide, Richard Manship said to Peter Godson -- you would prove my wife a witch. Signed: John Killey.

Liber - Patent Record F & B - 1640-1658

Margarett Herringe, age 23, deposed

f. 624 that Rich. Manship asked Peter Godson if he would prove his wife a witch.

Peter Godson & his wife convicted of defaming the wife of Richard Manship, as before Mr. Richard Preston.

Ismeall Wright demanded payment from the estate of Thomas Trumpeter.

Peter Godson demanded of Bartho. Herringe.

Letters of administration were granted to Ismael Wright on the estate of Thomas Trumpeter.

William Ewen attorney for Mr. Robert Clarke demanded

f. 625 from the estate of Thomas Trumpeter.

Elisabeth Manship, age 41, deposed that coming from the house of Peter Godson, she met Margaret Herringe, who said that Phillip Hyde had beaten her said Herringe.

Peter Godson deposed that he found Margaret Herring & she said she had been beaten by Phillip Hyde.

Thomas Gregory deposed that when he was at the house of Richard Manship, he saw Margaret Herringe in bad condition & the deponent's wife stayed with said Margaret.

Richard Manship deposed that Margaret Herringe was sick, & Phillip Hyde confessed to having beaten her.

Jane Godson deposed that she saw Margaret Herringe sick & she said Phillip Hyde had beaten her.

Per Richard Manship & Elisabeth Manship, Rich. Moore ordained his wife as sole executrix.

f. 626 Richard Collett attorney for Lawrence Ward vs. John Wakefield.

Thomas Gregorie & his wife were summoned in the cause between Bartho. Herringe & Phillip Hyde.

John Hammond vs. John Barriffe for rights to land.

Simon Bird, servant to Mr. Thomas Trueman & hired to Robert Taylor, filed a complaint.

Estate of Thomas Trumpeter to pay John Harford.

George Newman, age 20, deposed that he heard Mrs. Brookes

f. 627 relate that Mrs. Goulson had beaten her maid.

Margaret Pritchard, age 20, deposed that she heard Mrs. Brookes say that Mrs. Goulson had beaten her maid, & that Elisabeth Tennis would testify.

John Dumoid, age 28, deposed that February 2 years ago, he was with Mr. Phenwick, Mr. Eltonhead & his wife, & Mark Lucye Deponent heard Mr. Eltonhead & Mr. Phenwick report on killing of hogs.

John Sewell, age 20, deposed that February 2 years ago, he was at house of Mr. Hooper & saw a boat belonging to Mr. Phenwick with hog flesh.

Mrs. Brookes reported that Sarah Goulson punished her maid servant which cannot be proved.

Mr. Robert Brooke vs. Mr. Phenwick.

f. 628 Richard Manship deposed that the wife of Peter Godson said to deponent's wife that the eldest on of wife of Michael Baisey was not the son of Anthony Rawlins (her former husband), & knew the man in MD who was the father. Said the wife of Michael Baisey was a whore & that Thomas Ward (of Kent) had told her.

Elisabeth Manship deposed the same.

Margaret Herring deposed that the wife of Peter Godson affirmed that the son of Anthony Rawlins was the son of another man in MD.

Liber - Patent Record F & B - 1640-1658

Francis Brooke vs. (N) Fox.

Ann Pope deposed that the maid servant of Robert Taylor told the deponent that she the servant took sugar belonging to John Hambleton & that Mary Taylor beat her for it, & that Sarah & Mary Taylor drank it.

Barnaby Jackson deposed that David Thomas went to get wife of (N) Gregory to administer to Thomas' pregnant wife. Barnaby Jackson testified in the cause between Thomas Gregory & David Thomas.

Wife of Peter Godson convicted of slandering the wife of Michael Baisey & wife of Peter Godson is to be committed to the sheriff.

f. 629 Raph Beane vs. John Dandy. Cites a bill from Walter Beane.

Peter Underwood, age 18, deposed that Mr. Meese shipped him & chattel to MD, & Peter Johnson brought the deponent. The next day, the deponent met Mrs. Hooper with said chattel. Henry Hooper is to pay Peter Johnson for the chattel.

Bartholomew Herring vs. Phillip Hyde.

f. 630 Mr. Skippwith vs. Richard Ricknell.

Capt. John Smith exhibited a bill from Cornelius A Johnson.

John Hammond acknowledged a judgement to Capt. John Smith in case Cornelius Johnson doesn't pay.

(N) Salter vs. Capt. Vaughan.

Isack Iluice vs. Francis Brooke. Iluice to possess 200 a. Beaver Neck on Isle of Kent.

f. 631 Mark Pheboe vs. Mr. Beard.

Walter Peake vs. Thomas Bennett.

John Tennis & his wife did not perform the agreement with Mr. Johnson. Tennis' wife was a servant to Mr. Johnson.

Peter Joy, age 26, deposed that Mr. Hambleton came to the house of Samuell Griffin & told the deponent that he had bought 200 a. from Mr. Phenwick at the head of St. Cutbeard's Creek.

Cornelius Cannady, age 30, deposed that he asked Mr. Hambleton whether he had bought any land of Mr. Phenwick & he said yes.

f. 632 Friendship Tounge, age 26, deposed that he went with Mr. Phenwick & Mr. Hambleton to show them a tract of land at the head of St. Cutbeard's Creek.

John Hambleton demanded of Cuthbt. Phenwick.

The estate of Thomas Connery is to pay Mr. William Eltonhead.

Joseph Edwards has served his time to Mr. Arthur Turner.

Petition of John Sturman

f. 633 that there was a suit between the petitioner's father William Hardwich & Capt. Thomas Cornwalleys. Cites pardons by former governor Leo. Calvert, Esq., Mr. Thomas Greene, & Lord Baltimore.

f. 634 John Shanks registered a cattle mark. Amey Shanks registered a cattle mark. The wife of Robert Coles gave wife of John Shanks chattel. Ann Maynor gave John Shanks chattel. Thomas Dyneard gave Amey Shanks daughter of John Shanks chattel. John Shanks gave his daughter Amey Shanks chattel.

5 December 1654. Court. Attendees: Mr. Richard Preston, Mr. William Parker, Mr. Sampson Waringe, Mr. John Lawson, Mr. William Parrott.

Attachment was granted to Mr. Henry Coursey

f. 635 against the estate of Thomas Deanes.

Mr. William Ewen attorney for Mr. Robert Clarke acknowledged a judgement to Richard Collett on estate of Mr. Clarke.

Liber - Patent Record F & B - 1640-1658

Mr. Phenwick vs. William Warman.

Richard Collett attorney for John Pedro acknowledged judgement to William Chaplyn.

Attachment was granted to Richard Foster against the estate of Col. Francis Yardley.

William Barton vs. Richard Foster. Cites the parcel of land where Foster lives. Barton to survey said land according to lease granted to Jackson & Gwider.

Mary wife of Martin Kirke vs. Markes Phepo. Action of rape. Martin Kirke vs. Marks Phepo.

Andrew Warner was granted payment in cause between Mr. Bonifield & Martin Kirke.

Robert Brooke, Esq. (of Putuxent) appointed Mr. John Hamond as his attorney

f. 636 in actions with Mr. Robert Clarke & Richard Hoskings.

Mr. Robert Clarke vs. Robert Brooke, Esq.

Capt. John Smith attorney for Richard Beard vs. Markes Phepoe.

Martin Kirke is to remain in sheriff's custody.

Mrs. Rebecca Hall is dismissed.

Capt. John Smith testified that Bartho. Bloome had a warrant for 200 a. from Mr. Hatton.

Mich. Brooke vs. John Jarboe.

Henry Potter vs. Martyn Kirke.

f. 637 Martin Kirke vs. Mrs. Bonifield.

Administration was granted to Alice Griffine wife of Samuel Griffin (dec'd).

Francis Vandan vs. John Lewger.

Mr. Thomas Lund vs. Tho. Bennett.

Mrs. Godson was bound to wife of Michael Baisey, is remitted.

Andrew Keaton vs. Martin Kirke.

George Skipwith vs. Richard Ricknell. Mentions: Cornelius Cannadie is security to Ricknell.

Mr. Richard Preston ordered to pay John Shankes.

f. 638 Certificate of 375 a. granted to Daniell Goulson.

Walter Peake dismissed as witness for Francis Vandan.

Mr. Robert Brooke, Esq. vs. Mr. Cuthbert Phenwick.

Attachment was granted to Richard Foster against the estate of Col. Francis. Yardley.

John Hamond is to build a courthouse.

Alce Griffine vs. Cornelius Cannady.

John Hodgine & John Grammer were appointed constables for north side of Putuxent. Ishmeall Wright was appointed constable for south side of Putuxent. Francis Billingley was appointed constable for The Cliffs.

Ishmael Wright, age 40, deposed that Mr. Eltonhead was at the deponent's house & speaking with Phillip Hyde & Henry Bullin concerning land. Mr. Eltonhead said he had 5000 a. to take up.

f. 639 Peter Joy, age 26, deposed that he went to build a house for Cornelius Cannady which Samuell Griffine was to pay for.

Liber - Patent Record F & B - 1640-1658

Rebecca Hall, age 30, deposed that she saw the marks that the wife of Martin Kirke gave Mrs. Bonyfield.

Christian Bonifield, age 46, deposed that when she was at the house of Marke Phepoe & Mary Kirke wife of Martin Kirke said she would hang that rogue (N) Potter.

Rebecca Hall, age 30, deposed that Mary Kirke said she followed (N) Potter from her house through my ground where my husband was killed. The deponent said that Mary Kirke said that Marke Phepoe was a rogue.

f. 640 Elisabeth Potter, age 29, deposed that Mary Kirke came to the house of Henry Potter & Rebecca Hall & she had words. Rebecca Hall said, Mary Kirke you said Markes Phepoe came to your house & you beat him.

Richard Preston (of Putuxent) sold to James Gunion, Pratrick Mellegin, Thomas Ager, & Andrew Scott Scotland, between Capt. John Smith & John Felton. Date: 20 November 1654. Witnesses: John Smith, John Sutton.

Richard Preston assigned his right to land which Capt. John Smith lives on, between Scotland & John Tennis. Date: 20 November 1654. Witness: John Sutton.

f. 641 Griffith Beddo transcribed the aforesaid carefully. Mr. Joshua George examined it. Date: 24 February 1724. Signed: Joshua George, Griffith Beddoe, Sam. Young.

Liber - Patent Record Z & A - 1637-1651

f. 1   1637. Shipped for Isle of Kent on the St. Thomas by Thomas Cornwallis, Esq.

License to Thomas Cornwallis, Esq. to trade with the Indians. Date: 30 December 1637. Signed: Leonard Calvert.

Thomas Cornwallis, Esq. is discharged from all accounts to Lord Proprietor. Signed: John Lewger.

Shipped on the St. Thomas by Thomas Cornwallis, Esq. on behalf of Jerome Hawley, Esq. Said Thomas

f. 2   paid to John Lewger his Lordship's Collector. Came Thomas Cornwallis & delivered goods. Date: 30 March 1638. Signed: John Lewger.

f. 3   Order to take Mathew Price of Isle of Kent into custody, to answer the suit of William Clobery (merchant, of London). Date: 30 December 1637. Signed: Leonard Calvert.

To Capt. Geo. Evelin, warrants for: John Glantham, Robert Lake, John Russell, Nicholas Polentine, William Taber, John Pinwill, Thomas Smith, Samuel Smith & John Abbott & Richard Thompson.

Security by William Cox (gentleman, of Isle of Kent) in suit vs. William Clobery (merchant, of London).

Warrant for Mrs. Cartwright James.

f. 4   Warrant for Robert Phillpott.

Warrant for William Blizard.

Warrant against John Butler, Thomas Smith, & Edward Beekler (planters, of Isle of Kent).

Warrant to Capt. Evelin, regarding General Assembly of all freeman of the Province. Date: 30 January 1637.

f. 5   Leonard Calvert (Governor) to Capt. George Evelin (of Isle of Kent)

f. 6   to choose 6 men as advisors. Date: 30 December 1637.

Warrant against Andrew Chappell (marriner) at suit of Thomas Pasmore (carpenter). Signed: James Cauther.

f. 7   3 January. Warrant against Jo. Hillierd (planter) at suit of Roger Moy.

Commission of High Constable to Robert Vaughan (sergeant, of St. George's Hundred). Date: 5 January 1637. Signed: Leonard Calvert.

f. 8   Robert Nicholls (planter, of St. Maries Hundred) acknowledged a debt to John Lewger (Secretary).

f. 9   John Lewger on behalf of the Lord Protector vs. Capt. Henry Fleete (planter, of St. George's Hundred).

f. 10 Leonard Calvert vs. Rose Gilbert (widow) late wife of Richard Gilbert (planter, dec'd, of St. Maries Hundred).

f. 11 Robert Percy (marshall) is commanded to apprehend Rose Gilbert (widow). Date: 20 January 1637. Signed: Leonard Calvert.

f. 12 Capt. Henry Fleete appeared & testified. Signed: Henry Fleet.

22 January. Thomas Cornwallis, Esq. vs. Thomas Pasmore (carpenter, of St. Maries Hundred) & Roger Moy (planter, of same place). Defendants obliged themselves to John Neale (merchant, of Accomack Virginia). Said Neale assigned to plaintiff.

f. 13 Thomas Pasmore by his attorney James Cauther & Roger Moy acknowledged the debt.

25 January. Henry James & William Edwin (planters, of St. Maries Hundred) acknowledged debt to Mr. Leonard Calvert, Esq. Signed: Henrie James, William Edwine.

f. 14 Thomas Cornwallis, Esq. vs. Anum Benum (planter, of Metapanient).

Leonard Calvert, Esq. vs. Thomas Charington (planter, of St. George's Hundred).

Liber - Patent Record Z & A - 1637-1651

William Bretton (gentleman, of St. George's Hundred) acknowledged debt to Capt. Robert Wintour. Date: 25 January 1637.

f. 15   5 February. James Cauther attorney for Thomas Pasmore vs. Thomas Charinton & James Edlow & Anum Benum. Acknowledgement of bill.

John Lewger (Secretary) is commissioned

f. 16   as conservator of peace in St. Maries' Co. Date: 24 January 1637. Witness: Leonard Calvert.

f. 17   25 January 1637. General Assembly. Attendees: Lt. General, Capt. Thomas Cornwallis, Esq., Capt. Robert Wintour, Esq., Mr. John Lewger (gentleman, Secretary), Capt. Robert Evelin (gentleman, commander of Isle of Kent), Mr. Thomas Greene (gentleman), Mr. William Bretton (gentleman), Capt. Henry Fleete (gentleman), Mr. Robert Philpott (gentleman, of Isle of Kent), Mr. William Brainthwaite (gentleman), Mr. John Wyatt (gentleman), Mr. Robert Clerke (gentleman), Richard Garnett, Sr. (planter, of Mattapanient), Justinian Snow (planter, of St. Maries Hundred), Marmaduke Snow (planter, of St. Maries Hundred), Francis Rabnett (planter, of St. Maries Hundred), Sergt. Robert Vaughan (high constable of St. George's Hundred), James Baldridge (sheriff of St. Maries Co.), Francis Gray (carpenter, of St. Maries Hundred), James Cauther (planter, of St. Maries Hundred), William Lewis (planter, of St. Maries Hundred), Thomas Francklin (planter, of St. Maries Hundred), Thomas Nabbs (planter, of St. George's Hundred), Sergt. Thomas Baldridge (planter, of St. Maries Hundred), Edward Fleete (planter, of St. Maries Hundred), Robert Percy (marshall), John Price (planter, of St. Maries Hundred),

f. 18   Thomas Morrison (planter, of St. George's Hundred), Thomas Stent (planter, of St. George's Hundred).

Summoned by writs: Mr. Thomas Copley, Esq. (of St. Maries Hundred), Mr. Andrew White (gentleman, of St. Maries Hundred, sick) represented by Robert Clerke (gentleman), Mr. John Altham (gentleman, of St. Maries Hundred, sick) represented by Robert Clerke (gentleman), Joseph Edlow (planter, of Mattapanient), Anum Benum (planter, of Mattapanient), Nicholas Hervey (planter, of Mattapanient), William Broughe (planter, of Mattapanient), Randoll Revell (cooper, of St. George's Hundred), freemen of Isle of Kent represented by Mr. Robert Philpot, Roger Moy (planter, of St. George's Hundred) represented by Sergt. Robert Vaughan, John Wortly (planter, of St. George's Hundred) represented by Sergt. Robert Vaughan, Robert Nicholls (planter, of St. Maries Hundred) represented by Sergt. Robert Vaughan, James Courtney (planter, of St. George's Hundred) represented by Capt. Robert Evelin, Davie Wickliff (planter, of St. George's Hundred) represented by Capt. Robert Evelin, Ralphe Beame (planter, of St. George's Hundred) represented by Capt. Robert Evelin, Thomas Charington (planter, of St. George's Hundred) represented by Capt. Robert Evelin, Henry Lee (planter, of St. George's Hundred) represented by John Lewger (Secretary), John Norton (planter, of St. Maries Hundred) represented by John Lewger (Secretary), John Halfhead (brickmason, of St. Maries Hundred) represented by Justinian Snow, Robert Wiseman (planter, of St. Maries Hundred) represented by William Lewis, Davie Odcroft (planter, of St. Maries Hundred) represented by William Lewis, William Edwine (planter, of St. Maries Hundred) represented by William Lewis, Henry James (planter, of St. Maries Hundred) represented by William Lewis, John Smithson (planter, of St. Maries Hundred) represented by William Lewis, John Hillierd (planter, of St. Maries Hundred) represented by Francis Rabnett, Christopher Martin (planter, of St. Maries Hundred) represented by Francis Rabnett, Robert Smith (planter, of St. Maries Hundred) represented by Francis Rabnett, Thomas Pasmore (carpenter, of St. Maries Hundred) represented by James Cauther,

f. 19   John Medley (planter, of St. Maries Hundred) represented by Capt. Thomas Cornwallis, Henry Bishop (planter, of Mattapanient) represented by Richard Garnett, Sr., John Bryant (planter, of Mattapanient) represented by Richard Garnett, Sr., Richard Lusthead (planter, of Mattapanient) represented by Richard Garnett, Sr.

Summoned but did not appear: Nathaniel Pope (planter, of St. Maries Hundred), Henry Wood (planter, of St. Maries Hundred), John Medcalfe (planter, of St. Maries Hundred), John Courtis (planter, of St. George's Hundred), John Davies (planter, of St. Maries Hundred), John Richardson (planter, of St. George's Hundred), Thomas Hebden (planter, of St. George's Hundred).

Claim: John Robinson (carpenter).

f. 20   26 January. Morning. General Assembly. Attendees: Lt. General, Capt. Thomas Cornwallis, Capt. Robert Wintour, Capt. Geo. Evelin, Francis Rabnett, John Robinson, William Lewis, John Lewger, Thomas Green, John Wyatt, Robert Clerke, Tho. Francklin, James Baldridge, Edward Fleete, Robert Philpott, William

Liber - Patent Record Z & A - 1637-1651

Brainthwaite, Richard Garnett, Justinian Snow, Marmaduke Snow, Robert Percy, Sergt. Vaughan.

Summoned: Thomas Hebden represented by Capt. Tho. Cornwallis, John Richardson represented by Capt. Robert Evelin, Mr. Thomas Copley represented by Robert Clerke, Mr.. Andrew White represented by Robert Clerke, Mr. John Altham represented by Robert Clerke, John Price represented by Francis Rabnett, Nathaniel Pope represented by John Lewger (Secretary), John Medcalfe represented by William Lewis.

f. 21 Summoned but did not appear: Thomas Morrison, Henry Weed, John Courtis, Thomas Nabbs, John Davies, Mr. Bretton, Capt. Fleete, James Cauther, Thomas Stente, Thomas Baldridge, Francis Gray by John Robinson.

Claims by: Edward Bateman (ship carpenter, St. Maries Hundred) represented by Mr. John Lewger (Secretary), Roger Oliver (marriner) represented by Mr. William Brainthwaite (gentleman), Zachary Mottershead (gentleman), John Langford (gentleman, high constable of Isle of Kent).

f. 22 Afternoon. General Assembly. Attendees: Lt. General, Capt. Thomas Cornwallis, Capt. Robert Wintour, Capt. George Evelin, Mr. John Lewger (Secretary), Mr. Thomas Greene, Mr. William Bretton, Mr. Philpott, Mr. Langford, John Wyatt, Robert Clerke, Justinian Snow, Marmaduke Snow, Francis Rabnett, Thomas Nabbs, James Baldridge, Edward Fleete, Richard Garnett, Robert Percy, Sergt. Vaughan, Zachary Mottershead, William Lewis.

Summoned: John Robinson represented by Justinian Snow, William Brainthwaite represented by Lt. General, Roger Oliver (mariner) represented by Lt. General, John Davis represented by Francis Rabnett, Thomas Stente represented by Francis Rabnett, Thomas Franklin represented by Edward Fleete, Francis Gray represented by Justinian Snow, Thomas Baldridge represented by James Baldridge, James Cauther (did not appear).

Claim: Thomas Boys (mariner, of St. Maries Hundred) represented by Francis Rabnett.

Did not appear: Thomas Morrison, John Courtis, Capt. Fleet, Henry Weed, William Bretton, Thomas Nabbs, John Davis, Thomas Stente, Thomas Baldridge.

f. 23 29 January 1637. Morning. General Assembly. Attendees: President, Capt. Cornwalleys, Capt. Geo. Evelin, Mr. Lewger (Secretary), Mr. Thomas Greene, Mr. Clerke, Sergt. Vaughan, Capt. Henry Fleete, Justinian Snow, Francis Rabnett, James Baldridge, Edward Fleete.

Summoned & amerced: Capt. Robert Wintour, William Lewis, Thomas Maurice, Richard Garnett, Mr. Philpott, Mr. Langford.

Summoned: Mr. William Bretton represented by Capt. Fleete, John Courtis represented by Capt. Fleete, Thomas Nabbs represented by Capt. Fleete, Mr. John Wyatt represented by Mr. Clerke, Zachary Mottershead represented by Capt. Cornwallis, Robert Percy represented by Mr. Lewger, Marmaduke Snow & his brother for him.

Edmond Parrie (of Isle of Kent) revoked his proxy to Mr. Philpott & was admitted.

f. 24 Claim: John Fleete (planter, of St. George's Hundred) represented by Capt. Henry Fleete.

f. 25 Afternoon. General Assembly. Attendees: President, Capt. Cornwallis, Capt. Evelin, Mr. Lewger, Mr. Greene, Richard Garnett, Sergt. Vaughan, James Baldridge, Capt. Fleete, Francis Rabnett, Mr. Philpott, Mr. Langford, Edmond Parrie, Justinian Snow, Mr. Clerke, Edward Fleete.

Summoned: Capt. Wintour (sick), Marmaduke Snow by his brother, Thomas Maurice, James Cauther (amerced), William Lewis (amerced).

f. 26 James Baldridge commissioned as sheriff
f. 27 & coroner of St. Maries' Co. Date: 29 January 1637. Signed: Leonard Calvert.

Inquest before coroner at Mattapanient in St. Maries' Co. Date: 31 January 1637. To view the body of John Bryante (also John Briante, planter, of Mattapanient). Jury: Richard Garnett, John Wyatt, John Halfhide, Edward Fleete, Thomas Franklin, Christopher Martin, Randoll Revell, John Hillierd, Nicholas Harvey, Richard Lusthead, John Robinson, Zachary Mottershead (planters).

Liber - Patent Record Z & A - 1637-1651

f. 28 ...
- Joseph Edlow (planter, of Mattapanient) deposed regarding the death of John Bryant.
- Henry Bishop (planter, of Mattapanient) deposed the same as Joseph Edlow.

Thomas Maurice & John Hillierd acknowledged debt to Roger Moy (planter, of St. George's Hundred).

f. 29 Roger Moy assigned said interest to James Cauther.

James Cauther & Roger Moy reclaimed the right to chattel belonging to John Hillier which John Hillierd & Thomas Morris are bound. Date: 2 February 1638. Signed: Roger Moy by James Cauther, Tho. Morys. Witnesses: Bryan Kelly, Edwart Fleet.

1 February. Mr. Thomas Greene (gentleman) acknowledged debt to Capt. Robert Wintour, Esq. Mr. Thomas Green (gentleman) acknowledged debt to Mr. John Lewger (Secretary).

f. 30 6 February. Anum Benum, Joseph Edlow, & Thomas Charington (planters, of St. Maries' Hundred) acknowledged debt to Mr. Thomas Cornwallis, Esq.

Mr. Robert Philpott (gentleman, of Isle of Kent) & John Langford (high constable of Isle of Kent) acknowledged debt to Mr. Leonard Calvert, Esq.

f. 31 8 February 1637. Mr. Edmond Parry (planter, of Isle of Kent) acknowledged debt to Leonard Calvert, Esq. Signed: Edmond Parrie.

Administration granted to John Langford (gentleman, of Isle of Kent) of the estate of Michael Scott (planter, of Isle of Kent).

f. 32 Robert Philpott, William Coxe, & Thomas Allen (gentlemen, of Isle of Kent) commissioned as conservators of the peace. Date: 9 February 1637. Signed: Leonard Calvert.

f. 33 John Langford was commissioned as sheriff & coroner of Isle of Kent.

8 February 1637. General Assembly.

f. 34 Attendees: President, Mr. Hawly, Capt. Cornwallis, Capt. Wintour, Capt. Evelin, Mr. Lewger (Secretary), Henry Fleete, Robert Vaughan, Jame Baldridge, Francis Rabnett, Justinian Snow, Thomas Maurice, Thomas Philpott, John Langford, Edward Parrie, Robert Clerke, Edward Fleete, Jas. Cauther, Mr. Greene, William Lewis.

Summoned: Richard Garnett represented by Robert Clerke, Marmaduke Snow represented by Justinian his brother, Edmond Parrie (amerced), Richard Lusthead represented by Robert Clerke.

f. 35 Afternoon. General Assembly. Attendees: President, Mr. Hawley, Capt. Cornwallis, Capt. Wintour, Mr. Lewger (Secretary), Capt. Evelin, William Lewis, Capt. Fleete, Robert Vaughan, James Baldridge, Francis Gray, Francis Rabnett, Justinian Snow, Thomas Morris, Robert Philpot, John Langford, John Robinson.

Summoned: Robert Clerke, Edward Fleete, James Cauther, Andrew Chappell, Cyprian Throughgood, Anthony Cotton, John Halfhead, Edmond Parrie (amerced), Mr. Greene represented by Capt. Cornwallis.

Francis Gray, John Robinson, & John Halfhead revoked their proxies to Justinian Snow.

f. 36 Mr. Robert Philpott (gentleman, of Isle of Kent) & John Langford (high constable of Isle of Kent) acknowledged debt to Mr. Leonard Calvert, Esq.

f. 37 To: sheriff of Isle of Kent. Command to take into custody Richard Thompson, John Abbott, & Samuel Smith to answer to suit of William Clobery (merchant). Date: 9 February 1637. Witness: Leonard Calvert.

Thomas Games (mariner) commissioned for authority to trade with Dutch in Hutson's River or with the Indians

f. 38 on Cape Henry & Cape Charles. Date: 12 February 1637. Witness: Leonard Calvert.

10 February. Shipped on the St. Margett by Robert Clerke on behalf of his master Thomas Copley, Esq. goods.

12 February 1637. James Cauther & Thomas Pasmore acknowledged debt to Thomas Cornwallis, Esq.

Liber - Patent Record Z & A - 1637-1651

f. 39 Mr. Thomas Cornwallis executor of John Saunders (gentleman) exhibited inventory & accounts and gave several discharges by: Richard Gerrard, Thomas White, Roger Walton. Jerome Hawley, Esq. produced an assignment of the legacy of said Valentine Saunders to said Jerome & demanded accounting.

f. 40 John Richardson sold 50 a. on Wickliff's Creek to Capt. George Evelin to be paid to Ralph Beane.

George Evelin paid said bill with a bill from Thomas Stente which satisfied Ralph Beane & said John Richardson. Date: 29 April.

Proclamation

f. 41 regarding actions by inhabitants of Isle of Kent. Mentions: Sasquisahanoughes & other Indians, Capt. Thomas Cornwallis, Esq. Signed: Leonard Calvert, Jerome Hawley, John Lewger.

f. 42 Warrant to William Brainthwaite to seize all vessels trading with the Indians. Date: 8 February.

15 February 1637. William Upton (mariner) vs. Capt. Thomas Cornwallis. Said Thomas had received tobacco from John Medley. Roger Moy deposed that Robert Nicholls told him that the tobacco was "wetted" by John Medley. Robert Nicholls deposed that the tobacco was never "wetted" & he never

f. 43 told Robert Moy any such thing.

26 February 1637. Leonard Calvert, Esq. (Lt. General), Robert Nicholls, & John Medley (planters, of St. Maries' Hundred) acknowledged debt to Justinian Snow.

22 February 1637. Thomas Francklin & Robert Nicholls acknowledged debt to Leonard Calvert, Esq.

f. 44 25 February. Thomas Francklin (planter) acknowledged debt to Leonard Calvert, Esq.

Leonard Calvert (Lt. General), planning to go to Isle of Kent, authorizes Mr. John Lewger (Secretary) to hold the Assembly.

f. 45 26 February 1637. General Assembly. Attendees: Mr. John Lewger (Secretary), Capt. Robert Wintour, Edward Bateman, John Halfhead, Robert Percie, Thomas Hebden, Christopher Martin, John Price, John Richardson, John Hill.

Summoned: Mr. Thomas Greene, Nathaniel Pope.

James Clofton (mariner) vs. Anthony Cotton (planter, St. Maries' Hundred).

f. 46 Said James was servant to said Anthony. Signed: James Claughton.

f. 47 James Claughton (mariner) vs. Anthony Cotton.

Thomas Francklin & Edward Fleete acknowledged debt to Lord Proprietor. Said Thomas & Edward to appear as witnesses in action of Claughton vs. Cotton.

26 February. Anthony Cotton & Edward Fleet acknowledged debt to Lord Proprietor.

f. 48 James Claughton (mariner) posted bond before John Lewger (Secretary). Francis Gray (carpenter, of St. Maries' Hundred) posted security on said bond. Mentions: Anthony Cotton (planter, of same hundred).

f. 49 Francis Gray (carpenter) acknowledged debt to Lord Proprietor. Mentions: suit of James Claughton vs. Anthony Cotton.

28 February. Shipped on the Deborah by Capt. Henry Fleete goods.

f. 50 Capt. Henry Fleete acknowledged debt to Leonard Calvert.

f. 51 5 March 1637. General Assembly. Attendees: Mr. Secretary, Mr. Greene, Mr. Sherriff, Christopher Martin, John Hillierd, Francis Gray, Robert Percy, Nathaniel Pope, Thomas Baldridge, Edward Bateman, Zachary Mottershead.

12 March 1637. General Assembly.

f. 52 Attendees: President, Capt. Cornwallis, Capt. Wintour, Mr. Secretary, Mr. Greene, Mr. Sherriff, Edward Fleete, John Smithson, John Wyatt, Marmaduke Snow, Thomas Nabbs, Anthony Cotton, Francis Gray, Rainold Fleete, Francis Rabnett, John Robinson, John Price, John Halfehide, Robert Smith, John Medley, Isaac

Page 73

Liber - Patent Record Z & A - 1637-1651

Edwards, John Courtis, William Lewis.

Summoned: Andrew Chappell, Cyprian Throughgood, Robert Vaughan, William Lewis, James Cauther, Francis Rabnett, Robert Clerke represented by John Wyatt.

<u>13 March 1637. General Assembly.</u> Attendees: President, Capt. Cornwallis, Capt. Wintour, Mr. Secretary, Cyprian Throughgood, Cuthbert Fenwick, James Cauther, Anthony Cotton, Robert Vaughan, Edward Fleete, William Lewis, Rainold Fleete, Mr. Sheriff, John Wyatt, Zachary Mottershead, Francis Rabnett, Marmaduke Snow, Mr. Greene.

Summoned: James Courtney represented by Robert Vaughan, David Wickliff represented by Robert Vaughan, Ralphe Beane represented by Robert Vaughan, Andrew Chappell represented by Robert Vaughan, Francis Gray represented by Capt. Cornwallis, John Robinson represented by Capt. Cornwallis, John Courtis represented by Capt. Cornwallis, Thomas Daved.

f. 53 Appeared: Mr. Thomas Greene, Francis Rabnett, John Halfehide, Isaac Edwards, Thomas Maurice, Cuthbert Fenwick.

<u>14 March 1637. General Assembly.</u> Attendees: President, Capt. Cornwallis, Mr. Secretary, Mr. Greene, John Wyatt, Cyprian Throughgood, Sergt. Vaughan, Zachary Mottershead, Cuthbert Fenwick, Mr. Sherriff, Raynold Fleete, Francis Rabnett, John Halfehide, William Lewis, Isaac Edwards.

Summoned: James Cauther, Thomas Maurice, Edward Fleete, Christopher Thomas, Richard Loe.

f. 54 Summoned: Anthony Cotton (amerced), Marmaduke Snow represented by Francis Rabnett.

Claim: Christopher Thomas (of Isle of Kent), Richard Loe.

Bill read: attainder of William Cleyborne (gentleman).

<u>12 February 1637 at St. Maries'. Court.</u> Attendees: Lt. General, Capt. Robert Wintour, Mr. John Lewger (Secretary).

Freeman for Grand Inquest: Thomas Greene (gentleman), Marmaduke Snow (gentleman), Francis Rabnett, Henry James, Andrew Chappell, John Robinson, Henry Bishop, Thomas Francklin, John Medley, Francis Gray, John Halfehide, Christopher Martin, Thomas Nabbs, John Courtis, Thomas Morris, Thomas Baldridge, Nathaniel Pope, Robert Vaughan, John Smithson, Robert Percy, James Cauther, Rainold Fleete, Isaac Edwards.

f. 55 To testify: Capt. Cornwallis, Cutbert Fenwick, Anthony Cotton, Edward Fleete, John Nevill, William Lewis.

First inquest for Lord Proprietor in River Pocomoque on the Eastern Shore on 23 April 1635. Thomas Cornwallis, Esq. & others went in the ships St. Helen & St. Margarett. Ratcliff Warren (also Lt. Warren), Richard Hancock, Robert Lake, et. al. on a ship of William Cleyborne (of Isle of Kent) fired on ships of said Thomas Cornwallis.

f. 56 William Ashmore (apprentice, of St. Maries') died of gunshot.

Second inquest for Lord Proprietor in harbour of Great Wighcocomico in Bay of Chesapeak on 10 May 1635. Thomas Cornwallis, Esq. and Cutbert Fenwick & John Hollis cited as servants of said Thomas. Thomas Smith (gentleman, of Isle of Kent), Phillip Taylor, Thomas Duffill, and Richard Hancock (planters)

f. 57 in a ship of William Cleyborne (gentleman, of Isle of Kent), fired on ship of said Thomas. William Ashmore (apprentice, of St. Maries') died of gunshot. William Cleyborne encouraged Lt. Warren to make the assault.

f. 58 <u>14 March 1637. General Assembly.</u> Attendees: President, Capt. Cornwallis, Mr. Secretary, Mr. Greene, John Wyatt, James Cauther, Xopfer Thomas, John Nevill, Zachary Mottershead, Robobert Percy, Cutbert Fenwick, Rainold Fleete, Thomas Maurice, Richard Loe, Anthony Cotton, Isaac Edwards, Edward Fleete, Thomas Francklin, William Lewis, Sergt. Vaughan, Francis Rabnett, John Halfehide, Cyprian Throughgood.

Mr. Greene amerced, & John Wyatt & Cyprian Throughgood.

Claim: John Nevill.

Mr. Secretary for Lord Proprietor vs. Thomas Smith. Depositions by John Jackson & Arthur Brooks.

Liber - Patent Record Z & A - 1637-1651

f. 59 ...

f. 60 Departure by: Capt. Cornwallis, Cutbert Fenwick, William Lewis, John Nevill, Anthony Cotton, Edward Fleete, Cyprian Throughgood.

Inquiry into deaths of: William Ashmore, Ratcliff Warren, John Bellson, William Dawson. Cites assault on ships of Capt. Thomas Cornwallis.

f. 61 15 March 1637. Morning. General Assembly. Attendees: President, Capt. Cornwalleys, Mr. Secretary, Mr. Greene, Robert Clerk, Mr. Sheriff, Cyprian Throughgood, John Wyatt, Sergt. Vaughan, Reinold Fleete, Cutbert Fenwick, Anthony Cotton, James Cauther, Edward Fleete, Francis Rabnett, William Lewis.

Summoned: Christopher Thomas, Isaac Edwards, Capt. Wintour (amerced), John Nevill, Richard Lowe represented by Capt. Cornwalleys, John Halfehide represented by Capt. Cornwalleys.

Bill read: attainder of William Cleborne. Sentence of Thomas Smith.

Afternoon. General Assembly. Attendees: President, Capt. Cornwalleys, Mr. Secretary, Mr. Sheriff, Robert Clerk, Joh Wyatt, Cutbert Fenwick, Rainold Fleete, John Nevill, Edward Fleete, Anthony Cotton, Francis Rabnett, William Lewis, Isaac Edwards,

f. 62 Summoned: Capt. Wintour (amerced), Cyprian Throughgood represented by Robert Clerke, Sergt. Vaughan represented by Francis Rabnett, James Cauther represented by Francis Rabnett, Mr. Greene represented by Capt. Cornwalleys, Christopher Thomas (amerced), Richard Garnett represented by Thomas Cornwalleys.

Thomas Baldridge vs. Isaac Edwards.

16 March 1637. Morning. General Assembly. Attendees: President, Capt. Cornwalleys, Mr. Secretary, Mr. Greene, Mr. Sheriff, Sergt. Vaughan, Edward Fleete, Robert Percy, Francis Rabnett, Reinold Fleete, Anthony Cotton, Isaac Edwards, Robert Clerke, William Lewis, John Wyatt.

Claim: Richard Thompson (gentleman, of Isle of Kent).

Summoned: Capt. Wintour (amerced), John Nevill (amerced), Christopher Thomas represented by Tho. Cornwallis, Cutbert Fenwick represented by Tho. Cornwallis.

Bill read: sentence of Thomas Smith.

f. 63 Robert Clerke for Mr. Copley vs. administrator of John Bryant.

Afternoon. General Assembly. Attendees: President, Capt. Cornwallyes, Mr. Secretary, Mr. Greene, Mr. Sheriff, Mr. Thompson, Edward Fleete, Sergt. Vaughan, John Wyatt, Rainold Fleet, Anthony Cotton, Isaac Edwards, Robert Percy, Francis Rabnett, Robert Clerke, William Lewis.

Summoned: Capt. Wintour (amerced), John Nevill (amerced).

f. 64 Bill read: attainder of William Cleyborne.

17 March 1637. Morning. General Assembly: President, Capt. Cornwalleys, Mr. Secretary, Mr. Greene, Mr. Sheriff, Robert Clerke, John Wyatt, William Lewis, Francis Rabnett, Edward Fleete, Reinold Fleete, Sergt. Vaughan, Mr. Thompson, James Cauther, Anthony Cotton.

Summoned: Capt. Wintour, Anthony Cotton, Capt. Evelin represented by Lt. General, John Nevill represented by Robert Clerke.

Bill read: sentence of Thomas Smith.

f. 65 Memorandum before: Leonard Calvert, Esq. Lt. General, George Evelin (gentleman, of St. George's Hundred), Richard Thompson (gentleman, of Isle of Kent), Marmaduke Snow.

19 March 1637. Morning. General Assembly. Attendees: President, Capt. Cornwalleys, Mr. Secretary, Capt. Evelin, William Broughe, Robert Clerke, Mr. Sheriff, Robert Vaughan, William Lewis, Francis Rabnett, Edward Fleete, John Wyatt, John Halfehide, Reinold Fleete, Anthony Cotton, Cutbert Fenwick, John Robinson, Francis Gray, Richard Loe.

Summoned: Isaac Edwards, Mr. Greene.

f. 66 24 March. General Assembly. Attendees: President, Capt. Cornwallyes, Mr.

Liber - Patent Record Z & A - 1637-1651

Secretary, Robert Clerke, Mr. Sheriff, Thomas Franklin, William Lewis, Francis Rabnett, John Wyatt, John Halfehide, Francis Gray, Anthony Cotton, John Robinson, Thomas Hebden, Henry Crawley (of Isle of Kent), Thomas Bradnock (of Isle of Kent), Edward Beckler (of Isle of Kent).

Administration of estate of John Briant granted to Richard Garnett.

26 March. William Edwin granted a license to marry Mary Whitehead.

27 March. Administration of estate of Susan Sey granted to Cyprian Throughgood.

23 March. Inquest of death of Thomas Morris.

f. 67 24 March. Inquest into death of Thomas Cullamore.

27 March. to sheriff of Isle of Kent: notice to seize all chattel of William Cleyborne (gentleman).

6 April. Administration of estate of Zachary Mottershead granted to James Baldridge.

James Baldridge & Thomas Baldridge acknowledged debt to Lord Proprietor, bond on estate of Zachary Mottershead.

22 March 1637. Henry Crawley acknowledged debt to Lord Proprietor, bond on estate of

f. 68 William Blissard (planter, of Isle of Kent).

26 March 1638. William Edwin (planter) acknowledged debt to Lord Proprietor, for marriage to Mary Whitehead (spinster).

Richard Garnett, Sr. & Richard Garnett, Jr. acknowledged debt to Lord Proprietor, bond on estate of John Brian.

f. 69 30 March 1638. Randoll Revell (cooper) & James Cloughton (mariner) acknowledged debt to Leonard Calvert, Esq. for use of William Parry (of VA). Mr. Lewger received satisfaction 18 Ja. 1638. Tho. Cornwalleys satisfied

f. 70 on 4 March 1638.

Christopher Martin released James Claughton (mariner) of all debts.

Leonard Calvert, Esq. Lt. General, going to VA, appointed Mr. John Lewger (Secretary) as Lt. General. Date: 1 April 1638.

To Robert Wintour, Esq. Establishment of St. George's Hundred on west side of St. George's River and said Robert

f. 71 is commissioned as justice of the peace.

f. 72 31 March 1638. Witness: Leonard Calvert.

8 April 1638. Capt. Robert Wintour lent to Capt. George Evelin 5 servants, including: (N) Speed, (N) Browne.

9 April 1638. Capt. George Evelin to Phillip West, William Williamson, & John Hopson. Freedom of service to said Evelin for 1 year.

f. 73 Capt. George Evelin assigned debt to Capt. Thomas Cornwalleys, Esq. Witness: John Lewger (Secretary).

Thomas Morris deposed, regarding the inventory of estate of Zachary Mottershead (gentleman, dec'd, of St. Maries').

Capt. George Evelin acknowledged debt to Lord Proprietor.

f. 74 Said George to bring John Dandie into court.

John Dandie acknowledged debt to Capt. George Evelin.

10 April 1638. Andrew Chappell acknowledged debt to James & Thomas Baldridge.

f. 75 Jerome Hawley, Esq. acknowledged debt to Lord Proprietor. Said Jerome to bring John Norman into court. Mentions: Cyprian Throughgood.

Liber - Patent Record Z & A - 1637-1651

12 April. Capt. Henry Fleete brought goods in the ship Deborah

f. 76 traded with the Indians.

17 April. Mr. Sheriff appointed Robert Percy as his bailiff.

28 April 1638. Samuel Smith acknowledged debt to Lord Proprietor. Richard Thompson (gentleman, of Isle of Kent) acknowledged debt to Lord Proprietor. Henry Hawley (gentleman, of VA) acknowledged debt to Lord Proprietor.

f. 77 Samuel Smith posted bond in suit of William Clobery (merchant).

25 April 1638. Capt. George Evelin acknowledged debt to Lord Proprietor. John Lewger (Secretary) acknowledged debt to Lord Proprietor.
- Suit between said George & Samuel Smith.

Cutbert Fenwick (gentleman, of St. Maries') is authorized to question all persons unlawfully trading in Province. Date: 26 April 1638.

f. 78 29 April 1638. Inventory of estate of John Briant by Richard Garnett, Sr.

f. 79 List of debts: Richard Garnett, Sr. Received of Richard Garnett chattel of John Briant (planter, dec'd, of Mattapanient). Date: 22 September 1638. Signed: Thomas Copley.

28 April 1638. Richard Thompson (gentleman, of Isle of Kent) acknowledged debt to Lord Proprietor,

f. 80 bond against Thomas Stente.

29 April 1638. John Ormesby acknowledged debt to John Harris the elder.

Accounts of estate of John Briant by Richard Garnett, Sr. Payments to: Mr. Secretary, Mr. Copley.

Complaint exhibited against you in court

f. 81 by Randoll Revell. Date: 1 May 1638. Signed: John Lewger (Secretary).

3 May 1638. John Medley & Robert Nicholls (planters) acknowledged debt to Leonard Calvert, Esq. Assignment to James Baldridge. Date: 28 August 1638.

f. 82 Inventory of estate of Richard Bradley by Thomas Francklin. List of debts: Capt. Cornwalleys, Mr. Copley, Mr. Greene, Tho. Pasmore, Xpofer Martin, John Price, Ralphe Beane, the Governor, Mr. Hawley.

Accounts of Thomas Francklin. Payments to: Randoll Revell, Capt. Cornwalleys.

7 May 1638 at St. Maries'. Court. Attendees: (N) George, Capt. Evelin, Thomas Francklin, Robert Clerke, Cutbert Fenwick, Mr. Greene, John Price, Richard Garnett, William Edwin, Xpofer Martin, Thomas Gerard, Anthony Cotton, John Richardson, John Hill, Thomas Pasmore.

f. 83 Richard Garnett to pay all unaccounted-for residue of estate of John Briant to Mr. Thomas Copley.

Capt. George Evelin is to pay John Dandie wages & grant 1 year's freedom, against claims from said Evelin or Mr. Clobery (merchant). John Lewger (Secretary) is surety.

Capt. George Evelin acknowledged debt to Capt. Tho. Cornwalleys for amount assigned said Thomas from Capt. Robert Wintour.

Report of Cutbert Fenwick taken 8 May 1638. Inquiry about a boat

f. 84 on the Eastern Shore, which belonged to Rowland William (of Accomack), who was killed by Indians.

13 May 1638. Cyprian Throughgood for Mr. Tho. Copley chattel traded with the Indians. Signed: Cy. Throughgood.

Leonard Calvert, Esq. Lt. General, going to VA, appointed Capt. Thomas Cornwallyes, Esq. as Lt. General. Date: 27 May 1638.

f. 85 27 May 1638. Capt. Henry Fleete acknowledged debt to Lord Proprietor.

John Boteler (gentleman, of Isle of Kent)

Liber - Patent Record Z & A - 1637-1651

- f. 86 appointed as captain of military of Isle of Kent. Signed: Leonard Calvert.

- f. 87 30 May 1638. Capt. George Evelin (of Evelinton, St. Maries' Co.) acknowledged debt to his brother Lt. Robert Evelin. Said George assigned all interest of William Clobery (merchant) in the service of Andrew Baker, Thomas Baker, & John Hatche. Said George sold to said Robert his right in Pinie Point plantation (300 a.) in Mannor of Evelinton & 1 other plantation (50 a.) occupied by John Richardson.

- f. 88 7 June 1638. Capt. Henry Fleete is authorized to trade with Indians. Signed: John Lewger (Secretary). Same license granted to James Cloughton. Date: 9 July.

    19 June 1638. Tho. Baldridge (sheriff) acknowledged debt to Lord Proprietor, as surety to John Norton (sawyer). Signed: James Baldridge.

    20 June 1638. Goods & chattels seized from Capt. Cleyborne in Palmer's Island. Servants cited: Edmond Griffin, William Jones, William Freeman, Richard Reymont.

- f. 89 Signed: Robert Vaughan.

- f. 90 List of goods belonging to Thomas Smith (of Kent). Includes items belonging to Sergt. Howard (of Kent). Received by Sergt. Vaughan at Palmer's Island. Signed: John Fullwood (alias John Sands).

    1 July. Accounts of Sergt. Robert Vaughan. Mentions items of: Sergt. Howard, Thomas Smith. Mentions items & servants delivered to Mr. Lewger. Mentions items delivered to: Reinold Fleete, Mr. Perkins, Will. Cooke, Jack Harrington.

- f. 91 Process against William Lewis, Francis Gray, & Robert Sedgrave. On 1 July, William Lewis informed Capt. Cornwalleys that certain of his servants had drawn a petition to Sir John Hervey. The captain sent for Robert Sedgrave, who confirmed writing & delivering it to Francis Gray. Mentions: charges against William Lewis (of St. Inego's).

- f. 92 Signed: Christopher Carroll, Ellis Beache, Ro. Sedgrave, et. al. On 3 July, the sheriff was commanded by warrant to bring William Lewis,

- f. 93 Robert Sedgrave, Francis Gray, Christopher Carroll, & Ellis Beache to court. Mentions: Mr. Copley,

- f. 94 Mr. Smith (minister). Richard Duke (protestant), witness produced by Francis Gray,

- f. 95 deposed. Mentions: James Thornton.

- f. 96 3 July 1638. William Lewis, John Medcalfe, & Richard Browne acknowledged debt to Lord Proprietor.

- f. 97 Xpfer Martin & Edward Fleete acknowledged debt to Francis Gray in suit of John Robinson. Date: 1 May 1637. Signed: Christopher Martin.

    6 July. Thomas Murice & Thomas Pasmore acknowledged debt to Lord Proprietor, for his defense vs. Florentine Paine (of Accomack). Signed: Thomas Maurice.

    9 July. James Neale for Mr. Hawley, goods to be shipped on ship Saint Nicholas.

- f. 98 James Neale returned & requested discharge. Date: 10 September 1638. Signed: John Lewger (Collector).

    Administration of estate of Mr. Hawley granted to Capt. Mr. Thomas Cornwallis, Esq. Date: 2 August 1638.

    Administration of estate of Thomas Cullamore granted to same captain.

    7 August. Thomas Copley, Esq. by his attorney Cyprian Throughgood vs. John Norton. Mentions: covenant by defendant with Francis Gray.

- f. 99 Thomas Cornwalleys, Esq. administrator of Mr. Jerome Hawley, Esq. acknowledged debt to Lord Proprietor,

- f. 100 as bond on estate of Thomas Cullamore.

    John Lewger attorney for Lord Proprietor vs. Capt. Tho. Cornwalleys, Esq. Cites debt from estate of Jerome Hawley, Esq. (dec'd). Said Thomas is administrator

Liber - Patent Record Z & A - 1637-1651

f. 101 to Tho. Cornwallyes, Esq. Jerome Hawley, Esq. (dec'd, of St. Maries') in his last will & testament dated 20 October 1633 in England, named as his executors William Hawley, Esq. (of Grossmont in County Munmoth), Arthur Dodington, Esq., & Lewis Hele, Esq. Said Tho. to be administrator. Date: 14 August 1638. Signed: John Lewger, (Secretary).

f. 102 Thomas Cornwallyes, Esq. acknowledged debt to Lord Proprietor, bond on estate of Jerome Hawley, Esq. (dec'd).

14 August 1638. John Lewger (Secretary) vs. Thomas Cornwallyes. Cites goods conveyed by Mr. Hawley, Esq. (dec'd, of St. Maries') in England

f. 103 to John Sims (of Pounsford in County Somerset) delivered to Capt. Thomas Cornwallyes, Esq. for use of said John Sims. Inventory taken 9 September 1637 & testified by John Althome. Signed: Leonard Calvert.

Jerome Hawley, Esq. (dec'd, of St. Maries') on 17 December conveyed to Thomas Cornwallis, Esq. all his goods in the Province for debt due to John Sims, Esq. (of Pounsford in County Somerset).

f. 104 Said Thomas to hold land, save widow's 1/3rd.

Thomas Copley, Esq. vs. Tho. Cornwalleys, Esq. administrator of Jerome Hawley, Esq. (dec'd, of St. Maries').

f. 105 Thomas Cornwalleys acknowledged said bill. Date: 30 August 1638. Plaintiff to recover 1/2.

16 August. Creditors to estate of Jerome Hawley (dec'd): Mr. Sheriff appointed by Mr. Secretary, Robert Percy appointed by Mr. Copley, Tho. Hebden appointed by Mr. White.

18 August. Administration granted to Anne Smithson (widow) of her husband's estate. Inventory to be brought by Bartholomew Day.

23 August. Anthony Cotton (planter) vs. Thomas Cornwalleys, Esq. administrator of Jerome Hawley, Esq. (dec'd, of St. Maries').

f. 106 Tho. Cornwalleys acknowledged said debt. Date: 30 August.

22 August. Inventory of estate of Andrew Baker, appraised by Thomas Baldridge & Thomas Perry. List of debts: David Wickliff, Phillip West.

f. 107 26 August 1638. Cyprian Throughgood (gentleman) vs. Thomas Cornwalleys, Esq. administrator of Jerome Hawley, Esq. (dec'd, of St. Maries').

30 August. Thomas Cornwalleys acknowledged said debt.

26 August 1638. Cyprian Throughgood (gentleman) administrator of Susan Saye (spinster, of St. Maries') vs. Thomas Cornwallyes, Esq. administrator of Jerome Hawley, Esq. (dec'd).

f. 108 Cyprian Throughgood (gentleman) administrator of Susan Saye (spinster, of St. Maries') vs. Thomas Cornwallyes, Esq. administrator of Jerome Hawley, Esq. (dec'd). Said Susan was servant to said Jerome at time of her death.

30 August 1638. Thomas Cornwallyes acknowledged said debt. Tho. Cornwalleys, Esq. showed he is creditor to estate of Jerome Hawley

f. 109 & produced note from said Jerome to John Sims, Esq. (of County Somerset) & assigned to said Tho.

27 August 1638. Mrs. Eleanor Hawley (widow) & Thomas White, Esq. deposed that Jerome Hawley, Esq. (dec'd, of St. Maries') acknowledged receipt from Mr. John Sims (of Pounsford of County Somerset) & assignment to Thomas Cornwallyes, Esq. (of St. Maries').

29 August. John Halfehead vs. John Hill (fugitive).

f. 110 Inventory of estate of Zachary Mottershead (gentleman, dec'd, of St. Maries'), delivered by James Baldridge (sheriff) & appraised by Thomas Francklin & Anthony Cotton.

Accounts of said estate by James Baldridge. Payments to: accountant,

f. 111 2 men who brought the said Tho. Cullamore to the grave, the coroner, Capt. Tho. Cornwalleys.

Liber - Patent Record Z & A - 1637-1651

Thomas Hebden deposed on 8 September 1638 that on 11 April last, he was with Capt. Robert Wintour & heard him discharge Edward Parker & William Nanfin of all obligation of service, declaring he had received from the mother of Edward Parker goods in England.

<u>21 September</u>. Mr. Thomas Greene (gentleman) sold chattel to Leonard Calvert, Esq.

f. 112 Inventory of estate of Mr. William Smith (dec'd, of St. Maries'), appraised by Francis Rabnett & Robert Percy.

f. 113 List of debts: Mr. Gerard, Richard Duke,

f. 114 Jo. Hillierd, John Bryant, Tho. Allen. Signed: Anne Smith.

Accounts of said William Smith by Anne wife & executrix. Payments to: Mr. White, Capt. Cornwalleys, Mr. Pasmore, goodwife Gilbert, John Robinson, Thomas Willis, John Hillierd, Richard Bradley, Sergeant Vaughan, Robert Percy, Thomas Allen (legacy), Francis Rabnett, Richard Lusthead. Signed: Anne Smith.

<u>9 January 1639</u>. Thomas Gerard (gentleman) & Thomas Hebden (planter) deposed, at the request of John Lewger, Esq. executor of Richard Lee (gentleman), that they were present when the inventory was made.

f. 115 <u>3 November 1638</u>. Thomas Cornwalleys, Esq. refused to prove the will of his servant James Hitches. Administration was granted to Thomas Hebden. Said Thomas acknowledged debt to Lord Proprietor, bond on the estate of James Hitches.

f. 116 <u>4 February 1638</u>. Sergt. Thomas Baldridge was granted administration on the estate of Edward Bateman.

Marmaduke Snow was granted administration on estate of his brother Justinian Snow who died at sea intestate. Date: 19 March 1638. Witness: John Lewger (Secretary).

f. 117 <u>19 March 1638</u>. Marmaduke Snow (gentleman) & Mr. Giles Brent (gentleman) acknowledged debt to Lord Proprietor, bond on estate of Justinian.

f. 118 Marmaduke Snow was granted administration on estate of his brother Justinian Snow (planter, of St. Maries') & said Marmaduke is now "non compos mentis" and very ill, administration of said estate is now granted to Thomas Gerard (surgeon, brother-in-law of said Marmaduke).

f. 119 <u>24 April 1639</u>. Thomas Gerard (surgeon) & Thomas Baldridge (sheriff of St. Maries') acknowledged debt to Lord Proprietor, bond

f. 120 on the administration.

John Medley (planter, of St. Michael's Hundred) was granted administration on the estate of Richard Lee (planter, of St. Maries'). John Medley acknowledged debt to Lord Proprietor, bond on estate of Richard Lee. Date: 2 May 1639.

<u>2 December 1639</u>. Randoll Revell was granted administration on the estate of Andrew Chappell.

f. 121 Said Randoll Revell & Francis Gray (carpenter) acknowledged debt to Lord Proprietor, bond on said estate. Randoll Revell discharged of the administration. Date: 27 May 1640.

Several action by various creditors against Thomas Cornwalleys, Esq. administrator of Jerome Hawley, Esq. (dec'd, of St. Maries')

f. 122 & recovered in court. At the request of said Thomas, herein provided is an authentic certificate of the several judgements. Mentions: assignment from John Sims, Esq. (of County Somerset). On 27 August 1638, Eleanor Hawley (widow of said Jerome) & Thomas White, Esq. (age 60 & upwards, of St. Maries') deposed regarding said debt & assignment.

f. 123 Judgements cited against the estate: John Lewger, Thomas Copley, Esq., Andrew Cotton (mariner), Cyprian Throughgood (planter), Andrew Chappell (mariner), John Cook (carpenter & servant to said Jerome), Richard Hill (carpenter & servant to said Jerome), Edward Brent (ship carpenter), Ann Smithson (widow & servant to said Jerome).

f. 124 Cites petition by Richard Garnett the elder (husbandman, of Mattapanient) for price of a maid servant sold by him to said Jerome. Date: 3 January 1639. Signed: Leonard Calvert, Esq.

Page 80

Liber - Patent Record Z & A - 1637-1651

James Cauther (planter, of St. Michael's Hundred) was granted administration on the estate of William Wassell (planter, of same hundred, dec'd intestate). Date: 30 January 1639. Signed: Leonard Calvert.

f. 125 William Brainthwaite (gentleman, of Isle of Kent), whereas Henry Crawley (planter, of Isle of Kent, dec'd) did by his last will & testament dated 15 February 1639, bequeath to Catherine Smith daughter of John Smith (of Isle of Kent) all of his estate, as by deposition of

f. 126 Robert Lake, taken before William Brainthwate (gentleman) & by deposition of Thomas Kidd taken before Giles Brent, Esq. (commander of Isle of Kent), is granted administration of estate of said Crawley.

f. 127 The estate is to be preserved for use of said Catherine until she comes of age. Date: 16 March 1639. Witness: Leonard Calvert. William Brainthwaite & Thomas Gerard (gentleman) his surety acknowledged debt to Lord Proprietor. On 1 March 1640, administration is discharged.

John Lewger (gentleman, Secretary) deposed, as the request of Thomas Cornwalleys, Esq.

f. 128 regarding the certificate on judgements on the estate of Jerome Hawley, Esq. (dec'd, of St. Maries').

f. 129 John Lewger (gentleman, Secretary) deposed on 4 May 1640, at the request of Thomas Cornwallyes, Esq., regarding the certificate on judgements on the estate for which Thomas Cornwallis is administrator.

John Lewger (Secretary) granted to Robert Clerke (gentleman, of St. Maries')

f. 130 administration on estate of Thomas Cooper (carpenter, of St. Michael's Hundred, dec'd intestate). Date: 5 June 1640.

Administration was granted to John Russell on the estate of John Glantham. Date: 7 December 1640.

f. 131 Robert Vaughan was granted administration on the estate of Thomas Holt (planter, of VA, dec'd). Date: 19 January.

f. 132 4 March 1640. John Smith (of Kent) was appointed guardian of his daughter Katherine. Surety is his plantation at Crayford which he had of Mr. Will. Brainthwait. Said John Smith made Mr. Will. Brainthwaite (gentleman) his tenant for the plantation at Broadcreek, to hold until Katherine Smith comes of age 14 years.

8 October 1641. Leonard Calvert Lt. General granted Eleanor Martin (widow of Xpher Martin)

f. 133 administration of her husband's estate (dec'd intestate). William Howkins & Joseph Edlo agreed to pay all debts due from estate of Xpher Martin (tailor, of St. Maries', dec'd intestate).

f. 134 Giles Brent (of Isle of Kent) was granted administration on estate of Thomas Adams (gentleman, of Isle of Kent, dec'd). Date: 26 March 1642.

Richard Purlivant (of Isle of Kent) was granted administration on estate of Henry Wood. Date: 28 June 1642.

f. 135 John Abbott (planter, of Isle of Kent) was appointed administrator on estate of John Boteler (gentleman, of Isle of Kent, dec'd). Said Boteler made a will on 1 April last per Mathew Rodan & Thomas Allen, & appointed his brother as executor. Said brother lives in England & cannot execute the same. Date: 1 July 1642.

f. 136 Robert Vaughan was granted administration on estate of William Westlies.

f. 137 2 August 1642. Depositions by Robert Huett, Hannah Huett, & William Risbrook that William Westly (miller, of Isle of Kent, dec'd) did make a will:
- I give all to Henry Bellamy.

f. 138 Giles Brent was to grant administration to Henry Bellamy on the estate of William Westly. On 3 August, Robert Vaughan vowed to pay all debts.

Thomas Cornwalleys, Esq. was granted administration on the estate of Richard Lusthead, Thomas Charington, & John Machin (planter, of Mattapanient Hundred, dec'd).

f. 139 22 August 1642. Capt. Cornwalleys (gentleman) acknowledged debt to Lord

Liber - Patent Record Z & A - 1637-1651

Proprietor, bond.

Dame Jane Cockshutt (widow) was granted administration on estate of her husband John Cockshutt.

f. 140 Date: 13 October 1642. Witness: John Lewger, Esq. (Secretary). Said Jane Cockshutt acknowledged debt to Lord Proprietor, bond. George Bincks (gentleman, licentiate in Physick) administered the oath to Tho. Greene

f. 141 (gentleman) & Nathan Pope (planter) to appraise the estate of John Cockshutt (dec'd). Date: 15 October 1642. Witness: John Lewger. On 21 October 1642, oath was administered. Signed: George Binx. On 1 June, waiting word on debt of Mr. Herne.

Inventory of James Hitches by his administrator Thomas Hebden. Date: 12 December 1638. List of debts: Thomas Hebden, Richard Lusthead, Anum Benam,

f. 142 William Lewis, Thomas Francklin, the Governour. Signed: Tho. Hebden.

Inventory of Edward Bateman (carpenter, of St. Maries') by his administrator Thomas Baldridge. List of debts: Anthony Cotton.

Inventory of Richard Loe by his administrator Mr. Baldridge. Servants: James Moulins.

f. 143 Note: "the dogge is omitted" per John Cook given to John Hollis.

Inventory of Thomas Cullamore by his administrator Capt. Thomas Cornwalleys. Date: 7 August 1638. Appraisers: James Baldridge, Thomas Hebden.

f. 144 List of debts: estate of Jerome Hawley, Esq.

f. 145 Inventory of Mr. John Baxter by his administrator Justinian Snow. Date: 20 February 1637. Legacies: to his wife. List of debts: Mr. Thomas Greene, Mr. Lawes (mariner), Capt. Henry Fleete.

Inventory of Richard Lee (gentleman) by his executor John Lewger. Date: 31 March 1639. Appraisers: Thomas Gerard (gentleman), Thomas Hebden (planter).

f. 146 ...

f. 147 Servants: Humphrey Chaplin, Ann Norris,

f. 148 John Jones, Xpher Moreland.

f. 149 Inventory of Justinian Snow (planter, of St. Maries') by his administrator Thomas Gerard. Date: 24 May 1639. Appraisers: Giles Brent, Esq., James Baldridge (planter).

f. 150 ...

f. 151 Servants: John Langworth, Peter Heyward, Tho. Knight, Richard Scotfoord, Christopher Morland,

f. 152 ...

f. 153 ...

f. 154 Samuel Barrett.

f. 155 List of debts: Nicholas Hervey, Richard Lusthead, Randoll Revell, James Cauther, Roger Moy & Thomas Maurice, Mr. Lewger, Thomas Franklin, Ralphe Beane, Reinold Fleete, Enam Benam, Owen Phillips, the Governour, Mr. Britton, my brother Marmaduke Snow, executor of Richard Lee, accountant, Roger Oliver, John Cooke, Mathias Sousa, John Hullowes, Thomas Boys, John Hillierd, Francis Rabnett, Joseph Edlo,

f. 156 Thomas Stente, Xpher Martin, Richard Nevill, Richard Loe, Robert Smith, Mathias de Sousa, John Hallowes, John Dandie, Nathan Pope, Anth. Cotton, Mr. Thomas White, James Cauther, the Secretary, Thomas Francklin, Mr. Phillips.

f. 157 Inventory of Capt. Robert Wintour, Esq. (of St. Maries'). Appraisers: James Baldridge, Thomas Hebden. Date: 4 September 1638. Servants: George Tailor, Richard Browne, Simon Demibiel, Thomas White, Bartholomew Phillips, Rowland Morgan, Arthur Webb.

f. 158 ...

Liber - Patent Record Z & A - 1637-1651

f. 159 ...

f. 160 List of debts: Mr. Copley, Cyprian Throughgood, Thomas Hebden, Robert Nicholls, John Norton, the Governour, William Bretton, David Wickliff, Richard Garnett, Ralphe Beane, Capt. Evelin, Mr. Tho. Greene, William Lewis, Capt. Cornwalleys.

f. 161 Inventory of Mr. Thomas Egerton (gentleman, of St. Maries', dec'd intestate) by his administrator the Secretary. Mentions: Marmaduke Snow.

Inventory of Michael Lums by his administrator Cutbert Fenwick (gentleman). Date: 17 January 1639. Appraisers: Thomas Gerard, Thomas Baldridge.

f. 162 List of debts: the Governour, Capt. Cornwalleys, John Hallowes, Xpofer Martin. Signed: Cuthbart Fenwick.

Inventory of William Wassell (planter, of St. Michael's Hundred) by his administrator James Cauther. Date: 11 April 1640. Appraisers: Robert Percy, John Hillierd. List of debts: Mr. Purlivant (of Kent).

Inventory of Andrew Chappell (mariner, of St. Maries') by his administrator Randoll Revell. Date: 28 February 1639. Sales to: Jo. Foster,

f. 163 Andrew Marrow, Randoll Revell, Francis Gray, Fra. Gray, James Cauther. List of debts: accountant for goods brought out of New England, Mr. Parry (of VA), Thomas Brice (of VA), Thomas Games (of Isle of Kent).

Inventory of Henry Crawley taken in presence of Giles Basha (sheriff of Isle of Kent). Date: 2 April 1640. Delivered on 1 June 1640 by Capt. William Brainthwaite.

f. 164 Mentions: Phillip Conner, Thomas Keine.

Inventory of Lawrence Mullock (of Isle of Kent) by Mr. Phillpot. Date: 7 September 1640.

f. 165 Inventory of John Glantham by his administrator John Russell.

Inventory of Christopher Martin (tailor, of St. Maries') & of Joseph Edlo (planter). [1/2 belongs to said Xpofer Martin.]

f. 166 List of debts: Robert Percy & John Hillierd, John Harwood, Francis Gray. Appraisers: John Wepvill, William Howkins.

Inventory of Leonard Leonardson. Date: 18 April 1642.

f. 167 Inventory of Richard Lusthead (of Mattapanian). Date: 23 August 1642. In presence of Cutbert Fenwick & Richard Gardyner. Delivered on 3 December 1642.

f. 168 Second portion in presence of: Henry James, Thomas Franclin.

Inventory of Thomas Carinton in presence of Cutbert Fenwick & Richard Gardyner. Date: 23 August 1642. Delivered on 3 December 1642.

Inventory of John Machin (of Mattapanian). Delivered on 3 December 1642. List of debts: Robert Nicholls,

f. 169 Henry Bishop, Richard Gardner the elder, Richard Lusthead, Mr. Robert Clerke, John Harington, Mr. Robert Wiseman, William Lewis, Xpofer Carroll, Lewis Froman, Cutbert Fenwick, Mr. Thomas Gerard, Edward Cotton.

Inventory of Henry Woods by his administrator Richard Purlivant. Mentions: time served me praised by John Abbott & Tho. Keyne.

Inventory of Mr. John Cockshott in presence of Mr. Fenwick attorney for Capt. Cornwalleys & Mr. Geo. Binks. Appraisers: Mr. Tho. Greene, Nathan. Pope. Delivered on 28 October 1642 by Jane Cockshott (widow).

f. 170 ...

f. 171 ...

f. 172 ...

f. 173 Inventory of Mr. Adams. Signed: Thomas Dobbs. Cites: items due estate from Thomas Bradnox, items in the shallop & at house of Tho. Butler belonging to Mr. Tho. Adams (dec'd). Date: 6 February 1641. Signed: Franc. Rabnett.

f. 174 Accounts of Jerome Hawley, Esq. (of St. Maries') by Thomas Cornwalleys, Esq.

Liber - Patent Record Z & A - 1637-1651

delivered on 20 April 1639. Debts received: Thomas Hebden, John Dandie, John Wyatt, Cyprian Throughgood, Anthony Cotton, Capt. Evelin & Co., Thomas Bradnock & Richard Purlivant, William Medcalf, Ed. Comins & Thomas Pett, Robert Phillpott & Lawrence Mollock, William Coxe & John Smith.

f. 175 Payments to: Mr. Lewger for Tho. Cullamore, Mr. Lewger, Leonard Calvert, Esq., Robert Percy, John Halfehead, Randoll Revell, Anthony Smithson, Will. Lewis, accountant, Lord Baltimore, Andrew Chappell, Edward Brent, Xpofer Plunkett, John Cook, Richard Hill, Cyprian Throughgood, Anthony Cotton, Richard Garnett, Capt. Evelin & Co., Thomas Copley, Esq.

f. 176 on estate of Jerome Hawley, discharge

f. 177 of administration. Date: 29 April 1639.

On estate of Thomas Cullamore (of St. Maries'),

f. 178 discharge of administration. Date: 4 May 1639.

Accounts of Thomas Cullamore by Thomas Cornwalleys, Esq. delivered on 18 September 1638. Payments to: John Harris, James Neale (merchant), the Secretary.

Accounts of Mr. John Baxter (gentleman, of St. Maries') by his administrator Justinian Snow. Date: 20 February 1637. Payments to: Mr. Rolston,

f. 179 Mr. Rolston (of VA), John Briant, Mr. James Neale (merchant, of VA), Martin (N) (Mr. Rolston's man), Mr. Lewger, Mr. Wells (surgeon), Thomas Allen (legacy), Mr. Thomas White.

f. 180 Due from: John Bryant. Accounts of Mr. Lewger delivered to Capt. Thomas Cornwalleys assignee of Mr. Thomas White on 4 May 1639: received from Justinian Snow.

Accounts of Andrew Baker (carpenter) made 20 August delivered by John Lewger (Secretary). Received from: Thomas Pasmore.

f. 181 Payments to: John Halfehide, Ralple Beane, Rich. Browne (tailor), Will. Freeman, James Courtney.

Accounts of Capt. Robert Wintour, Esq. (of St. Maries') by John Lewger (Secretary). Date: 4 September 1639. Payments to: Mr. Copley, accountant, James Baldridge, Thomas Morris, Thomas Franclin, Randoll Revell, Capt. Tho. Cornwalleys, Jo. Halfehide, Tho. Pasmore, Mr. Gerard, William Nanfin, Edward Packer, George Tailor, Mr. Fulke Brent, Robert Percy, Mr. Giles Brent, Mr. Vavafor.

f. 182 Accounts of Mr. Egerton per the Secretary. Received from: Mr. Gerard, Lt. Vaughan, Isaac Edwards, James Price, Mr. Broadhurst, Edward Fleete, James Cauther, Christopher Martin, the Secretary, Marmaduke Snow, John Medley, John Robinson (barber). Payments to: Thomas Hebden, the Treasurer, the Secretary, Francis Gray,

f. 183 James Cauther, Mr. Gerard, Thomas Franclin, widow Briant, Jo. Robinson (barber), Capt. Giles Brent, William Asceter, Lt. Vaughan.

Accounts of Richard Lee (gentleman) by his executor John Lewger, Esq. Payments to: the sheriff for passage of Mr. Lee et. al. from VA, Capt. Cornwalleys, Mr. Gerard, Mr. Pulton, Francis Gray for coffins for dec'd & his wife, Robert Percy, the Treasurer,

f. 184 accountant, Mrs. Margaret Hubersley (for Ann Norris (maid servant)).

21 March 1639. Thomas Gerard administrator of Justinian Snow requested discharge. Mentions: Marmaduke Snow attorney of Abel Snow.

f. 185 Account of Justinian Snow (gentleman, of St. Maries') by his administrator Thomas Gerard (gentleman). Payments to: Walter Broadhurst (gentleman), Anthony Rawlins, executor of Richard Lee on judgement of 1 man servant Xpofer Moreland, Thomas Baldridge, Mrs. Throughton, my brother Marmad. Snow, John Price, Francis Rabnett,

f. 186 Thomas Franclin, Capt. Tho. Cornwalleys, Esq., Mr. Britton, Tho. Cooper, Francis Gray & Phillip West, the Secretary, the sheriff, James Baldridge, the Indian Emperor, Peter Heyward, the Treasurer of the Colony, my brother Marmaduke Snow for use of my brother Abel Snow. Mention: house at Snow Hill.

f. 187 Thomas Gerard (gentleman) administrator of Justinian Snow (gentleman, of St.

Liber - Patent Record Z & A - 1637-1651

Maries') is discharged. Date: 1 April 1640. Witness: Leonard Calvert, Esq.

f. 188 Accounts of Michael Lums by Cutbert Fenwick (gentleman). Received from: Capt. Cornwalleys, Xpofer Martin. Payments to: Capt. Cornwalleys, Mr. Gerard, Thomas Baldridge, Mr. Pulton, Jo. Harrison, Jo. Robinson (barber), Will. Asiter, John Norman, John Hallowes, the Secretary, accountant. On 7 May 1640, account allowed.

f. 189 Accounts of (N) by Randoll (N). Debts: accountant, Mr. Parry (of VA). Payments to: Mr. Augud (of ----mack), Andrew (N) (seaman), Thomas Games, Mr. Lewger, accountant, Thomas & James Baldridge, Capt. Thomas Cornwalleys, James Cauther, Francis Gray, Mr. Weyvill, Mr. Pasmore, David Wickliff, Richard Pinner, John Dandie.

f. 190 List of debts: Thomas Brice (of VA). Payments to: accountant, Jo. Norton, the Governour, John Hampton, Tho. Morris, Xpofer Martin, Thomas Cary, Thomas Baldridge, widow Bryant, Jo. Robinson, the Secretary,

f. 191 Robert Vaughan, Tho. Bradnox, Edw. Comins, Edm. Lemmin, John Malham, Tho. Pett, Robert Short, Walt. Joanes, Fran. Lumbard, Fran. Brookes, Joh. Ayres, Zach. Wade, Rich. Cotsford, Walter King.

Inhabitants of Isle of Kent who took oath of fealty to Lord Baltimore: Tho. Bradnock, Edward Comins, John Malham, Thomas Pett, Robert Short, Francis Lumbard, John Ayres, Zacharias Wade, Richard Cottsford, Edmund Lennin, Walter Joanes. Date: 16 April 1647. Signed: Leonard Calvert.

Leonard Calvert, Esq.

f. 192 appointed Robert Vaughan as commander of Isle of Kent, & authorized Capt. Robert Vaughan, William Coxe, Thomas Bradnoxe, Edward Comins, Phillip Conner & Francis Brookes (gentlemen) to try cases. Date: 18 April 1647. Signed: Leonard Calvert.

f. 193 13 May. To Capt. Robert Vaughan et. al. (of Isle of Kent). Concerning speeches of John Harwood near the Governour's house at St.

f. 194 Maries' in April last, being charged by Edward Packer.

14 May. Nicholas Cawsin demanded of John Court.

19 May. List of goods of Mrs. Margarett Brent.

28 May. Thomas Munday demanded 200 a. for transporting self, wife, & 1 child in 1646 & Edmund Hudson 100 a. for transporting self. Warrant for head of King's Creek in New Towne.

31 May. to: Capt. Robert Vaughan. Authorization to collect for the Lord Proprietor customs, confiscations, forfeitures, and escheats on Isle of Kent. Signed: L. Calvert.

f. 195 Mr. Francis Brookes is authorized to collect for the Lord Proprietor all neate cattle on Isle of Kent. Date: 31 May 1647. Signed: L. Calvert.

Mr. Francis Brookes is authorized to collect all estate belonging to John Abbott (of Isle of Kent). Signed: L. Calvert.

1 June. Robert Kedger demanded 300 a. for transporting self, wife, & 1 servant Miles Richards in 1641 & 100 a. on assignment from William Asseter. Warrant for northeast branch of Herring Creek.

William Marshall demanded from estate of Thomas Weston.

Nicholas Cawsin demanded from estate of Thomas Weston.

Edmond Smith (planter) is bound to

f. 196 George Rutland (alias George Mannors, planter). Date: 7 May 1647. Witnesses: Charles Rawlison, William Bretton.

Leonard Calvert, Esq. demanded of John Hollis from estate of Peter Draper. Mr. Fenwick is attorney for John Hollis.

Robert Kedger vs. William Lewis.

Thomas Greene, Esq. gave chattel to his son Leonard Greene. Witness: William Bretton.

Liber - Patent Record Z & A - 1637-1651

Cuth. Fenwick (gentleman) acknowledged debt to Leonard Calvert, Esq.

f. 197 as surety for John Hollis (planter, of Apamatuck).

Motion of John Shertcliffe. Robert Ford (age 9/10) was brought to this country by Nicholas Harvey (now dec'd). Said John is appointed guardian.

Edm. Hudson vs. Francis Posey.
* Joane Rawlins deposed.
* Anthony Rawlins deposed.

Edward Packer vs. John Dandy.

f. 198 William Stephanson vs. Robert Smith.

George Rutland vs. Capt. Edw. Hill.

3 June. John Dandy demanded of Henry Brookes.

On 21 January 1641, Robert Huett & Henry Bellamy (both of Isle of Kent) sold to Roger Baxter (of Isle of Kent)

f. 199 Crainey Point. Witness: John Bennett.

7 June. Thomas Bushell demanded 50 a. on assignment from William Smoote.

10 June. Commission of the Lord Proprietor to Leonard Calvert, Esq. of 18 September 1644.

f. 200 Said Leonard Calvert did orally on 9 June 1647 on his death bed appoint Thomas Greene, Esq. to be Governour, as per Mrs. Margarett Brent, Francis Anketill, & James Linsey.

12 June. John Dandy was convicted of various crimes. The late Governour Leonard Calvert, Esq.

f. 201 promised to pardon him. Thomas Greene, Esq. confirms the same.

James Linsey demanded of Francis Gray due to Marks Pheypo.

William Johnson & Walter Gweast (fort soldiers, of St. Inego's) are bound to James Lindsey (soldier). Date: 1 May 1647. Signed: Walter Geast, William Johnson. Witness: Charles Rawlinson.

Thomas Howard & John Metcalfe (both of St. Maries') are bound to James Lindsey. Date: 5 April 1647. Signed: Tho. Howard, John Metcalfe. Witness: John Price.

f. 202 William Hungerford is bound to James Lindsey. Date: 1 May 1647. Witness: Charles Rawlinson.

17 June. George Rutland demanded security of Edmond Smith.

Capt. John Price (captain of fort of St. Inego's) notified the Governour of need for corn.

f. 203 18 June. Corn of Cuth. Fenwick (gentleman) is to be delivered to Capt. John Price. Signed: Tho. Greene. Witness: Marke Pheypo.

Sergt. Pheypo delivered corn of Cuth. Fenwick (gentleman) to Capt. John Price. Signed: Marks Pheypo.

Francis Poesy demanded of Thomas (N) (servant of Edward Buddon (of Keketon)).

Henry Hooper (chirurgeon) received from Thomas Mathews attorney of Thomas Copley, Esq. chattel.

19 June 1647. Mrs. Margarett Brent requested a claim

f. 204 against the estate of Leonard Calvert. Mrs. Margarett Brent requested administration on said estate. Legacies paid to Rich. Willan & James Linsey by Mrs. Margarett Brent. Signed: Richard Willan, James Lendshy.

Edmond Hudson demanded warrant to bring Edward Wordly & his wife into court to answer suit.

Letter: Mentions Mr. Trussell, Mr. Hill. Signed: William Berkeley. Date: 12 June 1647.

Liber - Patent Record Z & A - 1637-1651

- **f. 205** Letter: Satisfaction of Sir William Berkley. Signed: Edward Hill. Date: 18 June 1646.

    Letter: reply

- **f. 206** to Capt. Edward Hill. Date: 19 June 1647. Signed: Thomas Greene.

    Mrs. Margarett Brent granted administration on estate of Leonard Calvert, Esq.

    20 June. Robert Holt demanded of John Bell.

    22 June. Letter: regarding rule of the Province.

- **f. 207** ...

- **f. 208** Date: 20 June 1647. Signed: Edw. Hill. To: Mr. Thomas Greene, Capt. Giles Brent.

    Letter: regarding rule of the Province. Date: 21 June 1647. Signed: Thomas Greene. To: Capt. Edward Hill.

- **f. 209** 23 June. Edmund Hudson demanded a warrant to bring Thomas Munday to court. Edmund Hudson demanded of Thomas Munday.

- **f. 210** 27 June. Survey of 300 a. for William Smoote near mouth of Herring Creek, surveyed by Robert Clerke. Patent for transporting self, wife, & 2 children in 1646, bounding Thomas Bushell, [metes & bounds], Smoote's Hollow, for 300 a. Date: 12 June 1647. Signed: Thomas Greene.

- **f. 211** William Smoote acknowledged debt to Cuth. Fenwick (gentleman) on assignment from Robert Clerke.

    Certificate for Robert Kedger on northeast branch of Herring Creek for 400 a. Patent to Robert Kedger (boatwright) for transporting self & 1 man servant in 1641 & 100 a. on assignment from William Asseter,

- **f. 212** on northeast branch of Herring Creek called Ichcombe Freehold, bounding Kedger's Bite, [metes & bounds], for 400 a. Date: 14 June 1647. Signed: Tho. Greene.

- **f. 213** Letter: concerning Capt. Hill. Signed: Tho. Greene. To: Sir William Berkely, Governour of VA.

- **f. 214** 30 June. Ellis Richarson (of Chiskuck, York Co. VA) demanded a servant man William Price (fugitive to MD). Warrant to Sergt. Pheypo to apprehend said man.

- **f. 215** Mrs. Margarett Brent requested further time to produce inventory of estate of Leonard Calvert.

    Ellis Richarson vs. William Price.

    2 July. Commission of the Counsell 1644. To: Leonard Calvert, Esq., Giles Brent, Esq., John Lewger, Esq., Thomas Greene, Esq., Thomas Gerard, Esq., James Neale, Esq.

- **f. 216** ...

- **f. 217** Date: 18 September 1644.

    John Hawlis (of MD) is bound to John Kemp (of VA). Date: 10 July 1646. Signed: John Hallowes. Witness: Robert Miles. John Kemp assigned to Walter Chyles bill of John Hollis. Date: 5 December 1646. Witness: Robert Beard. Satisfaction on 27 April 1647.

- **f. 218** 5 July. Humphrey Howell demanded of Mrs. Margaret Brent executrix of Leon. Calvert.

    Robert Kedger demanded of John Dandy.

    Proclamation: regarding Nanticoke Indians & Wickomick Indians.

- **f. 219** Capt. John Price to command force against those Indians. Date: 4 July 1647. Signed: Tho. Greene.

- **f. 220** 20 July. Richard Bennett demanded 450 a. for transporting self, wife, & 5 children in 1646. Warrant for 200 a. on Herring Creek to eastward of land of Thomas Bushell.

Liber - Patent Record Z & A - 1637-1651

15 July. Proclamation: regarding speeches of James Johnson to Richard Bennett.

f. 221 Mentions: Capt. Hill, Capt. Price.

Richard Bennett deposed that his life was in danger from James Johnson.

f. 222 Mr. Robert Clerke made certificate on 30 May 1647 to William Wheateley for 100 a. on east side of Black Creek. William Wheateley acknowledged debt to Cutt. Fenwick (gentleman) on assignment from Robert Clerke (surveyor). Signed: William Wheatley. Patent to William Wheateley (planter) for transporting self in 1643, on east side of Black Creek, called Sherwell, bounding White Oak Hollow,

f. 223 [metes & bounds], Wheately's Branch for 100 a. Date: 18 July 1647. Signed: Tho. Greene.

7 June 1647. Robert Clerke (surveyor) made certificate for Thomas Bushell on western branches of Herring Creek for 150 a. Patent

f. 224 to Thomas Bushell (planter) for transporting self in 1642 & 50 a. on assignment from William Smoote, on western branch of Herring Creek, bounding land of William Smoote, Turkey Branch, called Bushell's Rest.

f. 225 Date: 24 July 1647. Signed: Tho. Greene. Thomas Bushell acknowledged debt to Robert Clerke (surveyor).

28 July. William Lewis demanded a boat from Mr. Thomas Pasmore (of Chicacoan).
- Mr. Pasmore deposed that the boat was borrowed from Henry Moseley (of Chicacoan).
- Charles Maynard deposed that the boats was formerly of Mr. Lewis.
- Thomas Howard deposed the same.

Henry Moseley ordered to appear.

f. 226 Mr. Bretton (Registrar) is empowered to sign writs & warrants in absence of the Governour.

Richard Span, at the request of John Richard, deposed that the deponent recovered chattel from said John Richard at Isle of Kent last November, to transport it to VA & land it at shore of Capt. Cleyborne at Kiceton. Afterwards, Peter Knight received the chattel.

Thomas Greene, Esq. demanded chattel of Richard Span. Richard Spanne acknowledged debt to Tho. Greene, Esq.

f. 227 31 July. Thomas Jackson, at the request of John Harwood, deposed that Leonard Calvert (dec'd) killed chattel for the fort. Stanop Roberts deposed the same.

3 August. Mr. Robert Clerke (surveyor) made a certificate on 14 July 1647 for John Grimesditch for 100 a. on east side of Brittaine Bay.

Cuth. Fenwick (gentleman) attorney for Capt. Tho. Cornwalleys discharged John Pyle of debt, due for freight of chattel from Accomack.

5 August. Henry Spink, age 26, deposed that last June, the deponent was at the house of Mr. Gerard, when Mr. Broadhurst said to the deponent that there was no Governour in MD for Capt. Hill was Governour. Signed: Henry Spinke.

Charles Maynord attorney for Thomas Jackson demanded of Thomas Fidler.

f. 228 6 August. John Dandy, at the request of Henry Spink, deposed that the deponent heard Nicholas Harvey (now dec'd) say he left chattel with his man Henry Spink, when he departed to VA.

26 August. William Bretton (gentleman), being sick; Robert Clerk (gentleman) is appointed to take his place. Signed: Tho. Greene.

27 August. Cuthbert Phenwick (gentleman) executor of Nicholas Harvey vs. John Paulet. John Dandy deposed that about 8 years ago, he made chattel for Nicholas Harvey & it was taken in March 1644.

John Danda deposed that James Lindesey owed John Cooke.

f. 229 30 August. Robert Holt demanded 400 a. for transporting self, wife, & 4 children in 1646. Warrant for 200 a. on north side of Pato. River near Her. Creek & next to Will. Smoote.

Francis Posey is bound to Robert Holt. Date: 18 March 1646. Signed: Fra. Posey. Witnesses: Edmond Smyth, John Bell.

Liber - Patent Record Z & A - 1637-1651

3 September. John Medcalfe attorney for Edward Coles demanded a warrant to arrest Nicholas Pauhampton.

Nathaniell Pope demanded of Mrs. Margarett Brent due

f. 230 from estate of Leonard Calvert, Esq. (dec'd).

Robert Clerke (surveyor) made certificate on 14 July 1647 for 200 a. for James Johnson on west side of Poplar Hill Creek.

4 September. Walter Guest acknowledged debt to William Whittle.

Joseph Edlo demanded of John Dandy. Said Dandy paid Tho. Cornwallis, Esq.

7 September. Robert Clerke, at the request of John Dandy, deposed that he was present when the bill between Edward Packer & said Dandy was made, & said Packer did discharge said Dandy.

11 September. Walter Peakes acknowledged debt to Tho. Greene, Esq., in case he did not provide chattel demanded by Cuthbert Phenwick administrator of Nicholas Harvey.

f. 231 Robert Clerke (surveyor) made certificate on 14 July 1647 for Francis Pope & John Courts for 200 a. on west side of Poplar Hill.

Mr. William Whitby (of VA) demanded the return of Henry Potter (his servant) who fled out of VA.

13 September. Mr. William Whitby attorney for Thomas Moore demanded return of Walter Guest (his servant) who fled out of VA.

Walter Guest is bound to Edward Fisher

f. 232 as servant. Date: 14 December 1645. Witnesses: Thomas Harrote, Antho. Tiboult. Edward Fisher assigned his right to Mr. Tho. Moore. Date: 14 February 1645. Witness: Anth. Tiboult. Walter Guest came to Mr. Thomas Moore on 14 February 1645 & left in October 1646.

15 September. Order by Governour for oath by all persons involved in Rebellion,

f. 233 fealty to Lord Proprietor & Governour Thomas Greene, Esq.

Proclamation: The inhabitants of Appomatuck & Chickacoan have several suits pending, & persons who were involved in the recent Rebellion. Signed: Tho. Greene.

f. 234 18 September. Edmund Hudson demanded of William Stephanson.

Henry Potter acknowledged debt to William Lewes (gentleman).

f. 235 22 September. On 23 August 1647, Blanch Oliver (widow, of St. Maries') for estate left her by her husband Roger Oliver (dec'd) for use of his son William Oliver, & in consideration of her affection for her son said William Oliver & likewise to her daughter Mary Harrison, assigns chattel to said children. Signed: Blan. Oliver. Witnesses: Giles Brent, Marie Brent.

27 September. Jeoffrey Oliver vs. John Slynsby.

Robert Kadger vs. John Slynsby.

f. 236 Giles Brent, Esq. vs. Tho. Allen.

Mrs. Margarett Brent vs. Andrew Marrow.

Robert Sedgrave attorney for Edmund Parry vs. Walter Smyth.

John Hamton vs. Mrs. Marg. Brent for service to Isle of Kent last March from estate of Leonard Calvert, Esq.

Robert Holt vs. Cuthbert Phenick (gentleman), on wrongful attachment of chattel of Francis Posey made over to him.

Nathaniell Pope vs. Cuthbert Phenick (gentleman).

Marks Phepo vs. Francis Gray.

Liber - Patent Record Z & A - 1637-1651

John Horwood discharged of his fine imposed by Leonard Calvert, Esq.

Mrs. Marg. Brent vs. Andrew Marrow.

f. 237 Satisfaction on 24 February 1647.

William Stephanson vs. Robert Smith.

Cuthbert Phenicke vs. John Paulett. Mentions: estate of Nicholas Harvey. Walter Peakes delivered the chattel.

Anthony Rawlings executor of Richard Cox vs. Cuthbert Phenick (gentleman) attorney for Capt. Tho. Cornwallis.

John Nevill vs. John Halfehead.

Nicholas Cassine vs. Nathaniell Pope for charges the year Mr. Brent was Governour.

30 September 1647. Cuthbert Phenick (gentleman) received payment from John Hollis (of Apomatakes) due to Capt. Thomas Cornwallyes, Esq. Witness: John Rozier.

Robert Clerke vs. Nathaniel Pope

f. 238 on behalf of the Lord Proprietor, regarding the Rebellion on Isle of Kent. Said Nathaniell to post bond.

Richard White vs. John Roser (gentleman).

Henry Pomnly vs. William Carpenter.

Nicholas Cassine vs. Nathaniell Pope.

William Assiter vs. Tho. Thomas.

William Assiter vs. Richard Nevett & William Smithfield.

2 October. Edward Huddson attorney for Robert Kager vs. John Danda.

f. 239 John Hampton, at the request of Marks Phepo, deposed that he knows of no chattel brought into house of James Caughter by John Hollis tendered for Mr. Pursell in March 6 years ago.

John Hollis vs. estate of James Neale. John Hampton deposed that he heard Capt. Hill (then Governour) that John Hollis had recovered from the estate of Mr. James Neale. John Hack had affirmed regarding the recovery.

f. 240 Nathaniell Pope vs. Cuth. Fenwick.

Antho. Dawking vs. Cuth. Fenwick attorney for Richard Coxe.

Marks Phepo vs. John Hollis.

Warrant to warn John Hamp.

Cuthbert Phenwick vs. Antho. Rawlins executor of Richard Cox.

Nathan. Pope vs. Mrs. Margaret Brent.

Robert Clerke (gentleman) vs. Nathaniell Pope.

f. 241 John Hollis attorney for Mr. Speake demanded of Leonard Calvert, Esq.

Rich. White vs. John Rosser.

Nathaniell Pope vs. William Edwine.

Joseth Edlo, per request of Blanch Oliver late wife of Roger Oliver, deposed that he heard Leonard Calvert, Esq. say about a killed ox. Edward Packer deposed the same.

Richard White vs. John Hollis.

Francis Gray sold to Mr. John Hampton all his cattle in MD. Date: 17 April 1647. Witnesses: Will. Treake, Rest. Hollois.

f. 242 Capt. John Hampton assigned bill to Cuthbert Fenwick. Date: 28 May 1647.

Liber - Patent Record Z & A - 1637-1651

Witness: John Rosier.

4 October. John Hollis deposed in the cause of Mr. Speake.

John Hollis is to have chattel out of the stock of Leonard Calvert, Esq.

Cuthbert Phenicke demanded of John Hollis from estate of John Weyvell.

Jo. Hollis is authorized to take a cow from His Lordship's stock to satisfy debt due Tho. Speake. Date: 10 February 1646. Signed: L. Calvert.

Robert Holt vs. Cuthbert Phenick.

f. 243 Will. Edwine denies <torn>

Richard White vs. (N) Hollis.

Mr. Giles Brent appeared for Mrs. Brent at suit of John Hampton.

Markes Phypo assumed that he satisfied Mr. Giles Brent on account of Nathaniell Pope. Remainder from Mr. Pope due in question between Marmaduke Snow & Mr. Foulke Brent.

f. 244 John Dandy vs. Joseth Edlo.

Petition of Blanch Howell, desiring chattel from estate of Leonard Calvert, Esq. Mr. Giles Brent appeared as attorney for executrix.

Nathaniel Pope deposed on 4 October 1647 that before going to Kent last March, he advised the Governour to allow John Hampton some payment.

5 October. Francis Brookes (of Isle of Kent) demanded of John Hampton.

Francis Brookes (of Isle of Kent) demanded of Cuthbert Fenwick (gentleman) executor of Henry Brookes (merchant).

f. 245 Petition of Nicholas Ketin & James Linsey to Thomas Greene, Esq. & Capt. Grall. Petitioners were hired by Capt! Giles Brent, for Mr. Gilmot in 1643 & request payment.

Giles Brent, Esq. deposed that he & Mr. Lewger did contract with the petitioners for service to Mr. Gilmott & knows nothing of payment made.

Mr. Thomas Bradnox, age 40, deposed on 11 September 1647 that Mr. Nathaniell Pope, as agent for the Governour, tried to get people to avoid the Island and come to Apomatuck.

f. 246 Mr. Edward Comins, age 40, deposed on 11 September 1647 that Mr. Nathaniell Pope came to the Island as agent for the Governour, and made promises.

12 December 1646 at St. Inego's Fort. Court. Attendees: The Upper House: the Governour, Mr. Lewger, Mr. Greene. Signed: William Lewis, Jo. Jarbo, Robert Sharpe, John Salter, Will. Clare, Tho. Kingwell.

Discussion

f. 247 regarding the Rebellion.

6 October. Robert Clarke (surveyor) demanded of Robert Kager.

Robert Kager demanded of (N) Danda.

8 October. Robert Clark (surveyor) made certificate on 14 July for Christopher Carnoll for 100 a. on south side of Popler Hill Creek.

Robert Clarke (surveyor) made certificate on 14 July for John Nevell for 50 a. on south side of Popler Hill Creek.

f. 248 Robert Clarke (surveyor) made certificate on 14 July for James Johnson for 200 a. on west side of Popler Hill Creek.

Robert Clarke (surveyor) made certificate on 14 July for Richard Nevett for 100 a. on Breton's Bay.

Robert Clarke (surveyor) made certificate on 14 July for John Nun for 300 a. on Breton's Bay.

Liber - Patent Record Z & A - 1637-1651

11 October. George Acreeke demanded 100 a. for transporting self & his wife in 1646. Warrant for 200 a. on Wiccocomoke River next to Thomas Gerard, Esq.

Capt. John Price for self & all soldiers of Fort of St. Inego's demanded of Mrs. Marg. Brent administratrix of Mr. Calvert, Esq.

f. 249 12 October. William Edis (planter) demanded 100 a. by gift of his master Henry Lee. Warrant for land next to William Smoote.

William Stephanson demanded of Thomas Munday & Edward Hudson.

22 October. William Shiles demanded 100 a.: 50 a. for service & 50 a. from Capt. John Price. Warrant for head of Richard Nevett's Branch on Bretton's Bay.

16 October. George Manners demanded 150 a. for transporting self & 1 child in 1646. Warrant for south side of St. Jerome's Creek.

18 October. Francis Brookes (gentleman) demanded of executor of Richard Purlavant.

Robert Cadger vs. John Slymsby. Subpoenas to: Ed. Hudson, Thomas Munday.

20 October.
- Thomas Munday, at request of Robert Kadger, deposed.
- Edward Hudson deposed the same.

f. 250 27 October. Robert Kedger vs. William Lewis.

29 October. John Prichard discharged John Hilliard of all debts. Date: 26 January 1646. Witness: William Pindley.

Thomas White discharged John Hilliard of debt. Date: 11 April 1647. Witness: Charles Rawlinson.

30 October. John Wheatley demanded 200 a. for transporting his wife & 1 son in 1641. Warrant for 50 a. on west side of St. George's River near Packer's Creek.

2 November. Robert Clarke (surveyor) made certificate on 27 June 1646 for William Tomson for 500 a. near Namassconson in Patowmack River.

11 November. John Hollis demanded of Richard Duke.

John Hollis demanded of Thomas Waggott.

f. 251 John Hollis demanded of John Norman.

John Hollis demanded of Henry Boston.

John Hollis demanded of William Bretton.

John Hollis demanded 500 a. for transporting 5 servants in 1640. Warrant for east side of Cedar Point next to James Neale, Esq.

John Hollis demanded of Peter Mackewell.

3 November. Capt. John Price sold chattel to William Smoot bought of Leonard Calvert, Esq. Witnesses: Robert Clark, John Metcalfe.

William Stephanson demanded of Robert Sharpe.

4 November. Thomas Waggott demanded of George Acreeke.

Capt. Edward Hill

f. 252 (gentleman, of VA) appointed John Hollis as his attorney. Date: 26 January 1646. Witness: Sam. Taylor.

6 November. Robert Clarke (gentleman) gave chattel to his son John Clarke & his daughter Mary Clarke.

8 November. Proclamation by Lt. General concerning food supplies. Date: 10 November 1647. Signed: Tho. Green.

f. 253 9 November. Marks Phepo demanded of John Nevell.

Liber - Patent Record Z & A - 1637-1651

Marks Phepo demanded of William Edwin.

Nicholas Cassine demanded of Richard White.

10 November. Robert Clarke (surveyor) made certificate for Thomas Munday & Edward Hudson for 300 a. at head of King's Creek.

f. 254 Robert Clarke (surveyor) made certificate for William Shiles for 100 a. at head of Nevett's Branch.

Robert Clarke (surveyor) made certificate for William Edis for 50 a. near Herring Creek.

John Hanceford (gentleman, of VA) claimed against the estate of Thomas Weston (merchant, dec'd) & requested administration.

11 November. John Medly demanded 300 a. for transporting his wife & 2 servants in 1646: Lancelot Sleepe, Rowland Mace. Warrant for west of land of Mr. Neale.

John Thymble & William Brown demanded 100 a. for service. Warrant for Back Creek of Mr. Neale.

Christopher Russell demanded 100 a. for transporting self in 1647. Warrant for land near

f. 255 Back Creek of Mr. Neale.

14 November. Walter Smyth demanded of Francis Vandan.

Walter Smith demanded of Richard White. Subpoena to: (N) Posy.

Walter Smith demanded of Edward Hall administrator of Isack Edwards. Subpoena to: Thomas Petite.

Walter Smith demanded of Edward Packer.

19 November. Lt. William Evins & John Jerbo demanded 200 a. for transporting selves in 1646 & 200 a. on assignment from Walter Peakes (planter). Warrant for Isle of Kent in Great Thickett, sometime in possession of John Abbott.

Jeffry Power demanded of Mrs. Margaret Brent executrix of Leonard Calvert.

20 November. Anthony Rawlings demanded of Thomas Gerard, Esq.

f. 256 Subpoena to: Walter Broadhurst & James Walker.

Anthony Rawlins vs. Edward Hudson.

22 November. Marks Phepo demanded 400 a. for transporting self & 2 servants & on assignment from Owen Seymor, all in 1641.

Nicholas Keyting demanded 100 a. for transporting self & 100 a. on assignment from Edward Leonard & 100 a. on assignment from William Maclawghlin, all in 1641.

Marks Phepo demanded of William Edis.

23 November. Walter Peakes demanded of Thomas Waggot.

Walter Peakes demanded of George Manners.

24 November. Richard Banks demanded of William Shiles.

Walter Peakes demanded of Walter Smith.

John Hollis received of Capt. John Price chattel due Mr. Thomas Speake from His Lordship.

f. 257 Date: 9 November 1647. Signed: John Hallowes. Authorization given to John Hollis to take chattel from His Lordship's stock due Thomas Speake. Date: 10 February 1646. Signed: Leonard Calvert.

Mr. Thomas Thornbury (gentleman) appointed William Whitley as his attorney. Date: 11 November 1647. Signed: Thomas Thornborough. Witnesses: Adam Stavely, Gabriell Odgers.

26 November. Edward Hudson attorney for Edward Bland (merchant, of VA) demanded of John Waltham. Edward Bland (merchant) appointed Edward Hudson

Liber - Patent Record Z & A - 1637-1651

(planter) his attorney in suit with Walter Dewall & John Wallton. Date: 4 November 1647. Witness: John Gresham.

f. 258 Thomas Munday demanded of Humphrey Howell.

30 November. Mrs. Margaret Brent demanded further time for estate of Leonard Calvert, Esq.

Richard Bennett demanded of Mrs. Marg. Brent administratrix of Leon. Calvert, Esq.

1 December. Elisabeth wife of Francis Posey, at the request of Anthony Rawlins, deposed that last July, the deponent was with Goody Munday & Edw. Hudson as they walked through corn belonging to Mr. Clark & Richard Cox & returned to house of Thomas Munday.

Joseph Edlo (planter) demanded of John Hampton.

John Pyle demanded of Mrs. Marg. Brent administratrix of Leon. Calvert, Esq.

Francis Brookes vs. John Hampton.

f. 259 Walter Smith vs. Edw. Packer. Defendant paid Barn. Jackson.

Robert Kedger vs. (N) Slingsby.

George Manners attorney for John Hollis vs. Tho. Waggott.

Anthony Rawlins vs. Edward Hudson. Mentions: Rich. Coxe.

Edward Hudson attorney for Edward Bland (merchant, of VA) vs. John Wallton Mentions: boat brought out of VA. Arbitration by: Walter Peakes, Marks Phepo.

George Manners attorney for John Hollis vs. John Norman.

William Smithfield

f. 260 acknowledged debt to Thomas Greene, Esq. Witness: Thomas Gerard.

Anthony Rawlins vs. Tho. Gerard, Esq.

Walter Pakes vs. Walter Smith.

George Manners attorney for John Hollis vs. William Betton.

Marks Phepo vs. William Edis.

John Norman vs. William Shiles.

Nicolas Cawsin, at request of Marks Pheypo, deposed that when he first came to the Province, Thomas Pursall desired the deponent to speak to John Hollis & James Cauther regarding chattel owed. The deponent was to ask for it when he next went to VA. About 1 year after the deponent went to VA, he demanded of James Cauther, who replied that the chattel was at the house of John Hollis.

f. 261 2 December. Edward Hull, age 27, at the request of William Wheatley attorney for Mr. Thomas Thornborough, deposed that Governour Calvert said he had given chattel to Mr. Thorneborough.

Thomas Waggott demanded of George Manners.

Thomas Petite, at the request of Walter Smith, deposed that about 12 months ago, he was at the plantation of Goody Langsford.

Thomas Jackson, at the request of William Wheately, deposed that Governour Calvert indicated that the chattel did not belong to (N) Coleough, but to Mr. Thornborough.

Peter Makaill acknowledged debt to John Hollis. Witness: Tho. Gerard.

f. 262 Thomas Waggott vs. George Manners.

Walter Pekes vs. Thomas Waggott.

Walter Pekes vs. George Manners.

Marks Pheypo vs. John Hollis.

Liber - Patent Record Z & A - 1637-1651

Mrs. Margaret Brent administratrix of Leonard Calvert, Esq. vs. Thomas Gerard, Esq.

Cuthbert Fenwick (gentleman) attorney for Capt. Tho. Burbage demanded of George Manners.

Warrant for Tho. Jackson in suit of Mr. Gerard vs. Mrs. Brent.

Cuthbert Fenwick (gentleman) demanded of Mrs. Marg. Brent administratrix of Leonard Calvert, Esq.

Cuthbert Fenwick (gentleman) attorney for Capt. Cornwallis demanded of John Hampton.

Thomas Jackson, at the request of Thomas Gerard, Esq., deposed that Edward Packer received chattel on account of Governour Calvert in 1644

f. 263 which said Edward Packer would not receive.

Cuthbert Fenwick (gentleman) demanded of Anthony Rawlins.

Mrs. Margaret Brent vs. Tho. Gerard, Esq. Warrant to John Hatche (sheriff). Jury: Mr. Fenwick, Mr. Cawsine, Peter Makerell, Mr. Thompson, Mr. Brough, Geo. Manners, Mr. Beane, William Asseter, Robert Cadger, John Medly, John Halfhead, William Lewis. Mrs. Marg. Brent assigned the judgement to Edw. Packer.

Thomas Gerard, Esq., at request of Anthony

f. 264 Rawlins, deposed that in February 1644, the deponent was on board the ship of Mr. Ingle, near Heron Island, & saw chattel supposedly of Mr. Fenwick, but belonged to the Governour, Mr. Copley, Capt. Cornwalleys, or Mr. Fenwick. Signed: Tho. Gerard.

William Wheatly vs. Francis Anketill & James Langworth. Mentions Nicholas Harvey.

Cuthbert Fenwick (gentleman) attorney for Capt. Thomas Cornwalleys vs. John Hampton.

Jeoffrey Power vs. Mrs. Marg. Brent.

f. 265 Mr. Calvert promised the plaintiff chattel.

On 1 January, sequestration granted to Tho. Greene, Esq. on estate of Dr. George Binks. John Hatch (sheriff) had chattel appraised by Barnaby Jackson & Henry Adams, and other chattel appraised by Henry Adams & George Manners.

3 December. Thomas Gerard, Esq. attorney & administrator of Henry Brookes (merchant) demanded of Capt. Robert Vaughan.

John Hatch, at the request of John Thimbleby, deposed that when Capt. Hill was going to VA, the said John Thimbleby went with him. The deponent (as sheriff) demanded of said Thimblebly levy due Gov. Calvert. Said Thimbleby assigned it to John Medly.

f. 266 Edward Hudson demanded of William Stevenson.

Subpoena to: John Villaine & Hen. Clay.

Cuthbert Fenwick (gentleman), at the request of Tho. Gerard, Esq., deposed that he was the foreman in suit between the said Tho. Gerard, Esq. & Mrs. Marg. Brent. Cites assignment to Edward Packer to which assignment was in name of Gov. Calvert.
- Leon. Calvert, Esq. assigned chattel from Mr. Thomas Gerard (gentleman, of St. Clement's Hundred) to Edward Packer. Date: 15 September 1645. Signed: L. Calvert. Witnesses: Walter Smith, Nathaniel Pope.

Edward Packer, at the request of Tho. Gerard, Esq., deposed that this assignment was on a bill from Tho. Gerard to Leon. Calvert, Esq.

f. 267 Mrs. Marg. Brent deposed that she believed she had excess than what was assigned by Mr. Calvert to Edward Packer, & Mr. Calvert demanded of Mr. Gerard. Signed: Margarett Brent.

John Thimbleby demanded of the levy of Capt. Edw. Hill due Gov. Calvert. John Hallowes is attorney for defendant.

Liber - Patent Record Z & A - 1637-1651

Mr. Gerard vs. Mrs. Marg. Brent. Mr. Giles Brent to be present.

Walter Beane demanded of Mrs. Marg. Brent administratrix of Leon. Calvert, Esq.

To: Mr. Broadhurst. Notice of seizure of chattel of Mr. Lewis. Date: 18 November 1647. Signed: Tho. Greene.

f. 268 William Lewis demanded of Tho. Gerard, Esq.

William Lewis acknowledged debt to Tho. Gerard, Esq. Signed: William Lewes.

Walter Beane vs. Mrs. Brent. Mentions: Mr. Calvert.

Notice regarding rent of William Lewis tenant to Mr. Tho. Gerard. Said chattel belongs to Mrs. Eure, & to be delivered to Barth. Phillips. Signed: Tho. Greene.

Walter Beane demanded of William Smithfield.

On 14 January 1644, I sold to William Asseter (taylor, of St. Maries')

f. 269 chattel. Signed: William Brainthwaite. Witness: Barnaby Jackson.

Bartholomew Phillips, at the request of Nicholas Gwyther, deposed that said Nicholas sold deponent chattel.

Robert Smith demanded of William Stephenson.

Nicolas Cawsen demanded of Walter Pekes.

William Assiter (taylor), age 31, deposed that he never received chattel per Mr. Brainthwaite.

William Thompson, age 50, deposed that last Spring, he discussed with Gov. Calvert regarding chattel demanded by William Assiter.

4 December. Robert Clark (surveyor) demanded of Thomas Munday & Edward Hudson.

9 December. Ralph Beane demanded of John Nunne.

f. 270 Humphry Howell demanded of Richard Nevett as per judgement against said Richard on behalf of Blanch Oliver.

Thomas Gerard, Esq. demanded of William Lewis.

George Manners attorney for John Hallowes demanded of Francis Van Enden.

10 December. William Whitle attorney for Mr. Tho. Thornborough demanded of Mrs. Marg. Brent. Mentions: Leonard Calvert, Esq.

Thomas Munday attorney of Edward Hudson demanded of John Walton.

William Bretton demanded of Tho. Munday due from him & Edward Hudson.

13 December. Mrs. Margaret Brent vs. Thomas Gerard, Esq.

f. 271 Notice of General Assembly on 7 January. Date: 14 December 1647. Signed: Tho. Greene. Summons to Capt. Giles Brent.

18 December. Marks Phepo demanded of William Edwin.

Adam Stavely demanded of Humphry Howell.

Capt. John Price demanded of Tho. Thomas.

20 December. Mathias Briant demanded of James Walker.

William Edidis demanded of Marks Pheypo attorney of Mr. Hanceford administrator of Mr. Weston.

f. 272 William Marshall demanded of Marks Pheypo from estate of Mr. Weston.

Nicholas Cawsen demanded of Marks Pheypo from estate of Mr. Weston.

John Hollis by his attorney George Manners demanded of Hen. Boston.

Francis Van Enden demanded of John Norman.

Liber - Patent Record Z & A - 1637-1651

21 December. John Norman demanded of Robert Clarke (surveyor).

William Bretton (gentleman) demanded of Robert Clarke (surveyor).

Walter Pekes demanded of Peter Mackarill.

3 January. William Edwin demanded 50 a. Warrant for land in Mannor of West St. Maries' by plantation of Tom Surgeon.

Robert Taylor, age 17, at request of William Lewis, deposed that he was at the house of Mr. Lewis when some of Ingle's Company removed chattel. Mr. Gerard came with for of his men: John Wortley, Thom. Knight, James Walker, Nat. Joanes.

f. 273 James Walker, age 29, at request of Lt. William Lewis, deposed that he was with Mr. Thomas Gerard regarding the chattel.

Mrs. Margaret Brent on behalf of her brother Capt. G. Brent demanded of Tho. Allen.

Jury: Walter Beane, John Medley, Tho. Allen, George Saphyre, Rich. Banks, Mr. Clarke, John Halfhead, Walt. Peakes, Nic. Cawsen, William Lewis, John Norman, Mr. Robert Percy.

Capt. John Price vs. Mrs. Brent administratrix of Leon. Calvert, Esq.

Thom Allen, at the request of Capt. Giles Brent, deposed that the deponent assigned to Capt. Brent about Christmas 1644 certain bills of William Porter (of Kent Co.).

Question: Mr. Leon. Calvert &

f. 274 Mrs. Brent as administratrix.

Jeoffrey Power received from His Lordship's stock.

Edward Packer, age 33, at request of Capt. Giles Brent, deposed that in May 1643, a maid servant of Sir Edm. Plowden went to Kent with Mrs. Marg. Brent as her servant.

4 January. Capt. John Price, age 40, at request of Lt. William Evins, deposed that said Evins bargains with Gov. Calvert regarding his salary.

f. 275 William Tompson demanded 250 a.: 100 a. by assignment from the Governor, 100 a. as administrator of Robert Tuttey, & 50 a. for his wife, on east side of St. Clement's Bay, called Indian Quarters.

William Smoote demanded of Marks Pheypo attorney for Mr. Hansford administrator of Mr. Weston.

Thomas Hebden demanded of Marks Pheypo attorney for Mr. Hansford administrator of Mr. Weston for care of his servant John (N).

James Johnson demanded of John Cooke. Bill of James Johnson to be in hands of Walter Beane.

Charles Maynard, age 25, at request of William Lewis, deposed that while he was at the house of Mr. Gerard, Capt. Henry Fleete & Mr. Payne were there, discussing hogs, some of which belonged to Mr. Lewis.

f. 276 Henry Clay, age 24, at request of Thomas Munday, deposed that while he was at said Munday's house, the deponent heard Edward Hudson & Tho. Munday discuss with William Stevenson certain debts, & said Munday had to speak with Mr. Phillip Authur. Signed: Hen. Clay. John Villaine deposed the same.

Cuth. Fenwick (gentleman) vs. Anthony Rawlins. Mentions: payment by Walt. Gweast to Mr. Ingle.

Francis Van Enden acknowledged debt to John Hallowes. Satisfaction on 9 October 1648.

William Marshall vs. Marks Pheypo attorney for Mr. Hanceford.

f. 277 Giles Brent, Esq. demanded of Marks Pheypo attorney of administrator of Mr. Weston.
- Edward Packer, at request of Capt. Giles Brent, Esq., deposed that in 1643 he served a notice on estate of Mr. Weston.
- Giles Brent, Esq. demanded renewal of notice on administrator of Mr.

Liber - Patent Record Z & A - 1637-1651

> Weston.
> - Marks Pheypo attorney for administrator of Tho. Weston requested waiver.

Henry Spink vs. Cuth. Fenwick (gentleman) attorney for Nic. Harvey. Satisfaction on 22 December 1648.

f. 278 Marks Pheypo administrator of Tho. Pursall demanded of John Hallowes.

John Hallowes vs. Henry Boston.

Barnaby Jackson, at request of Francis Van Enden, deposed that the deponent was present when the bargain was made between said Francis & John Norman, & said Francis agreed to take Tho. Oliver as payment. Signed: Barnab Jackson.

John Hallowes demanded of William Lewis.

John Hallowes demanded of Robert Percy (gentleman).

Edmund Smith, age 30, at request of Stephen Salmon, deposed that Mr. Fenwick

f. 279 agreed to compensate said Salmon.

5 January. William Evans & John Garbo demanded of Mrs. Marg. Brent attorney for His Lordship.

Walter Pakes attorney for Francis Posey demanded of John Hatche.

Edward Packer, at request of Mrs. Brent, amended his earlier deposition to add: that Capt. Fleete knew that the chattel belonged to Mrs. Margaret Brent.

Hugh Dunne requested administration on estate of Richard Marshall.

Lawrence Marshall (yeoman), of Margottyefield of County Glocester, grandfather & guardian to Agnes Marshall (only child & daughter of my son Richard Marshall (dec'd)) appointed Hugh Dunne (mariner, of Bedeford of County Devon) as attorney. Date: 27 October 1646. Witnesses: John Tomlins, James Rowbotum, George Hartwell.

f. 280 Francis Van Dan vs. John Norman.

Lt. William Lewis vs. Thomas Gerard, Esq. George Manners deposed for the plaintiff that Tho. Gerard, Esq.

f. 281 took chattel per Charles Maynard.

Nicholas Cawsen vs. Walt. Pakes.

John Hollis vs. Robert Percy.

Edw. Hudson vs. William Stephenson.

Staveley Adam vs. Humphry Howell.

f. 282 Lt. William Evans & John Garbo vs. Mrs. Brent.

Marks Pheypo vs. William Edwin.

George Rutland vs. Capt. Edw. Hill. Attorney for defendant is John Hallowes.

John Hallowes vs. William Lewis.

John Hallowes vs. James Neale, Esq. Mentions: suit of Mr. Tues. Benjamin Gill is attorney for Mr. Neale.

Hugh Dunne is granted administration.

Thomas Greene, Esq. sold chattel to Henry Adams. Date: 12 December 1647. Signed: Tho. Greene.

f. 283 Walter Peckes is bound to Walter Beane. Date: 1 August 1647. Signed: Walter Pekes. Witnesses: Thomas Jackson, Richard Banks. Satisfaction given on 29 April 1650. Witness: Tho. Hatton.

7 January. John Hallowes demanded of John Hampton & Francis Gray.

John Hallowes demanded of Henry Brookes & Richard Cole.

Liber - Patent Record Z & A - 1637-1651

Edward Packer demanded of John Dandy.

Walter Peakes acknowledged satisfaction of George Manners. Witness: William Bretton.

f. 284 Walter Peake is creditor to the book on the soldier's account. Date: 19 November 1647. Signed: Margaret Brent. Witness: William Bretton. Walter Pekes assigned to Nicolas Cawsin. Nicolas Cawsin accepted assignment. Date: 5 January 1647.

John Deare demanded of Tho. Waggott.

William Bretton demanded of Mrs. Margaret Brent.

Nicolas Gwyther, at the request of William Bretton, deposed that Lt. Evans asked of Gov. Calvert if Mr. Bretton was to do duty as a soldier. Response was yes & order given to Sergt. Thomas Jackson.

10 January. Walter Smith demanded 400 a. Warrant for 100 a. on northeast branch of Herring Creek, near land of Robert Kedger.

Henry Boston demanded of John Hallowes.

22 January. Anthony Rawlings demanded of Adam Stauely.

f. 285 24 January. Margaret Brent sold to Walter Waterlin chattel. Date: 21 January 1647. Witnesses: Thomas Allen, John Hatch.

Leonard Calvert, Esq. sold to John Hatche chattel. Mrs. Margaret Brent administratrix of said Leon. Calvert, Esq. verified the sale. Date: 21 January 1647. Witnesses: Thomas Allen, Thomas Kingwell.

Mrs. Brent (gentlewoman) sold to Anthony Rawlins chattel.

George Manners demanded of John Slingsby.

George Manners demanded 500 a. on a grant from John Hallowes. Warrant given on 31 October 1649.

f. 286 John Hallowes had a grant (when Capt. Hill was present) for 500 a. on north side of Cedar Point. Assignment to George Manners. Date: 5 January 1647. Witness: William Bretton.

25 January. Lt. William Evans, at the request of Mr. Thornborough, deposed that Mr. Calvert forgave Mr. Thornborough for what had passed in MD, before the deponent and John Jarbo.

John Jarbo deposed that Mr. Calvert forgave Mr. Thornborough at York for what had passed in MD.

f. 287 29 January. John Jarbo deposed that in VA for Gov. Calvert, that Gov. Calvert was to send a boat, but none came.

At the Assembly on 7th, the assembly was adjourned to 7 February because the representatives of Kent Island were absent. Date: 11 January 1647. Signed: Thomas Greene.

17 January. Assembly adjourned due to absence of Mr. Bretton.

18 January. Assembly adjourned due to absence of Mr. Bretton.

20 January 1647. General Assembly at St. John's. Attendees: Governor, Capt. Robert Vaughan (with proxies of Kent Island), George Akerick (with proxies of St. Clement's Hundred), John Medley (with proxies of Newtowne & St. Michael's Hundred), Richard Banks (with proxies of Newtowne Hundred), Capt. John Price (with proxies of St. George's Hundred), John Halfhead (with proxies of St. Maries'),

f. 288 Barnaby Jackson, Mr. Cuth. Fenwick, Edward Packer, Thomas Allen (with proxies of St. Michael's Hundred), Walter Waterlin, Mr. Bretton (with proxies of Newtowne), George Manners, John Hatch, Mr. John Wyatt.

Act: Assembly to consist of: Governor & 10 of: Capt. John Price, Capt. Robert Vaughan, Mr. Fenwick, Mr. Bradnox, Mr. Conner, Mr. Thorneborough, Mr. Brookes, Tho. Allen, Richard Banks, Barnaby Jackson, George Saphyer, George Akerick, John Medley, Walter Waterlin, Walter Pekes, Edward Packer.

Liber - Patent Record Z & A - 1637-1651

21 January. General Assembly. Attendees: same, except Mr. Fenwick, Mr. Thornborough, Mr. Brookes, George Saphier.

f. 289 Summons to: George Saphyer.

Mrs. Margaret Brent demanded a vote in the assembly & was refused.

f. 290 22 January. Mr. Robert Clerk proxy for Wal. Smith. Mr. Clerk proxy for George Akerick & his proxies. Fran. Posey proxy for John Medley & his proxies. Attendees: same, except Georg Saphier.

24 January. General Assembly. Attendees: same, except Tho. Allen, Richard Banks, Mr. Fenwick, Mr. Brooks, Mr. Thorneborough, Walter Pekes. Mr. Robert Clerk proxy for William Lewis. John Hatch proxy for Tho. Hebden, Tho. Jackson, & Tho. Allen & their proxies. Attendees: same, except Richard Banks, John Hatch, Wal. Waterling.

f. 291 ...

f. 292 Adjournment. Mr. William Tompson proxy for Capt. John Price & his proxies.

25 January. General Assembly. Attendees: same, except Mr. Fenwick, Mr. Brookes. George Saphyer appeared.

26 January. General Assembly. Attendees: all. Nicholas Gwyther petitioned for a vote. Mr. Fenwick denied, saying he owed him service.

f. 293 27 January. General Assembly. Attendees: same, except John Medley, Walter Waterlin. Committee appointed, consisting of: Mr. Clarke, Rich. Banks, Wal. Pekes, George Saphier, Edw. Cotten, Edw. Packer.

28 January. Mr. John Wyatt proxy for Mr. Brookes. Mr. Percy proxy for John Medley & his proxies. Mr. Percy proxy for Tho. Math. & Mr. Crou. Tho. Allen proxy for John Hatch.

Act nullifying earlier acts: 28 January 1647. Signed:

f. 294 Robert Vaughan, Cuth. Fenwick, Robert Percy for John Medley, Phillip Conner, Rich. Bankes, Tho. Allen, George Saugher, Walter Waterlin, Robert Clarke for Geo. Akerick, Walter Pekes, William Tompson for Capt. Price, Tho. Bradnox, Tho. Thornborough, Edw. Packer, John Wyatt for Mr. Brookes, Edward Cotten for Bar. Jackson, William Bretton.

29 January. Nicholas Gwyther petitioned for his freedom. Mr. Fenwick, attorney for Capt. Cornwalleys, denied to him. Nicholas Gwyther to show account.

Thomas Oliver vs. Mr. Fenwick attorney for Capt. Cornwallis. Petitioner to be at his own disposal.

Francis Posey vs. John Hatch.

f. 295 Nathaniell Pope for Mr. James Neale gave land to Mr. Tho. Thorneborough, depositions regarding Mr. Calvert (late Governor).

f. 296 Adjournment. Francis Posey proxy for Walter Pekes & his proxies.

31 January. Nicholas Gwyther produced accounts. Mentions: Francis Posey, Bartholomew Rench, Bartholomew Phillips, Mousser Obert, William Marshall, Gov. Calvert.

f. 297 Tho. Thorneborough petitioned for chattel promised by Gov. Calvert.

Adjournment. Francis Posey proxy for Mr. Thorneborough.

3 February. General Assembly. Attendees: all except Tho. Allen. Francis Posey proxy for Mr. Thorneborough.

Adjournment. Mr. John Wyatt proxy for Walter Pekes.

10 February. General Assembly. Attendees: all except Mr. Bretton. Lt. William Lewis appointed to take his place.

14 February. General Assembly. Attendees: all except Francis Posey proxy for Mr. Thorneborough.

21 February. General Assembly. Attendees: Governor, Capt. Giles Brent, all except Mr. Bretton. John Lewger, Jr. appointed to take his place.

Liber - Patent Record Z & A - 1637-1651

f. 298 Capt. Giles Brent, Esq., Capt. Robert Vaughan, & Mr. Cuth. Fenwick appointed to draw up remonstrance on the grievances of the Province.

22 February. General Assembly. Attendees: all except Mr. Percy proxy for John Medley. Grievance brought forth. George Manners proxy for Mr. Thorneborough in lieu of Francis Posey.

23 February. General Assembly. Attendees: all except George Manners proxy for Mr. Thornborough.

Edward Packer assignee of Mrs. Margarett Brent vs. John Hatch attorney for Thomas Gerard, Esq. Bills of Thomas Thomas, Joseph Cadle, & Walter Beane, to be delivered to said Edward Packer.

f. 299 Mrs. Marg. Brent requested her case against Thomas Gerard, Esq. be heard by the House.

24 February. General Assembly.

26 February. General Assembly.

29 February. General Assembly. Morning. Attendees: all except Tho. Allen, George Saphyer, John Lewger proxy for Mr. Bradnox, Mr. Fenwick.

f. 300 General Assembly. Afternoon. Attendees: all except Tho. Allen, John Lewger proxy for Mr. Bradnox, Mr. Fenwick.

William Whittle, Stanop Roberts, & William Hungerford vs. estate of Mrs. Margaret Brent.

1 March. General Assembly. Attendees: all except Mr. Fenwick, Wal. Gwest proxy for G. Akerick, John Lewger proxy for Mr. Bradnox, Capt. John Price.

Committee appointed: Mr. Bretton, John Hatch, Bar. Jackson, Rich. Banks, Mr. Saphyer.

2 March. General Assembly. Morning. Attendees: all except Mr. Fenwick, Mr. Percy proxy for John Medley, John Lewger proxy for Mr. Bradnox, C. Price.

f. 301 General Assembly. Afternoon. Attendees: all except Mr. Fenwick, Walter Gweast proxy for G. Akerick, Mr. Percy proxy for John Medley, Capt. John Price.

John Hatch for William Edisse & Mr. John Rosier attorney for Capt. Stone vs. estate of Mr. Thomas Weston (dec'd).

3 March. General Assembly. Attendees: all except Capt. Brent, Mr. Fenwick, Mr. Percy proxy for John Medley, Capt. Price.

Clause engrossed by all except Mr. Saphier, Capt. Price, Barnaby Jackson, Mr. Bretton.

4 March. General Assembly. Attendees: all except Mr. Fenwick Mr. Percy proxy for John Medley.

f. 302 Clause engrossed by all except Mr. Saphyer, Bar. Jackson, Mr. Bretton.

Committee appointed: Capt. Brent, Capt. Vaughan, Capt. Price, Mr. Saphyer, Barnaby Jackson, Edward Packer.

Payments from the House to: Mr. John Lewger, Mr. Bretton, Robert Vaughan, Capt. Price, Francis Van Enden.

f. 303 Cause signed by: Giles Brent, Robert Vaughan, John Price, George Saphyer, Edward Packer, Barnaby Jackson.

Richard Banks, at request of Mr. Cuth. Fenwick attorney for Capt. Tho. Cornwalleys, age 35, deposed that in 1644 the deponent paid Mr. Fenwick for use of Capt. Cornwalleys. Said payment was forcibly taken by Rich. Ingle (mariner). Signed: Richard Bankes.

Walter Waterlin, age 40, deposed that in 1644 the deponent paid Mr. Fenwick. After Rich. Ingle (mariner) came to the Province, said Ingle took the payment.

31 January. Thomas Gerard, Esq. per John Hatch demanded of Henry Foxe.

Thomas Gerard, Esq. per John Hatch demanded of William Edwin.

f. 304 10 February. John Prichard demanded of Geoffrey Power.

Liber - Patent Record Z & A - 1637-1651

Henry Pountney demanded of Edward Hudson.

Mrs. Marg. Brent demaned of Francis Gray.

Stanope Roberts demanded of William Whitle for damages to cutlace claimed by John Prichard.

Richard Browne per Lt. William Evans demanded of John Prichard.

Francis Van Enden sold to Francis Pope & John Court chattel. Date: 24 December 1647. Witnesses: Richard Banks, James Johnson.

William Tompson (planter, of New Town Hundred) sold to Rich. Banks & William Wright chattel. Date: 29 January 1646. Witness: Francis Pope.

f. 305 Ralph Beane (planter, of Newtowne Hundred) sold to Richard Banks & William Wright chattel. Date: 11 July 1647. Witness: Francis Pope.

Francis Van Enden (planter, of Newtown Hundred) sold to Rich. Banks & William Wright chattel. Date: 22 December 1647. Witnesses: John Wyatt, William Bretton.

Mr. John Pyle sold to Marks Pheypo chattel. Date: 19 January 1647. Witnesses: Walter Smith, William Lewis.

f. 306 Edward Packer demanded of John Hatch attorney for Mr. Thomas Gerard, Esq.

Francis Posey demanded of Thomas Waggott.

Subpoena to Walter Waterlin.

Francis Pope, age 38, deposed that (at the request of Mr. Cuth. Fenwick attorney for Capt. Tho. Cornwallyes) that Mr. Fenwick received payment due Capt. Cornwallyes (after Capt. Ingle came to the Province). Ralph Beane demanded said payment taken aboard said Ingle's ship.

Walter Waterlin, at the request of Fran. Posey, deposed that last September Francis Posey paid Tho. Waggott.

John Waltham deposed the same.

James Lindsey, at the request of Capt. John Price, deposed that Lt. William Lewis brought an Indian woman & child from a house during the march on the Eastern Shore last July.

George Manners deposed the same.

f. 307 Walter Gweast deposed the same.

23 February. Mrs. Marg. Brent attorney for His Lordship sold to John Ward (soldier at St. Inego's Fort) chattel. Date: 16 February 1647. Witnesses: Giles Brent, Robert Vaughan.

Anthony Rawlins demanded of Robert Clarke (gentleman).

24 February. Thomas Greene (Governor) gave chattel to his son Robert Greene.

f. 308 26 February. John Wyatt (gentleman), at the request of Capt. Giles Brent, deposed that Anne Fletcher (servant of Sir Edmund Plowden sometime in Summer of 1643) was brought to house of Capt. Brent at Kent by John Lee, very ill & was cared for by Mrs. Brent.

Margaret Brent delivered to Thomas Allen chattel. Date: 24 February 1647.

Letter from Cecilius Lord Baltimore. To: my brother Leonard Calvert, Esq., Secretary John Lewger, Esq. Subject: Power to appoint to receive rents. Date: 15 November 1646.

f. 309 29 February. Capt. John Price deposed that Mr. Calvert said the charge should be paid out of his own estate.

Walter Pekes deposed that Elias Beach spoke to Mr. Calvert regarding pay to soldiers.

Lt. William Evans deposed that he heard Mr. Leon. Calvert say that, if necessary, he would defray charges for keeping soldiers.

f. 310 William Whitle deposed that he heard Mr. Calvert, say that His Lordship's

Liber - Patent Record Z & A - 1637-1651

estate & his own should be used to pay soldier's wages.

Marks Pheypo deposed the same.

Margarett Brent sold to George Manners (gentleman) Buttler's Land 100 a. in St. Michael's Manor. Date: 28 February 1647. Witnesses: Giles Brent, John Metcalfe.

Anthony Rawlins demanded of Mrs. Margaret Brent attorney for His Lordship, assignment

f. 311 from Nicholas Gwyther & Tho. Jackson & Adam Stauely.

Edward Hull demanded of Mrs. Marg. Brent attorney for His Lordship.

Hugh Donne (mariner) administrator of Richard Marshall sold to John Hatch & William Marshall chattel from estate of Richard Marshall (dec'd). Signed: Hugh Donn. Date: 11 February 1647. Witnesses: W. Ediffe, John Slingsby.

Lt. William Evans (lieutenant of Fort of St. Inego's), at the request of John Prichard, deposed that John Salter (after he came to the Province with Governor Calvert), claimed chattel of John Prichard.

f. 312 3 March. Francis Van Enden sold to Barnaby Jackson chattel. Date: 1 March 1647. Witnesses: Walter Pekes, Walter Gweast.

Walter Beane, at the request of Cuthbert Fenwick, deposed that he paid Rich. Ingle, due from Mr. Fenwick or Capt. Cornwallis.

f. 313 4 March. Thomas Weston (ironmonger, of London). Mentions: Thomas Stone. [passage is in Latin.] Date: 1641. Witnesses: Henr. Lawrence, John Hutton.

Mentions: Thomas Stone of Cateaten St., London.

Thomas Stone, age 68, merchant of London, deposed that Thomas Weston (ironmonger, formerly of London) is indebted

f. 314 to the deponent, per account of Capt. William Stone. Date: 10 August 1647. Witness: Robert Aylett.

Letter to: Capt. William Stone (of Accomack). From: Thomas Weston. Date: 3 January 1644. Mentions: your uncle, your brother Mr. John Stone.

Thomas Stone (haberdasher, of London) assigned to Capt. William Stone (merchant, of Accomac) PoA to receive of Thomas Weston (formerly of VA, dec'd). Date: 31 July 1647. Witnesses: Richard Chandler, John Edwards.

f. 315 Capt. William Stone (merchant, of Northampton), by virtue of a PoA of Thomas Stone (haberdasher, of London) constituted John Rosier (clerk, of Appomatucks) as attorney to receive of Thomas Weston (of VA, dec'd). Date: 22 February 1647. Witnesses: Mathew Stone, Rand. Revell.

f. 316 2 March. General Assembly. Attendees: all except Mr. Fenwick, Walter Gweast proxy for George Akerick, Mr. Percy proxy for John Medley, Capt. John Price.

William Ediffe, at the request of John Hatch, requested his cause be heard.

William Ediffe vs. administrator of Thomas Weston.

John Hatch deposed that William Ediffe had not received of Thomas Weston.

Capt. William Stone attorney for Mr. Thomas Stone (merchant, of London) per John Rosier demanded of administrator of Thomas Weston (merchant, dec'd).

Marks Pheypo attorney for Mr. Hansford administrator of Mr. Weston.

f. 317 Citation regarding rebellion lead by Rich. Ingle. Date: 4 March 1647. Signed: Tho. Greene.

Francis Pope & John Courts (planters) transported selves in 1645

f. 318 granted land on west side of Poplar Hill, 200 a. Date: 3 August 1647. Signed: Thomas Greene.

6 March. Mrs. Marg. Brent attorney for His Lordship sold to Edward Cotton (carpenter) chattel. Date: 5 March 1647. Witnesses: John Metcalfe, Signed: Margaret Brent.

Liber - Patent Record Z & A - 1637-1651

f. 319 1 April 1648. Capt. Thomas Cornw. per Cuth. Fenwick demanded of Thomas Sturman & his son John Sturman.

Mr. William Tompson was sworn in as high sheriff of St. Maries' Co.; Phillip Land as undersheriff.

5 April. William Harditch vs. Tho. Copley, Esq.

John Sturman per William Harditch vs. Tho. Copley, Esq.

Robert Clarke (gentleman) vs. John Sturman, regarding chattel bought of Mr. John Pyle.

Henry Hooper demanded of His Lordship's attorney.

Robert Sharp demanded of Mrs. Marg. Brent administratrix of Leonard Calvert, Esq.

4 April. Cause to be tried by jury:

f. 320 Edward Packer, Mr. Clarke, Fr. Posey, Mr. Wyatt, Robert Smith, Robert Sharpe, Mr. Pyle, Tho. Allen, Tho. Mathews, Tho. Hebden, Antho. Rawlins. Mentions: John Hatch, G. Manners, Mr. Wiseman, Nic. Ketin.

William Harditch vs. Thomas Copley, Esq. by his attorney Thomas Mathews. Mentions: Thomas Sturman, Gov. Mr. Leonard Calvert.

John Sturman deposed regarding chattel formerly of Thomas Sturman belonging to William Harditch.

f. 321 ...

f. 322 John Greenold, at the request of William Harditch, deposed of actions while of Mr. Sturman's.

Robert Clarke (gentleman) vs. John Sturman by his attorney William Harditch.

John Pyle deposed that he sold chattel to Robert Clarke (gentleman) about last November.

Robert Clarke (gentleman) deposed that the chattel is the same sold him by Mr. Pyle.

Thomas Waggot deposed that while at the house of Mr. Clark, that either Mr. Clark or his wife asked the deponent if he had taken the chattel.

William Harditch attorney for John Sturman vs. Robert Clark (gentleman). Robert Clark indicated that he bought chattel

f. 323 of Mr. John Pyle.

Antho. Rawlins vs. Robert Clark (gentleman).

Anth. Rawlins demanded of Phillip Auther.

6 April. Antho. Rawlins vs. His Lordship by his attorney Mrs. Margaret Brent.

Edward Hull vs. Mrs. Margaret Brent.

Richard Bennett vs. Mrs. Margaret Brent administratrix of Leonard Calvert, Esq.

Edward Packer vs. John Dandy.

Robert Smith demanded of Walter Beane.

Henry Hooper (chirurgeon) vs. His Lordship by his attorney Mrs. Margarett Brent.

f. 324 William Harditch vs. Tho. Copley.

Robert Smith deposed that Thomas Sturman had the chattel & by some means came into possession of (N) Pope.

Anthony Rawlins deposed regarding chattel in question between William Harditch & Mr. Copley.

Andrew Marrow deposed the same.

Liber - Patent Record Z & A - 1637-1651

John Sturman vs. Mr. Tho. Copley.

Thomas Sturman gave chattel to his son John Sturman. Date: 13 March 1646. Witnesses: William Pindley, Andrew Marrow.

John Pyle (gentleman) assigned to John Sturman chattel

f. 325 in return for chattel delivered by said Sturman to Robert Clarke. Date: 6 April 1648. Signed: John Pille, John Sturman.

6 April at St. Maries'. Court. Henry Adams demanded of Thomas Greene, Esq. William Bretton (gentleman) was appointed judge.

Charles Rawlinson, at request of Robert Smith, deposed that last Winter, the deponent & Capt. Price brought chattel from St. George's to St. Maries'. Said chattel having been seen at home of Walter Beane earlier.

f. 326 George Manners demanded of Nicholas Brown (gentleman) & Edward Commens (of Kent) for transporting out of St. Maries' Co.: Thomas Munday, John Deere, estate of Henry Boston.

7 April. Thomas Copley, Esq. demanded of Mrs. Margarett Brent administratrix of Leon. Calvert, Esq. (dec'd).

John Waltham demanded 100 a. for transporting self. Warrant for branches of Herring Creek, between Tho. Bushell & Robert Kedger.

25 April. Bartholomew Phillips demanded of William Lewis.

Bartholomew Phillips demanded of Paul Simpson.

29 April. John Hallowes demanded of Richard Duke.

John Hallowes demanded of William Styles 5 years service due by indenture.

John Hallowes demanded of John Warren.

Ralphe Beane demanded 100 a. bought of Mr. Calvert & 500 a. for transporting 5 men between 1640 & 1648: Tho. Jones,

f. 327 John Cole, Edward Shelly, Lancelot Sleepe, Joseph Durford & 100 a. for transporting self & 50 a. for his service & 150 a. for his brother Walter Beane who transported self & wife. Warrant for 1500 a. at Peyney Point commonly called plantation of Capt. Evelin or Peter Draper.

Barnaby Jackson vs. Humphrey Howell.

29 May. Lt. William Lewis acknowledged judgement to Bartholomew Phillips & bound self to Mr. William Tompson. Date: 29 April 1648. Witness: Phillip Land. 10 September, Lt. Lewis desired amendment to above.

Proclamation. Date: 22 May 1648. Signed: Tho. Greene.

f. 328 10 June at St. Inego's. Court. Attendees: Governor, Mr. Brent, Mr. Gerard.

Capt. Edward Hill demanded from Governor & Council due from Leonard Calvert, Esq. Payment to be made by Lord Proprietor's attorney.

13 June. Giles Brent, Esq. vs. Cuthbert Fenwick (gentleman). Cites wages due from administrator of James Cauther.

f. 329 Bond posted by Cuth. Fenwick.

14 June. Edward Packer deposed that in May or June 1644, Simon Richardson (then sheriff of Kent Co.), by warrant from Capt. Giles Brent, Esq. (then Governor of the Province) seized chattel in possession of Mr. William Cox, acknowledged pertaining to Capt. Will. Cleyborne for the use of Lord Proprietor.

f. 330 19 June. Thomas Mathews was sworn in as clerk of the court during his abode on the Isle of Kent.

Francis Brooke vs. Tho. Bradnox & Edward Commins.

Francis Brooke demanded of Edward Cummins.

Subpoena to Fran. Lumbard & Thomas Pett.

Liber - Patent Record Z & A - 1637-1651

William Lant, at the request of Capt. Giles Brent, deposed regarding chattel at Thomas Bradnox.

John Goneere deposed that he knew of no flesh at the house of Thomas Munday other than pigs, & he didn't know of Edw. Hudson bringing any flesh.

Edward Claxton deposed that Edward Hudson did kill chattel of Mr. Brent on Isle of Kent

f. 331 & the deponent went with Hudson to Tho. Munday & met with John Goneere.

John Goneere deposed that he heard Edward Hudson tell Tho. Munday that he had killed chattel.

Roger Baxter vs. Edw. Cummins.

f. 332 Subpoena to William Lant, Walter King, & John Bennett.

Richard Duke, age 35, deposed to Thomas Gerard, Esq. that Margaret South came to the deponent & desired him to sell him an Indian.

John Lancelot, age 19, deposed to Thomas Gerard, Esq. that Mr. Sowth asked Richard Duke to go with him to Wicocomoco to get him an Indian.

22 June at house of Henry Morgan at Kent. Court.

Thomas Mathewes on behalf of Lord Proprietor vs. John Goneere.

f. 333 Francis Brookes vs. Mr. Bradnox & Edw. Cummins.

Francis Brookes vs. Edward Cummins. Mentions: Capt. Robert Vaughan (commander of Kent).

Robert Short demanded of Francis Lumbard.

23 June at the house of Henry Morgan at Kent. Court.

Robert Holt demanded of the His Lordship's attorney.

f. 334 John Salter & Henry Clay demanded of His Lordship's attorney.

Capt. Giles Brent vs. Capt. Robert Vaughan.

Tho. Bradnox deposed that at a meeting at the house of Thomas Kain, he heard Capt. Vaughan demand of John Abbott.

f. 335 Zachary Wade deposed that chattel now in possession of Capt. Robert Vaughan given by the Governor (dec'd) to said Capt. Vaughan from His Lordship's stock, but was from the stock of Mr. Brent, having been allotted Mr. Brent out of the chattel of Capt. Cleyborne.

Capt. Giles Brent vs. Capt. Robert Vaughan.

Zachary Wade deposed that William Cox came to the deponent, in the field of Mr. Brent, & spoke of chattel of Mr. Brent.

Henry Morgan (sheriff of Kent Co.) vs. Tho. Munday.

f. 336 John Dandy vs. Edward Commins.

Zachary Wade vs. Capt. Robert Vaughan.

26 June. John Howard, age 22, deposed that last Summer, at the house of Mr. Bradnox in Kent, that John Palmer, Mr. Bradnox, William Lant, John Malham, & the deponent spoke of killing a steer.

f. 337 Thomas Mathewes attorney for Mr. Tho. Copley, Esq. demaned of John Howard.

Henry Morgan deposed that he heard Francis Brookes relate that Mr. Cox told him, just before his death, that he had chattel, given to his children & he heard Mrs. Cox on her deathbed state that Mary Martin should receive chattel.

27 June at the house of Edw. Commins. Court.

Henry Clay deposed that he new knew Tho. Munday or any of his household to kill chattel belonging to Henry Morgan.

Liber - Patent Record Z & A - 1637-1651

Robert Short deposed that he saw fresh bacon in the house of Thomas Munday in February or March last.

John Dandy vs. Edw. Commins.

f. 338 Henry Morgan demanded of Edmond Lenin (not resident in the country).

John Howard demanded of Tho. Bradnox.

William Lant deposed regarding the chattel of Mrs. Cox.

1 July. Henry Morgan (sheriff) demanded of Edward Hudson.

Cuthbert Fenwick (gentleman) demanded of William Lewis for self & for Capt. Cornwallyes.

John Hallowes demanded of John Dandy.

Roger Baxter (planter, of Isle of Kent) acknowledged a gift of chattel to his 2 sons John & Francis Baxter.

f. 339 3 July at house of Capt. Vaughan at Kent. Court.

Capt. Giles Brent attorney for Tho. Gerard, Esq. administrator of Henry Brookes (merchant, dec'd) & attorney for Henry Brookes, Sr. (the father) & request regarding the inventory of estate of said Hen. Brookes. Capt. Robert Vaughan delivered an account of the estate & payments to: Mr. Cox, John Bennett, Hen. Morgan, Fran. Lumbard, Mr. Giles Brent, accountant.

10 July. Lt. William Lewis acknowledged judgement to Capt. Cornwalleys & Mr. Fenwick (gentleman). Witness: Phillip Land.

11 July. Mrs. Margarett Brent demanded of Peter Knight (merchant).

f. 340 William Tompson (planter, of St. Clement's Hundred) acknowledged debt to His Lordship, regarding actions of Lt. William South (of Knoughton, VA) & Rich. Torney (of VA). Witnesses: Thomas Greene, Giles Brent.

15 July. Thomas Asbrook acknowledged a debt to William Whittington (of Accomack). Signed: Thomas Ashbrook.

17 July. Richard Jones (of Isle of Kent) per his attorney Marks Pheypo demanded of Robert Simkin.

18 July. William Tompson (gentleman) vs. Robert Smith.

3 August. John Dandy demanded of Tho. Ashbrook security for any claims as a result of transporting him from VA to MD.

Thomas War demanded 300 a. for transporting self & wife & 2 children in 1648. Warrant for north side of St. Clare's Creek.

f. 341 Giles Brent gives to the 2 children of William Cox, Elisabeth Coxe & William Coxe, chattel until either is 15 years old. Then each is to have equal share of chattel from Tho. Greene, Esq. Date: 30 June 1648. Witnesses: Paul Simpson, Robert Vaughan, Ralph Crouch.

Interrogation by George Manners of Edw. Commins (of Kent). Mentions: John Deere, Mr. Sturman.

f. 342 7 August. Subpoena to Robert Simkin. Robert Simkin deposed regarding the abovecited interrogations. Mentions: George Manners, Edward Commins, Thomas Munday.

William Harditch vs. Capt. John Price.

f. 343 8 August. Warrant to George Manners to impanel a jury regarding the death of Tho. Allen at Point Lookout.

9 August. Jury: Edward Cotton, William Edwin, Odoan James, Angel Simpson, John Lewger, Edw. Hull, Humphrey Howell, John Cage, John Harwood, Lewis Frooman, Richard Willan, George Dolle.

William Marshall demanded of Henry Lee.

22 August. Lt. Richard Banks apprehended 5 Indians suspected of felony.

Liber - Patent Record Z & A - 1637-1651

25 August. Thomas Copley, Esq. vs. John Hallowes. Mentions: John Kekeape (servant to said Copley).

f. 344 28 August. Cuthbert Fenwick (gentleman) demanded of William Witle.

John Hallowes & Richard Sedgrave certified that Capt. Francis Paytres is attorney for Capt. Edward Hill. Date: 14 July 1649. Signed: Fran. Poyteres.

7 September at St. Maries. Court. Jury: Mr. Fenwick, Bar. Jackson, John Holfhead, Walter Beane, Walter Peake, Thomas Warre, John Ward, Fran. Posey, Mr. Wiseman, Tho. Hamper, Rich. Willan, Mr. Lewger.

Richard Nevett complained regarding the action of Indians: Indian Takanine, Indian Mohotanco, Indian Anarsine,

f. 345 11 September. Henry Pountney vs. Edward Hudson (of Kent) regarding bill of Nicholas Pickett.

William Whitle demanded 100 a. for transporting self in 1646 & 100 a. for transporting William Hungerford & 100 a. for Jo. Ward for transporting themselves in same year. Warrant for south side of St. Hierom's Creek aka Poplar Creek.

13 September. William Smoote demanded of Mrs. Margarett Brent.

Thomas Mathews (of VA) by his attorney Francis Poetrosse demanded of George Akerick.

Robert West by his attorney Francis Poetrosse demanded of George Akerick.

f. 346 Oswin Hull by his attorney Fran. Poetrosse demanded of George Akerick.

William Thomas by his attorney Fran. Poetrosse demanded of George Akerick.

14 September. William Hardige discharged L. Calvert, Esq. & all his soldiers brought from VA of all debts. Date: 8 January 1646. Signed: William Hardich. Witnesses: Thomas Greene, John Wyatte.

15 September. Thomas Greene, Esq. demanded 2000 a. for transporting self & 2 able manservants: Thomas Cooper, Anam Benam in 1633; & on assignment from Mr. Nicolas Fairefax & Mr. William Smith for transporting themselves in the same year, & 300 a. for transporting a servant in 1634: Thomas Willis, & 100 a. in the right of his wife Mrs. Winifred Segborne for transporting herself in 1638 & 100 a. for transporting 2 children in 1644: Thomas & Leonard Greene. Warrant for the north side of St. Hierom's Creek.

Phillip Land demanded 100 a. for

f. 347 transporting self in 1647 & 400 a. on assignment from Tho. Greene, Esq. Warrant for near mouth of St. Hierom's Creek.

Nicolas Cawsin demanded of Mrs. Margarett Brent on assignment from Walter Peake.

18 September. George Manners (planter) vs. Edw. Hall.

John Hallowes attorney for Ralphe Horsely (of Chicacoan) vs. Owen James.

19 September. Nicholas Cawsin demanded 1000 a. for transporting self & 2 manservants: Julian Bernett, John Taylor, & 2 others: Arthur La Hay, Thomas Peteet in 1639 & 100 a. for transporting 1 manservant John Walter in 1642. Warrant for on south side of St. Hierom's Creek.

22 September. Walter Beane vs. John Waltham.

23 September. Anthony Rawlins vs. Mrs. Margarett Brent His Lordship's attorney on assignment from Adam Stauely.

f. 348 Edward Hull vs. Mrs. Margarett Brent His Lordship's attorney.

Henry Moosley by his attorney Robert Sharp vs. Lt. William Lewis.

25 September. William Styles vs. George Manners.

27 September. Subpoena to Robert Sharpe, Edward Hull, & Henry Potter to testify in cause between George Manners & Edward Hall.

Liber - Patent Record Z & A - 1637-1651

Subpoena to Robert Sharp to testify in cause between Robert Smith & Walter Beane.

30 September. Edward Hull, age 28, deposed that in last July, regarding the actions by George Manners to the chattel of Edward Hall.

2 October. Henry Potter, age 29, deposed regarding chattel of Edward Hall & actions of George Manners.

f. 349 Interrogations regarding G. Manners vs. Edward Hall. Henry Potter deposed.

On 1 July 1648, Edward Hudson deposed that Henry Clay said

f. 350 he may have injured chattel of Henry Morgan, who spoke of it to Thomas Munday.

Thomas Bushrode by his attorney Cuthbert Fenwick vs. Capt. Giles Brent.

Capt. Tho. Cornwalleys by his attorney Cuth. Fenwick demanded of Capt. Giles Brent.

Cuth. Fenwick (gentleman) demanded of Mrs. Marg. Brent His Lordship's attorney.

3 October at St. Maries. Court. Jury: Nicolas Cawsin, Stanope Roberts, Mr. John Lewger, William Styles, Walter Smith, William Hungerford, Nathan: Jones, Charles Rawlinson, George Manners, John Villaine, William Marshall, Mr. Browne, Mr. Hebden, Christ: Russell, Walt. Beane, Mr. Broughe, John Holfhead, Barn. Jackson, Mr. Fenwick.

William Harditch vs. Capt. John Price.

Anthony Rawlins vs. Mrs. Margarett Brent His Lordship's attorney

f. 351 regarding assignment from Adam Stauely.

Mrs. Margaret Brent acknowledged debt of His Lordship to Nicolas Cawsin assignee of Walter Peakes, less fees due Mr. William Bretton. Date: 2 December 1649. Satisfaction.

Thomas Greene, Esq. vs. John Trussell (gentleman, of Chicacoan).

John Hallowes vs. Robert Percy, regarding assignment from John Hilliard.

f. 352 Request certificate from magistrate in VA, regarding oath of John Hilliard.
- George Manners deposed that while he was at Appamatucks, John Hillard came to the deponent desiring him to be his attorney on a bill from Mr. Percy.
- Anthony Rawlins deposed that Mr. Clarke did promise to pay the deponent.

f. 353 ...
- John Tew, age 21, deposed at the request of Cuth. Fenwick (gentleman), that the chattel which John Hallowes carried to St. Maries' from Appamatucks was for the use of Mrs. Speake (of Chicacoane).

Robert Smith vs. Walter Beane. Viewers appointed: Capt. John Price, Robert Sharpe.

4 October at St. Maries'. Court. William Harditch vs. Capt. John Price. Jury: Wal. Beane, Mr. Broughe, Mr. Browne, Bar. Jackson, William Hungerford, Nat. Joanes, Charles Rawlinson, G. Manners, Stanope Roberts, Mr. Lewger, William Styles.

Capt. Giles Brent vs. Mr. Fenwick. Mentions: James Cauther.

f. 354 Edward Hull vs. His Lordship's Attorney.

Anthony Rawlins to testify in cause of William Harditch.

Cuthbert Fenwick (gentleman), at the request of Nicolas Cawsin, deposed that, in 1644, the deponent saw a bill of Esq. Yardley (of Accomack) made to Nicolas Cawsin.

Thomas Hebden, at the request of Capt. John Price, in the case vs. William Harditch, deposed that he was present when Gov. Calvert sent said captain to bring all items involved in the Rebellion to Fort of St. Inego's.

Mrs. Margaret Brent vs. Mr. Peter Knight (merchant). Cites bills of his [sic] brother Mr. Giles Brent,

f. 355 Gov. Mr. Leonard Calvert.

Liber - Patent Record Z & A - 1637-1651

<u>5 October at St. Maries'</u>. Court. Tho. Bushrode vs. Giles Brent. Mentions: Mr. John Lewger (son of Mr. John Lewger), Nath. Pope.

f. 356 Giles Brent replied that he was taken prisoner into England the day the bill was due. Mentions: Mr. Giles Brent (in VA), Mr. Fenwick.

f. 357 Richard Jones (of Kent) vs. Robert Simkin.

Cuthbert Fenwick vs. His Lordship's Attorney.

Mrs. Margarett Brent vs. Peter Knight.

John Hampton by his attorney John Hallowes vs. Mrs. Brent administratrix of Leon. Calvert, Esq.

Hilliard vs. Percy. Giles Brent, Esq. deposed.

John Cage, at the request of Mr. John Lewger, deposed regarding the chattel in suit between Mr. Lewger & Mr. Fenwick.

f. 358 Thomas Hebden deposed the same.

Walter Beane vs. Thomas Greene, Esq.

Thomas Hebden (gentleman) vs. Tho. Johnson.

Giles Brent, Esq. vs. Edmund Lennin. Subpoena to Hugh Hopewell.

Mrs. Margarett Brent, for Lord Proprietor, requested in case regarding chattel of Mr. Thomas Copley & claimed by William Harditch.

William Harditch vs. Capt. John Price.

Barnaby Jackson (one of the jurors in case of Capt. John Price vs. William Harditch) deposed.

f. 359 William Styles (one of the jury) deposed that he did not agree with the verdict given by the foreman.

Walter Beane (foreman) deposed. Others deposing: Mr. Browne, William Marshall, Mr. Broughe, Mr. John Lewger, William Hungerford, Stanope Roberts, Nath. Joanes.

George Manners deposed that he heard William Styles say no, but when it came to deliver the verdict, no one rose.

Joane, wife of Thomas Warre, deposed that she was in the room whent he jury returned, & after the foreman responded that all agreed, William Styles

f. 360 said no, but she did not know to what question.

William Styles is excused from being on a jury.

<u>6 October</u>. Nicolas Cawsine, age over 40, deposed on 13 June 1648 that Edw. <u>Commins</u> (of Isle of Kent), before Ingle's

f. 361 Rebellion, bought bacon.

Jane Hopewell, age 20, deposed on 13 June 1648 before Thomas Greene, Esq. (Governor) that, 2 or 3 months before Ingle's Rebellion, she heard John Waters, servant to Nicolas Cawsine, say that he had 6 years to serve his master & would never serve out the time.

Jane Hopewell deposed on 13 June 1648 that in Summer 1646, she heard Richard White say he was indebted to Nic. Cawsine.

Charles Rawlinson, at the request of Thomas Baker, deposed that, at the beginning of the Plunder, the deponent was at Crosse House, Walter Coterill & Tho. Baker approached & Coterill gave Baker chattel. Witness: Giles Brent.

f. 362 Blanch Oliver deposed the same. Witness: Giles Brent.

Charles Rawlinson, at the request of Cuth. Fenwick (gentleman), deposed that when he was at Chicacoan, he saw chattel of Mr. Fenwick for use of Mr. Speake. Witness: Giles Brent.

Thomas Baker, at the request of Blanch Oliver, deposed that chattel was killed at his master Pope's Fort, during the Rebellion, which belonged to Blanch

Liber - Patent Record Z & A - 1637-1651

Oliver. Witness: Giles Brent.

William Harditch demanded of John Hatch & Richard Banks administrators of Thomas Allen (dec'd).

William Harditch vs. William Styles (juryman).

f. 363 7 October at St. Maries'. Court. Lt. William Lewis requested his board be delivered, since the defendant Henry Moseley (of Chicacoan) had not appeared.

Barnaby Jackson demanded security of John Waltham, who is leaving for Appamatuck & no certainty of return.

John Hallowes vs. Francis Van Enden.

Humphrey Howell vs. Anthony Rawlins.

Humphrey Howell, husband of Blanch Oliver, vs. Nathaniel Pope.

William Smoote vs. Cuthbert Fenwick (gentleman), regarding chattel bought of Jeoffrey Power.

f. 364 Lt. William Lewis demanded of Robert Clarke (gentleman) on assignment from John Pyle.

Thomas Pasmore assigned to Anthony Rawlins 100 a. for servant Henry Baker. Witness: Rich. Browne.

William Harditch, at the request of Capt. Giles Brent, deposed that chattel sold by John Sturman to Anthony Rawlins does not come from Mr. Pyle, and of chattel sold by Thomas Sturman to Anthony Rawlins.

9 October. Cuth. Fenwick (gentleman) vs. Capt. John Price, said Price to deliver chattel to Mr. Tho. Speake.

Robert Clarke (gentleman) vs. Walter Smith.

f. 365 Giles Brent, Esq. vs. William Harditch & Anthony Rawlins, regarding chattel with mark of Thomas Sturman.

Giles Brent, Esq. vs. William Harditch, regarding sale of chattel to Anthony Rawlins, formerly taken by Tho. or John Sturman.

Charges of the Assembly in 1647: Mr. Bretton, Capt. Vaughan, Francis Van Enden,

f. 366 Walter Waterlin.

Mr. Thomas Copley moved regarding rent on East St. Maries'. Mrs. Margarett Brent (His Lordship's Attorney) gave her consent.

f. 367 14 October. Mathyas Briant deposed that, last April, he met an Indian named or Indian Moyke, living at Wiccocomoc, whi had actually killed chattel of Mr. Tompson.

16 October. Edward Cottam requested restraint of Tho. Baker (of Appamatucks). Subpoenas to Walter Coterill & George Manners.

Ralph Beane vs. William Styles.

f. 368 Ralph Beane demanded of Francis Van Enden.

Lt. Richard Banks demanded of Francis Van Enden.

18 October. Walter Coterill, at the request of Edward Cottam, deposed that he gave chattel to Tho. Baker at the time of the Rebellion. Further, neither Charles Rawlinson nor Blanch Oliver were present.

The Freeman of County of St. Maries' met regarding the levy & charges of imprisonment of the Indians.

f. 369 19 October. Edward Packer deposed on 14 June 1648 that he never delivered chattel of Capt. Thomas Cornwalleys for use of Mr. Leonard Calvert, Esq. assigned by Mrs. Margarett Brent.

Thomas Gerard, Esq. released Mrs. Margarett Brent administratrix of Leonard Calvert, Esq. of all debts. Date: 7 June 1648. Witnesses: Giles Brent, William Eltonhed.

Liber - Patent Record Z & A - 1637-1651

Lord Commissioners for Plantations. Petition of Capt. William Cleyborne & his partners vs. Lord Baltimore. At Whitehall, 4 April 1638. Present: Lord Archbishop of Canterbury, Lord Keeper, Lord Treasurer, Lord Privy Seal, Earl Marshall, Earl of Dorsett, Lord Cottington, Mr. Treasurer, Mr. Comptroller, Mr. Sec. Cooke, Mr. Windebanck.

f. 370 ...

f. 371 ...

f. 372 Signed: T. Meautys.

Mrs. Margarett Brent vs. Anthony Rawlins, regarding conveyance of chattel of William Harditch, said chattel never belonging to either Harditch or Tho. Sturman.

20 October. John Garbo (of Newtowne) acknowledged a gift to Mary, daughter of Walter & Frances Peaks. Signed: John Jarbo.

27 October 1648. Francis Van Enden conveyed to John Hallowes all salary for keeping my ordinary. Witness: James Johnson.

f. 373 30 October. George Manners, at the request of Edward Cottam, deposed that the bull claimed by Tho. Baker, as a gift from Walter Cotherill at the time of the beginning of the Rebellion, was a calf of a cow believed to be plundered from Edward Cottam by Rich. Hobin.

3 November. John Hatch demanded from estate of Tho. Allen (dec'd).

John Walton by his attorney George Manners demanded of Edward Hudson damages for said Hudson entrusted

f. 374 with goods by said Walton's wife.

Edward Commins vs. George Manners.

Humphrey Howell acknowledged a debt to Phillip Land.

3 November at St. Maries'. Court. John Medley, John Shertcliff, Walter Peake, William Browne, John Mansell, Stephen Salmon, Edward Packer, Phillip Auther, Mr. Robert Clarke, John Courts, John Warren, John Thimbleby, Dan. Clocker fined. Except: John Maunsell, John Warren, Dan. Clocker, Edward Packer, Mr. Clarke, John Courts, Stephen Salmon. Jury: John Maunsell, Edward Cottam, Antho. Rawlins, Robert Kedger, John Warren, Walt. Waterlin, Robert Sharpe, Humphrey Howell, Dan. Clocker, Edw. Hull, Hen. Pountney.
- Lt. Rich. Banks, George Manners.
- Edward Packer, Walter Smith.

f. 375 George Manners vs. Edward Commins & Nic. Browne (of Kent). Mentions: estate of Hen. Boston.

Robert Smith vs. Walt. Beane. Mentions: chattel bought of Mr. John Lewger.
- Edward Packer deposed that Mr. Lewger sold chattel to Walter Beane.
- Walter Beane deposed.

Henry Mosely (of Chicacoan) vs. William Lewis. Defendant is represented by William Bretton.

f. 376 Humphrey Howell vs. Anthony Rawlins. Mentions: payment to Francis Vanden.

Walter Waterlin vs. John Thimbleby administrator of Peter Mackarell.

Walter Beane demanded of Walter Coterill.

Humphrey Howell demanded of Anthony Rawlins.

William Smoote deposed that he sold to Jeoffrey Power (of VA) chattel & said Power claimed damages.

f. 377 4 November. Anthony Rawlins petitioned regarding his bill to John Sturman.

Robert Sharpe, at the request of Rich. Bennett, deposed regarding chattel that Rich. Bennett provided Gov. Calvert, et.al.

4 November at St. Maries'. Court. Thomas Burbage per his attorney Cuth. Fenwick vs. George Manners.

Liber - Patent Record Z & A - 1637-1651

George Manners, at the request of Edward Hudson, deposed that he heard Mr. Bretton demanded of Tho. Munday & said Munday demanded of Mr. Bretton an execution vs. John Walton in suit of Edward Hudson.

f. 378 William Bretton deposed the same.

Cuth. Fenwick (gentleman) vs. Capt. John Price.

Cuthbert Fenwick demanded of Edward Hudson.

Mrs. Margarett Brent vs. Peter Knight (merchant).

John Maunsell demanded of William Stiles.

f. 379 John Holfhead demanded of John Hatch or Richard Banks (administrators of Thomas Allen (dec'd)).

George Manners acknowledged an execution on chattel of Mr. Tho. Baldridge & delivered it to Mrs. Marg. Brent. Mrs. Margarett Brent acknowledged sale of said chattel to John Holfhead.

Henry Pountney demanded of Edw. Hudson.

Francis Brookes (gentleman) vs. Edward Commins.

6 November. Mrs. Margarett Brent His Lordship's Attorney vs. Edw. Commins.

Anthony Rawlins vs. Francis Poesy.

f. 380 Mrs. Margarett Brent vs. Edward Commins (of Kent). Mentions: Capt. Cleyborne. On 16 November 1649, Mrs. Margarett Brent vs. Edward Commins resolved. Signed: Marg. Brent, Edward Comins. Witness: Tho. Hatton.

6 November at St. Maries'. Court. Edward Cottham requested chattel which Tho. Baker was taking to Appamatucks on 16 October. Per Walter Coteril & George Manners.

f. 381 Blanch Oliver & Charles Rawlinson deposed for Tho. Baker.

Mrs. Margarett Brent vs. Thomas Bradnox.

Edw. Commins petitioned regarding the suit by the Lord Proprietor. Mrs. Marg. Brent

f. 382 His Lordship's Attorney vs. Edward Commins. George Manners deposed. Thomas Greene, Esq. (Governor) acknowledged receipt of Edward Commins. Mrs. Margarett Brent His Lordship's Attorney acknowledged receipt. Date: 16 November 1649.

7 November. Thomas Mathewes demanded of Richard Duke.

Subpoena to John Shertcliff (at the request of Edw. Commins)

f. 383 to testify in suit vs. Fran. Brookes.

Edward Packer demanded of Francis Van Enden.

Giles Brent sold to Mr. Thomas Bradnox (of Kent) chattel, some with the mark of John Abbott. Date: 25 June 1648. Witnesses: Thomas Mathewes, Phillip Conner.

Edward Commins (of Isle of Kent) acknowledged debt to Mrs. Margaret Brent. Signed: Edward Comins. Witness: William Bretton.

f. 384 Tho. Greene, Esq. (Governor) appointed Giles Brent, Esq. as judge in the cause against himself & Capt. Robert Vaughan.

Edward Commins acknowledged defaming Francis Brooks.

James Langworth vs. William Wheatley that said Wheateley in 1644 took chattel from Nicolas Harvey. Subpoena to Joseph Edlow & his wife.

Mrs. Margarett Brent His Lordship's Attorney demanded of Mr. Cuthbert Fenwick attorney of Capt. Thomas Cornwallyes, being 1/2 assumption of Rich. Ingle (mariner).

Robert Percy (gentleman) deposed for His Lordship that in 1643 that he was at St. Inego's when Capt. Thomas Cornwalleys before Mr. Giles Brent (Governor) assumed that

Liber - Patent Record Z & A - 1637-1651

f. 385 Richard Ingle (mariner) should pay for defense of the Colony.

8 November. Francis Brooks (gentleman) demanded of Francis Lumbard.

Francis Brooks (gentleman) demanded of Robert Short.

Francis Brooks (gentleman) demanded of Thomas Pett.

Francis Brooks (gentleman) demanded of Edward Cole.

Thomas Greene, Esq. (Governor) vs. Capt. Robert Vaughan (Commander of Isle of Kent).

f. 386 Subpoena to Mr. Francis Brooks to bring said Capt. Vaughan to court.
- Francis Brooks (gentleman), age 40, deposed that soon after the Governor's departure from Isle of Kent last Summer, he heard Capt. Vaughan make certain remarks. Mentions: Capt. Brent.
- Lt. William Evans deposed that last September, that at the house of Capt. Vaughan in Isle of Kent, Capt. Vaughan made certain remarks. Mentions: Governor Greene, Capt. Brent, Mr. Cox.

f. 387 Nicholas Cawsine demanded of Edward Commins (of Kent).

Francis Brooks (gentleman), at the request of Capt. Giles Brent, deposed that last Fall, he was present at the house of Henry Morgan & saw Edward Commins depose regarding the destruction of chattel of Capt. Brent.

Francis Brooks (gentleman), at the request of Capt. Giles Brent, deposed that he was present when Capt. Vaughan examined Roger Baxter last Fall regarding the destruction of chattel of Capt. Brent by Edw. Commins.

9 November. Francis Brooks (gentleman) vs. William Jones (of Kent).

f. 388 Notice: John Gressam (planter, of Kent) had participated in the Rebellion & was pardoned by general pardon on 16 April 1647 & lately by Thomas Greene, Esq. (Governor) on 3 March 1647 (except for Richard Ingle (mariner)). He persists in his attitude & is to be turned over as a rebel.

f. 389 Warrants to: William Tompson (sheriff of St. Maries'), Henry Morgan (sheriff of Kent).

10 November. Robert Clarke (gentleman) demanded of Edward Hudson.

11 November. Notice from the Governor: powers on Isle of Kent revoked from Capt. Robert Vaughan. Mr. Phillip Conner to administer justice. Signed: Thomas Greene.

Notice: added to your office of High Sheriff of Kent, command of the militia. Signed: Tho. Greene. To: Henry Morgan.

f. 390 14 November. Ralphe Beane demanded of William Smithfield.

Ralphe Beane demanded of John Nevell & Christopher Carnoll.

Ralphe Beane demanded of Joseph Edlow.

Ralphe Beane demanded of Walter Pekes.

18 November. Henry Pountney demanded 200 a. for transporting self & 1 manservant Tho. Payne in 1644. Warrant issued for head of Herring Creek in New Towne Hundred.

23 November. William Thompson demanded of Thomas Petite.

Thomas Pasmore by his attorney Rich. Browne demanded of Tho. Petite.

f. 391 John Hatch vs. John Hallowes (of Appamatucks) for transporting out of the Province John Wallton who was indebted to the complainants.

Barnaby Jackson vs. John Hallowes (of Appamatucks) for transporting out of the Province John Walton (cooper) who was indebted to the complainants.

27 November. Walter Smith vs. Robert Clarke (gentleman). Subpoena to John Brisco.

Thomas Oliver demanded an attachment to John Hallowes for transporting out of the Province John Walton who was indebted to the complainants.

Liber - Patent Record Z & A - 1637-1651

28 November. Thomas Copley, Esq. by his attorney Thomas Mathews vs. Tho. Speake (gentleman).

f. 392   29 November. Thomas Hebden vs. William Marshall & John Hatch. Subpoena to Robert Ward.

Notice from the Lord Proprietor. John Nunne (gentleman) transported self in 1640. On assignment from Tho. Bushell, he is due 200 a. per Mr. Lewger. Grant of land in Breton Bay west of William Assetter, south of William Browne,

f. 393   for 300 a. Date: 11 October 1647.

John Nunne (planter) sold to John Shertcliff & Henry Spinke (planters), land in New Towne on south side of Breton's Bay, 150 a. Date: 20 October 1648. Witnesses: William Bretton, Phillip Land.

f. 394   Grant to William Bretton (gentleman) who transported self, his wife, & 1 child & 3 manservants in 1637. Said Bretton is lawful heir of Thomas Nabbes who transported self & his wife in 1637. Grant is for land in Patowmeck River, near Heron Island,

f. 395   750 a., called Manner of Little Brittain. Date: 10 July 1640. Signed: Leonard Calvert.

1 December. John Mottrom (gentleman) by his attorney Thomas Speake (gentleman) demanded of Humphrey Howell.

Robert Clarke (gentleman) demanded of Walter Smith. Subpoena to: Wal. Beane, John Walton, John Greenold, Hum.

f. 396   Howell, Francis Poesy, Lt. William Evans.

Paul Simpson vs. Capt. Edward Hill.

4 December. His Lordship's Attorney vs. Tho. Bradnox (of Isle of Kent). Subpoena to John Howard.

4 December at St. John's. Court. Attendees: The Governor, Giles Brent, Mr. Tho. Gerard. Warrant for jury: John Medley, Rich. Nevett, John Court, William Assiter, Mr. Robert Clarke, William Browne, John Nunne, John Grimsditch, Hum. Howell, Robert Ward, Walter Peake, John Shertcliffe, WIlliam Whittle, Ant. Rawlins, Tho. Mathews, John Nevell, George Manners, Phill. Authur, John Norman, Fran. Poesy.

His Lordship's Attorney vs. Blanch Howell, regarding suit of Tho. Baker vs. Edward Cottham.

f. 397   John Medley demanded of Marks Pheypo.

John Nevell assigned chattel to Walter Bean.

Walter Smith vs. Robert Clarke (gentleman).

Thomas Gerard, Esq. attorney for Martin Johnson (mariner) demanded of estate of Thomas Allen (dec'd). John Hatch (administrator) denied the request.

f. 398   Walter Waterlin demanded of John Hatch administrator of Thomas Allen (dec'd).

Anthony Rawlins demanded an attachment to estate of John Hallowes (of Appamatucks) for transporting John Waltham out of the Province who was indebted to the complainants.

Mary, wife of Thomas Bradnox, demanded from the estate of William Coxe (of Isle of Kent, dec'd) chattel. Also she demanded chattel given by Francis Cox (dec'd) wife of said Cox. Summons to Capt. Vaughan.

5 December. Walter Gweast demanded of Anthony Rawlins. Subpoena to William Stevenson & Edward Hull (at the request of the defendant).

Robert Smith by his attorney George Manners demanded of John Thimbleby out of the estate of Peter Mackerell (dec'd).

John Hallowes demanded of John Thimbleby from estate of Peter Mackerell (dec'd), on assignment from Robert Heuett (of Chicacoan).

f. 399   5 December at house of Barnaby Jackson. Court. Attendees: The Governor, Giles Brent, Mr. Tho. Gerard. John Medley vs. Marks Pheypo per his attorney George Manners.

Liber - Patent Record Z & A - 1637-1651

William Ashbiston petitioned that he has served his indenture to his master Tho. Allen. John Hatch (administrator) acknowledged completion of service.

Cuth. Fenwick vs. Capt. John Price.
* William Bretton (gentleman) deposed.
* James Langworth deposed. Mentions: Charles Rawlinson.

Warrant for a grand jury: John Hatch, Wal. Waterlin, Rich. Browne, John Greenold, Anth. Rawlins, John Holfhead, Edw. Hull, Geo. Manners, Thomas War, Rich. Bennett, Henry Spinke, William Hungerford.

His Lordship's Attorney vs. Tho. Bradnox

f. 400 (of Isle of Kent). Mentions: John Howard, Mr. Bradnox, John Mallham, Mr. Bretton, John Palmer, Mr. Bradnox & his wife, Governor, Mr. Brent.

Edward Commins vs. Francis Brooks. Mentions: previous suit held at house of Henry Morgan on Isle of Kent on 22 June.

f. 401 Mr. William Thompson sold to Water Waterlin chattel. Signed: William Tompson. Witnesses: Rich. Browne, William Assiter.

Mrs. Margaret Brent His Lordship's Attorney sold to William Whitle (soldier of St. Inego's Fort) chattel. Date: 21 January 1647. Witnesses: John Mettcalfe, John Pritchett.

6 December at St. John's. Court. Attendees: Governor, G. Brent, Mr. Tho. Gerard. At the request of Giles Brent, Esq., whereas Thomas or John Sturman were to prove title to certain chattel, in question between said Brent & the said parties.

f. 402 Mrs. Margarett Brent requested continuance of her suit with Edw. Commins & her suit with Mr. Bradnox.

Governor vs. Capt. Robert Vaughan.

Edward Commins petitioned regarding the complaint by John Dandy.

Anthony Rawlins petitioned, producing a deposition by George Manners. Bill passed to John Sturman in exchange for chattel. The chattel was taken & delivered to Capt. Giles Brent.

f. 403 Edw. Commins vs. George Manners.

Robert Holt, age 28, deposed on 23 October 1648 that George Manners desired Henry Clay to speak to Edw. Commins.

Henry Clay, age 27, deposed on 27 October 1648 that in speaking with George Manners at his house, he asked the deponent if he saw chattel in Commin's boat.

f. 404 James Walker demanded of Nicholas Gwyther.

Thomas Jackson by his attorney Nicholas Gwyther demanded of William Bretton. James Walker deposed. William Bretton deposed.

Nicholas Cawsin vs. Edward Commins. Mentions: Capt. Vaughan.

Walter Smith vs. Robert Clarke. Rich. Browne & Humphrey Howell to adjudicate.

Edward Commins petitioned regarding the suit by Francis Brooks.

f. 405 Henry Morgan, age 30, deposed on 26 November 1648 that about 4 years ago, Francis Brooks received payment for use of Edward Commins, being due Commins from John Powell.

Thomas Keene, age 55, deposed that about 4 years ago, the deponent received an attachment of Mr. Wyatt in a suit concerning Francis Brooks & Edw. Commins, chattel in custody of Henry Morgan. Bill delivered to Francis Brooks by the wife of Edw. Commins. Witness: John Mottrom.

Robert Clarke (gentleman) vs. Walter Smith.

f. 406 Blanch Oliver alias Howell vs. Nat. Pope.

All suits vs. John Hallowes.

James Langworth vs. William Wheatley.
* Henry Spinke deposed that the defendant took chattel from house of Nic.

Liber - Patent Record Z & A - 1637-1651

Harvey.
- Defendant stated he was under command of Capt. Tho. Baldridge.

f. 407 Edward Commins vs. Robert Simkin.

Thomas Busrode per his attorney Thomas Mathewes vs. Capt. Giles Brent. Attorney of Cuth. Fenwick posted bond for the plaintiff. Mentions: Tho. Gerrard.
- Tho. Gerard, Esq. deposed.
- Capt. Giles Brent deposed. Mentions: his arrest in James Towne, Mr. Richards (judge in County Court).

f. 408 Mrs. Margaret Brent vs. Peter Knight (merchant).
- Nicolas Browne, age 40, deposed that in 1646, Mr. Peter Knight was at the deponent's house, when a shot was heard at the house of Capt. Brent.
- William Jones (of Isle of Kent), age 34, deposed on 25 September 1648 that in April 1646, he saw chattel loaded on a sloop belonging to Mr. Knight.

f. 409 ...
- Richard Cotsford deposed on 28 September 1648 that in July or August 1646, the deponent saw Mr. Peter Knight take chattel from Kent Mill, and other items during the Rebellion. Mentions: Governor Mr. Calvert, Mr. Browne, Mr. Brent, Mrs. Brent.

f. 410 Edward Smith petitioned in suit vs. William Bretton for his service. Subpoena to Francis Poesy.

William Wheatley demanded of Owen James. Subpoena to William Stevenson.

f. 411 7 December at St. Maries'. Court. Attendees: Governor, C. Giles Brent, Mr. Thomas Gerard. Motion regarding chattel of His Lordship's stock. Paid to Geoffrey Power who sold it to William Smoote & Mr. Cuth. Fenwick now owns.

Mrs. Margaret Brent petitioned regarding the patent of Mr. Leonard Calvert.

Walter Peakes demanded 100 a. on assignment from Geoffrey Oliver who transported self in 1646. Warrant for head of Nevell's Creek in Brittaine Bay.

Nicholas Gwyther demanded an attachment against the estate of Thomas Jackson.

f. 412 Giles Brent, Esq. demanded of Cuth. Fenwick attorney of Capt. Tho. Cornwallyes. Mentions: Richard Ingle (mariner) in 1643.

Francis Van Enden demanded of Francis Posey.

Francis Van Enden demanded of John Hatch.

Francis Van Enden demanded of Robert Clark.

Thomas Bradnox, age 40, deposed that in the Winter of 1644, Capt. William Cleyborne (one of the Councell of VA) came to Isle of Kent and incited a rebellion against Mr. Brent. They

f. 413 marched from the house of Edward Commins to the house of John Abbott.

f. 414 Capt. Cleyborne urged the inhabitants to go with his cozen Tompson.

9 December. Capt. Robert Vaughan petitioned the Governor to withdraw the action.

f. 415 Edward Commins demanded of Nicholas Browne.

Edw. Commins demanded of Robert Short.

Edw. Commins demanded of Thomas Pett.

Edw. Commins vs. Edw. Hudson regarding chattel due from John Deare.

Edward Commins demanded of Henry Clay.

Edward Commins demanded of William Lant.

11 December. Capt. Robert Vaughan vs. Tho. Bradnox.

f. 416 Proclamation by the Governor. Proclamation was sent to inhabitants of Isle of Kent on 11 November to suspend authority of Capt. Robert Vaughan. Authority is re-instated. Mentions: Mr. Phillip Conner. Appointment

Liber - Patent Record Z & A - 1637-1651

f. 417 of Mr. Nicholas Browne as assistant. Signed: Thomas Greene.

Mr. Nicholas Browne deposed on 20 November 1647, in an inquiry by Mr. Francis Brooks concerning chattel of the Lord Proprietor, that 5 weeks ago, he heard Henry Morgan declare that William Lant related there was chattel killed at Broad Creek which belonged to John Abbott.

Mr. Isaack Hine, age 28, deposed on 20 November 1647, in the case of Mr. Francis Brooks vs. Richard Span, that he was at Abbott's house last August when Richard Span killed chattel & additional chattel was killed by John Palmer.

Nicolas Browne deposed on 20 November 1647, in the case of Mr. Francis Brooks vs. Richard Span, that about 6 weeks ago, he was talking with Richard Span concerning chattel killed

f. 418 at Abbott's house.

Rich. Cotsford, age 20, deposed on 20 November 1647, in the case between Francis Brooks & Edm. Lennin & Andrew (N) (Mr. Commin's man of Kent) that 3 weeks ago, Edm. Lennin spoke of killing chattel of Abbott.

18 December. John Shertcliffe demanded 100 a. for transporting self in 1646. Warrant for 100 a. in Broad Neck at New Towne.

Capt. Giles Brent (attorney for administrator of Henry Brooks (merchant, dec'd)) demanded of Capt. Robert Vaughan, for chattel that Mr. Cox had from Mr. Tho. Weston due Mr. Henry Brooks.

Owen James demanded of Humphrey Attwicks.

19 December. John Shertcliffe registered a cattle mark.

f. 419 Mary daughter of John Shertcliffe registered a cattle mark.

Henry Spinke registered a cattle mark.

20 December. On 15 November 1648, Mr. Robert Clarke returned a survey for Phillip Land (gentleman) at the mouth of St. Hierom's Creek, containing 500 a.

Owen James by his attorney Phillip Land demanded of John Thimbleby administrator of Peter Mackarell (dec'd).

The surveyor returned a survey for William Edwin on the west side of St. George's River for 50 a.

f. 420 Patent registered for St. Williams.

Edward Cottham vs. Thomas Baker.

29 December. Walter Beans & Walter Peakes requested administration of the estate of William Smithfield (dec'd), being the greatest creditors. Smithfield died intestate & has no kindred in the Province. Appraisers: Richard Nevett, John Shertcliff, John Grimsditch.

f. 421 Warrant to Mr. William Tompson to empanel a jury to inquire into death of William Smithfield (who drowned in Bretton's Bay).

Indenture between Thomas Green, Esq. & Hanah Mathewes. Said Hanah is to serve 4 years. Date: 25 April 1647. Signed: Tho. Greene, Hannah Mathews. Witness: Nathaniel Pope.

f. 422 Walter Peakes demanded of William Smoote.

f. 423 Subpoena to: Humphrey Howell, John Grimsditch.

2 January. William Edwin demanded of John Hallowes (of Appamatucks).

8 January. Edward Hull, at the request of Anthony Rawlins, deposed that Walter Gweast was at the home of Anth. Rawlins about 1 year ago, when said Rawlins gave Gweast chattel for being his attorney against Mr. Fenwick.

William Bretton assigned to John Maunsell 50 a. for 1 able man servant Edward Smith.

Stephen Salmon assigned to John Maunsell 50 a. for transporting self in 1646.

John Maunsell demanded 100 a. Warrant for the head of Brittaine's Bay, against the plantation of John Grimsditch.

Liber - Patent Record Z & A - 1637-1651

Stephen Salmon demanded 50 a. Warrant for north side of Brittaine Bay.

f. 424 Robert Robins demanded of Ralph Beane. Subpoena to Mr. Tompson & John Maunsell.

William Stephenson deposed that last Summer, he was in the field of Robert Kedger, he heard Owen James & William Wheatley discussing a new plantation.

Humphrey Howell, age 35, deposed that he as a skipper on a vessell of Mr. Rosier, he heard Mr. Rosier speak to John Mallham at Chicacoane in March 1645.

Capt. William Stone demanded of John Hatch & Richard Banks administrators of Tho. Allen (dec'd).

George Manners demanded of John Hatch & Richard Banks administrators of Thomas Allen (dec'd).

Notice by the Governor on adjournment

f. 425 until 5 February. Signed: Tho. Greene.

Robert Sharpe assigned to Capt. William Hawley 100 a. for transporting self in 1646. Witness: John Hatch.

Marks Pheypo assigned all land to Capt. William Hawley: 100 a. from Tho. Pursall for James Lindsey, 100 a. due William Maclaughlin, 100 a. from Owen Seymore, 100 a. from William Macfenine, 100 a. in his own right, 100 a. from the late Governor.

Robert Clarke demanded 100 a. for transporting self in 1638 & 250 a. for transporting 3 servants in 1640: William Shepherd, Roger Pletso, Mary Shepherd. Assignment to Capt. William Haweley.

William Stone assigned his right for transporting 6 persons to Capt. William Hawley: James Morphew, Marke Blunfield, Michael Bassatt, Negro Phillis, William Watts, Nicolas Holmes.

Cuth. Fenwick (gentleman) assigned to Capt. William Haweley 2000 a. due self & Capt. Tho. Cornwalleys. In 1640: Lt. Nicolas Gwyther, Rich. Farmer, Edm. Jacus, Hierom Coote, John Mishell, George Winches, Morrice Froman. In 1641: Hen. Brooks, William Durford, John Cole.

John Shertcliff assigned to Capt. William Haweley 200 a.: 100 a. for transporting self & 100 a. on assignment from Edward Smith for transporting self in 1646.

f. 426 Capt. William Hawley demanded 4250 a. due on assignment from: Mr. Fenwick (2000 a.), Capt. Stone for transporting 6 men in this year (1100 a.), Marks Pheypo (500 a.), Mr. Clarke (350 a.), Robert Sharpe (100 a.), John Shertcliffe (200 a.). Warrant for 4250 a. on south side of Patuxent River between Machewetts Creek & Sacqueakitts.

9 January. Francis Vandan demanded of Charles Rawlinson.

Francis Vandan demanded of Marks Pheypo.

13 January. Capt. John Price demanded 100 a. for transporting 1 able man servant Richard Browne in 1637, & 200 a. for transporting 2 able man servants Tho. Jackson & William Hardidge in 1636, & 100 a. for transporting 1 able man servant Edward Williams in 1644, & 100 a. for transporting self about 11 years ago.

15 January. Thomas War by his attorney Robert Sharpe demanded of Tho. Ashbrooke.

Cuth. Fenwick demanded of John Shertcliff & Henry Spinke.

Cuth. Fenwick demanded of Walter Peakes.

Cuth. Fenwick demanded of Robert Smith.

Cuth. Fenwick demanded of Robert Wiseman.

f. 427 Cuth. Fenwick demanded of Joseph Edlow.

Robert Clarke demanded of Capt. William Hawely & Mr. John Wilkins.

Liber - Patent Record Z & A - 1637-1651

Francis Poesy demanded 100 a. for transporting self in 1640 & 100 a. for transporting 1 able man servant Joseph Gregory in 1640, & 100 a. on assignment from John Knott who transported self in 1643 & 100 a. on assignment from John Villaine who transported self in 1646. Warrant for Wicocomoco River on north side of Mr. Neale's Creek.

Thomas Ashbrook demanded 200 a. for transporting self & his wife in 1648 & 100 a. on assignment from his brother John Ashbrooke who transported self in the same year. Warrant for land adjoining grant for Francis Poesy on Wicocomoco River.

George Manners vs. Edward Hall.

Nicolas Keytin vs. Capt. Giles Brent.

f. 428 Robert Duglas by his attorney John Hallowes demanded of Gabriel Odgers attorney for Mr. Tho. Thorneborough.

Mr. Robert Clarke returned the survey for William Tompson, called Indian Quarters on east side of St. Clement's Bay in Patowmack River for 250 a. [See f. 477.]

Mr. Robert Clarke returned the survey of Walter Peakes on south side of Nevett's Creek in Bretton's Bay for 100 a., called St. Anne's.

Capt. William Stone demanded an execution against estate of Mr. Thomas Weston (dec'd).

f. 429 16 January. Sheriff reported that the estate of Mr. Weston is overpaid.

17 January. Notice for assessment of real estate of Mr. Tho. Weston.

Edward Langford assigned to Mr. Phillip Land all right for transporting self in 1648. Phillip Land demanded 100 a. Warrant for 100 a. at head of Deep Creek joining land of Gov. Calvert, known as Trinity Mannor.

24 January. John Gray demanded 100 a. for transporting self in 1640.

f. 430 John Gwy assigned the right to the aforesaid to Thomas Petite. Thomas Petite demanded 100 a. aforesaid & 100 a. on assignment from Nicolas Cawsin & 100 a. for transporting his wife in 1639 & 50 a. for transporting 1 child Catherine Petite in 1645.

Robert Ward demanded of Walter Waterlin due from Robert Simkin.

Capt. John Price demanded from the estate of Hen. Brooks (merchant).

William Broughe demanded of John Thimbleby from estate of Peter Mackerell.

8 February. George Manners deposed that he paid Abraham Johnson at Kent on 1 February last for the use of Capt. William Stone for a maid servant bought by deponent of said Stone, now in the possession of Tho. Greene (Governor).

George Manners attorney for Nicolas Keytin & Marks Pheypo demanded of Mrs. Margaret Brent.

George Manners demanded of Mrs. Margaret Brent for use of Capt. Edward Hill.

Robert Greane, Esq. demanded 100 a. for transporting self in 1648.

Walter Beane demanded of Lt. William Lewis.

f. 431 9 February. George Manners demanded of Edward Hudson 1 year's service.

Edward Packer acknowledged a debt to Rich. Lord (?) (merchant).

John Maunsell, at the request of Robert Robins, deposed that sometime last Summer, Ralphe Beane & William Stiles came to the house of Mr. Tompson.

Francis Van Enden acknowledged a debt to Edward Packer.

f. 432 9 February at St. John's. Court. Warrant for jury: Lt. William Lewis, Tho. Mathewes, John Maunsell, Nic. Gwyther, Robert Kedger, Hen. Spinke, Hen. Pountney, Rich. Browne, Tho. Hebden, John Lewger, Mr. Clarke, Jos. Edlow, Mr. Fenwick, Owen James, William Boreman, George Manners, Robert Sharpe, Robert Ward, Robert Robins, Robert Wiseman, Robert Simkin. Rich. Browne, Jos. Edlow, Richard Ward, & Robert Wiseman did not appear.

Liber - Patent Record Z & A - 1637-1651

Henry Spinke petitioned regarding the judgement against the estate of Nic. Harvey. George Manners, Robert Robins, John Maunsell, & Owen James appointed to value the chattel.

Thomas Hebden vs. Tho. Jackson.

f. 433 Mrs. Bradnox vs. estate of William Cox (of Kent). Mentions: George Manners, Capt. Robert Vaughan.

Blanch Oliver (alias Howell) vs. Nath. Pope. George Manners attorney for John Hallowes deposed that the chattel did not belong to Nath. Pope, but to John Hallowes. Walter Gweast attorney for said Blanch requested a continuance.

Mrs. Margarett Brent His Lordship's Attorney vs. Capt. Thomas Cornwallis. Cuthbert Fenwick attorney for Capt. Tho. Cornwalleys requested a continuance. Mentions: Mr. Percy, Capt. Giles Brent.

George Manners vs. Mrs. Margaret Brent. Payment for use of Capt. Edward Hill for Roanoke & Peake loaned to Gov. Calvert.

f. 434 Cuth. Fenwick (gentleman) vs. John Shertcliff & Henry Spinke.

William Wheateley vs. Owen James.
- Robert Kedger deposed that Owen James & the deponent had made a covenant with the plaintiff.
- Owen James deposed the same.

Barnaby Jackson vs. John Hallowes for transporting out of the Province John Walton. George Manners is attorney for the defendant.

Thomas Speake (gentleman) by his attorney Edw. Packer vs. Mr. Thomas Copley.

f. 435 10 February at St. John's. Court. John Nevell, at the request of Francis Van Enden, deposed that last Christmas at the house of Tho. Peteet, Mr. John Hallowes bargained with Francis Van Enden.

Thomas Hebden vs. Tho. Jackson.

Nicolas Gwyther vs. Tho. Jackson.

Mrs. Margaret Brent vs. Edward Commins. George Manners is attorney for defendant. Mentions: Capt. Giles Brent.

f. 436 Robert Clarke (gentleman) petitioned in suit by Walter Smith.

Suits of William Edwin, Anthony Rawlins, & John Hatch against John Hallowes were dismissed.

George Manners declared that he is the attorney for John Hallowes of Appamatucks in MD.

Nicolas Gwyther petitioned regarding payment for judgement to James Walker for the use of Tho. Jackson. Mentions: William Bretton.

f. 437 Cuthbert Fenwick (gentleman) assigned to Edmund Smith, a judgement against John Shertcliffe & Henry Spinke.

12 February. Margaret Brent (spinster) sold to Barnaby Jackson (taylor) chattel. Witness: William Bretton.

Margaret Brent executrix of Leonard Calvert, Esq. sold to Henry Pountney "John Norton's Plantation" in Trinity Creek, 90 a. Witnesses: Cuth. Fenwick, Edmund Smith.

f. 438 Thomas Gerard, Esq. appointed Capt. Giles Brent as his attorney. Date: 10 June 1648. Witnesses: Edw. Hill, Cuth. Fenwick. Endorsed for my sister Mrs. Margaret Brent.

Survey for John Shertcliff in New Towne, adjoining land of Rich. Hill, Piccomoco Creek, Patowmack River, Broad Creek, land formerly of John Nunn in possession of said Shertcliff, 100 a. [See f. 474.] Signed: Robert Clarke.

Survey for John Maunsell (planter) on west side of Bretton Bay, adjoining Maunsell's Marsh, 100 a. Signed: Robert Clarke.

Edmund Smith (gentleman) sold to

f. 439 Cuth. Fenwick (gentleman), all land & chattel in England. Date: 10 February

Liber - Patent Record Z & A - 1637-1651

1648. Witnesses: Phillip Land, William Bretton. Estate is in hands of his uncles: Mr. Lawrence Tuttersall of Odstock in Wiltshire, & Mr. Peter Tuttersall of Chideeck in Dorsetshire. Signed: Tho. Greene.

20 February. George Manners assigned to Mr. William Eltonhead 150 a. for transporting self & his son William Manners in 1646 & 250 a. on assignment from John Hallowes.

William Eltonhead (gentleman) demanded 2000 a. for transporting self in 1648 & transporting 6 able men: William Chappell, Joseph Edlow, Jeoffrey Gaunt, Edward Langton, Nicolas Smith, & John Charman & 1 maid servant Anne Davis & 1 boy

f. 440 (under age 16) Joseph Edlow & 1 freewoman wife to said Edlow & assignment from George Manners of 400 a. Warrant for Machewatts Creek on south side of Patuxent River downward to Cedar Poynt.

Lt. William Evans demanded 100 a. for transporting self in 1648. Date: 1 December 1648.

John Jarbo demanded 100 a. for transporting self in 1646. Date: 1 December 1648.

Warrant to lay out 100 a. for Lt. William Evans & John Jarbo in Bretton's Bay. Date: 4 December 1648.

Anthony Rawlins demanded 100 a. on assignment from Tho. Pasmore. Warrant for head of Gov. Calvert's Creek.

7 March. Ralph Beane demanded of Phillip Auther.

Ralphe Beane demanded of John Shertcliff & Henry Spinke.

Ralphe Beane demanded of John Wiseman.

Ralphe Beane demanded of John Nunne.

Ralphe Beane demanded of Joseph Edlow.

Ralphe Beane demanded of Elias Beach.

Ralphe Beane demanded of John Warren.

f. 441 Ralphe Beane demanded of Anthony Rawlins.

Ralphe Beane demanded of Henry Fox.

Ralphe Beane demanded of William Smoote.

Ralphe Beane demanded of Thomas Hamper.

Ralphe Beane demanded of William Edwin.

Ralphe Beane demanded of John Thimbleby administrator of Peter Mackerell (dec'd).

Ralphe Beane demanded of John Thimbleby.

Ralph Beane demanded of John Wheatley.

8 March. Thomas Gerard, Esq. by his attorney William Bretton demanded of John Thimbleby administrator of Peter Mackerell (dec'd).

Robert Kedger demanded of Cuth. Fenwick.

William Bretton demanded 200 a. for transporting 2 maid servants: Mary Field last year, & Martha Crab in 1648. Warrant for 100 a. adjoining his land in Brettaine Bay.

9 March. Ralphe Beane demanded of Edward Packer.

f. 442 Henry Morgan by his attorney George Manners demanded of Mrs. Margarett Brent attorney of Capt. Giles Brent.

18 March. John Warren demanded of John Thimbleby & William Browne.

Phillip Land demanded of Mrs. Margaret Brent.

Liber - Patent Record Z & A - 1637-1651

George Manners demanded of estate of Thomas Allen (dec'd).

Cuth. Fenwick (gentleman) demanded of estate of Thomas Allen (dec'd).

Robert Smith, Walter Waterlin, & Walter Beane demanded of estate of Thomas Allen (dec'd).

Thomas Ashbrook & John Ashbrooke (planters, of New Towne) assigned their rights to 300 a. in Wiccocomoco River to Francis Poesy & John Burlane (of New Towne). Date: 17 March 1648. Witness: Robert Clarke.

Henry Morgan, age 33, deposed that last October, Mrs. Cox was dangerously sick, & she desired certain chattel to go to Mrs. Bradnox. Witness: Phillip Conner.

f. 443 Phillip Andrey deposed on 23 November 1647, that when Mrs. Cox (now dec'd) was sick, she gave chattel to Mrs. Bradnox & her child. Witness: Giles Brent.

Phillip Conner, age 32, deposed that he heard Mrs. Cox say she gave chattel to Mrs. Bradnox. Witness: Robert Vaughan.

Margaret Winchester deposed that 2 days before she died, Mrs. Cox said she would give chattel to Mrs. Bradnox. Witness: Phillip Conner.

Edward Ebbs deposed that chattel belonging to Mrs. Cox was residing at Capt. Vaughan after the Governor & Capt. Brent left. Witness: Phillip Conner.

From Charles Rex. Thomas Copley (gentleman) is alien borne & may be subject to trouble because of his religion. He is given freedom to practice his religion. Date: 10 December 10th year of reign, at Westminster.

f. 444 Thomas Greene, Esq. demanded 500 a. in his wife's right Mrs. Ann Cox for immigrating in 1633 & 50 a. for 1 maid servant Ann Pyke in 1638 & 150 a. for 1 man & 1 maid servant Henry Adams & Anne Norrise in 1639 & 50 a. for 1 maid servant Margaret Nutbrowne in 1640 & 50 a. for 1 maid servant Alice Phillips in 1648 & 100 a. on assignment from his brother Robert Greene, Esq. Warrant for north side of St. Hierom's Creek.

Walter Peakes & John Slingsby have joined in partnership for 5 years. Mentions: Peake's wife, Peake's children. Date:14 March 1648. Witnesses: Jeoffrey Oliver, William Styles, John Jarbo.

f. 445 Survey for Ralphe Beane on north side of Patowmack River, bounding Herring Creek, St. George's Creek, land of John Prichyard, for 1500 a. Called Piney Point. [Patent f. 507] Signed: Robert Clarke.

Margarett Brent His Lordship's Attorney sold to Barnaby Jackson chattel, being part of wages of Nicolas Gwyther. Date: 28 March 1648. Witness: James Lindsey. Delivered on 10 March 1647. Date: 2 December 1647. Margarett Brent sold to Barnaby Jackson chattel, provisions regarding said Jackson or John Greenwell. Signed: Thomas Greene (Governor).

f. 446 Margarett Brent His Lordship's Attorney confirmed the sale.

Survey for Stephen Salmon (planter) on west side of Bretton Bay, bounding St. Stephen's Spring, land formerly granted to William Broughe & now owned by said Stephen, for 50 a. [Patent f. 481] Date: 24 January 1648. Signed: Robert Clarke.

Survey for John Wheateley on east side of Packer's Creek, on west side of St. George's River, bounding Wheatley's Fresh, St. John's Spring, for 50 a. [Patent f. 484] Date: 26 January 1648. Signed: Robert Clarke.

15 March at St. John's. Court. Warrant for jury: James Walker, Elias Beach, John Shertcliff, Rich. Banks, Nic. Keytin, Walt. Peeke, James Lindsey, William Hungerford, Rich. Willan, Geo. Akerick, John Lewger, Rich. Browne. Did not appear: James Walker, Rich. Browne, Rich. Banks, John Shertcliffe, Elias Beach, George Akerick, Walter Peake.

Ralphe Bene vs. Joseph Edlow.

f. 447 Ralph Beane vs. John Wiseman.

Ralph Beane vs. John Warren.

Henry Morgan by his attorney George Manners vs. Mrs. Margarett Brent attorney for Capt. Giles Brent.

Liber - Patent Record Z & A - 1637-1651

Phillip Land vs. Mrs. Marg. Brent.

Mrs. Margaret Brent vs. Edward Commins.

George Manners vs. Mrs. Margaret Brent, for Roanoke & Peake.

Thomas Hamper, at the request of George Manners, deposed that he never heard Mrs. Margaret Brent undertake to pay wages of His Lordship's garrison.

Mr. Phillip Land was appointed High Sheriff of St. Maries' Co.

f. 448 Nicho. Cossin assigned 100 a. to Thomas Petite. Date: 24 January 1648.

1649. Thomas Hatton His Lordship's Secretary received the book of entries. Date: 9 April 1649. On 16 April, Mr. William Bretton delivered 2 books to Tho. Hatton.

9 April. Tho. Petite demanded 100 a. on assignment from Walter Cotterill. Walter Cotterell demanded 100 a. for transporting self in 1640 & assigned to said Petite. Warrant for 450 a. for Tho. Petite on Patowmack River near Cedar Point.

f. 449 William Bretton (gentleman) & Walter Peakes (gentleman) are security to Phillip Land now High Sheriff. Date: 16 April 1649.

20 April. An extent issued to the sheriff of St. Maries' Co. on 17 January at suit of Capt. William Stone vs. lands of Mr. Thomas Weston.

Capt. William Stone appointed Thomas Greene, Esq. as Lt. General, etc.

f. 450 & Mr. Thomas Hatton as His Lordship's Secretary. Date: 2 May 1649.

William Stiles is bound to John Slingsby, payment due at house of Walter Peakes. Date: 9 March 1648. Witnesses: Jeoffrey Oliver, Walter Pakes.

Robert West is bound to George Akerick. Date: 4 March 1645. Witness: William Williams.

f. 451 George Akerick deposed that as per the agreement between himself & Robert West (of VA), the deponent paid him & a bill due the deponent from William Skiffen.

8 May. John Nunne gave chattel to Mary Shertcliffe for consideration which her mother took when I was sick. Date: 19 April 1649. Witnesses: David Prichard, Edmund Smith.

Henry Pountney vs. Mrs. Margaret Brent. Summons to: Henry Fox.

Marks Pheypo & Nicholas Keeten vs. Franciscu Pope. Subpoena to: Lt. Richard Banks, William Wright, William Tompson.

Marks Pheypo & <torn> vs. Jacobu Johnson. Subpoena to: Lt. Banks, William Wright, William Tompson.

f. 452 Robert Kedger vs. John Dandey.

William Bruffe vs. Johem Thimbleby administrator of Peter Mackerell.

William Bruffe vs. Richard Richard Nevett.

George Manners vs. Edrm. Hall. Subpoena to: George Sanghier, Henry Potter, Tho. Ware.

Robert Robins vs. Thomas Ebden. Subpoena to: Henr. Fox, Humfr. Atwick, Jo. Maunsell.

Walter Beane vs. Tho. Green, Esq.

John Hollis vs. William Browne.

Geo. Manners vs. Franc. Van Enden.

Jo. Malham vs. Edrm. Claxton.

Subpoena to Cloves Mace to testify for William Smoote in case against Ralph Beane.

Capt. Tho. Baldrich vs. Mrs. Margaret Brent.

Liber - Patent Record Z & A - 1637-1651

Fr. Vanenden vs. Ralph Beane. Subpoena to: Lt. Richard Banks.

Francis Jarvis vs. Franc. Brooks. Subpoena to: Jo. Nicholls, Jo. Dandey, Mr. Robert Clarke, Humphrey Howell.

Lewes Froman vs. Chas. Beach.

Walter <torn>

1 June 1649. Henry Adams deposed that about 1 year ago,

f. 453 he was a servant to Mrs. Margaret Brent, sent to fetch chattel from Anthony Rawlins.

By Governor of Maryland. Thomas Pasmore (of VA) desires to transport self & family to Maryland. Said Thomas is to have 1000 a. in place convenient to him & Capt. Henry Fleete. Date: 26 June 1634. Signed: Leonard Calvert, Jerome Hawley, Tho. Cornwallis.

Thomas Pasmore (carpenter, of St. Maries' Hundred) sold to James Cauther his lands. Date: 28 December 1638. Witnesses: Francis Rabnett, John Hallowes, Francis Gray.

f. 454 James Cauther (planter, of St. Maries' Hundred) assigned to Thomas Sturman (cooper, of Isle of Kent) Thomas Uells (planter) his property per Gov. Jeremy Hawley & Capt. Thomas Cornwalleys. Date: 1 November 1641. Witnesses: John Hampton, John Worrell.

Thomas Pasmore, age 65, deposed on 4 May 1644 before Mr. John Trussell (Commander of Northumberland Co. VA) that Capt. Leonard Calvert freely gave him 1000 a. where Thomas Sturman now lives.

John Sturman deposed that on

f. 455 9 June 1649 at the house of Mr. Fenwick, he examined certain chattel.

Capt. William Stone, Esq. received of Marks Pheypo (gentleman) the following debts due estate of Mr. Weston (dec'd): Thomas Peake, Dr. Binks, Peter Makarell, Mr. Lewger, Henry Brooks, Mr. Gerard, Mr. Sturman, Richard White, Mr. Pope, Mr. Phillpott, Robert Kadger, accountant. Date: 1 May 1649.

Marks Pheypo (attorney for Mr. Hansford executor of Mr. Weston (dec'd)) deposed that the above list is complete, & delivered to Capt. William Stone. Date: 1 June 1649.

8 June. Administration of estate of Mr. Henry Brooks (merchant) was granted to Mr. Cuthbert Fenwick.

2 June. Robert Robins deposed that in September 1647, he was at the house of Richard Grigson at

f. 456 Back River (VA) & said he had chattel belonging to Anthony Rawlins.

George Manners vs. Francis Van Enden. Elias Beach deposed that since last Christmas, the deponent was aboard the ship of Skipper Abraham, & heard Francis Vanenden desire George Manners to act as envoy.

Elias Beach appointed George Manners as his attorney.

Elias Beach vs. Henry Adams.

Gabriell Ozier demanded 100 a. for transporting self in 1647. Date: 7 April 1649.

Thomas Phillips demanded 100 a. for transporting self in 1647.

John Lancelott demanded 100 a. for transporting self in 1647.

George Sanghier demanded 400 a. for transporting self, his wife, & 3 children in 1647. Date: 1 May.

f. 457 Thomas Hamper demanded 100 a. for transporting self in 1646.

Warrant to Richard Bennett for 350 a. on north side of land of Mr. Neale.

Mr. Clarke. Christopher Russell assigned his right to land to George Akerick. Witness: James Walker.

Liber - Patent Record Z & A - 1637-1651

George Akericke demanded 200 a. for transporting self & his wife in 1647 & 100 a. on assignment from Christopher Russell. Date: 30 May. Warrant to George Akerick for east side of Wiccocomoco River.

Phillip Authur demanded 100 a. for transporting self in 1647. Warrant for east side of Wiccocomoco River.

William Hungerford demanded 100 a. for transporting self in 1647. Warrant for east side of Wiccocomoco River.

James Walker demanded 50 a. for being a servant to Mr. Thomas Gerrard for 4 years, which expired 3 years ago. Warrant for east side of Wiccocomoco River.

John Shanks demanded 50 a. as a servant to Mr. Thomas Gerard 8 years ago. Date: 3 May. Warrant for east side of Wiccocomoco River.

f. 458 James Hare demanded 100 a. for transporting self in 1647. Date: 30 May. Warrant for east side of Wiccocomoco River.

Mr. Richard Browne demanded 200 a. for transporting self & his wife last July. Warrant for east side of Wiccocomoco River.

Richard Ware demanded 100 a. for transporting self in 1645. Date: 1 June 1649. Warrant for west side of St. George's River.

Lt. Richard Banks demanded 100 a. for transporting self in 1646. Warrant for Poplar Hill.

James Johnson demanded 100 a. for transporting self in 1647 & 100 a. for transporting John Elliott his servant in 1642. Warrant for Wiccocomoco River.

Anthony Rawlins demanded 250 a. for transporting self, his wife & 1 child in 1645 & 50 a. due Richard Cox (dec'd) his service (which expired 5/6 years ago) to Mr. Copley & by assignment from Capt. John Price for transporting self & 50 a. due Rawlins as servant (expired 10 years ago) to Mr. Justinian Snow. Warrant to layout 400 a. for Anthony Rawlins on Patuxent River near Sakawakitt or Wiccocomoco River.

f. 459 William Bretton (gentleman) recorded a cattle mark.

William Bretton (gentleman, of Newtowne) sold to Richard Bennett (planter, of Newtowne) chattel. Witness: Richard Browne.

<u>1 June 1649 at St. Maries'.</u> Court. Thomas Greene, Esq. (Governor), Capt. John Price, Mr. Thomas Hatton (Secretary).

Phillip Land vs. Mrs. Marg. Brent.

Marks Pheypo & Nicolas Keeten vs. Francis Pope.

Marks Pheypo & Nicholas Keeten vs. James Johnson.

f. 460 Mrs. Margaret Brent for Mrs. Eure vs. Anthony Rawlins. Mentions: conveyance from William Hardwich, Thomas Sturman.

Marks Pheypo attorney for Mr. John Hansford administrator of Mr. Thomas Weston. Mentions: execution by William Stone, Esq. Accounts filed.

Anthony Rawlins administrator of Richard Cox (dec'd). Inventory filed.

Mrs. Margarett Brent vs. Edward Commins by his attorney George Manners.

f. 461 Capt. Thomas Baldrich by his attorney George Manners vs. Mrs. Margaret Brent.

Henry Pountney vs. Mrs. Margarett Brent.

George Manners vs. Francis Van Enden. Mentions: Skipper Abraham, John Hollis.

John Warren vs. John Thimbleby & William Browne. Mentions: Ralph Beane, William Smoote.

f. 462 Capt. Giles Brent attorney for administrator of Henry Brooks (merchant) vs. Capt. Robert Vaughan.

Ralphe Beane vs. Anthony Rawlins.

<u>2 June.</u> Robert Robins vs. Ralphe Beane.

Liber - Patent Record Z & A - 1637-1651

Lewis Froman vs. Elias Beach.

f. 463 John Hollis vs. William Browne.

William Bruffe vs. John Thimbleby administrator of Peter Makerell.

Thomas Gerard, Esq. by his attorney William Bretton vs. John Thimbleby administrator of Peter Mackerell. Deposition by George Manners citing suit of William Lewis vs. estate of Mr. Gerrad.

f. 464 Ralphe Beane vs. William Smoote.

Francis Van Enden vs. Ralphe Beane. Lt. Richard Banks deposed regarding chattel.

f. 465 Abraham Johnson (mariner) by his attorney John Hatch vs. Phillip Land.

Robert Robins vs. Thomas Hebden.
- John Maunsell deposed that he was present when Thomas Ebden sold chattel to Robert Robins.

f. 466 ...
- Humfrey Atwick should deliver.
- Humfrey Atwick deposed that Thomas Hebden last January delivered to Robert Robins chattel. Mentions: William Smoote.

William Smoote vs. Mr. Cuthbert Fenwick.

George Manners vs. Mrs. Marg. Brent.
- Mr. John Hallowes deposed that Mrs. Margaret Brent did write a letter indicating payment to be made to Capt. Edward Hill. Date: 4 May 1649. Witness: Thomas Baldridge.

f. 467 Robert Kadger vs. John Dandey.

Anthony Rawling registered a cattle mark. Cites chattel bought of Andrew Monroe, Capt. Stone, Mr. Greene, Walter Waterlin, Walter Beane.

f. 468 James Johnson registered a cattle mark.

William Tompson registered a cattle mark. Elisabeth daughter of William Tompson registered a cattle mark.

John Thimbleby registered a cattle mark.

Registration of cattle mark of Peter Mackarell (administrator is John Thimbleby).

Joseph Cadle registered a cattle mark.

Thomas Hamper registered a cattle mark.

Mathias Brian bought chattel of William Tompson.

John Nunne registered a cattle mark.

Ralphe Beane vs. William Smoote. Summons to: Henry Atwick.

Survey for Capt. William Haweley on south side of Putuxent River, bounding Hawley's Branch, St. Valentine's River, St. James' Creek, Chesepeack Bay, Scrutton's Plantation for 4250 a. Date: 15 January 1648. Signed: Robert Clarke.

f. 469 Survey for William Eltonhead (gentleman) near mouth of Putuxent River, bounding Capt. William Hawley St. James' Creek, Chesepeacke Bay, for 2000 a. Date: 8 March 1648. Signed: Robert Clarke. [Patent f. 487.]

Survey for Anthony Rawlins (planter) on south side of Trinity Creek, bounding St. Anthony's Hollow, [metes & bounds], for 100 a. called Whit Birch Freehold. Date: 12 March 1648. Signed: Robert Clarke. [Patent f. 478.]

Survey for Richard Banks (planter) in Popler Hill Creek, bounding land of John Courts, land of Francis Pope, land of said Banks, for 100 a. called Dunbar. Date: 14 March 1648. Signed: Robert Clarke. [Patent f. 460.]

Survey for Lt. William Evans & John Jarbo (planters) on Bretton's Bay, bounding land of John Grimsditch, land of Richard Nevett, for 100 a., called Clipping. Date: 15 March 1648. Signed: Robert Clarke. [Patent f. 479.]

Liber - Patent Record Z & A - 1637-1651

f. 470 Survey for Francis Posey & John Burlane (planters) on west side of Wiccocomoco River near Neale's Creek, bounding Posey's Creek, Posey's Runne, Burlane's Fresh, for 700 a. of which 300 a. is assigned to Thomas Ashbrooke, called Arthur's Hope. Date: 22 March 1648. Signed: Robert Clarke. [Patent f. 482.]

Survey for William Styles (planter, of Newtowne) at head of Nevett's Creek on Bretton's Bay, bounding Dorrell's Swampt, land of John Jarbo & William Evans, Styles' Oake, for 100 a. Date: 3 July 1649. Signed: Robert Clarke. [Patent f. 485.]

7 July 1649. Abraham Johnson (mariner) by his attorney John Hatch vs. Thomas Greene, Esq.

Francis Posey vs. John Hatch.

William Eltonhead (gentleman) vs. Lt. Richard Banks et. al. administrators of Thomas Allen (dec'd).

f. 471 Ralphe Beane vs. William Smoote. Summons to: Robert Kedger, Thomas Bushell.

Ralphe Beane vs. James Johnson.

Ralphe Beane vs. Richard Nevett.

Ralphe Beane vs. Francis Vanenden.

Ralphe Beane vs. Stephen Salmon.

Robert Smith vs. William Stevens.

Paul Simpson assignee of Capt. Baldridge vs. Jo. Thimbleby administrator of Peter Mackarell.

Thomas Baker by his attorney Rich. Brown vs. Edward Cotton. Subpoena to: Francis Vandan, Walter Waterlin.

Capt. John Price vs. Edward Williams.

Walter Gweast vs. Walter Beane.

Charles Rawlinson vs. William Brown.

f. 472 Walter Beane vs. Lt. William Lewis.

Hugh Lee vs. Lt. William Lewis.

Robert Kedger vs. Lt. William Lewis.

Walter Smith vs. Mr. Robert Clarke. Summons to: Humfrey Howell.

29 September. Thomas Dynyard registered a cattle mark.

Mr. Richard Brown registered a cattle mark.

22 October. Henry Adams registered a cattle mark.

Henry Adams vs. Fr. Vanenden.

24 October. Cuthbert Fenwick (gentleman) vs. Richard Duke.

John Hollis (gentleman) vs. Nicholas Gwyther.

Richard Cooll vs. Jo. Halfhead. Subpoena to: William Boreman, George Manners, Francis Poesy.

Subpoena to Thomas Sturman to testify for Thomas Copley, Esq.

22 October. Andrew Munrowe (of Appamattox) sold chattel to Elias Beach.

f. 473 Date: 6 April 1648. Witnesses: William Harditch, John Sturman.

John Hollis assignee of Anthony West vs. George Sanghier.

John Dandey assignee of Henry Bishop vs. Xpofer Carnoll.

John Hollis assignee of Tho. Boyce vs. Henry Fox.

Liber - Patent Record Z & A - 1637-1651

<u>29 October</u>. Joseph Edlow registered a cattle mark.

Paul Simpson vs. Rich. Floyd.

Paul Simpson vs. Phillip Authur.

Benjamin Gill attorney for Mr. James Neale vs. Gabriel Ozier.

<u>26 October</u>. Walter Pakes vs. William Smoote. Mentions: Henry Armes (servant of plaintiff).

William Tompson vs. Jo. Hatch attorney for Mr. Gerrard.

Francis Poesy demanded 100 a. for transporting a servant bought of Edward Budden (of VA) in 1646. Date: 23 June. Warrant for on Wiccocomoco River.

Account of appraisement of crop & servant of Francis Poesey. Date: 13 August 1647. Appraisers: Anthon Rawlins, George Manners.

f. 474 Francis Jarvise vs. Mr. Francis Brooks. Arbitrators: George Manners, William Smoote, Marks Pheypo, Nicholas Keyten. Date: 1 June 1649. Signed: Francis Brookes, Francis Jarvis. Witness: Richard Browne. Arbitration. Signed: Marks Pheypo, George Manners, William Smoote, Nicolas Keyten. Witnesses: Rich. Browne, John Wade. Subscribed by Nicholas Keyting before Thomas Hatton.

John Shercliffe granted land for transporting self in 1646 & providing service to Thomas Greene, Esq., bounding land of

f. 475 Richard Hills, Piccomow Creek, Patowmeck River, Broad Creek, land formerly of John Nunne now possessed by said Shercliffe, 100 a. Signed: Thomas Greene. [Certificate: f. 438]

William Tompson granted 100 a. on assignment from Thomas Greene, Esq. (Governor) & 50 a. due from his wife. Said Tompson is administrator of Robert Tovey (dec'd) who transported self,

f. 476 Indian Quarter, on east side of St. Clement's Bay in Patowmock River, bounding Tompson's Creek, [metes & bounds], St. Andrew's Fresh. Date: 8 June 1649. Signed: Thomas Greene. Amendment

f. 477 recorded. Date: 8 January 1648. Survey for William Tompson on east side of St. Clement's Bay on Patowmeck River, bounding Tompson's Creek, [metes & bounds], St. Andrew's Fresh, 250 a.

Walter Pakes granted, on assignment from Jeoffrey Oliver who transported self in 1646, 100 a. & to advise William Stone, Esq., on south side of Nevett's Creek in Bretton's Bay, bounding Style's Runne, Upper Path of Newtowne, Randall's Marsh. Date: 2 July 1649. Signed: William Stone.

f. 478 Anthony Rawlins granted, on assignment from Thomas Pasmore who transported Henry Baker (servant), 100 a. called White Birch Freehold, on south side of Trinity Creek, bounding St. Anthonies Hollow, Rawlins Pine, Baldridge Tree.

f. 479 Date: 3 July 1649. Signed: William Stone. [Certificate: f. 469.] Note: Joane Rawlins wife to Anthony Rawlins (dec'd) assigns right to Thomas Simmons & Michael McCrawleley. Date: 14 April 1654. Witnesses: William Edde, Tho. Junes.

Lt. William Evans & John Jarbo who transported selves in 1646

f. 480 were granted land in Bretton's Bay, bounding land of John Grimsditch, land of Richard Nevett, 100 a. Date: 1 July 1649. Signed: William Stone. [Certificate: f. 469.]

Lt. Richard Banks who transported self in 1646

f. 481 was granted & to advise William Stone, Esq., all the land in Popler Hill Creek, bounding land of John Courts & Francis Pope, land of said Banks, Court's Runne, for 100 a., called Dunbarr. Date: 1 July 1649. Signed: William Stone. [Certificate f. 469.]

Stephen Salmon (planter) was granted 100 a. for transporting self in 1646

f. 482 & to advise William Stone, Esq., on west side of Bretton's Bay, bounding St. Stephen's Spring, land of William Brough now in occupation of said Stephen, for 50 a. Date: 1 July 1649. Signed: William Stone. [Certificate f. 446.]

Liber - Patent Record Z & A - 1637-1651

Francis Poesey for transporting self in 1640 & Joseph Gregory (servant) & John Knott assigned

f. 483 to said Poesey 100 a. for transporting self in 1643 & John Villaine assigned to said Poesey 100 a. for transporting self in 1646 & 300 a. on assignment from Thomas Ashbrooke & to advise William Stone, Esq., is granted to said Francis Poesy & John Burlane (planters) land on west side of Wicokomoco River near Neale's Creek, bounding Poesey's Creek, Poesey's Runne, Burlane's Fresh, for 700 a. Date: 1 July 1649. Signed: William Stone.

f. 484 John Wheateley for transporting self in 1641 & to advise William Stone, Esq. was granted on east side of Packer's Creeke on west side of St. George's River, bounding Wheatley's Fresh, St. John's Spring, for 50 a. Date: 1 July 1649. Signed: William Stone. [Certificate f. 446.]

f. 485 William Styles was granted 50 a. on assignment from Capt. John Price & 50 a. for service & to advise William Stone, Esq., on Nevett's Creek, bounding Dorrell's Swampt, land of John Jarbo & William Evans, Styles' Oake, for 100 a. Date: 1 July 1649. Signed: William Stone. [Certificate f. 470.]

f. 486 13 July. George Manners on 10 February last satisfied claims by John Hallowes (of Appamatocks).

Abraham Johnson (mariner) by his attorney John Hatch vs. Phillip Land, from 2 June last. Mentions: land now in possession of William Tompson (of Newtowne). Date: 17 July 1649. Signed: John Hatche, Phillip Land.

f. 487 William Eltonhead (gentleman) for transporting self & 6 man servants, 1 maid servant, 1 boy, & 1 free woman in 1648 & 400 a. on assignment from George Manners & to advise William Stone, Esq., near mouth of Putuxent River, bounding land of Capt. William Hawley,

f. 488 St. James' Creek, Bay of Chesepeake, for 2000 a., called Mannor of Eltonhead. Date: 26 July 1649. Signed: William Stone. [Rights f. 439; Certificate f. 469.]

Francis Jarvis appointed his kinsman William Edwin as his attorney to sue Francis Brookes, & revoked a former PoA to Mr. Richard Browne. Date: 1 August 1649.

21 April 1649. General Assembly. Attendees: all, but Mr. Pile & Mr. Hatton.

f. 489 Payments to: Lt. Banks, Walter Pakes, Mr. Brown, John Maunsell, Mr. Thorneboroughe, George Manners, Mr. Fenwick, Mr. Bretton, Capt. Vaughan, Mr. Conner. Committee: Cuthbert Fenwick, Richard Banks, Phillip Conner, Richard Browne, Walter Pakes.

f. 490 Act concerning Religion.

f. 491 ...

f. 492 ...

f. 493 ...

f. 494 Signed: Freemen, Tho. Hatton, William Stone.

Act for Punishment of Counterfeit of Great Seal.

f. 495 Signed: Freemen, Tho. Hatton, William Stone.

Act for Purchasing Land from Indians.

f. 496 Signed: Freemen, Tho. Hatton, William Stone.

Act for Punishment of Certain Offenses.

f. 497 Signed: Freemen, Tho. Hatton, William Stone.

Act against Fugitives.

f. 498 Signed: Freemen, Tho. Hatton, William Stone.

Act touching Indians.

f. 499 Mentions: Andrewe Cusamazinah (servant to Mr. Fenwick). Signed: Freemen, Tho. Hatton, William Stone.

Liber - Patent Record Z & A - 1637-1651

Act touching Cattle Marks.

f. 500 Signed: Freemen, Tho. Hatton, William Stone.

Act for Planting Corn.

f. 501 Signed: Freemen, Tho. Hatton, William Stone.

Act for Support of the Lord Proprietor.

f. 502 Signed: Freemen, Tho. Hatton, William Stone.

Order touching the Lord Proprietor's Stock.

f. 503 Signed: Freemen, Tho. Hatton, William Stone.

Order for Defense of the Province.

f. 504 ...

f. 505 Signed: Freemen, Tho. Hatton, William Stone.

Order Providing for the Smith. Signed: Freemen, Tho. Hatton, William Stone.

6 August. Mr. Copley demanded 8500 a. for transporting 22 able men in 1633.

f. 506 Mr. Copley demanded 2000 a. more.

16 August. Thomas Copley, Esq. assigned to Mr. Thomas Mathewes 4000 a. for transporting 10 man servants in 1633.

Thomas Copley, Esq. assigned to Mr. Raphe Crough 4000 a. for transporting 10 man servants in 1633.

Thomas Copley, Esq. assigned to Mr. Robert Clarke 500 a. for transporting 2 man servants in 1633.

17 August. Mr. Ralphe Crouche demanded 4000 a. on assignment from Mr. Tho. Copley. Warrant for north side of Patowmeck River near PortTobacco.

Mr. Robert Clarke demanded 500 a. on assignment from Mr. Copley. Warrant for north side of Patowmeck River.

30 August. Warrant for 1000 a. for Nicholas Cawsin on Patowmeck River between Cedar Point & head of PortTobacco Creek.

Jane wife of Nicholas Cawsin late widow

f. 507 of John Cockshott demanded 2000 a. for Mary & Jane Cockshott her children by said John, due said John for transporting self & 7 persons in 1642, per Robert Clarke (surveyor). Warrant for Patowmeck River between Cedar Point & head of PortTobacco Creek.

Ralphe Beane bought of Leonard Calvert, Esq. 700 a. & transported self & 5 able men between 1640 & 1648 & 50 a. for his service & 150 a. due his brother Walter Beane for transporting self & his wife & to advise William Stone, Esq., land on north

f. 508 side of Patowmeck River, bounding Herring Creek, Heron Marsh, St. George's Creeke, land of John Prichard, for 1500 a., called Piney Point. Date: 20 August 1649. Signed: William Stone. [Certificate f. 445.]

3 September. Richard Hilles sold to Richard Browne his plantation in MD. Date: 29 June 1649. Witnesses: John Hallowes, William Withers.

6 September 1649. Mr. John Pile demanded 400 a. for transporting self & his wife in 1648 & for William Tattersall & Mary Tattersall

f. 509 in 1648. Warrant for Patowmeck River above Cedar Point.

9 September. John Court demanded for self & for Francis Pope 200 a. who were transported in 1639 by Capt. Fulk Brent. Warrant for Patowmeck River.

Richard Smith demanded 100 a. for his transportation in 1644. Warrant for Patowmeck River.

John Court & Francis Pope registered a joint cattle mark. Mentions: chattel bought of Francis Vanenden with His Lordship's mark, & of Ralphe Beane with

Liber - Patent Record Z & A - 1637-1651

mark of Walter Beane.

<u>13 September</u>. Warrant to Walter Smith for 100 a. near Patowmeck River.

Warrant to summons John Slingsby & James Johnson to testify in case of John Jarbo vs. Walter Smith.

Capt. William Stone

f. 510 appointed Thomas Greene, Esq. as Lt. General during his absence, or Mr. Thomas Hatton. Date: 20 September 1649.

<u>24 October</u>. Tho. Hatton assigned to Lt. William Lewis 50 a. for transporting Mary Forrell in 1648.

<u>29 September</u>. Barnaby Jackson registered a cattle mark.

John Greenwell registered a cattle mark.

Mr. John Lewger registered a cattle mark.

Richard Willin registered a cattle mark.

James Lindsey registered a cattle mark.

James Langworth registered a cattle mark.

John Hatch demanded 150 a. on assignment from Mr. Thomas Gerrard of 2 servants:

f. 511 Thomas Abbott, Ales Sponner. And 100 a. for transporting self about 45 [sic] years ago & 100 a. for transporting his wife about 2 years ago & 100 a. for transporting his servant Richard Roe in 1649.

Hugh Hopewell registered a cattle mark.

Humfrey Howell registered a cattle mark.

William Oliver & Mary Harrison (children of Roger Oliver & (N) Harrison (dec'd)) registered a cattle mark.

Mr. William Eltonhead registered a cattle mark.

Gartrude & Jane (daughters of Thomas Smith (gentleman, dec'd)) registered a cattle mark.

Thomas & Sarah (children of Capt. Phillip Taylor (dec'd)) registered a cattle mark.

Lt. Nicholas Guyther registered a cattle mark.

John Halfhead registered a cattle mark.

Thomas Copley, Esq. registered a cattle mark.

Thomas Mathewes registered a cattle mark.

Elias Beach registered a cattle mark.

Elias Beach (son of Elias Beach) has chattel given him by Mr. Nathaniell Pope

f. 512 & registered a cattle mark. Signed: Elias Beache the elder. Witness: Tho. Hatton.

<u>25 October</u>. Lt. William Lewis demanded 100 a. for self & his wife in service, 200 a. for transporting self & his wife in 1646, & 550 a. for 6 servants: Rowland Morgan, Rowland Mace, James Compton, Ralphe Hasleton, John Ashbrook, Penelope Brookes. And 100 a. on assignment from Mr. Nathaniell Pope for transporting his servant Francis Willis & 50 a. on assignment from Mr. Hatton.

Nathaniel Pope (gentleman, of Appamatocks) assigned 2000 a. bought of Mrs. Stratton at her going to England. Witnesses: John Metcalfe, William Evans.

Warrant to Lt. William Lewis at Portoback for 2000 a.

John Warren demanded 300 a.: 100 a. for his service bought of Capt. Giles Brent, 200 a. for transporting self & his wife in 1646. Warrant for Patowmeck River.

Liber - Patent Record Z & A - 1637-1651

f. 513 4 October 1649. Walter Beane & William Bruffe appointed to appraise chattel of William Wheatley (dec'd) per his administrator James Langworth. Signed: Tho. Greene. To: Mr. John Lewger, Jr. Date: 5 October 1649. Administered. Signed: John Lewger.

29 October. George Manners demanded 100 a. for transporting his servant Bartholomew Wrench in 1645. Warrant for Louise Creek in St. Michael's Hundred.

30 October. Anthony Rawlins gave chattel to his daughter Ann Rawlins (under age), bought of Capt. William Stone, in lieu of chattel given her by John Harrwood. Signed: Anthony Rawlings.

Anthony Rawlins gave chattel to his daughter Marg. Rawlins, in exchange for chattel given her by

f. 514 Edward Hull & Mary Edwin, until she comes of age.

John Norman demanded 100 a. due John Smithson (dec'd) for transporting self in 1635, said Norman married Smithson's widow, & 50 a. as a servant to Capt. Cornwallis, & 50 a. for his wife as a servant to Capt. Hawley. Warrant for Patowmeck River.

John Norman registered a cattle mark for his daughter Mary Norman, for chattel given her by Walter Beane.

John Norman registered a cattle mark.

21 September. Lt. Richard Banks registered a cattle mark.

Lt. Richard Banks demanded 200 a.: 100 a. on assignment from Ralphe Beane, & 100 a. for transporting a man servant last year. Warrant for Patowmeck River.

William Wright demanded 250 a.: 100 a. for transporting self in 1644, 100 a. on assignment from Ralphe Beane, & 50 a. for transporting a maid servant

f. 515 last year. Warrant for Patowmeck River.

29 September. Agreement between Mr. Cuthbert Fenwick administrator of Nicholas Harvey (dec'd) & John Dandy. Mentions: Frances Harvey daughter of said Nicholas.

Frances Harvey daughter of Nicholas Harvey (dec'd) registered a cattle mark.

Capt. Cornwalleys registered a cattle mark.

Mr. Cuthbert Fenwick registered a cattle mark. Thomas Fenwick son of Mr. Cuthbert Fenwick registered a cattle mark. Cuthbert Fenwick son of Mr. Cuthbert Fenwick registered a cattle mark. Ignacius Fenwick son of Mr. Cuthbert Fenwick registered a cattle mark. Teresa Fenwicke daughter of Mr. Cuthbert Fenwick

f. 516 registered a cattle mark.

Edward Packer registered a cattle mark.

John Warren registered a cattle mark.

John Dandy registered a cattle mark.

Thomas Petite registered a cattle mark.

Mr. William Durant demanded 850 a. for transporting self, his wife, 4 children, 2 man servants: William Warren, William Hogg & 1 woman servant & 2 freeman: William Pell, (N) Archer in 1648. Warrant for Chaptico or elsewhere on Wicocomoco or Patowmeck River.

Thomas Petite demanded 200 a. for transporting self & his wife about 4 years ago.

1 October 1649. Thomas Petite assigned to William Marshall his right to 200 a. above.

William Marshall demanded 100 a. for transporting his man servant Richard Morris in 1648, & 200 a. on assignment from Thomas Petite, & 100 a. from Walter Cotterell. Warrant

f. 517 for north side of Thomas Petite's Creek, joining land of George Manners.

Liber - Patent Record Z & A - 1637-1651

<u>29 September</u>. Walter Cotterell demanded 100 a. for transporting self 4 years ago. Walter Cotterell assigned to William Marshall.

<u>1 October 1649</u>. James Langworth was given administration of estate of William Wheately (dec'd). No known kindred to whom to give administration.

<u>11 October</u>. David Prichard demanded 100 a. for transporting self in 1649. Warrant for Holloweing Point on south side of Wicocomoco River.

Lt. Nicholas Gwyther demanded 250 a.: 50 a. each for transporting self & his wife for service, 100 a. by guift from Anslowe Simpson (dec'd) who transported self in 1646 to John Gwyther son of said Nicholas, & 50 a. on assignment from Charles Rawlinson.

Charles Rawlinson demanded 50 a. for service & assigned

f. 518 to Lt. Nicholas Gwyther.

Warrant to layout 250 a. for Lt. Nicholas Gwyther at mouth of Poplar Creek on branch of St. Jerome's Creek.

Margarett wife of Mr. Thomas Hatton (Secretary) & Mary Farroll servant to said Secretary testified that Anslowe Simpson said he gave to John Gwyther child of Lt. Nicolas Gwyther & his now wife land due for his transportation.

John Maunsell (planter) is granted 50 a. due on assignment from William Bretton (gentleman) & 50 a. on assignment from Stephen Salmon, on west side of Bretton Bay, bounding

f. 519 Maunsell's Marsh. Date: 20 October 1649. [Patent cancelled.]

Marks Pheypo attorney for Mr. John Hansford administrator of Mr. Thomas Weston (dec'd). Mentions: account against estate by William Stone, Esq. Accounts

f. 520 passed. Date: 1 June 1649.

f. 521 Anthony Rawlins administrator of Richard Cox (dec'd). Inventory accepted & accounts passed. Date: 1 June 1649.

f. 522 <u>15 October 1649</u>. Thomas Ashbrook acknowledged a debt to Mr. Cuthbert Fenwick.

<u>17 October 1649</u>. Paul Simpson (mariner) sold a bill from Capt. Edward Hill to George Manners last March/April.

Edward Hill appointed Mr. John Hollis as his attorney to recover any payments due in County of Northumberland & in MD. Date: 17 September 1649. Witnesses: Jo. Rosier, John Hillier.

<u>24 October</u>. Walter Pakes demanded 350 a.:

f. 523 150 a. for transporting his servant Henry Armes, Peter Pakes (under age 16) son of said Walter in 1646, 200 a. on assignment from Richard Butler & Edmund Wright who transported selves in the same year. Warrant for Walter Peakes on west side of Grimes Creek.

John Jarbo demanded 250 a. on behalf of Barkram Obert & his son Barkram Obert (under age 16) & Dominick (N) who transported themselves in 1646. Warrant for Barkram Obert & Dominick (N) on Patowmeck River.

Ralph Beane deposed that about 5 years ago when Richard Ingle (mariner) & his accomplices plundered the Colony, he saw John Rabley (of VA) et. al. take away chattel to Ingle's ship, formerly belonging to Mr. Cuthbert Fenwick or Capt. Thomas Cornwalles. Date: 4 November 1649.

John Medley deposed that about 5 years ago, when Richard Ingle & his accomplices plundered the Colony, certain persons took chattel from the deponent's house, chattel formerly belonging to Mr. Cuthbert Fenwick or Capt. Tho. Cornwallis. One of them was

f. 524 John Rabley (of VA). Date: 4 November 1649.

John Maunsell deposed that about 5 years ago, when Richard Ingle & his accomplices plundered the Colony, several persons took chattel from the deponent's house, chattel formerly belonging to Mr. Cuthbert Fenwick or Capt. Thomas Cornwallys, & John Rabley (of VA) was amongst them. Date: 5 November 1649.

Liber - Patent Record Z & A - 1637-1651

29 October. Robert Simpkins demanded 100 a. for transporting self in 1647. Warrant for Patowmeck River.

Humfrey Howell demanded 100 a. for transporting self in 1647. Warrant for Patowmeck River.

Mr. Robert Clark assigned to Thomas Mitchell 100 a. due for transporting his servant Roger Bletsoe in 1641. Signed: Rob. Clarke.

Thomas Mitchell demanded 100 a. due on assignment from Mr. Robert Clarke. Warrant for Patowmeck. Benjamin Gill demanded 1000 a. due

f. 525 for transporting self & 5 others in 1642. Warrant for Wiccocomoco River near plantation of Mr. Neale.

Richard Duke demanded 100 a. due on assignment from Thomas Copley, Esq. Warrant for Wiccocomoco River.

4 November. Warrant for George Akerick for 300 a. on St. Clement's Bay between land of Mr. Gerrard & head of the Bay.

Warrant for Nicholas Banister for 350 a. at Hollins Point on Wicocomoco River.

William Edwin registered a cattle mark. Elisabeth & Mary daughters of William Edwin registered a cattle mark.

Lt. William Lewis registered a cattle mark.

John Maunsell registered a cattle mark.

John Hallowes vs. George Manners. Mentions: bill due from Franc. Vandam demanded by Phillip Land his now attorney.

f. 526 Thomas Uell vs. Mrs. Marg. Brent.

O'Doughorty David [sic] vs. Lt. William Lewis.

Walter Beane registered a cattle mark.

Charles Maynard demanded 50 a. due as a servant to Mr. Cuthbert Fenwick & 50 a. on assignment from said Fenwick. Mr. Cuthbert Fenwick assigned 50 a. to Charles Minor for transporting him the said Charles Maynard his servant about 12 years ago. Warrant to Charles Minor for 100 a. on St. Clement's Bay above the rich land of Mr. Tompson.

5 November. Serjeant Marks Pheypo registered a cattle mark. Said Pheypo has chattel bought of Mr. Hansford executor of Mr. Weston (dec'd).

6 November. Thomas Gerrard, Esq. vs. Lt. William Lewis.

9 November. Paul Simpson vs. William Whittle.

Paul Simpson vs. Walter Guest.

William Assiter registered a cattle mark.

Robert Kedger attorney for Mordecai Cooke who married

f. 527 the widow & administratrix of (N) Peasley vs. John Dandy.

10 November. Thomas Greene, Esq. vs. Skipper Abraham Jonson.

Thomas Greene, Esq. demanded of Lt. William Lewis.

24 November. Robert Holt

f. 528 (planter) is bound to Paul Simpson (mariner, of St. Inego's). Date: 20 July 1649. Witnesses: Robert Clark, Edward Clayton.

14 November. John Nevill demanded 200 a. for transporting self in 1646 & his wife.

Xopher Carnoll demanded 100 a. for transporting self in 1646. Warrant for John Nevill & Xopher Carnall for 300 a. on Patowmeck River.

Walter Gwest sold to John Medley his crop. Date: 10 September 1649. Signed: Walter Guest. Witness: Richard Browne.

Liber - Patent Record Z & A - 1637-1651

f. 529 <u>15 November</u>. William Smoote vs. Mrs. Marg. Brent.

Marg. Brent acquitted Edward Commins of all debts to her & her brother Giles Brent. Signed: Margaret Brent. Witness: William Evans.

<u>16 November</u>. Edward Commins demanded 600 a.: 200 a. for transporting self & his wife about 10 years ago, 400 a. for 4 man servants: Edward Claxton in 1639, John Williams in 1640, Andrewe Kline & Richard Salter in 1644. Warrant for western shore of Chesepeack.

Edward Claxton demanded 50 a. for service to Edward Commins. Warrant for Isle of Kent between land of said (N) & land of Phillip Conner.

Motion of Capt. Robert Vaughan & request

f. 530 of John Hatch attorney for Skipper Abraham Jonson that Thomas Greene, Esq. (Governor) withdraw the action.

Jo. Dandy vs. Xopher Carnoll. Subpoena to: Walter Cotterell.

Mrs. Margaret Brent registered a cattle mark.

<u>10 November 1649</u>. Attachment to goods & chattel of Skipper Abraham Jonson until he answer to the suit of Thomas Greene, Esq.

f. 531 Attached by: Tho. Greene, Esq., Phillip Land, Geo. Manners, Henry Fox, Mrs. Marg. Brent, Edw. Commins.

<u>20 November</u>. Robert Robins appointed George Manners his attorney to prosecute against estate of Mr. Hebden.

Lt. William Lewis appointed George Manners his attorney to prosecute against Hugh Lee.

Tho. Hatton His Lordship's Attorney General vs. Gabriel Odgers. Mentions: land of Mr. Neale, Mr. Bretton.

<u>22 November</u>. Thomas Weston released Robert Cadger of all debt, & released Robert Cadger from debt to John Hansford (of VA). Date: 1 May 1641. Witnesses: William Palmer, Rich. Hansford.

George Manners is granted 500 a. due on assignment from John Hallowes

f. 532 & to advise Thomas Greene, Esq. Date: 25 October 1649. Survey on north side of Patomeck River near Cedar Point, bounding Petite's Creek, Manners' Branch. Signed: Robert Clarke.

f. 533 Thomas Pasmore deposed that he bought of Richard Tompson (dec'd, of VA) chattel for the deponent's wife (now dec'd). And the deponent never had dealings with Henry Lee (planter). Date: 26 November 1649.

<u>28 November</u>. Thomas Hebden gave Mr. Nicholas Cawseen, Barnaby Jackson, & Luke Gardiner all my estate. My wife Mrs. Katheren Hebden shall have use of estate during her lifetime. Mentions: chattel at home of Walter Beane to be given to Mr. Thomas Copley, Esq. Date: 13 June 1649. Witnesses: John Pile, William Boreman.

f. 534 Survey for John Courts & Francis Pope (planters) on north side of Patomeck River near Petite's Creek, bounding land of Thomas Petite, Pope's Vally, for 200 a. Date: 15 October 1649. Signed: Robert Clarke. [Called Bowler, Patent f. 546.]

Survey for William Bretton (gentleman) on Bretton Bay, bounding St. Clemens Bay, St. William's Creek, freehold of said William Bretton, for 100 a. Date: 25 October 1649. Signed: Robert Clarke.

Survey for Nicholas Causine (planter) on east side of Patomeck River near Portobacco Creek, bounding Ware Branch, [metes & bounds],

f. 535 for 1000a. Date: 25 October 1649. Signed: Robert Clarke. [Called Causine Mannor.]

Survey for Mary & Jane Cockshott on east side of Patomeck River, bounding land of Nicholas Causine, for 1200 a. Date: 25 October 1649. Signed: Robert Clarke. [Called Cockshott.]

Survey for Richard Smith (planter) on north side of Patomeck River on Petite's Creek, bounding Smith Bighte, Bennett's Branch, for 100 a. Date: 25 October

Liber - Patent Record Z & A - 1637-1651

1649. Signed: Robert Clarke. [Patent f. 541.]

Survey for Richard Bennett on Patomeck River on north side of Petite's Creek, bounding Manners' Branch, Bennett's Branch,

f. 536 for 350 a. Date: 25 October 1649. Signed: Robert Clarke. [Patent f. 544.]

Survey for Thomas Petite (planter) on north side of Patomeck River near Cedar Point, bounding Guyes Branch, Cotterell's Marsh, Petite's Creek, land of John Courts & Francis Pope, for 450 a. Date: 25 September 1649. Signed: Clarke Robert [Called Guise, Patent f. 539.]

Survey for William Hungerford on Hungerford's Branch, bounding Back Creek, Hungerford's Marsh, Prior's Bight, for 100 a. Date: 25 October 1649. Signed: Robert Clarke. [Called Hungerford, Patent f. 540.]

Survey for Thomas Mathewes on north side of Patomeck River near Portobacco Creek now called St. Thomas' Creek, bounding Naugen's Creek now called St. Raphael's Creek, St. Isadere's Creek, for 3500 a. & another on east side of St. Thomas' Creek,

f. 537 St. Mathewes' Branch, St. Nicolas' Branch, for 500 a. Date: 25 October 1649. Signed: Robert Clarke. [Called Saint Thomas' Mannor, Patent f. 372.]

Survey for Raphe Crouch (gentleman) on north side of Patomeck River, bounding St. Raphaell's Creek, Naugeny Creek, for 4000 a. Date: 26 October 1649. Signed: Ro. Clarke. [Relinquished.]

Survey for Lt. William Lewis on north side of Patomeck River near Portobacco Creek now called St. Thomas' Creek, bounding St. Ursulla Marsh, St. John's Branch, for 2000 a. Date: 26 October 1649. Signed: Robert Clarke. [Called Chandlor, Patent f. 367.]

Survey for Humphrey Howell (planter) on north side of Patomeck River, bounding land of Thomas Petite, land of Thomas Michell, Guyes Branch, for 100 a. Date: 25 October 1649. Signed: Ro. Clark. [Called Howell, Patent f. 547.]

f. 538 Survey for Robert Sympkin (planter) on north side of Patomeck River near Back Creek, bounding White Oak Marsh, [metes & bounds], Simpkins Branch, for 100 a. Date: 25 October 1649. Signed: Robert Clark. [Called Simpkine, Patent f. 548.]

Survey for Benjamin Gill on Wicocomoco River near land of James Neale (gentleman), bounding Neale's Marsh, St. James' Creek, for 1000 a. Date: 25 October 1649. Signed: Robert Clarke. [Called Gills Land.]

Survey for Richard Duke (planter) assignee of Thomas Copley, Esq. on Wicocomocco River near Poesey's Creeke, bounding Duke's Branch, for 100 a. Date: 25 October 1649. Signed: Robert Clarke. [Called Duke's Place, Patent f. 543.]

Survey for Thomas Michell (planter) on Patomeck River near Neale's Creek, bounding land of Humfrey Howell, Michell's Branch, land of Robert Simpkin, for 100 a. Date: 25 October 1649. Signed: Robert Clarke. [Called Mitchell, Patent f. 542.]

f. 539 Patent to Thomas Petite for 100 a. due on assignment from John Guy & 100 a. on assignment from Nicolas Cowsene & 100 a. on assignment from Walter Cotterell & 100 a. due for transporting his wife in 1639 & 50 a. for transporting 1 child Katheren Petite in 1645, & to advise Thomas Greene, Esq., on north side of Patomeck River near Cedar Point, bounding Guyes Branch, Cotterell's Branch, Petite's Creeke, land of John Court & Francis Pope, for 450 a. Date: 22 November 1649. Signed: Tho. Greene. [Called Guise, Certificate f. 536.]

f. 540 Patent to William Hungerford (planter) for transporting self in 1647 & to advise William Stone, Esq., on Hungerford's Branch, bounding Back Creek, Hungerford Marsh, Prior's Bight, for 100 a. Date: 1 December 1649. [Certificate f. 536.]

f. 541 Patent to Richard Smith (planter) for transporting self in 1644 & to advise William Stone, Esq., on north side of Patomeck River on Petite's Creek, bounding Smithe's Bight,

f. 542 Bennett's Branch, for 100 a. Date: last November 1649. [Certificate f. 535.]

Patent to Thomas Michell (planter) on assignment from Robert Clarke (gentleman) & to advise William Stone, Esq.,

Liber - Patent Record Z & A - 1637-1651

f. 543 on Patomeck River near Neale's Creek, bounding land of Humfrey Howell, Michell's Branch, land of Robert Simpkin, for 100 a. Date: 1 December 1649. [Certificate f. 558.]

Patent to Richard Duke (planter) on assignment from Thomas Copley, Esq. & to advise William Stone, Esq.,

f. 544 on Wicocomoco River near Poesey's Creeke, bounding Duke's Branch, for 100 a. Date: 1 December 1649. [Certificate f. 538.]

Patent to Richard Bennett (planter) for transporting self, his wife & 4 children in 1646 & to advise William Stone, Esq.,

f. 545 on Patomeck River on Petite's Creek, bounding Manners Branch, Bennett's Branch, for 350 a. Date: 1 December 1649. [Certificate f. 535.] Assigned by Richard Bennett to John Ward in 1650 & by John Ward to Henry Fox in the same year, & by Fox to Robert Robins & by him included in a grant to himself & Robert Hauley of 550 a.

f. 546 on 10 June 1651.

Patent to John Courts & Francis Pope (planters) for transporting selves in 1639 & to advise William Stone, Esq., on Patomeck River on Petite's Creek, bounding land of Thomas Petite, Pope's Valley, for 200 a. Date: 29 November 1649. [Called Bowler, Certificate f. 534.]

f. 547 Patent to Humfrey Howell for transporting self in 1647 & to advise William Stone, Esq., on north side of Patomeck River, bounding land of Thomas Petite, land of Thomas Michell, Guyes Branch, for 100 a. Date: 1 December 1649. [Certificate f. 537.]

f. 548 Patent to Robert Simpkin (planter) for transporting self in 1647 & to advise William Stone, Esq., on north side of Patomeck River & near Back Creek of Mr. Neale, bounding White Oak Marsh, [metes & bounds],

f. 549 Simpkins Branch, for 100 a. Date: 1 December 1649. [Certificate f. 538.]

25 February 1649. Capt. Abraham Johnson (of Edam, Holland) appointed Mr. John Hatch as his attorney. Date: 1 March 1648. Witnesses: Cuthbert Fenwick, Cleres Jacopson.

Mr. Hatton. Petition to allow John Shertcliff to have title to 200 a.

f. 550 Date: 20 February 1649. Signed: William Hawley. Witness: John Sherciffe. Land was for Shercliffe & Edw. Smith for transporting selves in 1646. John Shercliffe demanded 200 a. which he formerly assigned to Capt. William Hawley being re-assigned to him & 100 a. due on assignment from Nicolas Paulhampton & 50 a. in right of his wife for her service to Mr. Lewger & 50 a. for his own service to Mrs. Troughton & 50 a. due Henry Spinke as servant to Nicholas Harvey & 50 a. for Mathewe Crabbe a woman servant bought of William Stiles.

100 a. assigned to Jo. Shercliffe (of Newtowne). Date: 26 January 1649. Signed: Nich. Paulhampton. Witness: Robert Clarke.

Warrant to layout 500 a. for John Shercliffe & Henry Spinke on south side of Putuxent River at Newtowne.

23 March. Robert Holt by Edward Hudson demanded 400 a. for transporting self, his wife, & 4 children 3 years ago. Warrant to south of Putuxent River.

f. 551 Date: 6 September 1648. William Pack was bound to Robert Lewellin from then until his arrival in VA & after for 10 years. Witnesses: Richard Husbands, Arthur Ludford, Thomas Byam. Date: 17 February 1648. Assignment to Ralphe Beane. Date: 27 January 1649. Assignment to John Pille.

Capt. John Price demanded of estate of Thomas Hebden (dec'd).

Patent to James Johnson (planter) on assignment from William Assiter for transporting self & 1 servant in 1640 & to advise William Stone, Esq.,

f. 552 on Patomeck River, bounding Poplar Hill Creek, Johnson's Marsh, for 200 a. [Called Latchford.]

Mrs. Katheren Hebden administratrix of Thomas Hebden (dec'd) vs. Barnaby Jackson et. al. Mr. John Pile deposed on 22 April 1650 that he was present when Mr. Thomas Hebden (dec'd) delivered a guift to Barnaby Jackson et. al.

f. 553 Mr. William Eltonhead vs. Joseph Edlow.

Liber - Patent Record Z & A - 1637-1651

Mr. Cuthbt. Fenwick vs. Edm. Hall

Mr. John Hallowes assignee of Anthony West vs. George Sanghier.

Mr. John Hallowes assignee of Tho. Boyse vs. Henr. Fox.

Mr. Phillip Land vs. Humfr. Howell.

John Slingsly vs. Franc. Poesey.

Thomas Petite vs. Jo. Hansford.

Mr. Robert Clarke vs. John Nunne.

Lt. Richard Banks vs. James Johnson. Subpoena to: Richard Bennett.

George Berry (mariner) vs. John Earle.

Daniell Clocker vs. Cuthbert Fenwick (gentleman) attorney for Capt. Tho. Cornwalleyes. [Concerns Clocker's service.]

Anthony Rawlins vs. John Ashley.

Henry Pountney vs. Walter Pakes.

Mr. William Durant assignee of Mr. Phillip

f. 554 Bennett agent for Thomas Jenery (merchant) vs. David Prichard.

Mr. William Brough vs. Ricnd. Nevett.

Mr. William Brough vs. Barthol. Phillips.

James Lindsey vs. Barthol. Phillips.

Mr. Cuthbert Fenwick vs. Ricnd. Duke.

Tho. White vs. James Walker administrator of John Tompson for chattel sold 3 years ago.

William Smoote vs. Mrs. Margaret Brent.

Henry Packman vs. Waltern Pakes.

Joseph Edlowe vs. John Dandy.

Jo. Court vs. Ricnd. Husbands.

Jo. Court vs. Ricnd. Husbands. Subpoena to: Cuthbert Fenwick, William Marshall.

Anth. Rawlins vs. Marks Pheypo.

James Lindsey vs. estate of William Tompson.

Jo. Hatch vs. Robert Smith.

Jo. Hatch vs. Ricnd. Ware.

Jo. Hatch vs. William Hardwich.

Nichol. Gwyther assignee of Tho. Hamper vs. John Ashley.

Nichol. Gwyther assignee of Tho. Hamper vs. John Trigare.

Jo. Dandy vs. William Stephens & Jo. Burlane.

Jo. Dandy vs. Fr. Brooks.

f. 555 Thomas May vs. Walter Beane.

George Manners vs. Paul Simpson.

Henry Pountney vs. Jo. Ashley & Jo. Tigare.

William Brough vs. estate of William Tompson.

Liber - Patent Record Z & A - 1637-1651

Humfry Atwicks vs. Richard Smith.

Tho. Sturman vs. Mrs. Marg. Brent.

Jo. Medley vs. Ricnd. Browne.

Jo. Medley vs. Tho. Greene, Esq.

John Shercliffe vs. Stephen Salmon.

Henry Armes vs. Walter Pakes.

John Hatch vs. Walter Guest.

Jo. Underhill (mariner) vs. Henr. Fox.

Rich. Husbands (mariner) vs. (N) Cotton.

William Edwin attorney for Fr. Jarvis vs. Franc. Brooks.

Phillip Land vs. Ricnd. Browne.

Phillip Land vs. Ricnd. Stedman.

James Lindsey vs. Robert Smith. Subpoena to: Tho. Waggatte.

Nichol. Cawseene vs. Joseph Cadle.

Fr. Brooks vs. William Edwin. Subpoena to: John Nicholls.

Nichol. Cawseene vs. Capt. Edward Hill for man servant.

Robert Gourden vs. Ralph Beane. Subpoena to: Rowland Beanes, John Medley.

George Manners vs. Capt. Edw. Hill.

f. 556 Robert Kadger vs. Cuthbert Fenwick.

Robert Kadger vs. Mrs. Marg. Brent.

Edward Hudson vs. John Rosier (clarke).

Nichol. Gwyther vs. Mr. Cuthbt. Fenwick.

Mr. Richard Husbands vs. Phillip Land.

Tho. Hamper vs. Geoffrey Gaunt.

Mr. Robert Clarke vs. estate of William Tompson.

John Hatch administrator of Tho. Allen vs. Walter Waterling.

Mr. Robert Clark vs. Lt. William Lewis.

Mr. Robert Clark vs. Paul Simpson.

Francis Brookes vs. Charles Rawlinson.

John Greenway (planter, of St. Maries'), age 25, deposed that about 5 years ago, he was present when Mr. William Brainthwait (dec'd, of St. Maries') married Helenor Stephenson (who came from England with Sir Edmund Plowden as his servant). Date: 14 February 1649. Witnesses: William Stone, Tho. Stone, Tho. Hatton.

Thomas Waggatte, age 23, deposed that on 6 February 1649, that about 3 years ago, Robert Smith brought chattel to Chechacone from his house to be given to Smith's children by John Hilliard, which belonged to Serg. James Lendesey & currently at plantation of Mr. Mottrom at Checkacone.

f. 557 Witness: Tho. Hatton.

Richard Browne is bound to Phillip Land. Date: 4 November 1649. Witnesses: Jo. Wade, Fracis Vanenden.

Richard Brown is bound to Phillip Land. Date: 1 November 1649. Witnesses: John Wade, Fr. Vanenden.

Liber - Patent Record Z & A - 1637-1651

10 January 1648. William Tompson (of St. Clement's Hundred) is bound to William Brough. Witness: Bartholomew Phillips.

Margaret Brent attorney for her brother Giles Brent sold to Lt. William Evans chattel. Witness: Tho. Hamper.

f. 558 15 November 1649 at St. Maries'. Court. Attendees: Tho. Greene, Esq., Capt. John Price, Mr. Tho. Hatton, Mr. John Pile, Capt. Robert Vaughan.

William Eltonhead (gentleman) in right of his wife vs. Lt. Richard Banks & other administrators of Tho. Allen (dec'd). Mentions: that the plaintiff's wife is widow of (N) Smith (gentleman), Daniell Cugly, Giles Bashawe attorney for Capt. Phillip Taylor her former husband.

Inventory of estate of Tho. Allen accepted.

John Hollis by his attorney Phillip Land vs. Geo. Manners. Mentions: defendant was plaintiff's attorney, Francis Vanenden.

f. 559 William Smoote vs. Mrs. Margaret Brent. Mentions: William Stephenson, John Sturman, Mr. Fenwick, Geoffrey Power.

f. 560 Mrs. Marg. Brent vs. George Manners. Mentions: estate of Mr. Gerrard.

John Dandy vs. Xpofer Carnoll.

John Thimbleby administrator of Peter Mackarell (dec'd) acknowledged a debt due Walter Beane.

Tho. Gerrard, Esq. by his attorney Mr. Bretton vs. Jo. Thimblely administrator of Peter Mackarell. Mentions: deposition of George Manners.

Tho. Baker by his attorney Mr. Richard Browne vs. Edward Cotton by his attorney Barnaby Jackson.

Benjamin Gill vs. Gabriel Odgers. Mentions: house of Mr. Neale,

f. 561 Mr. Richard Browne attorney for defendant.

Elias Beach vs. Henry Adams.

f. 562 19 November 1649. Tho. Greene authorized William Bretton (gentleman) to administer oath to George Manners & Henry Adams.

George Manners deposed that Elias Beach desired the deponent said Elias' attorney

f. 563 to ask for continuance in case between said Elias & Henry Adams where Capt. Stone should act as judge.

David O'doughorty by his attorney Mr. Richard Browne vs. Lt. William Lewis. Mentions: Mr. Copley.

Thomas Gerrard, Esq. by his attorney Mr. William Bretton vs. Lt. William Lewis.

Thomas Uell vs. Mrs. Marg. Brent.

f. 564 Richard Cole vs. Jo. Halfhead. Witness: William Boreman.

John Hollis vs. Nicholas Gwiter.

Hugh Lee vs. Lt. William Lewis.

Paul Simpson vs. John Thimbleby.

Paul Simpson vs. Richard Lloyd.

Water Waterling vs. John Thimbleby administrator of Peter Mackarell.

Robert Robins vs. (N) Hebden. Mentions: Capt. John Price, wife of Mr. Hebden, John Hatch.

f. 565 William Bretton (gentleman), per Benjamin Gill, deposed that last week he heard Mr. Gabriell Odgers say he intended to leave the Province, to go to Wicocomoco to live near the plantation of Mr. Knight, Thomas Phillips went out with him. Mentions: Richard Duke, John Lanclott.

Liber - Patent Record Z & A - 1637-1651

22 November. Ralph Beane appointed George Manners as his attorney.

19 October 1649. John Hallowes appointed Mr. Phillip Land as his attorney. Witness: Tho. Copley.

29 November 1649. Last January, George Manners sold to Capt. Robert Vaughan a man servant Robert Atkinson, & to Mr. Phillip Conner another man servant. Witnesses: Tho. Hatton, William Bretton.

20 November 1649. Francis Vanenden acknowledged to George Manners

f. 566 a judgement. Witness: Tho. Hatton. Date: 13 February 1650. Satisfaction given.

John Malham deposed that in September 1648, he was with others who brought chattel from Indian Town named Machoatick into Matapania on south side of Patomeck River. John Hallowes said that that chattel that he had lent to Nicholas Gwyter.

Hugh Lee deposed that in September 1648, John Hallowes had instructed him to take certain chattel into his possession. The deponent was told by John Malham & Robert Honyborne that it was brought from Machoatick to Matapania.

f. 567 Capt. Robert Vaughan demanded 100 a. for transporting William Loader a man servant in 1642 & 100 a. for transporting James Courtney another man servant in 1638 & 100 a. for transporting James Atkinson another man servant in 1648 & 200 a. for transporting 4 women servants: Francis Woolhouse in 1640, Penelope Prince in 1644, Mary Field in 1644, & Frances Pinke in 1646. Warrant for Parson's Point & Poplar Neck on east side of Isle of Kent.

7 January. Richard Butler demanded 100 a. for transporting self in 1646. He assigned it to Walter Pakes. Date: 10 August 1646. Witness: John Polard.

9 January. Edmond Rite demanded 100 a. for transporting self in 1646. He assigned it to Walter Pakes. Date: 20 September 1646. Witness: Richard Ware.

7 January 1649. Warrant for 200 a.

f. 568 on Wicocomoco or Patomeck Rivert for John Hatch. On 1 April, warrant was renewed for 350 a.

Capt. John Price (Muster Master General) is bound to John Underhill. Date: 19 December 1649. Witnesses: Richard Browne, Geo. Sanghier. Date: 7 March 1650. George Manners attorney for Jo. Underhill acknowledged receipt.

21 January. Nicholas Gwither appointed George Manners as his attorney. Witness: Tho. Hatton.

Thomas Bushnell registered a cattle mark.

Francis Antell registered a cattle mark.

18 January. Warrant for 300 a. to Mr. Thomas Pasmore on Patomeck River. Assigned to Mr. Tho. Sturman or Jo. Sturman. Date: 18 February 1649.

11 February 1649. John Maunsell assigned to Stephen Salmon 50 a. due in right of his wife for service bought of Mr. Hatton.

f. 569 John Maunsell demanded 50 a. in right of his wife.

William Marshall assigned to William Pell 200 a.: 100 a. as a part of 400 a. due on record, 100 a. for transporting Ellen Jones his servant in 1650. Date: 17 December.

William Pell demanded 200 a. for transporting self & (N) Arther his man servant last March & 200 a. on assignment from William Marshall. Warrant for River Patapsco or other on western shore of Chesepeacke Bay.

Thomas Sturman registered a cattle mark.

Fred Johnson received of Nicholas Cawse by Mr. Richard Ingle for use of Mr. Thomas Herne. Date: 20 December 1644. More received by Mr. Ingle for said Thomas Hearne.

20 December. James Johnson gave chattel to Thomas Bennett. Should he d.s.p. before age 21, said chattel to be disposed of by Elisabeth Bennett to next eldest son of said Elisabeth & after

Liber - Patent Record Z & A - 1637-1651

f. 570 his decease to youngest son, then eldest daughter to youngest. If husband should outlive wife, then said Richard Bennett shall dispose of chattel. Date: 18 February 1648. Witnesses: Walter Smith, Jo. Cable.

Richard Lawrence sold to John Cage 100 a. Date: 18 December 1649. Witness: Tho. Oliver. Richard Lawrence demanded 100 a. for transporting self 7 years ago, assigned above.

last of December. John Cage demanded 100 a. on assignment from Richard Lawrence & 50 a. for service to Capt. Cornwallis. Warrant for north side of Patomeck River.

27 December. Warrant for 700 a. for Serg. Marks Pheypo & Nicholas Keeting at Point Patience on north side of Putuxent River. [Demand f. 256.]

7 January. Phillip Bagley demanded 100 a. for transporting self in 1649. Warrant for Patapsco River on western shore of Bay.

Mr. Joseph Rock demanded 100 a. for transporting

f. 571 self in 1649. Warrant for near Patapsco River on western shore of Bay.

9 January 1649. Richard Husbands (master of the ship "Hopefull Adventure") sold to John Hatch one man servant: Richard Rooe. Witnesses: Cuthbert Fenwick, Arthur Turnor.

Mr. Thomas Pasmore deposed on 18 January 1649 that he had a grant of 1000 a. from Leonard Calvert, Esq., subsequently conveyed to Mr. Thomas Sturman. Mentions: deponent's house in VA. Soon after the grant, Mr. Calvert appointed the deponent &

f. 572 Andrew Chappell (since dec'd) to select the land, bounding land occupied by Francis Martin.

George Manners deposed that he recently tried to serve a warrant to Paul Simpson, but said Paul was not available. Date: 11 February 1649.

12 February 1649. Stephen Salmon demanded 200 a.: 50 a. as a servant to Capt. Cornwallis, 50 a. in right of his wife who was a servant to Mrs. Troughton, 50 a. remaining due from a guift from Governor Calvert, 50 a. on assignment from John Maunsell.

f. 573 Warrant for Cedar Point on Patomeck River joining land of George Manners.

14 February 1649. In resolution of 2 actions between Francis Brookes & William Edwin concerning Francis Jarvis, said Brookes sold to said Edwin chattel. Witness: Tho. Hatton.

25 January 1649 at St. Maries'. Court. Attendees: William Stone, Esq., Mr. Tho. Hatton.

John Court vs. Mr. Richard Husbands (mariner). Deposition of Mr. Cuthbert Fenwick regarding speech between the plaintiff & defendant.

f. 574 Anthony Rawlins vs. Marks Pheypo. Mentions: George Manners, plaintiff's attorney Mr. Fenwick.

Daniell Clocker vs. Mr. Cuthbert Fenwick attorney for Capt. Cornwalleys. Mentions: plaintiff was servant to Capt. Cornwalleys.

Anthony Rawlins vs. John Ashley.

f. 575 20 February 1649. Mrs. Margaret Brent assigned to Zachary Wade 100 a. due for transporting him as her servant in 1641.

7 January. Mr. William Durand demanded 900 a. for transporting self, his wife, his daughter Elisabeth, Joseph Long, Thomas Marsh, Margaret Marsh, & 2 servants: William Warren & William Hoggins last March 8 & Anne Cole his servant. Warrant for Patapsco River on western shore of Bay or Isle of Kent.

Mr. Zephaniah Smith demanded 600 a. for transporting self & 5 servants in 1649: Robert Tompson, Robert Knight, James Cope, Richard Vaughan, Grace Wells. Warrant for Patapsco River on western shore of Bay.

14 February 1649 at St. Maries'. Court. Attendees: William Stone, Esq., Thomas Green, Esq., Mr. Thomas Hatton, Mr. John Pile.

Liber - Patent Record Z & A - 1637-1651

William Harwich vs. Mr. William Bretton. Mentions: cause between said Hardwich & Capt. John Price.

f. 576 John Hatch one of the administrators of Tho. Allen (dec'd). Mentions: charge of redeeming Allen's children from Indians.

John Hatch vs. William Hardwich. Mentions: transporting Edward Hull out of the Province.

John Sturman vs. Mrs. Margaret Brent attorney for Capt. Giles Brent. Mentions: Anthony Rawlins, father of the plaintiff.

f. 577 ...
- Thomas Youll deposed that the chattel that Anthony Rawlins had in his possession did not belong to Capt. Brent, & the chattel which did belong to Capt. Brent is dead. Witness: Ro. Sedgrave (of Northumberland Co.).
- George Watts deposed that the chattel which Capt. Brent received of Anthony Rawlins is not his, & that which Capt. Brent claims is dead. Witness: Ro. Sedgrave (of Northumberland Co.).

Mrs. Margaret Brent acknowledged that her brother Capt. Giles Brent never had chattel of Anthony Rawlins.

Mr. Richard Husbands (mariner) vs. Mr. Phillip Land. Mentions: John Treleague (servant of plaintiff).

f. 578 Thomas Sturman vs. Mrs. Margaret Brent. Mentions: grant to Thomas Pasmore of 100 a. by Leonard Calvert, Esq. (dec'd).

John Hatch attorney for Abraham Johnson (mariner) vs. Thomas Greene, Esq.

attorney for Abraham Johnson (mariner) vs. Phillip Land. The

f. 579 defendant assigned his whole estate to Mr. Bretton.

15 February. Thomas Greene, Esq. (of St. Maries') paid satisfaction to John Medley (planter, of Newtowne Hundred). Date: 26 September 1647. Witnesses: William Tompson, George Dolti.

27 February. John Halfhead demanded 100 a. as a servant to his Lordship, 100 a. in right of his first wife Anne (a freewoman), 50 a. in right of his now wife Julian (a servant to Mrs. White). Warrant between Capt. Dorrell's Quarter & Mattapania River on south side of Putuxent River.

Joseph Edlowe demanded 250 a. by grant from his Lordship to Simpkin Througood assigned to said Joseph & 50 a. as a servant to Leonard Calvert, Esq. (dec'd).

f. 580 Warrant between Capt. Dorrell's Quarter & Mattapania house on south side of Putuxent River.

Edward Tompson vs. Mrs. Marg. Brent. Defendant is executrix of estate of Leonard Calvert, Esq. (dec'd) to deliver to Joane Tompson (dec'd) & her children. Date: 9 March 1649.

16 March 1649. Edward Cotton registered a cattle mark.

Margarett Brent sold to Edward Cotton chattel suckled by wife of Nicholas Harvie. Date: 8 January 1648. Witness: Mary Brent.

18 March. Hugh Hopewell demanded 100 a. for transporting self in 1641 & 50 a. in respect of his wife's service to Mr. Copley.

Tho. White demanded 50 a. for his service to Capt. Clayborne which expired 9 years ago. Warrant for 200 a. for Hugh Hopewell & Thomas White at Hogpen Taverne Neck or Saccawakitt on south side of Putuxent River.

Tho. White registered a cattle mark.

f. 581 12 February 1649. Hunfrey Howell acknowledged a judgement to Mr. Phillip Land. Signed: Humfry Howell.

Mr. Isaac Ilive demanded 100 a. for transporting self in 1644. Zacharias Wade demanded 100 a. on assignment from Mrs. Brent. Warrant for 200 a. for Ilive & Wade on Isle of Kent on plantation where Jo. Gresham lived.

Francis Vandan vs. Nath. Pope.

23 March. Owen James demanded 100 a. for transporting self in 1645 & 200 a. for transporting 2 man servants: Richard Stanford in 1648, John Pascho in 1649.

Liber - Patent Record Z & A - 1637-1651

Warrant for Hog's Neck adjoining Bushell's plantation.

Daniell Clocker demanded 100 a.: 50 a. for self as servant to Capt. Cornwalleys, 50 a. in right of his wife (servant to Mrs. Margarett Brent). Warrant for western shore of Chesepeck Bay to southward of Putuxent River & next neck to northward of Peter Draper's Neck.

Elias Beach demanded 50 a. for service to Nicholas Cawseene & 100 a. in right of his wife who transported self about 10 years ago & 50 a. for a woman servant of Mr. Husbands about 1 year ago--she is now the wife of George Manners. Date: 2 September. Warrant for eastern side of St. George's River.

f. 582 20 February. William Freeman by his attorney Mr. Richard Husbands is bound to Mr. Thomas Sturman. Date: 7 September 1649 in London.

20 February 1649 at St. Michael's Hundred. Court. Attendees: William Stone, Esq., Capt. John Price, Mr. Thomas Hatton.

Mr. Thomas Sturman vs. Mr. Richard Husbands (mariner) attorney for Mr. William Freeman.

f. 583 Mentions: John Sturman (son of plaintiff).

f. 584 Tho. Sturman vs. Richard Husbands (mariner). John Dandy deposed that about 10 days ago, he heard said Thomas Sturman desire said Husbands to deliver up a bond. Mr. Husbands said the bond was at house of Mr. Fenwick. Date: 24 February 1649.

Tho. Sturman vs. Rich. Husbands (mariner). Concerns bond by plaintiff to Mr. Freeman. George Manners deposed that a day or 2 ago, the deponent heard said Sturman demand the bond of said

f. 585 Husbands, who said the bond was at house of Mr. Fenwick. Date: 27 February 1649.

25 February 1649 at St. Maries'. Court. Attendees: William Stone, Esq., Thomas Greene, Esq., Tho. Hatton (gentleman).

Mr. Phillip Land vs. Mr. Richard Brown by his attorney George Manners.

John Hatch administrator of Tho. Allen (dec'd) vs. Walter Waterling.

William Stone, Esq. demanded payment to estate of Mr. Weston (dec'd) from administrator of Peter Mackarell.

f. 586 Walter Waterling vs. John Thimbleby administrator of Peter Mackarel.

John Ward registered a cattle mark.

Elias Beach vs. Henry Adams.

George Manners acknowledged judgement to John Halfhead.

Mrs. Katheren Hebden requested confirmation of her administration of her husband's estate.
- William Boreman deposed that when Mr. Thomas Hebden (dec'd) declared via a deed dated 13 June last that Mrs. Hebden was to deliver chattel to Mr. Pile.
- William Marshall deposed that 3 weeks to a month ago

f. 587 ...
before the decease of Mr. Tho. Hebden, Mrs. Hebden complained that Mr. Hebden had made away with estate he had of her. Mentions: John Hatch, Mr. Cawseen.
- Deposition by Mr. John Pile. (see f. 559.)

Mr. Robert Clarke acknowledged debt to Skipper Jacob Derrickson.

Serg. James Lindsey vs. Robert Smith. Mentions: deposition of (N) Waggate, Mr. Greene.

f. 588 26 February 1649 at St. Maries'. Court. Attendees: Governor, Secretary.

Mr. John Hallowes vs. George Manners.

Hugh Lee vs. Lt. William Lewis.

Liber - Patent Record Z & A - 1637-1651

George Manners vs. Paul Simpson.

George Manners vs. Capt. Edward Hill.

Francis Vanenden vs. Nathaniell Pope.

William Smoote vs. Mr. Cuthbt. Fenwick. Mentions: William Stephenson, John Sturman.

f. 589 Giles Brent acknowledged debt to Tho. Weston (merchant, of VA). Date: 20 October 1640. Mrs. Margaret Brent attorney for Capt. Giles Brent deposed that she paid said debt. William Stone, Esq. (Governor) claimant to estate of Mr. Weston is satisfied.

25 February 1649. Lt. William Evans acknowledged a gift to Andrew Tompson (minor, son of William Tompson (of Little Brittaine, dec'd)) bought of Margarett Brent (gentlewoman) attorney for Capt. Giles Brent.

f. 590 Proclamation: regarding headrights.

f. 591 Date: 13 April 1649. Signed: William Stone.

Proclamation (further).

f. 592 ...

f. 593 Date: 30 October 1649. Signed: Thomas Greene.

Proclamation (further).

f. 594 Date: 25 March 1650. Signed: William Stone.

Proclamation of Charles II as King. Date: 15 November 1649. Signed: Tho. Greene.

Proclamation regarding general pardon.

f. 595 Date: 15 November 1649. Signed: Tho. Greene.

Mrs. Marg. Brent for Mrs. Eure vs. Anthony Rawlins.
- William Hardwich deposed.

f. 596 ...
- William Hardwich deposed that the other chattel he had of his father-in-law Thomas Sturman. Date: 18 February 1649.

Proclamation by Governor & Captain General of Virginia. Mentions: a petition to his Majesty that Isle of Kent & Palmer's Island

f. 597 belong to Lord Baltimore. Date: 4 October 1638 at James City. Witness: Rich. Kempe.

f. 598 Phillip Land (gentleman) made over to William Bretton (gentleman) all lands, etc., until 10 June 1650. Date: 20 June 1649. Witness: Rowland Maes.

Proclamation: Mr. Richard Husbands (mariner) is appointed admiral or vice admiral. Date: 23 February 1649. Signed: William Stone.

f. 599 John Russell (of Isle of Kent) deposed on 25 February 1649 that yesterday he was aboard the ship "Green Poppingay" now at St. George's River & heard John Dandy caution Mr. Husbands (mariner).

Charles Rawlinson declared that Francis Brookes made claim on chattel

f. 600 recently sold to Mr. John Hallowes, received from Mrs. Margaret Brent about 2 years ago, and said chattel never belonged to James Cauther or Francis Brookes. Date: 6 March 1649.

Charles Rawlinson deposed that about 2 years ago, Thomas Waggate told Mrs. Fenwick, wife of Mr. Cuthbert Fenwick, that there was chattel belonging to Capt. Cornwallyes. William Smoote recovered the chattel. Date: 6 March.

f. 601 Paul Simpson is bound to John Dandy. Witness: Tho. Maidwell.

John Ashley & John Tragare acknowledged a debt to Mr. Nicholas Gwither. Date: 8 February 1649. Witness: William Eltonhead.

Liber - Patent Record Z & A - 1637-1651

John Thimbleby & William Brown (planters) appointed

f. 602 George Manners (planter) as their attorney. Mentions: John Hollis (trader, of Appomatucks). Date: 4 February 1649. Witness: William Whittle.

William Tompson is bound to Raphe Beane. Date: 23 April 1649. Witnesses: Rowland Sissill, Tho. Thomas.

Walter Pakes is bound to Walter Beane. Date: 1 March 1649. Witnesses: Rich. Nevett, Rowland Sissell.

Walter Guest is bound to

f. 603 John Treleague. Date: 1 February 1649. Witness: Henry Bishop.

Phillip Land is indebted to John Underhill. Date: 20 December 1649. Witness: Robert Wiseman.

Richard Browne appointed George Manners as his attorney. Date: 2 February 1649. Witness: Jo. Wade.

Phillip Land appointed Lt. Nicholas Gwither as his attorney. Date: 6 March 1649. Witness: Tho. Hatton.

Nathaniell Pope (of Appamatox) assigned 1000 a. to William Lewis which was bought of Mrs. Straton at her going to England. Date: 21 January 1649. Witness: Phillip Chaddock.

f. 604 Mr. John Pile registered a cattle mark.

Luke Gardiner registered a cattle mark.

12 February. Robert Robins demanded 250 a. for transporting self, his wife & (N) Robins his child in 1648. Warrant for Cedar Point near George Manners & Stephen Salmon.

9 February. Henry Bishop demanded 100 a. for transporting self in 1640. Warrant for Patomeck River.

Simon Demeibilla demanded 200 a. for transporting self & Walter Waterson in 1640.

17 February. John Maunsell demanded 600 a.: 300 a. on assignment from John Warren, 300 a. on assignment from Mr. Robert Clarke. Warrant for Patomeck River.

Margaret Brent sold her rights to Barnaby Jackson for 500 a. due herself & her sister Mary Brent for transporting servants in 1638: Samuell Pursall, Tho. Ted, Francis Towers, John Stephen, John Delahay. Date: 26 January 1649.

5 February. Barnaby Jackson demanded 500 a. due by sale from Mrs. Brent, 100 a. for Henry More a man servant bought of Mr. Blount about 6 years ago, 50 a. due for his service to Mr. Lewger. Warrant between Cedar Point & Point Lookout on western shore of Chesepeack Bay.

Mrs. Margaret Brent & Mrs. Mary Brent demanded

f. 605 2000 a. for transporting selves & 4 maid servants: Mary Taylor, Elisabeth Guest, Mary Damghton, Elisabeth Brooke.

Mrs. Margaret Brent attorney for her brother Capt. Giles Brent demanded 6000 a. for transporting man servants: Thomas Rowney, William Snipe, James Price, Humfrey (N), William (N) in 1637, & Devoreux Goodwyn John Warren, Richard Pinner, John Robinson, Edward Berry in 1638 et. al.

John Medley assigned his right to 50 a. (in St. Clement's Hundred near Newtowne) to John Warrens, Date: 15 November 1647. Witnesses: Tho. Baylie, John Thimbleby. John Warren assigned to William Browne. Date: 3 June 1650. Witness: Tho. Hatton.

f. 606 28 February 1649. Walter Waterling gave to Robert Smith 100 a.: 50 a. for my freedom & 50 a. for a maid servant. Witness: William Asbeston.

Robert Smith demanded 50 a. for his service, 100 a. for Thomas Thomas a servant bought of Mr. Pasmore 15 years ago, 300 a. in right of Rose his now wife formerly the wife of Richard Gilbert, for transporting said Gilbert & his wife & Elisabeth & Grace their children, & 100 a. on assignment from Walter Waterling. Date: 2 September. Warrant for Putuxent River.

Liber - Patent Record Z & A - 1637-1651

John Nevill registered a cattle mark.

Survey for Charles Maynard on east side of St. Clement's Bay, bounding St. Charles' Branch, for 100 a. Date: 6 February 1649. Signed: Robert Clarke. [Called Newington.]

Survey for John Thimbleby & William Brown (planter, of Newtown) on north side of Potomock River, bounding Picokomoco Creeke, land of John Medley, land of John Shercliffe, Medley's Branch, for 150 a. Date: 28 January 1649. Signed: Robert Clarke. [Called Thimblebie, Patent f. 344.]

f. 607 Survey for Walter Pakes on east side of Bretton Bay, bounding Grymesditch Creek, St. Lawrence's Branch, for 300 a. Date: 29 January 1649. Signed: Robert Clarke.

Survey for Bartholomew Obert & Dominick (N) on east side of Bretton's Bay, bounding St. Lawrence's Branch, for 200 a. Date: 4 February 1649. Signed: Robert Clarke.

Survey for George Ackrick on west side of St. Clement's Bay, bounding Elisabeth's Branch, Ackrick's Fresh, for 300 a. Date: 11 February 1649. Signed: Robert Clarke. [Called Acricke.]

Survey for Barnaby Jackson called Streton near Bay of Chesapeack, bounding Jackson's Fresh,

f. 608 [metes & bounds], for 650 a. Date: 1 March 1649. Signed: Robert Clarke.

Survey for John Halfhead on south side of Putuxent River, bounding land of Joseph Edlowe, St. James' Creeke formerly Machewatts Creeke, St. Patrick's Creeke, St. Thomas' Creek, for 250 a. Date: 2 March 1649. Signed: Robert Clarke. [Called Halfhead on ye Hill.]

Survey for Joseph Edlowe (planter) on south side of Putuxent River, bounding Machchewatts Creek now called St. James' Creek, Halfhead Hollow, for 300 a. Date: 2 March 1649. Signed: Robert Clarke. [Called Sasquahana Point.]

15 March. Robert Burle demanded 700 a. for transporting self & 6 others in 1649: Mary his wife, Robert Burle, Jr., Stephen Burle, William Holman, Neal Clarke, Rebecca Kitteridge. Warrant.

Abraham Hollman demanded 100 a. for transporting self in 1650. Warrant.

f. 609 Thomas Munnes & Elkenath Bourne (seamen) deposed that 7 days ago, they were employed by Mr Richard Husbands (mariner) & received of John Jarbo chattel for Raphe Beanes. Date: 26 February 1649.

Notice to: My cousin Mr. John Pott (at Golden Quarter in VA). Deliver to Mr. Thomas Hatton chattel, a gift for his son Thomas Hatton. Date: 5 September 1648. Signed: Francis Pott.

f. 610 Grant to Nathaniell Pope (planter, of St. Maries') for transporting self & to advise Leonard Calvert, Esq., on north side of St. James' Creek, bounding St. Maries' Bay, townland of John Lewger, Esq., Pope's Swamp, St. John's Brooke, for 100 a. [Patent Liber F, f. 14.]

f. 611 Date: 27 February 1639. Nath. Pope assigned to Francis Vandan. Date: 17 November 1645. Francis Vandan assigned to Richard Willan & James Lindesey for chattel to remain in hands of Barnaby Jackson. Date: 16 January 1647. Witnesses: Robert Clarke, Edward Cotton. Richard Willan & James Lindesey assigned to Mr. Thomas Hatton. Date: 1 March 1649. Witness: William Evans. Agreement between Serg. James Lindesey & Richard Willan for themselves & for John Greeneway and Thomas Hatton (gentleman),

f. 612 sale of land near Snow Hill Mannor. Date: 6 February 1649. Witnesses: Nicholas Gwither, John Wade. John Greeneway agrees to sale. Date: 1 February 1649. Witness: James Langworth. Richard Willan James Lindesey, & John Greeneway accepted payment. Date: 1 March 1649. Witness: William Evans.

1 March 1649. Mr. Thomas Hatton

f. 613 demanded 1500 a. for transporting self, his wife, his 2 sons Robert & Thomas Hatton, Patrick Forrest, George Beckwith, Mary Forrell his servants in 1648 & for transporting Margarett Hatton (widow) his sister-in-law & her children William, Richard, Barbara, Elisabeth, Mary, Elinor, & her servant John Perryn in 1649.

Liber - Patent Record Z & A - 1637-1651

James Lindesey, Richard Willan, & John Greeneway acknowledge receipt. Date: 25 January 1650. Witness: Arthur Turnor.

25 March 1650. Lt. Nicholas Gwither was appointed high sheriff of St. Maries' Co. Signed: William Stone.

19 April 1650. John Medley demanded allowance for chattel delivered to Capt. John Price for the use of Gov. Calvert in St. Tho. Fort.

13 May 1650. Mr. Robert Clarke deposed that about 7 years ago, by warrant from Mr. Secretary Lewger, he surveyed 4000 a. on south side of Putuxent River for Mr. Cuthbt. Fenwick in right of Capt. Thomas Cornwalleyes.

f. 614 Mr. Cuthbert Fenwick on behalf of Capt. Tho. Cornwallis demanded said 4000 a. Warrant for south side of Putuxent River westward of land of Nicholas Havey (dec'd).

Mr. Cuthbert Fenwick demanded 200 a. formerly assigned to Capt. William Hawley who relinquished it. Warrant for said 2000 a. on south side of Putuxent River westward of land of Capt. Cornwallyes.

17 May. Mr. George Puddington demanded 800 a. for transporting self & 7 others: Jane Puddington, Elisabeth Robins, Mary Puddington, Comfort Puddington, Thomas Hippesty, John Burrage, Margaret Joye. Warrant for Parson's Neck on Isle of Kent or any part of Annarundell or Kent Counties.

Thomas Cole demanded 200 a. for transporting self & his wife Priscilla last year. Warrant for Parson's Neck on Isle of Kent or Annarundell County.

Mr. James Cox demanded 300 a. for transporting self & 2 others

f. 615 last year: James Hames, Francis Tappes. Witnesses: Richard Ewen, John Hall. Warrant for Parson's Neck on Isle of Kent or Annarundell County.

Richard Ewen demanded 1000 a. for transporting self & 9 others last year: Suffa his wife, Elisabeth Davy, Richard Ewen, Jr., John Ewen, Susanna Ewen, Ann Ewen, William Davis, John King, James Browne. Witnesses: James Coxe, John Hall. Warrant for Parson's Neck on Isle of Kent or Annarundell Co.

13 June. Daniell Clocker registered a cattle mark.

19 April. Mr. Phillip Land demanded 150 a.: 100 a. on assignment from Edward Langford, 50 a. in right of transportation of his late wife (dec'd). Warrant for 100 a. at Plumme Point on St. George's River above the land of Henry Adams.

Capt. William Stone appointed Thomas Hatton (gentleman, Secretary) as Lt. General. Date: 22 May 1650.

f. 616 Walter Beane demanded allowance for chattel delivered to Capt. Price for use of Governor Calvert in St. Thomas Fort.

William Boreman, age 20, deposed on 28 May 1650 that in 1645, the deponent was aboard a pinnace (in St. Inego's Creek) which contains items belonging to Mr. Cuthbert Fenwick who employed Andrew Monroe as its master. Mr. Richard Ingle came aboard and plundered the pinnace. Said Ingle during the insurrection commanded a pinnace belonging to Capt. Thomas Conwallies. Said Ingle also plundered the house of Mr. Copley at Portoback.

f. 617 3 June. William Hungerford registered a cattle mark.

Arthur Turnor registered a cattle mark.

John Harwood registered a cattle mark.

John Courts registered a cattle mark.

Francis Pope registered a cattle mark.

Richard Smith registered a cattle mark.

4 June. William Smoote demanded 100 a. for transporting 2 children in 1646. Warrant for southeast side of Herring Creek between land of Robert Kedger and Walter Beane.

5 June. Date: 24 May 1650. Walter Guest (planter, of Newtowne) delivered to William Johnson (planter, of St. George's Hundred) for bill of John Medley (planter, of Newtowne).

Liber - Patent Record Z & A - 1637-1651

f. 618 Witness: William Bretton.

Mathias Bryan registered a cattle mark.

2 April 1650. Thomas Green, Esq. gave chattel to his son Francis Greene & to his son Thomas Greene. Signed: Tho. Greene. Witness: Tho. Hatton.

26 April 1650. Francis Brookes (of St. Maries') assigned to Capt. William Stone, Esq. chattel. Witness: William Bretton.

27 April 1650. Francis Vanenden is bound to Barnaby Jackson, Walter Beane, & John Halfhead. Witness: Tho. Hatton.

f. 619 Leonard Calvert, Esq. is bound to deliver to Joane Tompson for use of children of Thomas Butler (dec'd). Date: 10 February 1646.

18 April 1650 at St. Maries'. Court. Attendees: Governor, Secretary, Capt. Robert Vaughan.

Humfry Tabb vs. Benedict Pearse & William Allen. Defendants cited as runaways. Benedict Pearse was servant to John Taylor & William Allen was servant to Bartholomew Wethersby in VA, per letter from Sir William Berclaye.

19 April 1650 at St. Maries'. Court. Attendees: Governor, Mr. Greene, Capt. Price, Secretary, Mr. Pile.

Mr. John Trussell vs. Walter Pakes. Mentions: boy taken by Indians in VA & given to Sir William Berclay.

f. 620 Boy was defendant's child.
- Hugh Lee, age 41, deposed that in August 1647, wife of Walter Pakes was at the house of James Claughton (dec'd). Mr. John Trussell was taking a boy home that had been a captive of the Indians. Pakes' wife, in the presence of the deponent, William Raynalds, & Thomas Haylls, said that her husband "should cure" the boy.
- William Raynalds, age 42, deposed that the above is correct.
- Thomas Haills, age 39, deposed that the above both are correct. Witnesses: Jo. Mottram, Tho. Speke.

f. 621 About last Easter, the defendant said to Thomas Greene, Esq. that he thought the child's father was John Winchester. Mr. John Pile deposed that the defendant's wife sent word to Mr. Trussell that the boy should be delivered to him.

John Trussell assigned all claim to the boy Peter (N) to Walter Pakes.

Mr. John Pile deposed on 19 April 1650 that he recently heard wife of Walter Pakes say that about 1 year ago, either she or her husband sent word to Mr. Trussell (of Checacone in VA) that he should pay her husband or John Sturman

f. 622 for her husband, the boy would be delivered to said Trussell.

22 April 1650 at St. Maries'. Court. Attendees: Governor, Secretary, Capt. Vaughan.

Thomas Bradnock by his attorney Zachary Wade vs. Edward Hudson.

2 March 1649. Thomas Bradnox (of Isle of Kent) appointed Zachary Wade (planter, of Isle of Kent) as his attorney. Witnesses: Robert Vaughan, Francis Lumbard.

Edward Hudson, age 25, deposed on 23 June 1649. Mentions: Goodman Munday. Witnesses: Robert Vaughan, Phillip Conner, Nicholas Browne.

f. 623 Sepert Derrickson, age 25, deposed on 28 February 1649, regarding Edward Hudson. Witness: Robert Vaughan.

Cornelius Cornelinson Van de Graft, age 22, deposed on 1 March 1649, regarding Edward Hudson. Witness: Robert Vaughan.

Proclamation: regarding killing of hogs & deer. Date: 29 April 1650. Signed: William Stone.

f. 624 13 May. Warrant to John Shercliffe on western side of Bretton's Bay between Davies Point & land of John Maunsell.

Nathaniell Hunt assigned his right to 100 a. for his transportation to Thomas Warr. Date: 26 April 1650. Nathaniell Hunt demanded 100 a. for his

Liber - Patent Record Z & A - 1637-1651

transportation.

20 June. Thomas Warre demanded 400 a.: 100 a. on assignment from Nathaniell Hunt, 300 a. on record [see f. 169]. Warrant to Thomas Warr on south side of River Putuxent from head of Macham's Neck, joining Gardiner's Neck to Mattapania.

21 June. Stephen Salmon demanded 50 a. in his right as a servant to Capt. Cornwallies, 50 a. in right of his wife bought of Mrs. Troughton, 100 a. for transporting self about 3 years ago, 50 a. on assignment from John Mansell, 100 a. due Thomas Howard for transporting self about 3 years ago. Warrant to Stephen Salmon & Thomas Howard at Cedar Point on Potomock

f. 625 River, joining land of George Manners.

Robert Hanley demanded 100 a. for transporting self in 1648. Warrant for Hollowing Point against Choptico on Wiccocomoco River.

24 June. Mr. Phillip Land registered a cattle mark.

Francis Brookes assigned chattel to Edward Hall. Date: 10 June 1650. Witnesses: Jeffrey Oliver, George Manners.

Edward Hudson registered payment to George Manners. Witness: Raphe Crouch.

Date: 2 February 1649. John Underhill appointed George Manners as his attorney. Witnesses: Benjamin Cowell, Arthur Turnor.

Margarett Brent (of St. Maries') appointed

f. 626 George Manners as attorney for herself, & her brother Giles Brent. Date: 13 April 1650. Witness: Mary Brent.

Date: 2 November 1646. Giles Brent, Esq. appointed his sister Mrs. Margaret Brent as his attorney. Witnesses: Richard Power, Mary Brent.

Richard Nevett appointed George Manners as his attorney. Date: 3 June 1650. Witness: Raphe Crouche.

25 June. Robert Kadger registered a cattle mark.

William Brough registered a cattle mark.

<none> Attestation by Griffith Beddoe & Richard Clagett to accuracy of copy. Date: 6 October 1725. Signed: Tho. Addison. Witnesses: D. Dulany, T. Bordley, Joh. Beale.

Liber - Patent Record A & B - 1650-1657

<none> Liber #3: transcribed from old Liber A Folio 340 to end & old Liber B Folio 240 to end. Signed: G. Beddoe.

f. 1 26 June 1650. Humphrey Atwicks registered a cattle mark.

Thomas White appointed George Manners as his attorney.

Francis Poesey appointed Mr. Richard Browne as his attorney.

Mr. Edward Tompson authorized Mr. Thomas Hatton (Secretary) to recover from Mrs. Margaret Brent chattel. Signed: Edward Thompson. Witness: Mathew Stone.

27 June. Thomas Cadger demanded 100 a. for transporting self in 1650. Warrant to Thomas Kadger for Potomock River.

Survey for Zephaniah Smith (planter, of Annarundell Co.) on west side of Chesepeack Bay near South River, bounding Inlargement Creeke, Smithe's Creek, for 585 a. Survey for said Smith in Town Neck of Severne, bounding said Bay, Town Branch of Severne, land of George Sanghier, land of Samuell Wills, for 15 a. Date: 21 June 1650.

f. 2 20 June 1650. William Bretton (gentleman, of Newtowne) sold chattel to Charles Maynard (planter, of Newtowne). Witness: William Evans.

Mr. Paul Simpson (mariner), age 60, deposed on 28 June 1650 that last March, he was with Lt. William Lewis at Appamattocks in Northumberland Co. VA & heard wife of Mr. John Hallowes say to said Lewis that he intended to carry away William Greenstead & Thomas Meredith (runaway servants). Said Lewis did take them away to Portoback. Said servants ran away, possibly to VA.

f. 3 14 May 1650. Survey for Owen James (planter) on Herring Creek on Hogs Neck, bounding land of Robert Kadger, land of Thomas Bushell, James' Swamp, for 100 a. Signed: Robert Clarke.

16 May 1650. Survey for John Shercliff (planter) on west side of Bretton's Bay, bounding Shercliffe's Hollow, Spinks Branch, for 150 a. Signed: Robert Clarke.

12 August. Warrant for 150 a. more for Shercliff in the same place.

16 July. Mr. Richard Budd demanded 400 a. for transporting self, his wife, & 2 man servants: William Harper, Simon Bowles in 1650. Warrant for furthest point of Chaptico.

Francis Poesey demanded 50 a. in right

f. 4 his now wife bought of Mr. Fenwick (she was his servant) for transporting 7 years ago, & 100 a. for Thomas (N) a man servant bought of Mr. Budden (of Kequetan) 5 years ago. Warrant for Swanne Point in Potomock River on further side of Weare Creeke from plantation of Mr. Neale.

18 July. Warrant for Robert Brooke, Esq. for 2000 a. or more on south side of Putuxent River near the plantation of Indians called Cinquack.

Grant to Charles Maynard (planter) who performed service to Mr. Cuthbert Fenwick & to advise William Stone, Esq., on east side of St. Clement's Bay, bounding

f. 5 St. Charles' Branch, for 100 a. Date: 1 February 1649. Signed: William Stone. Charles Maynard assigned to Thomas Thomas. Date: 1 September 1650. Witnesses: Joseph Cadle, Robert Hanly.

15 June 1650. Survey for Robert Burle (planter, of Annarundell Co.) on west side of Chesepeack Bay on Burle Banks, bounding

f. 6 Burle's Pounds, Holman's Marsh, for 450 a. Signed: Robert Clarke.

Survey for Abraham Holman (planter, of Annarundell Co.) called Holman's Hope on west side of Chesepeack Bay, bounding Abraham's Marsh, Holman's Marsh, for 100 a. Signed: Robert Clarke.

Grant to John Thimbleby & William Brown. [Certificate A:329] William Brown delivered a former grant to Richard Nevett for 100 a. dated 10 December 1641 & assigned it to Tho. Willis & delivered to said Brown as assignee of Willis. John Warren assigned 50 a. to said Browne & John Thimbleby & said Brown to advise William Stone, Esq., for 150 a. Date: 28 January 1649. Signed: William Stone.

Liber - Patent Record A & B - 1650-1657

f. 7   Lt. William Lewis (of Portobacco) conveyed chattel to Paul Simpson (mariner). Date: 10 July 1650. Witnesses: John Hallowes, Robert Spicer.

f. 8   Mr. William Wilkinson registered a cattle mark.

<u>25 June 1650 at St. Maries'. Court.</u> Attendees: Governor, Capt. John Price, Thomas Greene, Esq., Mr. Tho. Hatton.

Mr. William Broughe vs. Richard Nevett by his attorney George Manners.

Mr. William Broughe vs. Bartholomew Phillips by his attorney Mr. Phillip Land. Bartholomew Phillips appointed Mr. Phillip Land as his attorney. Date: 21 June 1650. Witness: William Bretton.

Mr. William Broughe vs. Lt. William Evans & his wife executrix of her late husband William Tompson (dec'd).

f. 9   Henry Brookes (planter, of Appamatocks) appointed George Manners (planter) as his attorney. Date: 26 April 1650. Witness: Nicholas Gwither.

<u>1 July.</u> Warrant for Mr. Thomas Hatton for 500 a. at Wicocomoco Point where Francis Poesey or George Akrick shall direct.

Henry Brookes by his attorney George Manners vs. Nichol. Cawseene.

f. 10   John Malham vs. Lt. William Lewis. Last March, plaintiff was sheriff of Northumberland Co. VA & had custody of William Greenestead & Thomas Merriday (runaway servants) & the defendant took them to Portoback. Subpoena to: Paul Simpson.

John Dandy vs. Mr. Rich. Husbands (mariner). Mr. William Eltonhead (gentleman) deposed that last February aboard a ship of Mr. Richard Husbands in St. George's River, he heard Mr. Husbands say he would punish John Dandy.

f. 11   George Manners vs. Marks Phepoe & Nichol. Keeeting and Nichol. Keeting vs. George Manners. Arbitrators: Mr. Cuthbert Fenwick, Mr. William Eltonhead, Mr. Richard Willan.

f. 12   Marks Phepo appointed Nicholas Keeting as his attorney Date: 4 June 1650. Signed: Marks Pheypoe.

William Hardwich vs. Walter Beane. Mentions: suit between plaintiff & Capt. John Price, Barnaby Jackson (juryman), William Stiles (juryman). William Hardwich made some "opprobious words" to Tho. Greene, Esq.

f. 13   Edward Tompson vs. Mrs. Marg. Brent. Plaintiff is guardian for children of Thomas Butler (dec'd). Defendant is executrix of Leonard Calvert, Esq. (dec'd). Defendant's attorney is George Manners. Edw. Tompson received satisfaction, signed 20 September 1653, Northumberland Co. VA. Witnesses: Samuell Smith, Tho. Willford.

f. 14   Lt. Gwiter (high sheriff) was given payment for apprehending runaways at the request of Humfry Tabb.

Richard Cole vs. Jo. Halfhead. Subpoenas to: Jo. Greeneway, James Langworth.

<u>12 August.</u> John Courts demanded 200 a. for transporting Margaret his now wife (service bought of Barnaby Jackson) & Joseph Letton in 1649. Warrant for Wicocomoco River in John Hatches' Neck.

Walter Beane sold chattel to John Ward. Date: 2 March 1649. Witnesses: William Assiter, Henry Fox.

Mr. Richard Brown assigned to Thomas Dynyard 100 a. for his transportation & that of his wife. Date: 15 August 1650. Signed: Richard Browne.

<u>15 August.</u> Thomas Dynyard demanded 50 a. for his service to Mr. Neale & 100 a. on assignment from Mr. Richard Browne.

f. 15   Warrant for west side of St. Clement's Bay.

Warrant for Mr. Richard Brown for 100 a. on west side of St. Clement's Bay or east side of Wicocomoco River.

Serg. James Lindesey demanded 100 a. for transporting self about 3 years ago & 50 a. for his service to Mr. Thomas Pursell.

Liber - Patent Record A & B - 1650-1657

William Newgent (gentleman) demanded 200 a. for transporting self & his servant Henry Moore in 1649. Warrant for 350 a. to Mr. William Newgent & Serg. James Lindsey on north side of Potomock or south side of Putuxent Rivers.

Questions for witnesses for plaintiff in case of Mr. Francis Brooks vs. Mrs. Margaret Brent attorney for Capt. Giles Brent.

f. 16 Subpoena to Shercliff. John Shertcliffe deposed on 19 June 1650 regarding said questions. Signed: Jo. Shertcliffe. Witness: William Bretton.

Bartholomew Phillips (planter, of Newtown Hundred) acknowledged debt to Thomas Mathewes (gentleman, of St. Maries'). Date: 16 June 1650.

James Langworth, age 20, & John Greenhold age 25, deposed on 19 June 1650. James Langworth deposed that 2 years ago

f. 17 he helped John Halfhead alter a cattle mark. Signed: Ja. Langworth. John Greenehold deposed the same. Signed: Jo. Greenehold.

17 August. Mr. Francis Brookes demanded 100 a. for transporting self 14 years ago & 100 a. for transporting his man servant John King at the same time, 200 a. for transporting 2 other man servants Tho. Rowney & William Snipe about 12 years ago. Warrant for Wicocomoco River.

Roger Harris demanded 100 a. for transporting self in 1650. Warrant for Wicocomoco River.

Hannah wife of Hugh Lee (of Checacone) demanded 800 a. as administratrix of her former husband Robert Hewett for transporting: Robert Hewett & his wife said Hanna, Elisabeth Phillips, Henry Bellamy, Henry Wood, Jonas Perkins, Elisabeth Clothworth, Davy Adcroft, Henry Cartwrights. [Cartwright's oath: f. 354.] Date: 9 April 1650.

f. 18 Warrant for western shore of Chesepeack Bay over against Kent.

Mathew Rhodon (planter, of Isle of Kent) has served his full time to William Clobbery & Co. (merchants, of London). Date: 28 October 1639. Signed: Leonard Calvert.

Hanna wife of Hugh Lee (of Checakone, VA) deposed that her son-in-law Mathew Rhodan transported self about 7 years ago & dwelled in MD for about 1 year with Francis Gray. Date: 9 April 1650.

Mathew Rhodan demanded 100 a. for transporting self 7 years ago & 50 a. as a servant to Governor Calvert. Warrant for western shore of Chesepeack Bay over against Kent. Date: 9 April 1650.

James Cloughton demanded 750 a. for transporting about 9/10 years ago: James Cloughton the elder & his wife Jane, himself their son, Andrew Barshaw their mate, Humphry Fulford, John Powell, Richard Pynner, Nicholas Porter man servants. James Cloughton the younger deposed that the aforesaid James Cloughton the elder & his wife Jane

f. 19 (deponent's parents) are both deceased. Deponent is their eldest son. Warrant for western shore of Chesepeack Bay over against Kent. Date: 9 April 1650.

George Crouch demanded 200 a.: 100 a. for transporting self about 10 years ago, 50 a. in right of his wife (former servant to Richard Howbyn (of Kent)), 50 a. for transporting his daughter Mary since. Warrant for western shore of Chesepeack Bay over against Kent. Date: 9 April.

William Tompson (of Newtown Hundred) sold chattel to Phillip Land. Date: 20 December 1648. Witness: William Bretton.

f. 20 William Bretton (gentleman, of St. Maries') sold chattel to Phillip Land (gentleman, of St. Maries'). Date: 27 June 1650. Witness: Nicholas Gwiter.

18 August. Francis Vandan demanded 50 a. for his service to Capt. Tho. Cornwallies, 100 a. for William (N) the Scott, a man servant bought of Robert Smith, 50 a. in right of

f. 21 his wife (former servant to Thomas Greene, Esq.). Warrant for Machams Creek forward Pynehill River on south side of Putuxent River.

22 August. Mr. Thomas Mathewes demanded 1000 a. for transporting self & 4 man servants in the 4th year: John Macham, Robert Hedger, Phillip Spurr, Richard Betham. And 100 a. in right of his wife who transported self about 7 years ago.

Page 154

Liber - Patent Record A & B - 1650-1657

Mr. Richard Willan demanded 100 a. for transporting self about 12 years ago & 100 a. for transporting self again 4 years ago. Witness: Leonard Calvert, Esq.

29 August. Warrant for Owen James for 100 a. between land of Mr. Weston & first branch of Herring Creek leading to Newtown.

3 September. John Hatch registered a cattle mark.

30 August. Tho. Harris demanded 300 a. for transporting self, his wife, his servant John Hamlington in 1650. Warrant for Thomas Harris on Potomock River.

f. 22 Edward Bowles demanded 500 a. for transporting self, his wife, his children William & Joane Bowles, his servant John Norman in 1650. Warrant for 400 a. on Potomock River.

9 September. Walter Bean demanded 300 a.: 100 a. on assignment from Raphe Beane for transporting Ralphe Lowe in 1649, 100 a. for transporting Richard Peirce a man servant in 1649, 100 a. for transporting his wife in 1648. Warrant for land recently bought of Francis Poesey on west side of Wicocomoco River.

John Slingesby demanded 100 a. for transporting self 4 years ago. Warrant for western side of Wicocomoco River adjoining land of Walter Beane bought of Francis Poesey.

11 September. John Wheatly registered a cattle mark.

Nicholas Banister registered a cattle mark.

Nicholas Banister demanded 200 a. for transporting self & his wife 2 years ago. Warrant for creek near land of John Hatch on west side of Wickocomoco River or at Wicocomoco Point.

Stanop Roberts demanded 100 a. for transporting self 5 years ago. Warrant for Drapers Neck on western shore of Bay of Chesepeack between Potomock & Putuxent Rivers.

f. 23 Mr. Benjamin Gill sold tract Rakepakobe to Francis Poesey & John Bolane. Date: 26 August 1650. Witnesses: Robert Robins, Thomas Harris, Edward Bowles.

13 September. Warrant for Francis Vanenden for 200 a. on Mattapanie River adjoining land of Thomas Warr on south side of Putuxent River.

19 September. Joseph Cadle demanded 100 a. for transporting self 4 years ago & 100 a. for transporting self 8 years ago. Warrant for northwest side of Bretton's Bay near house of said Joseph.

Thomas Gerrard, Esq. demanded 2100 a. for transporting before 1648 these servants: Jonell Gibbs, Nathaniell Jones, Richard Sabbell, Mathias Bryan, James Walker, John Goore, Robert Beard, Cornelius Cannady, William Empson, William Jones, Ann Knowles, Mary Braffe.

f. 24 Warrant adjoining his land at Mattapanie.

Thomas Gerrard demanded 2000 a. for transporting self, his wife & 5 children in 1650, Mr. Austen Hull, 8 man servants & 4 woman servants: Justinian, Susan, Frances, Temperance, & Elisabeth his children, John Gouldsmith, John Piper, Humphrey Chapman, George Symons, Robert Holmes, George Banck, Tho. Tongue, John Knott, Margarett Armstrong, Susan Fagel, Sarah Fidel. [Names entered on 8 September 1651.] Date: 10 February 1650. Warrant for Patomock or Wicococomoco Rivers.

23 September. Luke Gardiner demanded 500 a. on assignment from Francis Gray & 100 a. for transporting his servant Mary Toogood last Christmas.

William Johnson demanded 300 a. on assignment from Walter Guest & 100 a. for transporting self in 1646. Warrant for 1000 a. for William Johnson & Luke Gardiner on Bretton's Bay or Patomock River.

24 September. John Medley demanded 450 a. for transporting Lancelot Sleepe 4 years ago, Richard West 2 years ago, Rowland Mace 7 years ago, William Elliot 10 years ago his servants, & 100 a. for transporting his wife. Warrant for 300 a. on Potomock River. Another warrant for 50 a.

f. 25 John Thimbleby & William Browne demanded 300 a.: 100 a. for their service, 200 a. for transporting 2 man servants: John Perfitt 7 years ago, John Tovy 2 years ago. Warrant for Patomock River.

Liber - Patent Record A & B - 1650-1657

23 September. To: Mr. Brittaine. Obtain a warrant for 500 a. & give to Luke Gardiner. Signed: Francis Gray. Date: 12 September 1650.

Mr. Tho. Hatton registered a cattle mark.

28 September. Richard Bennet demanded 100 a. due to John Hollis (dec'd) for transporting self about 9 years ago. Claimed as greatest creditor per administration granted to him in VA. Warrant for Patomock River.

John Ward demanded 100 a. for transporting self 3 years ago. Warrant.

29 September. Warrant for 200 a. for Capt. John Price adjoining his plantation.

Mr. John Wade (chirurgeon) demanded 100 a. for transporting self & 50 a. for transporting his maid servant Ann Smith

f. 26 in 1648. Warrant for Patomock River.

1 October. Thomas Michell demanded 300 a. for transporting self, his wife & 2 children in 1648. Warrant for Patomock River.

Francis Pope demanded 100 a. for transporting his wife in 1649. Warrant for branch of creek near land of William Hungerford on north side of Patomock River. Date: 28 September.

Robert Robins demanded 400 a.: 250 a. as per record, 150 a. on assignment from Francis Poesey. Warrant for Patomock River on further side of Weare Creek from plantation of Mr. Neale & north side of Island Creek. Date: 28 September.

Warrant for Mr. Rich. Brown for 100 a. on Patomock River. Date: 28 September.

Henry Cartwright (of Checakone, VA), former servant to Robert Huett (dec'd), deposed that his master did transport all of aforenamed persons. Date: 9 April 1650.

15 September 1650. Richard Bancks paid for redemption of Thomas son of Thomas Allen (dec'd). Witnesses: Thomas Hatton, Barnaby Jackson.

f. 27 Last August. Thomas Maidwell vs. John Dandy & his wife. Thomas Maidwell (of St. Maries') deposed on 2 September 1650.

f. 28 23 September 1650. Thomas Maidwell vs. John Dandy. Terminated. Signed: Tho. Maidwell, John Dandy. Witnesses: Edward Packer, Raphe Crouch.

William Smoote vs. Mr. Cuthbt. Fenwick. Mary wife of Lt. Nichol. Gwither deposed on 7 October 1650.

f. 29 Acts of the Assembly. Date: 29 April 1650.

I. Act concerning Adultery.

II. Act concerning Cursing.

III. Act concerning Drunkeness.

f. 30 IV. Act concerning Strikeing.

V. Act concerning False Witness.

VI. Act concerning Prohibiting all compliance with Capt. William Cleyborne. Capt. William Cleyborne heretofore of Isle of Kent & now of VA.

f. 31 ...

f. 32 VII. Act concerning Deserted Plantations.

f. 33 VIII. Act concerning Secretaries' & sheriff's fees.

f. 34 ...

f. 35 IX. Act concerning Prohibiting any Indians to come into Kent or Annarundell Counties without notice.

f. 36 ...

f. 37 X. Act concerning Erecting that portion of the Province called Providence as Annarundell Co.

Liber - Patent Record A & B - 1650-1657

  XI. Act concerning Muster Master Generall's fee.

  XII. Act concerning Re-edifying Fort of St. Inego's.

f. 38 ...

f. 39 XIII. Act concerning A march on the Indians.

  XIV. Order against Ingressors.

f. 40 XV. Order for recording of cattle marks.

  XVI. Order on 9th Act & 10th, 11th, & 12th Orders of last Assembly.

f. 41 XVII. Order prohibiting foreigners to hunt.

f. 42 XVIII. Order for payment to Governor from every taxable person.

  XIX. Order for relief of poor.

  XX. Order concerning the charge of redeeming the 2 children of Thomas Allen (dec'd) from Indians. Children are under 21.

f. 43 XXI. Order made upon petition of Mr. Thomas Thornborough. Mentions: chattel in possession of Mr. Cuthbert Fenwick bought of Mrs. Margarett Brent executrix of Leonard Calvert, Esq. (dec'd).

f. 44 XXII. Order concerning assessment of this year's levy.

  <u>29 April 1650</u>. Certification of intent on passage of law in 1647 regarding payment of debts of an estate. Signed: John Price, Robert Vaughan, Cuthbt. Fenwick, Geo. Manners, William Bretton, John Hatch.

f. 45 Certification of intent for passage of bills in last year. Signed: William Stone, Tho. Greene, John Price, John Pille, Thomas Hatton, Robert Vaughan, Cuthbt. Fenwick, William Bretton, George Manners, Robert Clarke.

  Proclamation regarding summoning of the Assembly. Date: 24 January 1649. Signed: William Stone.

f. 46 <u>5 April 1650</u>. Freeman of Providence

f. 47 chose Mr. George Puddington & Mr. James Coxe as their burgesses. Signed: William Stone.

  <u>2 April 1650</u>. Burgesses from St. Maries' County (signed Nicolas Gwuther):
- St. George's Hundred: Mr. John Hatch, Mr. Walter Beane.
- Newtown Hundred: Mr. John Medley, Mr. William Brough, Mr. Robert Robins.
- St. Clement's Hundred: Mr. Francis Poesey.
- St. Maries' Hundred: Mr. Phillip Land, Mr. Francis Brooks.
- St. Inego's Hundred: Mr. Tho. Mathews.
- St. Michael's Hundred: Mr. Thomas Sturman, Mr. George Manners.

  <u>6 April 1650</u>. Assembly of the Burgesses. Mr. William Bretton chosen clarke of the House.
- St. Maries': Mr. Phillip Land, Mr. Francis Brooks.
- New Town: Mr. William Brough, Mr. John Medley, Mr. Robert Robins.
- St. Clement's: Mr. Francis Poesey.
- St. Inego's: Mr. Thomas Mathewes.
- St. Michael's: Mr. Tho. Sturman, Mr. Geo. Manners.
- St. George's: Mr. John Hatch, Mr. Walter Beane.
- Kent: Capt. Robert Vaughan.
- Providence: Mr. James Coxe, Mr. George Puddington.

f. 48 General Assembly. Attendees: all except Mr. Mathews, Mr. Hatch, & Mr. Beane. Mr. James Coxe chosen Speaker of the House.
- Oath for the burgesses.
- Oath for the clark.

f. 49 Act for settling of present assembly. Signed: William Stone.

f. 50 Act for better ordering of both Houses. Signed: William Stone.

f. 51 <u>8 April 1650</u>. General Assembly. Attendees: all present. Mr. Thomas Mathews (Burgess of St. Inego's Hundred) chose not to take the oath on grounds of religion. He departed the Assembly.

Liber - Patent Record A & B - 1650-1657

9 April Morning. General Assembly. Attendees: all except Mr. Mathews (expelled), Mr. Francis Brooks (sick).

f. 52 ...
- Act of Recognition read.

Afternoon. General Assembly. Attendees: same as before.
- Act of Rights read.
- Act of Oblivion read.

10 April Morning. General Assembly. Attendees: same as before.

Afternoon. Debate. Mentions: Mr. Tho. Greene, Mr. Tho. Mathewes.

f. 53 11 April Morning. General Assembly. Attendees: same as before.

Debate on Act of Recognition. Mentions: Mr. Robert Clarke.

Afternoon. General Assembly. Committee appointed. Lower House: Capt. Robert Vaughan, Mr. Puddington, Mr. Hatch, Mr. Land, Mr. Robins, Mr. Beane. Upper House: Mr. Secretary, Mr. Robert Clarke.

17 April Morning. General Assembly. Attendees: same as before.
- Act concerning trade with the Indians.
- Act for better support of Lord Proprietor.
- Act prohibiting transportation or sale of ordinances, amunition goods, etc.

f. 54 18 April Morning. General Assembly. Attendees: same, except Mr. Brooks (sick). Mr. Fenwick is Burgess of St. Inego's Hundred for Mr. Mathewes. Mr. Fenwick would take the oath of secrecy provided it not prejudice his religion or conscience. House voted that he might not have a place if he won't take the oath.

Afternoon. General Assembly. Attendees: same as before. Since no infringement was intended, Mr. Fenwick is sworn in.

19 April Morning. General Assembly. Attendees: same as before.

f. 55 Afternoon. General Assembly. Attendees: same as before.
- Act which prohibited compliance with Capt. Cleyborne passed.

20 April Morning. General Assembly. Attendees: same, except for Mr. Fenwick & Mr. Brooks (sick). Four Acts & 1 Order read.

Afternoon. General Assembly. Attendees: same, except for Mr. Brooks.

f. 56 22 April Morning. General Assembly. Attendees: same as before.

Afternoon. General Assembly. Attendees: same as before. Governor appointed Committee to prepare laws & orders to be sent in by the Burgesses: Mr. Speaker, Capt. Vaughan, Mr. Fenwick, Mr. Hatch, Mr. Puddington, Mr. Land.

23 April Morning. Committee. Attendees: all with Mr. Green & Capt. Price of Upper House. Mr. Fenwick appointed chairman. Four Acts & 1 Order read.

Afternoon. General Assembly. Attendees: same as before. Four Acts & 1 Order read.

24 April Morning. Committee. Attendees: all. One Act read. Order

f. 57 concerning petition of Mr. Thornborough read.

24 April Afternoon. General Assembly. Attendees: all except Mr. Brooks. Committee reported.

25 April Morning. General Assembly. Attendees: all except Mr. Brooks (sick), Mr. Fenwick, Mr. Robins, Mr. Hatch. Declaration concerning the Body of Laws & letter, signed by: Capt. Price, Mr. Secretary, Capt. Vaughan of the Upper House, & all of the Lower House except: Mr. Fenwick, Mr. Medley, Mr. Manners, Mr. Brooks.

Afternoon. General Assembly. Attendees: all except Mr. Brooks. Governor appointed a committee: Capt. John Price & Capt. Vaughan of the Upper House, & Mr. James Coxe, Mr. George Puddington, Mr. Phillip Land, Mr. John Hatch, Mr. William Brough, & Mr. Robert Robins of the Lower House.

Mr. John Medley requested to go home, as his wife was sick.

Liber - Patent Record A & B - 1650-1657

f. 58 26 April Morning. Committee. Attendees: as appointed. Capt. John Price appointed chairman.
- Order drawn up regarding petition of Mr. Thornborough.
- Order touching on 2 children of Thomas Allen.
- Order for supplies for the Governor.
- Petition of John Halfhead.
- Order for the poor.

26 April. General Assembly. Attendees: same as before.
- Petition by Lt. William Lewis.

27 April. General Assembly. Attendees: same as before.

f. 59 Charges brought forth by: William Lewis, Mathias Briant, Mr. Chappell, Francis Martinson.

29 April Morning. General Assembly. Attendees: same as before. Bills passed.

f. 60 Afternoon. General Assembly. Attendees: same as before. Bills passed.

Bill of charges:
- St. Maries': Robert Robins, Mr. William Brough, John Medley, Mr. Phillip Land, John Hatch, Walter Beane, Francis Poesey, George Manners, Mr. Thomas Sturman, Mr. Cuthbt. Fenwick.
- Kent, etc.: Capt. Robert Vaughan.
- Annarundell: Mr. Puddington, Mr. Coxe.

f. 61 Ralphe Beane assigned land due him by his servant Raphe Lowe to his brother Walter Beane. Date: 9 April 1650. Signed: Raphe Beane.

f. 62 Francis Poesey assigned 150 a. to Robert Robins. Date: 7 September 1650. Witness: David Prichard.

11 October 1650. Jane wife of Henry Brooks, at the request of William Lewis, deposed that her former husband David Wickliffe bargained with Capt. Cornwallis to received 200 a., which her husband assigned to Lt. William Lewis.

Richard Cole, at the request of William Lewis, deposed that about 12 years ago, David Wickliffe bargained with Capt. Thomas Cornwallis for 200 a. Signed: Rich. Cole.

9 September. Francis Martin demanded 700 a. for transporting his wife, William, Lodowicke, & Frances his children & his servants Tho. Waters & George (N) in 1649. Warrant for Putuxent River.

11 October. William Tarver demanded 100 a. for transporting self this year. Warrant for a branch on north side of Thomas Petite's Creek on Patomock River.

10 October. Mr. William Wilkinson (clerk) demanded 900 a. for transporting self, his wife, Mary, Rebecca, & Elisabeth Wilkinson his daughters, Elisabeth Budden her daughter, 2 man servants William Warren & Robert Cornish, & a woman servant Anne Stevens in 1650.

f. 63 Warrant for Patuxent River.

Arthur Turnor demanded 300 a. for transporting self, his wife & his servant Joseph Edwards last year. Warrant for Putuxent River.

Nathaniell Pope demanded 700 a. for transporting self, his wife, man servants Samuell Baruth, Thomas Baker, Edward Cane, Bartholomew Slaughter, & John Steven before 1648. Warrant to Mr. Nathaniell Pope for Patomock River. Date: 28 September.

Thomas Sturman demanded 650 a. for transporting self, his wife, Anne & Elisabeth his daughters, John Sturman his son, manservants George Watts & Thomas Simonds about 10 years ago, & wife of John Sturman about 2 years ago. Warrant for Putuxent River. Date: 28 September.

Thomas Pasmore assigned to John Sturman 300 a.

John Sturman demanded 300 a. on assignment from Thomas Pasmore. Warrant for Patomock River.

Grant to Lt. William Lewis (gentleman) for 2000 a.

f. 64 & to advise William Stone, Esq. [Certificate: f. 294.] Date: 26 October 1649. Signed: William Stone.

Liber - Patent Record A & B - 1650-1657

12 October. Joseph Edley is bound to Mr. William Eltonhead. Date: 8 January 1649. Witness: Nicholas Smith.

f. 65 Luke Gardiner demanded 100 a. for transporting self from VA in 1647 & desires his father's plantation Sacawaykitt.

Geoffrey Gant is bound to Mr. William Eltonhead. Date: 1 February 1649. Signed: Jeffrey Gant. Witness: Jo. Tragare. List of items. Mentions: Martin Kirk, H. Potter. Signed: Jeffrey Gant. Witness: Martha Conoway.

2 September 1650 at St. Maries'. Court. Attendees: Governor, Robert Brooks, Esq., Mr. Thomas Hatton.

George Manners is appointed his Lordship's attorney, to inquire into affairs of Capt. Giles Brent.

f. 66 10 October 1650 at St. Maries'. Court. Attendees: Governor, Mr. Tho. Greene, Esq., Capt. John Price, Mr. Secretary.

John Sturman vs. Tho. Copley, Esq. Mentions: chattel promised to Robert Sedgrave on 26 August 1646.

John Greeneway, age 25, deposed that last Michaelmas, Mr. Tho. Copley gave him an order to deliver chattel for use of Robert Sedgrave. The deponent told Charles Rawlins attorney for said Sedgrave that he should come & pick it up. Since the chattel was not claimed, it was tendered to Mrs. Margaret Brent & Mr. John Rookewood, & notice given to Charles Rawlins.

f. 67 Signed: Jo. Greeneway. Witness: John Pille. Date: 22 June 1650. Mrs. Margarett Brent averred the tender. Complainant disputed Charles Rawlinson to receive the chattel.

John Hatch vs. William Hardwich. Mentions: note given to defendant or Thomas Sturman for delivery of chattel, payment having been made to Tho. Greene, Esq.

f. 68 Lt. William Lewis appeared at the suit of John Malham.

Joseph Edlowe acknowledged debt to Tho. Copley, Esq. out of the estate of Robert Wiseman (dec'd).

11 October 1650. Court. Attendees: Governor, Tho. Greene, Esq., Capt. Price, Mr. Secretary.

Joseph Cadle vs. Robert Robins.

John Thimbleby administrator of Peter Mackarel produced an account of the estate.

Tho. Warr vs. Rich. Brown. Mentions: debt for Mr. Land.

Capt. John Price vs. Luke Gardiner.

f. 69 Richard Bennett, Esq. vs. Thomas Copley, Esq. & Raphe Crouch (gentleman).

Paul Simpson by his attorney Lt. William Lewis vs. Francis Poesey & John Villane by their attorney Mr. Richard Brown.

Richard Bennett vs. Rich. Browne. Mentions: plantation in Mr. Gerrard's mannor.

f. 70 Mrs. Katheren Hebden administratrix of her late husband vs. Barnaby Jackson & other trustees of the decedent's estate. Mentions: deposition by William Marshall.
- Mr. John Pile deposed on 11 October 1650. Mentions: when deponent was living at house of Mr. Cawseen.

f. 71 ...
- John Halfhead deposed on the same date, that he was at house of Mr. Hebden about 3 weeks before he died & Mr. Hebden would not release Barnaby Jackson of the trust.

12 October. Richard Browne acknowledged a judgement to George Manners.

Richard Browne acknowledged a judgement to George Manners formerly due to Richard Hill.

Nicholas Banister vs. Richard Browne. Plaintiff's wife heard wife of Francis Pope say that the King died justly. Mentions: wife of George Ackrik, Mr.

Liber - Patent Record A & B - 1650-1657

William Bretton, wife of plaintiff.

f. 72 George Manners acknowledged judgement to William Hardwich.

Thomas Copley, Esq. vs. William Hardwich.

12 October 1650. Court. Attendees: Governor, Capt. John Price, Mr. Secretary.

John Rosier (clerke) by his attorney William Hardwich vs. Arthur Turnor. John Rosier appointed William Hardwich his attorney. Date: 27 December 1649. Witnesses: Phillip Chaddock, John Hiller.

William Brough vs. Richard Nevett.

Raphe Beane vs. William Evans.

f. 73 Nathaniell Pope (gentleman, of Appamattocks) appointed William Hardwich as his attorney. Date: 4 October 1650. Witnesses: Phillip Silvestie, David Anderson.

Nathaniell Pope by his attorney William Hardwich vs. John Halfhead.

William Eltonhead, Esq. came into court.

Richard Nevett by his attorney George Manners vs. John Slingsby. Mentions: Walter Pakes,

f. 74 Walter Beane.

Mr. John Pile came into court.

Tho. White by his attorney George Manners vs. James Walker executor of Jo. Tompson by his attorney Richard Brown.

John Slingsby vs. Richard Brown.

George Manners vs. Paul Sympson by his attorney Lt. William Lewis.

f. 75 Tho. Greene, Esq. came into court.

Henry Brooks by his attorney George Manners vs. Nicholas Cawseene. Mentions: deposition of Richard Cole, Gov. Calvert (dec'd).

Robert Smith vs. Walter Beane.

John Halfhead vs. Tho. Green, Esq.

Richard Cottesford

f. 76 (planter) appointed Francis Brooks (gentleman) as his attorney to recover from Joseph Cadle. Date: 22 July 1650. Witnesses: Giles Brent, Temperance Jay.

Richard Cottesford by his attorney Francis Brookes vs. Joseph Caddle. Plaintiff was servant to defendant.

Nicholas Cawseene vs. Joseph Cadle.

Humfry Atwicks vs. George Manners.

John Malham vs. Lt. William Lewis.

f. 77 James Walker appointed Richard Brown as his attorney. Signed: Ja. Walker. Date: 3 June 1650. Witness: John Shancks.

12 October. Mr. William Newgent demanded 100 a. for transporting Henry Moore his servant in 1649. Warrant for land adjoining land bought of William Assiter at Bretton's Bay.

16 September. Warrant to Mr. Tho. Hatton for 200 a. at Chingomuxon.

16 September. Mr. John Metcalf demanded 800 a. for transporting self & his servant John Robinson 15 years ago. Warrant at Chingomaxon on north side of Patomock River.

18 October. Warrant for Tho. Greene, Esq. for 2500 a. on Chingomuxon Creeke.

Grant of a mannor to Tho. Mathews (gentleman) of 4000 a. on assignment from Thomas Copley, Esq. who

Liber - Patent Record A & B - 1650-1657

f. 78 transported 10 able man servants in 1633 & to advise William Stone, Esq., on north side of Patomock River near Portobacco Creek, now called St. Thomas' Creek, called St. Thomas Mannor. Date: 25 October 1649. Signed: William Stone.

f. 79 <u>Ultimate October</u>. Warrant to Lt. Nicholas Gwither for 250 a. on Chingomuxon Creek.

Robert Clarke (gentleman) appointed Nicholas Gwither (gentleman, of St. Inego's) as his attorney. Date: 27 May 1650.

Eliza Comins appointed Zachary Wade as her attorney. Date: 7 October 1650.

<u>1 November 1650</u>. Administration granted to Eliz. Comins (widow) on estate of her husband Edward Comins, sent to Mr. Phillip Conner at Kent.

<u>6 November 1650</u>. Francis Vanenden acknowledged judgement to Mrs. Mary Brent.

George Manners acknowledged judgement to Edward Hall,

f. 80 due from said Manners to Marks Pheipo.

Survey for John Hatch (planter) on west side of Wicocomoco River on south side of Hatches Creek, <metes & bounds>, for 100 a.; also, on north side of Hatches Creek, <metes & bounds>, for 250 a. [Called Hatchland.] Date: 22 October 1650.

Survey for John Courts (planter) on west side of Wicocomoco River, <metes & bounds>, bounding Courts Marsh,

f. 81 land of John Hatch, for 200 a. [Called Letton.] Date: 23 October 1650.

Survey for Francis Pope (planter), bounding Pope's Branch, <metes & bounds>, for 200 a. Date: 25 October 1650.

Survey for Walter Beane (planter) on west side of Wicocomoco River, bounding Hatches Creek, Poesey's Creek, for 700 a. [Called Beanland.] Date: 2 October 1650.

f. 82 Survey for John Slingsby (planter) on Poesey's Creek, <metes & bounds>, bounding land granted to said Poesy now in possession of Walter Beane, for 100 a. [Called Slingsby, Patent: Liber AB&H, f. 115.] Date: 2 October 1650.

Survey for John Shercliffe (planter) on north side of Bretton's Bay, <metes & bounds>, for 150 a. [Called Fearny Hill.] Date: 4 November 1650.

Survey for Joseph Cadle (planter) on north side of Bretton's Bay near Popler Creek, bounding Cadle's Creek, Bruff's Fresh, for

f. 83 250 a. [Called Long Neck.] Date: 4 November 1650.

Survey for Owen James (planter), on Herring Creek, bounding land granted to Mr. Thomas Weston, Kedger's Path, <metes & bounds>, for 100 a. [Called Mt. Sinai.] Date: 5 October 1650.

Survey for William Newgent (gentleman) near Newtowne, bounding Lee's Creek, Bretton's Bay, Patomock River, Broad Creek, land granted to William Assiter, for 100 a. [Called Huggin's Neck.] Date: 2 November 1650.

Survey for Thomas Warr on south side of Putuxent River, bounding

f. 84 Warrs Spring, Gardiners Creek, for 400 a. [Called Machens Neck.] Date: 2 October 1650.

Survey for Francis Vanenden on south side of Putuxent River, bounding land of Hugh Hopewell, <metes & bounds>, for 200 a. Date: 2 October 1650.

Survey for Thomas Hatton (gentleman, Secretary) on west side of Wicocomoco River, bounding Wicocomoco Point, <metes & bounds>, for 500 a. Date: 28 October 1650.

Survey for Hugh Hopewell & Thomas White (planters) on south side of Putuxent River, bounding Hogpen Creeke,

f. 85 <metes & bounds>, Sakawatts Creek, for 150 a. [Called Hogpen Neck.] Date: 6 October 1650. Additional for same on south side of Putuxent River, bounding Warrs Spring, land of Francis Vanenden, land of Thomas Warr, for 50 a.

Liber - Patent Record A & B - 1650-1657

Survey for Anthony Rawlins (planter) on north side of Putuxent River, bounding St. John's Creek, <metes & bounds>, for 400 a. [Called Stafford's Freehold.] Date: 8 October 1650.

f. 86 19 No. William Mitchell (gentleman, of City of Chichester, County of Sussex) travelled to MD or VA on ship Thomas & John. He transported several servants & 2 of his children. He chooses to remain in England. Those men transported (except children & cook) are discharged to: Mr. John Henshaw, Mr. Richard Hodgkins, & Xopher Gery. The women transported are discharged to: Anne Boulton (his servant). Date: 4 April 1650. Witnesses: Thomas Robinson, Richard Dorrington.

24 No. Mr. Thomas Sturman demanded 1000 a. per judgement against Mrs. Margaret Brent. Warrant for St. Michael's Hundred.

Warrant for Robert Brooke, Esq. for 2000 a. on Wicocomoco River. Date: 21 August.

f. 87 21 No. Warrant for Robert Brooke, Esq. for 1000 a. on north side of Putuxent River. Warrant for Robert Brooke, Esq. for 2000 a. on south side of Putuxent River at Aquaseake. Warrant for Robert Brooke, Esq. for 1000 a. on south side of Putuxent River at above Aquaseake.

Edward Hall recorded a cattle mark.

George Manners recorded a cattle mark.

20 November 1650 at St. Maries'. Court. Attendees: Governor, Tho. Green, Esq., Robert Brookes, Esq., Capt. John Price, Mr. Secretary, Mr. William Eltonhead.

Mr. Thomas Sturman vs. Mrs. Marg. Brent executrix of Leonard Calvert, Esq. Mentions: patent by Tho. Pasmore.

Marks Bloomefield vs. Francis Martin. Defendant was to pay plaintiff at Accomack.

f. 88 Mr. Michael Tamter (mariner) is to transport chattel belonging to Mattapania Indians.

Nathaniell Pope vs. John Halfhead.

Mr. John Rosier (clerke) vs. Arthur Turnor.

21 November 1650 at St. Maries'. Court. Attendees: Governor, Tho. Green, Esq., Robert Brookes, Esq., Mr. Secretary, Mr. Eltonhead.

f. 89 Erection of Charles County. Robert Brooks, Esq. to be the Commander. [Voided on 3 July 1654.]

Barnaby Jackson, et.al. vs. Katheren Hebden (widow). Mentions: estate of Tho. Hebden.

William Stone (Governor) vs. Mrs. Marg. Brent.

f. 90 George Manners vs. Nicholas Keeting. Mentions: Marks Pheypo.

Geo. Manners vs. Nicholas Keeting. Mentions: suit of Edward Hall. Mr. William Eltonhead deposed that Marks Pheypo promised & Nicholas Keeting did not dissent to save the plaintiff harmless from Edward Hall. Satisfaction given. Date: 26 November 1650.

George Manners vs. Paul Simpson.

f. 91 Edward Smith vs. Mr. Cuthbt. Fenwick.

John Halfhead vs. Tho. Green, Esq.

John Cooke deposed that Daniell Clocker demanded of his master Capt. Cornwallies the same year that he was freed. Before: William Stone. Date: 28 September 1650.

Maudlin Whittle (wife) deposed on 17 November 1650 that when she lived with Mr. Cuthbt. Fenwick, chattel belonging to William Smoote came to Mr. Fenwick's property. Before: William Bretton. Signed: Maudly Whittle.

f. 92 Petition by the inhabitants of County of Kent, regarding cattle running wild for last 5 years. Signed: John Winchester, Elisabeth Commins, Edward Claxton,

Liber - Patent Record A & B - 1650-1657

John Salter, Phillip Conner, John Phillips, Nicholas Brown, Henry Morgan, Tho. Bradnox, Francis Lumbard, Roger Baxter, John Deere, Tho. Pett, William Jones, Robert Martin, Richard Blunt, William Porter.

7 November 1650 at St. Maries'. Court. Attendees: Governor, Tho. Green, Esq., Capt. John Price, the Secretary.

Consideration of the petition.

f. 93 Mentions: Mrs. Margaret Brent for herself & her brother Giles Brent, Esq.

f. 94 Letter to: Mr. William Smith. Mentions: our meeting in London, Mr. Smith's daughter's departure, Mrs. Smith. Date: 21 February 1649 at London. Signed: William Mitchell.

25 December. Caveat entered for Susanna Porter widow of William Porter of Isle of Kent.

27 December. Thomas Hamper acknowledged judgement to Lt. Nicholas Gwither.

f. 95 28 December. William Marshall registered a cattle mark.

Robert Allen (son of Thomas Allen (dec'd)) registered a cattle mark.

27 December. Concerning the charge of the children of Thomas Allen (dec'd). William Marshall to pay for redemption of Robert Allen (the younger of the 2 children) & deposited a bill with Walter Waterling. Date: 27 May 1650.

30 December. Zephaniah Smith (of Providence in Anne Arundel Co.) sold to Robert Simpkin chattel. Date: 4 December 1650. Witnesses: Tho. Hatton, William Chappell.

8 January. Humphry Howell appointed George Manners attorney for self & his wife & on behalf of his wife's children.

f. 96 Henry Potter appointed George Manners his attorney in cause with Mr. Eltonhead.

10 January. Sergt. Richard Nevett demanded 100 a. on assignment from Richard Brown who received it on assignment from Thomas Phillips & 100 a. on assignment from said Brown who received it on assignment from John Walton. Warrant on Patomock River. Thomas Phillips assigned to Richard Browne his right to 100 a. for transporting self in 1648. Date: 21 October 1650. Witness: Gabriell Odger. Richard Browne assigned it to Richard Nevett. Date: 22 November 1650. John Walton assigned his right to 100 a. to Richard Browne. Date: 15 October 1650. Witness: Jo. Hallowes. Signed: Jo. Walton. Richard Brown assigned it to Sergt. Richard Nevett. Date: 22 November 1650.

Francis Poesy deposed that about 5 weeks ago, he was at the house where Richard Brown lately lived in St. Clemens Hundred, & where George Browne kept a store, & saw said George Brown & Mathew Williams

f. 97 assault said Richard Browne. Date: 11 January 1650.

Capt. William Hawley gave to Martin Kirke 200 a. called St. Jerome's Thickett on the north side of St. Jerome's plantation. Date: 4 January 1650. Witnesses: George Manners, Friendship Tounge.

Edward Hall gave to Henry Potter 1/2 of his land & houses. Date: 17 December 1648. Witness: Marks Pheypo.

Henry Potter sold to Martin Kirke 25 a. (1/2 of his dividend). Date: 13 November 1649. Witnesses: Marks Pheypo, Nicholas Keeting.

f. 98 16 December 1650 at St. Maries'. Court. Attendees: Governor, Capt. John Price, Mr. Tho. Hatton.

Henry Morgan was appointed guardian to Tabitha Short (daughter of Robert Short (dec'd)).

8 January 1650 at St. Maries'. Court. Attendees: Governor, Capt. John Price, William Mitchell, Esq., William Eltonhead, Esq., Mr. Tho. Hatton.

Debate on death of servant of Raphe Bean. Jury to meet at house of Luke Gardiner at Herring Creek.

Hugh Hopewell to detain chattel of Luke Gardiner & William Johnson.

Liber - Patent Record A & B - 1650-1657

Daniell Clocker vs. Mr. Cuthbt. Fenwick attorney for Capt. Tho. Cornwallies.

f. 99 John Slingsby vs. Richard Nevett.

3 February 1650. Katheren Hebden (widow) assigned to William Marshall her rights to 200 a.: 100 a. due Tho. Payne (dec'd), & 100 a. of her patent.

8 February. William Marshall demanded 300 a. of a former warrant (f. 282) & 200 a. on assignment from Mrs. Hebden. Warrant for west side of Wickocomoco River.

Warrant to John Cage for 150 a. on west side of Wickocomoco River.

Robert Clarke assigned to Mathias Brian 100 a., being part of 500 a. assigned from Thomas Copley, Esq. Mathias Bryan demanded 100 a. Warrant near the land of William Tompson on St. Clement's Bay.

f. 100 Thomas Greene, Esq. (of St. Maries') sold to Thomas Hawkins (mariner, of London) his right to mannor on Isle of Kent called Bobing Mannor of 500 a. & land on Popley's Island of 1000 a. Witnesses: Tho. Hatton, Robert Clarke.

10 February 1650. Richard Ware acknowledged a debt to Edward Scurffield (mariner). Signed: Walter Pakes.

f. 101 Capt. William Stone, Esq. sold chattel to Edward Hall. Date: 14 January 1650. Witness: Edmund Wormell.

11 February 1650. Walter Pakes acknowledged a debt to Raphe Beane.

Mr. Robert Clarke acknowledged a debt to John Hatch attorney for skipper Abraham Johnson being a debt of Mr. Phillip Land.

Sergt. Richard Nevett acknowledged a debt to Raphe Beane.

Richard Brown (gentleman) sold his right to house & plantation in mannor of Mr. Thomas Gerrard

f. 102 which he bought of Richard Hills, to George Manners. Date: 12 March 1650. Signed: Rich. Browne.

13 February. Warrant to John Maunsell for 600 a. on Patomock River.

14 February. Warrant to Thomas Harris for 300 a. on Thomas Petite's Creek, adjoining the land of Francis Pope.

Warrant to William Tarver for 100 a. on Thomas Petite's Creek on north side of Manners' Branch.

15 February 1650. William Bretton (gentleman) acknowledged a judgement to William Stone, Esq. (Governor).

13 February 1650 at St. Maries'. Court. Attendees: Governor, Secretary, William Eltonhead, Esq., William Mitchell, Esq.

Motion by Lewyn Bufkin, Esq. on behalf of self & Robert Kedger, Edward Hall, John Buttry, & other creditors of Robert Brookes, Esq.

f. 103 ...

f. 104 20 February. Warrant to Stephen Salmon for 250 a. [f. 339] on Patomock River.

Martin Kirk appointed George Manners as his attorney in the cause against Francis Antell.

15 February 1650. Henry Fox sold chattel to John Ward. Witnesses: John Wade, Charles Maynard.

20 February. William Johnson demanded 200 a. for transporting 2 servants: Thomas Tunnet, Edward Turner. William Johnson assigned 150 a. of above to Walter Guest. Walter Guest demanded 150 a. Warrant for

f. 105 Patomock River, between head of King's Creek & Huckleberry Swamp, on Robert's Neck.

Edward Packer demanded 100 a. for transporting self before 1648. Date: 28 September. Warrant for Patomock River.

Liber - Patent Record A & B - 1650-1657

Thomas Bushell had the right to 100 a. for transporting self before 1640, & assigned it to Henry Lee. Grant on south side of Bretton's Bay, bounding Blount Point, Lee's Creek. [Patent: Liber F, f. 145.]

f. 106 Date: 24 January 1642. Signed: Leonard Calvert.

Warrant to Cyprian Thorowgood for 300 a. Date: 22 May 1637. Cyprian Thorowgood assigned it to his brother-in-law Joseph Edlow. Date: 12 April 1643. Witness: Robert Farnham.

4 March. James Johnson demanded 200 a. for transporting his 2 servants in 1648: John Cable, John Hudson. Warrant for east side of Flood's Creek, adjoining land in his possession.

19 February 1650 at St. Maries'. Court. Attendees: Governor, William Mitchell, Esq., William Eltonhead, Esq., Secretary.

Levin Bufkin, Esq. vs. Robert Brookes, Esq.

f. 107 Mentions: Charles Brookes (gentleman, son of defendant) as his attorney, Elwyn Bufkin, Esq. (plaintiff), Robert Brooke (defendant), 2 servants (Edward Phillpott, Vincent Atkinson) of Mr. Mitchell,

f. 108 Mr. Henshaw.
- Vincent Atkinson, age 20, deposed on 11 February 1650 that he served Mr. Brooke of de la Brooke on account of Levin Bufkin, Esq. Mentions: Mrs. Brooke, son of Mr. Brooke, 3 other servants.

f. 109 ...
- Edward Phillpott, age 49, deposed on 11 February 1650, that he served Mr. Brooke of de la Brooke on account of Levin Bufkin, Esq.

Jury: Mr. Cuthbt. Fenwick, Mr. Richard Hoskins, Mr. Edward Warmell, Mr. Thomas Mathews, Mr. Phillip Land, Mr. Francis Brookes, Mr. John Hatch, Stephen Salmon, John Buttery, Edward Scurffield, William Johnson, Luke Gardiner.

Edward Hall vs. Robert Brooke, Esq.

f. 110 Robert Kadger vs. Robert Brooke, Esq. Mentions: defendant's son Mr. Charles Brooke.

f. 111 John Buttery (carpenter) vs. Robert Brooke, Esq.

William Andrews, Esq., skipper Jacob Derrickson, Lewis Froman, Henry Adams, Luke Gardiner, James Lindesey, Thomas Mathews, John Dandy vs. Robert Brooke, Esq. Mentions: John Dandy is assignee of John Hallowes.

4 March. Mr. Robert Clarke surveyed 1000 a.

f. 112 for Giles Brent, Esq. on Isle of Kent formerly conveyed from Leonard Calvert, Esq. (dec'd). Said Mr. Brent conveyed it to his sister Mrs. Brent. Mrs. Margarett Brent demanded 1000 a. on conveyance from her brother Giles Brent, Esq. Warrant for Isle of Kent.

William Mitchell demanded 2200 a. for transporting 22 servants in 1650. Warrant for Eastern Shore of Bay of Chesepeack.

7 March 1650. Raphe Beane revoked PoA to George Manners.

John Shercliff & Henry Spinke were bound to Raphe Beane. Date: 17 February 1650. Witness: Richard Willan.

f. 113 William Durand revoked PoA to Zephaniah Smith, & gave to Mr. Thomas Marsh. Date: 9 February 1650. Witness: Edward Lloyd.

12 March. L. Calvert authorized Thomas Bradnox & Edward Commins (gentleman) to acquire all of Neale's cattle on Isle of Kent. Date: 19 April 1647.

John Smith (planter, of Isle of Kent) received satisfaction from Thomas Bradnox on debt from Mr. William Brainthwait. Date: 19 July 1642. Witnesses: John Metcalf, Dirch Serritt. [Obligation in Latin.

f. 114 Date: 28 February 1639.] Cites goods bequeathed to Katherine Smith daughter of said John Smith by last will & testament of Henry Crawley. Witnesses: Francis Rabnett, John Gresham. John Smith (of Crayford, Isle of Kent) assigned to Mr. William Brainthwait (gentleman, Isle of Kent) all right to lands bequeathed to his daughter Katherine Smith by Henry Crawley (dec'd).

f. 115 Date: 28 February 1639. Witnesses: Francis Rabnett, John Gresham. John Smith (planter, Isle of Kent) acknowledged receipt of payment from Mr. Brainthwait (gentleman, Isle of Kent) due from estate of Henry Crawley (dec'd, Isle of Kent). Date: 19 February 1639. Witnesses: Robert Lake, William Lant. John Smith, father of Katherine Smith, acknowledged sale of bequest to his daughter from Henry Crawley to Mr. William Brainthwait,

f. 116 & said Smith to pay Robert Cowper (carpenter) & said Smith to receive the servant Henry Cartwright. Date: 18 February 1639. Witness: Phillip Conner.

20 March. Warrant for Richard Ware for 100 a. on Patomock River.

17 March. Mr. Francis Brookes demanded 200 a. for transporting George Scovell & for transporting his now wife Anne. Warrant for Western Shore of Bay of Chesepeack between Patomock & Putuxent Rivers.

John Halfhead appointed George Manners his attorney in cause against Mr. Nathaniell Pope. Date: 12 February.

Robert Robins appointed George Manners his attorney in cause against Arthur Turnor. Date: 12 February.

11 March 1650. Edward Scurffield received payment from Capt. John Price for use of John Underhill. Witnesses: Thomas Lugg, Daniell Clocker.

f. 117 20 March. Cuthbert Fenwick (gentleman) assigned all rights to chattel from estate of Nicholas Harvey to John Darby (blacksmith). Witness: William Bretton.

1 April 1651. Bartholomew Phillips registered a cattle mark.

Mrs. Margaret Brent revoked PoA to George Manners.

William Stone authorized Mr. Richard Browne to examine witnesses in case of Francis Poesy vs. Benjamin Gill. Date: 12 September 1650.

Richard Ware, Robert Holt, & Edward Hudson (planters, all of St. Michael's Hundred) were bound to Henry Pountnell. Date: 24 February 1650. Witness: John Metcalf, Thomas Leech.

Robert Simpkin (of Providence) was bound to

f. 118 Zephaniah Smith. Date: 4 December 1650. Witnesses: William Chappell, Tho. Coles.

10 February 1650 at St. Maries'. Court. Attendees: Governor, Thomas Greene, Esq., Capt. John Price, Mr. Thomas Hatton, Thomas Gerrard, Esq.

Edward Scurffield (mariner) vs. Raphe Beane. Mentions: chattel paid for in VA & for Walter Beane & Robert Kadger aboard ship of Mr. Husbands then in James River,

f. 119 to be transferred to ship of Mr. Ludlow in York River.

f. 120 Richard Bennett, Esq. vs. Thomas Copley, Esq. & Raphe Crouch (gentleman).

Richard Nevett vs. Walter Pakes. Mentions: John Slingsby.

List of debts due Richard Bennett (merchant): Mr. Copley, William Cooke & James Colelough, John Medley due Mr. Mottram & assigned to Mr. Chaddock, Mr. Lewger. Mr. Thomas Hatton to recover. Date: 25 May 1650. Witnesses: William Parker, John Bennett.

Richard Bennett conveyed to Mr. John Lewger the younger all right to the house & land at St. Maries' belonging

f. 121 to his father, who assigned it to me. Date: 28 August 1650. Witness: Mathew Stone.

Richard Bennett (merchant) deposed on 28 August 1650 that Mr. Copley sent to the deponent for certain goods. Mentions: Capt. Burbage & his wife, John Piper.

f. 122 Capt. William Mitchell vs. Mr. Thomas Hatton. Arbitration by: Mr. Cuthbert Fenwick, Barnaby Jackson. Date: 10 December 1650.

f. 123 Walter Waterling vs. John Hatch et.al. executors of Tho. Allen (dec'd).

Liber - Patent Record A & B - 1650-1657

11 February 1650 at St. Maries'. Court. Attendees: Governor, Tho. Green, Esq., Tho. Gerrard, Esq., Capt. John Price, Capt. William Mitchell, Mr. John Pille, Mr. William Eltonhead, Mr. Tho. Hatton.

Motion on arbitration between Mr. Thomas Hatton & Capt. William Mitchell.

f. 124 Thomas Ashbrooke vs. Nathaniell Hunt.

f. 125 George Manners vs. Thomas Warr.

John Lewger (gentleman) vs. Henry Fox. Mentions: Mr. Thomas Hatton attorney for Richard Bennett, Esq., who claimed estate from John Lewger, Esq. (father of the complainant).

f. 126 John Lewger, Jr. sold to Henry Fox Mannor of St. John's in St. George's River, received from his father & assignment from Mr. Richard Bennett. Date: 2 November 1650. Witnesses: Phillip Land, Henry Adams, Barnaby Jackson.

Motion by John Hatch for allowance to replenish cattle of Mrs. Eure. Mrs. Margaret Brent, who employed said Hatch, to pay fees.

Thomas Gerrard, Esq. vs. Benjamin Gill attorney for Mr. James Neale. Complainant is assignee of Arthur Whale

f. 127 & administrator of John Wortley.

(N) Fenwick vs. (N) Howell. Mentions: payment from defendant to Mr. Mottram, debt by Mr. Mottram to estate of Roger Oliver.

f. 128 Cuthbert Fenwick vs. Thomas Warr. Mentions: judgement by Tho. Ashbrooke.

William Eltonhead (gentleman) attorney for Mr. Edwyn Conoway vs. Marty Kirke.

12 February 1650 at St. Maries'. Court. Attendees: Governor, Tho. Gerrard, Esq., Capt. John Price, Capt. William Mitchell, Mr. William Eltonhead, the Secretary.

James Lindesey vs. Barthol. Phillips.

Phillip Land vs. Thomas Warr.

f. 129 Richard Browne deposed that he was a witness to an agreement on 19 November 1649 & Thomas Warr took the defendant as paymaster. With the agreement, Thomas Warr found fault with Mr. Phillip Land.

Paul Simpson, age 60, deposed to William Bretton on 24 September 1650 that he went to the house of Raphe Beane with Mr. Budd & they spoke of certain work on the plantation, and the

f. 130 death of one of the servants.

Jurors empanelled to inquire of the death of Raphe Loe, servant to Raphe Beane: William Newgent, Arthur Turner, Owen James, Tho. Bushell, William Smoote, Robert Cadger, William Edwyn, James Lindesey, Nich. Cawseen, Xpofer Bushell, William Broughe, Humfry Atwicks. Raphe Beane was discharged in the death of his servant Raphe Lowe.

Payment to chirurgeon's widow or administratrix now wife of Thomas Bushell.

f. 131 Mary wife of Francis Vanenden deposed on 21 March 1650 that when Mr. Land was sick in January, as sheriff he commissioned George Manners to do some business for him.

John Dandy vs. George Manners. Mentions: order between Paul Simpson & John Dandy, testimony of Francis Vanenden & his wife, Lt. Nicholas Gwither (deputy sheriff).

f. 132 Lt. Nicholas Gwither was appointed sheriff of St. Maries'.

8 March 1650 at St. Maries'. Court. Attendees: Governor, Tho. Gerrard, Esq., Mr. Tho. Hatton, Capt. Robert Vaughan, Mr. William Eltonhead.

Petition of Susan Porter (widow, of Isle of Kent) for items from estate of her husband William Porter.

"End of Liber"

f. 133 Zephaniah Smith (of Putuxent River) assigned all right to 15 a. on Town Neck in

Liber - Patent Record A & B - 1650-1657

County of Providence to Mr. Richard Bennett, Esq. (Governor of VA). Date: 5 December 1654. Witness: John Smith.

Henry Bishop assigned to John Medley chattel in the hands of John Greeneway. Date: 30 November 1654. Witness: John Greeneway, Zach. Wade.

Will. May registered a cattle mark.

Cornelius Cannadie (also Cornelius Cannady, bricklayer, of Putuxent) sold to Samuel Griffin (planter, of Putuxent) land on south side of Putuxent River, bound by land of Peter Joy. Date: 23 January 1653. Signed: Cornelius Cannedie. Witnesses: Cuthbt. Fenwick, Jane Fenwick.

f. 134 Michaell Brooke entered a caveat for 200 a. lying easterly in Hunting Creeke.

f. 135 John Domall registered a cattle mark.

Survey for Richard Smith (planter) on north side of Patomock River, <metes & bounds>, for 100 a. Signed: John Lugar. Date: 7 April 1654. [Called: Smith's Denn.]

William Nugent is bound to James Waker. Date: 2 March 1654. Witnesses: John Browne, Benjamin Gill.

24 April 1655 at Putuxent. Court. Attendees: Mr. Richard Preston, Mr. William Durand, Capt. Robert Sly, Capt. Sampson Waring, Mr. John Lawson, Mr. John Hatch.

f. 136 Commission for exercising the militia in Putuxent Co. given to Capt. John Smith & Capt. Peter Johnson.

Commission for exercising the militia in St. Maries' & Patomock River to Capt. John Sly & Capt. Richard Hodskeys. Capt. John Smith (mustermaster) shall be superintendent.

Establishment of countrey [sic] court in St. Maries' & Patomock River. President: Capt. John Sly. Commissioners: Mr. Richard Hodskeys, Mr. William Barton, Mr. James Johnson, Mr. Walter Beane, Mr. Edward Bolls, Mr. Daniell Clocker.

Appointment as commander of military forces on Herring Creek to Capt. Sampson Warring. Plantations included: Mr. Ayres, Capt. Carter, Mr. Richard Wells, Mr. Manning.

f. 137 Establishment of county court in Putuxent. Commissioners: Mr. James Berry, Mr. Michaell Brooke, Capt. Peter Johnson. Mr. Woodman Stockely, Mr. John Pott, Mr. Phillip Morgan.

Letters of administration granted to Mrs. Fenwick.

Mr. Evans convicted of high offense.

John Ashcombe fined.

Richard Collet convicted to high offense & is banished from the Province until he gives notice to Mr. Lawrence Ward (of VA).

f. 138 Letters of administration granted to Alice Griffin widow of Samuell Griffin (dec'd). Appraisers: Robert Taylor, John Knapp.

Phillip Hide has the right to 200 a. on north side of Putuxent, adjoining the land of Peter Godson.

William Stevens has the right to 300 a. next ot Phillip Hide.

Capt. Cornwallies, in a letter to Mr. John Wade, shipped goods on the Goulden Fortune. Mr. Richard Hodskeyes is agent for Capt. Cornwallies.

Lt. Richard Banks & Thomas Tunnell charged in armes against the present Government.

Francis Walton, a servant to Capt. William Stone, requests his freedom.

Letters of administration granted to John Tomkinson on estate of George Dolt. Mentions: debt to Phillip Land.

f. 139 Phillip Land is indebted to Henry Catlyn (gentleman).

Liber - Patent Record A & B - 1650-1657

Richard Reclesse is indebted to Mr. Richard Preston, part due from Cornelius Canneda.

Letters of administration granted to Daniell Gordon on estate of James Memois.

Phillip Land is indebted to Katheren Ebden for her charges on Richard Lawrence.

William Lewis is indebted to Samuell Parker.

Michael Brooke arrested John Jarbo,

f. 140 & said Jarbo to pay said Michaell Brookes.

William Lewis paid Mr. John Lawson.

John Medcalf, as sheriff, pressed a boat belonging to Phillip Land for the last insurrection, per Henry Fox.

Daniell Gourdon deposed that he, John Delahayes, & James Meines were indebted to Walter Beane, & William Lewis received for said Beane.

Capt. John Smith vs. John Homond (also John Hamond).

Henry Bullen was summoned as a witness for Peter Godson.

Susan Frizell was convicted of running away from her master Daniell Goulson.

f. 141 Mr. Luke Gardiner gave chattel to said Frizell, William Dorrington, Peter Achilles, Henry Cane, & William Stogden to pay said Goulson. John Seawell also gave.

April 1654. Court. Lt. William Lewis acknowledged a judgement to Capt. John Barriffe.

Henry Fox is a creditor to the estate of Francis Poesey (dec'd).

Cornelius Canada is indebted to George Skipwith for chattel which Skipwith borrowed from Thomas Davis for Richard Recklesse.

Henry Fox is granted an attachment to the estate of Thomas Hamond.

In order to administer justice,

f. 142 Capt. Robert Slye is admitted to Council of State. Capt. Robert Slye, Mr. John Hatch, & Mr. Lawson has power to issue writs.

Capt. John Smith shall be muster master for St. Maries', Potomock, & Putuxent Counties.

Capt. John Smith shall take proper measures regarding the estates of delinquents which

f. 143 are in Putuxent, Patomock, & St. Maries'.

Francis Brooke vs. Henry Fox.

Phillip Land issue a complaint.

Mr. Thomas Hebden (dec'd) sold to Nicholas Cawseen, Barnaby Jackson, & Luke Gardiner his whole estate on 13 June 1649. Lawrence Starkie, Esq. as successor to Thomas Copler, Esq. in the deed acknowledges

f. 144 receipt of Katherne relict of said Thomas Hebden full payment. Date: 9 December 1653. Signed: Nicholas Cawseene, Barnaby Jackson, Luke Gardiner. Witnesses: William Bretton, Benjamin Gill. Date: 18 May 1654.

Lawrence Starky (of St. Inego's), in PoA from Mr. Nicholas Cawseene & Barnaby Jackson, acknowledges receipt. Date: 9 December 1653. Witnesses: Samuell Harris, William Hurd.

f. 145 Henry Catchman to pay Capt. Peter Johnson.

26 June 1655. Provincial Court. Attendees: Capt. William Fuller, Mr. Richard Preston, Mr. Edward Lloyd, Capt. Richard Ewen, Mr. John Hatch.

MM Thomas Meares & Marsh were appointed commissioners.

Liber - Patent Record A & B - 1650-1657

<u>13 August 1655. Provincial Court.</u>

Capt. Sampson Waring,

f. 146 Mr. Michaell Brooke, Mr. Robert Pott, & Mr. Woodman Stockley were added as commissioners. Current commissioners: William Fuller, Edward Lloyd, Rich. Wells, Ri. Ewen, Tho. Meares, Tho. Marsh.

Capt. John Smith was appointed chief commander. Date: 24 April 1655. Signed: William Durand, Sampson Waring, John Lawson, Rich. Preston.

f. 147 <u>13 August 1655. Provincial Court.</u> Attendees: Capt. William Fuller (Governor), Mr. Edward Lloyd, Mr. Richard Wells, Capt. Richard Ewen, Mr. Thomas Marsh, Mr. Thomas Meares.

f. 148 Order to Captains of the Trayn Bands. Signed: William Fuller, Edward Lloyd, Richard Wells, Richard Ewen, Thomas Meeres, Thomas Marsh.

<u>22 August 1655. Provincial Court.</u> Attendees: Capt. William Fuller, Mr. Edward Lloyd, Capt. Ri. Ewen, Capt. Sampson Waring, Mr. Tho. Meeres.

Order for the sheriff. Signed: William Fuller.

Mary Hodger, executrix of John Hodger (dec'd), before her day of marriage, deeded to her son John Hodger chattel. Richard Kanery

f. 149 is to be the groom. Date: 12 July 1655. Signed: Richard Kanery, Mary Hoggen. Witnesses: James Veitch, William Stevens.

Richard True (boatwright) is bound to Arthur Turnor. Date: 21 February 1654. Witness: Walter Gest.

<u>3 October 1655. Provincial Court.</u> Attendees: Capt. WIlliam Fuller, Mr. Richard Preston, Mr. William Durand, Mr. Edward Lloyd, Mr. Thomas Meeres.

Henry Bullen vs. Mr. Michael Basy.

f. 150 Administration to William Stevens on chattel of John Crabtree.
- Edward Good sues for payment.
- William Steven claims payment.
- Alexander Magrudder claims payment.
- Basey Michael claims payment.
- Mr. Richard Preston claims payment.

Thomas Robinson deposed that the claim of Edward Good on the estate of his master John Crabtree is for his service.

f. 151 John Hawkins gave chattel to William Baten. Date: 4 October 1655. Witnesses: William Moffett, Richard Smith. William Batten discharges John Hawkins of all bills.

William Stevens claims payment from estate of John Crabtree.

Peter Johnson deposed that John Crabtree (son of John) said that payment was due Edward Good for service.

Michael Basy was convicted of swearing. William Stevens deposed that he went to the house of Michael Basey with James Veitch & recited a discussion between said Veitch & said Baisey.

f. 152 Peter Godson is to pay William Batten.

William Wilkinson (clerk) desired a certificate of death for John Crabtree & John Ramsey.

Phillip Land is indebted to Katherine Ebden.

William Dorrington is charged to investigate into the estate of Capt. William Stone. Signed: William Durand.

William Marshall deposed that Thomas Ashbrooke & his wife heard Walter Guest

f. 153 make a particular statement.

Petition of Elisabeth Smith suing for herself & her husband, for charges in cause between Bartholomew Herring & Phillip Hide.

Liber - Patent Record A & B - 1650-1657

Lt. William Evens confessed in open court.

John Sutton vs. estate of Capt. William Stone.

Michael Basy fined for swearing against James Veitch.

Mr. William Batten vs. estate of John Crabtree (dec'd).

Mr. William Ewen & Mathew Smith acknowledged as securities for Michael Basy.

f. 154 5 October 1655. Provincial Court. Attendees: Capt. William Fuller, Mr. William Durand, Mr. Edward Lloyd, Mr. John Hatch, Mr. Woodman Stockley, Mr. Thomas Meeres.

James Berry was convicted of several subscriptions against the Government. Capt. Peter Johnson is security to said James Berry.

Peter Godson was convicted of theft from wife of John Hambleton.

William Stockden vs. estate of John Crabtree.

Capt. Peter Johnson vs. estate of Capt. William Stone.

f. 155 William Bramhall was convicted.

John Wade & William Evans acknowledged a debt.

Peter Sharp vs. estate of Capt. William Stone.

Mr. Edmund Stokely is security for Robert Taylor.

Capt. John Price & Capt. Josias Fendall acknowledged chattel taken from Mr. Sharpe by soldiers under the command of Capt. Stone.

f. 156 Mr. James Berry fined.

Robert Clarke (gentleman) acknowledged to being a Roman Catholic. Said Clarke was fined; payment being a bill of James Veitch, & the plantation of said Clarke on Brittaine's Bay.

Lt. Banks was convicted. Capt. Peter Johnson is security.

Capt. Price had been fined in relation to his actions with Capt. Stone against the present Government.

Owen James was fined.

f. 157 William Chaplyn was given an attachment to estate of Capt. William Stone.

Servant, who was taken captive in the rebellion, of Mr. Batten is to be returned to his master.

Thomas Mathews confessed to being a Roman Catholic.

Ismael Wright was given an attachment on estate of Capt. William Stone.

Thomas Mathews is to find securities.

Robert Clarke (gentleman) assigned the land on Brittaine's Bay to public use.

William Mills is to be the security for Thomas Mathews.

William Boreman confessed to being a Roman Catholic.

f. 158 William Boreman was convicted of compliance with Capt. William Stone in the last rebellion.

Nathaniell Burroughes is security for William Boreman.

Mr. William Parker was given an attachment to estate of Capt. William Stone.

Richard Preston attorney for Thomas Potter (merchant, of London) was given an attachment on estate of Mathew Stone.

William Batten was given an attachment on estate of Mathew Stone.

Josias Fendall (gentleman) was charged

Liber - Patent Record A & B - 1650-1657

f. 159 with openly supporting Capt. William Stone.

Henry Parnell appeared in court on 8 October 1655 at Putuxent, on behalf of Edward Packer.

f. 160 Henry Parnell, on behalf of Job Chandler (gentleman), deposed that said Chandler shall be at the house of said Parnell in Wicocomoco River on 31 October.

James Waker acknowledged debts to George Burbage.

Phillip Land was arrested at the suit of John Barriffe attorney for Francis Emperor.

John Barriffe attorney for Francis Emperor arrested John Cornelius for debt.

f. 161 Richard Floyd vs. William Johnson.

John Dandy confessed to being a Roman Catholic.

John Dandy was convicted of compliance with Capt. William Stone in the late Rebellion.

Petition of William Ewen.

John Pyle confessed to being a Roman Catholic.

John Jarbo & James Langworth were convicted of compliance with Capt. William Stone in the late Rebellion.

Capt. John Smith vs. Cornelius Johnson.

Capt. William Fuller made payment for chattel taken from the shop of John Dandy.

f. 162 Signed: John Dandy. Date: 12 October 1655. Witnesses: William Durand, Josias Fendall.

Thomas Marsh was bound to William Allen. Signed: Tho. Marsh. Date: 17 February 1653. Witnesses: William Stone, Tho. Hatton.

Phillip Land appointed Mr. James Langworth as his attorney. Date: 20 December 1655. Witnesses: Robert Greene, Geo. Goodrick.

f. 163 Henry Coxe claimed 500 a. on assignment from Capt. John Barriffe granted to said John Coxe.

Walter Peake was granted administration on estate of Francis Vandan. Date: 30 December 1655.

26 December 1655. Provincial Court. Attendees: Mr. Rich. Preston, Mr. William Durand, Mr. Michael Brooke, Mr. Woodman Stockley, Mr. John Potts.

Petition of Mr. John Norwood (sheriff of Providence) for debts due him from: William Evans, Thomas Trueman, Capt. William Stone, Mr. Job Chandler, Edward Packer, Geo. Tompson, Robert Clarke, Henry William & John Losey. They were prisoners during the last Rebellion.

William Hunnington was given payment from the public account.

Griffin George vs. Thomas Trueman. Mentions: John Tawney.

f. 164 Estate of John Crabtree is to pay: Ismael Wright, Alexander Magrudder.

John Milam (merchant) assigned chattel in hands of William Ewen to the public.

Henry Kathman (also Henry Katchman) acknowledged a debt to William Batten.

Administratrix of Cuthbert Fenwick is to pay George Mees (merchant).

Lawrence Starcky was granted an attachment to Henry Mees.

John Davies was granted 100 a. on eastern side of Hunting Creek, near the house of John Little.

John Boone is to serve William Bramale.

Liber - Patent Record A & B - 1650-1657

Per the depositions of Richard Dawton, Martin Seuet, & Peter Grant & Katherine Hore, Francis Harvey is indebted to John Milam (merchant). John Danby, who undertook to justify any of his family, is to pay the debt.

f. 165 John Milam (merchant) is to pay charges in felony against Ann Danby.

Anne Danby acknowledged her offenses to John Milam.

Peter Sharp (chirurgeon) vs. Peter Godson. Mentions: death of Capt. John Smith supposedly at the hands of said Sharp.

Robert Taylor vs. Henry Keanie.

f. 166 John Hiat, servant to Thomas Trueman, is to pay debt.

John Hambleton sued for chattel due to his wife Temperance (daughter of Richard Moore (dec'd)).

John Corneliouson vs. Francis Emperor. Mentions: bill due John Albertson.

Alce Griffin (administratrix of her husband's estate) is to pay Richard Bennett, Esq.

26 December 1655. Court. Francis Emperor (merchant, of Elisabeth River) appointed Capt. John Barriffe as his attorney, to recover from Phillip Land & John Cornelison. Date: 14 December 1654 in VA. Witnesses: Geo. Swauley, William Whitby.

f. 167 Mr. Ri. Preston was granted an attachment on estate of Capt. William Stone, for chattel taken by Josias Fendall in the last Rebellion.

Thomas Orley was arrested on behalf of the Lord Protector.
- Elisabeth Potter deposed that about the end of September, Thomas Orley came to her husband's house. Mentions: land that the deponent's husband bought of Edward Hall. Thomas Orley indicated there was no government in MD.

f. 168 ...
- Martin Kirke & his wife Mary deposed that Thomas Orley indicated that there was no government in MD.

William Watson deposed that he had a warrant from Capt. William Stone, with (N) Medcalf, to publish a proclamation regarding the government. Mr. John Pott is security for William Watson.

Thomas Iger vs. Peter Godson.

Henry Foxe is indebted to Phillip Land.

Edward Lindsey is indebted to Phillip Land.

f. 169 (N) Floyd vs. William Johnson.

Stephen Benson was granted an attachment on estate of Capt. Stone.

Cornelius Johnson entered his right for 100 a.

Capt. Sampson Waring & James Veitch were elected as sheriffs. Mr. John Norwood & said Capt. Sampson Waring posted bonds for said office.

f. 170 Capt. Peter Johnson, Mr. Francis Brookes, & (N) are securities for said James Veitch.

Henry Coxe entered his right for 500 a. on assignment from Capt. John Barriffe. Land at the mouth of Putuxent River by William Stevens, on land formerly claimed by Mr. Eltonhead.

William Durand entered his right for 200 a., on land formerly claimed by Mr. Eltonhead.

Mr. Woodman Stokeley entered his right for 10 persons, transported 3-4 years ago. Land is on the south side of said land.

Mr. John Pott entered his right for 600 a. & 400 a. adjoining the land of said Pott near the land of Major Billingsley.

Petition of Mary Smith (widow), now wife of Capt. John Smith (sheriff), for fees. James Veitch (undersheriff) to provide such.

Liber - Patent Record A & B - 1650-1657

John Tawney, part of the estate of Tho. Trueman seized for his compliance with Capt. William Stone in the last Rebellion, is assigned to Capt. Peter Johnson.

f. 171 Simon Bird, servant to Thomas Trueman, has served his time & demands payment from the estate.

Phillip Land is indebted to Hugh Gale, & Francis Emperor, as administrator of estate of said Gale, has prosecuted said Land.

Francis Vandan is bound to William Brown & John Thimbleby. Witness: John Medle.

1 January. Thomas Read entered his right for 600 a. for transporting self, his wife, & 3 children.

f. 172 William Dorrington entered his right to 100 a. for transporting self.

Mr. Richard Preston entered his right to 1000 a.: 300 a. on land taken up by Mr. Eltonhead.

Recorded for John Medley. Lawrence Starcky (gentleman, of St. Inego's) was bound to Mr. Henry Corbyn (merchant, of London). Date: 13 May 1654. Witness: Raphe Crouch. Lawrence Starky acknowledged the debt. Date: 10 November 1654. Witness: Fr. Fitzheibet.

Job Chandler (merchant, of Portobacco) was bound to Henry Corbyn (merchant, of London). Date: 23 June 1654. Witness: Henry Coursey.

3 January 1654. John Norton entered his right for 200 a.

f. 173 for transporting self & his wife.

John Grammer entered his right for 100 a. for transporting William Acres.

John Grammer registered a cattle mark.

John Norton registered a cattle mark.

9 January 1655. William Durand (Secretary). James Berry entered this right for transporting self, Elisabeth his wife, William Berry, Roger Berry, Martha Berry, Thomas Skillinton, William Harbett, John Morth, John Pourtree, Mary Long, Elisabeth Howell, Garrett Comberton, William Burr.

Thomas Seamer entered his right for 100 a. for transporting self, land on Leonard's Creek adjoining Cornelius Abrams.

Sir Hen. Chicheley (knight, of Rapehanock, VA) was bound to Thomas Cornwallies, Esq. (of MD). Date: 7 November 1653. Witnesses: Richard Hotchkeys, John Antderton.

Robert Tinsbury entered a claim for 200 a.

f. 174 George Bussey entered a claim for 200 a.

William Turner entered a claim for 400 a.

Henry Keene entered a claim for 50 a.

Edward Keene entered a claim for 100 a.

18 January 1655. Arthur Wright entered a claim for 100 a. for transporting William Squire.

John Bagbey entered a claim for 200 a.

Abdeloe Martin entered a claim for 200 a. for transporting self & his wife.

William Marshall entered a claim for 200 a. for transporting John Dudlesse & Margaret Brunt.

Thomas Redolphus entered a claim for 100 a. for transporting self.

20 March 1655. Court. Attendees: Capt. William Fuller, Mr. Richard Preston, Mr. Thomas Meers, Mr. Michael Brooke.

Capt. William Mitchell vs. Francis Brooke.

f. 175 Walter Peake administrator of Francis Vandan shall be satisfied from his

Liber - Patent Record A & B - 1650-1657

estate.

John Crabtree died possessed of chattel belonging to Peter Johnson (son of Capt. Johnson).

John Bagby was granted an attachment on the estate of Daniel Morley.

Thomas Orley was arrested.

Bassill Little (merchant) is to receive compensation from the sheriff for theft from his store. Daniell Morley accused Cornelius Cannady as a conspirator in the theft from the store of Mr. Little (merchant).

f. 176 Peter Godson has not cared for Thomas Ager. Therefore, said Peter to repay.

Peter Sharp vs. Mr. William Battin.

Mr. William Batten vs. Bartholomew Bloome.

21 March 1655 at Putuxent. Court. Attendees: Capt. William Fuller, Mr. Richard Preston, Mr. Michael Brooke, Mr. John Hatch, Mr. Woodman Stockley, Mr. William Parrett.

Mrs. Ann Johnson was granted administration on the estate of her husband Capt. Peter Johnson (dec'd).

David Stevens is to be punished for abusing his master Mr. Richard Preston.

Capt. Waring (sheriff) had an attachment to Edward Booker on behalf of John Hawkins.

f. 177 Mr. Thomas Daynes was granted administration on estate of George Manners.

Capt. John Smith (dec'd) was indebted to: Leonard Strong (merchant) for use of William Scapes (merchant), John Brown (merchant), Ishmael Wright & Guy Whittle.

John Dandy vs. Christopher Cornell.

James Veitch complaint of John Hawkins that he received chattel at Clifts to be delivered at Putuxent from John Knapp.

f. 178 James Linsey petitioned for administration of estate of Benjamin Gill (dec'd). Thomas Gerrard, Esq. requested continuance.

Henry Fox attorney for Zachary Wade vs. estate of Capt. John Smith (dec'd).

Judgement for Henry Fox attorney for Capt. Mitchell is to be vacated.

John Hambleton vs. William Turner. Deferred to Mr. William Parrett & Mr. Michael Brooke.

Robert Clarke (gentleman) petitioned for relief for self & children.

f. 179 Geo. Mee was granted administration on estate of William Edie & John Preuce (dec'd).

22 March 1655 at Putuxent. Court. Attendees: Capt. William Fuller, Mr. Richard Preston, Mr. John Hatch, Mr. Thomas Meeres, Mr. William Parrett, Mr. Michael Brooke.

Walter Peake attorney for James Langworth vs. John Dandy.

John Dandy vs. Walter Peake.

Sheriff is to obtain & transport 2 runaway servants from VA to the commander of Cicacone. Col. William Claiborne has an interest in them.

John Hambleton is empowered to take the estate of Richard Moore (dec'd), & to make improvements for the use of the children.

Mrs. Ann Johnson received from Mr. William Ewen.

Mrs. Johnson was granted an attachment to the estate of Henry Catchmey.

Mr. Durand (Secretary) is out of the Province. Mr.

f. 180 Richard Preston is to perform the duties during his absence.

Liber - Patent Record A & B - 1650-1657

Bassill Little (merchant) vs. Mr. William Barrett (merchant, of London). Witnesses: William Fuller, Richard Preston, Tho. Meeres, Woodman Stockley, Michael Brooke, William Parrett, John Hatch.

Covenant between Mr. William Barrett (merchant, of London) & Capt. William Watts (mariner of ship Hopewell of London). Thomas Jordon for Mr. William Barrett (merchant, of London) protests for non-performance. Date: 21 March 1655. Witnesses: William Fuller, Richard Preston, John Hatch, Thomas Meeres, Michael Brooke, William Parrett, Woodman Stockley.

f. 181 John Dandy appointed his wife Anne Dandy as his attorney. Date: 17 May 1655. Witnesses: John Mettcalfe, John Shercliffe.

Mary Smith (widow of Capt. John Smith) sold to George Newman her plantation bought of Mr. Richard Preston. Date: 9 January 1655. Witnesses: Mich. Brooke, Thomas Semar, Frances Abramson.

Sir William Courtney (baronet, of Newhouse in Wiltshire) appointed Robert Thimbleby (gentleman)

f. 182 as his attorney for lands accrued by death of his mother Mrs. Elinor Hawley by the name of Mannor of St. Jerome & Mannor of St. Helen. Date: 25 November 1655 Witnesses: Bridg, Roger Corham, George Pultiott.

1 April 1656. John Bagby registered a cattle mark.

John Sutton registered a cattle mark.

WIlliam Harper registered a cattle mark.

f. 183 Roger Berry registered a cattle mark.

10 April 1656 at Putuxent. Court. Attendees: Mr. Richard Preston, Mr. William Parrett, Mr. Michael Brooke, Mr. Woodman Stockley.

Cites the PoA from Capt. William Mitchell to William Johnson & Henry Fox. Date: 25 April 1653.

Thomas Orley disclaimed the estate of George Manners unadministered by Edward Hall (dec'd).

Capt. Mitchell was bound to Jane Whitten.

Mr. Leonard Paid (merchant) vs. Capt. John Barriffe. Mentions: chattel sold by Mr. Enoch Derrick to Daniell Morley, to be received at John Bagby & Thomas Robinson is to mark it.

f. 184 Mr. John Knap was granted an attachment on the estate of Daniell Morley.

Emperor Smith was granted an attachment on estate of Will. Rump.

Joan Whitten, age 22, deposed that she agreed with Capt. William Mitchell for her transportation to this country & to serve his children in MD.

William Johnson appointed his brother James Langworth as his attorney, for any estate in MD or VA. Date: 9 April 1656. Witnesses: Robert Clarke, Thomas Sampson.

f. 185 Richard Preston sold to John Tennis (of Putuxent) land on eastern side of Leonard's Creek, part of 1000 a. belonging to me, [metes & bounds]. Witnesses: Woodman Stockley, Sampson Waring, John Sutton.

Message to: Mr. Richard Preston in Putuxent. From: Samuell Groome. Date: 29 March 1656. Mentions: Mr. Cranneg.

f. 186 Michael Brooke (of Putuxent) was bound to William Batten. Date: 27 April 1656. Security: bills by George Newman & Thomas Seamor. Witnesses: John Saffin, Will. Stockden.

f. 187 William Batten (of Putuxent) received of Michael Brookes. Date: 9 November 1656. Witnesses: George Newman, Henry Keene.

William Young (planter, of Nominy) for love & affection gives to Richard Bennett the younger (son of Richard Bennett the elder (planter, living in Poplar Neck)) chattel. Should said Richard Bennett the younger die, then the chattel is to belong to Mary Bennett the daughter of said Richard Bennett the elder & sister to said Richard Bennett the younger. Date: 27 December 1655. Witnesses: Henry Spinke, Emperor Smith.

Liber - Patent Record A & B - 1650-1657

f. 188 John Bagbee (planter, of Putuxent) sold to James Godgrace 200 a. at Bagbee's Branch. Date: 22 May 1656. Witnesses: William Harper, John Sutton.

f. 189 William Stockden (of Putuxent) for love & affection gave to Joseph Wright the younger (son of Ishmaeal Wright the elder (of Putuxent)) chattel. Date: 24 May 1656. Witnesses: William Harper, John Bagbee, John Sutton.

16 June 1656 at Putuxent. Court. Attendees: Mr. Richard Preston, Mr. Woodman Stockley, Mr. John Hatch, Mr. Michael Brooke, Mr. William Parrott.

John Bagbee deposed that he did not receive chattel from Daniell Morley. John Sutton & Thomas Robinson deposed that Daniell Morley agreed to the account.

John Bagby was granted 200 a. at the mouth of Hunting Creek, on land formerly of John Turner.

f. 190 Richard Collett had letters of administration on the estate of Thomas Connery. Mr. Eltonhead is to deliver the estate.

William Pritchard was granted 100 a. on Hunting Creek, next to land of Mr. Michael Brooke.

Mr. Thomas Trueman was granted a continuance.

Susan Cannady vs. Cornelius Cannady. Arbitrators: Mr. Richard Preston, Mr. Michael Brooke.

Ishmael was granted 200 a., joining his current land.

Henry Fox vs. Walter Pakes attorney for Mrs. Ann Hamond.

Henry Keene was granted 150 a., joining Cornelius Neck & 100 a. elsewhere.

f. 191 James Jolly was granted 200 a. for transporting 4 persons.

John Knap was granted an attachment on estate of Henry Catchmey.

Richard Shippey assigned a bill to Mary Catchmey.

Cornelius Abramson had an attachment on the estate of Mr. Edmund Scarburgh.

Alice Griffin (widow of Samuell Griffin (dec'd)) paid fees.

William Johnson vs. Capt. William Mitchell.

f. 192 Edward Keene vs. William Turner. Mentions: Edward Keene sold 200 a. to William Turner in Matopony Town.

Caveat of 500 a. was granted to Timothy Gunton for 7 rights bought of Mrs. Parr & 3 rights bought of Mr. Hugh Standly & his own transportation. The land is on the north side of Putuxent River, adjoining Qwastoe of Mrs. Brooke.

James Linsey was possessed of the estate of Benjamin Gill (dec'd). Robert Cole appeared & said that he was akin to said Gill. Linsey is to deliver the estate to said Cole, with an account to Mr. John Hatch.

Francis Vandan was indebted to Walter Pake administrator of said Vandan (dec'd).

f. 193 Non-suit was granted to William Johnson, James Langworth, & Luke Garner in cases against Capt. Mitchell.

Non-suit was granted to Mrs. Fenwick in case against Capt. Mitchell.

Cuthbert Fenwick (gentleman) was indebted to Skipper Jacob Derrickson. Mrs. Fenwick administratrix of said Mr. Fenwick (dec'd) is to pay Mr. John Hatch attorney for Skipper Jacob Derrickson.

17 June 1656 at Putuxent. Court. Attendees: Mr. Richard Preston, Mr. John Hatch, Mr. William Parrott, Mr. Michael Brooke, Mr. Woodman Stockley.

Agnus Norman was granted administration on estate of John Norman (dec'd).

Robert Taylor presented Thomas Holland (servant) which said Tailor bought of Mr. Thomas Bennett (merchant). Said Holland deposed his age as 20.

f. 194 At Court on 10 April 1656 at Putuxent, Capt. William Mitchell vs. James Langworth & a servant in the possession of said Langworth bought of Will.

Liber - Patent Record A & B - 1650-1657

Johnson. Mentions: family & children of Capt. Mitchell.

Capt. John Smith (dec'd) is indebted to Edward Booles.

Certificate for 200 a. was granted to Edward Wood on assignment from Timothy Gunton.

George Willard (dec'd) is indebted to William Stevens.

Caveat of 200 a. was granted to Henry Pope on east side, between said Pope & Mr. Woodman Stockley.

f. 195 Mr. Hugh Standly vs. Mr. John Pott. Jury: Phillip Morgin, Will. Ewen, John Hambleton, John Bagbee, John Day, Tho. Seamore, Arthur Wright, William Jonnes, Robert Taylor, Henry Foxe, Walter Pake, Geo. Mee, Rich. True.

Marks Pheypo vs. Richard True & William Smoote. Continuance granted.

Mr. Standly is to return the servant from Mrs. Hooper to Mr. Norton.

Francis Vandan is indebted to John Jarbo. Walter Pake administrator of estate of Francis Vandan is to pay.

Lord Protector vs. Thomas Orley. Elisabeth Potter & Martin Kirke & his wife subpoenaed.

f. 196 William Nugent (dec'd) is indebted to Henry Fox.

John Crabtree (dec'd) is indebted to Mr. Phillip Morgan attorney of John Thurmar.

George Manners (dec'd) is indebted to Mr. John Hatch. Edward Hall married the relict of said Manners. Thomas Orley married the relict of said Hall.

Thomas Seamore petitioned for security for bill from William Jonnes.

f. 197 John Hatch appointed Capt. Sampson Waring as his attorney in the case against Thomas Orley. Date: 17 June 1656. Witness: John Sutton.

Alice Griffin, age 35, deposed that Cornelius Cannady asked John Sallisbury whether certain chattel had been sold. John replied that he had to ask his mother. Mentions: chattel of mother of John Sallisbury in VA.

George Bussey, age 34, deposed that Edward Keene sold his right to 200 a. to William Turner, that he bought of Mr. Parrott. Signed: Richard Keene.

Henry Keene, age 30, deposed that he made the bill of William Jonnes for Thomas Seamore.

f. 198 James Jolly deposed the same.

Markes Pheypoe deposed that he heard Edward Hall say that he had to pay Mr. John Hatch for his wife's clothes.

Elisabeth Potter deposed that she heard Edward Hall say he would pay Mr. Hatch for his wife's clothes. Mentions: estate of Mr. Manners.

Marks Pheypoe deposed that Edward Hall undertook to fulfill the conditions.

Thomas Ashbrooke deposed that Richard True sent the deponent to Mr. Hatton to determine if Marke Pheypoe had been there for his bill. Mentions: Goodman True, Goodman Smoote.

John Nevill deposed that he heard Goodman Smoote & Marke

f. 199 Pheypoe at the landing place of Richard True making a bargain. Date: 14 June 1656.

Cornelius Cannady assigned to John Knap all his right to land which is unsold within the indenture. Date: 2 June 1656. Witnesses: Richard Sheppey, William Ewen.

Thomas Hebden transported self in 1635, his wife Katherine in 1640, & received on assignment from James Neale, Esq. (for transporting 5 men in 1640) 1000 a. on advice of Giles Brent, Esq.,

f. 200 was granted the neck of land on the west side of St. George's River, bounding St. George's Creek, Beane's Creek, for 700 a. Date: 7 February 1643.

Liber - Patent Record A & B - 1650-1657

Katherine Marshall, wife of William Marshall, late wife of Thomas Hebden (dec'd) assigned her right to 600 a. on St. George's Creek to James Hall. Date: 10 June 1646. Witnesses: Peter Libar, John Douglas.

f. 201 Lt. Col. Samuell Smith administrator of Robert Duglasse (dec'd) assigned 500 a. on Cedar Point to William Batten. Date: 24 May 1655. Witness: William Thomas. Lt. Col. Samuell Smith sold to Mr. WIlliam Batten the tract Cedar Point. Mr. Michael Brooke is to acknowledge this in court. Date: 24 May 1656. Witness: Thomas Spekes.

Francis Pakes authorized James Langworth (of St. Winifred's) as attorney for the case against John Dandy. Date: 10 June 1656. Witnesses: Walter Guest, John Green.

f. 202 Thomas Lewis gave chattel to Ishmael Wright, Jr. & Ishmael Wright, Sr. gave chattel to his son Ishmael Wright.

Thomas Hussey (planter) authorized Walter Pake (gardner) as his attorney. Witnesses: Tho. Jordan, John Greene.

22 September 1656 at Putuxent. Court. Attendees: Capt. William Fuller, Mr. Richard Preston, Mr. Edward Lloyd, Mr. John Pott, Mr. Michael Brooke.

Judith Catchpole is accused of murdering her child.

f. 203 James Jolly deposed that he was at the house of John Grammer a week before the death of the servant of William Bramhall. The servant said that Judith Catchpole "cut a maid's skinn off her throat & she never felt it."

Elisabeth Norton deposed that the servant (dec'd) of William Bramhall said that Judith Catchpole "cut a maid's skinn off her throat & she never felt it."

Andrew Wilcox deposed that the servant (dec'd) of William Bramhall said that when the murder was done, all were asleep.

Elisabeth Norton deposed that the servant (dec'd) of William Bramhall said that he & Judith Catchpole ground a knife & said Judith "prickt a seaman in the back" & that Judith was to kill 3 or 4 more men.

f. 204 Jury to examine Judith Catchpole: Rose Smith, Mrs. Belcher, Mrs. Chaplin, Mrs. Brooke, Mrs. Batten, Mrs. Cannady, Mrs. Bussey, Mrs. Brooke [sic], Elisabeth Claxton, Elisabeth Potter, Dorothy Day.

Judith Catchpole, servant to William Dorrington, was brought to court on charges of murdering a child on her voyage on the Mary & Francis from England about October 1655 & arriving the following January. Her accuser is deceased. Acquittal.

George Me demanded from the estate of Capt. John Barriff (dec'd).

f. 205 John Bagbee deposed that Daniell Morley desired last December that the deponent pay a bill to William Stogden for the use of Guye White.

Ishmael Wright deposed that Daniell Morley came to the deponent's house last Christmas for Mr. Willard. William Stogden asked about payment & Morley relied that John Bagbee was to pay.

Capt. William Fuller attorney for Leo. Payd (merchant) vs. Guy White. Mentions: payment by Daniel Morley.

f. 206 Francis Brooke vs. Martin Kirke.

John Grammer, vs. John Felton.

Cornelius Abramson vs. Henry Keene.

Mr. Symon Overzee (merchant) demanded from the estate of Capt. John Barriffe (dec'd). Mentions: Capt. William Ewens administrator of the estate, bill of Phillip Land, bill of Walter Pakes, bill of John Cornelius, bill of Edmund Lindsey.

23 September 1656 at Putuxent. Court. Attendees: Capt. William Fuller, Mr. Richard Preston, Mr. Edward Lloyd, Mr. John Pott, Mr. Mich. Brooke.

f. 207 Martin Kirke deposed that Henry Potter desired the deponent to assess chattel bought of Mr. John Hatch.

Liber - Patent Record A & B - 1650-1657

George Mee deposed that Mr. Friendship sold part of his land (between George Manners & said Friendship) to Edward Hall. Signed: George Me.

Henry Potter vs. Capt. William Mitchell attorney for Tho. Orley.

Elisabeth Claxton deposed that Henry Potter went to the house of Thomas Orley & demanded his bond.

Henry Keene vs. Mrs. Ann Dorrington. Assessment by:

f. 208 Mr. Mich. Brooke, Capt. Sampson Waring, Mr. Henry Osborne, Mr. Tho. Thomas.

Marke Pheypoe vs. Richard True.

Emperor Smith vs. John Nevill.

Capt. William Evens vs. Capt. Richard Banks.

Elisabeth Potter deposed that 6 years ago, Mrs. Eltonhead & Mr. Scarbrough bargained for chattel for her children. Attachment was granted to Mrs. Jane Eltonhead on the estate of Col. Edmund Scarbrough in MD.

Capt. William Mitchell vs. James Langworth attorney for William Johnson. Mentions:

f. 209 servant maid sold by said Johnson, children of Capt. William Mitchell.

Thomas Greene & Jane Greene, widow of Nicholas Harvie (dec'd), sold to Mr. Edward Lloyd all right to 1 parcel of land in Putuxent.

24 September 1656 at Putuxent. Court. Attendees: Capt. William Fuller, Mr. Richard Preston, Mr. Edward Lloyd, Mr. John Pott, Mr. Michael Brooke.

Capt. Mitchell vs. James Langworth. Mentions: John Gee (servant of said Mitchell) sold by Will. Johnson agent of Capt. Mitchell to said Langworth.

f. 210 Andrew Wilcox deposed that he went with Mr. John Hawkins to the house of Cornelius Abramson. Mr. Hawkins was to receive payment from Mr. Robert Taylor. The wife of Cornelius Abramson said that Thomas Seamore had damages some of the chattel.

Robert Taylor vs. John Felton. Mentions: chattel received by said Felton & Mr. Morgan at the house of Cornelius Abramson, Phillip Morgin. Some of said chattel was damaged.

Nicholas White deposed that Richard True & Goodman Smoot agreed with Markes Pheypoe to repair a shallop.

f. 211 Marks Pheypoe vs. Richard True.

Capt. William Mitchell vs. Luke Gardnor. Mentions: manservant John Spurdance sold by William Johnson agent for said Mitchell to said Gardnor.

Capt. Josias Fendall took an oath.

25 September 1656 at Putuxent. Court. Attendees: Capt. William Fuller, Mr. Richard Preston, Mr. Edward Lloyd, Mr. John Pott, Mr. Mich. Brooke.

James Veitch demanded from Thomas Cager for service

f. 212 done to Capt. John Barriffe (dec'd).

William Johnson vs. Capt. William Mitchell.

Walter Pakes administrator of estate of Francis Vandan (dec'd). Estate is overpaid.

Ann Hamond petitioned for execution against the estate of Capt. John Barriff (dec'd).

Capt. Sampson Waring attorney for Mr. John Hatch vs. Capt. Mitchell attorney for Thomas Orley. Mentions: Orley is the administrator of estate of Edward Hall (dec'd).

f. 213 Elisabeth Claxton deposed that when Mr. Francis Brooke brought his wife to the deponent's house, he beat her. She went into labor & gave birth to a child.

Liber - Patent Record A & B - 1650-1657

Rose Smith deposed that she was sent to help the wife of Francis Brooke

f. 214 give birth & it was a premature male.

Francis Brooke was brought to court on charge of murder.

William Bretton deposed that 5/6 years ago, Capt. William Ewens delivered the calf to John Norman for a young girl cited as his daughter-in-law & said Norman brought the calf in the deponent's boat with his own son & Cladrueny Maze. The calf

f. 215 went on the lands of Mr. Gerrard.

Mr. Gerrard deposed.

Luke Gardnor deposed that the cattle mark on the particular cow was not the same as the rest of the cattle shown by Mr. Gerrard & his son & Mr. Slye.

Walter Pake deposed that he went to the house of Capt. Mitchell & found Mr. Francis Brooke with his head in his wife's lap, very sick. Capt. Mitchell wanted Mr. Brooke to go to court to sue for his wife's service.

f. 216 Thomas Greene (planter, of Elisabeth River VA) deposed that Leonard Calvert, Esq. (Governor) granted to Nicholas Harvie 1000 a. on southwest side of Putuxent River, bounding St. Thomas his Point. Thomas Greene & his wife Jane Greene (late wife of said Nicholas) sold said patent to Edward Lloyd. Date: 8 March 1654. Witnesses: William Greene, Robert Langley.

f. 217 Edward Lloyd assigned his right to his patent to Ishmael Wright & William Stogden. Date: 26 September 1656. Witnesses: Sampson Waring, Richard Smith. Before: William Fuller, Rich. Preston. Witness: William Gibbins.

Mr. Edward Lloyd was put in possession of St. Thomas his Point, formerly owned by Jane Greene widow of Nicholas Harvie (dec'd).

f. 218 Date: 25 September 1656. Signed: William Fuller. Sampson Waring (sheriff of Putuxent) put Mr. Edward Lloyd in possession of said land. Witnesses: Richard Smith, William Gibbins.

Francis Brooke (gentleman, of St. Maries') was bound to Thomas Hinson (of Isle of Kent) for Beaver Neck & to be delivered to Mr. Collett (of Putuxent). Date: 26 September 1656. Witnesses: John Sutton, Will. Mitchell.

f. 219 Mr. Pott vs. Mr. Standly. Arbitrators: Francis Brookes, James Langworth.

Barnaby Jackson (planter, of St. Maries') sold to Timothy Gudridge (planter, of Putuxent) 100 a. on northwest side of said Jackson's land Fresh Pond Neck. Date: 31 December 1655. Signed: Barnaba Jackson. Witnesses: John Metcalfe, John Chocoy, John Loul.

f. 220 20 October 1656 at Putuxent. Court. Attendees: Mr. Richard Preston, Mr. Woodman Stockley, Mr. Mich. Brooke, Mr. John Pott, Mr. William Parrott.

George Mee demanded of the estate of Capt. John Barriffe (dec'd). Capt. John Barriffe (dec'd) was indebted to Mr. Nicholas Gwider & is to be paid to Mr. Mathewes.

William Ewens vs. William Phillips.

Ann Hamond vs. John Miles.

f. 221 Emperor Smith vs. Mr. William Battin.

Ann Hamond attorney for John Hamond vs. John Lewger.

Capt. William Mitchell vs. Mrs. Fenwick.

21 October 1656. Court (con't).

Henry Potter vs. Thomas Orley by his attorney Capt. Mitchell.

f. 222 Emperor Smith vs. John Nevill. Mentions: said Smith applied physick & chirurgery to said Nevill's wife.

John Cornelius deposed that June 2 years ago, the deponent was at the house of John Nevill, where he heard Nevill's wife say that if it had not been for the Dutch doctor, she had not been her own woman.

Liber - Patent Record A & B - 1650-1657

Mr. Francis Brooke deposed that 7 years ago, the deponent carried chattel from Mr. Cuthbert Fenwick to Col. Thomas Burbage.

William Sinclare deposed that 4 years ago, there was chattel sent down from Mr. Fenwick to Col. Burbage via a ship of Capt. Hinfield.

f. 223 Richard Collett attorney for Capt. Edward Streeter who married the relict of Col. Thomas Burbage (dec'd) vs. Mrs. Jane Fenwick widow & administratrix of Mr. Cuthbert Fenwick (dec'd). Mentions: deposition by Francis Brooke, deposition by William Sinclare.

Edward Good deposed that he heard John Crabtree (dec'd) say that half of the mill belonged to George Sutton. John Ramsden (a servant) was between the two & said servant was with Crabtree until the servant died about June 1655.

f. 224 Mr. John Hatch vs. Capt. William Mitchell attorney for Thomas Orley. Jury: Thomas Hinson, Thomas Trueman, Hugh Standly, Walter Peake, John Cornelius, Michael Basey, Richard Bankes, John Tilton, William Marle, John Lightfoot, John Nevill, George Sutton.

Capt. Richard Banks vs. Capt. Evens.

John Cornelius vs. Richard Bennitt.

Paul Simpson vs. Mr. Symon Overzee.

Walter Pake vs. Paul Simpson.

Mr. John Pott vs. Mr. Standley.

Robert Taylor petitioned for satisfaction for transporting people over the Putuxent River.

f. 225 The sheriff is to make a list of inhabitants of Putuxent & Potomack.

Mr. Rich. Preston demanded of James Veitch on a bill by Richard Bennett, Esq.

Michael Brooke gave to Mary Smith, Jr. (heir of Capt. John Smith (dec'd)) chattel & 100 a. which Mr. Richard Preston gave to Capt. John Smith. Date: 20 October 1656. Witness: John Pott.

Cornelius Cannady vs. his wife Susan Cannady. Arbitrators: Richard Preston, Mr. Michael Brooke. Mentions: said Susan came from VA. Date: 24 June 1656. Signed: Cornelius Cannady, Susanna Cannady. Witnesses: Richard Preston, William Berrey.

f. 226 William Wildye received of Cuthbert Fenwick (dec'd) chattel for use of Capt. Thomas Burbage. Date: 13 October 1656. Witness: Robert Vaughan.

John Hamond appointed his wife Ann Hamond his attorney, granted to her & Walter Pake.

f. 227 Date: 16 April 1655. Witnesses: M. Fantleroy, Christo. Brounridge. Ann Hamond revoked the joint PoA to her & Walter Pake by her husband John Hamond. Date: 18 November 1656. Witnesses: John Lawson, Walter Pakes.

Robert Clarke (gentleman) sold to Ann Hamond, wife of John Hamond, all interest in the plantation on east side of Bretton's Bay, for 1000 a. Date: 27 May 1656.

f. 228 Witnesses: John Lawson, Robert Thimbleby. Ann Hamond, wife & attorney of John Hamond, sold to Richard Hotchkeyes a plantation on east side of Bretton's Bay, conveyed to me by Robert Clarke (gentleman), for 1000 a.

f. 229 Date: 18 November 1656. Witnesses: Walter Peake, John Lawson, Robert Thimbleby. Revocation by Ann Hamond wife of John Hamond of the joint PoA

f. 230 given to Walter Peake. Signed: John Lawson. I was present when the deed was delivered to Richard Hotchkeyes by Ann Hamond. Signed: Robert Thimbleby.

Thomas Hopkins & Robert Hopkins registered cattle marks.

12 January 1656 at Putuxent. Court. Attendees: Mr. Richard Preston, Michael Brooks, Mr. Woodman Stockley, Mr. John Potts, Mr. William Parrott.

William Meares, servant to Mr. William Parker, deposed his age as 20 next May.

Liber - Patent Record A & B - 1650-1657

Mr. Robert Taylor & John Read appraised the estate of Mr. Cuthbert Fenwick (dec'd).

Hennery Chappoon demanded of David Parrea per the oaths of Henry Hooper & Clement Hinton.

f. 231 Henry Hooper deposed regarding the demand of Henry Chappoon of David Farrea. Signed: Henery Hooper. Clement Hinton deposed the same.

Robert Kingsbury is indebted to David Brown. Mentions: Kingsbury is engaged for said Brown to Cornelius Abraham.

The wife of Friendship Toungue (dec'd) refused administration on his estate. Administration was granted to Mrs. Jane Fenixe.

Elisabeth Jolly was accused of slander of Mrs. Turner & Mrs. Bassey.

Richard Bennett vs. John Cornelius.

f. 232 13 January 1656. Court (con't).

Mr. William Parker was granted an attachment on the estate of Maj. John Billingsly.

Michaell Basey is to receive from the estate of John Crabtree (dec'd).

Henry Billsbury, a servant to John Little, complained of cruel treatment.

f. 233 Timothy Guttridge vs. John Knap.

Mr. Woodman Stockley attorney for Thomas Cole vs. John Knap.

Henry Keen was granted payment for attendance at court for Thomas Semare.

James Veitch is to pay William Wilkinson attorney for William Cooper.

David Farrea vs. Richard Garford. Arbitrators:

f. 234 Mr. Harrisse, Mr. Stockley.

George Sutton deposed regarding the mill of John Crabtree.

John Williams vs. Michael Basey. Said Williams is to pay Henry Bullin & his wife.

David Farera vs. Tim. Guttridge.

David Farera vs. Emperor Smith.

f. 235 William Bramalll (planter) vs. Mr. John Potts.

Hubert Patee vs. William Turner.

Maj. John Billingsley vs. Thomas Semer (also Thomas Seamor). Mentions: Thomas Seamor is indebted to David Farrea.

Peter Joy vs. Henry Catchma (non-resident).

David Farrea (planter) vs. James Jolly.

Emperor Smith vs. Mr. Battin.

f. 236 Henry Potter (planter), in consideration of assignment between Thomas Orley & Samuell Scott, agrees with Thomas Orley (of Chickakane VA) & his attorney William Mitchell (of MD) to defend the plantation of Thomas Allen according to the covenant with John Hatch & Richard Banks (overseers) by Thomas Warr & Robert Sharp. Date: 7 November 1656. Witnesses: Nicholas Barcholest, Edmond Lemond.

f. 237 Mr. Bassill Little deposed that Elisabeth Jolley replied, in answer to the question of missing chattel, that none was there except for the wife of William Turner & the wife of George Bussey.

Mrs. Dorrington deposed the same, and that said Jolley should swear that Gooddy Turner was a thief.

Mary Damaell deposed the same.

Liber - Patent Record A & B - 1650-1657

George Bussey deposed that there was a bargain between Thomas Seamer & Edward Keen. James Jolley deposed the same.

Clement Hinton deposed that David Farrea promised Mr. Ewens payment.

f. 238 Edward Good deposed that John Crabtree promised Goodman Bassey payment for chattel Crabtree had of Michael Bassey.

Clement Hinton deposed that David Farrea hired of Mr. Henry Hooper the store that was Mr. Jordan.

Edward Good deposed that Thomas Seamer should say that John Tennis was a thief.

Timothy Gunton deposed that Mr. John Potts was to give chattel to William Brammaell.

John Merthe deposed that Mr. John Pott was to give chattel to William Brammaell.

James Veitch deposed regarding a bargain between William Turner & Hubert Pattee. George Bussey deposed the same.

William Mitchell, Esq. discharged James Gunnion of all debts. Date: 8 January 1656. Witnesses: Pa. Simpson, Robert Thimelby.

f. 239 James Gunnion & Patrick Mulligan requested administration on estate of Andrew Scott & Thomas Ager (dec'd). Date: 22 January 1656.

Sampson Waring (sheriff of Putuxent, St. Maries', and Potomack Cos.) shall dutifully execute said office. Signed: Sampson Waring, John Norwood, Ri. Preston. Witnesses: William Durand, William Owen, James Langworth, Peter Jonson.

f. 240 James Veitch (sheriff of Putuxent, St. Maries', and Potomack Cos.) shall dutifully execute said office. Signed: Sampson Waring, John Norwood, Ri. Preston. Witnesses: William Durand, William Owen, James Langworth, Peter Jonson.

George Bussey requested administration on estate of Edward Beasly (dec'd). Date: 20 January 1656.

Thomas Hopkins demanded 50 a., joining his land in St. John's Creek.

James Veitch, Peter Johnson, & Francis Brookes acknowledged a debt to Oliver Lord Protector. Date: 10 December 1655. Mentions: said James as sheriff under Capt. Sampson Waring (high sheriff),

f. 241 Capt. John Smith. Witnesses: William Durand, James Langworth, John Barriffe.

William Stogden requested administration on estate of William Gibbins (dec'd). Date: 28 January 1656.

William Stephens demanded 200 a., adjoining his current land on Putuxent River. Date: 27 January.

David Farrera vs. Henry Hooper. Jury: Capt. William Mitchell, John Knap, Mr. Hugh Stanly, Robert Tayler, Mich. Basey, John Hamleton, Thomas Reed, Mr. Thomas Thomas, Henry Keen, Edward Keen, William Turner, George Bussey.

f. 242 Henry Hooper vs. David Farrera.

Timothy Goodridge assigned to Bassill Little chattel of Mr. Knap in the house of John Cornelius. Witness: Edward Keene.

10 March 1656 at Putuxent. Court. Attendees: Mr. Richard Preston, Mr. Michael Brookes, Mr. Woodman Stockley, Mr. John Potts.

f. 243 David Farrera vs. Cornelius Canedy.

Thomas Robinson vs. James Attchison. Mentions: said James is indebted to said Thomas for chattel assigned to Henry Osborne.

David Ferrara vs. Henry Pope.

Timothy Guttridge vs. James Attchison.

Mr. Battin vs. Mr. Morgan.

Liber - Patent Record A & B - 1650-1657

Hubert Patee was accused of slander by George Bussey & James Veach (also James Veatch).

f. 244 William Stokden was granted administration on estate of William Gibbins (dec'd).

Emperor Smith demanded of the estate of William Gibbins (dec'd).

John Bagbey was granted 200 a. on north side of land adjoining Thomas Thomas.

John Dammarell demanded 200 a., adjoining the abovementioned land of John Bagbey.

Henry Bills vs John Little.

Mr. Rich. Harris vs. James Attchison & Tim. Guttridge

f. 245 Richard Harris vs. Timothy Guttridge.

Peter Johnson registered a cattle mark.

Timothy Guttridge vs. James Attchison.

George Bussey was granted administration on estate of Edward Beasley (dec'd).

David Farrera vs. Mr. Hen. Hooper.

William Muffett vs. John Hawkins.

f. 246 David Farrera vs. Henry Hooper.

Mathew Smith vs. David Farrera.

Will. Battin vs. Walter Carre.

Robert Kingsberry deposed that Hubert Patee slandered the witnesses of William Turner: George Busse, James Veatch. William Thomas deposed the same.

Robert Taylor deposed that Capt. Johnson killed a steer.

f. 247 John Dammarell deposed that last October, Capt. Johnson desired the deponent to kill a steer & James Wilson & John Boone went with the deponent.

William Howse deposed that he heard John Little call his servant Billsberry on the Sabbath to beat him.

Stephen Harloe deposed that 2 years ago at the house of John Little, on the Sabbath, the deponent heard him call his servant Henry Billsberry to beat him.

Richard Garford deposed that he was employed by John Little to bring his servant Billsberry. When the servant was brought, he was beaten. Billsberry requested Henry Pope as his security. Before: Woodman Stockley.

f. 248 Thomas Binkes deposed that William Gibbins (dec'd) gave chattel to Julian Hyell. Before: Richard Preston.

Michael Farmer deposed that William Gibbins promised Julian Hyell chattel that was between him & Thomas Binkes. Before: Richard Preston.

Edward Good deposed that Michael Basey had chattel of John Crabtree.

f. 249 Clement Hinton deposed that when we went to Potomack River to received goods from a ship of John Cornelius via Col. Smith, the deponent told Capt. Mitchell that there should be damage to the chattel.

Henry Chapin deposed that when Capt. Mitchell took a shipment of good from John Cornelius, the deponent told Capt. Mitchell that it would cost extra.

Elisabeth Manship relinquished to

f. 250 Bartholomy Herring all rights to chattel given him in exchange for bequest by her husband Richard Manship. Date: 23 March 1656. Witnesses: Richard Smith, Thomas Belcher, Thomas Turner.

20 March 1656 at Putuxent. Court. Attendees: Capt. William Fuller, Mr. Rich. Preston, Mr. Edward Lloyd, Mr. Michael Brooke, Mr. William Parratt.

Mrs. Sarah Marsh administratrix of her husband Mr. Thomas Marsh (dec'd) sued for administration of estate of Valerius Leo & Andrew Hanson (dec'd). Per Mr. Thomas Ringgold, said Valerius & Andrew were debtors to Mr. Marsh.

William Berry vs. John Little. John Little scandalized Mrs. Elisabeth Potts by the depositions of Henry Pope & Richard Garford.

f. 251 William Berry vs. John Little. Cause: John Little scandalized Berry's father & mother in depositions by Henry Pope & Richard Garford. Said Henry & Richard were paid for their time on behalf of John Little.

Hen. Pope to be paid for his time on behalf of Henry Billsberry.

f. 252 Phillip Hyde vs. John Williams. Mentions: testimony by Michael Basey.

21 March 1656 at Putuxent. Court. Attendees: same as before.

Order to Mr. Francis Brookes.

Aron Jacobsen is to be paid for his time by Henry Billsberry.

John Little was given punishment.

f. 253 Mentions: Little's wife.

Richard Harris vs. Michael Basey.

Michael Basey vs. Phillip Hyde.

Timothy Guttridge vs. John Knap.

Mr. Henry Hooper (attorney of Mr. Meese) was granted administration on estate of Mr. Lawrence Starkey (dec'd).

f. 254 Mr. John Harris (merchant of London) vs. John Grammer.

James Veitch is indebted to Cinnamon Barbury.

Mr. William Battin by his attorney James Veitch vs. Mr. Phillip Morgan.

Mr. Phillip Morgan vs. Maj. John Billingsley. Mentions: chattel received by said Billingsley of Nicholas Dixon.

f. 255 Maj. John Billingsly is indebted to Mr. William Parker.

William Moffett vs. John Hawkins.

Walter Peake vs. Mr. Paul Simpson.

Paul Simpson vs. Walter Peake.

f. 256 David Farrera vs. John Read.

William Wardiff vs. John Waide.

Capt. Peter Johnson (dec'd) was security to James Veitch, & William Dorrington is married to relict of said Johnson.

William Dorrington registered a cattle mark.

Order regarding the gauge of casks.

f. 257 Paul Simpson was granted an attachment on the estate of John Pritchard (non-resident of the Province).

Order for the replenishment of Militia. Date: 23 March 1656. Appointments:

f. 258 Mr. Woodman Stockley as captain of Putuxent north of plantation of Mr. Brooke. Lt. Henry Keen as captain of Putuxent south of plantation of Mr. Brooke & up as high as the plantation of Henry Cox. Mr. Phillip Morgan as captain of bay side of the plantation. Signed: Capt. William Fuller, Mr. Richard Preston, Mr. Edward Lloyd, Mr. Tho. Meeres, Mr. Michael Brookes, Mr. William Parker, Mr. WIlliam Parratt.

Mr. John Lord exhibited a bill due from John Hamond to Nicholas Watkins. Order on 6 December 1650 at Jamestown for bill to be paid. Said Lord desires Ann Hammond to pay.

Liber - Patent Record A & B - 1650-1657

f. 259 Mr. Thomas Ringhold sued Capt. Joseph Weekes for defamation at County Court of Kent. Appealed.

Mathew Smith, who married the relict of Richard Manship, was granted 50 a. on right of said Manship's transportation, lying between land of Mr. Hamstead & Cornelius Cannedy in Indian Towne.

Mr. Michael Brookes was granted 300 a. in Indian Town, joining the land of John Damaell.

Francis Abraham vs. Mr. William Dorrington. Mentions: chattel killed by Capt. Johnson.

f. 260 David Farrera vs. Henry Hooper.

Order for new commissioners: Capt. Phillip Morgan, Mr. William Ewens, Mr. Thomas Thomas, Lt. Phillip Thomas, Mr. Samuell Vethers, Lt. Richard Woolman.

James Gunnion & Patrick Mulligan were granted administrations on the estates of Andrew Scott & Thomas Ager (dec'd).

William Mill attorney for Luke Barber vs. Ann Hammond.

Mrs. Jane Fenwick vs. Capt. William Mitchell.

Mathew Smith deposed that Henry Carlien & Elisabeth Garnier posed as husband & wife.

f. 261 Elisabeth Smith deposed the same.

Markes Clare deposed that when the deponent came from Holland, he had 12 indentures which Maj. John Billingsly had out of Holland. Markes Clare, Jr. deposed the same.

Henry Pope deposed that John Little said that the church was burnt in which Mr. Berry & his wife were married, and that his wife had another husband. Richard Garford deposed the same.

Henry Hooper gave chattel to Phillip Harwood. Date: 20 April 1657. Witnesses: Richard Preston, Thomas Turner.

f. 262 Henry Pope deposed that John Little said that Mrs. Potts was dishonest with said Little's Indian boy. Richard Garford deposed the same.

Francis Abraham deposed that Ann Seamer wife of Thomas Seamer told the deponent that she had 7 years to serve when she first came.

Michael Basey deposed that John Williams desired the deponent to take a barrel of beer at the Jewes store for use of said Williams & Phillip Hyde.

Jane Eltonhead deposed that she went with her brother & sister Fenwick to St. Inego's to Capt. William Mitchell. Said Mitchell was indebted to the deponent's brother Fenwick. Date: 6 January 1653.

f. 263 John Cammell deposed that Mr. John Wade agreed with William Woodriff for 1 year's service. Before: John Lawson.

Thomas Tunnell, age 27, deposed that last year, William Wardriffe engaged to serve Mr. John Waide for 1 year. Signed: Tho. Tunnell. Date: 9 January 1656. Before: Richard Preston.

f. 264 Thomas Bennett (of London) assigned a bill of Mr. James Berry (of Putuxent) to James Cary (of London), which bill Henry Hooper was to receive. [Recorded for Mr. William Berry.] Witnesses: Andrew Paynter, Robert Hyll. James Cary received payment from James Berry via Mr. Robert Tayler.

Ishmael Wright (planter) & his wife Ann sold to Anthony LeCompte (planter)

f. 265 the plantation occupied by Henry Bullen & Alexander Mayrobe on Point Patience on Putuxent River, for 75 a., between plantations of John Ascombe & William Stephens. Date: 13 January 1656. Witnesses: Will. Mitchell, Sampson Warring.

William Eltonhead (gentleman) sold to John Anderson (gentleman)

f. 266 the plantation, island, & neck, adjoining John Wakefield. Witnesses: John Anketill, John Pedro, Francis Anketill.

Liber - Patent Record A & B - 1650-1657

Richard Nevett sold

f. 267 1/2 of 300 a. to Peter Achilles. Date: 15 May 1657. Witnesses: Thomas Turner, Thomas Carye.

Giles Glover was bound to Thomas Belcher or Richard Smith. Date: 5 May 1657. Witnesses: Richard Preston, Henry Osborne.

f. 268 Paul Simpson (gentleman) discharged Walter Peake (gardiner) of all debts. Signed: Pau. Simpson. Date: 15 May 1657. Witnesses: John Lightfoote, Peter Achilles.

Christopher Russell (planter) sold chattel to Henry Kente. Date: 11 May 1657. Witnesses: Robert Ome, Arthur Turnor.

f. 269 Phillip Harwood, age 40, deposed that chattel of Mr. Hooper was with the Jewes goods. Date: 20 April 1657. Before: Richard Preston.

14 May 1657 at Putuxent. Court. Attendees: Mr. Richard Preston, Mr. Mich. Brookes, Mr. John Hatch, Mr. Phillip Morgan, Mr. William Parratt.

Mr. Peter Sharpe vs. Robert Harwood. Mentions: plaintiff is suing on behalf of his daughter-in-law Elisabeth Gary.

Elisabeth Gary, age 24, deposed that 3 years ago, Robert Harwood first expressed his intentions. A year later, she was raped by him. Date: 3 May 1657. Before: Phillip Morgan.

f. 270 Sarah Benson, age 26, deposed that last August at Mr. Sharp's Landing with Elisabeth Gary talking about Robert Harwood, Elisabeth replied she would never be married to him if her mother had her way. Before: William Fuller, Samuell Withers.

Thomas Bellcher vs. Giles Glover. Said Giles is engaged with Richard True.

f. 271 An attachment was granted to Thomas Bellcher & Richard Smith on the estate of Richard True in the hands of Giles Glover.

Capt. Sampson Waring attorney for Mr. John Brown vs. William Dorrington administrator of Capt. Peter Johnson for debt of Abraham Holman.

Thomas Davis, age 50, deposed that he was present when the agreement between John Scottcher & Nicholas Carr was made, regarding 100 a. in Clifts exchanged for 100 a. at Patapsco.

Sampson Waring, age 38, deposed that he was present when the agreement between John Scottcher & Nicholas Carr was made, regarding 100 a. in Clifts exchanged for 100 a. at Patapsco.

f. 272 David Farrera vs. Phillip Harwood & Thomas Robinson.

John Court vs. Richard True.

John Cornelius vs. William Marshall.

Arthur Turner vs. Giles Glover.

f. 273 Walter Peake vs. Thomas Cary (merchant).

Nicholas Carr is to take possession of the land acquired from John Scottcher.

Elisabeth Robins vs. her husband Robert Robins. Mr. John Hatch is to take depositions.

f. 274 Thomas Seamer vs. Maj. John Billingsly.

Zacherah Waide vs. William Woodriffe.

The fine of Hubert Patee was rescinded.

Mr. John Lawson vs. William Stiles.

Henry Moore vs. William Smoote. Mentions: Robert Robins

f. 275 confessed a judgement on behalf of said Moore.

John Court vs. Giles Glover.

Liber - Patent Record A & B - 1650-1657

Mrs. Jane Eltonhead was granted administration on the estate of her husband Mr. William Eltonhead (dec'd).

Arthur Turner was granted an attachment on estate of Richard True.

William Marshall, age 50, deposed that at Easter, he was at Pukewaxen at home of Goodman Boell where Robert Robins was, & they spoke of how said Robert & his wife lived. Robins replied that "she is a common whore, and I have good witness that William Herde rid her from stump to stump. Further this deponent sayth ye Francis Pope tooke Samuell Parker, fucking of his wife."

f 276 William Hinson, age 28, deposed that he was in the field of William Marshall & heard Robert Robins say to William Herde "Herde, you rogue, you swived your sister from tree to tree."

Thomas Michell, age 43, deposed that in June 1655 at the house of Robert Robins with others, the wife of Robert Robins & Robert Hunley had a disagreement.

Thomas Davis, age 50, deposed that he was present when the agreement between John Scottcher & Nicholas Carr was made, regarding 100 a. in Clifts exchanged for 100 a. at Patapsco.

John Bogg, age 30, deposed that Mr. Lawson received chattel of William Stiles,

f. 277 promising to send his bill to said Stiles via Zaccery Wade.

William Hinson, age 28, deposed that he heard Elisabeth Robins say to her husband Robert Robins that he spent his means on others.

Edward Bowles, age 59, deposed that an accounting of the chattel to be delivered to his attorney Capt. Sampson Waring was complete. Date: 11 May 1657. Before: John Hatch.

15 May. Attendees: Mr. Richard Preston, Mr. Michael Brookes, Mr. John Hatch, Mr. William Parratt.

Tho. Wright deposed that he was induced by John (N), servant to Mr. Thomas Thomas, for said Wright to runaway from his master Mr. Thomas Cary. They left one of their company in Kent on the Eastern Shore.

Francis Troteene deposed that he was induced to run away from his master Mr. Cary by Thomas Wright, & one of the company was lost.

f. 278 John Bealle deposed that he had no reason to run away from his master, & the man that was lost went out from the rest of the group with Mr. Morgan's man Samuell (N).

Capt. William Mitchell attorney for Thomas Orley presented evidence that Edward Hall (dec'd) did administer the estate of George Manners (dec'd). Said estate was overpaid. Mentions: Thomas Orley married Rebecca (relict of George Manners).

Mr. Paul Sympson was granted administration on estate of John Pritchard (dec'd), said Simpson being the greatest creditor.

Thomas Markeen, servant to Mr. William Chaplin, complained to the court that because of his master, he was disabled.

f. 279 John Tawney vs. William Dorrington. Mentions: said Tawney was servant to said Dorrington.

Robert Tayler vs. Capt. Waring attorney for Mr. John Browne.

Edward Bowell vs. John Slingsby.

John Slingsby vs. Edward Bowell.

James Veitch vs. Phillip Hyde.

John Nevill & Susan Attcheson were accused of adultery & fornication. Mentions: depositions by Mary Gillford & Johanna Watts, petition by Mr. Nathaniel Burrowes.

f. 280 Mary Gillford, age 30, deposed that she was at her husband's house, & looked out the door and saw the wife of James Attcheson go over the fence. The deponent & Susan Barbary went to investigate, & saw said Susan Attcheson & John Nevill. The wife of Sanders Watts also came & observed.

Liber - Patent Record A & B - 1650-1657

Johanna Watts, age 25, deposed the same.

f. 281 Alexander Watts, age 25, deposed that he desired John Nevill to go along with his wife, to help her with chattel from Mrs. Fenwick. Said Nevill was staying at the house of Susan Attcheson. At night, said Susan went to bed in the bed of Cornelius Canneday & called for Nevill to join her.

f. 282 Thomas Plott, age 20, deposed that hew as in the house of his master George Reed where also was John Nevill & Susan now the wife of James Attcheson. Mentions: wife of George Reed.

f. 283 Mary Gillford deposed further about John Nevill & Susan Attcheson.

Ann Dorrington, age 37, deposed that when Maj. Billingsly came to her house, she heard Thomas Seamer demand a bill of him, which said Billingsly had received for said Seamer's wife.

f. 284 William Marshall vs. Emperor Smith. Mentions: Emperor Smith is indebted to Henry Fox & said bill was assigned to William Marshall by Phillip Land.

Patrick Forrest petitioned regarding the probate of the wills of Mr. Thomas Hatton & Mrs. Hatton (dec'd). Mr. John Hatch or Mr. John Lawson to prove the will.

James Jolly was bound to David Farrera. Date: 31 March 1657. Witnesses: Robert Tayler, Giles Sadleir.

f. 285 Thomas Seamer was bound to David Farrera. Date: 10 May 1657. Witnesses: Jacob Lumbrozo, Michael Basey.

Timothy Goodridge (planter, of Putuxent) assigned to Peter Godson (phistion, of Putuxent) 100 a. bought of Barnaby Jackson called Fresh Pond Neck, adjoining Mr. William Eltonhead.

f. 286 Date: 18 November 1655. Witnesses: William Ewen, Ambross Bigge. Peter Godson & his wife Sarah Godson assigned to John Cheron (planter, of St. Maries') said 100 a. bought of Timothy Goodridge. Signed: Pierre Dieufil, Sarah Godson. Date: 18 November 1655. Witnesses: Edmond Cannoway, Tobias Mathew.

16 June 1657 at Putuxent. Court. Attendees: Mr. Richard Preston, Mr. Michael Brookes, Mr. William Ewens, Mr. Tho. Thomas.

John Robinson, servant to Mr. Tho. Thomas, deposed that after Robert Chessick has been brought back home, the deponent heard him say that if Mr. Dorrington's man would run away with him to

f. 287 Sweades, he would leave Mr. Thomas immediately. Said Chissick declared that Mr. Chaplin's man William Touy would let the others know: John (N) at Mr. Chaplin, the Frenchman at Mr. Cary, 2 at Mr. Bellcher, 1 at Mr. Osbourne. About 2 days later, he told the said Chissick that his master & Richard Blinks had gone fishing. Mentions: Stephen (N) servant to Mr. Thomas.

f. 288 Francis Spencer, servant to Mr. William Ewens, deposed on 16 June 1657 that on the 14th, William Touy, servant to Mr. Chaplin, came to his master's house & told me that he & his fellow servant John (N) intended to go away immediately with other servants. Later that day, the deponent met with Stephen (N) Mr. Thomas' boy & asked me to go.

Stephen Chaplin deposed that last Sunday Mr. Chaplin's man William Touy came to the deponent's master's house & spoke to Robert Chissick (servant of Mr. Thomas). If Mr. Cary's Frenchman

f. 289 would go, he would go. And he spoke to Mr. Ewen's man Frances (N). They intended to go to Sweades, and use a boat of Mr. Osbourne.

William Touy deposed that he intended to run away & Mr. Thomas' man Robert Chessick also, and one Chaplin, Mr. Ewen's man Francis (N). They intended to use a boat of Mr. Osbourne. Said Chessick desired the deponent to speak to 2 servants at Mr. Bellcher.

John Beall deposed that William Touy asked the deponent if he would run away with him, & replied "No." Said William told the deponent that he & Robert (N) Mr. Thomas' man had spoken to Mr. Ewen's man Francis (N), and

f. 290 Stephen Chaplin said they were going to take a boat of Mr. Osbourne.

Punishment cited for: Robert Chessick, Stephen Chaplin, John Beall, William Touy.

Liber - Patent Record A & B - 1650-1657

f. 291 Henry Pope (planter, of Putuxent) sold to Robert Kingsberry (planter, of Putuxent) 1/2 of demesne, adjoining Robert Tayler. Date: 17 May 1652. Witnesses: Robert Tayler, Daniell Barwick.

f. 292 Henry Pope (planter, of Putuxent) sold to John Senclare (planter, of Putuxent) land, adjoining Edward Basley, Robert Kingsberry. Date: 11 August 1655. Witnesses: Cornelius Abraham, Andrew Willcox.

Mrs. Mary Harris (of Putuxent) requested administration on estate of her husband Mr. Richard Harris (dec'd). Date: 30 June 1657.

John Sutton & William Harper sold their plantation to Arthur Wright.

f. 293 Date: 24 July 1657. Witnesses: Thomas Turner, John Bagbey. Richard Preston was engaged by Arthur Wright to see that this obligation was performed.

William Asbeston acknowledged payment by Robert Smith. Date: 1 January 1654. Robert Smith gave to his daughter Elisabeth Asbeston & her children all right to this bill. Signed: Robert Smithe. Witnesses: John Bisco, Marke Bloomfied.

f. 294 25 July 1657 at Putuxent. Court. Attendees: Mr. Richard Preston, Mr. William Ewens, Mr. William Parratt, Mr. Thom. Thomas.

Alexander King came to the Province about 3 months ago with Mary his pretended wife. They were suspected fugitives and emprisoned. Said King has escaped. Said Mary confessed she is not the wife of said King, but of John Butler (of York VA).

f. 295 Concerns about 2 fugitive servants from York VA: Peter Key servant to Mr. Nathaniell Bacon, Huntington Ayes servant to Mr. Fran. Wheeler.

John Davis, age 40, deposed that Alexander King & Mary King stayed at the deponent's house & lived as husband & wife.

Mary Davis, age 28, deposed the same. Before: Woodman Stockley.

Jane Pauldin deposed on 25 July 1657 that last March, John Norton (planter), when his wife was abroad, came to the house of the deponent and desired her to be "dishonest with him". The deponent is pregnant by said Norton.

f. 296 7 August 1657 at Putuxent. Court. Attendees: Mr. Richard Preston, Mr. Michael Brookes, Mr. William Ewens, Mr. Woodman Stockley, Mr. Thom. Thomas.

Capt. Phillip Morgan vs. Thomas Hobson & James Shaklady (2 servants to Mr. William Parker). Charged with forging a certificate by Mr. Richard Wells as their master & Thomas Boone as witness.

James Veitch gave chattel to Richard Keene son & heir of Richard Keen (planter, of Putuxent). Said chattel is on the plantation of Ishmael Wright. Date; 30 September 1657. Witnesses: Thomas Turner, Robert Blinkome.

Mary Jarbo gave

f. 297 chattel to the youngest child of Mrs. Ann Hammond. Said Mary is his godmother. Date: 3 June 1656. Witnesses: Peter Mills, Jacques Coullott, John Jarbo.

22 August 1657 at Putuxent. Court. Attendees: Mr. Richard Preston, Mr. John Pott, Mr. William Parratt, Mr. Tho. Thomas.

William Berry, son & heir of James Berry (late of Accomack, both now of Putuxent), sold to Capt. Fran. Pott (of Northampton) 2 tracts of land (from my father): 350 a. on the Magguthy Bay in Northampton Co. (granted to said Berry by patent in the time of Sir John Harvey, Knight, 22 August 1637); 250 a. adjoining said land & land of Francis Pott called Golden Quarter (granted to Sir Francis Wyatt, 10 October 1640). Date: 14 May 1655. Witnesses: Rich. Preston, Will. Johnson, John Pott.

f. 298 William Silverthorne, age 23, deposed that he never heard Hanna Wise, or anyone else, say that Mrs. Elisabeth Berry had another husband in England besides Mr. James Berry.

f. 299 22 September 1657 at Putuxent. Court. Attendees: Mr. Rich. Preston, Mr. Ed. Lloyd, Capt. Rich. Ewen, Mr. John Hatch, Mr. Mich. Brooke, Mr. Sam. Withers, Mr. John Pott, Mr. Will. Ewens, Mr. Will. Parratt, Mr. John Lawson, Capt. Phill. Morgan.

Mrs. Mary Harris was granted administration on estate of her husband Richard Harris (dec'd). Appraisers appointed: John Halfhead, Mr. GouldSmith, Mr.

Liber - Patent Record A & B - 1650-1657

William Stephens. Mr. William Chaplin & Mr. William Ewens to administer the oath.

Elisabeth Robins vs. her husband Robert Robins. Mentions: motion by William Whittell.

William Chaplin vs. John Day. Mentions: request for accounting of estate of William Walwoorth by said Day.

Nathaniell Pope vs. William Robinson.

f. 300 Nathaniell Pope vs. Edward Hall.

Nathaniell Pope vs. Abram Holman (also Abraham Holman) attorney for Thomas Hawkins.

Nathaniell Pope vs. Richard Watson.

f. 301 John Lewger by this attorney Walter Hall vs. Thomas Mitchell.

William Ireland (servant to Mr. William Parker) vs. Capt. Morgin.

Capt. Mitchell vs. Mr. Gerrard.

23 September 1657 at Putuxent. Court. Attendees: same as before.

James Attcheson vs. John Nevill & wife of said Attcheson.

f. 302 Thomas Seamer vs. Maj. John Billingsly. Arbitrators: Mr. Michael Brookes, Mr. William Ewen.

Order for inquest into death of Henry Gouge, servant of John Dandie.

Mary Gillford vs. wife of Alexander Watts.

Phillip Land vs. John Cornelius & Walter Pecke. Mentions: wife of said Land.

Maj. John Hollis vs. John Nevill. Mentions:

f. 303 said Nevill confessed to debt to Mr. John Hatch.

William Styles is indebted to Edward Williams.

Thomas Seamor vs. Maj. John Billingsley.

Mrs. Jane Eltonhead vs. estate of Mr. Edmond Scarborough (of Accomacke).

Mr. George Guttridge was granted administration on estate of Capt. William Lewis (dec'd). Said Guttridge married the relict.

William Dorrington vs. Abram Holman (also Abraham Holman). Mentions: 2 servants of said Dorrington, said Holman to receive chattel of Capt. Peter Johnson.

f. 304 Peter Underwood deposed that he had runaway from his master's service & came to Kent & stayed at the house of Abraham Holman. Said Holman took the deponent & John Boone and gave them supplies & showed them how to steer to Elk River. John Boon deposed the same.

Inquest into death of Henry Gouge,

f. 305 who supposedly met an untimely death by his master John Dandy. Mr. James Veitch to take 2 chirurgeons (Mr. Richard Maddocks & Mr. Emperor Smith) to view the body.

24 September 1657 at Putuxent. Court. Attendees: Mr. Richard Preston, Mr. Ed. Lloyd, Mr. Sam. Withers, Mr. William Ewens, Mr. John Lawson, Mr. Thom. Thomas, Mr. William Parratt, Mr. John Pott.

Baslean Protestant, age 20, deposed that he lived for 1 year with James Linsey. Deponent had runaway from his master (N) Hollis.

Report on inquiry into death of Henry Gouge.

f. 306 Date: 25 September 1657. Signed: William Barton, Richard Lloyd, Christopher Russell, Thomas Bassett, Richard Nevett, Christopher Goodicker, Henry Lilly, Edward Turner, Richard Bennett, William Whittle, William Young.

Liber - Patent Record A & B - 1650-1657

Edward Turner was granted an attachment on the estate of Capt. Samuell Tillman.

Mr. Roger Groce vs. Roger Scott. Mentions: said Scott was accused of fathering a child by Frances Smith a maid servant to said Groce. Examinations are to be taken by Mr. Edward Lloyd.

f. 307 John Lord vs. Ann Hamond. Mr. John Lord attorney for Margaret Myles is due payment from John Hamond per court order at Jamestown.

Mr. Richard Smith attorney for Mrs. Sarah Marsh vs. Mr. Robert Clarke. Mentions: Mr. Abbott, Mr. Thomas Marsh.

Mr. John Hatch vs. Mr. John Lewger by his attorney Mr. Edward Hall.

f. 308 James Veitch is indebted to Mrs. Ann Dorrington.

William Thomson is indebted to Ann Hamond.

Paul Simpson vs. Ann Hamond.

Aron Jacobson vs. Tobias Norton.

25 September 1657. Court (con't). Attendees: Mr. Rich. Preston, Mr. Ed. Lloyd, Mr. John Hatch, Mr. Sam. Withers, Mr. John Lawson, Mr. John Pott, Mr. Will. Ewens, Mr. Thom. Thomas.

John Salter vs. Francis Brooke.

Edward Hostkeys vs. Capt. Josias Fendall. Mentions: Michael Basey.

f. 309 John Lord, age 28, deposed that he heard Col. Smith say he had lent Capt. Josias Fendall a boy named Edward Hostkeys. Also that Mr. Cooke affirmed that his master set him free on his deathbed in Jameco.

Samuell Bonam, age 36, deposed that he heard Col. Smith say that he had lent Capt. Fendall a boy.

Nicholas Oliver, age 35, deposed before Mr. William Parratt on 13 July 1657 that Edward Hostkeys was hired for 1 year to William Smith for payment to his own master Samuell Broadstreet.

Margaret Herring vs. John Little.

f. 310 Michael Basey vs. Robert Hopkins.

John Little vs. Mr. John Pott.

John Little vs. Mr. John Pott.

Mrs. Ann Hamond acknowledges a debt to Mr. John Lord (of New England).

Mr. John Cornelius vs. William Denby.

Samuell Parker vs. Richard Foster.

Appointment of new commissioners: Mr. Edward Lloyd, Mr. Michael Brookes, Mr. John Hatch.

Petition of Capt. William Mitchell.

f. 311 Edward Turner deposed that he never received any payment from Capt. Tillman.

Richard True deposed that he heard Edward Turner demand payment from Capt. Tillman.

Umphrey Attookes, age 38, deposed that he heard Edward Turner demand something of Capt. Tillman.

f. 312 John Hart received payment from Edward Turner for the use of Capt. Tillman. Date: 30 April 1656. Witness: William Johnson.

John Lawson deposed on 23 September 1657 about the transaction between Edward Turner and Capt. Tillman.

John Davis, age 41, deposed that Allbert (N)

f. 313 came to the deponent's house & asked me to go to the house of John Little to assess some chattel. Before: John Pott.

Liber - Patent Record A & B - 1650-1657

Sepharinah Hack, age 21, deposed that Aron (N) came to him & said he had lost chattel at John Little's. John Little & Richard (N) were shown the damaged chattel. Signed: Sepharina Hack. Before: John Pott. ["Depositions inter Aron (N) & Tobias Norton."]

Henry Pope, age 46, deposed about the chattel of ould Little.

Henry Billsberry, age 34, deposed that Aron (N) helped with the chattel & Aron (N) & his mate told John Little about its condition.

f. 314 Articles of Agreement between Peter Sharpe (chirurgeon, of Putuxent) & Robert Harwood (planter, of Putuxent). Date: 24 September 1657. Mentions: suit by said Peter on behalf of Elisabeth Gary daughter of Judith wife of said Peter, promise of marriage between said Robert & said Elisabeth. Said Elisabeth to be conveyed to house of Mr. Thomas Davis at Clifts,

f. 315 said Robert to have free discourse with her.

f. 316 Signed: Peter Sharpe, Robert Harwood, Date: 26 September 1657.

f. 317 26 September 1657. Court (con't). Attendees: same as before.

Mr. William Durand was granted an attachment on the estate of Capt. Josias Fendall for a boy servant. Said boy is in the employment of Thomas Emmerson. Valuation by Mr. Roger Groce, Lt. Richard Woolman, William Pell, Thomas Miles.

Mr. Robert Clarke proved delivery to James Veitch (sheriff), some as payment to Mr. John Norwood (sheriff of Providence).

f. 318 Mr. Michael Brooke was granted administration on the estate of Bartholomy Bloome (dec'd).

Inquest into the death of Henry Gouge supposedly by his master John Dandy, per Richard Furbear. Depositions taken by Richard Preston & William Ewens.
- William Wood, age 20, deposed about finding John Dandy's man dead & reporting to said Dandy.

f. 319 ...
- Said Dandy & Robert Cole & 2 men went to inspect. Date: 6 August 1657.
- Inspection of the body of Henry Gouge. Dandy's maid servant said that the boy Darbey (N) said his master was beating Harry (N). Darby Canneday reported what he heard. Date: 7 July 1657. Signed: Will. Thomson, Anthony Webb, Nich. Oliver, Robert Shelle, Robert Cole, Richard Furbear, John Howerd, John Jarbo.
- Richard Furbear, age 40, deposed

f. 320 ...
of his examination of the body. Date: 6 August 1657.
- Sarah Midleton, (servant to John Dandie), age 21, deposed that Darby Canneday (fellow servant) told her he heard Dandy beating Henry Gouge.

f. 321 ...
- John Harwood, age 30, deposed that John Dandy did not inquire of his servant that evening, & of his examination of the body.
- Mr. John Jarbo, age 38, deposed of his examination of the body of Henry Gouge.

f. 322 ...
- Darbey Canneday (servant to John Dandy), age 14, deposed that he & fellow servant Sarah Middleton heard Henry Gouge cry out.
- Thomas Carpender, age 51, deposed on his examination of the body of Henry Gouge,

f. 323 ...
and that the wife of John Dandy told the deponent that said Dandy said he should be hanged for said Gouge.
- Ann Dandy wife of John Dandy, age 34, deposed that on the same day that

f. 324 ...
Henry Gouge was missing, she & her husband discussed him.

f. 325 ...
- Anthony Webe, age 53, deposed on 8 August 1657 on his examination of the body of Henry Gouge.

f. 326 ...
- John Dandy deposed that he escaped & fled to VA, was re-apprehended & brought back to court, regarding the death of Henry Gouge. Mentions:

Liber - Patent Record A & B - 1650-1657

Robert Cole,

f. 327 ...

Nicholas Oliver. Date: 14 August 1657.
- Walter Peake, age 49, deposed that he had seen Dandy's man last Spring and asked about his injuries. The deponent spoke to Dandy's wife at the house of John Shircliffe.
- Maj. John Hallowes, age 41, deposed that when John Dandy came over the Patomack River to the deponent's house, the deponent & said Dandy went to the house of Mr. Bradhorst, where said Dandy commented on the death of his servant.

f. 328 28 September 1657. Court (con't). Attendees: Mr. Richard Preston, Mr. Edward Lloyd, Mr. Sam. Withers, Mr. John Lawson, Mr. Will. Ewens, Mr. Will. Parratt.

Lt. Richard Smith was appointed Attorney General.

29 September 1657. Court (con't). Attendees: Mr. Richard Preston, Mr. Ed. Lloyd, Mr. Sam. Withers, Mr. John Lawson, Mr. Tho. Thomas, Mr. Rich. Ewens, Mr. Mich. Brooke, Mr. John Pott, Mr. Will. Parratt, Mr. Will. Ewens.

Petition of Richard Smith (Attorney General). About 7 July, Henry Gouge servant to John Dandy was found dead by William Wood. It was believed that the deceased was murdered by John Dandy. Request he be brought to trial.

f. 329 Grand Jury: Mr. John Knape, Mr. Hugh Stanly, Mr. Thomas Cary, Robert Harwood, Mr. John Adbor, William Turner, George Bussie, John Felton, William Muffett, Richard Keene, John Day, Mr. William Chaplin, Mr. William Dorrington, Mr. John Abeington, John Gramer, Daniell Goulson, Mr. John Cornelius, Arthur Wright, Henry Coxe, Thomas Reed, William Stockden.

f. 330 John Dandy indicted.

30 September. Court (con't). Attendees: same as before.

f. 331 Trial Jury: Mr. Robert Blinkhorn, Mr. John Ashcomb, Mr. Stephen Gary, Mr. Henry Osborne, Mr. John Hambleton, George Newman, Richard Blinks, Griffin George, John Tayler, John Bagbey, Mr. Nathaniell Burrowes, Mr. William Berry. The prisoner challenged George Newman, who was replaced with Thomas Bellcher.

f. 332 Verdict: guilty. Sentence: execution on 3 October 1657 on Island at the mouth of St. Leonard's Creek in the Patuxent River.

Julian Hyell vs. William Stockden.

f. 333 1 October 1657 at Putuxent. Court. Attendees: Mr. Richard Preston, Mr. Ed. Lloyd, Mr. Sam. Withers, Mr. Will. Ewens,

George Beckwith petitioned on behalf of self & Francis Harvie daughter of Nicholas Harvie (dec'd) for chattel in the hands of John Dandy.

Ann Dandy wife of John Dandy petitioned for relief for herself & the 2 orphans in her charge. She is pregnant with a 3rd child.

f. 334 Mr. Thomas Sprige vs. John Nevill.

Mr. Emperor Smith & Mr. Rice Maddookes (chirurgeons) petitioned for payment for examining the body of Henry Gouge.

Richard Furbar petitioned for payment due from John Dandy.

Peter Joy petitioned to be relieved as security for John Dandy.

5 October 1657. Court (con't). Attendees: Mr. Rich. Preston, Mr. Ed. Lloyd, Mr. Sam. Withers, Mr. Will. Ewens.

f. 335 Mr. James Veitch (sheriff) & the clerk of the court petitioned for payment from the estate of John Dandy.

Thomas Bellcher petitioned for payment from the estate of John Dandy.

Richard Smith attorney for Maj. John Hallowes (VA) petitioned for payment from the estate of John Dandy.

Mr. Richard Smith (Attorney General) petitioned for payment from the estate of John Dandy.

f. 336 Jane Green wife of Thomas Green (of Eliz. River, Lower Norfoulke Co. VA)

Liber - Patent Record A & B - 1650-1657

deposed that she is the widow of Nicholas Harvey (planter, of Patuxent, dec'd) & agrees to the sale by her husband Greene to Edward Lloyd (of Seaverne) called St. Thomas his Point. Signed: Jane Greene. Date: 20 August 1657. Witness: Edmond Bouman.

George Beckwith (planter, of Patomocke River) for self & his wife Frances daughter & heir of Nicholas Harvey (planter, dec'd) demanded chattel that was in the hands of John Dandy.

f. 337 John Balaen sold chattel to Edward Williams. Date: 15 June 1656. Witness: Christopher Russell.

William Odeom received payment from Mr. Hooper for the use of Mr. John Laramor. Date: 18 January 1648.

21 May 1655 at Providence. Court. Attendees: Capt. General Fuller, Mr. William Durand, Mr. Edward Lloyd, Capt. Richard Ewens.

Mr. Thomas Hatton (late Secretary) is to have power of distress for such fees due him prior to the resignation of the government by Capt. William Stone in July 1654.

3 November 1657 at Putuxent. Court. Attendees: Mr. Richard Preston, Mr. Michael Brookes, Mr. Thom. Thomas, Mr. Will. Ewens, Mr. William Parratt, Mr. Phillip Morgin, Mr. Woodman Stockly.

Mr. Henry Coursey vs. Thom. Seamor.

f. 338 Mary Cole deposed that Joseph Edlow & she did lie together at the house of said Edlow, at the advice of Thomas Seamor & Thomas Breamstead (husband of said Mary) was present.

Samuell Gosey, age 23, deposed that he heard Thomas Seamor read "the prayer and the Matrimonie".

Thomas Walton, age 25, deposed that the day after Mary Cole was married, the deponent went to the house of Joseph Edlow to see if Mary Cole was there, & Thomas Seamor came out & requested that it not be known that he & Mary Cole were there. Thomas Breamstead also came to Joseph Edlow's.

f. 339 The deponent also said that on another occasion, Richard Norton called Mary Cole out & said that Thomas Seamor "would speake with her to go a little way with him". Signed: Thomas Wallton.

Robert Price, age 35, deposed that he heard Richard Norton called Mary Cole out & said that Thomas Seamor "would speake with her to go a little way with him".

Richard Norton, age 79, deposed that Thomas Seamor was reading the prayer & marriage from the Common Prayer Book, & Joseph Edlow & Mary Cole came in & Thomas read it to them.

Edward Dixter, age 18, deposed that Thomas Wallton asked Richard Norton, when he came back from the house of Joseph Edlow, why he brought the maid & Norton answered that Thomas Seamor had sent him. Thomas Wallton & Richard Price affirmed the same.

Julian Haffhead, age 34, deposed

f. 340 that Mary Cole told her that Thomas Seamor would have lain with her in his own room. John Haffhead affirmed the same.

Arthur Ludford, age 37, deposed that Thomas Seamor was drunk the night Mary Cole was carried to the house of Joseph Edlow. At the inquiry of Mr. Coursey, said Thomas responded in uncivil language unfit for an overseer. Patrick Forrest affirmed the same.

Patrick Forrest demanded of the estate of Mr. Thomas Hatton (dec'd) & from the estate of John Pritchard (dec'd) due to Capt. Price.

f. 341 Mr. William Wilkinson, age 50, deposed on 13 April 1657 that he asked John Pritchard, then sick, if he owed Capt. John Price.

Roger Scott vs. Tobias Norton. Mentions: debt due Mr. Henry Hooper.

Mr. Thomas Sprige vs. John Nevill.

John Reed, age 28, deposed that Mr. Thomas Sprige sold chattel to John Nevill.

Liber - Patent Record A & B - 1650-1657

f. 342 Hugh Johnson, age 17, deposed that Mr. Thomas Sprige sold chattel to John Nevill.

Thomas Boothe, age 21, deposed that Mr. Sprige came to the house of Mr. Burroughes & spoke to John Nevill about some chattel.

Mr. Richard Smith attorney for Mrs. Sarah Marsh vs. Mrs. Jane Eltonhead administratrix of Mr. William Eltonhead (dec'd).

Mr. Robert Clarke, age 46, deposed on 4 November 1657 that the deponent bought a servant of Mr. William Eltonhead which he turned over to Mr. Thomas Marsh.

f. 343 Capt. Sampson Waring, age 39, deposed that the day Mr. Eltonhead died, the deponent heard him say to one of his sons-in-law: to see that Mr. Marsh paid the debt.

Walter Peake attorney for Fran. Peake demanded from the estate of Richard Lawrence given said Fran. by the lwt of said Richard. The chattel of John Dandy is to be examined.

4 November 1657. Court (con't). Attendees: Mr. Rich. Preston, Mr. Mich. Brookes, Mr. William Ewens, Mr. Wood. Stockley, Mr. Phillip Morgin.

Mr. George Peake who married the relict of Mr. Robert Parr (dec'd) was summoned to provide an accounting of the estate of said Parr.

f. 344 Capt. Henry Keene demanded from the estate of Bartholomy Bloome (dec'd).

The estate of Bartholomy Bloome is indebted to Mr. Thomas Bellcher & Mr. Richard Smith.

Walter Peake & John Cornelius vs. Phillip Land.

Robert Robins informed the court that his estranged wife Elisabeth Robins was pregnant & requested an inquiry.

Mr. John Pott vs. John Little.

f. 345 William Muffett, age 36, deposed that Tobias Norton & Mary Little came from Accomack in Spring of last year. Mary requested the deponent to read some papers of Mr. James Berry & his wife. The papers purported that they were never married & Mary Little said she would prove that Berry's children were bastards. Signed: William Moffett.

f. 346 Bartholomy Herring affirmed the same.

James Veitch was granted administration on the estate of John Drueman (dec'd).

Mr. Nathaniell Burroughes was fined for misdemeanors in Court at the suit between John Nevill & James Attcheson.

Aron Jacobson vs. John Little. Jury: Walter Peake, Capt. Hen. Keene, Edward Keene, Patrick Forrest, Thomas Reede, James Gunnell, Robert Robeson, Mathew Smith, Nathaniell Burroughs, John Cornelius, John Hambleton, Alexander Watts.

f. 347 Richard Smith attorney for Mrs. Sarah Marsh vs. Patrick Forrest executor of Mr. Thomas Hatton (dec'd). Mr. Marsh obtained at Kent an order against the estate of Fran. Lumber due Mr. Hatton & a note of Mr. Medcalfe.

f. 348 Capt. Henry Keene petitioned for payment for expenses during the trial & execution of John Dandy.

William Sinckler petitioned for attachment against the estate of Joseph Edlow (supposedly fled the Province).

John Nevill & Susan Attcheson punished.

Robert Clarke vs. James Veitch.

5 November 1657. Court (con't). Attendees: same as before.

f. 349 Roger Scott fined.

Patrick Forrest demanded of the estate of John Dandy (dec'd) due to the estate of Mr. Thomas Hatton (dec'd).

Order for the sheriff to secure the estate of John Dandy, his wife having embezzled some of the estate.

Liber - Patent Record A & B - 1650-1657

f. 350 Thomas Stagwell attorney for John Battar vs. Richard True.

Capt. Sampson Waring demanded of the estate of John Dandy (dec'd).

Mr. Richard Hostkeys demanded of the estate of John Dandy (dec'd) on assignment from Markes Bloomfield.

The punishment for John Nevill was changed to a fine.

f. 351 Mrs. Jane Eltonhead, age 40, deposed that she heard Capt. Fendall say that Col. Smith had a boy aboard.

Aron Jacobson, age 27, deposed on 4 November 1657 that he heard John Little say that about last July that if Mr. Fran. Stockley were alive, he would testify that Elisabeth Potts was dishonest with said Little's Indian boy, & the deponent heard (Mrs.) Mary Little say of her husband John Little that if the deposition of the little boy Cornelius (N) (his servant) could be taken, then there would be more information.

Abdelo Martin, age 34, deposed

f. 352 that Aron Jacobson came to the deponent's house & said he had received damaged chattel from John Little.

William Squire, age 25, deposed on 4 November 1657 that he saw the chattel that John Little paid Aron Jacobson & it was good, & from Mr. Jordan.

John Cornelius, age 36, deposed that George Reede made payment for Maj. John Billingsly & it was good.

John Harwood, age 50, deposed that George Reede made payment for Maj. John Billingsly & it was good.

f. 353 William Cannaday, age 30, deposed that George Reede made payment for Maj. John Billingsly & it was good. Before: Mich. Brooke, Phill. Morgan. Date: 24 September 1657. Witness: John Lawson.

John Knap (of Putuxent) relinquished his title to land bought of Thomas Cole to said Cole, land adjoining Mr. Richard Preston. Date: 4 November 1657.

Peake Walter administrator for Fran. Vandan (dec'd)--the estate is overpaid. Date: 6 November 1657.

f. 354 6 November 1657. To: Mr. Thomas Stone. "your father" desired me to speak to William Empson to pay Mr. Robert Slye. Signed: Job Chandler. Date: 27 January 1656 at Portoback. Received payment of William Empson for the Governor per Math. Slye. Signed: Peter Machin. Date: 2 March 1653. Witness: Daniell Mills.

Mary Empson registered a cattle mark.

John Billingsley (planter, of Chucatuch VA) sold chattel to George Reede (planter, of Putuxent). Date: September 1657. Witnesses: William Mitchells, Griff. Standen.

f. 355 16 November. James Attcheson (planter, of Putuxent) assigned his plantation to Timothy Guttridge on exchange for a bill in the hands of Mr. Harris. Date: 1 May 1657. Witnesses: Tho. Bellcher, John Knape.

Abdele Martin discharged Edw. Wood of all debts. Witnesses: John Bagbey, John Sutton. Recorded for William Wood on 23 November.

f. 356 Thomas Phillips was bound to Mr. John Hatch or Zacharias Wade, for the use of John Baley (son of John Baley (dec'd)) & Elinor Baley (widow). Date: 27 May 1656. Witnesses: John Wade, Richard Browne.

Elinor Baley (widow & late wife of John Baley (dec'd)) gave chattel to her son John Baley. Mr. John Hatch & Mr. Sacrey Wade were appointed overseers of her son's estate. Date: 16 May 1656. Witnesses: John Wade, William Right, Walter Peake, Richard Brown.

f. 357 5 December 1657 at Putuxent. Court. Attendees: Mr. Richard Preston, Mr. Michaell Brookes, Mr. William Parratt, Mr. Thom. Thomas, Mr. Phill. Morgin, Mr. William Ewens.

Mr. Bassill Little (merchant), being aboard the ship Concord & sick as per John Runting & Robert Makey, in case of his death, appointed Capt. Robert Morris as master of the ship & Mr. Henry Meese as merchant.

Liber - Patent Record A & B - 1650-1657

f. 358 John Runting, age 50, deposed the above. Robert Makey, age 21, deposed the above.

Mr. James Veitch (sheriff) petitioned for fees

f. 359 regarding the estate of Mr. Bassill Little (dec'd).

Robert Morris & Henry Meese (merchants) are to provide an accounting of the debts, goods, & estate of Mr. Bassill Little (dec'd). Witnesses: Sampson Waring, Phill. Morgin.

Mr. Thomas Webb (merchant, of London) consigned 4 servants to me on the ship Role of Capt. John Tully.

f. 360 Signed: Richard Preston. Date: 10 December 1657. Witnesses: Walter Censerfe, Thomas Carye, Henry Meese, Tho. Jordan, Robert Young.

William Barton, Sr. (mariner, of St. Clement's Manor) gave chattel to his grandchild William Thomas. Date: 27 December 1657. Witnesses: William Barton, Jr., Robert Joyner.

John Malum assigned John Poore (age 13, an Irish lad) to

f. 361 John Lawson. Date: 19 November 1655. Witnesses: Richard Cole.

William Barton, Jr. registered a cattle mark.

29 December 1657 at Putuxent. Court. Attendees: Mr. Richard Preston, Mr. John Hatch, Mr. [name omitted], Mr. William Parratt, Mr. William Ewens.

Richard Smith was granted an attachment on the estate of John Cockerel.

Capt. William Mitchell vs. Thom. Gerrard, Esq.

Capt. Thomas Cornwallis vs. Capt. William Mitchell.

f. 362 Jacob Lumbrozo was granted an attachment on estate of John Cockerell.

Joshua Stedd attorney for Mr. Morris vs. George Peake.

Capt. William Ewens administrator of Capt. Barriffe (dec'd) vs. Robert Coberthat.

Capt. William Ewens administrator of Capt. John Barriffe (dec'd) vs. John Makinney.

Capt. William Ewens administrator of Capt. John Barriffe (dec'd) vs. William Lucas.

Mr. Richard Smith attorney for Mrs. Marsh vs. Mrs. Jane Eltonhead.

f. 363 Mrs. Jane Eltonhead vs. estate of Mr. Edmund Scarbrough.

30 December. Court (con't). Attendees: Mr. Rich. Preston, Mr. Michaell Brookes, Mr. John Hatch, Mr. John Lawson, Mr. Thom. Thomas, Mr. William Ewens.

Mr. Edward Parks vs. John Jenkins.

Jacob Lumbrozo vs. William Gillford.

Robert Macklin was granted an attachment on estate of Mr. Thomas Hatton (dec'd). Patrick Forrest is executor.

John Sewell acknowledged a judgement to William Berry.

Capt. William Stone was granted an attachment on the estate of Capt. William Lewis (dec'd).

f. 364 Samuell Parker was granted an attachment on the estate of Capt. William Lewis (dec'd).

Mr. John Lawson was granted an attachment on the estate of Capt. William Lewis (dec'd).

Mr. George Guttridge administrator of Capt. William Lewis (dec'd) petitioned for an inventory of the estate.

Liber - Patent Record A & B - 1650-1657

Mr. Nicholas Gwyther vs. estate of Mr. Thomas Marsh. Mentions:

f. 365 oath by Henry Coursey.

Tobias Norton vs. Henry Hooper. Jury: Mr. Robert Tayler, Thomas Stagwell, Edmond Hinshman, Patrick Milligan, William Young, Thomas Read, Mr. Peter Sharpe, Robert Harwood, Henry Coxe, William Turner, Patrick Forrest, George Bussey.

William Howse, age 25, deposed that 2 years ago, Mr. Henry Hooper sold to Tobias Norton a servant, as able as Richard (N) was Mr. Stockley's man.

f. 366 Ann Howse, age 27, deposed that 2 years ago, Mr. Henry Hooper sold to Tobias Norton a servant, as able as Richard (N) was Mr. Stockley's man.

Roger Scott attorney for Mr. Henry Hooper vs. Tobias Norton.

Petition of Robert Mackey concerning his freedom.

Mr. Henry Osborne, age 30, deposed that he demanded of Mr. Bassill Little a servant & the deponent could have any servant except Robert Mackey.

f. 367 Mr. Peter Sharpe, age 34, asked Mr. Bassill Little about purchasing his servant Robert Mackey.

Timothy Guttridge vs. Alexander Watts.

Thomas Davis vs. Elisabeth Frame (maid servant bought of John Hawkins by said Davis.)

Robert Harwood, age 30, deposed that he was at the house of Mr. Thomas Davis November a year ago, when William Kempe bought Elisabeth Frame of Mr. John Hawkins for Mr. Thomas Davis.

f. 368 Adam Stavelay, age 30, deposed on 29 December 1657 that he went from Manadose to Rapahanock with John Hawkins to the house of Rice Jones. Said Hawkins had a manservant with 1.5 years to service in exchange for Elisabeth Frame.

Thomas Speake vs. George Reynolds.

Order for the sheriff for Robert Cole to acquire the estate of Benjamin Gill (dec'd)

f. 369 now in the hands of James Linsey.

Mr. Walter Senserfe was granted an attachment on the estate of Maj. John Billingsley.

Thomas Brandson acknowledged a judgement to Thomas Jordan (merchant).

William Gillford acknowledged a judgement to Thomas Jordan (merchant).

William Barton, Sr., age 52, deposed regarding the conditions of a servant from Thomas Batchelor by Mr. Parks.

Maurice Smith, age 40, deposed that he heard Mr. Stevenson offer Mr. Trueman to hire a servant.

f. 370 John Hyatt, age 27, deposed that he heard his master Mr. Trueman & Mr. William Stevenson bargain for the hire of the deponent's time.

Richard Tarling, age 23, deposed concerning a servant that Mr. Sparks hired to Mr. Batchelor.

31 December 1657. Court (con't). Attendees: Mr. Richard Preston, Mr. Michael Brookes, Mr. John Hatch, Mr. William Ewens, Mr. John Lawson, Mr. Wood. Stockely, Mr. Thomas Thomas, Mr. William Parratt.

Capt. William Mitchell vs. Thomas Phillips.

f. 371 Capt. William Mitchell vs. Thomas Gerrard, Esq.

Cornelius Abram acknowledged a judgement to Jacob Lumbrozo.

Capt. Sampson Waring attorney for Mr. John Brown vs. estate of Richard Moore (dec'd).

Liber - Patent Record A & B - 1650-1657

Richard Nevett acknowledged a judgement by Robert Taylor to Cornelius Johnson.

Mr. Henry Coursey vs. Capt. William Mitchell attorney for Thomas Seamor & Joseph Edlow.

f. 372 Capt. Sampson Waring deposed that 9 months ago, he demanded a debt of Richard True for Thomas Stagwell, being a bill of Thomas Knoles.

Capt. William Mitchell vs. Thomas Innes.

Mr. Luke Gardiner freed a maid servant for use of Daniell Goulson to James Veitch (sheriff).

Richard True vs. Thomas Stagwell.

David Farera vs. Thomas Seamor.

Thomas Seamer vs. Henry Coursey.

f. 373 Edmond Linsey was indebted to William Empson.

Mrs. Jane Fenwick administratrix of Friendship Thoungue was granted "Quietus Est".

Patrick Forrest attorney for Capt. John Price & William Huse petitioned for payment from the estate of Mr. Thomas Hatton (dec'd) & the estate of John Dandy (dec'd).

William Turner vs. John Sewell.

1 January 1657. Court (con't). Attendees: Mr. Richard Preston, Mr. Mich. Brookes, Mr. John Lawson, Mr. William Ewens, Mr. Wood. Stockley, Mr. William Parratt, Mr. Thom. Thomas.

f. 374 David Farera vs. James Jolly.

Ann Dandy wife of John Dandy (dec'd) & now wife of Mr. Rice Maddocks is to give surety on the estate of said Dandy.

Mr. William Wilkinson petitioned for relief for supporting an orphan of John Pritchard (dec'd).

f. 375 Paul Sympson administrator of said Pritchard is to deliver all estate of said Pritchard to said Wilkinson for the use of said child.

Mr. Richard Preston vs. estate of William Clawson.

Stephen Gary was granted an attachment on the estate of Richard Moore (dec'd).

Jane Palldin, servant to William Dorrington, had a bastard

f. 376 child by John Norton, as per depositions on 25 July 1657.

William Dorrinton deposed that said Jane Palldin did not want to return home from court without the deponent. When they got home, she went inside, & Goodman Norton went outside after the deponent went in, & then returned & went to his wife Elisabeth as if to stab her. The deponent stopped him. Signed: William Dorrington.

Griffin George deposed that he lived at the house of John Norton & about the time that Jane Palldin "quickned", Elisabeth Norton

f. 377 told the deponent that the servant was pregnant. When questioned, said Palldin indicated that the father was Goodman Norton. Mentions: discussions with William Brammall, William Dorrington.

f. 378 Mr. Dorrington brought his maid home.

Mary Hebborne deposed that Jane Palldin, when she was first pregnant, went to her mistress Mrs. Dorrington. Mrs. Dorrington inquired as to the father & said Palldin said she didn't know. When asked by John Buckstone, she said John Norton.

f. 379 Said Jane told the deponent she was to be sold to Goodman Goulson.

f. 380 Goodwife Norton desired Palldin to say the father was George Hardestie.

Liber - Patent Record A & B - 1650-1657

Peter Underwood, age 21, deposed that when he was at the house of John Norton, he saw John Norton & Jane Palldin "intimate".

Thomas Turner deposed that he was sent

f. 381 by his master William Dorrington to John Norton to mark cattle. The deponent demanded what said Norton would do with Jane Palldin, as she was pregnant. He replied that he must suffer the law.

Edmond Hinshman deposed that when Mr. Preston sent a warrant for Jane Palldin, the deponent went with the constable & Andrew Willcox to John Norton's. Said Palldin resisted arrest. Signed: Edmond Hinchman.

f. 382 Mr. Luke Barber deposed that he went to Mr. Gerrard's after Capt. Mitchell came to the Province, & Mr. Gerrard asked the deponent to remember him to Capt. Mitchell.

Edmond Phillpott, age 60, deposed that at the end of April 1656, Capt. William Mitchell sold the deponent to Mr. Thomas Gerrard, & said Mitchell was to be paid on his return from England. Should he not return, payment was to be made to Mitchell's children.

Mr. Henry Coursey, age 29,

f. 383 deposed that Capt. Nicholas Gwither was bound to Mr. Thomas Marsh (dec'd, of Severne).

Mr. Thomas Trueman, age 29, deposed that he made an indenture between Edward Hostkeys & Capt. Josias Fendall. Mentions: Col. Smith.

Richard Garill, age 50, deposed that he was present when John Little & Tobias Norton were making their accounts, with Aron Jacobson & his partner Allbert Johnson. Signed: Richard Garrill.

f. 384 Sepharin Hach deposed that he heard Allbert Johnson say that he was to bring payment from the Manadose for John Little. Signed: Sepherin Hach.

Inquiry of Elisabeth Robins, she supposing herself pregnant by her husband Robert Robins. Jury: Margaret Banks, Darcos Lawson, Barbara Johnson, Mary Wright, Ann Smith, Jane Robinson.

Thomas Sherriden, age 40, deposed that last Spring, he lost chattel that usually wandered to the land of Robert Hopkins & his brother.

f. 385 Mentions: Michael Basey (bad neighbor), wife of Henry Bullen, wife of Michael Basey.

f. 386 Aron Jacobson petitioned to receive all debts of his partner Allbert Johnson.

Henry Hooper & his wife Sarah sold to John Taylor & William Jones (planters), 1 neck of land in their tenure on the north side of Putuxent River, called

f. 387 Tom's Point. Date: 6 January 1657. Witnesses: Walter Censerfe, Thomas Turner.

Edmond Phillpott, by assignment, is to serve Thomas Gerrard, Esq. (of St. Clement's) for the time he was to serve Capt. William Mitchell. Date: 27 May 1652. Witnesses: Roger Isham, Thomas Hawkines.

f. 388 26 January 1657. Owen James demanded of the estate of Paul Simpson (dec'd).

Thomas Stone released Soliman Barbarah of all service due to Capt. William Stone. Date: 13 November 1657. Witness: Sam. Bonam. Recorded: 11 February 1657.

30 January 1657 at Putuxent. Court. Attendees: Mr. Richard Preston, Mr. Mich. Brooke, Mr. William Euens, Mr. John Hatch, Mr. William Parratt.

Mr. Peter Sharpe (chirurgeon) vs. Capt. Robert Morris & Mr. Henry Meese executors of Bassill Little (dec'd).

f. 389 Mr. William Dorrington vs. estate of Mr. Bassill Little (dec'd, merchant). Mentions: Mr. Stedd.

Mr. Richard Smith presented a woman servant of Mr. Bassill Little (dec'd) named Elisabeth Lee (under age 16) bought of Mr. Henry Meese executor of said estate.

Mr. Morris executor of estate of Bassill Little (dec'd) vs. John Sutton.

Liber - Patent Record A & B - 1650-1657

Christopher Cary vs. Thomas Letchworth.

f. 390 Mr. Morris executor of estate of Bassill Little (dec'd) vs. Henry Cox.

John Bonam vs. William Lawrel (also William Lawrell).

Mr. Morris executor of estate of Bassill Little (dec'd) vs. George Bussey.

Mr. Morris executor of estate of Bassill Little (dec'd) vs. Mr. John Pott. Mentions: assignment from Thomas Seamor to said Little.

f. 391 Mr. Henry Meese vs. Phill. Harwood.

Mr. Henry Osborne vs. Mr. Morris executor of estate of Bassill Little (dec'd).

Mr. Robert Morris & Mr. Henry Meese executors of estate of Bassill Little (dec'd) vs. Edward Keene.

Mr. Morris executor of estate of Mr. Bassill Little (dec'd) vs. Mr. Henry Hooper.

Mr. Morris executor of estate of Mr. Bassill Little (dec'd) vs. Ishmael Wright.

Capt. Robert Morris & Mr. Henry Meese executors of estate of Mr. Bassill Little (dec'd) vs. John Reede.

f. 392 Mentions: receipt of Mr. Richard Harris (dec'd).

Mr. Morris executor of estate of Mr. Bassill Little (dec'd) vs. John Bagbey.

Mr. Morris executor of estate of Mr. Bassill Little (dec'd) vs. William Turner.

Capt. Robert Morris & Mr. Henry Meese executors of estate of Bassill Little (dec'd) vs. Robert Tayler.

f. 393 Mr. Morris executor of estate of Bassill Little (dec'd) vs. John Grammer.

Mr. Robert Morris executor of estate of Mr. Bassill Little (dec'd) vs. Phill. Morgin.

Capt. Henry Keene was granted a judgement against the estate of Mr. Bassill Little.

Per testimony of Mr. Henry Osborne & Mr. Peter Sharpe, Robert Makey (servant of Mr. Bassill Little) was granted his freedom.

12 January 1657. John Piper, age 30, deposed that in the middle of last October, Thomas White came to the deponent's house & said that he was to gather some nuts for Margaret (N)

f. 394 William Marshall's maid, & that said White & said Margaret "had passed their faith & troth together".

Richard Tarling, age 23, deposed that 9 weeks ago, he was talking with Thomas White on the plantation of William Marshall. Said White said he "had been in leage with William Marshall's maid" for 2 or 3 years.

Peter Carr, age 33, deposed that at the end of last December, Thomas White came to the deponent & said that Margaret (N) William Marshall's maid had said she loved him. He (White) was going to buy her off, with chattel at Edward Swan & John Piper.

25 January 1657. William Empson, age 35, deposed that Thomas White told the deponent

f. 395 on 27 December 1657 that if he died before he married Margaret (N) William Marshall's maid, he would leave her all he had.

Thomas Lomax, age 27, deposed on 22 January 1657 that on 13 January 1657, John Slingsby at the now dwelling of William Marshall, said Slingsby desired to be maintained by said Marshall.

John Dougles, age 21, deposed on 22 January 1657 that on 13 January 1657, John Slingsby at the now dwelling of his master William Marshall, said Slingsby desired to be maintained by said Marshall. Signed: John Duglas.

f. 396 Luke Barber (gentleman, of Newtown) is indebted to Mrs. Jane Fenwick (of Putuxent). Date: 7 June 1657. Signed: L. Barber. Witnesses: Will. Mill,

Liber - Patent Record A & B - 1650-1657

Richard Lloyd.

London, 21 September 1657. Capt. John Tully (master of the Reliefe bound for VA, MD, & Providence) was bound to Thomas Webb (merchant, of London).

f. 397 Date: 23 September 1657. Witness: James Bagnall. Thomas Webb assigned to Mr. William Parratt (of Patuxon River VA). Date: 24 September 1657. Recorded for Mr. Parratt on 15 March 1657.

Robert Kingsborough gave chattel to

f. 398 Edward Wells (under age) son of Edward Wells, Elisabeth Wells (under age) daughter of Edward Wells, his own son Samuell Kingsborough (age 4). Recorded for the use of Robert Kingsborough's children. Date: 16 February 1657.

16 February 1657 at Putuxent. Court. Attendees: Mr. Rich. Preston, Mr. Mich. Brooke, Mr. Thom. Thomas, Mr. William Parratt, Mr. William Euens.

Jacob Lumbrozo vs. William Gillford.

f. 399 Mr. Symon Oversee vs. Walter Peake & John Cornelius. Mentions: bill to Phillip Land assigned to said Overzee.

Owen James petitioned for administration on estate of Paul Simpson (dec'd). Walter Peake deposed that there is a will.

Walter Peake demanded of estate of Paul Simpson (dec'd), due as surety for said Simpson to Mr. Simon Overzee.

Mr. Thomas Cary (merchant) vs. Mr. Henry Hooper. Mentions: Mr. Thomas Jordan (merchant).

f. 400 Richard Collett vs. William Hammington.

Hugh Standley vs. James Veitch.

Mr. John Lord vs. John Tennis.

Ann Barbery vs. Thomas Stone.

17 February 1657. Court (con't). Attendees: same as before.

John Harwood vs. William Edin. Mentions:

f. 401 Henry Fox, wife of said Edin.

Capt. William Ewens administrator of estate of Capt. John Barriffe (dec'd) vs. Cornelius Johnson. Mentions: Arthur Wright.

Thomas Bellcher vs. John Cockrell. Mentions: Richard Smith.

Thomas Seamor vs. Mrs. Jane Eltonhead.

f. 402 Mr. Thomas Stone on behalf of Capt. William Stone vs. John Cornelius.

Mr. Richard Smith & Mr. Thomas Bellcher vs. Hugh Standley.

Aron Jacobson vs. Hugh Standley. Mentions: Allbert Johnson.

Thomas Caiger vs. estate of Capt. John Barriff (dec'd).

f. 403 Mr. John Lawson vs. Mr. Emperor Smith. Mentions: Mr. Lawson is attorney to this brother Mr. John Collins.

Richard Smith vs. Mrs. Jane Eltonhead.

James Mullekin vs. Mr. Henry Coursey.

Richard Smith vs. Mr. Michaell Brooke.

Mr. Henry Hooper vs. Mr. Tobias Norton.

Timothy Guttridge vs. James Jolly.

Capt. Sampson Waring attorney for Thomas Stagewell vs. Capt. Phillip Morgin.

George Beckwith vs. Ann Maddocks.

Liber - Patent Record A & B - 1650-1657

Capt. Sampson Waring attorney

f. 404 for Thomas Stagwell vs. James Tompson.

Thomas Plott, age 21, deposed that the chattel in dispute between Alexander Watts & William Dorrington belongs to said Watts.

Mr. Michael Brooke attorney for William Barrett vs. Phillip Harwood.

Robert Patterson, age 40, deposed that he was present when David Farera reviewed the chattel of Mr. William Berry last May.

Phillip Harwood deposed that 2 months after Tobias Norton bought a servant Christopher (N) of Mr. Henry Hooper, he said that Norton liked the servant.

Mr. William Berry attorney for Aron Jacobson vs.

f. 405 John Cornelius. Mentions: Capt. Henry Keene, John Tayler, Allbert Johnson.

John Cornelius fined.

Mr. Henry Hooper fined.

Mary Dammarell petitioned for an inventory of the estate of her late husband. Appraisers: Mr. Richard Collett, Mr. George Gollding.

f. 406 Thomas Jordan (merchant, of London) appointed Richard Hix (carpenter, of Putuxent River) as his attorney. Date: 13 February 1657. Witnesses: Rich. Smith, Giles Sadleir.

Walter Senserfe (mariner, of London, master of King David of Yarmouth) appointed

f. 407 William Berry (planter, of Putuxent) as his attorney. Date: 1 February 1657. Signed: Walter Senserf. Witnesses: Richard Preston, Thomas Turner, William Sinclere.

24 March 1657. Writ to John Norwood (sheriff of Anne Arundel Co.) for burgesses to the Assembly on 27 April at St. Leonard's in County of Calverton. Same to John Coursey (gentleman) for Isle of Kent. Same to William Coursey (gentleman) for County of Calverton. Same to Nicholas Gwither for County of St. Mary's.

f. 408 Warrant to William Mitchell, Esq. for 3000 acres for transporting self & family, & over 30 persons.

f. 409 ...

f. 410 Date: 1 January 1649.

Warrant to Sergt. James Lindsey & Richard Willan for 1000 acres, called the Mannor of Snow Hill. Mentions: Richard Ingle. Date: 28 August 1649.

f. 411 Warrant to John Jarbo & Lt. William Evans

f. 412 for a plantation on Isle of Kent, formerly belonging to John Abbott, for 400 acres. Date: 18 August 1649.

f. 413 Warrant to William Eltonhead, Esq. (partner with Edward Eltonhead, Esq. (master of High Court of Chancery in England)) for 10,000 acres. [Grant to Edward Eltonhead.]

f. 414 Date: 29 September 1649.

f. 415 Recorded: 24 January 1652. Warrant to Robert Brooke, Esq. for transporting self, wife, 8 sons, & family.

f. 416 For 2000 acres.

f. 417 ...

f. 418 Date: 1 September 1649.

Warrant to Edward Eltonhead, Esq.

f. 419 extended to 7 years. Date: 16 June 1651.

f. 420 20 October 1654. General Assembly. Attendees: Capt. William Fuller, Mr.

Liber - Patent Record A & B - 1650-1657

Richard Preston (Speaker), Mr. Leo. Strong, Mr. John Hatch, Mr. Richard Wells, Mr. Richard Ewen, Mr. William Durand, Mr. Tho. Hinson, Mr. Edward Lloyd, Mr. Arthur Turner, Mr. William Parker, Mr. John Wade, Mr. Sampson Waring, Mr. James Berry, Mr. Joseph Weekes, Mr. William Ewen.

I. Act of Recognition. Mentions: Richard Bennett, Esq., Col. William Cleyborne. Commission: Capt. William Fuller, Mr. Richard Preston, Mr. William Durand, Mr. Edward Lloyd, Mr. Leonard Strong, Mr. John Hatch, Mr. John Lawson, Mr. Richard Wells,

f. 421 Mr. William Parker, Mr. Richard Ewen.

II. Mr. Thomas Hatton & Mr. Job Chandler were chosen burgesses for County of St. Mary & Potomock River. They refuse to sit.

f. 422 New writ ordered. Mr. Arthur Turner & Mr. John Wade were chosen.

III. Act concerning Religion. [Catholics were no longer protected.]

f. 423 IV. Inhabitants of Herring Creek & The Clifts are to pay county charges to Providence (formerly Annarundell).

V. Putuxent County erected.

VI. Assembly to be called every 3 years.

f. 424 VII. Publique Levies.

VIII. Act concerning Drunkeness.

f. 425 IX. Act concerning Swearing.

X. Act concerning False Reports Slandering & Talebearing.

f. 426 XI. Act concerning Sabboth Day.

XII. Act concerning Theft.

f. 427 XIII. Act concerning Fencing of Ground.

XIV. Act concerning Adultery & Fornication.

XV. Act concerning a Register of Births, Marriages, & Burials.

f. 428 XVI. Providence County erected. [formerly Annarundell Co.]

XVII. Act concerning Ship or Vessells.

XVIII. Act concerning War with Indians.

XIX. Act concerning Killing of Wolves.

f. 429 XX. Act concerning Stealing of Indians.

XXI. Act concerning Selling of Guns, Powder, & Shot to Indians.

XXII. Act for Discounting.

XXIII. Act concerning Weights & Measures.

f. 430 XXIV. Act concerning County of Maryes in Patomake.

XXV. Act concerning the Records.

XXVI. Act concerning the Militia.

f. 431 XXVII. Act concerning Rights of Lands.

XXVIII. Act concerning Indians Trespass.

f. 432 XXIX. Act against Fugitives.

f. 433 XXX. Act concerning Delivery of Guns to Indians.

XXXI. Act concerning Planting Corn.

f. 434 XXXII. Act concerning Striking Officers & Other Offences.

Liber - Patent Record A & B - 1650-1657

f. 435 XXXIII. Act against Ingrocers.

XXXIV. Act prohibiting Foreigners to Trade in the Province.

f. 436 XXXV. Acts repealed.
- Concerning religion.
- Concerning attachment & executions.
- Concerning Col. Cleyborne.
- Concerning deserted plantations & seatings.
- Concerning Inego's Fort.
- Concerning mutinies & seditious speeches.

XXXVI. Act concerning Accompts without Specialty.

XXXVII. Act concerning all Servants coming into the Province with Indentures.

f. 437 XXXVIII. Act concerning Treating with Indians. Authorization to: Mr. Richard Preston, Mr. William Parker, Mr. John Lawson, Mr. John Hatch, Mr. Sampson Waring, Mr. Cuthbt. Phenwick, Mr. John Wade, Mr. Arthur Turner, Mr. William Parrott.

f. 438 XXXIX. Act concerning Administration.

XL. Act concerning Mr. Robert Brooke's Petition for his Charge on the Publique.

XLI. Act for Charges from the Assembly.

f. 439 XLII. Act concerning Orphan's Estates.

XLIII. Act repealing proclamation by Lord Baltimore.

f. 440 XLIV. Accompts of Levies:
- County of Providence: Mr. Sprye, Mr. Strong, Mr. Durand.
- County of Kent: Mr. Wells on assignment from Mr. Fox.
- County of Putuxent: Hugh Hopewell, Esq. Brooke assigned by him & Mr. Fox to Mr. Wells, Cornelius, Mrs. Eltonhead,

f. 441 ...
 Richard Collett, Mr. Harris, James Veitch, Mr. Utie.
- County of Potomack: James Veitch, Governor Bennett, John Shanks, Mr. Wells, Capt. Smith, Mr. Chandler, Mr. Hammond, Mr. Johnson, Mr. Richard Preston.

24 September 1657. General Assembly at Putuxent. Attendees: Capt. Richard Ewens (Speaker), Capt. Richard Vaughan, Capt. Robert Slye, Capt. Joseph Weekes, Mr. Robert Taylor, Capt. Tho. Besson, Mr. Peter Sharpe, Capt. Phillip Morgin, Mr. Mich. Brooks, Mr. James Johnson.

I. Act of Recognition.

f. 442 II. Acts repealed.
- Concerning public levies on the visible estate of inhabitants.
- Concerning theft.
- Concerning births, marriages, & burials.
- Concerning sheriff's & clerk's fees.

III. Act concerning Pub. Charge.

IV. Act concerning Ground Leaves.

f. 443 V. Act concerning Sheriff's & Cherk's Fees.

VI. Act concerning Regulating of Attachments & Executions.

f. 444 VII. Act concerning Popler's Island.

VIII. Order of Assembly. Mentions: Capt. Josias Fendall, Mr. Parr.

IX. Order of Assembly. Capt. Richard Ewen, Capt. Thomas Besson, & Capt. Joseph Weekes

f. 445 appointed to committee.

X. Order of Assembly. Mentions (servants): (N) Stockden, (N) Guneen.

f. 446 XI. Order of Assembly. Mentions: Mr. John Hatch, Capt. Robert Sley.

XII. Order of Assembly. Accompts of: Capt. Fendall, execution of Mr. Parr, Mr. Spry, Mr. Hostkeys, John Cobreth, widow Besley & her 4 small children,

Liber - Patent Record A & B - 1650-1657

f. 447 Capt. Henry Keen, John Wallcott, Robert Francklin, John Underhill, George Whittle, Mr. Preston.
- To be paid at Providence: widow Besley, John Underhill, Thomas Besson, Mr. Norwood.
- To be paid at Kent: Mr. Spry, Andrew Skinner, Mr. Norwood.
- To be paid at Putuxent River: Mr. Bellcher, Mr. Sprye, John Wallcott, George Whittle, Mr. Belcher, (N) Gassaway & (N) Fisher, Mr. Preston, Henry Ashley, Mr. Norwood, John Cobreth, Capt. Fuller.
- To be paid at Potomack River: widow Beasley, Robert Francklin, John Underhill, Mr. Beard,

f. 448 ...
Mr. Belcher, Mr. Dorrington, Capt. Waring, Mr. Hostkeys, Capt. Keene, Capt. Fuller.
- Other charges: Mr. William Berry, George Newman, Richard Preston, Jr., Anthony LeCompte, John Bagbey, Hugh Hopewell, Fran. Billingsly, Mr. Stockley, James Veitch (sheriff), Capt. Waring, Robert Harwood, Mrs. Fenwick.

<none> Griffith Beddoe transcribed & Mr. John Lawson verified the contents. Date: 21 November 1726. Signed: G. Beddoe, J. Lawson, Benj. Tasker, Samuell Young, D. Dulany.

INDEX

Companies
    Capt. Evelin & Co. 84

(no surname)
    Allbert 194
    Andrew 85, 118
    Aron 195
    Bridgett 1
    Charles 3, 5
    Christopher 206
    Cornelius 17, 199
    Daniel 4
    Darbey 195
    David 22
    Deborah 2
    Dominick 134, 148
    Elisabeth 3
    Ellen 64
    Frances 191
    Francis 191
    Franissco 2
    Frannsco 4
    George 159
    Harry 195
    Humfrey 147
    Humphrey 2
    James 17
    Jane 3
    Jeremy 27
    John 64, 97, 190, 191
    Josias 3
    Julian 3
    Margaret 204
    Martin 84
    Peter 150
    Randoll 85
    Richard 195, 201
    Robert 191
    Samuel 12
    Samuell 190
    Small 4
    Stephen 191
    Thomas 86, 152
    William 17, 147, 154
    York 4

Abbington
    John 39
Abbott
    George 55
    John 9, 10, 54, 69, 72, 81, 83, 85, 93, 106, 113, 117, 118, 206
    Mr. 55, 194
    Thomas 132
Abeington
    John 196
Abell
    Robert 27, 37
Abotts
    John 9
Abraham
    Cornelius 48, 184, 192
    Francis 188
    Skipper 24, 125, 126
Abram
    Cornelius 201
Abrams
    Cornelius 175
Abramson
    Cornelius 178, 180, 181
    Frances 177

Acheson
    Vincent 29
Achilles
    Peter 170, 189
Ackcrek
    George 32
Ackrick
    George 148
Ackrik
    George 160
Acreeke
    George 92
Acres
    William 175
Acricke 148
Adames
    Henry 60
Adams
    Henry 2, 19, 25, 26, 29, 31, 46, 49, 59, 61, 95, 98, 105, 123, 125, 128, 141, 145, 149, 166, 168
    Mr. 83
    Tho. 83
    Thomas 10, 15, 16, 51, 57, 81
Adbor
    John 196
Adcroft
    Davy 154
Addison
    Tho. 151
Ager
    Thomas 68, 176, 185, 188
Akerick
    G. 101
    Geo. 100, 123
    George 99, 100, 103, 108, 123, 124, 125, 126, 135
Akericke
    George 126
Akrick
    George 153
Albertson
    John 174
Allder
    Phillip 45
Allen
    James 50
    John 31, 61
    Mr. 51
    Robert 164
    Tho. 80, 89, 97, 99, 100, 101, 104, 107, 112, 116, 119, 140, 141, 144, 145, 167
    Thom 97
    Thomas 5, 7, 10, 13, 72, 80, 81, 84, 99, 102, 111, 113, 115, 119, 123, 128, 156, 157, 159, 164, 184
    William 51, 53, 64, 150, 173
Alling
    Arthur 27
Allser
    Phillip 45
Altain
    Jo. 17
Altham
    John 70, 71
Althem
    John 2

Althome
    John 79
Altome
    John 4
Ancketill
    Francis 22
Anderson
    David 161
    John 188
Andrews
    Mr. 26
    William 26, 38, 166
Andrey
    Phillip 123
Angood
    John 16
Anketell
    Mr. 52
Anketill
    Francis 35, 86, 95, 188
    John 188
Antderton
    John 175
Antell
    Francis 30, 142, 165
Archer
    (N) 133
Armes
    Henry 129, 134, 140
Armesby
    John 8
Armstrong
    Margarett 155
Arther
    (N) 142
Arthur's Hope 128
Asbeston
    Elisabeth 192
    William 147, 192
Asbrook
    John 20
    Thomas 20, 107
Asceter
    William 84
Ascombe
    John 188
Ashbiston
    William 116
Ashbrook
    John 132
    Tho. 107
    Thomas 18, 107, 120, 123, 134
Ashbrooke
    John 120, 123
    Tho. 119, 168
    Thomas 35, 128, 130, 168, 171, 179
Ashcomb
    John 39, 43, 61, 64, 196
Ashcombe
    John 37, 43, 169
Ashley
    Henry 209
    Jo. 139
    John 20, 139, 143, 146
Ashmore
    John 13
    William 2, 4, 5, 17, 74, 75
Ashton
    John 14
Asiter
    Will. 85
    William 2, 4, 16, 21, 23
Asitor

William 17
Askew
    John 13
Askue
    John 2
Asseter
    William 85, 87, 95, 96
Assetter
    William 115
Assiter
    William 24, 30, 90, 96,
        115, 116, 135, 138,
        153, 161, 162
Atcheson
    Vincent 25, 44
Atkins
    Xpofer 17
Atkinson
    James 142
    Robert 142
    Vincent 166
Attcheson
    James 190, 191, 193,
        198, 199
    Susan 190, 191, 198
Attchison
    James 185, 186
Attookes
    Umphrey 194
Attwicks
    Humphrey 118
Atwick
    Henry 127
    Humfr. 124
    Humfrey 127
    Humphrey 32
Atwicks
    Humfrey 54
    Humfry 37, 43, 140, 161,
        168
    Humphrey 152
Atwix
    Humphrey 35
Atwixe
    Humphrey 32, 35, 43
Augud
    Mr. 85
Auther
    Phillip 28, 45, 104,
        112, 122
Author
    Phillip 28
Authur
    Phill. 115
    Phillip 97, 126, 129
Ayes
    Huntington 192
Aylett
    Robert 103
Ayres
    Joh. 85
    John 17, 85
    Mr. 169

Bacon
    Nathaniell 192
Bagbee
    John 178, 179, 180
Bagbey
    John 175, 186, 192, 196,
        199, 204, 209
Bagby
    John 176, 177, 178
Bagley
    Phillip 143
Bagnall
    James 205
Bailey
    John 40

Baily
    John 32, 33, 45, 51, 53
Bailye
    John 45
Baisey
    Michael 28, 38, 54, 57,
        59, 62, 65, 66, 67
    Michaell 27
Baker
    Andrew 2, 78, 79, 84
    Henry 8, 111, 129
    Tho. 59, 110, 111, 112,
        113, 115, 141
    Thomas 2, 46, 51, 78,
        110, 118, 128, 159
Balaen
    John 197
Baldrich
    Tho. 124
    Thomas 126
Baldridge
    Capt. 128
    Dorothy 21
    Jame 72
    James 70, 71, 72, 76,
        77, 78, 79, 82, 84,
        85
    Mr. 82
    Mrs. 21
    Tho. 47, 78, 113, 117
    Thomas 16, 38, 70, 71,
        73, 74, 75, 76, 79,
        80, 82, 83, 84, 85,
        127
Baley
    Elinor 199
    John 199
Balmer
    Thomas 50
Banck
    George 155
Bancks
    Richard 19, 28, 29, 57,
        58, 156
Banister
    Nicholas 135, 155, 160
Bankes
    Rich. 32, 100
    Richard 101, 183
Banks
    Lt. 124, 130, 172
    Margaret 203
    Margarett 45
    Rich. 37, 97, 100, 101,
        102, 112, 123
    Richard 14, 21, 25, 30,
        31, 32, 36, 37, 44,
        45, 49, 53, 93, 98,
        99, 100, 101, 102,
        107, 111, 113, 119,
        124, 125, 126, 127,
        128, 129, 130, 133,
        139, 141, 169, 181,
        183, 184
Bannester
    Nicholas 17
Barbarah
    Soliman 203
Barbary
    Susan 190
Barber
    John 52
    L. 204
    Luke 188, 203, 204
Barbery
    Ann 205
Barbury
    Cinnamon 187
Barcholest
    Nicholas 184

Barock
    John 17
Barratt
    Samuel 14
Barrett
    Samuel 4, 5, 82
    William 177, 206
Barriff
    John 34, 180, 181, 205
Barriffe
    Capt. 200
    John 59, 65, 170, 173,
        174, 177, 180, 181,
        182, 185, 200, 205
Barshaw
    Andrew 154
Barton
    William 67, 169, 193,
        200, 201
Baruth
    Samuell 159
Barwick
    Daniell 52, 192
Barwicke
    Daniell 52
Barwyck
    Daniell 52
Bary
    Garrat 39
Basey
    Mich. 185
    Michael 40, 171, 183,
        184, 186, 187, 188,
        191, 194, 203
    Michaell 184
Basha
    Andrew 9, 10
    Giles 5, 9, 10, 12, 83
Bashawe
    Giles 141
Basley
    Edward 192
Bassatt
    Michael 119
Bassett
    Thomas 193
Bassey
    Goodman 185
    Michael 185
    Mrs. 184
Basy
    Michael 171, 172
Batchellor
    Thomas 61, 62
Batchelor
    Mr. 201
    Tho. 60
    Thomas 58, 62, 201
Bateman
    Edward 71, 73, 80, 82
Baten
    William 171
Battam
    John 3
Battan
    Mr. 39
    William 39
Battar
    John 199
Batten
    Mr. 172
    Mrs. 180
    William 29, 42, 47, 171,
        172, 173, 176, 177,
        180
Battin
    Mr. 184, 185
    Will. 186
    William 176, 182, 187
Batts

Nathaniell 51, 56, 57
Baxter
   Francis 107
   John 82, 84, 107
   Richard 14
   Roger 2, 86, 106, 107, 114, 164
Baylie
   Tho. 147
Baysey
   Michael 28
Beach
   Ann 46
   Chas. 125
   Elias 6, 17, 102, 122, 123, 125, 127, 128, 132, 141, 145
Beache
   Elias 132
   Ellis 78
Beale
   Joh. 151
Beall
   John 191
Bealle
   John 190
Beame
   Ralphe 70
Bean
   Raphe 164
   Walter 115, 155
Beane
   Mr. 95, 157, 158
   Ralph 5, 20, 21, 22, 23, 45, 47, 73, 96, 102, 111, 119, 122, 123, 124, 125, 126, 134, 140, 142
   Ralphe 74, 77, 82, 83, 105, 114, 120, 122, 123, 126, 127, 128, 131, 133, 138, 159
   Ralple 84
   Raph 66
   Raphe 147, 155, 159, 161, 165, 166, 167, 168
   Wal. 109, 115
   Walt. 109, 112
   Walter 14, 18, 19, 20, 21, 27, 31, 32, 34, 35, 37, 40, 45, 47, 52, 53, 54, 56, 58, 59, 60, 66, 96, 97, 98, 101, 103, 104, 105, 108, 109, 110, 112, 120, 123, 124, 127, 128, 131, 132, 133, 135, 136, 139, 141, 147, 149, 150, 153, 155, 157, 159, 161, 162, 167, 169, 170
   William 34
Beanes
   Raphe 148
   Rowland 140
Beanland 162
Beans
   Walter 118
Beard
   Mr. 66, 209
   Richard 14, 67
   Robert 87, 155
Beasley
   Edward 186
   widow 209
Beasly
   Edward 185
Beaver Neck 66, 182

Beckler
   Edward 76
Beckley
   Richard 9
Beckwith
   Frances 197
   George 148, 196, 205
Beckworth
   Thomas 12
Beddo
   Griffith 68
Beddoe
   G. 152, 209
   Griffith 68, 151, 209
Beekler
   Edward 69
Belamy
   Henry 8
Belcher
   Mr. 209
   Mrs. 180
   Thomas 57, 186, 189
Bell
   John 87, 88
Bellame
   John 32
Bellamy
   Henry 8, 16, 81, 86, 154
Bellcher
   Mr. 191, 209
   Tho. 199
   Thomas 189, 196, 198, 205
Bellson
   John 75
Benam
   Anam 1, 5, 108
   Anum 82
   Enam 82
Bence
   William 35, 36
Bene
   Ralphe 123
Bennet
   Richard 156
Bennett
   Elisabeth 142
   Governor 208
   John 86, 106, 107, 167
   Mary 177
   Phillip 139
   Ri. 64
   Rich. 112, 116
   Richard 19, 28, 34, 40, 42, 50, 51, 64, 87, 88, 94, 104, 125, 126, 137, 138, 139, 143, 160, 167, 168, 169, 174, 177, 183, 184, 193, 207
   Sarah 19
   Tho. 61, 67
   Thomas 19, 39, 46, 51, 54, 58, 66, 142, 178, 188
Bennit
   Richard 36, 43, 50
Bennitt
   Richard 183
Benson
   Sarah 189
   Stephen 174
Benum
   Anum 69, 70, 72
Berclay
   William 150
Berclaye
   William 150
Berkeley
   William 86

Berkely
   William 87
Berkley
   William 87
Bernett
   Julian 108
Berrey
   William 183
Berry
   Edward 4, 17, 147
   Elisabeth 175, 192
   George 139
   James 169, 172, 188, 192, 198, 207
   Martha 175
   Mr. 188
   Roger 175, 177
   William 175, 187, 188, 192, 196, 200, 206, 209
Berwick
   Richard 2
Besley
   widow 208, 209
Besson
   Tho. 208
   Thomas 208, 209
Betham
   Richard 154
Bettam
   John 4, 5
Betton
   William 94
Bigge
   Ambross 191
Biggs
   Ambrose 17
Billingley
   Francis 67
Billingsley
   John 56, 184, 187, 193, 199, 201
   Major 174
Billingsly
   Fran. 209
   John 184, 187, 188, 189, 193, 199
   Maj. 191
Bills
   Henry 186
Billsberry
   Henry 186, 187, 195
Billsbury
   Henry 184
Bincks
   George 82
Binge
   Anthony 50
Binkes
   Thomas 186
Binks
   Dr. 125
   Geo. 83
   George 95
Binx
   George 82
Bird
   Simon 65, 175
Bisco
   John 61, 192
Biscoe
   John 61
Bish
   Ursula 16
Bishop
   Henry 2, 4, 5, 15, 16, 17, 37, 43, 45, 49, 52, 54, 63, 70, 72, 74, 83, 128, 147, 169
Biskoe

John 61
Bland
   Edward 93, 94
Bletsoe
   Roger 135
Blinkhorn
   Robert 196
Blinkome
   Robert 192
Blinks
   Richard 191, 196
Blissard
   William 76
Blizard
   William 9, 69
Bloff
   William 31
Blomefield
   Marke 16
Blomfield
   Marke 43
Bloome
   Bartho. 67
   Bartholomew 176
   Bartholomy 195, 198
Bloomefield
   Marke 61
   Marks 163
Bloomfied
   Marke 192
Bloomfield
   Markes 199
Blount
   Mr. 147
   William 16
Blunfield
   Marke 119
Blunt
   Richard 27, 164
Boarman
   William 28, 30
Boate
   William 9
Bobing Mannor 165
Boell
   Goodman 190
Bogg
   John 190
Bolane
   John 155
Bolls
   Edward 169
Bolton
   Ann 63
   Elisabeth 63
   Stephen 17
Bonam
   John 204
   Sam. 203
   Samuell 194
Bonifield
   Christian 68
   Mr. 67
   Mrs. 67
Bonyfield
   Mrs. 68
Booker
   Edward 176
Booles
   Edward 179
Boon
   John 193
Boone
   John 173, 186, 193
   Thomas 192
Boothe
   Thomas 198
Bordley
   T. 151
Boreman

Richard 7, 14
William 28, 29, 30, 32,
   36, 37, 38, 47, 54,
   59, 63, 120, 128,
   136, 141, 145, 149,
   172
Boston
   Hen. 96, 112
   Henry 92, 98, 99, 105
Bosworth
   John 63
Boteler
   John 15, 77, 81
Boules
   Edward 63
Boulton
   Ann 38, 46, 63
   Anne 163
   Elisabeth 63
   John 40
   Mrs. 33, 38
Bouman
   Edmond 197
Bounday
   William 46
Bourne
   Elkenath 148
Bousey
   Michael 25
Bouth
   Rob. 26
Bowcock
   John 62
Bowell
   Edward 190
Bowen
   David 17
   Davy 30
Bowler 136 138
Bowles
   Edward 57, 62, 155, 190
   Joane 155
   Simon 152
   William 155
Bowman
   William 17
Boyce
   Tho. 128
Boys
   Thomas 15, 71, 82
Boyse
   Tho. 139
Brackitt
   Peter 51
Bradhorst
   Mr. 196
Bradley
   Richard 77, 80
   William 32
Bradney
   William 17
Bradnock
   Tho. 85
   Thomas 4, 16, 76, 84,
     150
Bradnox
   Mary 115
   Mr. 99, 101, 106, 116
   Mrs. 121, 123
   Tho. 85, 100, 105, 106,
     107, 115, 116, 117,
     164
   Thomas 18, 38, 49, 83,
     91, 106, 113, 115,
     117, 150, 166
Bradnoxe
   Thomas 85
Braffe
   Mary 155
Brainthwait

Mr. 4, 167
Will. 81
William 8, 15, 140, 166,
   167
Brainthwaite
   Mr. 96
   Will. 81
   William 9, 38, 70, 71,
     73, 81, 83, 96
Brainthwate
   William 81
Bralley
   Richard 45
Bramale
   William 173
Bramalll
   William 184
Bramhall
   William 172, 180
Brammaell
   William 185
Brammall
   William 202
Brandson
   Thomas 201
Branthwait
   Mr. 10
Brasington
   Robert 5
Brasinton
   Robert 14
Breamstead
   Thomas 197
Brent
   Capt. 49, 97, 101, 102,
     114, 117, 123, 144
   Edward 80, 84
   Foulke 91
   Fulk 21, 131
   Fulke 1, 84
   G. 97, 116
   Giles 1, 2, 4, 5, 12,
     14, 15, 16, 17, 18,
     20, 26, 29, 35, 53,
     54, 60, 80, 81, 82,
     84, 87, 89, 91, 96,
     97, 100, 101, 102,
     103, 105, 106, 107,
     109, 110, 111, 113,
     114, 115, 116, 117,
     118, 120, 121, 122,
     123, 126, 132, 136,
     141, 144, 146, 147,
     151, 154, 160, 161,
     164, 166, 179
   Marg. 89, 90, 92, 94,
     95, 96, 97, 98, 101,
     102, 103, 104, 109,
     113, 124, 126, 127,
     135, 136, 140, 141,
     144, 146, 153, 163
   Margaret 1, 16, 17, 23,
     24, 29, 32, 42, 60,
     87, 90, 93, 94, 95,
     96, 97, 98, 99, 100,
     101, 102, 103, 104,
     109, 113, 116, 117,
     120, 121, 122, 124,
     125, 126, 127, 136,
     139, 141, 143, 144,
     146, 147, 151, 152,
     154, 160, 163, 164,
     167, 168
   Margarett 3, 4, 5, 18,
     23, 24, 26, 85, 86,
     87, 89, 95, 101, 103,
     104, 105, 107, 108,
     109, 110, 111, 112,
     113, 116, 121, 122,
     123, 126, 144, 145,

146, 151, 157, 160, 166
Marie 89
Mary 1, 3, 4, 5, 29, 31, 34, 53, 54, 56, 144, 147, 151, 162
Mr. 90, 105, 106, 116, 117, 166
Mrs. 91, 95, 96, 97, 98, 99, 102, 110, 117, 144, 147, 166

Bretton
Mr. 20, 23, 71, 88, 99, 100, 101, 111, 113, 116, 130, 136, 141, 144
William 21, 30, 37, 38, 46, 47, 49, 52, 57, 58, 61, 70, 71, 83, 85, 88, 92, 96, 97, 99, 100, 102, 105, 109, 112, 113, 115, 116, 117, 118, 121, 122, 124, 126, 127, 134, 136, 141, 142, 144, 146, 150, 152, 153, 154, 157, 161, 163, 165, 167, 168, 170, 182

Brian
John 76
Mathias 127, 165

Briant
John 4, 5, 76, 77, 84
Mathias 96, 159
Mathyas 111
widow 84

Briante
John 71

Brice
Thomas 83, 85

Bridges
(N) 23

Bright
Fra. 49
Francis 49

Brisco
John 114

Brisely
Edward 50

Brisley
Edward 48, 50, 55

Brittaine
Mr. 156

Britten
William 57

Britton
Mr. 7, 21, 82, 84
William 2, 6, 7

Broadhurst
Mr. 84, 88, 96
Walter 2, 8, 20, 84, 93

Broadstreet
Samuell 194

Brock
Richard 3

Brodhurst
Walter 16

Broff
William 31

Brome
Margaret 48

Broof
William 31

Brook
Frances 12
Francis 18
Richard 13
Robert 17, 39

Brooke

Anna 17
Baker 17
Charles 17, 166
Elisabeth 147
Esq. 208
Francis 17, 31, 66, 105, 170, 175, 180, 181, 182, 183, 194
John 3, 17
Mary 17
Mich. 67, 177, 180, 181, 182, 192, 196, 199, 203, 205
Michael 170, 173, 175, 176, 177, 178, 180, 181, 183, 186, 195, 206
Michaell 169, 171, 205
Mr. 30, 42, 166, 182, 187
Mrs. 166, 178, 180
Robert 17, 18, 26, 28, 29, 30, 31, 32, 33, 34, 39, 42, 43, 44, 46, 47, 50, 57, 59, 64, 65, 67, 152, 163, 166, 206, 208
Roger 17
Tho. 42
Thomas 17, 30, 42
William 17

Brookes
Ann 61
Charles 166
Fr. 62
Fracis 51
Fran. 85, 113
Francis 10, 18, 27, 28, 32, 35, 38, 44, 46, 47, 54, 57, 61, 62, 63, 85, 91, 92, 94, 106, 113, 129, 130, 140, 143, 146, 150, 151, 154, 161, 166, 167, 174, 182, 185, 187
Hen. 107
Henry 22, 86, 91, 95, 98, 107, 153
Mich. 189, 198, 202
Michael 177, 185, 187, 188, 190, 191, 192, 193, 194, 197, 201
Michaell 170, 199, 200
Mr. 30, 99, 100
Mrs. 65
Penelope 132
Robert 53, 57, 163, 165, 166

Brooks
Arthur 74
Elisabeth 1, 4
Fr. 139, 140
Fra. 40
Fracis 41
Franc. 125, 140
Francis 35, 38, 39, 46, 113, 114, 116, 118, 129, 154, 157, 158, 161
Hen. 119, 120
Henry 118, 125, 126, 159, 161
Jane 159
Mich. 208
Michael 183
Mr. 43, 100, 158
Robert 39, 160, 163

Broome
Margret 48

Brough
(N) 37
Mr. 34, 35, 95
William 6, 16, 20, 22, 32, 34, 37, 40, 129, 139, 141, 151, 157, 158, 159, 161

Broughe
Mr. 109, 110
William 6, 8, 13, 16, 22, 70, 75, 120, 123, 153, 168

Brounridge
Christo. 183

Brown
David 184
George 164
John 176, 189, 201
Mr. 130
Nicholas 56, 105, 164
Rich. 128, 156, 160
Richard 2, 3, 19, 20, 128, 140, 145, 153, 160, 161, 164, 165, 199
William 22, 59, 93, 128, 147, 148, 152, 175

Browne
(N) 76
George 164
James 149
John 38, 169, 190
Margaret 48
Mr. 109, 110, 117
Nic. 112
Nicholas 117, 118, 150
Nicolas 117, 118
Rich. 46, 84, 111, 114, 116, 120, 123, 129, 160, 165
Richard 17, 78, 82, 102, 119, 126, 129, 130, 131, 135, 140, 141, 142, 147, 152, 153, 160, 164, 167, 168, 199
Ricnd. 140
William 12, 23, 112, 115, 122, 124, 126, 127, 147, 155

Bruffe
William 124, 127, 133

Brunt
Margaret 175

Bryan
Mathias 150, 155, 165
Matthias 28

Bryant
John 2, 17, 70, 72, 75, 80, 84
widow 85

Bryante
John 71

Bryon
Matthias 28

Buckston
Thomas 59

Buckstone
John 202

Budd
Mr. 168
Richard 152

Budden
Edward 129
Elisabeth 159
Mr. 152

Buddon
Edward 86

Bufkin
Elwyn 166

Leavin 38
Levin 17, 30, 35, 166
Lewyn 165
Maj. 17
Bufkins
Major 35
Bugbye
John 50
Bullen
Henry 41, 170, 171, 188, 203
Bullin
Henry 67, 184
Burbage
Capt. 42, 167
Col. 183
George 173
Tho. 52, 95
Thomas 53, 61, 112, 183
Burgess
Joane 2
Burlane
Jo. 139
John 123, 128, 130
Burle
Mary 148
Robert 148, 152
Stephen 148
Burr
William 175
Burrage
John 149
Burroughes
Mr. 198
Nathaniell 172, 198
Burroughs
Nathaniell 198
Burrowes
Matthew 12
Nathaniel 190
Nathaniell 196
Burwell
Lewis 53
Busbie
Elisabeth 41
Bushell's Rest 88
Bushell
Ales 59
Tho. 45, 47, 50, 105, 115, 168
Thomas 13, 14, 20, 26, 36, 43, 54, 86, 87, 88, 128, 152, 166, 168
Xpofer 168
Bushnell
Ales 59
Thomas 59, 142
Bushrode
Tho. 110
Thomas 53, 109
Busrode
Thomas 117
Busse
George 186
Bussey
George 175, 179, 184, 185, 186, 201, 204
Mrs. 180
Bussie
George 196
Butler
John 10, 69, 192
Richard 134, 142
Tho. 83
Thomas 9, 20, 150, 153
Buttery
John 60, 166
Buttler's Land 103
Buttrice

John 53
Buttry
John 165
Byam
Thomas 138

Cable
Jo. 143
John 166
Caddle
Joseph 161
Cadell
Joseph 37
Jozyph 36
Cadger
Robert 49, 52, 92, 95, 136, 168
Thomas 152
Cadle
Jeziph 35
Joseph 28, 29, 32, 35, 37, 101, 127, 140, 152, 155, 160, 161, 162
Cage
John 22, 29, 31, 35, 37, 51, 63, 107, 110, 143, 165
Cager
Thomas 51, 54, 61, 181
Caiger
Thomas 205
Calvert
Gov. 24, 95, 96, 97, 99, 100, 109, 112, 120, 121, 149, 161
Governor 43, 103, 143, 149, 154
Governour 94, 95
L. 85, 91, 95, 108, 166
Leo. 66
Leon. 87, 94, 95, 96, 97, 99, 102, 105, 110
Leonard 1, 4, 5, 7, 10, 11, 13, 14, 15, 16, 20, 22, 24, 69, 70, 71, 72, 73, 75, 76, 77, 78, 79, 80, 81, 84, 85, 86, 87, 88, 89, 90, 91, 92, 93, 94, 95, 96, 99, 102, 104, 105, 109, 111, 115, 117, 121, 125, 131, 143, 144, 148, 150, 153, 154, 155, 157, 163, 166, 182
Mr. 92, 95, 96, 99, 100, 102, 105, 117, 143
Cammell
John 188
Canada
Cornelius 43, 46, 170
Cane
Edward 159
Henry 170
Canedy
Cornelius 38, 185
Cannaday
Cornelius 46
William 199
Cannadie
Cornelius 67, 169
Cannady
Cornelius 66, 67, 155, 169, 176, 178, 179, 183
Mrs. 180
Susan 178, 183
Susanna 183

Canneda
Cornelius 170
Canneday
Cornelius 191
Darbey 195
Darby 195
Cannedie
Cornelius 169
Cannedy
Cornelius 63, 188
Cannoway
Edmond 191
Canoda
Cornelius 42
Cant
W. 1
Cardell
Joseph 22
Carey
Thomas 3
Carington
John 44
Carinton
Thomas 83
Carlien
Henry 188
Carnall
Xopher 135
Carnock
Christopher 2
Carnoll
Christopher 28, 91, 114
Cr. 34
Xopher 135, 136
Xpofer 4, 17, 28, 128, 141
Carpender
Thomas 195
Carpenter
Thomas 44, 47, 57
William 90
Carr
Nicholas 189, 190
Peter 204
Carre
Walter 186
Carrington
John 34, 44, 47, 49
Carroll
Christopher 78
Xpofer 83
Carter
Capt. 169
Cartwright
Henry 156, 167
Cartwrights
Henry 154
Cary
Christopher 204
James 188
Mr. 190, 191
Thomas 85, 189, 190, 196, 205
Carye
Thomas 189, 200
Cassine
Nicholas 90, 93
Caszeene
Nicholas 31
Catchma
Henry 184
Catchman
Henry 170
Catchmay
Mr. 48
Catchmey
(N) 48
Geo. 48
George 48, 59
Henry 48, 59, 176, 178

Mary 48, 178
Mr. 48
Catchpole
   Judith 180
Catlyn
   Henry 17, 169
Caughter
   James 90
Causine Manor 136
Causine
   Nicholas 136
Cauther
   James 22, 23, 60, 69, 70, 71, 72, 74, 75, 81, 82, 83, 84, 85, 94, 105, 109, 125, 146
   Jas. 72
Cavert
   William 17
Cawse
   Nicholas 142
Cawseen
   Mr. 145, 160
   Nich. 168
   Nicholas 26, 40, 51, 136, 170
Cawseene
   Nichol. 140, 153
   Nicholas 37, 53, 58, 145, 161, 170
Cawsen
   Nic. 97
   Nicholas 96, 98
   Nicolas 96
Cawsin
   Jane 131
   Nicholas 85, 108, 116, 131
   Nicolas 94, 99, 108, 109, 120
Cawsine
   Mr. 95
   Nic. 110
   Nicholas 114
   Nicolas 110
Cedar Point 180
Cedger
   Robert 37
Censerfe
   Walter 200, 203
Chaddock
   Mr. 167
   Phillip 147, 161
Chair
   John 14
Chamberlaine
   Christopher 22
Chambers
   Christopher 35
Chandler
   Job 33, 34, 35, 36, 37, 39, 41, 42, 44, 52, 53, 55, 56, 173, 175, 199, 207
   John 45
   Mr. 40, 62, 208
   Richard 103
Chandlor 137
Chapin
   Henry 186
Chaplin
   Humphrey 2, 82
   Mr. 191
   Mrs. 180
   Stephen 191
   William 190, 193, 196
Chaplyn
   William 67, 172
Chapman
   Humphrey 155
Chappell
   Andrew 15, 69, 72, 74, 76, 80, 83, 84, 143
   Mr. 159
   William 47, 122, 164, 167
Chappoon
   Hennery 184
   Henry 184
Charington
   Thomas 69, 70, 72, 81
Charinton
   Thomas 2, 4, 11, 70
Charman
   John 122
Cheron
   John 191
Chessick
   Robert 191
Chicheley
   Hen. 175
Chifford
   John 17
Chipsham
   Mr. 63
   Robert 64
Chissick
   Robert 191
Chocoy
   John 182
Chyles
   Walter 87
Chynne
   Thomas 28
Cinquack 152
Clagett
   Richard 151
Claiborne
   W. 64
   William 64, 176
Clapborne
   Capt. 8
Clare
   Markes 188
   Will. 91
Clark
   Mr. 94, 104
   Ro. 137
   Robert 1, 28, 31, 34, 91, 92, 96, 104, 117, 135, 137, 140
   Thomas 23
Clarke
   John 92
   Mary 92
   Mr. 43, 52, 62, 66, 97, 100, 104, 109, 112, 119, 120, 125
   Neal 148
   Richard 56
   Ro. 137
   Rob. 135
   Robert 7, 28, 38, 40, 43, 46, 52, 53, 54, 63, 65, 66, 67, 91, 92, 93, 97, 100, 102, 104, 105, 111, 112, 114, 115, 116, 118, 119, 120, 121, 123, 125, 127, 128, 131, 135, 136, 137, 138, 139, 140, 145, 147, 148, 149, 152, 157, 158, 162, 165, 166, 172, 173, 176, 177, 183, 194, 195, 198
Claughton
   James 73, 76, 150
Clawson
   William 202
Claxton
   Edrm. 124
   Edward 32, 35, 40, 41, 57, 59, 62, 106, 136, 163
   Elisabeth 180, 181
Clay
   Francis 50
   Hen. 95, 97
   Henry 41, 97, 106, 109, 116, 117
Clayborne
   Capt. 8, 9, 10, 21, 144
   William 1, 8, 9, 31, 64
Clayton
   Edward 135
Cleborne
   William 75
Clerk
   Eleanor 3
   Mr. 100
   Nicholas 22
   Robert 5, 6, 7, 8, 75, 88, 100
   Thomas 23
Clerke
   Mr. 71
   Robert 8, 70, 71, 72, 74, 75, 76, 77, 81, 83, 87, 88, 89, 90
Cleyborne
   Capt. 9, 78, 88, 106, 113, 117, 158
   Col. 208
   Will. 105
   William 9, 34, 74, 75, 76, 112, 117, 156, 207
Cleybourne
   Capt. 1
Clifford
   John 30
Clifton
   James 4
Clipping 127
Clobbery
   William 154
Clobery
   Mr. 77
   William 69, 72, 77, 78
Clocker
   Dan. 112
   Daniel 29, 32, 33
   Daniell 42, 49, 52, 54, 139, 143, 145, 149, 163, 165, 167, 169
   Mary 21, 29, 32, 33, 34
Clofton
   James 73
Clothworth
   Elisabeth 154
Cloughton
   James 2, 9, 10, 76, 78, 154
   Jane 154
Cobbie
   Benjamin 2
Cobby
   Benjamin 1
Coberthat
   Robert 200
Cobreth
   John 208, 209
Cocke
   John 9
Cockerel
   John 200
Cockerell
   John 200

Cockrell
    John 205
Cockshott 136
    Jane 3, 7, 83, 131, 136
    John 3, 83, 131
    Mary 3, 131, 136
Cockshutt
    Jane 82
    John 82
Codd
    Baltasar 2, 7, 16
Cole
    Anne 143
    Edward 61, 114
    John 14, 22, 23, 105, 119
    Mary 197
    Priscilla 149
    Rich. 159
    Richard 2, 3, 4, 5, 14, 23, 61, 98, 141, 153, 159, 161, 200
    Robert 178, 195, 196, 201
    Thomas 32, 43, 44, 149, 184, 199
    William 35, 36, 39, 41, 45
Colelough
    James 167
Coleman
    John 61
Coleough
    (N) 94
Coles
    Edward 61, 89
    Robert 66
    Tho. 167
Colesford
    Richard 4
Collet
    Richard 58, 169
Collett
    Mr. 182
    Rich. 58
    Richard 58, 64, 65, 66, 67, 178, 183, 205, 206, 208
Collins
    Jasper 3
    John 205
Comberton
    Garrett 175
Comins
    Ed. 84
    Edw. 85
    Edward 8, 9, 85, 91, 113, 162
    Eliz. 162
    Eliza 162
Commens
    Edward 105
Commins
    Edw. 106, 107, 110, 113, 114, 116, 117, 136
    Edward 40, 105, 106, 107, 112, 113, 114, 116, 117, 121, 124, 126, 136, 166
    Elisabeth 163
    Mr. 41, 118
Compton
    James 2, 3, 5, 132
Conception Mannor 12
Conner
    Mr. 99, 130
    Phillip 8, 36, 83, 85, 100, 113, 114, 117, 123, 130, 136, 142, 150, 162, 164, 167

Conners
    Phillip 35
Connery
    Thomas 40, 52, 54, 59, 60, 62, 66, 178
Connerye
    Thomas 39, 41
Conoway
    Edwyn 168
    Martha 160
Conwallies
    Thomas 149
Cook
    John 21, 80, 82, 84
Cooke
    Edward 17
    Elisha 56
    John 1, 82, 88, 97, 163
    Miles 45, 46, 47, 56, 57
    Mordecai 135
    Mr. 194
    Richard 56
    Will. 78
    William 167
Cooll
    Richard 128
Coopar
    Walter 42
Cooper
    Ann 25, 29
    Robert 10
    Sam. 41
    Tho. 84
    Thomas 1, 4, 5, 81, 108
    Walter 25, 31
    William 25, 184
Coote
    Hierom 119
Cope
    James 143
Copler
    Thomas 170
Copley
    Mr. 1, 17, 23, 26, 27, 35, 57, 75, 77, 78, 79, 83, 84, 95, 104, 126, 131, 141, 144, 149, 167
    Tho. 77, 104, 105, 106, 131, 142, 160
    Thomas 1, 2, 3, 4, 12, 13, 14, 16, 17, 18, 19, 27, 28, 34, 50, 56, 60, 62, 70, 71, 72, 77, 78, 79, 80, 84, 86, 104, 105, 108, 110, 111, 115, 121, 123, 128, 131, 132, 135, 136, 137, 138, 160, 161, 165, 167
Coply
    Mr. 2
    Thomas 14
Corbett
    Hutton 11
Corbyn
    Henry 63, 175
Corbyne
    Henry 63
Corham
    Roger 177
Cornelinson Van de Graft
    Cornelius 150
Corneliouson
    John 174
Cornelison
    John 174
Cornelius
    John 39, 40, 47, 51, 53,

173, 180, 182, 183, 184, 185, 186, 189, 193, 194, 196, 198, 199, 205, 206
    Mrs. 53
Cornell
    Christopher 176
Cornish
    Robert 159
Cornw.
    Thomas 104
Cornwaleys Cross 12
Cornwaleys
    Capt. 1, 11, 16
    Thomas 3, 4, 6, 7, 10, 12, 16, 56
Cornwalleis
    Thomas 38
Cornwalles
    Thomas 134
Cornwalleyes
    Tho. 139
    Thomas 42, 44, 149
Cornwalleys
    Capt. 54, 58, 71, 75, 77, 78, 80, 81, 83, 84, 85, 95, 100, 101, 107, 133, 143, 145
    Tho. 76, 77, 78, 79, 84, 88, 101, 109, 119, 121
    Thomas 37, 46, 47, 52, 53, 54, 55, 56, 58, 59, 62, 63, 64, 66, 75, 76, 78, 79, 80, 81, 82, 83, 84, 85, 95, 111, 113, 125
Cornwallies
    Capt. 151, 163, 169
    Tho. 154, 165
    Thomas 37, 38, 60, 175
Cornwallis
    Capt. 40, 42, 43, 58, 60, 71, 72, 73, 74, 75, 95, 100, 103, 133, 143, 159
    Tho. 42, 60, 71, 75, 89, 90, 125, 134, 149
    Thomas 1, 35, 36, 37, 38, 39, 40, 41, 42, 44, 50, 55, 58, 60, 61, 62, 63, 69, 70, 71, 72, 73, 74, 75, 78, 79, 81, 121, 159, 200
Cornwallyes
    Capt. 46, 75, 102, 107, 146, 149
    Tho. 46, 79, 102, 117
    Thomas 43, 44, 50, 53, 60, 63, 77, 79, 81, 90, 113
Cornwallys
    Thomas 36, 134
Corwaleys
    Thomas 3
Corwalleys
    Thomas 51
Cossin
    Nicho. 124
    Nicholas 10, 11, 23
Coteril
    Walter 113
Coterill
    Walter 110, 111, 112
Cotesford
    Richard 17
Cotherill
    Walter 112
Cotsford

Rich. 85, 118
Richard 117
Cottalls
   Walter 9
Cottam
   Edward 2, 3, 4, 5, 111, 112
Cotten
   Edw. 100
   Edward 47, 100
Cotterell
   Walter 124, 133, 134, 136, 137
Cotterill
   Walter 124
Cottesford
   Richard 161
Cottham
   Edward 113, 115, 118
Cotton
   (N) 140
   Andrew 15, 80
   Anth. 82
   Anthony 72, 73, 74, 75, 76, 77, 79, 82, 84
   Edward 28, 47, 56, 83, 103, 107, 128, 141, 144, 148
Cottsford
   Richard 85
Coughan
   Lawrence 54
Coullott
   Jacques 192
Coursey
   Henry 25, 27, 29, 31, 32, 36, 39, 41, 42, 43, 45, 47, 49, 50, 54, 55, 56, 57, 59, 60, 61, 66, 175, 197, 201, 202, 203, 205
   John 47, 206
   Mr. 197
   William 42, 46, 47, 206
Court
   Jo. 139
   John 85, 102, 115, 131, 137, 143, 189
Courte
   John 12
Courtis
   John 70, 71, 74
Courtney
   James 15, 70, 74, 84, 142
   William 177
Courts
   John 20, 89, 103, 112, 127, 129, 136, 137, 138, 149, 153, 162
   Margaret 153
Coventrie
   Tho. 1
Cowdrey
   Mr. 49
Cowell
   Ben 34
   Ben. 56
   Benja. 57
   Benjamin 151
   Benjamine 47
Cowper
   Ann 18
   Robert 167
   Walter 18
Cowsene
   Nicolas 137
Cox's Neck 10
Cox
   Ann 123

Francis 115
Hen. 40
Henry 24, 28, 31, 42, 187, 204
James 26, 149
Mr. 56, 106, 107, 114, 118
Mrs. 106, 107, 123
Richard 1, 2, 3, 5, 90, 94, 126, 134
William 10, 69, 105, 106, 107, 121
Coxe
   Elisabeth 107
   Henry 38, 173, 174, 196, 201
   James 149, 157, 158
   John 173
   Mr. 159
   Rich. 94
   Richard 4, 90
   William 72, 84, 85, 107, 115
Crab
   Martha 122
Crabbe
   Mathewe 138
Crabtree
   John 61, 171, 172, 173, 176, 179, 183, 184, 185, 186
Crainey Point 86
Crane
   Robert 18
Cranneg
   Mr. 177
Crawley
   Henry 9, 76, 81, 83, 166, 167
Cromwell
   Oliver 61
Crou
   Mr. 100
Crouch
   George 154
   Mary 154
   Ralph 23, 27, 28, 60, 61, 107
   Raph 52
   Raphe 61, 137, 151, 156, 160, 167, 175
Crouche
   Ralphe 51, 131
   Raphe 151
Crough
   Raphe 131
Cuersyaente
   Crersyen 38
Cugly
   Daniell 141
Cullamore
   Tho. 79, 84
   Thomas 1, 76, 78, 82, 84
Cummins
   Edw. 106
   Edward 105, 106
Cusamazinah
   Andrewe 130
Cuseen
   Nicholas 40
Cuszeen
   Nicholas 30
Cuzeen
   Nicholas 40
Cuzeene
   Nicholas 47

Daines
   Thomas 36, 42

William 36, 42, 61
Damaell
   John 188
   Mary 184
Damghton
   Mary 147
Dammarell
   John 186
   Mary 206
Danbe
   John 31, 32
Danbey
   John 32
Danby
   Ann 174
   Anne 174
   John 58, 62, 174
Danda
   (N) 91
   John 88, 90
Dandey
   Jo. 125
   John 124, 127, 128
Dandie
   John 6, 76, 77, 82, 84, 85, 193, 195
Dandy
   Ann 29, 195, 196, 202
   Anne 177
   Jo. 136, 139
   John 20, 25, 29, 35, 36, 37, 38, 39, 40, 41, 44, 46, 47, 52, 55, 59, 60, 61, 66, 86, 87, 88, 89, 91, 99, 104, 106, 107, 116, 133, 135, 139, 141, 145, 146, 153, 156, 166, 168, 173, 176, 177, 180, 193, 195, 196, 197, 198, 199, 202
Darby
   Francis 63
   John 167
Darcy
   Richard 5
Darsy
   Richard 3
Daved
   Thomas 74
David
   O'Doughorty 135
Davies
   John 70, 71, 173
Davis
   Anne 122
   James 49
   John 58, 71, 192, 194
   Mary 192
   Thomas 48, 170, 189, 190, 195, 201
   William 149
Davison
   Thomas 1, 2, 3, 5
Davy
   Elisabeth 149
Dawking
   Antho. 90
Dawson
   William 75
Dawton
   Richard 174
Day
   Bartholomew 79
   Dorothy 180
   John 50, 179, 193, 196
Daynes
   Mr. 25, 31
   Thomas 25, 26, 27, 29,

    31, 32, 34, 47, 56,
       59, 176
    William 25, 32
de Sousa
    Mathias 82
Deanes
    Thomas 66
Deara
    John 20
Deare
    John 56, 99, 117
Deer
    John 29
Deere
    John 105, 107, 164
Delahay
    John 3, 147
Delahayes
    John 170
Delammonda
    Morrene 38
Demar
    Thomas 12
Demeibilla
    Simon 147
Demibel
    Simon 16
Demibiel
    Simon 82
Denby
    William 194
Denwood
    Levin 39
Derickson
    Jacob 31
    Seabrant 62
    Skyper Jacob 43
Derrick
    Enoch 177
    Mary 6, 17
Derrickson
    Jacob 58, 145, 166, 178
    Seabrant 62
    Sepert 150
    Skipper Jacob 54
Dewall
    Walter 94
Dieufil
    Pierre 191
Dirickson
    Seigar Jacob 43
Dirrickson
    Suppar Jacob 31
Dixon
    Nicholas 187
    Richard 13
    Robert 13, 22, 23
Dixter
    Edward 197
Dobbs
    Thomas 83
Dodington
    Arthur 79
Dodson
    Gervis 49, 57
Doe
    Thomas 7, 14
Dolle
    George 107
Dolt
    George 169
Dolti
    George 144
Dolty
    George 24, 26, 27, 57
Domall
    John 56, 169
Donn
    Hugh 103
Donne

    Hugh 103
Dorrington
    Ann 181, 191, 194
    Mr. 191, 202, 209
    Mrs. 33, 184, 202
    Richard 163
    William 170, 171, 175,
       180, 187, 188, 189,
       190, 193, 196, 202,
       203, 206
Dorrinton
    William 202
Douglas
    John 63, 180
    Robert 20, 61
Dougles
    John 204
Draper
    Peter 2, 7, 13, 85, 105
Drueman
    John 198
Dudlesse
    John 175
Due
    Jo. 47
Duffill
    Thomas 74
Duglas
    John 204
    Robert 45, 53, 120
Duglasse
    Robert 180
Duke's Place 137
Duke
    Richard 2, 4, 5, 21, 78,
       80, 92, 105, 106,
       113, 128, 135, 137,
       138, 141
    Ricnd. 139
Dulany
    D. 151, 209
Dumoid
    John 65
Dunbar 127
Dunbarr 129
Dunne
    Hugh 98
Durand
    Elisabeth 143
    Mr. 176, 208
    William 64, 143, 166,
       169, 171, 172, 173,
       174, 175, 185, 195,
       197, 207
Durant
    William 133, 139
Durford
    Joseph 3, 105
    William 3, 119
Dyneard
    Thomas 66
Dynyard
    Thomas 53, 128, 153

Eale
    William 61
Earle
    John 139
Ebbs
    Edward 4, 123
Ebden
    Katheren 170
    Katherine 171
    Thomas 124, 127
Eddce
    William 61
Edde
    William 39, 129
Eddey

    William 40
Edidis
    William 96
Edie
    William 176
Ediffe
    W. 103
    William 103
Edin
    William 205
Edis
    William 29, 30, 92, 93,
       94
Edisse
    William 101
Edley
    Joseph 160
Edlo
    Joseph 81, 82, 83, 89,
       94
    Joseth 90, 91
Edloe
    Joseph 16
Edlow
    James 70
    Jos. 120
    Joseph 70, 72, 113, 114,
       119, 122, 123, 129,
       138, 166, 197, 198,
       202
Edlowe
    Barnaby 19
    Joseph 19, 20, 139, 144,
       148, 160
Edward
    Robert 2
Edwards
    Isaac 3, 11, 74, 75, 84
    Isack 93
    John 103
    Joseph 66, 159
    Robert 2, 4, 5, 20, 21
Edwin
    Elisabeth 135
    Mary 133, 135
    William 4, 5, 20, 37,
       40, 46, 47, 51, 69,
       76, 77, 93, 96, 97,
       98, 101, 107, 118,
       121, 122, 130, 135,
       140, 143
Edwine
    Mary 40
    Will. 91
    William 40, 46, 49, 69,
       70, 90
Edwn
    William 31
Edwyn
    Mary 52
    William 2, 27, 28, 35,
       51, 52, 54, 62, 168
Egerton
    Mr. 2, 84
    Thomas 83
Eglesfield
    Ann 2
Elkin
    John 2, 4, 5
Ellesmore
    Daniell 59
Elliot
    William 155
Elliott
    John 126
Ellis
    John 49
Elstone
    Thomas 17
Elton

Ann 1
Eltonhead
  (N) 41
  Edw. 63
  Edward 63, 206
  Jane 181, 188, 190, 193,
    198, 199, 200, 205
  Mr. 25, 30, 43, 46, 50,
    53, 62, 65, 67, 163,
    164, 174, 175, 178,
    198
  Mrs. 35, 181, 208
  William 17, 20, 24, 25,
    26, 27, 28, 29, 30,
    33, 35, 36, 37, 38,
    39, 40, 46, 47, 50,
    51, 52, 53, 54, 55,
    56, 60, 66, 122, 127,
    128, 130, 132, 138,
    141, 146, 153, 160,
    161, 163, 164, 165,
    166, 168, 188, 190,
    191, 198, 206
Eltonhed
  William 111
Emmerson
  Thomas 195
Emperor
  Francis 173, 174, 175
Empson
  Mary 199
  William 2, 3, 5, 16, 37,
    38, 39, 51, 155, 199,
    202, 204
Euens
  William 203, 205
Euing
  Rich. 64
Eure
  Mrs. 30, 50, 96, 126,
    146, 168
Evans
  Ann 26
  John 19
  Lt. 31, 99
  Mr. 169
  William 19, 26, 28, 35,
    46, 49, 57, 98, 99,
    102, 103, 114, 115,
    122, 127, 128, 129,
    130, 132, 136, 141,
    146, 148, 152, 153,
    161, 172, 173, 206
Evelin
  Capt. 69, 71, 72, 75,
    77, 83, 105
  Geo. 69, 70, 71
  George 2, 41, 69, 71,
    73, 75, 76, 77, 78
  Monjoy 38, 39
  Robert 16, 70, 71, 78
Evens
  Capt. 183
  William 172, 181
Evins
  William 93, 97
Ewen
  Ann 149
  John 149
  Mr. 191
  Ri. 171
  Rich. 192
  Richard 64, 149, 170,
    171, 207, 208
  Suffa 149
  Susanna 149
  Will. 179
  William 50, 65, 66, 172,
    173, 176, 179, 191,
    193, 207

Ewens
  Mr. 185
  Rich. 196
  Richard 197, 208
  Will. 192, 194, 196, 197
  William 56, 180, 182,
    188, 191, 192, 193,
    195, 198, 199, 200,
    201, 202, 205
Fagel
  Susan 155
Fairefax
  Nicolas 108
Falconer
  Henry 34
Fantleroy
  M. 183
Farera
  David 184, 202, 206
Farmer
  Michael 186
  Rich. 119
Farnham
  Robert 166
Farrea
  David 184, 185
Farrera
  David 185, 186, 187,
    188, 189, 191
Farroll
  Mary 134
Fearny Hill 162
Felton
  John 68, 180, 181, 196
Fendall
  Capt. 194, 199, 208
  Josias 172, 173, 174,
    181, 194, 195, 203,
    208
Fenixe
  Jane 184
Fenwick
  (N) 168
  brother 188
  Cutbeard 10
  Cutberd 12
  Cutbert 12, 15, 16, 18,
    74, 75, 77, 83, 85
  Cutbert. 12
  Cuth. 20, 27, 86, 87,
    88, 90, 97, 98, 99,
    100, 101, 102, 104,
    105, 109, 110, 111,
    112, 113, 116, 117,
    119, 121, 122, 123
  Cuthb. 42, 43, 49, 53,
    54, 55
  Cuthbart 83
  Cuthbert 18, 23, 27, 30,
    35, 36, 37, 38, 39,
    42, 43, 44, 47, 52,
    74, 90, 91, 95, 103,
    105, 107, 108, 109,
    110, 111, 113, 121,
    125, 127, 128, 130,
    133, 134, 135, 138,
    139, 140, 143, 146,
    149, 152, 153, 157,
    167, 168, 173, 178,
    183, 184
  Cuthbt. 57, 58, 59, 60,
    61, 62, 139, 140,
    146, 149, 156, 157,
    159, 163, 165, 166,
    169
  Cutt. 88
  Ignacius 133
  Jane 169, 183, 188, 202,
    204
  Mr. 27, 30, 43, 44, 53,
    55, 59, 63, 83, 85,
    95, 98, 99, 100, 101,
    102, 103, 107, 108,
    109, 110, 118, 119,
    120, 125, 130, 141,
    143, 145, 152, 158,
    178, 183
  Mrs. 32, 146, 169, 178,
    182, 191, 209
  sister 188
  Thomas 133
Fenwicke
  Mr. 43
  Teresa 133
Ferfax
  Mr. 1
  Nicholas 5
Ferfex
  Nicholas 5
Feriner
  Richard 3
Ferrara
  David 185
Fidel
  Sarah 155
Fidler
  Thomas 17, 88
Field
  Mary 122, 142
Finch
  John 16
Firfax
  Nicholas 5
Fisher
  (N) 209
  Edward 89
  Katherine 17
Fitter
  William 12
Fitters
  William 10
Fitzheibet
  Fr. 175
Fitzwalters
  Garrett 17
Fleet
  Capt. 55, 71
  Edward 73
  Edwart 72
  Henry 2, 10, 62, 69
  Rainold 75
Fleete
  Capt. 71, 72, 98
  Edward 70, 71, 72, 73,
    74, 75, 78, 84
  Henry 10, 39, 47, 55,
    62, 69, 70, 71, 72,
    73, 77, 78, 82, 97,
    125
  John 71
  Rainold 73, 74, 75
  Raynold 74
  Reinold 75, 78, 82
Fletcher
  Anne 102
Floyd
  (N) 174
  Rich. 129
  Richard 173
Ford
  Mary 12, 23
  Robert 14, 86
Forrell
  Mary 132, 148
Forrest
  Patrick 61, 148, 191,
    197, 198, 200, 201,
    202

Foster
    Jo. 83
    Rich. 56
    Richard 28, 56, 57, 61, 67, 194
    Urmston 49
Fox
    (N) 66
    Henr. 124, 139, 140
    Henry 28, 30, 31, 38, 44, 45, 46, 47, 52, 53, 54, 55, 58, 59, 61, 62, 63, 64, 122, 124, 128, 136, 138, 153, 165, 168, 170, 176, 177, 178, 179, 191, 205
    Mr. 208
    Mrs. 33
Foxe
    Henry 44, 46, 101, 174, 179
    John 41
Foxery
    William 29
Frame
    Elisabeth 201
Francis
    James 38
Francklin
    Robert 209
    Tho. 62, 70
    Thomas 70, 73, 74, 77, 79, 82
Francklyn
    Thomas 62
Franclin
    Thomas 83, 84
Franklin
    Thomas 1, 71, 76, 82
Freeman
    Brigges 56
    Charles 56
    Elisabeth 56
    Morris 3
    Mr. 145
    Will. 84
    William 78, 145
Freman
    Lewis 17
Fremond
    Lewis 4, 5
Fremonds
    Lewis 2
Fresh Pond Neck 182, 191
Fridd
    John 4
Friendship
    Mr. 33, 181
Frizell
    Susan 170
Froman
    Lewes 125
    Lewis 19, 57, 83, 127, 166
    Morrice 119
Frooman
    Lewis 107
Fulford
    Humphry 154
Fuller
    Capt. 209
    General 197
    William 32, 34, 36, 38, 64, 170, 171, 172, 173, 175, 176, 177, 180, 181, 182, 186, 187, 189, 206, 207
Fullford
    Humphrey 4

Fullwood
    John 78
Furbar
    Richard 196
Furbear
    Richard 195
Fursdon
    Thomas 2
Furston
    Thomas 1

Gale
    Hugh 175
Games
    Richard 39
    Thomas 15, 72, 83, 85
Gant
    Geoffrey 160
    Jeffrey 160
Garbo
    John 98, 112
Gardiner
    Elisabeth 17
    John 17
    Julian 17
    Jullian 17
    Luke 2, 17, 25, 41, 45, 47, 53, 57, 61, 63, 136, 147, 155, 156, 160, 164, 166, 170, 202
    Richard 17
Gardner
    Richard 83
Gardnor
    Luke 181, 182
Gardyner
    Richard 83
Garford
    Richard 184, 186, 187, 188
Garie
    John 28
Garill
    Richard 203
Garner
    Luke 178
Garnett
    Elisabeth 6
    John 6
    Julian 6
    Luke 1, 3, 4, 5
    Richard 1, 6, 70, 71, 72, 75, 76, 77, 80, 83, 84
Garnier
    Elisabeth 188
Garreson
    Phillip 17
Garrill
    Richard 203
Gary
    Elisabeth 189, 195
    Stephen 196, 202
Gassaway
    (N) 209
Gaunt
    Geoffrey 140
    Jeoffrey 122
Gay
    John 3
Geary
    Mr. 44
Geast
    Walter 86
Geathar
    John 35
    Mary 35
Gee

    John 181
Geiries
    Mr. 56
Geiry
    Mr. 56
George
    (N) 77
    Griffin 173, 196, 202
    Joshua 68
Gerard
    Mr. 80, 84, 85, 88, 95, 96, 97, 105, 125
    Tho. 94, 95, 96, 98, 107, 115, 116, 117
    Thomas 46, 77, 80, 81, 82, 83, 84, 87, 92, 93, 94, 95, 96, 97, 98, 101, 102, 106, 111, 115, 117, 121, 122, 126, 127
Gerrad
    Mr. 127
Gerrard's Freehold 6
Gerrard
    Elisabeth 155
    Frances 155
    John 6, 14
    Justinian 155
    Mr. 6, 14, 20, 21, 38, 43, 58, 62, 129, 135, 141, 182, 193, 203
    Richard 4, 73
    Susan 155
    Temperance 155
    Tho. 46, 117, 141, 168
    Thom. 200
    Thomas 2, 5, 6, 8, 12, 14, 15, 16, 17, 18, 25, 28, 29, 37, 38, 39, 42, 43, 44, 46, 47, 52, 53, 55, 56, 57, 61, 126, 132, 135, 141, 155, 165, 167, 168, 176, 201, 203
Gery
    Xopher 163
Gest
    Walter 35, 45, 171
Gibbins
    William 182, 185, 186
Gibbons
    Edward 57
    Oliver 6, 8, 14
Gibbs
    Jonell 155
Gibons
    Edward 51
    Major Edward 53
Gifford
    Ursula 15
Gilbert
    Elisabeth 147
    goodwife 80
    Grace 147
    Richard 13, 69, 147
    Rose 15, 69, 147
Gill
    Benjamin 37, 58, 98, 129, 135, 137, 141, 155, 167, 168, 169, 170, 176, 178, 201
    Benjamine 18
Gillford
    Mary 190, 191, 193
    William 200, 201, 205
Gills Land 137
Gilmot
    Mr. 91
Gilmott

Mr. 91
Gladdus
    Dousbell 9
Glahay
    Arthur 31
    Mary 31
Glantham
    John 69, 81, 83
Glayhay
    Auther 31
    Mary 31
Glover
    Giles 189
Godgrace
    James 178
Godson
    Jane 65
    Mrs. 67
    Peter 64, 65, 66, 169, 170, 171, 172, 174, 176, 191
    Sarah 191
Godwin
    Devereux 4
Golden Quarter 192
Gollding
    George 206
Goneere
    John 106
Good
    Edward 171, 183, 185, 186
Goodicker
    Christopher 193
Goodrick
    Geo. 173
Goodridge
    Timothy 185, 191
Goodwin
    (N) 1
Goodwyn
    Devereux 59
    Devereuxand 17
    Devoreux 55, 62, 147
Gooken
    Daniell 49
Gookins
    Daniell 49
Goore
    John 155
Gordon
    Daniell 170
Gore
    John 20
    Stephen 12
Gosey
    Samuell 197
Gouge
    Henry 193, 195, 196
Gouldsmith
    John 155
    Mr. 192
Goulson
    Daniell 67, 170, 196, 202
    Goodman 202
    Mrs. 65
    Sara 48
    Sarah 47, 48, 65
Gourden
    Robert 140
Gourdon
    Daniell 170
Governor's Field 22
Gowther
    Nathaniell 50
Graft
    Cornelius Cornelinson Van de 150
Grall
    Capt. 91
Gramall
    William 48
Gramer
    John 42, 196
Grammer
    John 47, 48, 67, 175, 180, 187, 204
Grant
    Peter 174
Gray
    Fra. 83
    Francis 15, 17, 20, 21, 22, 23, 60, 70, 71, 72, 73, 74, 75, 76, 78, 80, 83, 84, 85, 86, 89, 90, 98, 102, 125, 154, 155, 156
    John 120
    Stephen 1, 3
Graye
    Francis 15
Greane
    Robert 120
Green's Rest 55
Green
    Francis 19
    Jane 196
    John 180
    Leonard 19
    Mr. 20, 23, 30, 158
    Robert 19
    Tho. 92, 124, 161, 163, 164, 168
    Thomas 4, 5, 17, 19, 21, 26, 29, 31, 61, 70, 72, 118, 143, 150, 196
    Winifred 19
Greene
    Francis 150
    Governor 114
    Jane 181, 182, 197
    John 180
    Leonard 85, 108
    Mr. 58, 71, 72, 73, 74, 75, 77, 91, 127, 145, 150
    Robert 49, 60, 61, 102, 123, 173
    Tho. 23, 82, 83,
    Tho. 86, 87, 88, 89, 95, 96, 98, 103, 105, 107, 108, 113, 114, 118, 119, 120, 122, 133, 136, 137, 140, 141, 146, 150, 153, 157, 158, 160, 161
    Thomas 1, 19, 43, 66, 70, 71, 72, 73, 74, 80, 82, 85, 86, 87, 88, 89, 91, 94, 98, 99, 102, 103, 105, 107, 108, 109, 110, 113, 114, 118, 123, 124, 126, 128, 129, 132, 135, 136, 137, 144, 145, 146, 150, 153, 154, 165, 167, 181, 182
    William 182
Greenehold
    Jo. 154
    John 154
Greenestead
    William 153
Greeneway
    Jo. 153, 160
    John 148, 149, 160, 169
Greenhold
    John 154
Greenold
    John 104, 115, 116
Greenstead
    William 152
Greenway
    John 28, 140
    Mary 28
Greenwell
    John 63, 123, 132
Gregorie
    Thomas 65
Gregory
    (N) 66
    Joseph 120, 130
    Tho. 39
    Thomas 39, 65, 66
Gresham
    Jo. 144
    John 8, 94, 166
Gressam
    John 114
Griffin
    Alce 174
    Alice 47, 169, 178, 179
    Edmond 78
    Frances 16
    Samuel 67, 169
    Samuell 66, 169, 178
Griffine
    Alce 48, 67
    Alice 67
    Samuell 67
Grigson
    Richard 125
    Thomas 5
Grigston
    Thomas 4
Grimesditch
    John 20, 21, 88
Grimsditch
    John 115, 118, 127, 129
Gripwood
    Richard 23
Griysta
    Thomas 2
Groce
    Roger 194, 195
Groome
    Samuell 177
Groves
    Symon 54
Gudridge
    Timothy 182
Guesse
    Elisabeth 4
Guesst
    Elisabeth 1
Guest
    Elisabeth 147
    Rob. 64
    Robert 59
    Walter 19, 52, 89, 135, 140, 147, 149, 155, 165, 171, 180
Gugnis
    Capt. 36
Guise 137
Guither
    Nicholas 3
Guneen
    (N) 208
Gunion
    James 68
Gunnell
    James 198
Gunnion
    James 185, 188
Gunton
    Timothy 178, 179, 185

Gutridge
    Thomas 25
Guttridge
    George 193, 200
    Tim. 184, 186
    Timothy 184, 185, 186,
        187, 199, 201, 205
Guy
    John 3, 137
Guyther
    Mr. 36
    Nicholas 36, 132
Gweast
    Walt. 97
    Walter 86, 101, 102,
        103, 115, 118, 121,
        128
Gwest
    Wal. 101
    Walter 135
Gwider
    Nicholas 182
Gwiter
    Lt. 153
    Nicholas 141, 154
Gwither
    Mary 156
    Nichol. 156
    Nicholas 22, 60, 61, 62,
        63, 142, 146, 147,
        148, 149, 153, 162,
        164, 168, 203, 206
Gwuther
    Nicolas 157
Gwy
    John 120
Gwyter
    Nicholas 142
Gwyther
    John 134
    Mr. 23
    Nic. 120
    Nichol. 139, 140
    Nicholas 24, 26, 27, 31,
        32, 44, 49, 52, 56,
        58, 59, 60, 96, 100,
        103, 116, 117, 128,
        134, 201
    Nicolas 99, 119, 121,
        123, 134

Hach
    Sepharin 203
    Sepherin 203
Hack
    John 90
    Sepharina 195
    Sepharinah 195
Hacker
    Michael 3
Haffhead
    John 197
    Julian 197
Hager
    Robert 18
Haills
    Thomas 150
Hales
    Thomas 9, 23
Halfehead
    John 30, 79, 84, 90
Halfehide
    Jo. 84
    John 73, 74, 75, 76, 84
Halfhead on ye Hill 148
Halfhead
    Anne 144
    Jo. 128, 141, 153
    John 13, 58, 61, 70, 72,
        73, 95, 97, 99, 132,
        144, 145, 148, 150,
        154, 159, 160, 161,
        163, 167, 192
    Julian 144
Halfhide
    John 71
Hall
    Edm. 139
    Edrm. 124
    Edw. 108
    Edward 20, 25, 26, 27,
        32, 36, 37, 40, 41,
        50, 93, 108, 109,
        120, 151, 162, 163,
        164, 165, 166, 174,
        177, 179, 181, 190,
        193, 194
    James 180
    John 149
    Rebecca 39, 42, 67, 68
    Thomas 25
    Walter 38, 40, 50, 193
    William 3
Halley
    Capt. 41
Hallis
    J. 23
Hallowes
    Jo. 17, 23, 164
    John 3, 15, 16, 21, 22,
        23, 26, 39, 44, 46,
        47, 54, 55, 58, 61,
        62, 82, 83, 85, 87,
        93, 95, 96, 97, 98,
        99, 105, 107, 108,
        109, 110, 111, 112,
        114, 115, 116, 118,
        120, 121, 122, 125,
        127, 130, 131, 135,
        136, 139, 142, 145,
        146, 152, 153, 166,
        196
    Mr. 26, 47
    Restituta 22
Hallows
    John 20
Hambleton
    John 47, 54, 55, 59, 66,
        172, 174, 176, 179,
        196, 198
    Mr. 66
    Temperance 174
Hamelton
    John 52
Hames
    James 149
Hamleton
    John 42, 185
Hamlington
    John 155
Hammington
    William 205
Hammon
    Benjamine 32
Hammond
    Ann 187, 188, 192
    Benjamin 17
    John 41, 49, 52, 65, 66
    Mordecue 41
    Mr. 208
Hamon
    Ann 49
Hamond
    Ann 49, 57, 178, 181,
        182, 183, 194
    Bardnard 57
    Bernard 49
    Daniell 49, 57
    John 46, 49, 55, 56, 57,
        59, 62, 67, 170, 182,
        183, 187, 194
    Mordecai 57
    Mordecay 49
    Thomas 170
Hamp
    John 90
Hamper
    Tho. 108, 139, 140, 141
    Thomas 18, 30, 31, 34,
        36, 37, 40, 122, 124,
        125, 127, 164
Hampstead
    William 34, 41
Hampsted
    William 33
Hampton
    John 20, 21, 22, 85, 90,
        91, 94, 95, 98, 110,
        125
Hamstead
    Anne 33
    Mr. 188
    William 33
Hamsted
    William 33
Hamton
    John 21, 22, 89
Hanceford
    John 93
    Mr. 96, 97
Hancock
    Richard 74
Handwich
    William 42
Haniford
    Richard 3
Hanington
    William 49
Hanley
    Robert 63, 151
Hanly
    Robert 152
Hanneford
    Mr. 56
Hansford
    Jo. 139
    John 126, 134, 136
    Mr. 97, 103, 125, 135
    Rich. 136
Hanson
    Andrew 187
Harbett
    William 175
Hardedige
    William 21
Hardestie
    George 202
Hardich
    William 26, 108
Hardidge
    William 119
Hardie
    Thomas 3
    William 49
Hardige
    William 21, 108
Harditch
    William 104, 107, 109,
        110, 111, 112, 128
Hardwich
    William 37, 42, 44, 66,
        126, 139, 144, 146,
        153, 160, 161
Hardwick
    William 18, 44, 53
Hare
    James 20, 126
Harellton
    Raph 35

Harford
  John 65
Harington
  John 83
  Thomas 5
Harloe
  Ann 52
  Stephen 186
Harlow
  Ann 52
Harper
  William 152, 177, 178, 192
Harrington
  Jack 78
  Jo. 12
  John 15
  William 4
Harris
  Ales 55
  John 7, 77, 84, 187
  Mary 50, 192
  Mr. 199, 208
  Rich. 186
  Richard 7, 29, 34, 56, 58, 186, 187, 192, 204
  Roger 154
  Samuell 170
  Tho. 155
  Thomas 61, 155, 165
Harrison
  (N) 132
  Jo. 85
  John 24
  Mary 24, 89, 132
  Thomas 58, 60
  William 55
Harrisse
  Mr. 184
Harrote
  Thomas 89
Harrwood
  John 133
Hart
  John 194
Hartwell
  George 98
Harvey
  Frances 133
  Francis 174
  John 192
  Nic. 98, 117, 121
  Nicholas 46, 71, 86, 88, 89, 90, 95, 133, 138, 167, 197
  Nicolas 113
  Richard 17
Harvie
  Francis 196
  Nicholas 144, 181, 182, 196
Harvy
  Richard 60
Harwich
  William 26, 144
Harwood
  John 20, 83, 85, 88, 107, 149, 195, 199, 205
  Phill. 204
  Phillip 17, 30, 42, 47, 188, 189, 206
  Robert 189, 195, 196, 201, 209
Hasleton
  Ralphe 132
Hatch 144
  Jo. 34, 129, 139
  John 2, 14, 19, 20, 26, 27, 28, 31, 32, 39, 43, 52, 54, 58, 63, 64, 95, 99, 100, 101, 102, 103, 104, 111, 112, 113, 114, 115, 116, 117, 119, 121, 127, 128, 130, 132, 136, 138, 140, 141, 142, 143, 144, 145, 155, 157, 158, 159, 160, 162, 165, 166, 167, 168, 169, 170, 172, 176, 177, 178, 179, 180, 181, 183, 184, 189, 190, 191, 192, 193, 194, 199, 200, 201, 203, 207, 208
  Mr. 157, 158, 179
Hatche
  John 2, 78, 95, 98, 99, 130
Hatchland 162
Hatton
  Barbara 148
  Elinor 57, 148
  Elisabeth 148
  Margarett 134, 148
  Mary 53, 148
  Mr. 17, 26, 31, 40, 54, 67, 130, 132, 138, 142, 179, 198
  Mrs. 54, 191
  Richard 19, 45, 49, 148
  Robert 19, 148
  Tho. 28, 38, 39, 41, 42, 47, 49, 50, 52, 53, 98, 113, 124, 130, 131, 132, 136, 140, 141, 142, 143, 145, 147, 150, 153, 156, 161, 164, 165, 168, 173
  Thomas 18, 19, 20, 23, 24, 25, 26, 29, 30, 31, 33, 34, 35, 36, 37, 39, 40, 41, 42, 43, 44, 45, 46, 47, 49, 50, 51, 52, 53, 54, 56, 57, 58, 59, 60, 63, 64, 124, 126, 129, 132, 134, 143, 145, 148, 149, 152, 153, 156, 157, 160, 162, 167, 168, 191, 197, 198, 200, 202, 207
  William 19, 45, 148
Hauley
  Robert 138
Hausford
  John 23
Havey
  Nicholas 149
Haweley
  William 119, 127
Hawely
  William 119
Hawkines
  Thomas 203
Hawkins
  John 171, 176, 181, 186, 187, 201
  Matthew 17
  Mr. 181
  Thomas 165, 193
  William 13
Hawley
  Capt. 133
  Eleanor 79, 80
  Elinor 177
  Henry 16, 77
  Ja. 16
  James 16, 44
  Jeremy 125
  Jerome 1, 16, 44, 69, 73, 76, 78, 79, 80, 81, 82, 83, 84, 125
  Mr. 72, 77, 78, 79
  William 16, 43, 52, 61, 79, 119, 127, 130, 138, 149, 164
Hawlis
  John 87
Hawly
  Mr. 72
Hay
  Arthur 3
Haylls
  Thomas 150
Hayward
  Tho. 58
Hazelton
  Ralph 53
Hearne
  Thomas 142
Heath
  Thomas 2, 4, 5, 17
Hebborne
  Mary 202
Hebden
  (N) 141
  Katheren 36, 60, 136, 138, 145, 160, 163, 165
  Katherine 26, 179
  Katherne 170
  Kathorne 37, 43
  Mr. 109, 136, 141, 145, 160
  Mrs. 35, 145, 165
  Tho. 79, 82, 100, 104, 120, 145, 163
  Thomas 2, 11, 12, 22, 36, 70, 71, 73, 76, 80, 82, 83, 84, 97, 109, 110, 115, 121, 127, 136, 138, 145, 170, 179, 180
Hebdon
  Capt. 21
Hedger
  Richard 4
  Robert 1, 2, 3, 4, 5, 154
Hele
  Lewis 79
Hempted
  Anne 33
  William 33
Hen
  Edward 23
Henry
  John 42
Henshaw
  (N) 34
  John 163
  Mr. 166
Henshawe
  John 25
Henshome
  Mr. 44
Herde
  William 190
Herne
  Mr. 82
  Thomas 142
Herring
  Bartholomew 66, 171
  Bartholomy 186, 198

Margaret 65, 194
Herringe
    Bartho. 64, 65
    Margaret 65
    Margarett 65
Hervey
    Frances 14
    John 78
    Nicholas 2, 4, 14, 15, 70, 82
Heuett
    Robert 115
Hewett
    Hanna 154
    Hannah 154
    Robert 154
Heyward
    Peter 5, 14, 82, 84
Hiat
    John 174
Hide
    Henry 43
    Phillip 38, 64, 169, 171
Hill
    Capt. 22, 87, 88, 90, 95, 99
    Edw. 86, 87, 95, 98, 121, 140
    Edward 20, 23, 26, 87, 92, 105, 108, 115, 120, 121, 127, 134, 140, 146
    John 2, 4, 5, 17, 73, 77, 79
    Mr. 86
    Rich. 121
    Richard 80, 84, 160
Hillard
    John 109
Hiller
    John 161
Hilles
    Richard 131
Hilliard
    Jo. 17
    John 20, 29, 92, 109, 140
Hillier
    John 72, 134
Hillierd
    Jo. 69, 80
    John 2, 5, 70, 71, 72, 73, 80, 82, 83
Hills
    Richard 4, 13, 21, 129, 165
Hinchman
    Edmond 203
Hine
    Isaack 118
Hinfield
    Capt. 183
Hinman
    John 38
Hinshman
    Edmond 201, 203
Hinson
    Tho. 207
    Thomas 182, 183
    William 17, 190
Hinton
    Clement 184, 185, 186
Hippesty
    Thomas 149
Hitchcocke
    James 50
Hitches
    James 80, 82
Hix
    Richard 206
Hoare
    Daniel 51
    Daniell 56, 57
Hobie
    Richard 23
Hobin
    Rich. 112
    Richard 22
Hobson
    Thomas 192
Hockley
    James 13
Hockly
    James 7
Hodger
    John 171
    Mary 171
Hodges
    Benjamin 4, 5
    Thomas 2
Hodgine
    John 67
Hodgkeys
    Richard 64
Hodgkins
    Richard 25, 34, 37, 38, 40, 163
Hodskeyes
    Richard 169
Hodskeys
    Richard 169
Hodskins
    Richard 40
Hogg
    William 133
Hoggen
    Mary 171
Hoggins
    William 143
Hogpen Neck 162
Holdern
    John 3, 10
Holfhead
    John 108, 109, 113, 116
Holland
    Thomas 178
Hollis
    (N) 91, 193
    Jo. 23, 91
    John 2, 15, 17, 20, 74, 82, 85, 86, 87, 90, 91, 92, 93, 94, 96, 98, 124, 126, 127, 128, 134, 141, 147, 156, 193
    Mr. 21
Hollman
    Abraham 148
Hollois
    Rest. 90
Hollowes
    John 38
Holman's Hope 152
Holman
    Abraham 152, 189, 193
    Abram 193
    William 148
Holmes
    Nicolas 119
    Robert 155
Holt
    Dorothy 24
    Richard 24
    Robert 17, 24, 27, 40, 51, 87, 88, 89, 91, 106, 116, 135, 138, 167
    Thomas 81
Homewood
    James 17, 24
Homond
    John 170
Honyborne
    Robert 142
Hooper
    Hen. 186
    Henery 184
    Henry 2, 3, 5, 18, 20, 21, 34, 52, 54, 60, 61, 62, 66, 86, 104, 184, 185, 186, 187, 188, 197, 201, 204, 205, 206
    Mr. 65, 189, 197
    Mrs. 66, 179
    Robert 17, 62
    Sarah 203
Hopewell
    Hugh 110, 132, 144, 162, 164, 208, 209
    Jane 110
Hopkins
    Robert 183, 194, 203
    Thomas 183, 185
Hopson
    John 76
Hore
    Daniell 53, 64
    Katherine 174
Horney
    Mr. 1
Horsely
    Ralphe 108
Horwood
    John 4, 90
Hoskings
    Richard 67
Hoskins
    (N) 34
    Richard 29, 33, 40, 44, 49, 53, 166
Hostkeys
    Edward 194, 203
    Mr. 208, 209
    Richard 199
Hotchkeyes
    Nich. 59
    Richard 50, 59, 183
Hotchkeys
    Richard 61, 63, 175
Hotchkins
    Richard 38
Hotchkyes
    Richard 46
Hoult
    Goodman 40
Hoults
    Richard 35
Howard
    Hugh 2
    John 3, 106, 107, 115, 116
    Sergt. 78
    Tho. 86
    Thomas 3, 50, 86, 88, 151
Howbyn
    Richard 154
Howell 137
    (N) 168
    Blanch 24, 50, 91, 115, 116, 121
    Elisabeth 175
    Hum. 115
    Humfr. 139
    Humfrey 58, 128, 132, 135, 137, 138
    Humfry 144
    Humphrey 24, 87, 94, 105, 107, 111, 112,

115, 116, 118, 119, 125, 137
Humphry 24, 50, 96, 98, 164
Hunfrey 144
Howerd
John 195
Howes
George 40
Howkins
William 14, 81, 83
Howper
Henry 18
Howse
Ann 201
William 186, 201
Hubersley
Margaret 84
Huddson
Edward 90
Hudson
Ed. 92
Edm. 86
Edmond 86
Edmund 85, 87, 89
Edw. 94, 98, 106, 113, 117
Edward 18, 24, 27, 40, 92, 93, 94, 95, 96, 97, 102, 106, 107, 108, 109, 112, 113, 114, 120, 138, 140, 150, 151, 167
John 166
Thomas 34
Huett
Hannah 81
Robert 8, 81, 86, 156
Huggin's Neck 162
Hughs
William 61
Hull
Austen 155
Edw. 107, 112, 116
Edward 94, 103, 104, 108, 109, 115, 118, 133, 144
Oswin 108
William 14
Hullowes
John 82
Hungerford 137
William 20, 35, 86, 101, 108, 109, 110, 116, 123, 126, 137, 149, 156
Hunley
Robert 190
Hunnington
William 173
Hunt
Edmond 31
Francis 35, 41
Katherine 25
Margaret 35, 41
Nathaniel 34, 36
Nathaniell 18, 34, 150, 151, 168
Hurd
William 170
Husband
Richard 35
Husbands
Mr. 29, 44, 47, 145, 146, 153, 167
Rich. 140, 145, 153
Richard 30, 36, 46, 47, 51, 53, 57, 63, 138, 140, 143, 144, 145, 146, 148, 153

Ricnd. 139
Huse
William 202
Hussey
Thomas 180
Hutford
Humphrey 17
Hutton
John 103
Hyatt
John 201
Hyde
Phillip 26, 65, 66, 67, 187, 188, 190
Hyell
Julian 186, 196
Hyll
Robert 188
Hynson
Thomas 49

Ichcombe Freehold 87
Iger
Thomas 174
Ilive
Isaac 144
Isaack 41
Iluice
Isaac 20
Isack 66
Indian Quarter 129
Indian Quarters 97, 120
Indian
Anarsine 108
Couna-weza 49
Marks 111
Mohotanco 108
Moyke 111
Skigh-tam-mongh 49
Takanine 108
Tauarine 108
Warcope the Emperor 49
Indians
Anarsine 108
Couna-weza 49
Mohotanco 108
Moyke 111
Takanine 108
Ingle
Capt. 38, 102
Mr. 95, 97, 142
Rich. 101, 103, 113
Richard 23, 38, 39, 42, 44, 55, 58, 60, 114, 117, 134, 142, 149, 206
Innes
Thomas 19, 202
Ireland
William 193
Isham
Roger 46, 203

Jackson
Bar. 100, 101, 108, 109
Barn. 94, 109
Barnab 98
Barnaba 182
Barnaby 2, 19, 38, 46, 57, 59, 66, 95, 96, 98, 99, 101, 103, 105, 110, 111, 114, 115, 121, 123, 132, 136, 138, 141, 147, 148, 150, 153, 156, 160, 163, 167, 168, 170, 182, 191
Barneby 22

John 74
Tho. 22, 95, 100, 103, 119, 121
Thomas 22, 28, 88, 94, 95, 98, 99, 116, 117
Jacobsen
Aron 187
Hans 58
Jacobson
Aron 194, 198, 199, 203, 205, 206
Jacopson
Cleres 138
Jacus
Edm. 119
James
Cartwright 69
Henrie 69
Henry 4, 5, 20, 69, 70, 74, 83
Odoan 107
Owen 25, 43, 108, 117, 118, 119, 120, 121, 144, 152, 155, 162, 168, 172, 203, 205
Tho. 60
Thomas 15, 52
Jarbo
(N) 25
Jo. 91
John 20, 24, 36, 57, 61, 99, 112, 122, 123, 127, 128, 129, 130, 132, 134, 148, 170, 173, 179, 192, 195, 206
Mary 192
Jarboe
John 67
Jarvis
Fr. 140
Francis 125, 129, 130, 143
Jarvise
Francis 129
Jay
Temperance 41, 161
Jelfe
James 7
Jenery
Thomas 139
Jenkins
John 200
Jenman
Abraham 17
Jennings
Mary 2, 17
Jerbo
John 93
Jermogan
Thomas 1
Jermogangout
Ellen 1
Mary 1
Jerry
Robert 50
Joanes
Nat. 97, 109
Nath. 110
Walt. 85
Walter 85
Johnson
Abraham 26, 27, 120, 127, 128, 130, 138, 144, 165
Allbert 203, 205, 206
Ann 47, 48, 176
Barbara 19, 203
Capt. 176, 186, 188
Cornelius 66, 173, 174,

202, 205
 Cornelius A 66
 Fred 142
 Hugh 198
 Ja. 21
 Jacobu 124
 James 9, 13, 19, 20, 25,
  88, 89, 91, 97, 102,
  112, 126, 127, 128,
  132, 138, 139, 142,
  166, 169, 208
 John 51, 63
 Martin 115
 Mr. 66, 208
 Mrs. 48, 176
 Peter 43, 47, 48, 55,
  66, 169, 170, 171,
  172, 174, 175, 176,
  185, 186, 187, 189,
  193
 Tho. 110
 Thomas 24
 Will. 179, 181, 192
 William 3, 17, 19, 25,
  27, 32, 46, 47, 49,
  52, 60, 61, 62, 63,
  86, 149, 155, 164,
  165, 166, 173, 174,
  177, 178, 181, 194
Jolley
 Elisabeth 184
 James 185
Jolly
 Elisabeth 184
 James 178, 179, 180,
  184, 191, 202, 205
Jones
 Ellen 142
 John 2, 6, 82
 Mary 35, 41
 Nath. 20
 Nathan: 109
 Nathaniell 155
 Rice 201
 Richard 107, 110
 Ro. 45
 Robert 44, 45, 50, 53
 Tho. 105
 William 17, 30, 35, 40,
  44, 78, 114, 117,
  155, 164, 203
Jonnes
 William 179
Jonson
 Abraham 135, 136
 Peter 185
Jordan
 Mr. 185, 199
 Tho. 180, 200
 Thomas 201, 205, 206
Jordon
 Thomas 177
Joy
 Peter 66, 67, 169, 184,
  196
Joyce
 Thomas 17
Joye
 Margaret 149
Joyner
 Robert 200
Junes
 Tho. 129

Kadger
 Robert 25, 89, 92, 125,
  127, 140, 151, 152,
  166, 167
 Thomas 152

Kager
 Robert 90, 91
Kain
 Thomas 106
Kale
 John 52
Kanery
 Richard 171
Katchman
 Henry 173
Kathman
 Henry 173
Keane
 Thomas 2
Keanie
 Henry 174
Keating
 Nicholas 35
 Nicolas 50
Keaton
 Andrew 67
Kedger
 Robert 2, 20, 21, 29,
  37, 85, 87, 92, 94,
  99, 105, 112, 119,
  120, 121, 122, 124,
  128, 135, 149, 165
Keeeting
 Nichol. 153
Keen
 Edward 185
 Henry 184, 185, 187, 209
 Richard 192
Keene
 Capt. 209
 Edward 175, 178, 179,
  185, 198, 204
 Hen. 198
 Henry 175, 177, 178,
  179, 180, 181, 198,
  204, 206
 Richard 179, 192, 196
 Thomas 116
Keeten
 Nicholas 124, 126
 Nicolas 126
Keeting
 Nichas 28
 Nichol. 153
 Nicholas 26, 27, 53, 60,
  62, 64, 143, 153,
  163, 164
Keine
 Thomas 83
Kekeape
 John 108
Kelley
 Bryan 8, 16
Kelly
 Bryan 72
 John 3
Kemp
 Jo. 23
 John 22, 87
Kempe
 Rich. 146
 William 201
Kente
 Henry 189
Ketchmay
 George 47, 58, 59
 Henry 47, 59
 Mary 47
Ketchmey
 George 59
 Henry 55
Ketin
 Nic. 104
 Nicholas 91
Key

 Peter 192
Keylin
 Nicholas 22
Keyne
 Tho. 83
 Thomas 8
Keyten
 Nicholas 129
 Nicolas 129
Keytin
 Nic. 123
 Nicholas 14
 Nicolas 120
Keyting
 Nicholas 93, 129
Kidd
 Thomas 81
Killey
 John 64
Killy
 John 64
King
 Alexander 192
 John 149, 154
 Marke 17
 Mary 192
 Walter 1, 2, 3, 4, 5,
  85, 106
 William 12
Kingsberry
 Robert 186, 192
Kingsborough
 Robert 205
 Samuell 205
Kingsbury
 Robert 184
Kingwell
 Tho. 91
 Thomas 99
Kirk
 Ales 30
 John 27
 Martin 27, 30, 35, 41,
  160, 165
Kirke
 John 27
 Martin 27, 30, 41, 50,
  53, 67, 68, 164, 174,
  179, 180
 Marty 168
 Martyn 67
 Mary 67, 68, 174
Kitchin
 Anthony 17, 30, 43
Kitteridge
 Rebecca 148
Kline
 Andrewe 136
Knap
 John 177, 178, 179, 184,
  185, 187, 199
 Mr. 185
Knape
 John 196, 199
Knapp
 John 169, 176
Knight
 Mr. 117, 141
 Peter 88, 107, 109, 110,
  113, 117
 Robert 18, 143
 Tho. 22, 82
 Thom. 97
 Thomas 5, 14, 21
Knipe
 William 4
Knoles
 John 2
 Thomas 202
Knolls

Page 227

John 1, 4
Knott
   James 39, 41
   John 120, 130, 155
Knowles
   Ann 155

La Hay
   Arthur 108
Lake
   Robert 69, 74, 81, 167
Lambe
   William 18
Lancelot
   John 106
Lancelott
   John 125
Lanclott
   John 141
Land
   Mr. 31, 37, 158, 160, 168
   Phillip 20, 24, 26, 27, 28, 29, 30, 31, 32, 38, 40, 45, 46, 47, 49, 51, 52, 53, 54, 55, 56, 60, 61, 62, 63, 104, 105, 107, 108, 112, 115, 118, 120, 122, 124, 126, 127, 130, 135, 136, 139, 140, 141, 142, 144, 145, 146, 147, 149, 151, 153, 154, 157, 158, 159, 165, 166, 168, 169, 170, 171, 173, 174, 175, 180, 191, 193, 198, 205
Landesdesdale
   Peter 54
Langdell
   Mr. 39
   Peter 39
Langfield
   Francis 28
   John 28
Langford
   Edward 120, 149
   John 16, 20, 71, 72
   Mr. 71
Langley
   Robert 182
Langsdale
   Peter 51
Langsford
   Goody 94
Langton
   Edward 122
Langworth
   Ja. 154
   James 12, 19, 20, 22, 25, 28, 49, 61, 63, 95, 113, 116, 132, 133, 134, 148, 153, 154, 173, 176, 177, 178, 180, 181, 182, 185
   John 82
Lant
   William 106, 107, 117, 118, 167
Laramor
   John 197
Latchford 138
Lavger
   John 9
Lawes
   Mr. 82

Lawne
   Mary 1, 4, 15
Lawrel
   William 204
Lawrell
   William 204
Lawrence
   Henr. 103
   Richard 143, 170, 198
Lawson
   Darcos 203
   J. 209
   John 18, 28, 32, 34, 47, 49, 60, 66, 169, 170, 171, 183, 188, 189, 191, 192, 193, 194, 196, 199, 200, 201, 202, 205, 207, 208, 209
   Mr. 64, 170, 190, 205
Leatherborow
   Thomas 13
LeCompte
   Anthony 188, 209
Lee
   Elisabeth 203
   Hanna 154
   Hannah 154
   Henry 2, 3, 11, 14, 70, 92, 107, 136, 166
   Hugh 42, 46, 128, 136, 141, 142, 145, 150, 154
   John 9, 102
   Mary 63
   Mr. 84
   Richard 2, 12, 80, 82, 84
Leech
   Thomas 167
Leefe
   Mary 1
Lehay
   Arthur 54
Leigh
   James 17
   Thomas 17
Lemmin
   Edm. 85
Lemond
   Edmond 184
Lendesey
   James 140
Lendshy
   James 60, 86
Lenin
   Edmond 107
Lennin
   Edm. 118
   Edmund 85, 110
Leo
   Valerius 187
Leonard
   Edward 93
Leonardson
   Leonard 83
Letchworth
   Thomas 204
Letherborow
   Thomas 7
Letton 162
   Joseph 153
Leveson
   Epaphroditus 40
Lewellin
   Robert 138
Lewes
   William 39, 41, 61, 89, 96
Lewgar

John 1
Lewger
   Ann 2
   Jo. 2, 21
   John 1, 2, 3, 4, 5, 6, 7, 10, 11, 13, 14, 16, 25, 28, 42, 49, 67, 69, 70, 71, 72, 73, 74, 76, 77, 78, 79, 80, 81, 82, 84, 87, 100, 101, 102, 107, 109, 110, 112, 120, 123, 132, 133, 148, 167, 168, 182, 193, 194
   Mr. 6, 7, 20, 71, 72, 76, 78, 82, 84, 85, 91, 108, 109, 110, 112, 115, 125, 138, 147, 167
   Secretary 149
Lewis
   Barth. 20
   Lt. 53, 105
   Mr. 88, 96, 97
   Thomas 3, 21, 180
   Will. 84
   William 5, 7, 15, 18, 21, 27, 32, 34, 35, 37, 40, 44, 45, 53, 57, 59, 61, 70, 71, 72, 74, 75, 76, 78, 82, 83, 85, 88, 91, 92, 95, 96, 97, 98, 100, 102, 105, 107, 108, 111, 112, 120, 127, 128, 132, 135, 136, 137, 140, 141, 145, 147, 152, 153, 159, 160, 161, 170, 193, 200
Libar
   Peter 180
Lightfoot
   John 183
Lightfoote
   John 189
Lilly
   Henry 193
Linch
   James 15
Lindesey
   Edmond 25, 58, 59
   James 27, 54, 58, 88, 148, 149, 153, 166, 168
Lindsey
   Edmond 57
   Edmund 29, 180
   Edward 174
   James 19, 86, 102, 119, 123, 132, 139, 140, 145, 154, 206
Linnen
   Edmond 2
Linnie
   Phillip 2
Linnis
   Phillip 1
Linsey
   Edmond 202
   James 40, 42, 86, 91, 176, 178, 193, 201
Lisle
   Thomas 30
Little Brittain 115
Little Thickett 10
Little
   Bassill 176, 177, 184, 185, 199, 200, 201,

203, 204
John 173, 184, 186, 187, 188, 194, 195, 198, 199, 203
Mary 198, 199
Mr. 176
ould 195

Littleton
Col. 38
Esq. 32
Nathaniel 35
Nathaniell 44

Livesey
Marke 27

Lloyd
Cornelius 34, 61
Ed. 192, 193, 194, 196
Edward 17, 28, 32, 34, 36, 38, 64, 166, 170, 171, 172, 180, 181, 182, 186, 187, 194, 196, 197, 207
Francis 34
Richard 25, 60, 141, 193, 205

Loader
William 142

Loe
Raphe 168
Richard 13, 74, 75, 82

Lomax
Thomas 204

Lone
John 56

Long Neck 162

Long
Joseph 143
Mary 175
William 58

Longworth
James 24
John 5, 14, 21

Lord
John 187, 194, 205
Rich. 120
Robert 50

Losey
John 173

Loul
John 182

Lovesay
Marke 17

Lowe
Mr. 23
Ralphe 155
Raphe 159, 168
Richard 10, 75

Loyd
Cornelius 25

Lucas
Mich. 10
William 59, 63, 200

Lucye
Mark 65

Luddington
William 16

Ludford
Arthur 138, 197

Ludlo
Esq. 31

Ludlow
Mr. 167

Lugar
John 169

Lugg
Thomas 167

Lumbard
Fran. 85, 105, 107
Francis 19, 35, 41, 85, 106, 114, 150, 164

Lumber
Fran. 198

Lumbrozo
Jacob 191, 200, 201, 205

Lums
Michael 83, 85

Lund
Thomas 67

Lusted
Richard 17

Lusthead
Richard 2, 3, 70, 71, 72, 80, 81, 82, 83

Lustick
Richard 17

Luthead
Richard 4, 5

Mace
Cloves 47, 60, 61, 62, 124
Rowland 3, 93, 132, 155

Macfenin
William 16

Macfenine
William 119

Macham
John 154

Machens Neck 162

Machin
John 2, 3, 4, 5, 81, 83
Peter 199

Mackall
George 18

Mackarel
Peter 145, 160

Mackarell
Peter 112, 118, 127, 128, 141, 145

Mackarill
Peter 97

Mackerell
Peter 115, 120, 122, 124, 127

Mackewell
Peter 92

Mackey
Robert 201

Mackin
John 1

Macklin
Robert 200

Macklyn
Robert 59

Maclaughlin
William 119

Maclawghlin
William 93

Maddocks
Ann 205
Rice 202
Richard 193

Maddookes
Rice 196

Maes
Rowland 146

Magnett
Charles 1

Magrudder
Alexander 171, 173

Maidwell
Tho. 146, 156
Thomas 24, 26, 27, 28, 29, 156

Makaill
Peter 94

Makarell
Peter 125

Makerell
Peter 95, 127

Makey
Robert 199, 200, 204

Makinney
John 200

Malham
Jo. 124
John 85, 106, 142, 153, 160, 161

Mallham
John 116, 119

Mallot
Cyprian 21

Malum
John 200

Manchester
W. 1

Manestry
Fran. 38

Manfeeld
John 37

Maning
John 56

Manners
G. 104, 109
Geo. 42, 95, 116, 124, 136, 141, 157, 163
George 17, 18, 20, 24, 25, 26, 27, 28, 30, 32, 33, 35, 37, 39, 92, 93, 94, 95, 96, 98, 99, 101, 102, 103, 105, 107, 108, 109, 110, 111, 112, 113, 115, 116, 119, 120, 121, 122, 123, 124, 125, 126, 127, 128, 129, 130, 133, 134, 135, 136, 139, 140, 141, 142, 143, 145, 146, 147, 151, 152, 153, 157, 159, 160, 161, 162, 163, 164, 165, 166, 167, 168, 176, 177, 179, 181, 190
Mr. 158, 179
Rebecca 20, 24, 25, 26, 27, 28
widow 26, 27
William 122

Manning
Joseph 25, 42, 46, 47, 58
Mr. 169

Mannor of Eltonhead 130
Mannor of Evelinton 78
Mannor of Kent Fort 12
Mannor of Snow Hill 12, 206
Mannor of St. Helen 177
Mannor of St. Jerome 177
Mannor of St. John's 168
Mannor of West St. Maries' 10, 97

Mannors
George 85

Mannsfield
John 28

Manor of Kent Fort 5
Manor of Little Brittain 7
Manor of Snow Hill 6
Manor of St. Richard's 6

Mansell
Jo. 21
John 7, 20, 22, 61, 112, 151

Mansfield
John 32

Manship
Elisabeth 64, 65, 186

Rich. 65
Richard 64, 65, 186, 188
Manyard
    Charles 37
Markeen
    Thomas 190
Marlburgh
    John 4, 5
Marle
    William 183
Marrow
    Andrew 83, 89, 90, 104, 105
Marsh
    Margaret 143
    Mr. 187, 198
    Mrs. 200
    Sarah 187, 194, 198
    Tho. 28, 57, 171, 173
    Thomas 17, 34, 36, 41, 143, 166, 170, 171, 173, 187, 194, 198, 201, 203
Marshall
    Agnes 98
    Ann 17
    Katherine 180
    Lawrence 98
    Richard 98, 103
    William 3, 23, 24, 29, 30, 31, 36, 37, 43, 45, 52, 53, 59, 63, 85, 96, 97, 100, 103, 107, 109, 110, 115, 133, 134, 139, 142, 145, 160, 164, 165, 171, 175, 180, 189, 190, 191, 204
Martin
    Abdele 199
    Abdelo 199
    Abdeloe 175
    Christopher 16, 70, 71, 73, 74, 76, 78, 84
    Frances 159
    Francis 16, 34, 35, 56, 143, 159, 163
    John 61
    Lodowick 34
    Lodowicke 159
    Mary 106
    Robert 164
    William 34, 159
    Xpfer 78
    Xpher 81, 82
    Xpofer 3, 77, 83, 85
Martine
    Francis 36
Martinson
    Francis 159
Martyn
    John 59
Math.
    Tho˜ 100
Mathew
    Thomas 1, 58
    Tobias 191
Mathewes
    Hanah 118
    Mr. 158, 182
    Tho. 120, 158
    Thomas 40, 59, 106, 113, 117, 131, 132, 137, 154, 157
Mathews
    Edward 58
    Hannah 118
    Mr. 157, 158
    Tho. 47, 104, 115, 157, 161

Thomas 37, 50, 56, 57, 64, 86, 104, 105, 108, 115, 157, 166, 172
Mattax Neck 8
Matthew
    Thomas 2
Matthews
    Edward 3
    Mr. 29
    Thomas 3, 4, 5, 29, 34
Maunsell
    Jo. 37, 124
    John 39, 40, 112, 113, 118, 119, 120, 121, 127, 130, 134, 135, 142, 143, 147, 150, 165
Maurice
    Thomas 71, 72, 74, 78, 82
May
    Thomas 139
    Will. 169
Maynard
    Charles 28, 29, 37, 46, 88, 97, 98, 135, 148, 152, 165
Mayne
    Job 22
Maynor
    Ann 66
Maynord
    Charles 88
Mayrobe
    Alexander 188
Maze
    Cladrueny 182
    Rowland 20
McCrawleley
    Michael 129
Me
    George 180, 181
Meantys
    T. 1
Meares
    Tho. 171
    Thomas 17, 170, 171
    William 183
Mears
    Tho. 28
Meautys
    T. 112
Medcalf
    (N) 174
    John 18, 24, 170
    William 2, 8, 9, 84
Medcalfe
    John 28, 70, 71, 78, 89
    Mr. 198
Medlap
    Henry 36
Medle
    John 175
Medley 13
    Goodman 54
    Henry 53
    Jo. 21, 140
    John 3, 13, 23, 26, 28, 37, 43, 45, 49, 53, 54, 59, 60, 61, 70, 73, 74, 77, 80, 84, 97, 99, 100, 101, 103, 112, 115, 134, 135, 140, 144 147, 148, 149, 155, 157, 158, 159, 167, 169, 175
    Mr. 158
Medly

John 93, 95
Medwell
    Tho. 35
    Thomas 31
Mee
    (N) 25
    Geo. 42, 176, 179
    Georg 53
    George 19, 25, 26, 27, 31, 37, 39, 40, 47, 61, 181, 182
    Mr. 39
Meeres
    Tho. 171, 177, 187
    Thomas 171, 172, 176, 177
Meers
    Thomas 175
Mees
    George 173
    Henry 173
Meese
    Henry 63, 199, 200, 203, 204
    Mr. 66, 187
Mego
    William 58
Meines
    James 170
Mellegin
    Pratrick 68
Memois
    James 170
Meredith
    George 60
    John 25, 27
    Thomas 152
Merriday
    John 23
    Thomas 153
Merryman
    James 17
Merson Freehold 9
Merthe
    John 185
Metcalf
    Gilbert 3
    John 26, 31, 63, 161, 166, 167
Metcalfe
    John 31, 38, 45, 47, 49, 50, 53, 57, 59, 86, 92, 103, 132, 182
    Mr. 58
Methin
    Thomas 39
Mettcalfe
    John 116, 177
Michell
    Capt. 40
    John 14
    Thomas 137, 138, 156, 190
Middleton
    Charles 13
    Sarah 195
Midleton
    Sarah 195
Milam
    John 173, 174
Miles
    John 62, 182
    Nicholas 62
    Peter 62
    Robert 87
    Thomas 195
Mill
    Will. 204
    William 188
Miller

Tho. 59
Milligan
   Patrick 201
Mills
   Daniell 199
   John 51
   Peter 192
   William 172
Minor
   Charles 135
Mishell
   John 119
Mitchell 137
   Capt. 29, 31, 32, 33, 35, 40, 44, 46, 54, 63, 176, 177, 178, 179, 181, 182, 186, 193, 203
   Joane 32, 34
   Mr. 166
   Mrs. 33, 40
   Thomas 20, 135, 193
   Will. 182, 188
   William 18, 25, 27, 29, 30, 31, 32, 33, 34, 35, 36, 37, 38, 40, 41, 42, 43, 44, 46, 47, 50, 54, 55, 61, 62, 63, 163, 164, 165, 166, 167, 168, 175, 177, 178, 181, 182, 183, 184, 185, 188, 190, 194, 200, 201, 202, 203, 206
Mitchells
   William 199
Modly
   John 22
Moffett
   William 171, 187, 198
Molita
   Fra. 17
Mollock
   Lawrence 84
Monroe
   Andrew 58, 127, 149
Moor
   Richard 59
Moore
   Henry 154, 161, 189
   Jane 64
   Rich. 65
   Richard 54, 64, 174, 176, 201, 202
   Roger 64
   Tho. 89
   Thomas 89
   Timothy 64
Moosley
   Henry 108
More
   Henry 147
   Richard 59
Moreland
   Christopher 6
   Xpher 82
   Xpofer 2, 84
Moreman
   Alice 1, 15
Morgan
   (N) 2
   Frances 1
   Francis 26
   Hen. 107
   Henry 10, 18, 49, 106, 107, 109, 114, 116, 118, 122, 123, 164
   Hoell 2
   Mr. 181, 185, 190
   Phill. 192, 199

Phillip 169, 179, 187, 188, 189, 192
   Roger 3
   Rowland 82, 132
Morgin
   Capt. 193
   Phill. 199, 200, 204
   Phillip 179, 181, 197, 198, 205, 208
Morgon
   Henry 36
Morland
   Christopher 82
Morley
   Daniel 176, 180
   Daniell 176, 177, 178, 180
   Walter 5
Morly
   Mr. 1
Morphew
   James 39, 119
Morris
   Mr. 200, 203, 204
   Richard 133
   Robert 199, 200, 203, 204
   Tho. 85
   Thomas 6, 14, 15, 16, 72, 74, 76, 84
Morrison
   Thomas 70, 71
Morth
   John 175
Morys
   Tho. 72
Moseley
   Henry 88, 111
Mosely
   Henry 112
Moss
   Thomas 21
Mosse
   Thomas 4
Motham
   Thomas 19
Motram
   Mr. 30
Mott
   John 21
Mottershead
   Zachary 71, 73, 74, 76, 79
Mottram
   Jo. 150
   John 21
   Mr. 30, 167, 168
Mottrom
   John 50, 115, 116
   Mr. 140
Moulins
   James 2, 13, 82
Moulson
   Edward 22
Mounkes
   Edward 41
Mountague
   Abigael 17
Moy
   Anne 15
   Robert 73
   Roger 15, 69, 70, 72, 73, 82
Mt. Sinai 162
Muffett
   William 186, 196, 198
Mullekin
   James 205
Mulligan
   Patrick 185, 188

Mullock
   Lawrence 83
Munday
   Goodman 150
   Goody 94
   Tho. 96, 97, 106, 113
   Thomas 85, 87, 92, 93, 94, 96, 97, 105, 106, 107, 109
Munnes
   Thomas 148
Munns
   Thomas 4, 5, 30
Munrowe
   Andrew 128
Muns
   Thomas 40
Murice
   Thomas 78
Myles
   Margaret 194

Nabbes
   Thomas 115
Nabbs
   Mary 7
   Thomas 70, 71, 73, 74
   William 2
Nanfin
   William 11, 80, 84
Nash
   Hugh 2
Neale
   Agnes 17
   James 11, 12, 18, 23, 58, 78, 84, 87, 90, 92, 98, 100, 129, 137, 168, 179
   John 69
   Mr. 37, 93, 98, 125, 135, 136, 138, 141, 152, 153, 156
Negroes
   Phillis 119
Nevell
   John 31, 91, 92, 114, 115, 121
   Richard 4
Nevett
   (N) 20
   Rich. 115, 147
   Richard 3, 13, 22, 23, 90, 91, 96, 108, 118, 127, 128, 129, 151, 152, 153, 161, 164, 165, 167, 189, 193, 202
   Richard Richard 124
   Ricnd. 139
Nevill
   John 13, 20, 23, 28, 74, 75, 90, 135, 148, 179, 181, 182, 183, 190, 191, 193, 196, 197, 198, 199
   Richard 2, 5, 7, 13, 82
Nevitt
   John 32
   Rich 21
   Richard 25
Newchan
   Robert 19
Newchant
   Robert 19
Newgent
   William 37, 154, 161, 162, 168
Newington 148
Newman

George 65, 177, 196, 209
Robert 55
Nicholas
   John 37
Nicholes
   John 50
Nicholls
   Jo. 125
   John 19, 25, 26, 27, 29, 31, 36, 47, 49, 53, 57, 58, 140
   Robert 16, 69, 70, 73, 77, 83
Nichols
   John 31
Norman
   Agnus 178
   John 20, 32, 57, 62, 76, 85, 92, 94, 96, 97, 98, 115, 133, 155, 178, 182
   Mary 133
Norris
   Ann 2, 82, 84
Norrise
   Anne 123
Norten
   John 3
Norton
   Elisabeth 180, 202
   Goodman 202
   Goodwife 202
   Jo. 85
   John 70, 78, 83, 175, 192, 202, 203
   Mr. 179
   Richard 197
   Tobias 194, 195, 197, 198, 201, 203, 205, 206
Norwood
   John 173, 174, 185, 195, 206
   Mr. 209
Nott
   John 2
Nottingham
   Richard 49
Nugent
   Robert 59
   William 34, 56, 58, 59, 61, 169, 179
Nun
   (N) 45
   John 45, 91
Nunn
   John 18, 23, 44, 45, 47, 53, 121
Nunne
   John 22, 25, 28, 30, 42, 44, 45, 96, 115, 122, 124, 127, 129, 139
Nutbrowne
   Margaret 123

O'Doughorty
   David 27, 141
Obert
   Barkram 134
   Bartholomew 148
   Mousser 100
Obesto
   William 61
Odcroft
   Davie 70
Odeom
   William 197
Odger
   Gabriell 164

Odgers
   Gabriel 120, 136, 141
   Gabriell 93, 141
Odoughorty
   David 37
Oliver
   Blan. 89
   Blanch 21, 22, 23, 24, 89, 90, 96, 110, 111, 113, 116, 121
   Geoffrey 117
   Geoffry 34
   Jeffrey 151
   Jeffry 47
   Jeoffrey 89, 123, 124, 129
   Nich. 195
   Nicholas 194, 196
   Roger 7, 24, 71, 82, 89, 90, 132, 168
   Tho. 98, 143
   Thomas 4, 100, 114
   William 24, 89, 132
Ome
   Robert 189
Onley
   Thomas 4
Orchard
   Nathaniel 2
Orley
   Rebecca 190
   Tho. 181
   Thomas 2, 174, 176, 177, 179, 181, 182, 183, 184, 190
Ormesby
   John 77
Orms
   John 16
Osbaston
   William 36, 61
Osborne
   Henry 181, 185, 189, 196, 201, 204
   Mrs. 48
Osbourne
   Mr. 191
OSulivt.
   Cornelius 16
Oversea
   Symon 49, 52
Oversee
   Symon 205
Oversey
   Symon 52, 55, 63
Overzee
   Simon 205
   Symon 180, 183
Owen
   William 185
Ozier
   Gabriel 129
   Gabriell 125

Pack
   William 138
Packe
   Edward 20
Packer
   Edw. 94, 95, 100, 121
   Edward 11, 21, 22, 23, 31, 36, 39, 46, 47, 49, 51, 53, 55, 56, 57, 58, 59, 60, 62, 63, 84, 85, 86, 89, 90, 93, 95, 97, 98, 99, 101, 102, 104, 105, 111, 112, 113, 120, 122, 133, 156, 165, 173
Packes
   Walter 37
Packman
   Henry 139
Paid
   Leonard 177
Paine
   Florentine 78
   Thomas 60
Painter
   Andrew 27, 61
Pake
   Walter 178, 179, 180, 182, 183
Pakes
   Francis 180
   Peter 57, 134
   Walt. 98
   Walter 18, 19, 20, 21, 25, 28, 34, 35, 37, 47, 49, 52, 54, 55, 56, 57, 59, 62, 94, 98, 124, 129, 130, 134, 139, 140, 142, 147, 148, 150, 161, 165, 167, 178, 180, 181, 183
   Walter. 52
   Waltern 139
   William 41
Palldin
   Jane 202, 203
Palmer
   John 106, 116, 118
   William 3, 136
Parfitt
   William 45
Parker
   Edward 10, 63, 80
   Samuel 62
   Samuell 170, 190, 194, 200
   William 66, 167, 172, 183, 184, 187, 192, 193, 207, 208
Parks
   Edward 200
   Mr. 201
Parnell
   Henry 173
Parr
   Mr. 208
   Mrs. 178
   Robert 198
Parratt
   Mr. 205
   Will. 192, 196
   William 186, 187, 189, 190, 192, 193, 194, 197, 199, 200, 201, 202, 203, 205
Parrea
   David 184
Parrett
   William 176, 177
Parrie
   Edmond 2, 71, 72
   Edward 72
Parrott
   Mr. 179
   William 66, 178, 182, 183, 208
Parry
   Edmond 72
   Edmund 89
   Elisabeth 24
   Mr. 83, 85
   William 76
Pascho

John 144
Pasmore
   Mr. 19, 80, 85, 88, 147
   Tho. 77, 84, 122, 163
   Thomas 1, 3, 7, 8, 16, 19, 69, 70, 72, 77, 78, 84, 88, 111, 114, 125, 129, 136, 142, 143, 144, 159
Patee
   Hubert 184, 186, 189
Pattee
   Hubert 185
Patterson
   Robert 206
Patty
   Hubart 59
Paty
   Hubart 59
Pauhampton
   Nicholas 89
Pauldin
   Jane 192
Paulet
   John 88
Paulett
   John 20, 90
Paulhampton
   Nich. 138
   Nicolas 138
Paulus
   Deborah 16
Payd
   Leo. 180
Payne
   Mr. 97
   Tho. 114, 165
Paynter
   Andrew 188
Paytres
   Francis 108
Peake
   Fran. 198
   George 198, 200
   Thomas 125
   Walter 66, 67, 99, 108, 112, 115, 123, 173, 175, 176, 183, 187, 189, 196, 198, 199, 205
Peakes
   Francis 32
   Walt. 97
   Walter 30, 32, 34, 35, 37, 46, 49, 52, 89, 90, 93, 94, 99, 109, 117, 118, 119, 120, 123, 124, 134
Peaks
   Frances 112
   Mary 112
   Walter 46, 49, 112
Peare's Plantation 12
Peare
   John 12
Peares Plantation 9
Pearse
   Benedict 150
   Edward 64
Peasley
   (N) 135
Pecke
   Walter 193
Peckes
   Walter 98
Ped
   Thomas 4
Pedro
   John 67, 188
Peeke
   Walt. 123
Peere
   Henry 17
Peirce
   Richard 155
Pekes
   Wal. 100
   Walter 94, 96, 97, 98, 99, 100, 102, 103, 114
Pell
   William 133, 142, 195
Penraddock
   Anthony 3
Percie
   Robert 73
Percy
   Mr. 100, 101, 103, 109, 121
   Robert 6, 7, 8, 69, 70, 71, 73, 74, 75, 77, 79, 80, 83, 84, 97, 98, 100, 109, 113
   Robobert 74
Peres
   Frannsco 5
Perfaite
   William 20
Perfett
   William 17
Perfitt
   John 155
Perkins
   Jonas 154
   Mr. 78
Perrie
   Robert 6
Perry
   Robert 15
   Thomas 79
Perryn
   John 148
Peteet
   Tho. 121
   Thomas 108
Petit
   Tho. 23
   Thomas 3
Petite
   Catherine 120
   Katheren 137
   Tho. 114, 124
   Thomas 20, 93, 94, 114, 120, 124, 133, 136, 137, 138, 139
Pett
   Tho. 85, 164
   Thomas 8, 41, 84, 85, 105, 114, 117
Petts
   Thomas 10
Pheboe
   Mark 66
Pheipo
   Marks 14, 20, 21, 22, 23, 27, 28, 162
Phenick
   Cuthbert 89, 90, 91
Phenicke
   Cuthbert 90, 91
Phenwick
   Cuthbert 67, 88, 89, 90
   Cuthbt. 66, 208
   Mr. 65, 66, 67
Phepo
   Mark 37, 40
   Marke 46
   Markes 67
   Marks 40, 67, 89, 90, 92, 93, 94, 96, 153
Phepoe
   Marke 68
   Markes 67, 68
   Marks 153
Pheypo
   Marke 86
   Markes 47
   Marks 40, 41, 42, 50, 53, 56, 59, 60, 63, 86, 94, 96, 97, 98, 102, 103, 107, 115, 119, 120, 124, 125, 126, 129, 134, 135, 139, 143, 163, 164, 179
   Sergt. 86, 87
Pheypoe
   Marke 179, 181
   Markes 179, 181
   Marks 153, 179, 181
Phillips
   Alice 123
   Barth 21
   Barth. 96
   Barthol. 139, 168
   Bartholomew 2, 17, 82, 96, 100, 105, 141, 153, 154, 167
   Elisabeth 154
   John 10, 22, 36, 164
   Mr. 82
   Owen 2, 7, 82
   Thomas 125, 141, 164, 199, 201
   William 48, 182
Phillipso
   Ann 15
Phillpot
   Mr. 83
Phillpott
   Edmond 203
   Edward 166
   Mr. 125
   Robert 69, 84
Philpot
   Robert 70, 72
Philpott
   Edward 44
   Mr. 8, 71
   Robert 8, 70, 72
   Thomas 72
Phypo
   Markes 91
Pickett
   Nicholas 108
Pike
   Ann 1, 2, 3
   John 3
   Robert 13
Pile
   John 23, 25, 29, 35, 58, 60, 131, 136, 138, 141, 143, 145, 147, 150, 160, 161
   Mr. 45, 130, 145, 150
Piles
   Jo. 22
   Mr. 53
Pille
   John 24, 25, 28, 29, 45, 57, 61, 105, 138, 157, 160, 168
Pills
   John 56
   Mr. 47
Pindley
   William 92, 105
Piney Point 123, 131
Pinie Point 78
Pinke

Frances 142
Pinley
  Will. 4
  William 8, 14
Pinly
  Will. 22
  William 6, 20, 21
Pinner
  Richard 4, 17, 85, 147
  Roger 23
Pinwill
  John 69
Piper
  John 155, 167, 204
Pletso
  Roger 119
Plott
  Thomas 191, 206
Plowden
  Edm. 97
  Edmund 102, 140
  Edward 32
Plunkett
  Xpofer 84
Poesey
  Franc. 139
  Francis 37, 55, 61, 129, 130, 152, 153, 155, 156, 157, 159, 160, 170
Poesy
  Fran. 115
  Francis 86, 113, 115, 117, 120, 123, 128, 129, 130, 164, 167
Poetrosse
  Fran. 108
  Francis 108
Polard
  John 142
Polentine
  Nicholas 69
Polhampton
  Nicholas 4
Pollin
  Roger 23, 25
Pomnly
  Henry 90
Poore
  John 200
Pope's Freehold 6
Pope
  (N) 104
  Abraham 25
  Ann 50, 66
  Anne 48
  Francis 12, 20, 22, 63, 89, 102, 103, 126, 127, 129, 131, 136, 137, 138, 149, 156, 160, 162, 165, 190
  Franciscu 124
  Hen. 187
  Henry 48, 179, 185, 186, 187, 188, 192, 195
  Mr. 91, 125
  Nat. 116
  Nath. 12, 20, 21, 22, 110, 121, 144, 148
  Nathan 21, 82
  Nathan. 83, 90
  Nathaniel 6, 20, 21, 70, 71, 73, 74, 90, 91, 95, 111, 118, 132
  Nathaniell 2, 38, 62, 89, 90, 91, 100, 132, 146, 147, 148, 159, 161, 163, 167, 193
Popeler's Island 9
Poplar Hill 64
Poplars Island 9
Porescourt
  William 3
Pork Hall 12
Porter
  Nicholas 154
  Susan 168
  Susanna 164
  William 97, 164, 168
Posey
  Elisabeth 94
  Fr. 104
  Fra. 20, 52, 88
  Fran. 100, 102, 108
  Francis 52, 54, 55, 58, 62, 86, 88, 89, 94, 98, 100, 101, 102, 117, 128
Posie
  Francis 2, 21
Posy
  (N) 93
Pott
  Fran. 192
  Francis 19, 50, 148, 192
  John 148, 169, 174, 179, 180, 181, 182, 183, 185, 192, 193, 194, 195, 196, 198, 204
  Mr. 182
  Robert 171
  Thomas 41
Potter
  (N) 68
  Awdrey 50
  Elisabeth 30, 41, 50, 68, 174, 179, 180, 181
  H. 160
  Henry 25, 27, 30, 36, 41, 42, 43, 50, 52, 67, 68, 89, 108, 109, 124, 164, 180, 181, 182, 184
  Thomas 172
Potts
  Elisabeth 187, 199
  John 173, 183, 184, 185
  Mrs. 188
Pounsney
  Henry 35
Pountnell
  Henry 43, 52, 167
Pountney
  Hen. 112, 120
  Henry 18, 24, 26, 27, 60, 61, 102, 108, 113, 114, 121, 124, 126, 139
Pourtree
  John 175
Powell
  Jo. 22
  John 116, 154
Power
  Geoffrey 101, 117, 141
  Jeffry 93
  Jeoffrey 95, 97, 111, 112
  Richard 151
Poyteres
  Fran. 108
Presto
  Richard 42
Preston
  Mr. 40, 43, 47, 48, 50, 203, 209
  Ri. 42, 47, 48, 49, 174, 185
  Rich. 48, 55, 64, 171, 173, 182, 183, 186, 192, 194, 196, 198, 200, 205
  Richard 33, 39, 42, 46, 47, 48, 64, 65, 66, 67, 68, 169, 170, 171, 172, 175, 176, 177, 178, 180, 181, 182, 183, 185, 186, 187, 188, 189, 190, 191, 192, 193, 195, 196, 197, 199, 200, 201, 202, 203, 206, 207, 208, 209
Prestone
  Richard 36
Prettiman
  John 8
Preuce
  John 176
Price
  C. 101
  Capt. 21, 30, 44, 62, 88, 100, 101, 105, 149, 150, 158, 160, 172, 197
  James 2, 4, 17, 84, 147
  John 4, 5, 18, 25, 26, 28, 29, 30, 36, 37, 39, 41, 42, 43, 44, 45, 46, 49, 51, 52, 53, 56, 57, 64, 70, 71, 73, 77, 84, 86, 87, 92, 93, 96, 97, 99, 100, 101, 102, 103, 107, 109, 110, 111, 113, 116, 119, 120, 126, 128, 130, 138, 141, 142, 144, 145, 149, 153, 156, 157, 158, 159, 160, 161, 163, 164, 167, 168, 172, 197, 202
  Lodowick 13
  Mathew 69
  Richard 197
  Robert 197
  Thomas 3, 8
  William 87
Prichard
  David 124, 134, 139, 159
  John 92, 101, 102, 103, 131
Prichyard
  John 123
Prince
  John 25, 26, 27, 35, 52
  Penelope 142
Prior's Mannor 10
Pritchard
  John 20, 187, 190, 197, 202
  Margaret 65
  William 178
Pritchett
  John 116
Prosser
  Tho. 10
Protestant
  Baslean 193
Puddington
  Comfort 149
  George 17, 26, 149, 157, 158
  Jane 149
  Mary 149
  Mr. 158, 159
Pultiott
  George 177
Pulton

Alexius 13
Ferdinand 4, 5
Ferdinando 5, 12
Mr. 1, 5, 84, 85
Purlavant
 Richard 92
Purlivant
 Mr. 83
 Richard 9, 81, 83, 84
Pursall
 Samuel 3, 4
 Samuell 21, 147
 Tho 22
 Tho. 22, 98, 119
 Thomas 14, 15, 22, 23, 94
Pursell
 Mr. 90
 Thomas 153
Pye
 George 3, 11, 16
Pyke
 Ann 123
Pyle
 John 88, 94, 102, 104, 105, 111, 173
 Mr. 104, 111
Pynner
 Richard 23, 154

Qwastoe 178

Rabley
 John 134
Rabnett
 Franc. 83
 Francis 4, 5, 70, 71, 72, 73, 74, 75, 76, 80, 82, 84, 125, 166
Rakepakobe 155
Ramsden
 John 183
Ramsey
 John 171
Raper
 George 30
Rapier
 George 49, 63
Rawling
 Anthony 127
Rawlings
 Anthony 18, 38, 54, 90, 93, 99, 133
 John 38
Rawlins
 Ann 133
 Ant. 115
 Anth. 104, 116, 118, 139
 Antho 21, 22
 Antho. 90, 104, 112
 Anthon 129
 Anthony 8, 17, 25, 26, 65, 84, 86, 93, 94, 95, 97, 99, 102, 103, 104, 108, 109, 111, 112, 113, 115, 116, 118, 121, 122, 125, 126, 127, 129, 133, 134, 139, 143, 144, 146, 163
 Charles 160
 Joane 86, 129
 Marg. 133
Rawlinson
 Charles 86, 92, 105, 109, 110, 111, 113, 116, 119, 128, 134, 140, 146, 160

Rawlison
 Charles 85
Raynalds
 William 150
Read
 Ananias 8
 Geo. 63
 John 34, 56, 184, 187
 Thomas 175, 201
 Walter 10
Recklesse
 Richard 52, 56, 64, 170
Reclesse
 Richard 170
Redolphus
 Thomas 175
Reed
 George 191
 John 197
 Thomas 185, 196
Reede
 George 199
 John 204
 Thomas 198
Rench
 Bartholomew 21, 100
Resurrection Manner 63
Revell
 John 7
 Rand. 103
 Randal 7
 Randall 2, 3, 7
 Randell 7
 Randol 7
 Randoll 10, 13, 60, 70, 71, 76, 77, 80, 82, 83, 84
 Rebecca 7
Reymont
 Richard 78
Reynolds
 Ann 2
 George 201
Rhodan
 Mathew 154
Rhodon
 Mathew 154
Richard
 John 88
Richards
 John 51
 Miles 85
 Mr. 117
Richardson
 John 2, 70, 71, 73, 77, 78
 Simon 3, 105
Richarson
 Ellis 87
Richins
 Robert 54, 59, 60
Ricketts
 Miles 4
Ricknell
 Richard 66, 67
Right
 William 199
Ringe
 Thomas 57
Ringgold
 Thomas 36, 187
Ringgould
 Thomas 49
Ringhold
 Thomas 188
Ringold
 Thomas 41
Ringould
 Thomas 41
Risbrook

Mary 19
 William 81
Risbrooke
 Mary 19
Rite
 Edmond 142
Roach
 Henry 27
Roadham
 Matthew 2
Roads
 John 39
Roberts
 Stanhop 46, 47, 60
 Stanop 88, 101, 155
 Stanope 102, 109, 110
Robeson
 Robert 198
Robines
 William 45
Robins
 (N) 147
 Elisabeth 149, 189, 190, 193, 198, 203
 Mr. 158
 Obedience 30
 Robert 119, 120, 121, 124, 125, 126, 127, 136, 138, 141, 147, 155, 156, 157, 158, 159, 160, 167, 189, 190, 193, 198, 203
Robinson
 Edward 3, 41
 Henry 17
 Jane 203
 Jo. 84, 85
 John 1, 4, 10, 11, 12, 14, 15, 16, 17, 70, 71, 72, 73, 74, 75, 76, 78, 80, 84, 147, 161, 191
 Richard 17
 Thomas 49, 163, 171, 177, 178, 185, 189
 William 193
Roch
 Henry 27
Rock
 Joseph 143
Rodam
 Matthew 4
Rodan
 Mathew 81
Roe
 Richard 132
Rogers
 Francis 17
 Mr. 2, 4
Rolston
 Mr. 84
Rooe
 Richard 143
Rookewood
 John 60, 160
Roper
 George 60
 widow 60
 William 38
Roser
 John 90
Rosier
 Jo. 134
 John 91, 101, 103, 140, 161, 163
 Mr. 119
Rosser
 John 90
Rouney
 Thomas 2

Rowbotum
  James 98
Rowney
  Tho. 154
  Thomas 4, 17, 147
Rozier
  John 90
Rump
  Will. 177
Runting
  John 199, 200
Rushell
  Christopher 63
  William 63
Russell
  Christ: 109
  Christopher 20, 93, 125, 126, 189, 193, 197
  John 49, 69, 81, 83, 146
  Nicholas 3, 5
Rutland
  Geo. 23
  George 22, 23, 85, 86, 98
Rutlidge
  John 15

Sabbell
  Richard 155
Sacawaykitt 160
Sachell
  William 50
Sadleir
  Giles 191, 206
Saffin
  John 177
Saint Thomas' Mannor 137
Sallisbury
  John 179
Salman
  Steeven 35
Salmon
  Stephen 20, 25, 60, 98, 112, 118, 119, 123, 128, 129, 134, 140, 142, 143, 147, 151, 165, 166
Salter
  (N) 66
  John 20, 22, 37, 42, 91, 103, 106, 164, 194
  Richard 136
Sammion
  Stephen 12
Samon
  Stephen 24
Sampson
  Thomas 177
Samson
  Steven 32
Sanders
  Cornelius 56
  John 4
Sands
  John 78
Sanford
  John 56
Sanghier
  Geo. 142
  George 124, 125, 128, 139, 152
Saphier
  Georg 100
  George 100
  Mr. 101
Saphyer
  George 99, 100, 101
  Mr. 101
Saphyre
  George 97
Sasquahana Point 148
Saugher
  George 100
Saunders
  Cornelius 56
  John 73
  Valentine 73
Saye
  Susan 79
Scapes
  William 176
Scarborough
  Edmond 193
Scarbrough
  Edmund 181, 200
  Mr. 181
Scarburgh
  Edmund 178
Scot
  Andrew 42, 48
Scote
  Sarah 31
  William 32
Scotfoord
  Richard 82
Scotland 68
Scotsford
  Richard 14
Scott
  Andrew 48, 68, 185, 188
  Michael 9, 72
  Roger 194, 197, 198, 201
  Samuell 184
  Sarah 34, 37
  Tho. 41
  William 29, 34, 55, 56, 57
Scottcher
  John 189, 190
Scotte
  Andrew 48
Scovell
  George 167
  Sam. 4
  Samuel 2
Scrutton's Plantation 127
Scurfeeld
  Edward 40
Scurffield
  Edward 165, 166, 167
Scurfield
  Edward 37, 40
Seamer
  Ann 188
  Thomas 175, 185, 188, 189, 191, 193, 202
Seamor
  Thom. 197
  Thomas 177, 184, 193, 197, 202, 204, 205
Seamore
  Tho. 179
  Thomas 179, 181
Seawell
  John 170
Sedgrave
  Richard 108
  Ro. 78, 144
  Robert 2, 3, 5, 21, 78, 89, 160
Segborne
  Winifred 108
Semar
  Thomas 177
Semare
  Thomas 184
Semer
  Thomas 184
Senclare
  John 192
Senserf
  Walter 206
Senserfe
  Walter 201, 206
Serle
  Robert 1, 2
Serritt
  Dirch 166
Seuet
  Martin 174
Severne
  Thomas 22
Sewell
  John 65, 200, 202
Sey
  Susan 76
Seymor
  Owen 93
Seymore
  Owen 119
Shaklady
  James 192
Shancks
  John 161
Shankes
  John 67
Shanks
  Amey 66
  John 7, 14, 43, 66, 126, 208
Sharp
  Judith 28
  Peter 172, 174, 176
  Robert 21, 22, 104, 108, 109, 184
Sharpe
  Judith 195
  Mr. 172
  Peter 189, 195, 201, 203, 204, 208
  Richard 49
  Robert 91, 92, 104, 108, 109, 112, 119, 120
Sheale
  Robert 17, 57
Sheercliff
  John 1
Sheld
  Robert 45
Shelle
  Robert 195
Shelly
  Edward 105
Shepherd
  Mary 119
  William 119
Sheppey
  Richard 179
Sherciffe
  John 138
Shercliff
  John 152, 166
Shercliffe
  Jo. 138
  John 129, 138, 140, 148, 150, 162, 177
Sherley
  Robert 4, 5, 17
Sherly
  Robert 2
Sherriden
  Thomas 203
Shertcliff
  Anne 26
  John 28, 29, 112, 113, 115, 118, 119, 121, 122, 123, 138
Shertcliffe
  Jo. 154

John 20, 28, 86, 115,
    118, 119, 121, 123,
    154
  Mary 118, 124
Sherwell 88
Sherwood
  Francis 20
Shiles
  William 92, 93, 94
Shippey
  Richard 178
Shircliffe
  John 196
Short
  Robert 9, 85, 106, 107,
    114, 117, 164
  Tabitha 164
Shurtcliff
  John 46
Shurtcliffe
  John 38
Silverthorne
  William 192
Silvestie
  Phillip 161
Simkin
  Robert 107, 110, 117,
    120
Simmons
  Thomas 129
Simonds
  Thomas 159
Simons
  Thomas 35, 36
Simpe
  William 17
Simpkin
  Robert 18, 137, 138,
    164, 167
Simpkine 137
Simpkins
  Robert 135
Simpson
  Angel 107
  Anslowe 134
  Pa. 185
  Pau. 189
  Paul 18, 19, 27, 28, 29,
    31, 34, 35, 37, 45,
    61, 105, 107, 115,
    128, 129, 134, 135,
    139, 140, 141, 143,
    146, 152, 153, 160,
    163, 168, 183, 187,
    189, 194, 203, 205
  Robert 2, 4, 5, 17
  Thomas 63
Sims
  John 79, 80
Simson
  Paul 32, 35
Sinckler
  William 198
Sinclair
  W. 61
Sinclare
  W. 64
  William 183
Sinclere
  William 206
Sissell
  Rowland 147
Sissill
  Rowland 147
Skiffen
  William 124
Skillinton
  Thomas 175
Skinner
  Andrew 209

Skippwith
  Mr. 66
Skipwith
  George 67, 170
Slater
  Barth. 2
  Bartholomew 13
Slaughter
  Bartholomew 159
Sleepe
  Lancelot 93, 105, 155
Sley
  Robert 208
Slingesby
  John 54, 155
Slingsbie
  John 32
Slingsby 162
  (N) 94
  John 32, 54, 99, 103,
    123, 124, 132, 161,
    162, 165, 167, 190,
    204
Slingsly
  John 139
Sly
  John 169
  Robert 169
Slye
  Math. 199
  Mr. 182
  Robert 170, 199, 208
Slymsby
  John 92
Slynsby
  John 89
Smith's Denn 169
Smith
  (N) 141
  Alice 19
  Ann 156, 203
  Anne 80
  Capt. 208
  Catharine 9
  Catherine 81
  Col. 186, 194, 199, 203
  Edmond 85, 86
  Edmund 98, 121, 124
  Edw. 138
  Edward 3, 117, 118, 119,
    163
  Elisabeth 171, 188
  Emperor 177, 181, 182,
    184, 186, 191, 193,
    196, 205
  Frances 194
  Gartrude 132
  Henry 6, 14
  Herbert 9
  Jane 132
  Jo. 10
  John 2, 4, 5, 9, 49, 64,
    66, 67, 68, 81, 84,
    166, 167, 169, 170,
    171, 173, 174, 176,
    177, 179, 183, 185
  Katharine 9
  Katherine 9, 81, 166,
    167
  Mary 174, 177, 183
  Mathew 172, 186, 188,
    198
  Maurice 201
  Mr. 1, 33, 78
  Mrs. 164
  Nicholas 160
  Nicolas 122
  Rich. 206
  Richard 4, 9, 131, 136,
    137, 140, 149, 169,

    171, 182, 186, 189,
    194, 196, 198, 200,
    203, 205
  Robert 15, 20, 21, 22,
    25, 43, 70, 73, 82,
    86, 90, 96, 104, 105,
    107, 109, 112, 115,
    119, 123, 128, 139,
    140, 145, 147, 154,
    161, 192
  Rose 24, 147, 180, 182
  Samuel 69, 72, 77
  Samuell 153, 180
  Thomas 4, 5, 69, 74, 75,
    78, 132
  Wal. 100
  Walter 18, 19, 93, 94,
    95, 99, 102, 109,
    111, 112, 114, 115,
    116, 121, 128, 132,
    143
  William 5, 9, 18, 27,
    31, 33, 36, 40, 41,
    44, 46, 47, 50, 61,
    80, 108, 164, 194
  Zeph. 18
  Zephania 37, 43, 46
  Zephaniah 18, 23, 26,
    143, 152, 164, 166,
    167, 168
Smithe
  Robert 192
Smithfield
  William 18, 19, 21, 22,
    90, 94, 96, 114, 118
Smithson
  Ann 16, 80
  Anne 79
  Anthony 84
  John 70, 73, 74, 133
Smoot
  Goodman 181
  William 25, 92
Smoote
  Goodman 179
  Will. 88
  William 18, 26, 40, 53,
    60, 86, 87, 88, 92,
    97, 108, 111, 112,
    117, 118, 122, 124,
    126, 127, 128, 129,
    136, 139, 141, 146,
    149, 156, 163, 168,
    179, 189
Smote
  William 37
Smyth
  Edmond 88
  Walter 89, 93
Snipe
  William 147, 154
Snow Hill Mannor 148
Snow Hill 12, 84
Snow
  (N). 2
  Abel 6, 12, 84
  Abell 12
  Justinian 6, 70, 71, 72,
    73, 80, 82, 84, 126
  Marmad. 84
  Marmaduke 2, 70, 71, 73,
    74, 75, 80, 82, 83,
    84, 91
  Marmd. 2
Sousa
  Mathias 2, 82
  Mathias de 82
  Matthias 4, 5
South
  Margaret 106

Sowth
  William 107
  Mr. 106
Sowther
  Nathaniell 56
Span
  Richard 88, 118
Spanne
  Richard 46, 88
Sparks
  Mr. 201
Speak
  Thomas 21
Speake
  Mr. 90, 91, 110
  Mrs. 109
  Tho. 91, 111, 115
  Thomas 93, 115, 121, 201
Speed
  (N) 76
  John 2
Speke
  Tho. 150
Spekes
  Thomas 180
Spencer
  Francis 191
Spicer
  Robert 153
Spink
  Henry 14, 20, 88, 98
Spinke
  Hen. 120
  Henry 88, 115, 116, 118, 119, 121, 122, 138, 166, 177
Sponner
  Ales 132
Sprige
  Mr. 198
  Thomas 196, 197, 198
Spry
  Mr. 208, 209
Sprye
  Mr. 208, 209
Spurdance
  John 181
Spurr
  Phillip 2, 3, 4, 5, 154
Squire
  William 175, 199
St. Ann's 11
St. Anne's 120
St. Clement's Mannor 12, 14
St. Clement's Manor 5
St. Elisabeth's 12
St. Gabriel's Mannor 13
St. Gabriel's Manor 22
St. Inigo's Mannor 12
St. Inigo's 12
St. Jerome's Thickett 35, 164
St. John's Freehold 6
St. Michael's Mannor 13
St. Michael's Manor 22, 103
St. Peter's Field 55
St. Richard's Mannor 14
St. Thomas his Point 182, 197
St. Thomas Mannor 162
St. Williams 118
Stafford's Freehold 163
Stagewell
  Thomas 205
Stagwell
  Thomas 199, 201, 202, 206
Standen
  Griff. 199
Standley
  Hugh 205
  Mr. 183
Standly
  Hugh 178, 179, 183
  Mr. 179, 182
Stanford
  Richard 144
Stanly
  Hugh 185, 196
Starcky
  Lawrence 173, 175
Starkey
  Laurence 43, 44, 47
  Lawr. 59
  Lawrence 34, 55, 187
  Mr. 43, 59
Starkie
  Lawrence 170
Starky
  Lawrence 34, 57, 62, 170, 175
Statham
  Thomas 2, 4, 17
Stauely
  Adam 99, 103, 108, 109
Stavelay
  Adam 201
Stavely
  Adam 93, 96
Stedd
  Joshua 200
  Mr. 203
Stedman
  Ricnd. 140
Steerman
  Thomas 16
Steg
  Thomas 4
Stent
  Thomas 11, 12, 70
  Thomas for 100 a. 12
Stente
  Thomas 71, 73, 77, 82
Stephans
  John 4
Stephanson
  William 20, 86, 89, 90, 92
Stephen
  John 147
Stephens
  John 3, 60
  William 43, 46, 60, 139, 185, 188, 193
Stephenson
  Helenor 140
  William 43, 44, 54, 96, 98, 119, 141, 146
Steven
  John 159
  William 171
Stevens
  Anne 159
  David 176
  William 43, 50, 128, 169, 171, 174, 179
Stevenson
  Mr. 201
  William 35, 37, 95, 97, 115, 117, 201
Steward
  Charles 9
Stiles
  William 2, 13, 113, 120, 124, 138, 153, 189, 190
Stills
  William 52
Stockden
  (N) 208
  Will. 177
  William 172, 178, 196
Stockely
  Wood. 201
  Woodman 169
Stockley
  Fran. 199
  Mr. 184, 201, 209
  Wood. 198, 202
  Woodman 171, 172, 173, 176, 177, 178, 179, 182, 183, 184, 185, 186, 187, 192
Stockly
  Woodman 197
Stogden
  William 170, 180, 182, 185
Stokden
  William 186
Stokeley
  Woodman 174
Stokely
  Edmund 172
Stone
  Capt. 31, 38, 101, 119, 127, 141, 172, 174
  John 103
  Mathew 39, 46, 51, 52, 55, 62, 64, 103, 152, 167, 172
  Tho. 140
  Thomas 46, 52, 103, 199, 203, 205
  William 17, 18, 23, 24, 25, 26, 27, 28, 29, 30, 31, 32, 33, 34, 36, 38, 39, 40, 41, 42, 43, 45, 46, 48, 49, 50, 51, 52, 53, 54, 55, 56, 57, 58, 60, 61, 62, 63, 64, 103, 119, 120, 124, 125, 126, 129, 130, 131, 132, 133, 134, 137, 138, 140, 143, 145, 146, 149, 150, 152, 157, 159, 162, 163, 165, 167, 169, 171, 172, 173, 174, 175, 197, 200, 203, 205
Stour
  Francis 16
Stower
  Francis 3, 4
Stradder
  William 25
Straton
  Mrs. 147
Stratton
  Mrs. 132
Streeter
  Edward 183
Streton 148
Stringar
  John 61
Stringer
  John 51, 53, 54, 57, 58, 60, 61, 62, 64
  Mr. 54
Strong
  Leo. 30, 207
  Leon. 64
  Leonard 28, 34, 64, 176, 207
  Mr. 208
Stubbs
  Sheffield 63
Sturman

Anne 159
Elisabeth 159
Jo. 142
John 16, 21, 24, 25, 26, 27, 31, 35, 36, 37, 38, 39, 42, 43, 44, 49, 53, 56, 66, 104, 105, 111, 112, 116, 125, 128, 141, 144, 145, 146, 150, 159, 160
Mr. 104, 107, 125
Richard 42
Tho. 111, 112, 140, 142, 145, 157
Thomas 20, 21, 22, 31, 39, 44, 53, 56, 104, 105, 111, 116, 125, 126, 128, 142, 143, 144, 145, 146, 157, 159, 160, 163

Styles
William 105, 108, 109, 110, 111, 123, 128, 130, 193

Surgeon
Tom 97

Sutton
Francis 7, 14
George 183, 184
John 68, 172, 177, 178, 179, 182, 192, 199, 203

Suype
William 2

Swan
Edward 52, 204

Swanne
Edward 52

Swauley
Geo. 174

Symonds
Thomas 39, 58

Symons
George 155

Sympkin
Robert 137

Sympson
Paul 44, 49, 50, 52, 53, 54, 55, 60, 61, 62, 161, 190, 202
Paule 49
Tho. 49

Sypson
Paule 49

Tabb
Humfry 150, 153

Taber
William 69

Tailor
George 82, 84
Henry 8
John 19
Sam. 21
Sarah 19

Tamter
Michael 163

Tappes
Francis 149

Tarling
Richard 201, 204

Tarver
William 159, 165

Tasker
Benj. 209

Tattersall
Mary 131
William 131

Tawney
John 173, 175, 190

Tayler
John 196, 206
Robert 185, 188, 190, 191, 192, 201, 204

Taylor
Dr. 27
George 2
John 7, 14, 19, 30, 31, 32, 42, 47, 49, 50, 57, 59, 108, 150, 203
Mary 1, 4, 48, 55, 59, 66, 147
Phillip 74, 132, 141
Robert 39, 42, 46, 47, 48, 54, 55, 58, 59, 65, 66, 97, 169, 172, 174, 178, 179, 181, 183, 184, 186, 202, 208
Sam. 92
Sarah 19, 66, 132
Thomas 132

Ted
Tho. 147

Tennis
Elisabeth 65
John 48, 66, 68, 177, 185, 205

Tennison
John 55

Tetersel
Edm. 3

Tetersell
Edward 5

Tew
John 109

The Hollow 11

Thimbellby
John 45

Thimblebie 148

Thimbleby
Jo. 128
Johem 124
John 36, 45, 49, 53, 61, 95, 112, 115, 118, 120, 122, 126, 127, 141, 145, 147, 148, 152, 155, 160, 175
Robert 177, 183

Thimblely
Jo. 141

Thimelby
Robert 185

Thomas Poteet's 28

Thomas
Christopher 74, 75
David 56, 59, 66
Mr. 191
Phillip 188
Tho. 43, 90, 96, 147, 181, 191, 192, 196
Thom. 192, 193, 194, 197, 199, 200, 202, 205
Thomas 8, 20, 28, 35, 43, 101, 147, 152, 185, 186, 188, 190, 201
William 108, 180, 186, 200
Xopfer 74
Xpofer 9

Thompson
Edward 152
John 9, 14, 20
Mr. 32, 75, 95
Richard 4, 5, 8, 9, 16, 69, 72, 75, 77
William 22, 24, 36, 96, 114, 116

Thomson
Edward 21
John 14
Richard 16
Will. 195
William 13, 21, 23, 194

Thornborough
Mr. 94, 99, 100, 101, 158, 159
Tho. 96, 100
Thomas 37, 93, 94, 157

Thornbury
Capt. 21
Thomas 93

Thorneborough
Mr. 94, 99, 100, 101
Tho. 100, 120

Thorneboroughe
Mr. 130

Thornton
James 2, 4, 5, 78

Thoroughgood
Cyprian 16

Thorowgood
Cy. 16
Cyprian 13, 166

Thoungue
Friendship 202

Throughgood
Cy. 77
Cyprian 72, 74, 75, 76, 77, 78, 79, 80, 83, 84

Throughton
Mary 7
Mrs. 1, 84

Througood
Simpkin 144

Thurmar
John 179

Thurston
Capt. 28
Charles 50, 51, 57
Richard 50, 57

Thurstone
Capt. 56
Richard 47

Thwaite
Francis 13

Thwaytes
Francis 2

Thymble
John 93

Tiboult
Anth. 89
Antho. 89

Tidd
Thomas 3, 16

Tigare
Jo. 139

Tillman
Capt. 64, 194
Samuell 194

Tilsley
Thomas 17

Tilton
John 183

Tinney
Thomas 30

Tinsbury
Robert 175

Toast
Joane 32

Tom's Point 203

Tomkinson
John 169

Tomlins
John 98

Tompkinson
    John 39, 59, 62
Tompson
    Andrew 146
    cozen 117
    Edw. 153
    Edward 144, 152, 153
    Elisabeth 127
    Geo. 173
    James 206
    Jo. 161
    Joane 144, 150
    John 139
    Mr. 111, 119, 120, 135
    Richard 136
    Robert 143
    William 13, 20, 36, 97,
        100, 102, 104, 105,
        107, 114, 116, 118,
        120, 124, 127, 129,
        130, 139, 140, 141,
        144, 146, 147, 153,
        154, 165
Tomson
    John 2
    William 92
Tongue
    Friendship 18, 24, 26,
        27
    Tho. 155
Toogood
    Mary 155
Topping
    Henry 17
Torney
    Rich. 107
Toung
    Friendship 38, 40, 41,
        43
Tounge
    Friendship 39, 66, 164
Toungue
    Friendship 53, 184
Touy
    William 191
Tovey
    Robert 129
Tovy
    John 155
Towers
    Francis 147
Trafford
    Col. 16
Tragare
    Jo. 160
    John 146
Treake
    Will. 90
Treleague
    John 144, 147
Trenton
    Mary 2
Trew
    Richard 32, 34
Trewe
    Richard 32, 34
Trigare
    John 139
Triggs
    Joane 1
    William 1
Trinity Mannor 13, 120
Trinity Manor 22
Troteene
    Francis 190
Troughton
    Mary 2
    Mrs. 138, 143, 151
True
    Goodman 179

Rich. 179
Richard 36, 56, 59, 60,
    171, 179, 181, 189,
    190, 194, 199, 202
Trueman
    Mr. 201
    Tho. 175
    Thomas 65, 173, 174,
        175, 178, 183, 203
Trumpeter
    Tho. 64
    Thomas 64, 65
Trussell
    John 109, 125, 150
    Mr. 86, 150
Tue
    John 1, 2, 3, 4, 5, 20
    Restituta 15
Tues
    Mr. 98
Tully
    John 200, 205
Tunnell
    Tho. 188
    Thomas 169, 188
Tunnet
    Thomas 165
Turner
    Arthur 25, 58, 66, 168,
        189, 190, 207, 208
    Edward 165, 193, 194
    Gooddy 184
    John 178
    Mrs. 184
    Thomas 24, 186, 188,
        189, 192, 203, 206
    William 60, 175, 176,
        178, 179, 184, 185,
        186, 196, 201, 202,
        204
Turnor
    Arthur 54, 143, 149,
        151, 159, 161, 163,
        167, 171, 189
    Edward 25
Tuttersall
    Lawrence 122
    Peter 122
Tuttey
    Robert 97
Tutty
    Robert 32
Tynney
    Thomas 28

Uell
    Thomas 135, 141
Uells
    Thomas 125
Underhill
    Jo. 140, 142
    John 142, 147, 151, 167,
        209
Underwood
    Peter 66, 193, 203
Upton
    William 73
Utie
    Mr. 208

Vallane
    John 32
Van Dan
    Francis 98
Van de Graft
    Cornelius Cornelinson
        150
Van Enden

Franc. 124
Francis 96, 97, 98, 101,
    102, 103, 111, 112,
    113, 117, 120, 121,
    125, 126, 127
van Eynden
    Francis 3
    Francisco 22
Vandam
    Franc. 135
Vandan
    Fran. 199
    Francis 37, 67, 93, 119,
        128, 144, 148, 154,
        173, 175, 178, 179,
        181
Vanden
    Francis 112
Vanenden
    Fr. 125, 128, 140
    Fracis 140
    Francis 26, 29, 30, 31,
        38, 44, 46, 125, 128,
        131, 141, 142, 146,
        150, 155, 162, 168
    Mary 168
Vanender
    Francis 26
Vaughan
    Capt. 10, 35, 66, 101,
        106, 107, 111, 114,
        115, 116, 123, 130,
        150, 158
    Lt. 84
    Richard 143, 208
    Robert 11, 12, 16, 17,
        18, 19, 24, 26, 32,
        34, 35, 37, 38, 40,
        41, 42, 47, 55, 56,
        69, 70, 72, 74, 75,
        78, 81, 85, 95, 99,
        100, 101, 102, 106,
        107, 113, 114, 116,
        117, 118, 121, 123,
        126, 136, 141, 142,
        150, 157, 158, 159,
        168, 183
    Sergeant 80
    Sergt. 71, 74, 75, 78
Vavafor
    Mr. 84
Veach
    James 186
Veatch
    James 186
Veich
    James 46, 54
Veitch
    James 57, 171, 172, 174,
        176, 181, 183, 184,
        185, 187, 190, 192,
        193, 194, 195, 196,
        198, 200, 202, 205,
        208, 209
Vethers
    Samuell 188
Villaine
    John 95, 97, 109, 120,
        130
Villane
    John 60, 160

Wade
    Jo. 140, 147
    John 18, 19, 26, 27, 28,
        29, 31, 35, 45, 129,
        140, 148, 156, 165,
        169, 172, 188, 199,
        207, 208

Mr. 31
Sacrey 199
Zaccery 190
Zach. 85, 169
Zacharias 85, 144, 199
Zachary 26, 49, 55, 106, 143, 150, 162, 176
Waggate
  (N) 145
  Thomas 146
Waggatte
  Tho. 140
  Thomas 140
Waggot
  Thomas 93, 104
Waggott
  Tho. 94, 99, 102
  Thomas 20, 22, 92, 94, 102
Waide
  John 187, 188
  Zacherah 189
Wakefield
  John 59, 65, 188
Waker
  James 169, 173
Waldron
  Dr. 27, 31, 32, 38
Walgrave
  Marm. 21
Walker
  Ja. 161
  James 20, 93, 96, 97, 116, 121, 123, 125, 126, 139, 155, 161
  John 2
  Richard 7, 14
Wallcott
  John 209
Wallton
  John 94, 114
  Thomas 197
Walter
  Christopher 30
  John 108
  Peake 199
  Roger 3
Walterlin
  Walter 3
Waltham
  John 93, 102, 105, 108, 111, 115
Waltom
  John 62
Walton
  Francis 48, 49, 169
  Jo. 164
  John 18, 20, 96, 112, 113, 114, 115, 121, 164
  Roger 73
  Thomas 197
Walwoorth
  William 193
Walworth
  William 50
War
  Thomas 107, 116, 119
Ward
  Jo. 108
  John 4, 5, 102, 108, 138, 145, 153, 156, 165
  Lawrence 58, 65, 169
  Mr. 58
  Richard 120
  Robert 20, 31, 38, 115, 120
  Tho. 41
  Thomas 40, 41, 65

Wardiff
  William 187
Wardner
  Andrew 40, 49
Wardnor
  Andrew 52
Wardriffe
  William 188
Ware
  Richard 27, 35, 49, 60, 126, 142, 165, 167
  Ricnd. 139
  Tho. 124
Wareing
  William 51
Wareman
  William 55
Waring
  Capt. 176, 190, 209
  Sampson 169, 171, 174, 177, 179, 181, 182, 185, 189, 190, 198, 199, 200, 201, 202, 205, 206, 207, 208
Waringe
  Sampson 66
Warman
  William 59, 67
Warmell
  Edmund 45
  Edward 166
Warner
  Andrew 67
Warr
  Tho. 160
  Thomas 20, 28, 29, 34, 36, 41, 43, 58, 150, 151, 155, 162, 168, 184
Warre
  Joane 110
  Thomas 108, 110, 151
Warren
  Humphrey 33
  John 4, 17, 47, 105, 112, 122, 123, 126, 132, 133, 147, 152
  Lt. 74
  Mrs. 32, 33, 40, 46
  Ratcliff 74, 75
  Robert 54, 60
  Susan 18, 29, 31, 32, 33, 34, 38, 46, 50, 63
  Susanna 32, 33
  William 51, 133, 143, 159
Warrens
  John 147
Warring
  Sampson 169, 188
Warron
  Jacob 49
  Mary 49
Wassell
  William 81, 83
Waterlin
  Wal. 116
  Walt. 112
  Walter 21, 43, 99, 100, 101, 102, 111, 112, 115, 120, 123, 127, 128
  Water 116
Waterline
  Walter 61
Waterling
  Wal. 100
  Walter 51, 57, 58, 59, 61, 64, 140, 145,

147, 164, 167
  Water 141
Waterlyn
  Walter 54
Waters
  John 110
  Tho. 159
Waterson
  Walter 147
Watkins
  Evan 13
  Nicholas 187
Watson
  Andrew 20, 24, 58
  Rich. 32
  Richard 50, 56, 58, 59, 193
  William 174
Watts
  Alexander 191, 193, 198, 201, 206
  George 144, 159
  Johanna 190, 191
  Margarett 17
  Sanders 190
  William 119, 177
Waughop
  John 58, 61
Wavell
  John 23, 38
Wavill
  Ja. 22
Webb
  Anthony 195
  Arthur 2, 82
  Marke 33
  Martha 29, 33, 63
  Tho. 46
  Thomas 200, 205
Webber
  Capt. 51
  Thomas 51, 52, 63
Webe
  Anthony 195
Weed
  Henry 71
Weekes
  Joseph 188, 207, 208
Weeks
  Joseph 40, 41, 49
Welds
  Thomas 18
Welles
  Richard 64
Wells
  Edward 205
  Elisabeth 205
  Grace 143
  Mr. 84, 208
  Rich. 171
  Richard 64, 169, 171, 192, 207
  Thomas 1
  William 25
Wepvill
  John 83
West's Valley 4
West
  Anthony 128, 139
  Jo. 27
  John 37
  Phillip 2, 4, 6, 7, 8, 10, 76, 79, 84
  Richard 155
  Robert 108, 124
Westbury Manor 3
Westlies
  William 81
Westly
  William 81

Weston
   Mr. 16, 54, 96, 97, 98, 103, 120, 125, 135, 145, 146, 155
   Tho. 98, 118, 120, 146
   Thomas 2, 3, 11, 23, 24, 56, 85, 93, 101, 103, 120, 124, 126, 134, 136, 162
Wethersby
   Bartholomew 150
Weyvell
   John 91
Weyvill
   Mr. 85
Whale
   Arthur 168
Whealey
   William 35
Wheateley
   John 123, 130
   William 88, 121
Wheately
   William 94, 134
Wheatley
   John 20, 29, 60, 92, 122
   Mrs. 38
   William 20, 22, 37, 88, 94, 113, 116, 117, 119, 133
Wheatly
   John 155
   William 95
Wheeler
   Fran. 192
   John 40
Whettle
   William 40
Whight
   Nicholas 34
   Richard 34
Whit Birch Freehold 127
Whitby
   William 89, 174
White Birch Freehold 129
White
   Andrew 2, 4, 17, 70, 71
   Francess 3
   Geaye 64
   George 1, 2, 3, 4, 5
   Guy 180
   Guye 180
   Mr. 79, 80
   Mrs. 144
   Nicholas 27, 181
   Rich. 90
   Richard 90, 91, 93, 110, 125
   Tho. 60, 139, 144, 161
   Thomas 2, 6, 14, 15, 73, 79, 80, 82, 84, 92, 144, 152, 162, 204
Whitehead
   Mary 1, 2, 76
Whitle
   William 96, 102, 108, 116
Whitley
   William 93
Whittell
   William 193
Whitten
   Jane 177
   Joan 177
Whittington
   Arthur 22
   William 49, 107
Whittle
   George 209
   Guy 176

Maudlin 163
Maudly 163
   William 28, 35, 37, 41, 42, 55, 58, 61, 89, 101, 115, 135, 147, 193
Wickiliff
   David 2
Wickliff
   David 11, 74, 79, 83, 85
   Davie 70
Wickliffe
   David 159
Wilcox
   Andrew 180, 181
Wildman
   John 46, 63
   Major 46
Wildye
   William 183
Wilford
   Mr. 54
   Thomas 50
Wilkins
   John 119
Wilkinson
   Elisabeth 159
   Mary 159
   Mr. 18, 32, 33, 36
   Rebecca 159
   William 32, 51, 53, 153, 159, 171, 184, 197, 202
Willan
   Rich. 86, 108, 123
   Richard 19, 25, 28, 29, 49, 86, 107, 148, 149, 153, 155, 166, 206
   Robert 61
Willane
   Richard 37
Willard
   George 52, 179
   Mr. 180
Willarde
   George 52
Willcox
   Andrew 192, 203
Willford
   Tho. 61, 153
William
   Henry 173
   Rowland 77
Williams
   (N) 2
   Betty 33
   Edward 10, 19, 119, 128, 193, 197
   Eleanor 17
   Elisabeth 29, 33
   John 136, 184, 187, 188
   Mathew 164
   Mrs. 29, 33, 40
   Richard 3, 8
   Rowland 16
   Thomas 4, 17
   William 124
Williamson
   Alexander 53
   Elisabeth 17
   Martha 1, 2
   William 2, 76
Willin
   Richard 132
Willis
   (N) 2
   Francis 132
   Tho. 152
   Thomas 23, 80, 108

Wills
   Samuell 152
   Thomas 5
Willsfoard
   Bridgit 52
   Tho. 52
Wilson
   James 186
   Tho. 62
Winbridge
   John 64
Winches
   George 119
Winchester
   John 150, 163
   Margaret 123
Windebanke
   Mr. 1
Winifride
   Mr. 1
Winter
   Capt. 2, 17
Wintour
   Capt. 71, 72, 73, 74, 75
   Edward 4
   Frederick 4
   Robert 2, 70, 71, 72, 73, 74, 76, 77, 80, 82, 84
Wise
   Hanna 192
Wiseman
   John 122, 123
   Mr. 104, 108
   Robert 20, 70, 83, 119, 120, 147, 160
Witby
   William 42
Withers
   Sam. 192, 193, 194, 196
   Samuell 189
   William 131
Witle
   William 108
Wolfe
   William 9
Wollaston Manner 58
Wollaston Mannor 12
Wood
   Edw. 199
   Edward 179
   Henry 70, 81, 154
   William 195, 196, 199
Woodriff
   William 188
Woodriffe
   William 189
Woods
   Henry 83
Woolhouse
   Francis 142
Woolman
   Richard 188, 195
Wordly
   Edward 86
Wormell
   Edm. 54
   Edmond 25
   Edmund 32, 165
Worrell
   John 125
Wortley
   John 2, 6, 16, 97, 168
Wortly
   John 70
Wrench
   Bartholomew 133
Wright 178
   Ann 188
   Arther 52

    Arthur 53, 175, 179, 192, 196, 205
    Edmund 134
    Ishmaeal 178
    Ishmael 67, 176, 180, 182, 188, 192, 204
    Ishmaell 42
    Ishmeall 67
    Ismael 37, 65, 172, 173
    Ismaell 39, 47
    Ismeall 43, 65
    John 8
    Joseph 178
    Mary 203
    Richard 7, 14
    Tho. 190
    Thomas 190
    William 14, 20, 64, 102, 124, 133

Wyatt
    Capt. 21
    Francis 192
    Joh 75
    John 70, 71, 73, 74, 75, 76, 84, 99, 100, 102
    Mr. 104, 116

Wyatte
    John 108

Yardley
    Argall 38, 58, 60
    Argol 35
    Col. 56, 58, 63
    Esq. 109
    Franc. 37
    Francis 30, 33, 34, 35, 36, 37, 51, 55, 56, 63, 67
    Francis. 67

Yardly
    Francis 59

Yaulle
    Thomas 26

Yeardley
    Francis 55

Yewell
    Thomas 8, 9, 21
    William 20

Youll
    Thomas 144

Young
    Robert 200
    Sam. 68
    Samuell 209
    William 177, 193, 201

Zacharis
    Zachay 51

Zause
    Mathias 17

Other Heritage Books by Vernon L. Skinner, Jr.:

Abstracts of the Administration Accounts of the Prerogative Court of Maryland, 1718–1724, Libers 1–5

Abstracts of the Administration Accounts of the Prerogative Court of Maryland, 1724–1731: Libers 6–10

Abstracts of the Administration Accounts of the Prerogative Court of Maryland, 1731–1737: Libers 11–15

Abstracts of the Administration Accounts of the Prerogative Court of Maryland, 1737–1744: Libers 16–20

Abstracts of the Administration Accounts of the Prerogative Court of Maryland, 1744–1750: Libers 21–28

Abstracts of the Administration Accounts of the Prerogative Court of Maryland, 1750–1754: Libers 29–36

Abstracts of the Administration Accounts of the Prerogative Court of Maryland, 1754–1760: Libers 37–45

Abstracts of the Administration Accounts of the Prerogative Court of Maryland, 1760–1764, Libers 46–51

Abstracts of the Administration Accounts of the Prerogative Court of Maryland, 1764–1768, Libers 52–58

Abstracts of the Administration Accounts of the Prerogative Court of Maryland, 1768–1771, Libers 59–66

Abstracts of the Administration Accounts of the Prerogative Court of Maryland, 1771–1777, Libers 67–74

Abstracts of the Balance Books of the Prerogative Court of Maryland: Libers 2 and 3, 1755–1763

Abstracts of the Balance Books of the Prerogative Court of Maryland: Libers 4 and 5, 1763–1770

Abstracts of the Balance Books of the Prerogative Court of Maryland: Libers 6 and 7, 1770–1777

Abstracts of the Inventories and Accounts of the Prerogative Court of Maryland, 1674–1678, 1699–1703

Abstracts of the Inventories and Accounts of the Prerogative Court of Maryland, 1679–1686

Abstracts of the Inventories and Accounts of the Prerogative Court of Maryland, 1685–1701

Abstracts of the Inventories and Accounts of the Prerogative Court of Maryland, 1688–1698

Abstracts of the Inventories and Accounts of the Prerogative Court of Maryland, 1697–1700: Libers 16, 17, 18, 19, 19½A, 19½B

Abstracts of the Inventories and Accounts of the Prerogative Court of Maryland, 1699–1704: Libers 20–24

Abstracts of the Inventories and Accounts of the Prerogative Court of Maryland, 1708–1711: Libers 29, 30, 31, 32A, 32B

Abstracts of the Inventories and Accounts of the Prerogative Court of Maryland, 1711–1713: Libers 32C, 33A, 33B, 34

Abstracts of the Inventories and Accounts of the Prerogative Court of Maryland, 1712–1716: Libers 35A, 35B, 36A, 36B, 36C

Abstracts of the Inventories and Accounts of the Prerogative Court of Maryland, 1715–1718: Libers 37A, 37B, 37C, 38A, 38B, 39A, 39B, 39C

Abstracts of the Inventories and Accounts of the Prerogative Court of Maryland, 1699–1708: Libers 25–28

Abstracts of the Inventories of the Prerogative Court of Maryland, 1718–1720

Abstracts of the Inventories of the Prerogative Court of Maryland, 1720–1724

Abstracts of the Inventories of the Prerogative Court of Maryland, 1724–1727

Abstracts of the Inventories of the Prerogative Court of Maryland, 1726–1729

Abstracts of the Inventories of the Prerogative Court of Maryland, 1728–1734

Abstracts of the Inventories of the Prerogative Court of Maryland, 1733–1738

Abstracts of the Inventories of the Prerogative Court of Maryland, 1738–1744

Abstracts of the Inventories of the Prerogative Court of Maryland, 1744–1748

Abstracts of the Inventories of the Prerogative Court of Maryland, 1748–1751

Abstracts of the Inventories of the Prerogative Court of Maryland, 1751–1756

Abstracts of the Inventories of the Prerogative Court of Maryland, 1755–1760

Abstracts of the Inventories of the Prerogative Court of Maryland, 1760–1763

Abstracts of the Inventories of the Prerogative Court of Maryland, 1763–1766

Abstracts of the Inventories of the Prerogative Court of Maryland, 1766–1769

Abstracts of the Inventories of the Prerogative Court of Maryland, 1769–1772

Abstracts of the Inventories of the Prerogative Court of Maryland, 1772–1774

Abstracts of the Inventories of the Prerogative Court of Maryland, 1774–1777

Abstracts of the Proceedings of the Orphans' Court of Sussex County, Delaware: Libers 1, 2, 3, 4, A (1708–1709, 1728–1777)

Abstracts of the Proprietary Records of the Provincial Court of Maryland, 1637–1658

Abstracts Worcester County, Maryland Estate Docket, 1742–1820

Other Wills in the Prerogative Court for Somerset and Worcester Counties, 1664–1775

Provincial Families of Maryland, Volume 1

Somerset County Will Books, 1750–1772

Somerset County Will, 1667–1748: Liber EB9

Somerset County Wills, 1770–1777 and 1675–1710: Liber EB5

Supplement Abstracts Inventories and Accounts, Prerogative Court, 1691–1706

Worcester County Inventories and Accounts, 1694–1742: Inventory Book JW15

Worcester County Wills: Will Book MH3, 1666–1742

www.ingramcontent.com/pod-product-compliance
Lightning Source LLC
Chambersburg PA
CBHW060312240426
43661CB00059B/2740